JOHN CAPGRAVE'S
ABBREUIACION OF CRONICLES

EARLY ENGLISH TEXT SOCIETY

No. 285

1983

JOHN CAPGRAVE'S ABBREUIACION OF CRONICLES

EDITED BY

PETER J. LUCAS

Published for
THE EARLY ENGLISH TEXT SOCIETY
by the
OXFORD UNIVERSITY PRESS
1983

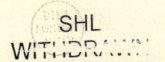

Oxford University Press, Walton Street, Oxford OX2 6DP

London Glasgow New York Toronto
Delhi Bombay Calcutta Madras Karachi
Kuala Lumpur Singapore Hong Kong Tokyo
Nairobi Dar es Salaam Cape Town
Melbourne Auckland

and associated companies in
Beirut Berlin Ibadan Mexico City Nicosia

Published in the United States
by Oxford University Press, New York

British Library Cataloguing in Publication Data

Capgrave, John 1393–1464
Capgrave's Abbreuiacion of Cronicles. —(Publications/Early
English Text Society; 285).
I. World history—Early works to 1800
I. Lucas, Peter J   II. Series
909   D17   80–41856
ISBN 0–19–722287–0

548212P.

Printed in Great Britain
at the University Press, Oxford
by Eric Buckley
Printer to the University

FOR

ANGELA

Receyue þis bok þouȝ it be simpil

PREFACE

JOHN CAPGRAVE's *Abbreuiacion of Cronicles* (completed *c.*1462–1463) is a substantial contribution to Medieval English historical literature. It is a Universal Chronicle, beginning with Adam and Eve, proceeding through biblical and ancient classical history to the birth of Christ, then progressively narrowing its focus to the Holy Roman Empire and the kingdom of England, and ending in 1417. The only previous edition, by F. C. Hingeston, misleadingly entitled *The Chronicle of England*, was the first volume of the Rolls Series (1858). It was an inauspicious start. The introduction is worthless, the text inaccurate, the glossary inadequate, and notes virtually non-existent. Its best feature, the index, suppresses the names of persons or places that Hingeston was presumably unable to identify. Even in the nineteenth century it was described as 'Ueber alle Begriffe unkritisch'—by A. Potthast in his *Bibliotheca Historica Medii Aevi* (Berlin, 1896 edn., i. 185)—and 'with its publication began what is perhaps the most distressing episode in the history of the series' (M. D. Knowles, *Great Historical Enterprises* (London, 1963), p. 112). Hingeston 'was a self-confident, naïve, mercurial young man' who probably gained the commission to edit Capgrave via engagement to J. Stevenson's daughter (whom he subsequently threw over). For the *Abbreuiacion of Cronicles* he used a transcript 'made by old Mr. Twycross, who certainly did his work well' (Hingeston's letter to the Master of the Rolls, PRO 37/44), but, whatever the merits of this transcription, the compositors, unfamiliar with the necessity of preserving Capgrave's spelling, proceeded to adapt it to modern practice. The result was a proof-reader's nightmare. Although Hingeston claimed to 'have taken an infinity of pains with them [the proofs]' the published edition produced what T. D. Hardy, who was 'annoyed', called 'general disappointment'. After publication Hingeston wrote abjectly trying to explain away the errors in the text. His further association with the Rolls Series was short-lived. After two more volumes and another which had to be suppressed he was relieved of further duties by the Master of the Rolls.

The present edition offers a new Text based on a transcription of the author's autograph manuscript (a fair copy), M, collated with the only other known manuscript, P, which must be a copy of an earlier autograph (or holograph). Since Hingeston (wrongly) thought P to be a copy of M the importance of this manuscript (P) and the contribution it could make to the establishment of the text has never before been recognized. In the Textual Notes are recorded alterations made by the original scribe of M (the author) and all substantive errors and variants from P. A particular feature of the Text is the extreme care exercised in the expansion of abbreviations and contractions so that no word occurs in a spelling which does not correspond to the author's own full spelling of that word. To this end a complete *Index Verborum*, made with the aid of a computer, was utilized: see my 'Computer Assistance in the Editorial Expansion of Contractions . . .'. In addition to the Textual Notes the Text is also accompanied by Source References so that a source version may be readily consulted when it is available and so that the passages for which no source has been found will be readily identifiable.

To accompany the Text and textual apparatus the volume is provided with a critical apparatus. In the Introduction the section on The Author and his Works summarizes the known facts and sets the *Abbreuiacion of Cronicles* within a new interpretation of Capgrave's over-all literary purpose. The Manuscripts are then described and The Relationship of the Principal Manuscripts assessed. The sections on Language offer the first full analysis of Capgrave's phonological and morphological usage based on the author's autograph manuscript, written and corrected in his own hand. The Capgrave material probably constitutes the single most important corpus of linguistic evidence for the West Norfolk area in the fifteenth century. There is also a section on the innovative element in Capgrave's vocabulary. In the section on Sources Capgrave's use of Martinus Polonus's *Chronicle of Popes and Emperors* and of the St. Albans Chronicles by Thomas Walsingham is carefully analysed, and Capgrave's reliance on a version of Walsingham's Chronicles antecedent to and slightly fuller than any that survives is demonstrated. Any future work on Walsingham's *Chronica Maiora* and *Short History* will have to take the evidence from Capgrave's *Abbreuiacion of Cronicles* into account. The final section of the Introduction, on Historiographical Value, discusses Capgrave's work in the context of the philosophy of history current in the Middle Ages. There is also a Commentary, which attempts to deal with points of difficulty and notes where Capgrave's text diverges from that of his sources. In the preparation of the Glossary I have drawn on the complete *Index Verborum* of the text made with the aid of the computer facilities available in University College, Dublin: see *Computers and the Humanities*, ii (1968), 241, no. L202, and v (1971), 295, and *Computers and Medieval Data Processing*, ii (1972), 35–6, no. 60. There is also a complete Glossarial Index.

I have great pleasure in thanking the many friends, colleagues, and advisers who have helped me while the work was in progress. This edition has its origins in a thesis begun in 1964 and awarded the degree of Ph.D. by the University of Leeds in 1973. My principal debt is to my then supervisor, Professor A. C. Cawley (Leeds), but for whose wisdom, guidance, and meticulous attention to detail this edition would have been the worse. Professor N. Davis (Oxford) first drew my attention when I was still an undergraduate to Capgrave as a possible topic for research. Mr M. B. Parkes (Oxford) and Dr Betty Hill (Leeds) gave encouragement during the earlier stages of my work on Capgrave. Professor R. M. Wilson (Sheffield), my examiner with Professor Cawley in 1973, corrected some points of detail. Professor A. J. Bliss (Dublin) assisted in the elucidation of specific points, notably in regard to numerological theory. Mr J. Taylor (Leeds) advised me on the possible sources of Capgrave's *Abbreuiacion of Cronicles*. Fr A. de Meijer, osa (Utrecht), and Professor the Revd. F. X. Martin, osa (Dublin), have shown exceptional interest in my work on Capgrave as it has progressed. I have also benefited from discussing the *Abbreuiacion of Cronicles* with students taking an optional course in Medieval English Historical Literature at University College, Dublin. Dr Anne Hudson (Oxford) has given encouragement while I was preparing the work for publication. Dr Pamela Gradon (Oxford) has also been supportive and most helpful. Other more specific debts are acknowledged in the Commentary or in footnotes. My wife, to whom this edition is dedicated, has tolerated Capgrave as a disembodied presence in the household, and, as a fellow medievalist, contributed valuable advice from time to time.

I should also like to thank Dr F. Anderson (then Director),

Mrs Phil Moriarty (Operations Controller), Mr M. Marr and Mr G. Clark (Software Advisers) of the computer laboratory in University College, Dublin, for their helpfulness and co-operation. The staff of libraries that hold manuscripts of the *Abbreuiacion of Cronicles* were unfailingly courteous and helpful, notably Mr A. E. B. Owen of Cambridge University Library, Dr R. Vaughan (then Librarian) and his assistant Mrs J. Rolfe of Corpus Christi College, Cambridge, and Mr C. W. Ringrose of Lincoln's Inn, London. Mrs Anne Coogan typed virtually the whole of this edition (except the Text) with great accuracy. My thanks are also due to the Twenty-Seven Foundation for making me an award which facilitated the preparation of this edition for publication, and to the School of English (University of Leeds) and the Library (University College, Dublin) for bearing part of the cost of purchasing photographs. The reproductions of Plates I–IV and VI–VII are by courtesy of Cambridge University Library and of Plate V by courtesy of the Masters and Fellows of Corpus Christi College, Cambridge.

PETER J. LUCAS

Dublin
Feast of St. Norbert 1979

CONTENTS

PREFACE   vii

PLATES   xii

LIST OF ABBREVIATIONS   xiii

CHRONOLOGICAL TABLE   xv

INTRODUCTION

    THE AUTHOR AND HIS WORKS   xix

    THE MANUSCRIPTS   xxix

    THE RELATIONSHIP OF THE PRINCIPAL MANUSCRIPTS   xl

    DATE   xliii

    LANGUAGE

      External Evidence   xliii

      Previous Studies   xliv

      Phonology   xlv

       Vowels   xlv

       Consonants   liii

      Morphology   lvii

      Vocabulary   lxvii

    SOURCES   lxxi

    HISTORIOGRAPHICAL VALUE   xciii

SELECT BIBLIOGRAPHY   xcix

THE TEXT   1

    Establishing the Text   2

    Editorial Procedure   3

    Source References   5

    Dedicatory Preface, with Textual Notes   7

    ABBREUIACION OF CRONICLES, with Textual Notes and Source References   11

COMMENTARY   251

SELECT GLOSSARY   315

GLOSSARIAL INDEX   363

PLATES

I. Cambridge, University Library, MS Gg.4.12, fol. 89ʳ   *frontispiece*

II. Cambridge, University Library, MS Gg.4.12, fol. 1ᵛ   *facing p.* 7

III. Cambridge, University Library, MS Gg.4.12, fol. 2ᵛ   „   9

IV. Cambridge, University Library, MS Gg.4.12, fol. 3ʳ ⎫ *between*

V. Cambridge, Corpus Christi College, MS 167, p. 1 ⎬ *pp.* 10 *and* 11

VI. Cambridge, University Library, MS Gg.4.12, fol. 35ʳ   *facing p.* 47

VII. Cambridge, University Library, MS Gg.4.12, fol. 61ʳ   „   116

LIST OF ABBREVIATIONS

Abbreviated bibliographical references are also to be found in square brackets at the end of the relevant entries in the Select Bibliography (pp. xcix–cvii, below).

AL	*Archivum Linguisticum*
ALLC	Association for Literary and Linguistic Computing
AN	Anglo-Norman
AS	Anglo-Saxon
AV	Authorized Version (of Bible)
BJR(U)L(M)	*Bulletin of the John Rylands (University) Library (of Manchester)*
BMQ	*The British Museum Quarterly*
BRUC	*A Biographical Register of the University of Cambridge to 1500*, A. B. Emden (ed.) (Cambridge, 1963)
BRUO	*A Biographical Register of the University of Oxford to A.D. 1500*, A. B. Emden (ed.) (Oxford, 1957–9)
C	Capgrave
compl.	complement(ary)
condit.	conditional
CSEL	Corpus Scriptorum Ecclesiasticorum Latinorum (Vienna)
DNB	*Dictionary of National Biography*
E	East
E&GS	*English and Germanic Studies*
E&S	*Essays and Studies*
ecclL	ecclesiastical Latin
EETS	Early English Text Society
EHR	*English Historical Review*
erron.	erroneous
hist.	historic
HLQ	*Huntington Library Quarterly*
indir.	indirect
interrog.	interrogative
L	Latin
loc.	locative
MÆ	*Medium Ævum*
M&H	*Medievalia et Humanistica*

ME	Middle English
MED	*Middle English Dictionary*
medL	medieval Latin
MGH	Monumenta Germaniae Historica
MLQ	*Modern Language Quarterly*
MnE	Modern English
MS	*Mediaeval Studies*
N	North
N&Q	*Notes and Queries*
Neophil.	*Neophilologus*
NM	*Neuphilologische Mitteilungen*
ODan.	Old Danish
OE	Old English
OED	*Oxford English Dictionary*
OF	Old French
ON	Old Norse (Old Icelandic)
ONF	Northern dialects of Old French
PBA	*Proceedings of the British Academy*
PL	Patrologia cursus completus, series Latina
predic.	predicative(ly)
PresE	Present English
PRO	Public Record Office
REED	*Records of Early English Drama*
RES	*The Review of English Studies*
RS	Rolls Series
S	South
SB	*Studies in Bibliography*
SE	South-East(ern)
sim.	similar(ly)
SN	*Studia Neophilologica*
SP	*Studies in Philology*
STC	*A Short-Title Catalogue of Books Printed . . . 1475–1640*
TCBS	*Transactions of the Cambridge Bibliographical Society*
TRHS	*Transactions of the Royal Historical Society*
W	West
WMid	West Midland
WS	West Saxon

SIGNS

<	developed from
/ /	enclose phonemic symbols
*	is prefixed to forms theoretically reconstructed

CHRONOLOGICAL TABLE

YEAR	CAPGRAVE'S LIFE	LITERARY EVENTS	POLITICAL EVENTS
1393	Capgrave born, probably at Lynn		
1399			Deposition of Richard II Henry IV king
1400		Chaucer dies	
1403			Henry IV defeats Percies at Shrewsbury
1404			Unlearned Parliament
1406	Witnesses departure of Princess Philippa from Lynn to wed the king of Denmark		Long Parliament
1408		Gower dies	
1409			Council of Pisa begins
c.1410	Enters Augustinian Order		
1412		Hoccleve, *Regement of Princes*	
1413			Henry IV dies Henry V king
1414		*Chronicles of London*	Council of Constance begins
1415			Henry V defeats French at Agincourt
1416–17	Ordained priest		
1417–22	Studies theology in London		
1417		*Gesta Henrici Quinti*	Oldcastle burnt
1420		Lydgate, *Troybook*	Treaty of Troyes Henry V marries Catherine of Valois
Before 1422	*Life of St. Norbert*		
1422	Qualifies as Lector in Theology Begins studies in Cambridge Delivers a sermon, later *Tretis*, at Cambridge	Walsingham, *St. Albans chronicles* Lydgate, *Life of Our Lady* Caxton born (?)	Henry V dies. Henry VI (aged 1) king, Bedford regent

YEAR	CAPGRAVE'S LIFE	LITERARY EVENTS	POLITICAL EVENTS
1423–5	Continues studies in Cambridge		
1423	B.Th. (Cantab.)	James I of Scotland, *Kingis Quair*	
1425	D.Th. (Cantab.)	*Castle of Perseverance* Paston Letters begin	
1426		Hoccleve dies	
c.1428		Lydgate, *Pilgrimage of the Life of Man*	
c.1430		Henryson born Adam of Usk, *Chronicon*	
1431		Christine de Pisan dies	Joan of Arc burnt Council of Basle begins
1432		*Book of Margery Kempe* written up	
1434		Lydgate, *Life of St. Edmund*	
1435		Misyn, *Fire of Love*	Bedford dies
1436			French recover Paris
Before 1437	*In Regum* (lost)		
1437–8	*In Genesim*	Lydgate, *Fall of Princes*	
1439	At Woodstock to deliver presentation copy of *In Genesim* to Humphrey duke of Gloucester		
1439–40	*In Exodum*	Lydgate, *Life of St. Albon*	
1440	*Life of St. Norbert* completed	*Promptorium Parvulorum* Invention of printing in Germany	
1441	Present at laying of foundation stone of King's College, Cambridge		
1441–5	*Concordia* (lost) *In Leviticum* (lost) *In Numeros* (lost) *In Deuteronomium* (lost) *Life of St. Katharine*		
1443–6		Bokenham, *Legendys of Hooly Wummen* Pecock, *Donet*	

YEAR	CAPGRAVE'S LIFE	LITERARY EVENTS	POLITICAL EVENTS
1445			Peace negotiations with France Henry VI marries Margaret of Anjou
1446	Visit of Henry VI to Augustinian Friary at Lynn		
1446–7	*De illustribus Henricis* completed		
Before 1447	*Super epistolas Pauli* (lost)		
1447		Bokenham dies	Humphrey, duke of Gloucester dies
c.1449		Lydgate dies	War with France resumed Rouen and eastern Normandy lost
c.1450	In Rome, probably for the Jubilee	Hardyng, *Chronicle* Bible printed at Mainz	Cherbourg lost
Before 1451	*Life of St. Augustine*		
c.1451	*Solace of Pilgrimes*		
1451	*Life of St. Gilbert* Revises *Tretis*		Gascony and Guienne lost Complaints in Norfolk against Sir Thomas Tuddenham
c.1452	*Manipulus doctrinae christianae* (lost)		
1453	Prior Provincial, Augustinian Order in England		English possessions in France reduced to Calais and the Channel Islands Constantinople falls to Turks
1454		Pecock, *Follower to the Donet*	Cardinal Kemp dies
1455	Re-elected Prior Provincial		Wars of the Roses begin
1456	Present in Oxford for the reception of Sir Edmund Rede	Shirley dies	
1457	Vacates position as Prior Provincial		
After 1457	*In Actus Apostolorum*		
c.1460	*In Apocalypsim Joannis* (lost)	Pecock dies Skelton and Dunbar born Wakefield plays MS written	Battles at Northampton and Wakefield

YEAR	CAPGRAVE'S LIFE	LITERARY EVENTS	POLITICAL EVENTS
1461		Ashby, *Poems*	Deposition of Henry VI Edward IV king
c.1462	*De Fidei symbolis*		Margaret of Anjou invades Northumberland Tuddenham executed
c.1462–3	*Abbreuiacion of Cronicles* completed		Margaret of Anjou goes to Flanders
1464	Dies at Lynn		Somerset rebels and is executed

INTRODUCTION

THE AUTHOR AND HIS WORKS[1]

NOTHING is known of John Capgrave's family.[2] *Capgrave* is probably a locality name from the place *Copgrove* in the West Riding of Yorkshire.[3] Except in this instance, the surname is not found in Norfolk (or Suffolk) in the Middle Ages.[4] In the *Abbreuiacion of Cronicles*, under the entry for the seventeenth year of Richard II, Capgrave wrote, *In þis ʒere, in þe xxi day of Aprile, was þat frere bore whech mad þese annotaciones* (203/12–13); thus, according to his own testimony, he was born on 21 April 1393. If his place of birth was not Lynn[5] he was almost certainly brought up there, as he refers to himself as a native of the town, *My cuntre is Northfolke, of þe town of Lynne*,[6] and in 1406 he witnessed the departure from Lynn of Princess Philippa, *quam ego oculis conspexi*,[7] on her voyage to marry King Eric IX of Denmark. Since 'candidates to the Order . . . could join only that monastery [i.e. friary] in whose district their parental home was located',[8] Capgrave presumably entered the Augustinian order in Lynn, probably c.1410, as six or seven years' training were required before ordination and Capgrave was ordained priest—*ad sacerdotium promotus sum*[9]—in 1416/17.

---

[1] This account owes much to de Meijer, summarized by Roth, but some new points are added.

[2] Unless he was the nephew of his namesake mentioned in an entry for 1390 in the Augustinian General Archives: see de Meijer, pp. 405–6.

[3] On which see A. H. Smith, *The Place-names of the West Riding of Yorkshire*, v. 90, English Place-Name Society, vol. xxxiv (Cambridge, 1961 for 1956–7).

[4] I owe this information to the kindness of Mr R. A. McKinley, whose *Norfolk and Suffolk Surnames in the Middle Ages* (London and Chichester, 1975) does not record the name *Capgrave*. It is also not recorded in his *Norfolk Surnames in the Sixteenth Century* (Leicester, 1969).

[5] Lynn was known as 'Bishop's Lynn' from 1201 (i.e. mostly within the control of the bishop of Norwich) and as 'King's Lynn' after the town was alienated to the Crown by Henry VIII. See F. Blomefield and C. Parkin, *An Essay towards a Topographical History of the County of Norfolk*, vols. i–xi (London, 1805–10), viii. 482. On the growth of the town see also V. Parker, *The Making of Kings Lynn* (London, 1971). [6] *Katharine*, p. 16, line 240.

[7] *De illustribus Henricis*, p. 109. See also *Abbreuiacion of Cronicles*, 229/30–230/4, and the notes to these lines in the Commentary.

[8] Roth, i. 47. [9] *De illustribus Henricis*, p. 127.

From 1417 to 1422 he studied theology at London, and on the completion of his course in 1422 he was made a lector in theology by the Provincial.[1] It was probably during this period, certainly before 1422, that he wrote his verse *Life of St. Norbert*, a free translation of the *Vita Sancti Norberti* formerly attributed to Hugh of Fosse, at the behest of the abbot of the Premonstratensian abbey at West Dereham, Norfolk.[2] In 1422 he was appointed by the Prior General to study at Cambridge,[3] where, in the same year, he delivered a sermon concerning the twelve orders who followed the Augustinian Rule. This sermon was later written up and revised as the *Tretis of the Orders þat be vndyr þe Reule of oure Fader Seynt Augustin*.[4] In 1423 Capgrave took a B.Th. (Cantab.), and he remained in Cambridge to take a D.Th. there in 1425, and probably to act as master-regent for a further two years. His progress from ordination to the *magisterium* was 'the fastest promotion on record'.[5] After 1427 and before 1437 there is no information about Capgrave, but, to judge from the large number of works, now lost, which are attributed to him by his biographers,[6] he was presumably engaged in literary activity. Certainly his lost commentaries *In Regum*, apparently dedicated to Humphrey duke of Gloucester (1 Sam. and 1 Kgs.) and his fellow Augustinian John Lowe, bishop of St. Asaph, were written before 1437 because Capgrave refers to them in the preface to his commentary *In Genesim*;[7] those presumably dedicated to Lowe must have been completed after 1433, when Lowe became bishop of St. Asaph.[8] Nearly all of these lost works were theological, so possibly Capgrave was also engaged in teaching the subjects upon which he wrote.

[1] de Meijer, p. 408.

[2] See my 'On the Date of . . . Capgrave's . . . *Norbert*', pp. 328–30.

[3] de Meijer, p. 409. On Cambridge University in the later Middle Ages see T. H. Aston, G. D. Duncan, T. A. R. Evans, 'The Medieval Alumni of the University of Cambridge', *Past and Present*, lxxxvi (1980), 9–86.

[4] Ed. Munro, pp. 145–8, quot. (from the *incipit*) on p. 145. Revisions include the reference at 147/26–7 to Capgrave's *Life of St. Gilbert* (1451) and the reference at 148/26–7 to the appropriation to Walsingham of Peterston, Norfolk, which took place in 1449.   [5] Roth, i. 174.

[6] As listed by de Meijer, p. 573, there were twenty-eight such works. Of these it is improbable that Capgrave ever wrote a *Vita Humphridi Ducis Gloucestriae*: see my 'Scribe and "Publisher" ', p. 15 and n. 5, also my 'Capgrave and the *Nova Legenda Anglie*', p. 8 and n. 6.

[7] de Meijer, p. 537, no. 9, note b.

[8] de Meijer, p. 538, no. 10, note a.

In 1437–8 Capgrave wrote his commentary *In Genesim*,[1] and on 1 January 1439 personally delivered the presentation copy to Humphrey duke of Gloucester at Woodstock.[2] Just over a fortnight later Capgrave began his commentary *In Exodum* which he completed the following year[3] and which is also dedicated to Duke Humphrey. Later in 1440 he completed his *Life of St. Norbert* (before 1422) by the addition of a two-verse envoy dating the completion of the work to the week of 15 August and dedicating it to John Wygenhale, the then incumbent abbot of the Premonstratensian abbey at West Dereham,[4] a village some fifteen miles from Lynn. Capgrave was probably at Lynn at the time. On 2 April 1441 he was present at the laying of the foundation stone of King's College, Cambridge.[5] His *Concordia*, or *De Augustino et suis Sequacibus*, dedicated to John Watford, abbot of the Canons Regular at St. James's abbey, Northampton, has not survived, but was presumably written at least as early as *c*.1442, since Watford died in 1445.[6] It was *mad to reforme charite betwix Seynt Augustines heremites and his chanones*[7] and Capgrave's concern for *vnyte* among *religious men* has been well remarked by Smetana.[8] By 1445 Capgrave had also written his verse *Life of St. Katharine*, for it is mentioned as *newly compylyd* by Osbern Bokenham in the prologue to his own life of St. Katharine (in his *Legendys of Hooly Wummen*)[9] written soon after 1445, the date of the preceding legend.

In 1446 Capgrave was presumably resident in Lynn as he was there on 1 August for the visit of King Henry VI to the Augustinian friary, of which, since he acted as host, Capgrave was presumably prior. Since it describes that event, his *De illustribus Henricis*, dedicated to Henry VI, must have been completed after the king's

[1] According to the colophon, quoted in my 'Scribe and "Publisher" ', p. 4, note 6, the work was begun 11 October 1437 and completed 21 September 1438.

[2] As recorded in the note added to the manuscript on f. 187ᵛ by Duke Humphrey, printed by de Meijer, p. 532, note b.

[3] According to the colophon, quoted in my 'Scribe and "Publisher" ', p. 4, note 4, the work was begun 17 January 1439 and completed 6 May 1440.

[4] See my 'On the Date of . . . Capgrave's . . . Norbert', pp. 328–30.

[5] *De illustribus Henricis*, p. 133.

[6] de Meijer, pp. 547–8, no. 26.

[7] *Tretis*, 146/6–7.

[8] *Norbert*, note to line 65. So also Pearsall, 'Capgrave's *Life of St Katharine*', *M&H*, NS, vi (1975), p. 122 and n. 21.

[9] Ed. M. Serjeantson, EETS 206 (1938), p. 173, lines 6354–60, quot. from line 6356, cited by de Meijer, p 564, no. 42, note a. See also line 4982.

visit to Lynn,[1] but, since it mentions Humphrey duke of Gloucester as being still alive,[2] it was probably finished before his death in February 1447. Capgrave would almost certainly have been still based at Lynn when Sir Thomas Tuddenham, lord of the manor of Oxburgh (under twenty miles from Lynn), financed his visit to Rome,[3] probably for the celebration of the Holy Year in 1450.[4] Following this visit to Rome Capgrave wrote *The Solace of Pilgrimes*, a description of the city. His *Life of St. Augustine*, a free translation of the *Vita Sancti Augustini* of Jordan of Saxony, must have been written earlier than 1451, as it is referred to in his *Life of St. Gilbert*[5] (1451). Both the *Life of St. Gilbert*, a translation of the *Vita Sancti Gilberti Confessoris* of Roger of Sempringham, and the *Tretis of tho Orderes þat be vndyr þe Reule of oure Fader Seynt Augustin* (written up and revised in 1451 from the sermon of 1422) were dedicated to Nicholas Reysby, master-general of the Order of Sempringham, a village about forty miles west of Lynn. About 1452 Capgrave wrote his *Manipulus Doctrinae Christianae*, now lost, dedicated to Cardinal John Kempe, archbishop of Canterbury (1452–4).

On 22 July 1453, at the chapter in Winchester, Capgrave was elected Prior Provincial of the Augustinian Order in England, and on 6 August 1455 he was re-elected at Lynn for a further two years.[6] On 21 April 1456 he was present in Oxford for the reception of Sir Edmund Rede of Borstall, and the recognition of his rights.[7] After vacating his position as Prior Provincial in 1457—*a sollicitudine officii mei penitus absolutus*[8]—Capgrave wrote his commentary *In Actus Apostolorum* and dedicated it gratefully to William Gray, bishop of Ely, who, when King's Proctor, had visited Capgrave during an illness in Rome *c*.1450. Capgrave's lost commentary *In Apocalypsim Joannis* (*c*.1460) may also have

[1] *De illustribus Henricis*, pp. 137–8. See also my 'Scribe and "Publisher" ', pp. 12–16.   [2] *De illustribus Henricis*, p. 109, cited by de Meijer, p. 417.
[3] 'vndyr whos proteccioun my pylgrimage was specialy sped', *Solace*, p. 1. Tuddenham, a powerful figure in Norfolk and a noted extortionist, was also Keeper of the Great Wardrobe in the royal household from 1446 to 1450.
[4] The Jubilee of 1450 was a very famous one. See H. Thurston, SJ, *The Holy Year of Jubilee* (London, 1900), pp. 65–72. Fredeman, 'Life', pp. 231–2, suggests that Capgrave went to Rome in 1449.
[5] Ed. Munro, pp. 61 and 142.   [6] de Meijer, pp. 400–1.
[7] W. Kennet, *Parochial Antiquities*, ed. B. Bandinel (Oxford, 1818), ii. 401.
[8] Quoted from the Dedicatory Preface to *In Actus Apostolorum*, printed by Hingeston, *De illustribus Henricis*, p. 221.

been dedicated to Bishop Gray. A little later, probably *c.* 1462, Capgrave wrote his book about the creeds, *De fidei symbolis*; it too was dedicated to Bishop Gray. In the Dedicatory Preface, quoting Job 17: 1, he speaks of approaching death, *Spiritus meus attenuatur dies breuiantur et solum mihi superest sepulcrum.*[1]

The *Abbreuiacion of Cronicles* was probably an earlier work,[2] completed *c.*1462–3. On the accession of King Edward IV in 1461 it was decided to prepare a copy of it for the new king and the Dedicatory Preface was added. In it Capgrave refers to himself as *a pore frere of þe Heremites of Seynt Austyn in þe conuent of Lenne* (7/2–3), where, on 12 August 1464, he died.[3]

The *Ordo fratrum eremitarum Sancti Augustini*, now known as the Order of St. Augustine, to which Capgrave belonged, was founded by papal decree in 1256 as an amalgamation of separate communities already following the rule of St. Augustine.[4] They were known as Hermits to distinguish them from Augustinian Canons.[5] Before the formal ratification of the Order their predecessors had already come to England where they got *leue for to edifie couentis in . . . Clare and Wodous* (119/27–30), that at Clare, Suffolk, being established under the patronage of Richard de Clare, duke of Gloucester, in 1248 and that at Woodhouse, Salop, in 1250. By the end of the thirteenth century there were twenty-two houses and by the end of the fifteenth century thirty-nine. Most of these English houses were in the Midlands or eastern part of the country and they were organized within limits, Cambridge, Oxford, Lincoln, and York. Capgrave's house at Lynn was in the limit of Cambridge, hence the fact that he went to Cambridge rather than Oxford.

The Augustinian friars had a reputation for education and learning. Most houses in England had their own *studium grammaticale*, and it may be assumed that Capgrave studied in the one at Lynn. Next a candidate for the Order went to a *studium*

---

[1] Printed by Hingeston, *De illustribus Henricis*, p. 213.

[2] See below, p. xliii.

[3] J. Leland, *Commentarii de scriptoribus britannicis*, ed. A. Hall (Oxford, 1709), ii. 454.

[4] On the history of the order in England see A. Gwynn, SJ, *The English Austin Friars in the Time of Wyclif* (London, 1940), and Roth, vol. i 'History', vol. ii 'Sources'.

[5] On whom see J. C. Dickinson, *The Origins of the Austin Canons and their Introduction into England* (London, 1950).

particulare of which there was one in each limit, that in the limit of Cambridge being at Norwich; possibly Capgrave went there.[1] Before going on to university Capgrave studied at the *studium generale* at London, though later there was such a *studium* at Lynn. In the later Middle Ages the mendicant friars were 'the principal exponents of dogmatic, moral and biblical theology'[2] and a number of Augustinian friars were well known as scholars and literary men. Among them Capgrave was pre-eminent. His literary output was phenomenal. He was a kind of latter-day Church Father, writing commentaries on most of the Old Testament (Genesis, Exodus, Leviticus, Numbers, Deuteronomy, Joshua, Judges, Ruth, 1 and 2 Samuel, 1 and 2 Kings, Psalms, Ecclesiastes, Isaiah, Daniel, the Twelve Prophets) and the whole of the New Testament (the Gospel, Acts, the Letters of Paul, the other Letters, Revelations) as well as other theological works, a chronicle, two works *de viris illustribus* (*Henricis* and *Augustinianis*), saints' lives, and a guide to the antiquities of Rome. This collection of works is very similar in scope to those produced by some of the early Church Fathers, such as St. Jerome. Capgrave was indeed, as he says himself, *a man sumwhat endewid in lettirure*.[3] Playing on his name he refers to himself as 'Johannes de Monumento Pileato'[4] —a *pileus* was a round cap worn by scholars.

Because Capgrave wrote at the end of an era his works could never have been widely read and many of the Latin ones have been lost. Apart from the surviving manuscripts our knowledge of them is largely due to the work of the sixteenth-century antiquaries John Leland and John Bale.[5] Most of the twelve surviving works are preserved in a small number of manuscripts closely associated

---

[1] So Fredeman, 'Life', p. 209. Cf. Commentary, note to 238/25-6.

[2] Roth, i. 176.   [3] *Augustine*, 1/9.

[4] Preface to *De Fidei Symbolis*, printed by Hingeston, *De illustribus Henricis*, p. 213.

[5] J. Leland (d. 1552), *Commentarii de scriptoribus britannicis*, ed. A. Hall (Oxford, 1709), ii. 453–4, repr. de Meijer, p. 119. J. Bale (d. 1563), *Illustrium Maioris Brytanniae Scriptorum summarium* (Wesel/Ipswich, 1548), fols. 201ᵛ–202ʳ (*STC* 1295/6); *Scriptorum illustrium Maioris Brytanniae catalogus* (Basle, 1557), pp. 582–3; *Index Britanniae scriptorum*, ed. R. L. Poole and M. Bateson (Oxford, 1902), pp. 188–9; all three repr. de Meijer, pp. 121–4. On Leland see T. D. Kendrick, *British Antiquity* (London, 1950), ch. iv. On Bale see W. T. Davies, 'A Bibliography of John Bale', *Oxford Bibliographical Society Proceedings*, v (1936–9), 201–79. Bale and (to a lesser extent) Leland are not always entirely reliable: see, for example, my 'Capgrave and the *Nova legenda Anglie*', pp. 1–10, esp. p. 8.

with Capgrave himself.[1] Seven works, (1) *Norbert*, (2) *In Genesim*,
(3) *In Exodum*, (6) *Augustine*, (7) *Solace*, (9) *Tretis*, (10) *In Actus
Apostolorum*, each survive in only a single manuscript written
or revised by the author, four of these, (1), (2), (3), and (10)
being presentation copies and another, (7), possibly so.[2] Three
works, (5) *De illustribus Henricis*, (8) *Gilbert*, and the *Abbreuiacion
of Cronicles*, survive in just two manuscripts each, one written
by the author and one copied by another scribe; in the case of the
Abbreuiacion of Cronicles the manuscript written by the author
was probably intended as a presentation copy. Another work,
(11) *De Fidei Symbolis*, also survives in just two manuscripts,
both revised by the author and one of which was a presentation
copy. The one remaining work, (4) *Katharine*, differs from the
others in that it survives in more manuscripts (four) than any of
the others and in that none of these manuscripts has any direct
association with Capgrave himself. All of them, however, were
probably written in East Anglia.

Most of Capgrave's works seem to have been written at the
behest of a particular individual or are addressed to a specific
dedicatee. The *Augustine* was written *to þe plesauns and consola-
tion of* a certain *gentil woman þat hath so willed me with sundry
[r]etribucione[s] þat I coude not disobeye hir desire.*[3] Having seen
this work, Nicholas Reysby, master-general of the Gilbertine
Order of Sempringham, commissioned Capgrave's *Gilbert* (also
the *Tretis*) so that, in the author's words to Reysby, it could be
made available to *the solitarye women of ȝour religioun whech
unneth can vndyrstande Latyn, þat þei may . . . red . . . þe grete
vertues of her maystyr.*[4] By dedicating the work to the head of a
religious order Capgrave apparently hoped that it would at least

---

[1] These works are listed below in the Bibliography, pp. xcix–cvii, esp. xcix–cii, where they are provided with the numerical designations used here.

[2] A fragment of (7) *Solace* also survives bound in as end-leaves in two other manuscripts. See Bibliography, part III, below, and my 'Fifteenth-century Copyist at Work', pp. 66–95. As the copy was evidently abandoned half-way through the third quire it cannot be classified as a separate manuscript of the whole work.   [3] 1/24–6. See also 1/15–16 and *Gilbert*, 61/7.

[4] Since the presentation copy of the *Gilbert* and *Tretis* in the author's handwriting is bound up with the *Augustine*, also in Capgrave's handwriting, in a fifteenth-century binding (British Library, Add. MS 36704) *þis gentil woman* for whom the *Augustine* was written may have had some connection with the double monastery at Sempringham. Cf. Fredeman, 'Capgrave's "Augustine" ', pp. 288–9, n. 1.

come to the attention of the other members of the house. This implication is spelt out more clearly in the prologue to the *Norbert*, which was written *So I plese him þat ʒaue me comaundment | To make þis werk* (14–15), i.e. the abbot of the Premonstratensian abbey at West Dereham:[1]

> And if ʒe list þat þis book present
> May be receyued in ʒoure fraternyte,
> Onto ʒoure name dedicate þan schal it be. (61–3)

Capgrave's *Concordia* was also dedicated to the head of a religious house, John Watford, abbot of the Canons Regular at St. James's Abbey, Northampton. Although this work has not survived, since it was *mad to reforme charite betwix Seynt Augustines heremites and his chanones*[2] it was presumably intended at least for the attention of all the Canons Regular at Northampton.

Besides heads of religious houses Capgrave also dedicated works to bishops. His lost commentaries *In Regum II* and *IV* were for John Lowe, OSA, bishop of St. Asaph.[3] Immediately before his selection for the episcopacy Lowe had been Prior Provincial of the Augustinian Order in England (1427–33) and Capgrave must have known him before that in London as Lowe came to the Augustinian house there in 1420 and Capgrave did not leave it until 1422. Capgrave probably also knew John Kempe, cardinal archbishop of Canterbury, to whom he dedicated his lost *Manipulus Doctrinae Christianae* (c.1452), in London when he was bishop there from 1421 onwards. Capgrave certainly knew William Gray, bishop of Ely, to whom he dedicated his commentaries *In Actus Apostolorum* and (possibly) *In Apocalypsim Joannis* (lost) and his work on the creeds, *De Fidei Symbolis*, because when he was ill in Rome (c.1450) Gray visited him there.[4] Capgrave's purpose in dedicating his commentary *In Actus Apostolorum* to Gray was *ut sic liber, a dominatione vestra praecedens, asterisco vel obelo consignatus, securius ad alios descendat, tanta auctoritate vallatus*.[5] He seems to have seen the dedicatee as conferring on the book a kind of glorified *imprimatur* which would

---

[1] Pearsall, 'Capgrave's *Life of St. Katharine*', *M&H*, NS, vi (1975), p. 136, n. 68, notes that the 'circumstances of the commission are . . . very similar to those of Lydgate's *Life of St. Albon* (1439)'.

[2] *Tretis*, 146/6–7.   [3] On whom see Roth, i. 104–8.

[4] See above, p. xxii.

[5] Printed by Hingeston, *De illustribus Henricis*, p. 222.

secure a wider audience for it. This consideration may be the reason why the second copy of the *De Fidei Symbolis* (All Souls MS XVII), which was prepared in Capgrave's scriptorium under his supervision but was not the presentation copy for Bishop Gray, also contained the Dedicatory Preface addressed to Gray.

The other dedicatees of Capgrave's works were aristocrats, with one exception the highest ranking in the land. The exception was Sir Thomas Tuddenham for whom Capgrave may have written his *Solace* as a kind of thanks-offering for Tuddenham's sponsorship of his visit to Rome. However, Capgrave seems to have had a wider audience than just Tuddenham in mind as the work is addressed *Onto all men of my nacioun þat schal rede þis present book and namely onto my special maystir Sir Thomas Tudenham vndyr whos proteccioun my pylgrimage was specialy sped. . . .*[1] Capgrave presumably wrote his *De illustribus Henricis* with King Henry VI in mind and after the king's visit to Lynn added a new chapter about the king and prepared the work to be copied.[2] The *Abbreuiacion of Cronicles* was also dedicated to a king, Edward IV, but when Capgrave says in the Dedicatory Preface *These reules had in mynde þe reder schal more parfitely vndirstand þis book* (8/6–7), he seems to have had in mind a more general readership besides the king. Three of the five works dedicated to Humphrey duke of Gloucester are lost, the commentaries *In Regum I* and *III* and *Super Epistolas Pauli*. Of the other two, the commentaries *In Genesim* and *In Exodum*, the Dedicatory Preface to the former yields interesting information about the process of dedication and 'publication'. Although Duke Humphrey had already seen Capgrave's commentaries *In Regum I* and *III* the author states that he knew the duke only by report and is sending the new one on Genesis to him because 'studiosissime *ut fertur* in scrutandis veterum auctorum opusculis indulgetis' and because 'ad eam [sacram scripturam] specialissime inuisendam spiritus ille supremi patris nos *ut audiui* inspirauit'.[3] Notwithstanding this lack of personal contact Capgrave says, 'Meditationes meas . . . *aliis* . . . *communicare cupiens* nulli . . . mellius destinandas putabam . . . quam Dominationi vestrae'.[4] When on

---

[1] *Solace*, p. 1.　　　　　　[2] See my 'Scribe and "Publisher" ', pp. 12–16.

[3] Printed by Hingeston, *De illustribus Henricis*, p. 229, italics mine; see also my 'Scribe and "Publisher" ', p. 31. For the passage referring to Capgrave's earlier commentaries *In Regum* see Hingeston, op. cit., p. 231.

[4] Printed by Hingeston, op. cit., p. 229, italics mine.

1 January 1439 Capgrave personally delivered the presentation copy to Duke Humphrey the author must have been encouraged, since a fortnight later he began his commentary *In Exodum*, also dedicated to the duke. Whether Capgrave was justified in feeling encouraged is another matter. Despite a promise in the Preface to *In Genesim* to go on to the rest of the Pentateuch he apparently stopped dedicating works to Duke Humphrey after his *In Exodum*.[1] Although Duke Humphrey was a famous book collector, Capgrave's commentaries were not typical of the books that really interested him.[2]

From this survey of Capgrave's dedications it is possible to discern a fairly clear over-all picture. He wrote the lives of saints who inspired the foundation of, or themselves founded, religious orders, and other works concerned with religious orders, for the heads of religious houses to be read by the inmates of those houses. His *Katharine*, in the Prologue to which no specific dedicatee is mentioned, may have been similarly directed, without the restriction of any one particular order, though Capgrave apparently envisaged that *It schall be know of man, mayde and of wyffe*,[3] and Pearsall has shown that in it Capgrave 'availed himself to some extent of the traditional style of romance'.[4] It would appear from the surviving manuscripts that it was read in nunneries; one manuscript, Arundel 396, was at the Augustinian nunnery of Campsey, Suffolk,[5] and another, Arundel 168, 'presumably also belonged, judging from its contents (lives of St. Christina and St. Dorothea, Lydgate's *Life of Our Lady*, etc.), to a nunnery'.[6] Works written for the religious orders had a ready-made, if limited, audience. For his commentaries and some other theological works Capgrave tried to reach a wider audience by dedicating these works to bishops and Duke Humphrey. He began with his

[1] See Lucas and Dalton, 'Capgrave's Preface Dedicating . . . *In Exodum* to Humfrey . . .', pp. 24–5.

[2] See, for example, *Duke Humfrey and English Humanism in the Fifteenth Century, Catalogue of an Exhibition held in the Bodleian Library* (Oxford, 1970). Cf. Fredeman, 'Life', pp. 224–5.

[3] *Katharine*, Prologue 66. In line 46 Capgrave says it was to be known *of woman and of man*. A large audience seems to be envisaged in lines 247–8.

[4] 'Capgrave's *Life of St. Katharine*', *M&H*, NS, vi (1975), 121–37, quot. on p. 130.

[5] N. R. Ker, *Medieval Libraries of Great Britain* (London, 1964 edn.), p. 28, also *Katharine*, pp. xxix–xxx.

[6] Pearsall, art. cit., p. 137, n. 76.

fellow Augustinian John Lowe, then dedicated five commentaries
to Duke Humphrey (d. 1447), one work to Cardinal Kempe
(d. 1454), and finally two, possibly three, works to Bishop Gray.
The bishops Capgrave probably knew before he dedicated works to
them, but at least two works were dedicated to Duke Humphrey
before the two men met. Similarly with the biographical and
historical works Capgrave dedicated to kings. The *De illustribus
Henricis* must have been largely composed before Henry VI's
visit to Lynn, and although the *Abbreuiacion of Cronicles* was
dedicated to Edward IV, author and king probably never met.
Evidently Capgrave remained throughout his career to a large
extent an author in search of a public.

THE MANUSCRIPTS

'Few [medieval chronicles] were written with an outside audience
in mind' or, if they were, few had a wide appeal. 'The majority
of chronicles survive now only in one or two manuscripts.'[1] Capgrave's *Abbreuiacion of Cronicles* is no exception, being preserved
in two manuscripts, designated M and P, both of which, apart
from minor later additions, contain only this text, P lacking the
Dedicatory Preface.

M: Cambridge, University Library, MS Gg. 4. 12.[2]

(1) *History.* The manuscript was completed, presumably in
Lynn, now King's Lynn, Norfolk, c.1462–3, after the accession
to the throne of Edward IV (to whom the work is dedicated)
on 4 March 1461, and before the author's death on 12 August
1464. Its history between this period and the end of the seventeenth century is unknown, but before 1697 it was in the library
of John Moore (1646–1714), bishop successively of Norwich
(1691–1707) and Ely (1707–14).[3] We know this because in his
Catalogus of 1697 (II. i. 362) Bernard, who was the first to refer
to the manuscript, lists it as no. 40 in Moore's collection; the
number '40' is written twice on fol. 1r. Where Moore got the
manuscript from is not known.[4] After Moore's death in 1714

---

[1] Quotations from J. Taylor, *The Use of Medieval Chronicles*, Historical
Association Helps for Students of History 70 (London, 1965), p. 5.

[2] For a brief description see *A Catalogue of Manuscripts in the Library of
the University of Cambridge*, iii (Cambridge, 1858), p. 152, no. 1511.

[3] On whom see *DNB*, s.n. Moore, John (1646–1714).

[4] Possibly this might be discovered when Moore's diaries, letters, and
private accounts are edited for publication.

the whole of his library was bought by George I (whose arms, originally attached to fol. 1ʳ, now appear on the front flyleaf) and in 1715 was given by him to Cambridge University,[1] where it has remained, in the University Library, ever since.

(2) *Binding*. In 1977 the manuscript was provided with a new binding of cardboard covered with paper, with a leather-reinforced spine and new paper flyleaves. It formerly had a binding of cardboard covered with pigskin (dating from *c*.1800) with three paper flyleaves at both front and back. The gold-tooled inscription from this binding is preserved on the inside back cover of the 1977 binding. From the fact that the outsides of the original end-leaves (fols. 1ʳ and 106ᵛ) are rubbed it would appear that the manuscript was not previously (before *c*.1800) bound between covers.

(3) *Material*. The manuscript is parchment throughout except for the paper flyleaves. The dimensions of each leaf are: outer edge approx. 306 × 217 mm.; written area approx. 221 × 145 mm., each column of text being 65 mm. wide.

(4) *Foliation*: [i]+106+[i]. There are 106 parchment leaves now numbered 1–106. Prior to 1977, when the manuscript was re-bound, a leaf was omitted from the numbering between fols. 79 and 80. In works published before 1977[2] this unnumbered leaf was referred to as fol. 79*bis*; it is now fol. 80 and the following folios (81–106) all carry a number one higher than before 1977. The pre-1977 numbers were erased when the new numbers were added. Fols. 101–6 (100–5 prior to 1977) had previously been numbered 20–5 but these numbers were subsequently crossed out or altered; in 1977 they too were erased. The roman numbers in square brackets refer to the paper flyleaves, one at the beginning and one at the end, added when the manuscript was re-bound. The manuscript has also been paginated in black ink at the top outer corner of the text area on each page. These page numbers may be by the hand which wrote '40' on fol. 1ʳ; certainly the style of writing the numbers and the colour of the ink do not accord with that of the text. The pagination does not include the Dedicatory Preface and therefore begins on fol. 3ʳ. On pages 9

[1] See J. C. T. Oates, *A Catalogue of the Fifteenth-century Printed Books in the University Library Cambridge* (Cambridge, 1954), pp. 14–16.

[2] e.g., my 'Scribe and "Publisher" ' (1969), and my 'Sense-Units and the Use of Punctuation-Markers' (1971).

(fol. 7^r), 11 (fol. 8^r), and 13 (fol. 9^r) the number is written twice, (*a*) normally, at the top outer corner of the text area, and (*b*) again, above and to the right of the column of dates at the left of the right-hand column. Pages 88–93 (fols. 46^v–49^r) have had their numbers altered from 89–94, in a darker ink. Pages 134–40 (fols. 69^v–72^v) were previously numbered 133–9; fol. 69^r is wrongly numbered '132' and not corrected. The pagination ends at p. 204 (fol. 104^v).

(5) *Collation*. There are fourteen quires, all regular quires of eight except the first, which contains the Dedicatory Preface, as follows:

1^{1+1},	fols. 1–2	8^8,	fols. 51–8
2^8,	fols. 3–10	9^8,	fols. 59–66
3^8,	fols. 11–18	10^8,	fols. 67–74
4^8,	fols. 19–26	11^8,	fols. 75–82
5^8,	fols. 27–34	12^8,	fols. 83–90
6^8,	fols. 35–42	13^8,	fols. 91–8
7^8,	fols. 43–50	14^8,	fols. 99–106

(6) *Catchwords and signatures*. Unfortunately the leaves were cropped by the binder (of *c*.1800) and only two catchwords and four signatures have survived (or partially survived) the binder's guillotine. Catchwords occur in the bottom right-hand corner of the verso page at the end of Quires 2, 'An 1328' (fol. 10^v) and 4, '3965' (fol. 26^v, slightly cut away at the bottom); the relevant part of fol. 34, the last leaf of Quire 5, has been eaten away. Signatures occur in the bottom right-hand corner of the recto page as follows: '+iii' (clear under ultra-violet light) on fol. 5^r in Quire 2; 'k' (clear under ultra-violet light) on fols. 83^r, 84^r, 85^r, 86^r in Quire 12—on fol. 85^r the 'k' is followed by the tops of three minims and the original reading was evidently 'k iii'.

(7) *Pricking*. Many prick-marks have not survived the binder's guillotine. Some of those that have survived occur at the bottom and top of pages; in Quire 3 (fols. 11–18) there are prick-marks at both top and bottom, the only quire of which this is so, whereas in Quire 9 (fols. 59–66) there are no surviving prick-marks at all. These prick-marks occur as follows:

Quire 1: fols. 1–2, bottom only
Quire 2: fols. 3–10, bottom only
Quire 3: fols. 11–18, top and bottom

Quire 4:   fols. 19–26, top only
Quire 5:   fols. 27–34, top only
Quire 6:   fols. 35–42, top only
Quire 7:   fols. 43–4 (leaves 1–2) top only, 47–8 (leaves 5–6)
           and 50 (leaf 8) bottom only
Quire 8:   fols. 51–7 (leaves 1–7), top only
Quire 10: fols. 67–74, top only
Quire 11: fols. 75–82, top only
Quire 13: fol. 96 (leaf 6), bottom only
Quire 14: fols. 100 and 102–5 (leaves 2 and 4–7) top only,
           fol. 101 (leaf 3) bottom only.

The prick-marks correspond to the four vertical rules of the frame
of the written area, never to the additional vertical rules used for
guidance in writing the dates. Besides these prick-marks which
correspond to the vertical rules there are also, at the top of some
pages, outer edge only, two prick-marks which correspond to the
two principal horizontal rules, one for the heading, one to mark
the top of the written area. These prick-marks occur as follows:

Quire 4:   fols. 21–3 (leaves 3–5)
Quire 5:   fols. 27–34
Quire 6:   fols. 35–42
Quire 12: fols. 83–90
Quire 14: fols. 100–5 (leaves 2–7).

From the facts that the prick-marks corresponding to the horizontal rules occur only at the outer edge and that all prick-marks seem
to have been inserted downwards (i.e. from recto to verso) it is
evident that the pricking was done by the quire, with the sheets
folded. This finding is confirmed by the fact that in contrast
with the surrounding leaves all the leaves in Quire 12 retain the
prick-marks corresponding to the horizontal rules. In Quire 14
there are no prick-marks on the outer sheet and on the three
inner sheets the position of the prick-marks corresponding to the
horizontal rules becomes progressively further from the outer
edge as the centre of the quire is approached; similarly in Quire
4 only the central leaves retain these prick-marks. Evidently,
when the pricking was done the inner leaves were not pulled in as
tightly as they were later to be by the binders.

(8) *Ruling*. The ruling is done with crayon, occasionally so

heavily that, on fol. 95 for example, there is a clear groove and ridge effect. There is a frame ruling with two columns to a page (*a* and *b*), and an extra line across the top of each recto page for headings. Normally each page has forty-two lines divided into seven sections. These sections are marked by every sixth line being ruled especially heavily or by a slightly elliptical horizontal stroke immediately outside the outer vertical rule. Exceptions to this pattern are as follows: fol. 24^r has forty-three lines (an extra line ruled in the second section); fol. 33^r has forty-three lines (an extra line ruled in the second section), though in column *a* the text has one line less than the ruling, so that two irregularities cancel each other out; fol. 80^r has forty-three lines in column *a* (an extra line ruled in the second section where one rule was attempted twice); fols. 80^v, 81^{rv}, 82^{rv}, and 85^r have forty-three lines (an extra line ruled at the bottom of the page). Occasionally the text does not conform to the ruling: fol. 18^v col. *b* has forty-one lines (five lines of text in the sixth section); fol. 34^v col. *a* has forty-one lines (five lines of text in the fifth section); fol. 85^r col. *a* has forty-four lines (seven lines of text in the second section in addition to the extra ruled line at the bottom of the page). Normally there are four vertical rules, but on fols. 3–36^r there is an additional vertical rule in each column as a guide for the Anno Mundi year numbers; fol. 17^r col. *b* has a further additional rule as a guide for the names of a pedigree. Fols. 36^v–58^v have two additional vertical rules to each column as a guide for the Anno Mundi followed by the Anno Domini year numbers. After fol. 58 an additional vertical line is ruled as required, though sometimes no rule for guidance in writing the Anno Domini year numbers is to be seen. The fact that the ruling on fols. 36^r and 58^v follows the pattern on fols. 35^v and 58^r, respectively, even though the circumstances dictating the ruling requirements change on fols. 35^v (Anno Domini year numbers begin) and 58^r (year numbers cease, allowing text to occupy the full width of the columns) suggests that the scribe ruled one or two pages ahead at a time. Accordingly, although the text finished on fol. 104^v, fol. 105^r is ruled as the preceding part of the quire but contains no text.

(9) *Handwriting*. The text is almost certainly written in Capgrave's own hand and there are also corrections by him.[1]

---

[1] See my 'Scribe and "Publisher" ', pp. 1–35. According to E. Colledge, 'The Capgrave "Autographs" ', *TCBS*, VI. iii (1974), 137–48, only the textual

The Dedicatory Preface ends with Capgrave's personal mark, a triquetra, with characteristic 'pendant', and is signed 'ʒoure seruaunt Capgrave': see Plate III. It is therefore autograph. There are also thirteen instances of the triquetra placed in the margin to draw attention to the subject-matter of the text it stands alongside.[1] The manuscript is written in a Fere Textura script, a modification of Capgrave's more cursive style of handwriting (on which the predominant influence is Secretary script) on the model of Textura, but it lacks the regularity and calligraphy associated with Textura.[2]

(10) *Rubrication.* The rubrication was evidently done by the scribe, Capgrave himself. Headings in red ink, such as 'Secunda etas' in the text on fol. 16[r], and 'Etas vi' in the text on fol. 35[r] (Plate V), are in the same hand as the text. The rubricator/scribe has also written 'Fy' in the margin on fol. 95[r] beside the entry describing how, after Glendower's defeat of Mortimer (p. 219 below), the Welsh women cut off the dead men's penises and put them in the dead men's mouths. There are also some corrections in red ink (see textual notes). On two occasions guide corrections were inserted suprascript in red ink and later erased when the final correction was written in brown ink on the line where the original word had been erased: see textual notes to 41/8 and 42/5. Most of the rubrication is punctuation—full and lesser paragraph marks, oblique strokes, shading, and points—

corrections are by Capgrave, the main body of the text being by another scribe whose handwriting is 'similar [to Capgrave's] to the point of identity' (p. 146). While it is theoretically possible that two men with indistinguishable handwriting wrote in the same manuscript, in practical terms it is highly improbable; the modern 'analogy' cited by Colledge involves slavish calligraphic imitation for its own sake and the two hands do not occur in the same document. Most of the examples Colledge cites from the Capgrave manuscripts are from San Marino, California, Henry E. Huntington Library, MS HM 55, containing Capgrave's 'Life of St. Norbert', but C. Smetana, co-author with Colledge of another article on Capgrave's *Norbert* [*MS* xxxiv (1972), 422–34], thinks these corrections are in the main hand and that Capgrave was responsible for both text and corrections: see his *The Life of St. Norbert by John Capgrave, O.E.S.A. (1393–1464)* (Toronto, 1977), esp. pp. 4–7, and my review in *MÆ* xlviii (1979), 316–19, esp. p. 316.

[1] For the instance beside the statement of Capgrave's birth see Plate I. For a discussion of this mark and an analysis of its uses see my 'Scribe and "Publisher" ', pp. 10–11, 19–23, and 27–35. I referred to it there as a 'trefoil' but more properly it is a triquetra.

[2] See further my 'Scribe and "Publisher" ', pp. 5–7.

the primary effect of which is to indicate the structure and meaning of the text.[1]

(11) *Illumination.* The only illumination is the first letter of the text, at the beginning of the Dedicatory Preface on fol. 1^v (Plate II). It is a capital T in gold leaf, infilled with blue and within a magenta square which is 42 mm. sq. and extends through six lines of text as well as protruding about 12 mm. above the top line of text. From the square a vine-stem in the form of a double bar in gold leaf and blue extends down the left-hand margin. Attached to the square and to the stem are sprays and branchlets with spoon-shaped leaves and (?)lotus flowers. The effect is to provide a border to the top and left-hand side of the page.

(12) *Contents*: John Capgrave, 'Abbreuiacion of Cronicles', including the Dedicatory Preface to Edward IV. The text finishes on fol. 104^v in col. *a* at line 17 and rubrication is lacking on this page. Fol. 105^r is headed in readiness for more text but does not contain any. Throughout the text there are annotations added probably in the sixteenth century. On fols. 105–6 there are a number of verses and proverbs, the first 'In papam Calixtum', beginning 'O bone Calixti nunc omnis clerus odit te . . .', also extracts from the prophecies of St. Bridget and others, and some lines in French. On fol. 106^v some verses in English occur, 'If love be not O Lord what fele I so . . .' (Chaucer, *Troilus and Criseyde*, i. 400 ff., the beginning of the 'Canticus Troili'; Brown–Robbins, *Index Supplement*, 1422.1), the unique text of 'Whan fishes in the water leve their swymmyng . . .' (Brown–Robbins, *Index*, 3946, printed by Person, *Cambridge ME Lyrics*, no. 50), and the unique text of 'Hiegh towers by strong wyndes full' lowe be cast . . .' (Brown–Robbins, *Index*, 1218, printed by Person, *Cambridge ME Lyrics*, no. 60). On fol. 105^v there are also some names, John Welshe and John Campynett (or Campynell'), but so far these men have eluded identification.[2] The removal of George I's arms from fol. 1^r in 1977 revealed the name 'FytzWylliam'.

---

[1] See my 'Sense-Units and the Use of Punctuation-Markers', pp. 1–24, also my 'Scribe and "Publisher" ', p. 8.

[2] Cf. the name 'William Campinet of Kilworty (?) Yorks' recorded in the margin of a manuscript of the Brut Chronicle in the John Rylands Library, Manchester: M. Tyson, 'Hand-List of the Collection of English Manuscripts in The John Rylands Library, 1928', *BJRL* xiii (1929), 152–219, esp. p. 185, no. 206.

(13) *Page Headings*. After the Dedicatory Preface each recto page is headed as follows:

fols. 3–8:	col. a 'Mill' I', col. b 'Etas I'
fols. 9–15:	col. a 'Mill' II', col. b 'Etas I'
fols. 16–22:	col. a 'Mill' III', col. b 'Etas II'
fols. 23–6:	col. a 'Mill' III', col. b 'Etas III'
fol. 27:	col. a 'Mill' IIII', col. b 'Etas III'
fols. 28–31:	col. a 'Mill' IIII', col. b 'Etas IIII'
fols. 32–4:	col. a 'Mill' IIII', col. b 'Etas V'
fols. 35–48:	col. a 'Mill' V',[1] col. b 'Etas VI'
fols. 49–60:	col. a 'Mill' VI', col. b 'Etas VI'
fol. 61:	col. a 'Mill' VI', col. b 'Etas VI Henricus 3'
fols. 62–4:	col. a 'Mill' VI', col. b 'Etas VI' and 'Henr' III'
fols. 65–7:	col. a 'Mill' VI', col. b 'Etas VI' and 'Edwardus I'
fols. 68–73:	col. a 'Mill' VI', col. b 'Etas VI' and 'Edwardus II'
fols. 74–83:	col. a 'Mill' VI', col. b 'Etas VI' and 'Edwardus III'
fols. 84–93:	col. a 'Mill' VI', col. b 'Etas VI' and 'Ric' II'
fol. 94:	col. a 'Mill' VI', col. b 'Etas VI' and 'Henr' IIII'
fol. 95:	col. a 'Mill' VI', col. b 'Etas VI' and 'Henricus IIII'
fol. 96:	col. a 'Mill' VI', col. b 'Etas VI' and 'Henr' IIII'
fol. 97:	col. a 'Mill' VI', col. b 'Etas VI' and 'Henricus IIII'
fols. 98–9:	col. a 'Mill' VI', col. b 'Etas VI Henr' IIII'
fol. 100:	col. a 'Mill' VI', col. b 'Etas VI' and 'Henr' IIII'
fols. 101–5:	col. a 'Mill' VI', col. b 'Etas VI' and 'Henr' V'.

In the transcription of such headwords contractions have been expanded only where they denote an obvious inflexion: thus *Henr'* remains but *Henric'* is transcribed *Henricus*. *Mill'* presumably stands for *Millenarius* 'millennium' and the numbers relate to the Anno Mundi dates. Since the third millennium is covered by fols. 16–20, fols. 21–6 have 'Mill' III' erroneously for 'Mill' IIII'. It follows that fols. 27–34 have 'Mill' IIII' erroneously for 'Mill' V', that fols. 35–48 have 'Mill' V' (or 'Mill' 5') erroneously for 'Mill' VI' (or 'Mill' 6'), and that fols. 49–104 have 'Mill' VI' erroneously for 'Mill' VII'.

(14) *Purpose*. Since 'marginal additions in the hand of the text are a characteristic feature of autograph MSS of chronicles'[2]

---

[1] Fol. 38, col. *a* is headed 'Mill' 5', i.e. with arabic '5' rather than roman 'V'.

[2] R. Vaughan, 'The Handwriting of Matthew Paris', *TCBS*, I. v (1953), 376–94, quot. on p. 383 n. 3, cited with some supplementary references in my 'Scribe and "Publisher"', p. 13 and n. 2, and see also p. 24.

the lack of such additions, apart from a short one on fol. 37^r, suggests that the manuscript was a fair copy. This suggestion is confirmed by the variety and exhaustiveness of the textual revisions and also by one tell-tale corrected error right at the beginning. On fol. 3^r col. *a* (Plate IV) the entry concerning Eve's twin babies is written in one year too soon because the scribe started to write the text continuously instead of entry by entry, just the kind of mistake anyone could make at the beginning of a fair copy, and an angled stroke in red is required to provide the correction. The fact that the manuscript is written wholly in Capgrave's superior Fere Textura script, the only manuscript so written, suggests that he intended it for some very important purpose, probably for presentation to someone of high social position.[1] In the event, the manuscript appears to have been completed hastily. The writing of the text ceases abruptly halfway down fol. 104^v, col. *a*, the text in this last column is not rubricated, and fol. 105^r is ruled and headed ready to receive more text. It is evident from the collation that the Dedicatory Preface (fols. 1–2) was added to the beginning of the manuscript and, since it refers to the fact that the text ends in 1417 (7/18), this Dedicatory Preface must have been written after it was decided to finish the text in that year. The provision of this Dedicatory Preface with an illuminated initial suggests that the manuscript was intended for presentation. As the Dedicatory Preface refers to Edward IV's accession (8/14–15) on 4 March 1461, it was presumably written not long after that event. Everything conspires to suggest that here was a manuscript already written as a fair copy in a formal script, and that on the new king's accession, the author hastily prepared to 'send' it to him (7/16) as a presentation copy. Whether it was ever actually dispatched there is no evidence.

P: Cambridge, Corpus Christi College, MS 167.[2]

(1) *History*. The manuscript was written *c*.1500, certainly not much earlier. Its place of origin is not known. At some time probably between *c*.1560 and 1575 it came into the possession of

---

[1] For a fuller statement of this argument see my 'Scribe and "Publisher" ', p. 25.

[2] For a brief description see M. R. James, *A Descriptive Catalogue of the Manuscripts in the Library of Corpus Christi College, Cambridge* (Cambridge, 1912), i. 378.

Matthew Parker (1504–75), archbishop of Canterbury (1559–75), and was bequeathed by him to Corpus Christi College, where it has remained ever since.[1] On p. 1 the manuscript's class-mark in the Parker library, 'E. 6', is written at the top.

(2) *Binding*. The present binding of cardboard covered with parchment and backed with pigskin dates from *c.*1700, when the paper flyleaves were added.

(3) *Material*. The manuscript is paper throughout, fairly thin, and worn in places at the edges. The dimensions of each leaf are: outer edge 301 × 205 mm.; written area 255–76 × 155–70 mm.

(4) *Foliation*: [ii]+98+[ii]. Like other manuscripts in the Parker collection the manuscript has been paginated in red crayon at the top right-hand corner of each recto page only; the numbers range from 1 to 195. The roman numbers in square brackets refer to the flyleaves, two at the beginning and two at the end, added when the manuscript was bound.

(5) *Collation*. The manuscript does not consist of regular quires. The sheets are drawn in by the sewing between pp. 36 and 37, 118 and 119, and 182 and 183. On the assumption that this sewing indicates the way the manuscript was made up the collation is 1^{36}, pp. 1–72; 2^{46}, pp. 73–164; 3^{1+1+14}, pp. 165–96.

(6) *Catchwords and Signatures*. None.

(7) *Pricking*. None.

(8) *Ruling*. The ruling is done with hard-point and is often difficult to see; p. 143 is clearer than most. Each page appears to be ruled separately. There is a vertical rule near the outer edge and also on the hinge side (though this line is not always visible) and the horizontal lines vary in number from 23 to 39, generally sloping upwards from left to right (though on p. 4 they slope downwards from left to right). The margin on the left-hand side of each page (recto and verso) is generally wider than that on the right-hand side.

(9) *Handwriting*. The text is written in one clear hand which generally gets progressively larger through the manuscript.

[1] On Parker's book-collecting activities see C. E. Wright, 'The Dispersal of the Monastic Libraries and the Beginnings of Anglo-Saxon Studies. Matthew Parker and his Circle: a Preliminary Study', *TCBS*, I. iii (1951), 208–37; also W. W. Greg, 'Books and Bookmen in the Correspondence of Archbishop Parker', *The Library*, IV. xvi (1935), 243–79, and M. Murphy, 'Religious Polemics in the Genesis of Old English Studies', *HLQ* xxxii (1969), 241–8.

(10) *Rubrication.* None.

(11) *Illumination.* None.

(12) *Contents*: John Capgrave, 'Abbreuiacion of Cronicles', lacking the Dedicatory Preface. There are no dates except for 'ii M ccc' at 19/5 within the (long) entry for AM 2242 and except for those incorporated in the text,[1] and the text is therefore written out continuously so that in the earlier part there are no gaps beside the years for which there are no entries. Throughout the text there are annotations added probably in the sixteenth century. One annotator displays the virulent side of Tudor (probably Elizabethan) Protestantism in his aversion to St. Thomas Becket, since the passage dealing with him (110/16–23) has been deleted and the instances of his name at 110/3, 111/6, 111/10, 111/24, and 135/18 have also been deleted.[2] On p. 196, an annotator has added 'anno 1418' beside the penultimate line of text, but there is no entry for that year and from the fact that in both M and P the text breaks off at the same point in the entry for 1417 it would appear that the author never completed the entry for 1417, let alone began one for 1418.

Two other manuscripts require brief mention.

B: Cambridge, University Library, MS Mm. 1. 44 (Baker 33).[3] This manuscript is in the hand of the antiquary Thomas Baker and was written between 1728 and 1732. It consists of 476 pages

---

[1] Only twenty dates are incorporated in the text, as follows: AM 5157, Octavian's accession to the empire (46/31–47/1); AM 5199, Christ's birth (47/28–9); AD 14, Tiberius's accession to the empire (48/6); AD 165, the first sending of missionaries to Britain (54/17); AD 808, the creation of one Anglo-Saxon kingdom (86/21–2); AD 855, Æthelwulf's accession to the kingdom of the West Saxons (86/24); AD 872, Alfred's accession to the kingdom of the West Saxons (89/27); AD 1066, the Norman Conquest of England (101/8); AD 1086, the accession of William II to the English crown (103/10–11); AD 1100, the accession of Henry I to the English crown (104/30); AD 1120, Henry I's return to England (105/14); AD 1170, the murder of St. Thomas Becket (110/20–1); AD 1172, the burning of Norwich cathedral (111/20); AD 1203, the foundation of the Dominican order (113/6); AD 1193, the capture of Acre (114/30); AD 1230 (erron. for 1250), the establishment of the Augustinian order in England (119/27); AD 1273, the accession of Edward I (126/29); AD 1376, the fiftieth year of the reign of Edward III (180/11); AD 1399, the accession of Henry IV (214/8); AD 1413, the accession of Henry V (238/17).

[2] Cf. M. McKisack, *Medieval History in the Tudor Age* (Oxford, 1971), pp. 96, 119, 121.

[3] See *A Catalogue of Manuscripts in the Library of the University of Cambridge,* v (Cambridge, 1867), p. 370.

316 × 200 mm., written area 295 × 185 mm. The second item, on pp. 23–5, is an extract from Capgrave's *Abbreuiacion of Cronicles* copied 'from a M̃S . . . in the Royal Library, Cambridge', i.e. M, the autograph.[1] This manuscript therefore has no independent textual value.

L: London, Lincoln's Inn, MS Hale 100.[2]

As Dr N. R. Ker kindly tells me,[3] this manuscript is in the hand of the Elizabethan antiquary Thomas Talbot (*fl.* 1580).[4] It consists of 113 folios 305 × 195–200 mm., written area 260–80 × approx. 155 mm. on the pages concerned. On fols. 46^{rv} (the last part of § 32 in Hunter's classification) and 49^{rv} (§ 36 in Hunter's classification) are notes relating to Anglo-Saxon history, mainly records of kings' reigns, and fols. 46^r, 46^v, and 49^r are headed 'Capgrave'; fol. 49^v may also have had this heading but the original top line of writing has been cut off when the leaves were cropped by a binder. Hingeston claimed these notes to be 'extracts from' Capgrave's *Abbreuiacion of Cronicles*,[5] but they contain many details not found in that work or in any other work by Capgrave. Why these notes should have been attributed to Capgrave is a mystery. They are of no authority for establishing the text of the *Abbreuiacion of Cronicles*.

THE RELATIONSHIP OF THE PRINCIPAL MANUSCRIPTS

Although M is autograph the relationship between M and P is important for establishing the text. According to Hingeston, followed by M. R. James, P was 'a copy' of M.[6] This claim is incorrect. A complete collation of the two manuscripts reveals

---

[1] Baker also made notes from the same manuscript, including Capgrave's reference to his date of birth (203/12–13) and an extract from the Dedicatory Preface, on pp. 671–2 of the copy of John Pits's *Relationum historicarum de rebus anglicis tomus primus*, ed. W. Bishop (Paris, 1619), now in the Bodleian Library (Gough Gen Top 208a) at Oxford.

[2] See J. Hunter, *Catalogue of Manuscripts in the Library of The Honourable Society of Lincoln's Inn* (London, 1838), p. 336, no. XCIII (C).

[3] Private communication dated 23 January 1965.

[4] On whom see *DNB*, s.n. Talbot, Thomas (*fl.* 1580), and M. McKisack, *Medieval History in the Tudor Age* (Oxford, 1971), p. 78, also R. J. Schoeck, 'The Elizabethan Society of Antiquaries and Men of Law', *N&Q* cxcix (1954), 417–21, supplemented 544, esp. 420.

[5] *De illustribus Henricis*, p. li, n. 1.

[6] Hingeston, *Chronicle*, p. xxvii; James, *Catalogue of MSS in CCCC*, i. 378.

that both derive independently from a common exemplar, presumably an earlier holograph or autograph (designated *A) as indicated in Fig. 1. This discovery makes Capgrave's *Abbreuiacion of Cronicles* specially interesting from a textual-critical point of view since what survives is an autograph copy by the author and a later copy by another scribe of a now-lost autograph or holograph

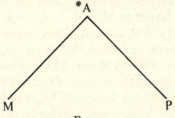

FIG. 1

manuscript, also by the author, of the author's work. The main evidence for the independence of M and P is the 206 corrections to M's text provided by P.[1] Although the adoption of some of these corrections is a matter of editorial judgement there can be little doubt about the vast majority.[2] The main evidence for M and P having a common exemplar is the fifty-five instances of common error.[3] Again, while a few of these errors are the result of editorial

[1] These corrections occur at 13/22, 15/21, 16/2, 17/23, 27/9, 29/12, 26, 30/21, 34/8, 35/24, 36/10, 39/4, 13, 41/11, 43/3, 44/5, 45/1, 3, 50/32, 52/7, 54/8, 12, 56/13, 22, 24, 57/8, 9, 11, 58/10, 59/13, 26, 30, 61/17, 18, 63/7, 66/7, 75/2, 12, 28, 76/31, 78/3, 17, 28, 80/20, 81/5, 12, 82/17, 83/5, 9, 32, 88/8, 19, 21, 90/3, 92/2, 29, 93/29, 94/33, 99/25, 101/12, 102/15, 103/22, 104/1, 106/12, 19, 109/8, 14, 111/17, 113/5, 114/30 (2), 115/8, 18, 119/17, 33, 35, 122/30, 123/1, 125/33, 126/27, 128/6, 129/5, 130/21, 132/4, 24, 27, 30, 134/17, 18, 135/30, 137/9, 27, 143/7, 144/30, 145/14, 20, 146/1, 151/7, 164/5, 165/20, 169/4, 170/1, 6, 25, 172/27, 175/9, 177/12, 181/15–16, 16, 182/5, 24, 183/6, 25, 184/2, 18, 185/3–4, 186/21, 22, 26, 187/3, 6, 189/2, 6, 7, 29, 190/11, 15, 15–16, 17, 20, 192/8, 10, 13, 15–16, 18, 24, 193/13, 16, 29, 194/9, 20, 195/16, 198/12, 28, 199/1, 3, 21, 25, 200/2, 9 (2), 201/19, 31, 202/11, 27, 203/3, 18, 204/4, 25, 206/3, 13, 26, 207/29, 208/23–4, 209/13, 211/7, 18, 213/4, 215/12, 16, 217/17, 24, 218/4, 219/4, 5, 17, 24, 220/13, 19, 221/11, 222/2, 225/18, 30, 226/10, 227/17, 228/3, 24, 230/2, 231/18, 24, 234/12–13, 31, 235/13, 236/12, 18, (2), 237/23, 238/2, 239/23, 240/1, 10, 11, 246/26, 249/8, 21.

[2] In view of the length of the text (approx. 85,000 words) the number of corrections adopted from P is not large, about one every 413 words.

[3] Common errors occur at 37/4, 41/11, 53/22, 62/24, 64/4, 65/16, 66/25, 70/23, 73/6, 75/17, 82/2, 91/21, 94/6–8, 95/31, 98/10, 100/26, 102/19, 103/25, 105/19, 106/5, 117/30, 118/18, 119/29, 122/3, 124/12, 125/25, 126/23, 132/6, 135/29, 136/7, 137/29, 139/24, 140/25, 142/28, 145/13, 148/2, 153/8, 155/17, 156/29, 160/13, 166/7, 167/16, 173/11, 179/21, 180/23, 193/16, 209/9, 221/15, 222/11, 223/22–3, 237/1, 239/4, 27, 242/13, 244/14.

judgement the vast majority are indisputable. There are only two
instances of M and P having a different error in the same place
(30/22 and 174/25). The closeness of M and P is confirmed by
eleven instances where the variant reading from P is identical
with, or suggests, the reading (from the common exemplar *A)
which has been amended or corrected in M.[1]

There is some evidence to suggest that the common exemplar
*A was similar in layout to M, with double columns of the same
width. A few errors in P occur at places corresponding to a line
division in M.[2] Some omissions in P correspond exactly to the
amount of text in a column line in M.[3] One erroneous addition
(at 15/16) corresponds to the amount of text in a column line in M.
This impression, that the layout of *A was in some respects
identical to that of M, is confirmed by other factors. In some proper
names in P the spacing corresponds to a line division in M.[4]
Punctuation occasionally occurs in P in places corresponding to a
line, column, or page division in M and for which there seems
to be no obvious explanation other than that of correspondence
to a line division in the exemplar (*A).[5] However, other evidence,
of the same kind, shows that *A was similar rather than identical
in layout to M, for punctuation also occasionally occurs in places
for which there seems to be no obvious explanation other than
that of correspondence to a line division in the exemplar (*A)
and yet there are no corresponding line divisions in M.[6] If some
of the errors common to M and P are anything to go by[7] *A was
also a copy, not the author's original.

---

[1] These instances occur at 16/21, 64/2, 65/32, 68/27, 69/28–9, 79/26, 91/4,
92/25, 126/31 (see note), 161/31, 167/16.

[2] Those at 35/4, 91/21, and 156/14.

[3] Those at 180/7–8, 202/15, 209/23, 222/20.

[4] *The odoricus* (68/30), *Ale mane* (90/21), *Ger uase* (158/9), *Abrust with*
(232/12).

[5] *Formose . put* (89/18–19), *kyngis . coronacion* (135/27), *erle . of* (138/15–16),
whech . he (240/20), *sacrament . of* (240/24).

[6] *lost . his* (94/12), *cam . of* (109/34), *tyme . was* (114/31), *took . of* (133/10),
onto . her councell (136/22), *fest . was* (143/4), *ʒork . walles* (144/30), *þerfor . he*
(161/13), *lederis . of* (195/24), *power . was* (203/16–17), *instructouris . of* (204/6),
him . with (214/11), *Cherch . hath* (226/5). Some of these instances are close
to line divisions in M, notably those at 114/31, 143/4, 144/30, 161/13, 214/11,
226/5.

[7] Notably those at 37/4, 62/24, 64/4, 65/16, 66/25, 82/2, 95/31, 98/10,
100/26, 103/25, 106/5, 117/30, 119/29, 122/3, 132/6, 139/24, 145/13, 153/8,
155/17, 166/7, 180/23, 193/16, 239/4, 242/13.

DATE

The autograph manuscript, M, consists of two parts, the text of the *Abbreuiacion of Cronicles*, and the Dedicatory Preface which was added at the beginning.[1] This Dedicatory Preface can be dated fairly precisely. Since it refers to Edward IV's accession to the throne (8/14–15), which occurred on 4 March 1461, it must have been written after that date. It must also have been written before Capgrave's death on 12 August 1464. But the compilation of material for the chronicle itself is unlikely to have been done within three years and may have begun much earlier than 1461, perhaps before 1438. In the Dedicatory Preface to his commentary *In Genesim* (1437–8) Capgrave wrote,

Sed et annualia mea reuoluens aliud inueni quod me monet. Scriptum enim in hiis reperi quod anno Domini M.CC.xlviii fundatus fuerat ordo heremitarum Sancti Augustini in Anglia per Ricardum de Clara filium Gilberti de Clara comitemque Glouernie.[2]

Since Capgrave refers to this event in the *Abbreuiacion of Cronicles* (119/24–32), *annualia mea* may refer to that work or an earlier draft of it. There are also possible signs of a change in spelling habits such as might have occurred if the work was compiled over a period, notably an increase in the use of *-þ'* at the expense of *-thir* in words like *othir/oþir*.[3] I have shown above (pp. xl–xlii) that another (or possibly two) holograph or autograph manuscript(s) must have preceded M, the autograph manuscript that has survived, which is presumably a final fair copy. But, as the date of these preceding manuscripts cannot be ascertained, all we can say is that the *Abbreuiacion of Cronicles* was written before *c.*1461, and that it was perhaps begun before *c.*1438.

LANGUAGE

EXTERNAL EVIDENCE

In the Dedicatory Preface Capgrave refers to himself as *a pore frere of þe Heremites of Seynt Austyn in þe conuent of Lenne* (7/2–3). Evidently he was at Lynn when he wrote it *c.*1462–3. Apart from a period when he went away to study in London (1417–22) and Cambridge (1422–7) he seems to have spent most

---

[1] See above, p. xxxvii.
[2] Printed in Hingeston, *De illustribus Henricis*, pp. 230–1.
[3] See my 'Orthographic Usage', pp. 332–4, § 3.

of his life in Lynn. He was certainly there in 1406, 1446, 1455, c.1462–3, and 1464 (the year of his death). He was probably there in 1393 (the year of his birth), 1440, and c.1450 (whence he travelled to Rome). Perhaps most importantly, he was almost certainly brought up there and did not go away for any length of time until he was twenty-four. This evidence convincingly localizes Capgrave in Lynn, so his language must be derived from that of Lynn except in so far as it was affected by extraneous factors such as literary influences or other dialects or any inchoate movement towards standardization.

The linguistic study of English in the two or three centuries before the introduction of printing ultimately has its foundations in the data available from those texts which were written by a known author or scribe (from a known background) at a known time in a known place. From the historical linguist's point of view autograph or holograph manuscripts that can be precisely dated and localized, and some facts about whose author are known, represent an ideal since they provide an opportunity to study the language of a specific man writing at a specific time in a specific place. Such ideal texts are provided by the autograph and holograph manuscripts of vernacular works by Capgrave, of which the fair copy of the *Abbreuiacion of Cronicles* (M) is the latest. The Capgrave material probably constitutes the single most important corpus of linguistic evidence for the W. Norfolk area in the fifteenth century.[1]

PREVIOUS STUDIES

Owing, partly, to the lack of good editions Capgrave's language has not been much studied. For his 'John Capgrave und die englische Schriftsprache', published in 1901, Dibelius drew mainly on Hingeston's edition of the *Abbreuiacion of Cronicles* (on the deficiencies of which see above, p. vii), supplementing it only with rhyme-evidence from the *Katharine*, which has not survived in an autograph or holograph manuscript. This work is therefore unreliable as far as the citation of forms from Capgrave's *Abbreuiacion of Cronicles* is concerned. A similar reservation must be entered for Rettger's *Development of Ablaut in the Strong Verbs*

---

[1] For other evidence see McIntosh, 'The Language of Havelok', pp. 43–7. Apart from London, Lynn is linguistically one of the best-documented towns in late medieval England.

of the East Midland Dialects (1934), a work which contains a number of ghost-forms from Hingeston's edition. Some aspects of Capgrave's language were studied as comparative material by Meech in his edition of *The Book of Margery Kempe* (1940), but he in turn relied heavily on Dibelius. The only previous editor of a Capgrave text to include a section in his Introduction on the language was Munro in his edition of the *Augustine, Gilbert,* and *Tretis* (pp. xiv–xxi). More recently, there has been Colledge and Smetana's article on 'Capgrave's *Norbert*: Diction, Dialect and Spelling' (1972), and my own study of the 'Orthographic Usage' of the *Abbreuiacion of Cronicles* (1973).

PHONOLOGY

In this summary Capgrave's general usage in regard to spelling(s) for the Middle English sounds established in the phonological histories of the English language[1] is given first followed by select representative examples of specific words; sometimes exceptions only are noted. A number in brackets after a word indicates how many times the word occurs with the spelling cited; a word not so followed may be assumed to occur once only.

Vowels

1. ME a   Spelt *a*

1.1   OE a + C (not N and not in length. comb.) in closed S: *mark* 'monetary unit' (29).

1.2   OE a/o + N

1.2.1 OE a/o + N in closed S: *man* (251).

1.2.2 OE a/o + N + C (not *b, d,* or *g*): *þank(id)* (4).

1.3   OE *æ* in closed S: *had(de)* (488).[2]

1.4   OE *a/ea* by Retraction/Breaking

1.4.1 OE *a/ea* + *l* + C (not *d*): *half(-)* (17).

1.4.2 OE *a/ea* + *r* + C: *harm(-)* (19).[3]

---

[1] Notably those by Luick, Jordan, and Dobson. The fullest collection of material for comparison is Kihlbom's *Fifteenth Century English* (1926), also Kökeritz, *Suffolk Dialect* (1932). The following abbreviations are used: C *for* consonant; length. comb. *for* lengthening combination; N *for* nasal consonant; pal. *for* palatal; S *for* syllable(s); + *for* coming before.

[2] Exceptions in this group owe their *e* to other origins or influence: (-)*messe(s)* (23), beside (-)*masse(s)* (19), may have *e* from the SE, or from OF *messe* or from ON *messa*; *gres(se)* (2) has probably been influenced by ODan. *græs* (*æ* = *ę*); *heruest* presumably descends from a SE or possibly a WMid form.

[3] The only exception is *merk* 'sign' (2) and *merkid* (2) beside *markyd*, from OE WS *mearc(ian)*. Forms with *e* are the reflex of OE *merc* (due to Anglian

1.4.3   OE *ea* + *h* + C: *wax* n. (3) and v.
1.5   OE *æ/ea* (after initial pal. C) in closed S: *scharp(ly)*.
1.6.1   OE *ā* shortened: *ask(-)* (36). See also § 13.1.
1.6.2   OE *ǣ²* shortened: *lasse* (2); cf. *lesse* (4) and § 7.1.
1.7   ON *a* in closed S: *want(-)* (4).
1.8   OF/L *a*: *artic(u)les* (15).

2. ME ā   Spelt *a*

2.1   OE *a* + C (not N) in open S: *make* (77).
2.2   OE *a/o* + N in open S: *name(s)* (85).
2.3   OE *æ* + C in open S: *graue(s)* (15).
2.4   OE *æ/ea* (after initial pal. C) in open S: *schaue*.
2.5   ME *a* (from shortening of OE *ǣ²*) in open S: *lady* (43). Cf. § 7.2 and note.
2.6   ON and MLG *a* + C in open S: *same* (376); *talow*.
2.7   OF *a* and L *ā*: *age* (58); *coronacio(u)n* (8).
2.8   OF *a(u)* + labial C: *saue* 'with the exception of' (25).

3. ME ai   Spelt *ai* (6%), *ay* (19%), *ei* (39%), *ey* (36%)

3.1   OE *æ* + pal. *g*: all spellings but predominantly *ay* (61%) as in *day(es)* (212).
3.2   OE *e* + pal. *g*: all spellings but predominantly *ey* (84%) as in *wey(es)* (22).
3.3   OE *ea/e* + *ht*: only in *streit(e)* (6), *streith* (2), *streyt(e)* (2).[1]
3.4   OE *ǣ²* + pal. *g*: *ey* (15), as in *neythir* (6), and *ei* (3).
3.5   OE *ē* (of various origins) + pal. *g*: *ey* only, in *grey* (3), *neybour* (OE *nēahgebūr*). Cf. § 11.6.
3.6   ON *ei*: all spellings but predominantly *ei* (98%) as in *þei* (886); *ey* before *k* in *ouyrweyk*.
3.7.1   OF *ai*: all spellings, *ey* commonest (46%), as in *meynte(y)n(-)* (15), also *ay* (31%), as always in *pay(-)* (50).
3.7.2   AN *ai* + palatalized C: usually *ai*, as in *failed* (5), but once *ereyne* 'spider'.
3.8.1   OF *ei*: all spellings but predominantly *ey* (68%), as in *seynt(is)* (170).
3.8.2   AN *ei* + palatalized C: *ey* only, as in *feyne* (11).[2]

Smoothing). Forms with *a* may descend likewise and have been modified in accordance with the shift of *er* to *ar* in IME, or such forms may descend from WS. Possibly the form with *e* was preferred to distinguish the word from *mark* 'monetary unit'.

[1] I have distinguished these forms from those derived from OF *(e)streit* by strict reference to their meanings in context.

[2] Thus there is a spelling distinction between *feyne* 'feign' and *fayn* (14) 'fain'.

4. ME au Spelt *au* (once only before vowel) and *aw* (rarely before C)

4.1   OE *a* + velar *g*: *draw*(-) (24).

4.2.1   OE *ā* + *ht*: see § 16.3.

4.2.2   OE *æ*, *ea* + velar *h*: *lawh*(*ing*) 'laugh' (2) (OE Angl. *hlæhhan*); *faut* (21).

4.3   OE *ēa* + *w*: *raw*.

4.4.1   OF *au*: *cause*(-) (78); *aw* occurs only in *sawtes* 'assaults' beside *saute* (2).

4.4.2   AN *a*(*u*) + N: predominantly *au* (88%)[1]—never *aw*—as in *graunt*(-) (54), also *a*, as in *chambir* (5) beside *chaumbir* (2), sometimes perhaps due to L influence as in *angel*(*lis*) (2) beside *aungel*(-)(18). The PresE suffix -*ance* is almost invariably spelt -*auns* (101), once -*ans*,[2] and once -*aunce*.

5. ME e Spelt *e*

5.1   OE *e* (not + length. C comb.) in closed S: *went* (146); *weel* 'well' (11) beside *wel* (22) is evidently a variant with *ē*.

5.2   OE *e*/*ie* (after initial pal. C; and not + length. C comb.) in closed S: *ȝet* (27).

5.3   OE *eo* (by Breaking) + *r* + C (not *d*, *l*, *n*, or *þ*-): *hert*(-) (19).

5.4   OE *e*/*ie*(by *I*-mutation; and not + length. C comb.) in closed S: *felled*.

5.5   ON *e*: *leggis* (2).

5.6   OF/L *e*: *consent*(-) (40).

6. ME ę Spelt *e*, in some words *ee*. Vowel-length is also frequently indicated by final -*e* (or equivalent) as in *fede* inf. (2) beside *fed* pp. (2)

6.1   OE *æ*[2] (by *I*-mutation): *se* 'sea' (62) beside *see* (6), *lede*(*r*) (12); see also § 1.6.2.

6.2.1   OE *ēa*: *ded* 'dead' (72) beside *deed* and *dede* (5), *gret* (137) beside *grete* (270).[3]

6.2.2   OE *ea* + length. C comb.: *berd*(*is*) 'beard(s)' (2); (after initial pal. C) *cherchȝerd*.

6.3   OE *e*, *eo* + C in open S: *mete*(*s*)(21); *heuene* (14). Cf. § 10.2.1.

6.4   ON *æ*: *sete*(*s*) (10).

6.5   OF *e*: *beste* (5),[4] *bestes* (17) beside *beest*(*is*) (2); *cese*(*d*) (6).

---

[1] Also *a*/*v* twice over line division, as in *coma*/*vnded*.
[2] Or possibly -*aus* erroneously for -*aŭs*.
[3] The form *chase* p.t. sg. (3) (beside *chose*) must be from OE *ceās*.
[4] Distinguished from *best* superl. adj. and adv. (18).

6.6   AN *e* (from OF *ai, ei*): *pes* (46) beside *pees* (15); *ese* (2).

6.7   L *e* in open S: *mediacio(u)n* (7).

7. ME $\bar{\text{e}}$ Spelt *e*, in some words *ee* or *e(Ce)* as in § 6

7.1.1   OE $\bar{e}$: *he* (2085); *feet* (13) and *fete*; *qwen* (13) beside *qween* (57), and *qwene* (2).

7.1.2   OE *e* + length. C comb.: *feld(is)* (14); (after initial pal. C) *ʒeld(e)* (3).

7.2   OE Angl. $\bar{e}$ (= WS $\bar{æ}^1$): *ded* beside *dede* (19);[1] (after initial pal. C) *ʒer(-)* (919).

7.3.1   OE $\bar{e}/\bar{\imath}e$ (by *I*-mutation): *ten* (15).

7.3.2   OE $\bar{e}/\bar{\imath}e$ (by *I*-mutation) + length. C comb.: *herd(e)* (47).

7.4.1   OE $\bar{e}o$: *se* (25), *held* (50); also *mek(-)* (from ON **miúkr*) (7).

7.4.2   OE *eo* + length. C comb.: *(h)erl(-)* (237), *erd(-)* (25).

7.5   OE *i/y* + C in open S: spellings in *e* and *i/y*, as *abiden, abydyn* (2) beside *abedyn, biried* (32), *byried* (40) beside *beried* (3).[2]

7.6   ON *œ*: *semeth* (3).

7.7   OF *e*: *beste(s)* (22) beside *beest(is)* (2).

7.8   OF *ué* (in stressed S): *remeue(d)* (18) and all forms (8) of *meve*; see also § 17.5.2. and note to § 14.7.

8. ME ęu   Spelt *eu* and *ew* (before vowel or *m*)

8.1   OE $\bar{e}a$ + *w*: *few(e)* (20).

8.2   OE $\bar{æ}^2$ + *w*: *lewed*.

8.3   OF *eau*: *beuté*; before a labial *rewme* (2) beside *rem* (8), *reme* (11), *remes* (2).

9. ME ęu /iu/   Spelt *eu* (before C), *ew* (uncommon before C) and *u* (mostly in words of French origin)

9.1   OE $\bar{e}o$ + *w*: *new(e)* (49), *treuth* (12); *truse* beside *treus* (4), *trews* (13).

9.2   OE *i* + *w*: *steward* (5).

9.3   AN *eu, iu*: *jeweles* (3) from AN *j(e)uel* whence also *joweles*; *reule(s)* (16).[3]

9.4   OF *iv*: *pursewed* (15).

9.5   OF *ü* /y:/: usually spelt *u*, as in *duke(s)* (248); *deuté* (4), *dewté* (3), and *dew* (6) from OF *deü* perhaps belong in § 9.3.[4]

9.6   OF *üi*: *frute(s)* (6); also *endewe* (2), *endewid*.

---

[1] The one form with *a*, *blod-last* 'letting of blood' (second element from OE *læs*), presumably shows shortening of OE $\bar{æ}^1$.

[2] For a full treatment of this feature see my 'Orthographic Usage', pp. 342–4, § 13.

[3] Note also *Hareflw* beside *Harflew* (2).

[4] But *ew* occurs in *issew* (10), *retenew* (2), *valew* (4). Note also *agw*.

10. **ME ĭ** Spelt *i* (most commonly), *y* (usual next to *m*, *n*, and *u*), sometimes *e*,[1] in three words in § 10.4 *u*

10.1   OE *i* (not + length. C comb.) in closed S: *i/y* only, as in *drink* (3), *drynk* (4); *sitte* (3); *wyntir* (10).

10.2.1   OE *io/eo* (by back mutation) in closed S: *i/y* only, as in *siluir* (9), *syluir* (3). Cf. § 6.3.

10.2.2   OE *ēo* shortened: only in *pirtene*; see also § 7.5.

10.3   ON *i*: *i/y* only, as in *clipped*, *wyndowe*.

10.4   OE *y* (not + length. C comb.) in closed S: all spellings, as in *sinne*(-) (7), *synne* (11); *first* (186); *chirch* (3) beside *cherch*(-) (167); *u* in *busch* (2), *cut*(-) (8), and *sundry* (5); *e* in *mech*(*il*) (136), *swech*(*e*) (89), *w*(*h*)*ech* (608) beside *which* (2).

10.5   ON *y*: mostly *i/y*, as in *bigge* (2) and *biggid* (7), *bygge*; *sistir* (19); *i* and *e* in *lift*(*e*) 'elevated' (5) beside *left* (2).

10.6.1   OE *ĭ* shortened: mostly *i*, in *fift* (2) and *fifte* (6), *wisdam* (2); probable shortening in reduced stress in *Chestirschere* (2), *Wiltschere* (2), *Lancastirschere*—also *-sc*(*h*)*ire* (7)—beside *schire*, *schiris*.

10.6.2   OE *ȳ* shortened: *i* in *hid* pp. (14), *hidde*; perhaps here too belongs *litil* (16), *lytil* (4).

10.7   OF *i*: *i/y*, as in *miracle*(*s*) (6) and *miracules*, *myracle*(*s*) (4); occasionally *e*, as in *merour*.

10.8   L *i*: *i/y*, as in *diuision* (2), *dyuysion*; *diuided*, *dyuyded* (5).

11. **ME ī** Spelt mostly *i/y* and *iCe*, *yCe*, but also *ei/ey* (§§ 11.6.1, 11.7.1, and 11.9.1); *e/ee* spellings in § 11.2 probably indicate variant pronunciations

11.1.1   OE *ī*: *i/y* only, as in *wif* (28), *wyf* (13), *wyues* (6); *time* (8), *tyme*(*s*) (462); *side*(*s*) (63), *syde*.

11.1.2   OE *i* + length. C comb.: *i/y* only, as in *child*(*e*) (46); *wind*, *wynd*(*e*) (11), *wyndes* (2).

11.2.1   OE *ȳ*: *i/y/e*(*e*), as in *hired* beside *hered*, *heres* 'wages'; *fire* (14), *afir*, *firy* (2), *fyre* (4) beside *fer*, *feer*.

11.2.2   OE *y* + length. C comb.: *i/y/e*, as in *onkind*, *onkynd*, *vnkynde* beside *onkende*.

11.3.1   OE *i* + pal. *g*: *i/y*, as in *twies* (2), *twyes* (3).

11.3.2   OE *ī* + pal. *g*: *i* only, in *thries* 'thrice' (3), *pries*.

11.4.1   OE *y* + pal. *g*: only in *by*(*e*) 'buy' (4), *biere*, and *lyes* 'untruths' (2).

11.4.2   OE *ȳ* + pal. *g*: only in *drie*, *dry*(*e*) (7), and *dried*, *dryed* (3).

---

[1] For a full account of the instances in §§ 10.4, 10.5, 10.7 see my 'Orthographic Usage', pp. 342–4, §§ 13–14.

11.5.1   OE *i* + *ht*: *i/y* only, as in *mite* p.t. (24), *myte* (68).[1]

11.5.2   OE *y* + *ht*: *i* only, in *flite* (2).

11.6.1   OE Angl. *ē* (of various origins) + pal. *g* (originally belonging to next S): *ey* in *bewreyed* (2); *y* in *nyhyng* 'neighing', cf. § 3.5. In this category too perhaps belong forms of the verb *die*: *i(e)*, *y(e)*, and *ei(e)*, *ey(e)* in *dye*, *died* (2), *dyed*, beside *deie*, *dey* (4), *deye* (12), *deieth* (6), *deyeth* (2), *deied* (120), *deyd*, *deyed* (67), also *deyng* vbl. n.

11.6.2   ON *ǣ* + pal. *g*: only in *sly* (2).

11.7.1   OE *ēa/ē* + pal. *g* or *h*: *i(e)*, *y(e)*, and *ei/ey*, as in *hie* (4), *hy(e)* (5), *hier*, *hiest* (3), beside *hey* (2), *heyer*, *heith* (2);[2] *yʒe* beside *eyne* (10), *eyeledes*; only *i/y* in *ni* 'near' (3), *ny* (24), *nyher*; only *ey* in *fley* 'fled'.

11.7.2   OE *ēo/ē* + pal. *g* or *h*: only in *thi* 'thigh'.

11.8   ON *ī*: *i* in *liknesse(s)* (6), *likned*; *y* in *dykes*.

11.9.1   OF *i*: mostly *i/y*, as in *exile(d)* (42); *ydol(es)* (9), *ydolatrie* (6); *diuers(e)* (3) and *dyuers* (32); also sporadic *ei/ey* as in *galeies* (3), *galey(es)* (3).

11.9.2   OF *i* + palatalized C: *i/y/ig*, as in *resine(d)* (6), *resyne(d)* (3), *resigne(d)* (8).

11.10   L *i*: *i/y* only, as in *diuulgid* (2), *dyuulged*.

12. ME o   Spelt *o*

12.1   OE *o* (not + length. C comb.) in closed S: *god(-)* (136);[3] (after initial pal. C) *schort(ly)* (9).

12.2.1   OE *ō* shortened: probably in *go(d)spel(l)* (13) (cf. § 14.1).

12.2.2   ME *ǭ* (< (i) OE *ā* or (ii) *a* + *mb*, *nd*, *ng*) shortened: no clear examples of (i); for (ii) see § 13.2.2.

12.3   ON *o*: *-scot* in *Romescot*.

12.4   OF and L *o*: *robbe(d)* (12); *fortunat* (3).

13. ME ǭ   Spelt mainly *o*, *oCe*, and *oo*; some spellings in *a* in §§ 13.1–2, especially § 13.2.1 and § 13.2.3–4

13.1   OE *ā*: *rod* (20), *rode* (4), *rood* (12); (after historical *w*) *to* 'two' (72), *too* (95); *a*-spellings are rare and probably show shortening, in *haliwatir*, beside *holy* (60); *halowid* (3), *halowmesse*, *Al(l)-halow* (2); and (in reduced stress) *wedlak* beside *wedlok* (2); see also § 1.6.1.

13.2.1   OE *a/ea* + *ld*: mostly *o*, also *a*, as in *cold* (5), *(be)hold(e)* (11),

---

[1] For further examples see my 'Orthographic Usage', pp. 338–9, § 9.

[2] The only spelling for 'height', perhaps to distinguish it from *hite* 'called' (55), always so spelt.

[3] The one instance of *good* is probably a mistake; cf. § 14.1.

and *(be)hald* (3); *e* in *eld(e)* (30) beside *old(e)* (26), *seld* (9) beside *sold* (3), *teld* beside *(told)* (21).[1]

13.2.2 OE *a/o* + *mb*: only in *lomb*, *wombe(s)* (4).

13.2.3 OE *a/o* + *nd*: more frequently *o*, as in *lond(e)* (200), also *a*, as in *hand(-)* (62); no words in this group show variation between *o* and *a*.[2]

13.2.4 OE *a/o* + *ng*: more frequently *o*, as in *among(is)* (46), *strong* (19), also *a*, as in *hang(-)* (24); no words in this group show variation between *o* and *a*.[2]

13.3 OE *o* + length. C comb.: *gold* (23), *word(es)* (24).

13.4 OE *o* + C in open S: mostly *oCe*, as in *chose(n)* pp. (38).

13.5 ON *ā*: only in *fro* (235), *lone* 'loan'.

13.6 OF and L *o*: *cote* (6), *(h)ost* 'army' (17), and *(h)oost* (29); *notarie(s)* (4).

14. ME ǭ   Spelt *o*, *oCe*, and *oo*

14.1 OE *ō*: *god* (2), *gode* (2), *good* (84);[3] *tok* (19), *toke* (5), *took* (139); (after initial pal. C) *schotyng*.

14.2 OE *u* + C in open S: possibly a long vowel in *wood* (3); other possible examples, such as *loue(d)* (18), *com* inf. and pp. (38) and *come* (44), are unhelpful because ME *u* was often spelt *o* before a letter composed of minims (*m, n, u*): *dore(s)* (14) may be from OE *duru* fem. or *dor* neut.

14.3.1 ME *ū* (OE *u* + length. C comb.) lowered before *r*: possibly in *morned*; see also § 18.5.

14.3.2 OE *eo* (< *u* after initial pal. C) + *ng*: in *ȝong(-)* (48).

14.4 ON *au*: *trost(id)* (8), *losed* p.t. 'set free' (2).

14.5 OF *o*: probably in *fool*.

14.6 OF *ov*: *pore(ly)* (18).

14.7 OF *ou* /u/ (= *ué* in stressed S): *reproue*, *proue*, and (with expanded contraction)[4] *proue(d)* (5), *prouyd*; cf. § 7.8 and § 17.5.2. [For the phonology see Dobson, § 36, n. 3.]

[1] For a full discussion of this feature see my 'Orthographic Usage', pp. 347–8, § 22.

[2] For a full discussion of this feature see my 'Orthographic Usage', p. 348, § 22.

[3] Cf. § 12.1. The words *god* and *good* are thus with three exceptions (one probably erroneous) always distinguished in spelling. Cf. also my 'Orthographic Usage', p. 342, § 12.

[4] This proviso is important because the same contraction is used for *pro-* and *pre-*. The expansion *pro-* is used in conformity with the majority of full spellings: *pro-* in *proue* and *reproue* beside *pre-* in *appreued* (which belongs in § 7.8); but *appreued* is so expanded to conform to the one full spelling of this word.

15. **ME oi and ui** Spelt *oi* and (more frequently) *oy*

15.1.1 OF *ǫi*: *joy(e)* (9); *noised* and *noyse(d)* (12).

15.1.2 OF *ǫi*: *boiling* (2); *anoynted* (13); *poison(ed)* (2) and *poyson(ed)* (2).

15.1.3 OF *oi* + palatalized C: *soile* 'land'; *oyle* (10); *voide(d)* v. (2) and *voyde(d)* (5).

16. **ME ǫu** Spelt *ou* (rare finally and never before vowel) and *ow*; *o* once in § 16.2.1 suggests possible monophthongization (Jordan, § 287). The *au* and *aw* spellings in § 16.3 probably indicate ME **au**

16.1   OE *o* + velar *g*: only in *bowe* n.

16.2.1 OE *ā* + velar *g*: *ow* in *owne* adj. (33) and derivatives but *o* once in the phrase *be her one* 'on their own'.

16.2.2 ON *ā* + velar *g*: only in *lower* compar.

16.3   OE *ā* + *ht*: *au/aw* only, in *taute* (3), *tawt*; *aute*, *awte*; also *nawt* beside *nowt* (17) from OE *nā(wi)ht* and *nō(wi)ht*. These *au* and *aw* spellings probably indicate a northern dialectal pronunciation with ME **au**;[1] they are included here rather than in § 4.2.1 to emphasize their dialectal quality.

16.4.1 OE *ǒ* + *ht*: *ou/ow* only, as in *þoute* (14); *nowt* (17); *brout(e)* (80), *browt(e)* (15); *doutir(is)* (63), *dowtir(es)* (15).

16.4.2 ON *ǒ* + *h*: only in *þouʒ* (20), *þou* (5), *þow* (2), *thow*.

16.5   OE *ā* + *w*: *ou/ow* only, as in *soule(s)* (14); *know(e)* (10) and derivatives (15); no words in this group show variation between *ou* and *ow*.

16.6   OE *ō* + *w*: *ou/ow* only, as in *foure* (29); *grow(e)* (8); variation between *ou* and *ow* is shown only (after initial pal. C) in *ʒou* (10), *ʒow*, but always *ʒour(e)* (28).

16.7   OF *ou*: *soudioures* (2); *scrowis* 'scrolls'.

17. **ME u** Spelt *u* usually, but also sometimes *o*; two instances of *vu* are recorded in § 17.8

17.1.1 OE *u* + C (not N and not in length. comb.) in closed S: *u* is usual, as in *ful* (77), *turne(d)* (31); *o* regularly in *borowes* (2), *þor(o)w(oute)* (38).

17.1.2 OE *u* after *w*: *o* in *woman(nes)* (40); *wolf* (2), *woluys*; and *wolle(-)* (8), *wolles* (2), *wolland*; *wonne* p.t. pl. (2), pp. (2) beside *wunne* pp.

17.2.1 OE *u* + N in closed S: *u* only, as in *sum(me)* 'some' (111); but the prefix from OE *un-* is usually spelt *on-*, as in *onwisely*, with occasional variation as in *onrithfully* beside *vnritefully*.

[1] Cf. Dobson, § 240.

17.2.2   OE *u* + N + C (not *d* or *g*): *u* (more frequently) and *o*, as in
         munk(is)(25) and *monk(is)*(16); *hunte(r)*(2), *huntid*(2), *hunting*(2).

17.3   OE *ū* shortened: probably in *dust*, *husband*, *-bond* (2), *us* (8)
         and *vs* (5), *vttir(ly)* (2) and *vtterest*.

17.4   ON *u*: *u* in *cunnyng* (3), *gunn(er)es* (2).

17.5.1   OF *u*: usually *u*, as in *suffered* (11), but also *o*, as in *soper* (2),
         and variation (rare), as in *corteyn*/*curteyn*.

17.5.2   ONF *u* (< *ué*): in *puple(s)* (149). See also § 7.8 and cf. § 14.7.

17.6   OF *ü* /y/: *u*, as in *juge(s)* (25).

17.7   OF *ui* + *sh*: *u* in *buschel*.

17.8   L *u*: *u*, as in *frustrat(e)* (3); initially spelt *vu-* in two proper
         names, *Vurbane* beside *Urbane* (3), *Vrban(e)* (15), and *Vulpianus*
         'Ulpianus Domitius'.

18. ME ū   Spelt *ou* (before C only) and *ow* (finally and before vowel, sometimes before C)

18.1.1   OE *ū*: *ou* and *ow*, as in *þousand(is)* (89), *now* (41); *out(e)* (109)
         and *owt(e)* (12), *toun* (2) and *town(es)* (90).

18.1.2   OE *u* + length. C comb.; *ou* (predominantly) and *ow*, as in
         found(e) (41), *ground(e)* (9) and *grownd* (2); *u*-spellings probably
         indicate a short vowel, as in *hungir* (16), and (with *o* after *w*)
         wondir (5). The forms *bonde* p.t. pl. and *bond* pp., beside
         bound(e) (4) and *bownde* (2), may be by analogy with *bond* p.t.
         sg. (2).

18.2   OE *u* + velar *g*: *ou* and *ow*, as in *foules* (2), *fowler* (2).

18.3.1   OE *u* + *h*: in *foutyn* p.t. pl., and *þorow* 'th(o)rough' (4).

18.3.2   OE *ū* + *h*: only in *row* 'rough'.

18.4   OE *ō* + velar *g*, *h*: *ow* only, as in *(with)drow* (10), *low* 'laughed'.

18.5   OF *u*: *ou* and *ow*, as in *councel(l)* (90), *power(e)* (43); *tour(e)*
         (26) and *towre(s)* (2); *o* in *corses*, beside *cours* (2), and *cort(is)*
         (5), beside *court(e)* (13), probably indicates ǭ as in § 14.3.1.

Consonants

19. **b**   A glide consonant *b* between *m* and a following *r* is apparently
           shown in *hambir* (2), *hamberes*, and *Mambre*.[1]

20. **ch** OE medial -*cc*- is usually represented by *cch*.

21. **d**   An excrescent *d* is sometimes added after *n* and *l*, as in *lynand*
           (4), *ild(e)* (5), *yld(e)* (20) beside *ile*, *yle(s)* (5). Conversely, *d* is lost
           in *an* (13) beside *and* (2651 including 10 with *d* suprascript),
           and *schul* p.t. (16) beside *schuld* (649), *schulde* (6), both words no
           doubt subject to reduced sentence stress.[1]

---

[1] See further my 'Orthographic Usage', p. 347, § 21.

Unvoicing of final -*d* in the past of weak verbs is indicated sporadically by the following: *clepit* (2) beside *cleped* (285), *delyueret* beside *delyuered* (15), *lettet* beside *letted* (9), *promittet*, *purposit* beside *purposed* (18), *scippit* beside *scippid* (2). The same process, combined with contraction, probably accounts for *visit* and *visite*, both p.t., beside *visited* (3).

22. f There is a good deal of variation between final *f* and *ue*, as in -*self* (17) beside -*selue* (14), *lif* and *lyf* sb. (42) beside *lyue* (6), but the adj. (and sb.) ending that gives PresE -*ive* always occurs as -*if*, as in *natif*.[1]

23. ġ Beside usual *g*, *j* is occasionally used medially for /dʒ/ in loanwords: *majesté* beside *magesté*; *trajedi(es)* (2) beside *tragedies*; *venjauns* (7), *venjabil* beside *venge* (9), *venged* (5); *Jene* 'Genoa' beside *Gene*.

The spelling *ch* occurs for /dʒ/ in *lichmen* and *lychmen*, beside *ligemen* (5); it is presumably a hypercorrect attempt to avoid showing the voicing of /tʃ/ to /dʒ/ that occurred in words like PresE *knowledge*.[2]

24. ġh The only word with MnE -*gh* which is spelt with *ȝ* is *þouȝ* (20) beside *þou* (5), *þow* (2), *thow*. Words with MnE -*ght* are never spelt with *ȝ* or *gh*, as *brout(e)* (80), *browt(e)* (15), *knyt(e)* (44), *rite* (46). In this group of words spellings with -*th* also occur, as *rith*(-) (11), *ryth*.[3]

25. h Omission of historical *h* sometimes occurs, as in *it* (394), *oseled* beside *hoseled* (2), *exortacion* (2) beside *exhorted*. Addition of unhistorical *h* occurs rather more frequently, as in *herl*(-) (5) beside *erl*(-) (232), *hys* 'ice', *hooth* (2) beside *o(o)th* (25), *wrecchidhest*.[4]

26. k Initially *k*, beside usual *c*, is sometimes used before *a*, in *karding*, *kalend(is)* (7), *kam* beside *cam* (240), *karikis*, also *skaped* beside *scape(d)* (10), once before *o*, in *kowardly*, and once before *l*, in *kleped* beside *cleped* (286). In other positions there is variation, in *mark* 'monetary unit' (16) beside *marc* (13), *reuoke(d)* (3) beside *reuoced* and *reuocacion*, *serkil* beside *sercle*, *vnkil* and *vnkik* (erroneous for *vnkil*) beside *vncil* (7) and *vncle* (6).

For the double letter *kk* is commonest, as in *wikkid(nes)* (9);

---

[1] For a full discussion of this feature see my 'Orthographic Usage', pp. 337–8, § 8.

[2] See further my 'Orthographic Usage', p. 332, § 2.

[3] For a full discussion of this feature see my 'Orthographic Usage', pp. 338–9, § 9.

[4] For a full discussion of this feature see my 'Orthographic Usage', pp. 339–40, § 10.

cc is rare, occurring in *saccis* beside *wollesakkes*, *occasiones* (2), *occupie(d)* (17) and *occupacion* (2), but presumably it has a different phonic significance in *occean* (4) and in words like *subjeccion* (9), where it is used regularly (hence, probably, Capgrave's evident reluctance to use it as an alternative for *kk*); *ck* occurs but twice, in *arck* beside *arke*, and in *patriack* (*r* before *ck* presumably omitted by mistake) beside *patriark(e)* (8), *patriarkes* (2), and is thus used as an alternative to single rather than double *k*.

Hesitation between *c* and *k* may be a cause of scribal error in *patriack* (for *patriarck*) and *vnkik* (for *vnkil*).

Occasionally *ch* is used for /k/, as in *lich* (18) beside *liknes(s)* (7), *likid*, *likned*.[1]

27. l   Apparent loss of *l* occurs once in *word* beside *world(is)* (29), and once in *schud* beside *schuld(e)* (655).

28. n   In general, avoidance of final *n* seems to have been preferred, as the following figures for verb endings indicate:

Infinitive	with -*n* (7)	without -*n* (over 1000)
Pr. pl.	with -*n* (6)	without -*n* (over 150)
P.t. pl.	with -*n* (32)	without -*n* (over 190)
Strong pp.	with -*n* (176)	without -*n* (340)
All forms 'be'	no forms with -*n*	

A very large proportion of the instances with -*n* occur before a vowel or *h*.[2]

In adjectives such as *my*, *no*, *o* 'one', *þi*, final -*n* is generally lost except when a vowel follows (whilst the equivalent pronoun forms are *myn*, *non*, *on*, *þin*). Retention of -*n* before a consonant or absence of -*n* before a vowel are both extremely rare. Lack of -*n* occurs sporadically in a few proper names, as *Mylforth Haue*, beside *hauene* (3), and *Burton upo Trent*, *Newcastell upo Tyne*. Intrusive *n* occurs in *Octones*, pl. of the proper name *Octo*.

29. p   A glide consonant *p* between *m* and a following voiceless consonant is apparently shown in *dempt* (2) p.t. of 'deem'. Other possible examples, such as *condempned* (19), probably reflect historical variants.[3]

In two words *p* alternates with *b*: *opteyned* beside *obteyne*, and *puplischid* beside *publisced*; in the latter case the variation may reflect variant OF forms.

---

[1] See further my 'Orthographic Usage', pp. 331–2, § 2.

[2] For a full discussion of this feature see my 'Orthographic Usage', pp. 344–6, §§ 15–20.

[3] See further my 'Orthographic Usage', p. 347, § 21.

30. **q** Initially there is a strong preference for *qw-* (88%) over *qu-* (12%). Medially there is roughly equal distribution with a slight preference for *-qu-*.

31. **s** For /s/ *c* is used beside *s*. In initial position there is variation only in *cenewes/senewis* 'sinews' and *Cistewis/Sistewes* 'Cistercians' (1/3). In other positions, for every three words which show variation there are eight spelt only with either *c* or *s*; an example of variation is *malice* (12) and *malyce* beside *malys* (3). In the ending which is now *-tion c* is usual, as in *nacio(u)n* (10), but *s* (usually *ss* after a vowel) does occur, as in *possession* (16); only one such word shows variation, *extorciones* beside *extorsion*.

32. **sh** Initially always spelt *sch*, except once in *scryues*. Normally the spelling *sc* indicates /s/, as in *scepter*, or /sk/, as in *scape*. Medially *sch* is in variation with *sc* in *bischop/biscop* (287/10) and *-schire/ -scire* (11/1). The spelling *ch* occurs in *marchale* (14) and in the suffix MnE *-ship*, where it usually follows a dental, as in *frendchip*, *lordchip(is)* beside *lordschippis*, *worchip(-)* (50) (eME *woröschipe*), but not in *felawchip* (12). Finally *sch* is in variation with *ch*, as in *fresch/frech* (2/1). In words with MnE *-ish*, representing OF *-iss-*, an extension of the stem of verbs in *-ir*, there is a tendency to suppress the vowel and spell with *ch*, as in *norched* (5).[1]

33. **t** Occasionally *d* is written instead of *t* after *n*: *acoundith*, *-id* beside *acountid* (2), and *marchaund(is)* (5) beside *marchaunt(is)* (3).

34. **th** The *y*-form of *þ* alternates with *th* in many words. Initially *th/þ* spellings occur in the ratio 1 : 9. Most of the instances with *th* in fact have *Th* as they occur at the beginning of a sentence or other important syntactic unit. The word *thre* (29) never has *þ-*. In other positions *þ* (in its *y*-form) is commoner than *th*, variation occurring only in *anothir*, *brothir*, *bretherin*, *clothis*, *othir*, *whethir*, *worthi*. The words *eythir* (2) and *neythir* (5) are never spelt with *þ*, probably because the juxtaposition of *þ* (in its *y*-form) and *y* was felt to be undesirable, the two being indistinguishable.[2] The spelling *tʒ* occurs in *witʒ* (3) beside *with* (667), *wyth* and *wᵗ* (8). Some words with historical *th/þ* between vowels show *d*-spellings, as *fedir-*, *leddir*, *eydir* (2) beside *eythir* (2), *eithir*. The medial consonant-sound in such words has presumably fallen together with that in words like *fader(-)* (96), which never show *th/þ*. Other words, like *opir*, *bropir*, never have medial *d*. Two words with historical *rth/rþ* always

---

[1] For a full discussion of this feature see my 'Orthographic Usage', pp. 330–1, § 2.

[2] For a full discussion of this feature see my 'Orthographic Usage', pp. 332–4, § 3.

have *d*-spellings, *erd*(-) (25) (possibly influenced by the reflex
of OE *eard*), and *morder* (2), *mordred* (possibly influenced by
OF *murdre*), but other words, like *ferper*, never have medial *d*.[1]

35. **v**   Spelt *w* in *dowe*(*s*) (2) and *nowil* 'navel'.

36. **w**   Spelt *v* in *avayte* sb. beside *awayte*.

37. **wh** The reflex of OE *hw-* is regularly spelt *wh* apart from three
isolated exceptions, *qwan* beside *whan*(*ne*) (263), *wech* beside
whech (608), *which* (2), *wite* beside *white* (6), *whiting*. Apparently
the avoidance of spellings with initial *qw*, which is a characteristic
idiosyncrasy of Norfolk writers, was deliberate; the one tell-tale
exception suggests as much. Spellings with *q* are also avoided in
sware 'square' and *swier*(*e*) 'squire' (4), *swyere*(*s*) (5), and *swieres*
(6). Besides the two isolated exceptions with *w* for normal *wh*
there are two reverse spellings of initial *wh* for historical *w*,
whas beside *was* (2004), and *white* 'weight'. Evidently there was a
deliberate attempt, largely successful, to distinguish *wh* from *w*.[2]

38. **y**   MnE initial *y* is always spelt *ʒ-*, never *y-*, as in *ʒe* (25), *ʒour*(*e*)
(26), *ʒer*(-) (917), *ʒong*(-) (48). The only exceptions are where an
alternative with *g-* was available, as *gyuer* beside *ʒiuer*. By
always using *ʒ-*, never *y-*, potential confusion with initial *þ*, in
its *y*-form, was avoided.[3]

39. **z**   Always used in words derived from medL *-izāre*: *baptize*(*d*)
(23), *canonized* (4), *intronized*, *practized*, *solempnyzed*; also
Helize (3) beside *Helise*.

40.   Doubling of the letter representing the last consonant of a word-
stem sometimes occurs, as in *summe* (99), *schippes* (35), *putting*
(2). These double consonantal letters evidently had the effect
of indicating that the preceding vowel was short.[4]

MORPHOLOGY

In this summary Capgrave's usage in regard to the main features
of Middle English morphology is given. Unless it is a page and line
reference a number in brackets after a word indicates how many
times the word occurs in the form cited; a word not so followed
may be assumed to occur once only.

[1] For a full discussion of this feature see my 'Orthographic Usage', p. 337,
§ 7.
[2] For a full discussion of this feature see my 'Orthographic Usage', pp. 340–1,
§ 11.
[3] For a full discussion of this feature see my 'Orthographic Usage', p. 330,
§ 1.
[4] For a full treatment of this feature see my 'Orthographic Usage', pp. 341–3,
§ 12.

Nouns

The plural of nouns is generally indicated by *-es/-is/-ys*.[1] On three occasions the plural is marked by simple *-s*: *mocions*; *sermons* beside *sermones* (2); *suggestions* beside *suggestiones* (2)—all words of French origin and having final *n* in the uninflected form. In *tribus* 'tribes' (3) the *-us* plural is presumably due to Latin influence. Besides *eyne* (10) there are the usual weak plurals in *-(e)n*: *hosen* (2); *oxen* (2); *schon*. This ending has been taken over and is used regularly in *bretheren*, *bretherin* (4), *breþerin* (11) (OE *brēþer*), and also in *childirn* (20), *childyrn* (9), *childryn*, but not regularly, as *childir* (3), *childyr* (OE *cildru*) occur as well. There are also the usual mutation plurals: *feet*, *fete*; *lys*; *men* (289), *-men* (10), poss. pl. *mennes* (5), *mennis* (2); *teeth*; *women* (14). The uninflected plural of the Old English strong neuter nouns with a long stem-vowel is retained in *sche(e)p* (5), though the sense is generally collective. Other uninflected plurals, as *goot* (13/10), *ox* (141/27), *wepun* (15/8), *ȝer(e)* (frequent), and *þing* (17), indicate collectiveness or number. In *sciens* 'fields of knowledge' (4), beside *sciensis*, and *vers* 'lines of verse' (6) the uninflected plural has been taken over with the borrowing of the word from French.

The possessive singular of nouns is generally indicated by *-es/-is/-ys*, but occasionally zero-inflections occur. Some of these unmarked possessives are nouns (*a*) which historically had no distinct genitive ending in Old English, as *broþir*, *fader* (12) beside *faderes* (3), *modir* beside *moderes*, (*b*) which were feminine in Old English and had the genitive marked only by *-e*, as *qween* (2) beside *qwe(e)nes* (3) and *qwenis*, or (*c*) which were declined weak in Old English, as *dogge*. Others are nouns to which the unmarked possessive has been extended where historically the *-es* genitive belongs, as *abbot*, *kyng* (3, all in group genitives) beside *kingis* (14, including 2 in group genitives), *kyngis* (97, including 10 in group genitives), and *kyngis* poss. pl. (2), also (although Middle English formations) *carter*, *sadeler*, or nouns borrowed from French, as *duke* (5, including 4 in group genitives) beside *dukes* (4, including 1 in a group genitive) and *dukis* (in a group genitive), *emperour* (3) beside *empero(u)res* (7), *erle* (in a group genitive)

---

[1] For the proportional distribution of these endings in the pl. and poss. sg. see my 'Orthographic Usage', p. 335, § 5.

beside *erles*.[1] As far as proper nouns are concerned the uninflected possessive is much the commoner construction, some seventy-two instances occurring,[2] as against twenty with *-es/-is*. Variation occurs in the following: *Arthure sistir | Arthures body* (117/9–10 | 110/24); *Edward broþir/hous/fader/dowtir/tyme/day | Edwardes deth* (101/15, 126/4, 133/31, 192/2, 203/8, 214/21 | 156/15); *Richard men/power/baner/tent | Richardis tyme/councel/ere* (114/10 and 12, 114/14, 194/20, 206/16 | 181/23, 212/24, 217/6). Only a few of the proper nouns with the uninflected possessive end in *s*: *Bris* (2), *Gilis*, *Laurens*, and *Thomas* (3). Two such nouns always show the inflected form: *Cristis* (10), and *Poules* (2).

Adjectives

The demonstrative adjectives are (*a*) *that* (10), *þat* (329) sg. and *tho, þo* (24), *þoo* (33) pl., and (*b*) *this* (227), *þis* (888), *þus* sg. and *these* (19), *this, þese* (136), *þes, þis* pl.

Pronouns

The demonstrative pronouns are (*a*) *that* (10), *þat* (65) sg. and *tho, þo* (2), *þoo* (12) pl., and (*b*) *this* (49), *þis* (94) sg. and *these* (9), *þese* (19) pl.

The personal pronouns are as follows:

First person

	sg.	pl.
nom.	*I* (61)	*we* (71)
obl.	*me* (9)	*us* (12), *vs*
poss. adj.	*my* (23), *mi, myn* (4)	*oure* (118), *our* (3)
(absol.)	*myn* 'mine' (2)	*oure* 'ours'

Second person

	sg.	polite sg.	pl.
nom.	*þou* (25), *thou* (7)	*ȝe* (15)	*ȝe* (10)
obl.	*þe* (15), *the* (2)	*ȝou* (7), *ȝow*	*ȝou* (3)
poss. adj.	*þi* (9), *þin* (3)	*ȝoure* (20), *ȝour* (2)	*ȝoure* (4)
(absol.)	*þin* 'yours'		
refl.	*þiself*	*ȝoureselue*	

[1] I have excluded two instances where the noun that could be possessive is more probably used adjectivally: *þe monasteri dores* (239/27); *þe parlement tyme* (232/20).

[2] I have excluded three instances where the noun that could be possessive is more probably used adjectivally: *London gates* (241/30), *ȝork walles* (144/30); *Rome wallis* (73/30).

Third person

	masc. sg.	fem. sg.	neut. sg.	pl.
nom.	*he* (2079)	*sche* (101)	*it* (236), *he* (6)	*þei* (829), *thei* (57), *they* (7), *þe* (4), *þai*
obl.	*him* (771), *hym* (5)	*hir* (48), *hire* (2)	*it* (157), *him*	*hem* (362), *þem*
poss. adj. (absol.)	*his* (1247)	*hir* (55)	*his* (8)	*her* (272), *here* (17) *her* 'theirs'
refl.	*himself* (9), *himselue* (7)	*hirselue*	*himself*	*hemself* (6), *hemselue* (5)

In the first and second person singular, forms of the possessive adjective in *-n*, *myn* and *þin*, are used in absolute position and occasionally before a vowel or *h*, but *myn* occurs before a consonant once, in an apostrophe, *O myn benigne lord . . .* (8/8). In the third person note the regular distinction between *hir* 'her' and *her* 'their'. The instance of *her* 'theirs' (97/21) is the latest use recorded by *MED her(e* pron. poss. pl. 2. Of the 829 instances of *þei* in the nominative plural of the third person six have *þe*[i] with suprascript *i* (probably entered as a correction) and suggest a desire to distinguish the pronoun from the definite article: two occurrences of *þei* 'the'—beside *þe* (5538)—are presumably hypercorrect spellings resulting from this desire. The solitary instance of *þai*, like that of *þem* in the oblique case, suggests both a knowledge of this spelling (or form) and an attempt, presumably conscious, to avoid it.

Verbs

The infinitive is normally written without final *n* (over 1,000). Spellings with *-n* (7) are due to special circumstances: three occur before a vowel, two occur in rhyme, and three (including one of those before a vowel) may reflect a vestigial use of the inflected infinitive, in *þat is to seyn* (2) and by analogy in *here is for to noten þat* (beside *note* (4) in similar constructions).[1]

The second person singular of the present tense generally ends in *-ist* (4), once *-est*; *hast* (7) and *seist* show contraction or syncopation. In *tredis* (123/22) final *t* is lacking before a dental consonant.

---

[1] For a full discussion of this feature see my 'Orthographic Usage', p. 344, § 15. For the proportional distribution of the endings *-en/-in/-yn* see ibid., pp. 346–7, § 20.

The third person singular of the present tense generally ends in *-ith* (56), also *-eth* (31), *-yth* (6); *(be)comth* (2) and *stant* (13), beside *standith*, show syncopation, as do verbs with stems ending in a vowel or diphthong, *doth* (2), *goth* (5), *lith* (31), *seith* (23); *hath* (18) shows contraction. All the instances of *-yth* occur after *n* or *u* 'v' where the use of *y* rather than *i* made for greater clarity (though *-ith* is used nine times in the same circumstance). The same consideration may also account for the twenty-two instances of *-eth* after *i, y, m, n, u*. In *beginnit* the lack of final *h* is probably to be accounted for by the common alternation between *-t* and *-th* in words with MnE *-ght* (see Phonology, § 24), also in *Japhet* (2) beside *Japheth* (2).[1]

The plural of the present tense is normally written without final *n* (over 150). Spellings with *-n* (6) occur in short native words, *longin, longyn* (3), *writyn* (before *h*), and in a longer foreign word, *trespasin* (before a vowel).[2]

The present participle usually ends in *-ing* (100) or *-yng* (75); *prayng* (4), beside *praying* (5), and *seyng*, beside *seying* (2), show syncopation. There are also a small number of instances in *-and*: *folowand* (once, plus 9 other instances used adjectivally) beside *folowing/-yng* (2, plus 3 other instances used adjectivally), *lyuand* (2) beside *lyuyng* (4) and *leuyng, lyand, seiand* beside *seying* (2) and *seyng*.

In the treatment of the past tense and past participle endings it will be convenient to deal with the strong verbs first. From Table 1 on pp. lxii–lxiv, which gives the principal parts of the strong verbs, it can be seen that the historical classes of strong verb remained fairly distinct. The greatest loss of distinctiveness is in class V where the p.t. pl. (also pp.) forms *begotin* etc., *gote, forgoten, goue, spoke, trode, woue*, if not from Old Norse, are developed analogically from class IV, so that the historical vowel of the p.t. pl. in class V (OE Angl. *mēton*) is not preserved, unless in *ete*. Other instances of one verb class influencing another occur in class IV, where p.t. sg. *cam* is by analogy with forms in class III like *began*, and in class VI, where p.t. sg. and pl. *drew* is by analogy with forms in class VII like *grew*, but both these instances affect only individual verbs rather than a whole class. In many verbs the vowel of the sg. and pl. of the past tense have become identical, either through

---

[1] Cf. also *bitumen/bithumen, cateloge/cathologe*.
[2] See further my 'Orthographic Usage', p. 344, § 16.

TABLE 1. *Strong verbs: principal parts*

Class	inf.	p.t. sg.	p.t. pl.	pp.
I	abide (2), abyde (2)	abod (3), abood	abiden, abydyn (2), abode (2)	abedyn
				bityn
	dryue	drof, droue (3)		dryue, dryuyn (2)
	ride (6), ryde	rod (20), rode (3), rood (9)	ride, ryde, riden, ouirridin, ridyn, ouyrrydin, rydyn, rood (3)	ouyrrydyn
	rise (5)	ros (20), rose (3), roos	rise (3), ryse, risen (7), risin (5), rysin, rysyn	rysen
				schriue, schryue
	smite, smyte (5)	smet (18)	smet (4)	smet (14)
	write (13)	wrot (14), wrote (28)	writin, writyn (2), wrytyn, wrote	wretin, writen, writin (10), writyn, wrytin (3), wrytyn (7)
II	chese (11)	chase (3), chose (coll. sg.)	chose (23)	chose (21), chosen (15)
	fle (13)	fley	Also *fled* (60), *fledde*	
	forbedyng pr. p.	forbad (4), forbade (2)		forbode (2)
III	beginne, begynne (2)	began (58), beganne	begun, begunne (2), began (3)	begunne (6)
		bond (2)	bonde	bond,[1] bound (2), bounde (2), bownde (2)
		drank		
	fite (27)	faut (3), fawt, faute (8), fawte (2)	foutyn, faut, faute (9), fawte	
	fynde (5)	fond (21), fonde (2)	fond (16), fonde (2), found, founde (7)	found (6), founde (27)
		gan		
	ȝelde (2)	ȝald	ȝold (2), ȝolde	ȝolde, ȝoldyn (2)
	help (26), helpe	halp	holp, holpe	holpen
		malt		molten (2)
	renne pr. 3 pl. (3)	ran (5)	runne (2)	
	sing, singe (2)	sang (3)	songin	songe (2), songen, sunge (2)
		sprang (3)	sprong	
	wyn	wan (7)	wonne (2)	wonne, wunne

[1] See Commentary, note to 41/13.

Class	inf.	p.t. sg.	p.t. pl.	pp.
IV	bere (4)		bore (2)	bor, bore (29), born (36)
	breke (3), forbreke	brak (11), brake	broke (11)	brok, broke (4), broken (2), brokyn, tobroken
		brast		
	com (29), come (30), ouircom	cam (172), kam, ouyrcam (12), com (also coll. sg.), come (also coll. sg.)	cam (71), came, com (18), come (28)	com (9), come (15), ouyrcom, ouyrcome (3)
	stele	stal	stole	stole (2)
V		bad (4)		
	begete	begat (27)	begotin	begoten, begotin, begotyn
		beqwath, beqwathe (2)	beqwathe	
	ete (2)	ete (5) fret (coll. sg.)	ete (2)	ete
	geue, gyue (18), forgyue	gaf (17), forgaf, gaue (26) ȝaue	gaue (3), ȝoue	goue (10)
	gete (8)	gat (3)	gote	get, forgete, gote (2), forgoten
	ly (wk pr.)	lay (23)	lay	
	mete (5)	met (9), mette (2)	met (9), mette (3)	
	se (22)	say (5), sei (4), sey (28)		sey, seyn (7), seyne
	sitte (3) (wk pr.)	sat (6)	sat (3)	
	speke (7)	spak (4)	spak, spoke	spoke, spokyn (adj.)
	trede (2)			trode woue
VI	drawe (4), withdrawe (6)	drew (2), drow (5), withdrow	drew, drow (3), drowe, withdrow	draw, drawe (11), drawen (5)
		flay		flayn
	forsake (5)	forsok (2), forsoke (3), forsook (2)	forsoke	
	lawh	low		
				schaue
	sle (4)			slayn (38)
	stand (11), stande (2), vndirstand (5), withstand	vndirstod (3), vndirstood (3), withstood	stod (5), stood (21), vndirstod	vndirstand (3)
	swere (wk. pr.)	swore (7)	swore (6)	swore (9), sworne

TABLE I *(cont.)*

Class	inf.	p.t. sg.	p.t. pl.	pp.
VI (cont.)	*take* (21), *vndirtake*	*tok* (12), *took* (97), *vndirtook* (2)	*took* (41)	*tak, take* (81), *taken* (9), *takyn* (3), *vndirtake*
		wook		
VII		*beet*	*bet*	*beten*
		blew (5), *blewe*		
	falle (6)	*fel* (34), *fell* (14), *felle* (3)	*fel* (4), *fell* (5), *felle*	*falle* (3)
		ouyrflew		*ouirflowe*
	grow, growe (3)	*grew* (6)	*grew*	*growe* (4)
	hald (3), *behald*, *hold* (4), *holde* (2)	*held* (44)	*held* (6)	*hald* (5), *hold* (3), *holden, holdyn*
	hange	*hing* (4)	*hing*	*hang* (3), *hange* (2), *hangen* (4), *hangin*, also *hanged* (7), *hangged, hangid* (3)
		hew		
	hite pr. 3 sg. (2)	*hite* (50), *behite*, *behote*		*hite* (4), *behite*, *behote* (2)
	knowe (4)	*knew* (9), *knewe* (2)	*knew* (3)	*knowe, aknowe* (2), *onknowe, knowyn*
	let	*let, lete* (3)	*let, lete*	*let*
	rede pr. 1 pl. (7)	*red* (7)		*red* (7)
	þrow (2), *þrowe* (2)	*threw, þrew*		*þrow* (2), *þrowe*, *ouirthrowe*
	wax	*wex* (2)		

the vowel of the p.t. sg. being extended to the pl., as in (class I) *abode, rood, wrote*, (class III) *faut(e), fawte, began*, (class IV) p.t. pl. *cam(e)*, (class V) *beqwathe, gaue, sat, spak*, or through the vowel of the p.t. pl. and pp. being extended to the p.t. sg., as in (class I) *smet*, (class III) *bond, fond(e)*, or through the vowel of the pp. being extended to the p.t. sg. and pl., as in (class V) *fret, met(te)*, (class VI) *flay* (pl. not recorded). In some verbs the vowel of the pp. has been extended to the p.t. pl., as in (class III) *ȝold(e), holp(e)*; in the standard type of class IV verb this extension is general, as in *bore, broke, stole*, also in p.t. pl. *com(e)*. In *hite* (VII) the vowel of the p.t. has been extended to the inf. and pp. Only two verbs show weak as well as the (historically correct) strong forms: *fle* (II) with its p.t. forms *fled(de)*, and *hange* (VII) with its pp. forms in -*ed*. One verb shows the opposite tendency, strong pp. forms beside the other (historically correct) weak ones: *dronch(in)* beside p.t. *drenchid*, perhaps through the influence of the cognate pp. *drunken (from *drink), or perhaps by analogy with class III strong verbs like *help/holpen*. In class II the root vowel of p.t. *chase* presumably descends from OE *eá*, and p.t. *forbad(e)* is probably by analogy with *bad* (class V).

In the past tense and past participle of weak verbs some 80 per cent of all instances end in -*ed*, 17.75 per cent in -*id*, 0.5 per cent in -*yd*, and 1.75 per cent in -*d*. Most of the uses of -*id* may have been induced either by the letter(s) preceding the ending, as with -*chid* (49) beside -*ched* (7), or by the spelling or pronunciation of the vowel in the verb-stem, as with *killid* (98), *kyllid* (5), *killyd* beside *killed* (2). Endings in -*d* are commonest after *r*, as in *answerd* (17) beside *answered* (10), but even after this letter occur in only about 7.5 per cent of all possible instances. They also occur rarely after *n*, as in *somound*, and once after *l*, in *strangild* beside *strangeled*, *strangillid*. After vowels -*d* is regular in *leyd(e)* p.t. and pp. of 'lay' (14), *leid(e)* (11), *layd(e)* (5), *laid*, but usually the ending is given in full, as in *payed* (24).[1] In the irregular weak verbs (class I) the only feature of note is the variation in the p.t. and pp. of *selle*, p.t. *seld* (8), *sold*, pp. *seld*, *sold* (2), and *telle*, p.t. *teld*, *told* (15), pp. *told* (6). *Cac(c)h*, a French loan-word, has p.t. *cacchid*, *caut*, *caute* (3), pp. *caute*. The forms of *haue* and *say* (class III) are given in Table 2 below. The infinitive form *a* occurs only

TABLE 2. *Weak verbs class III*

	HAVE	SAY
inf.	*haue* (120), *a* (19), *ha* (4)	*say*, *sei* (5), *sey* (44), *seye* (2), *seyn*
pr. 2 sg.	*hast* (7)	*seist*
pr. 3 sg.	*hath* (18)	*seith* (23)
pr.p.	*hauing* (2), *hauyng* (5)	*saying* (2), *seyng*
p.t.	*had* (468), *hadde*	*said* (5), *saide* (26), *sayd* (2), *sayde* (3), *seid* (47), *seide* (52), *seyd*, *seyde* (7)
pp.	*had* (16)	*said* (2), *saide* (3), *seid* (35), *seide* (15), *seyd* (3)

[1] For a full discussion of the endings of the p.t. and pp. of weak verbs see my 'Orthographic Usage', pp. 336–7, § 6.

after *schuld* (9) and *wold* (10), and *ha* only after *myte, mite* (2), and *wold* (2). The present participle form *seyng* occurs also on three occasions for 'seeing'. Many past participles (and some past tense forms) taken over from Latin past participles have not been fully assimilated to the weak class and end in *-t(e)* rather than *-ted*: *abrogat* (2), *consecrat* (2), *consecrate* (2) also p.t., *contracte, conuicte* (2) also p.t., *correct, correcte* but *corrected* p.t., *depauperat, detect, detecte, deuolute, distribut* p.t., *eject, frustrat, frustrate, induct, infect* (3), *infecte* (3), *inhibite, legittimat, porrect, rejecte, sublimat, suffocat, translat* (4) also p.t., *translate* (8) also p.t. (7) but also *translated* p.t.; *consecrate* (2) and *infecte* also occur as infinitives.

The forms of the preterite-present and anomalous verbs are given in Table 3.

TABLE 3. *Preterite-present and anomalous verbs*

BE	inf. *be* (332), *bee*; pr. 1 sg. *am* (3), 3 sg. *is* (302), pr.pl. *be* (50), *ar* (6), *are*; pr. p. *being*; p.t. sg. *was* (2004), *whas*, pl. *were* (523), *wer* (6); pp. *be* (32)
CAN	pr. 1 sg. *can* (3), pr.pl. *can* (2); p.t. *coude* (13), *coud*
DARE	pr.pl. *dare*; p.t. *durst* (12)
DO	inf. *do* (30), *doo* (2); pr.pl. *do, doo*; imper. sg. *do* (4), pl. *do*; p.t. *ded* (85), *dede* (3); pp. *do* (28), *doo* (7), *don* (3)
GO	inf. *go* (53), *goo* (5), *forgo*; p.t. *went* (146); pp. *go* (7), *goo*
MAY	pr. 2 sg. *may*, 3 sg. *may* (11), pr.pl. *may* (9); p.t. *myte* (68), *mite* (23), *mith*
MOTE	pr.pl. *mote* (3); p.t. *must* (10)
OWE	pr.pl. *owe*; p.t. *aute, awte*
SHALL	pr. 1 sg. *schal* (6), 2 sg. *schal* (7), *schalt*, 3 sg. *schal* (33), *schall*, *schul* (2), pr.pl. *schal* (16), *schul* (13); p.t. *schuld* (649), *schulde* (6), *schul* (16), *schud*
WILL	pr. 1 sg. *wil* (3), pr.pl. *wil* (10), *will* (2); p.t. *wold* (131), *wolde* (4), 2 sg. *woldist*
WITE	inf. *wete* (3), *wite* (2); p.t. *wist* (6), *wyst*

VOCABULARY

In this section some sixty-four words (and phrases) which apparently occur for the first time in English in the *Abbreuiacion of Cronicles* are listed, whether this occurrence is recorded in the dictionaries or not. At the time of writing *MED* has reached the letter N, so it is possible that subsequent fascicules of this dictionary will produce earlier instances of some words beginning with the letters O to Z (also 3 = Y). Words already in use but which occur in the *Abbreuiacion of Cronicles* in a sense not recorded earlier in English are not dealt with.[1]

abrogat pp. 'annulled' 140/27, 200/20 [L *abrogāt-us*]. Instance at 140/27 cited by *OED Abrogate* a. and pple and *MED abrogat* as earliest occurrence.

had in age 'was aged' 24/7. Not recorded by *OED* or *MED*; cf. *MED age* n. 1c.

annotacio(u)n n. 'chronological reckoning, notation' 7/34, 30/18, 116/30; **annotaciones** pl. 'historical records' 203/13 [L *annotātiōn-em*]. Instance at 30/18 cited by *OED Annotation* as earliest occurrence, also cited, together with that at 116/30, as only ME occurrences by *MED annotacion*. The L etymology is confirmed by the pl. instance, where the sense is taken from medL.

forth anon 'promptly' 196/27. Not recorded by *OED* or *MED*; cf. *MED an-on* adv. and conj. 1(b).

Bauaris n. pl. 'people of Bavaria' 84/24 [f. L *Bavāria*]. Not recorded by *OED* or *MED*.

Benedictines n. pl. 'regulations made by Pope Benedict XII' 158/26 [f. L *Benedictus*]. The only recorded instance in English, cited by *MED Benedictin*, but not by *OED*.

þe betir part 'the upper hand' 232/25. Not recorded by *OED* or *MED*; cf. *OED Better* a. A.5.

bit(h)umen n. 'pitch' 20/22, 26/24 [L *bitūmen*]. Instance at 26/24 cited by *OED Bitumen* as earliest occurrence, also cited, together with that at 20/22, as only ME occurrences by *MED bitumen*.

Bulgaris n. pl. 'inhabitants of Bulgaria' 77/14 [medL *Bulgārus*]. Recorded by *OEDS Bulgar* from 1759; not recorded by *MED*.

Chestirreres n. pl. '(rough) men from Chester' (adherents of Richard II) 211/23 [f. ME *Chestir* (OE *Legaceaster*) prob. by analogy with medL *Cestrenses*]. Not recorded by *OED* or *MED*.

[1] For such words beginning with letters in the first half of the alphabet see my 'Additions, Antedatings, Postdatings and Corrections to *OED* and *MED*, A–L', pp. 232–5, §§ 1.2 and 2.2.

cianeus n. 'lapis lazuli' 22/5 [L *cyanus*]. Not recorded by *OED* or *MED*.

collocucion n. 'conversation' 93/14 [L *collocūtiōn-em*]. Cited by *OED Collocution* as earliest occurrence, also cited together with an instance from Capgrave's *Gilbert*, as only ME occurrences by *MED collocucion*.

completori n. 'compline' 82/5 [ecclL *complētōri-um*]. *OED Completory* B.2 and *MED completorie* cite an instance from *Miroure of Mans Saluacionne* which may be earlier.

at his consent 'by compliance with his request' 150/16. Not recorded by *OED* or *MED*; cf. *OED Consent* sb. 2b.

Constantinopolitan adj. 'of Constantinople' 184/1–2 [L *Constantino-polītān-us*]. Recorded by *OED Constantinopolitan* from *c*.1568; not recorded by *MED*.

costfully adv. 'expensively' 244/1. Cited by *OED Costful* a. as earliest occurrence, also by *MED costfulli* as only ME occurrence.

depauperat pp. 'impoverished' 83/12 [medL *dēpauperāt-us*]. Cited by *OED Depauperate* ppl. a. as earliest occurrence, also by *MED depauperat* as only ME occurrence.

deuolute pp. 'transferred' 42/21 [L *dēvolūt-us*]. Cited by *OED Devolute* ppl. a. as earliest occurrence, also by *MED deuolute* as only ME occurrence.

diuulgid pp. 'made generally known' 7/6, 11/19, **dyuulged** 175/23 [L *dīvulgāre*]. Instance at 7/6 cited by *OED Divulge* v. as earliest occurrence, also cited, together with that at 175/23 and another instance from Capgrave's *Solace*, as only ME occurrences by *MED divulgen*.

domicelles n. pl. 'young ladies' 206/21 [medL *domicella*]. Cited by *OED Domicelle* as the only instance in English, but *MED* cites it under *damisele* where it is the only instance with *o* in the first syllable. Since Capgrave's word clearly derives from L, not OF, *OED* was right to treat it as a separate word.

Dominic adj. 'Dominican' 170/26 [f. L *Dominicus*]. Recorded by *OED Dominic* a. and sb. from 1674; not recorded by *MED*.

Dominices n. pl. 'Dominicans' 195/19 [as prec.]. Recorded by *OED Dominic* a. and sb. from *c*.1540; not recorded by *MED*.

edifieres n. pl. 'builders' 20/29 [f. OF *édifier*]. Cited by *OED Edifier* and *MED edifiere* as earliest occurrence.

had eleccion of 'was the choice of', 'was elected by' 70/24. Not recorded by *OED* or *MED*.

enchete v. 'confiscate for royal treasury' 226/16 [f. OF *encheoite*]. Cited by *OED Encheat* v. and *MED encheten* as earliest occurrence.

enchetyng vbl. n. 'confiscation for the royal treasury' 232/31 [f. prec.].

Cited by *MED encheting* as only ME occurrence; not recorded by *OED*.

enormes n. pl. 'wicked acts' 118/16 [f. OF *énorme*, L *ēnorm-is*]. Cited by *MED enorme* adj. as n. as only ME occurrence; recorded by *OED Enorm* from 1535 (adj. from 1481).

fayre-spokyn adj. 'eloquent' 65/1 [OE *fægre* + pp. of *sprecan*]. Cited by *OED Fair-spoken* and by *MED fair(e* adv. 3(a), together with an instance from Capgrave's *Augustine*, as earliest occurrences.

in so fer þat 'to the extent that' 222/18. Recorded by *OED In* prep. 38 from 1596; not recorded by *MED in* prep. 27.

flagellid p.t. 'scourged' 76/17 [L *flagellāre*]. Cited by *MED flagellen* as only ME occurrence; recorded by *OED Flagelle* v. from 1550.

forum n. 'forum' 25/22 [L *forum*]. Cited by *OED Forum* as earliest occurrence, also by *MED forum* as only ME occurrence.

ȝeringis n. pl. 'yearlings' 13/12 [f. OE *gēr*]. Cited by *OED Yearing* sb. as earliest occurrence.

holy fro 'reverently set apart from' 155/10. Not recorded by *OED* or *MED*; cf. *OED Holy* a. 1 and *MED holi* adj. (2) 3b.(a).

innoumbred pp. adj. 'countless' 92/28 [f. L *innumerātus*]. Cited by *MED innombred* as earliest occurrence; recorded by *OED Innumered* from 1471.

instructoures n. pl. 'teachers' 204/6 [L *instructor*]. Cited by *OED Instructor* as earliest occurrence, also by *MED instructour* as only ME occurrence.

insulane n. 'islander' 161/13 [L *insulān-us*]. Cited by *OED Insulan* as earliest occurrence, also by *MED insulane* as only ME occurrence.

karding vbl. n. 'carding or combing of wool, cotton, etc.' 13/30 [f. medL *cardāre*, OF *carder*]. Cited by *MED carding* ger. (1) as earliest occurrence; recorded by *OED Carding* vbl. sb.[1] from 1468.

legittimacion n. 'official declaration of legitimacy' 206/31 [medL *lēgitimātiōn-em*]. Cited by *OED Legitimation* as earliest occurrence, also by *MED legitimacion* as only ME occurrence.

lym-whiting n. 'whitewash' 181/13 [OE *lim* + vbl. n. f. OE *hwītian*]. Cited by *MED lim* n. (2) 4.(c) as only ME occurrence; not recorded by *OED* but cf. *Lime* sb.[1] 5.

for his lyue 'for the remainder of his lifetime' 114/2. Recorded by *OED Life* sb. 8b in similar phrase from 1576; not recorded by *MED lif* n. 2.(b).

mateyns and houres of oure Lady 'Little Office of our Lady' 100/30. Not recorded by *OED* or *MED*; cf. *MED matin* 1.(c).

Maundé Þursday 'Maundy Thursday' 56/29, 234/1. Instance at 56/29 cited, together with an instance from Capgrave's *Norbert*, as only ME occurrences by *MED maunde* n. (2); recorded by *OED Maundy Thursday* from 1517.

Moises-werk n. 'mosaic designs' 78/26 [tr. L *moseo opere* (abl.) and prob. from confusion of medL *mōsaicus* and *Mōsāicus* or OF derivs.]. Not recorded by *OED* or *MED*; cf. *OED Mosaic work*, recorded from 1606.

monstrows adj. 'unnatural' 24/1 [L *monstrōs-us*]. Cited by *OED Monstrous* as earliest occurrence. *MED* does not distinguish between *monstrous* and *monstruous* (L *monstruōs-us*); cf. *OED Monstruous*.

obloqui n. 'obloquy' 221/1 [lateL *obloqui-um*]. Cited by *OED Obloquy* as earliest occurrence.

patently adv. 'openly' 175/23 [f. OF *patent* adj.]. Recorded by *OED Patently* from 1863; cf. *OED Patent* a. 7.

Pelagianes n. pl. 'adherents of Pelagius' 66/24 [lateL *Pelagiān-us* adj.]. Recorded by *OED Pelagian* sb.[1] from 1532.

do plesauns to 'please' 142/30. Not recorded by *OED Pleasance*[1]; cf. *Pleasing* vbl. sb. 1.

porphiri-ston n. 'porphyry' 102/20 [medL *porphyri-um* + OE *stān* tr. L *porphyrius lapis*]. Cited by *OED Porphyry* 5b as earliest occurrence.

postiled p.t. 'commented upon' 121/1 [medL *postillāre*]. Cited by *OED Postil* v. as earliest occurrence.

rebaptized pp. 'baptized again' 62/2, 6 [lateL *rebaptizāre*]. Instance at 62/2 cited by *OED Rebaptize* as earliest occurrence.

reformeres n. pl. 'persons disposed to change the attitude of others' 160/13 [f. OF *reformer* or L *reformāre*]. Recorded by *OED Reformer*[1] from 1526.

regner n. 'ruler' 42/18 [f. OF *regner* or L *regnāre*]. Cited by *OED Reigner* as earliest occurrence.

rejeccion n. 'rejection' 192/3 [L *rējectiōn-em*]. Recorded by *OED Rejection* from 1552.

repayrer n. 'one who restores' 73/12 [f. OF *reparer* or L *reparāre*]. Recorded by *OED Repairer*[2] from 1504.

Scicilianes n. pl. 'Sicilians' 129/25 [f. L *Sicilia*]. Recorded by *OED Sicilian* sb. from 1513.

Sey-euel n. 'verbal detraction', as name for Pope Benedict XI 134/21 [OE *secgan* + OE *yfel* tr. L *maledic*]. Not recorded by *OED*; cf. *Say-well*.

semigoddes n. pl. 'demigods' 41/6 [L *sēmi* + OE *god* tr. L *sēmideus*]. Cited by *OED Semigod* as earliest occurrence.

to his seruyse 'at his disposal' 237/10. Not recorded by *OED*: cf. *Service*[1] 25.

sublimat pp. adj. 'exalted' 74/24 [L *sublimāt-us*]. Cited by *OED Sublimate* pa. pple and ppl. a. as earliest occurrence.

suffocat pp. 'killed by suffocation' 210/6 [L *suffōcāt-us*]. Cited by *OED*
  Suffocate pa. pple and ppl. a. as earliest occurrence.
ternaries n. pl. 'sets of three' 8/31 [lateL *ternārius* adj.]. Cited by *OED*
  Ternary sb. as earliest occurrence.
thurifie v. 'offer incense' 60/32 [ecclL *thūrificāre*]. Cited by *OED*
  Thurify, together with another instance from Capgrave's *Katharine*,
  as earliest occurrences.
zelator n. 'defender', 'supporter' 244/4; **zelato(u)ris** pl. 152/3,
  235/2 [ecclL *zēlātor*]. Instance at 152/3 cited by *OED Zelator*
  as earliest occurrence.

Of these sixty-four words (or phrases) which apparently occur
for the first time in English in the *Abbreuiacion of Cronicles*
some thirty-six (56.25 per cent) are borrowed from Latin.

SOURCES

Excluding the Dedicatory Preface Capgrave's *Abbreuiacion of
Cronicles* may be said to consist of three parts. These divisions,
which are inferred from the content of the work and are not
indicated by the layout of the manuscripts, are as follows:

Part I (11/1–47/24) deals with events up to the birth of Christ.
Part II (47/26–116/27) focuses on the reigns of the Roman and
  holy Roman emperors.
Part III (116/28–249/29) focuses on the reigns of the kings of
  England.

It will be convenient to keep these divisions in mind during the
discussion of the sources providing it is remembered that, besides
notices of the holy Roman emperors, Part II also contains notices
of the contemporary English kings.

About three-quarters of the *Abbreuiacion of Cronicles* can be
accounted for by derivation from one source or another. The
two major sources are the *Chronicon Pontificum et Imperatorum* of
Martinus Polonus and the St. Albans Chronicles of Thomas
Walsingham. From Capgrave's use of these two sources it would
appear that his method was to follow one main source at a time,
borrowing wholesale from it, but possibly adding to it occasionally
from his own knowledge or from some other source. Although his
work is a compilation in the larger sense there is no evidence that
he put together his account of a given topic or period from a
variety of sources.

For Part I, from the Creation to the birth of Christ, no major source is known, though there is considerable general correspondence with Isidore of Seville's *Chronica Maiora*, and a few passages are close to treatments of the same subject-matter in Higden's *Polychronicon*. Like Isidore, but unlike Higden, Capgrave employs a very rigid chronological scheme beginning with the Creation in Anno Mundi 1 and placing the birth of Christ in Anno Mundi 5199. He attributes this chronological scheme to Bede (47/27), in whose *Chronica Minora*, part of his *De Temporibus* (703), there occurs the following entry relating to Christ's birth:

> Huius anno XLII dominus nascitur conpletis ab Adam annis IIIDCCCCLII, iuxta alios VCXCVIIII.[1]

Later, in his *Chronica Maiora*, part of his *De Temporum Ratione* (725), Bede adopted his preferred scheme (not that *iuxta alios*), as a result of which he became the object of a charge of heresy.[2] Bede inherited his earlier alternative scheme from that handed on by Isidore from Jerome's translation of Eusebius's *Chronicon*.[3] Isidore's *Chronica Maiora*, or something very much like it, could have provided the framework of dates and events for Part I of Capgrave's work. Many of the dates coincide, e.g. at 30/27–33/7, and 35/2–36/31, and a considerable proportion of the events and personages dealt with by Capgrave occur in Isidore, albeit more briefly, and usually in the same order.[4]

For Part II, which focuses on the Roman and holy Roman emperors, the major source is the *Chronicon Pontificum et Imperatorum* of Martinus Polonus.[5] This source also accounts for the entry on Augustus at the end of Part I and for some entries concerning popes in Part III.[6] Martinus Polonus is the usual name of the

---

[1] Bede, *Chronica Minora et Maiora*, ed. T. Mommsen, MGH auct. antiq. xiii (Berlin, 1898), pp. 247–327, quot. on p. 281, §§ 175–6.

[2] See P. H. Blair, *The World of Bede* (London, 1970), pp. 266–7.

[3] Isidore, *Chronica Maiora*, ed. Mommsen, MGH auct. antiq. xi. 394–488, esp. 454. Eusebius, *Chronicon*, tr. Jerome, PL xxvii. 223–508. Eusebius/Jerome says 'Colliguntur omnes . . . Ab Adam usque ad Christum, [anni] quinque millia ducenti duo minus' (439–40).

[4] For instances where Capgrave diverges from Isidore see the relevant notes in the Commentary between 13/32 and 46/17 inclusive. In some places C's reading agrees with a variant given in some manuscripts of Isidore's work: see the notes in the Commentary to 13/22, 27/20, 28/30, 42/14.

[5] Ed. Weiland, MGH, script. xxii. 377–475.

[6] This source was identified by W. Matthews in *Medieval Literature and Civilization*, ed. Pearsall and Waldron (London, 1969). As noted in my review of this book in *Studies*, lix (1970), p. 426, Matthews's claim (p. 278) that Mar-

Dominican Martin of Troppau (d. 1278).[1] A native of Troppau in Silesia, then part of the kingdom of Bohemia, he was ordained in Prague but spent most of his life in Rome where he became papal chaplain and apostolic penitentiary. At the behest of Clement IV (1265–8) he compiled his *Chronicon Pontificum et Imperatorum*, intended as a practical handbook for canonists and as an aid for preachers. No critical research or scholarship went into its making: important events are omitted and trivial legends included. The work seems to have gone through three editions in Martinus's lifetime.[2] He sent an autograph of the first edition to his *confrères* in Prague. The second edition (up to 1268) was so compiled that each page contained two columns, one for popes and one for emperors, and fifty lines, one for each year. In the third edition he added a summary of ancient history and continued the text to 1277, where Weiland's printed edition formally ends. After Martinus's death, continuations were added, some printed by Weiland.[3] Perhaps because it was so handy and so easy to use as a work of reference and perhaps because of its origin in the curia the *Chronicon* enjoyed an extraordinary circulation. There are apparently over a thousand manuscripts of the work still in existence.[4]

In the *Abbreuiacion of Cronicles* Capgrave nowhere refers to Martinus by name but *þe cronicle* cited as a source at 107/14 is his.[5] Capgrave's use of Martinus's *Chronicon* extends from the treatment of the Emperor Augustus (47/1 ff.) to the notice of Pope John XXI (128/1). Evidently Capgrave followed the fuller AC

tinus is 'unmentioned by . . . [the] editor' is inaccurate (see Hingeston's edn., p. 125 n. 1), though Hingeston did not realize that Capgrave used Martinus as a major source. With this reference as a clue I identified Martinus as a source myself independently in 1965.

[1] On whom see *Allgemeine deutsche Biographie* (Leipzig, 1884), s.n. *Martinus Polonus, New Cath. Enc.*, s.n. *Martin of Troppau*, and H. Grundmann, *Geschichtsschreibung im Mittelalter* (Göttingen, 1965), pp. 22–3.

[2] For a more detailed account of the genesis and development of the work see Weiland, 'Ausgabe', pp. 1–79.

[3] MGH, script. xxii. 476–82, immediately after the *Chronicon*, and script. xxiv. 251–65, separately.

[4] For this information I am indebted to my colleague Fr J. E. Chisholm, CSSp., who made inquiries on my behalf in Fribourg (Switzerland) and Munich in 1967. In 1965 I was informed by Dr Isa Sanfilippo of the Repertorio delle Fonti Storiche de Medio Evo in Rome that the entry on Martinus for the new edition of Potthast's *Bibliotheca Historica Medii Aevi* was being prepared by Professor H. Schmidinger (Fribourg), but I have been unable to contact him. There is apparently no complete list of manuscripts containing Martinus's *Chronicon*.   [5] Cf. also Commentary, notes to 57/21, 58/27.

rather than the B recension.[1] Moreover his version must have included a continuation, as one continuation is the source for the entries for Popes Nicholas III (128/2) and Martin IV (129/16–28). The Continuation followed is that printed by Weiland at the end of the *Chronicon*; none of the Continuations I–IV printed separately contains the entry for Pope Martin IV used by Capgrave. Nevertheless, Capgrave's text agrees with Continuation III in one detail, and another statement, otherwise unaccounted for, is comparable with Continuation III's treatment of the same subject-matter.[2] Yet another passage, also otherwise unaccounted for, is comparable with Continuation IV's treatment of the same subject-matter.[3] The version of Martinus's *Chronicon* used by Capgrave may also have included some minor additions and alterations not included in Weiland's edition of the AC recension, as there is sporadic occurrence of details not in his text of Martinus[4] as well as sporadic agreement with variants cited by Weiland from different manuscript versions.[5]

The manuscript of Martinus's *Chronicon* used by Capgrave would almost certainly have been set out either with two columns to each page, one for emperors and one for popes, or with each two-page opening having one page for emperors and one for popes. It was therefore possible for the reader's eye to alternate between the treatment of the emperor and the treatment of the pope for the same period. Capgrave was writing a single integrated narrative so he incorporated the notices of each emperor and pope in turn. Sometimes, however, statements explicitly grouping several popes together within one emperor's reign are introduced, as, for example, *In his time were seuene popes*.[6] There is little attempt to integrate the treatment of emperor and pope. On one occasion what looks like attempted integration turns out not to be so. As Pope Gregory I is mentioned in the account of

[1] See Commentary, note to 56/27–31.

[2] See Commentary, notes to 128/2 and 132/4–5, respectively.

[3] See Commentary, note to 134/30–135/2.

[4] See Commentary, especially notes to 51/3–4, 52/15–17, 53/18–20, 54/31–2, 55/9–10, 17–18, 26–8, 56/13, 16–17, 57/10–11, 12–14, 16–17, 58/2, 19, 30, 59/5, 28–30, 61/12, 62/21–2, 64/11–15, 68/32, 33–4, 74/11–14, 75/11, 11–14, 76/6–7, 78/4–5, 80/19–20, 81/28, 82/5, 83/19–20, 87/3, 96/10, 100/21, 108/28–32, 117/2–3, 125/4, 28–9.

[5] See Commentary, especially notes to 54/30, 55/19, 56/15, 58/29, 67/26, 68/6, 69/21, 75/29–30, 80/17, 22, 85/6, 88/8, 96/3, 129/20.

[6] 75/18. Similarly 89/8, 97/32–3, 100/20, 108/6, 111/25.

the reign of Emperor Mauricius (74/3–22) Gregory is not accorded
an individual entry; Martinus's account of him is not used. The
only instance where information from the separate treatments of
the popes and emperors is woven together with any, even small,
degree of success is in the account of the reign of Emperor
Henry V (104/13–27), where Capgrave was virtually forced to
attempt some sort of integration by the fact that the narrative
deals with the strife between the emperor and the pope. Another
similar attempt in the reign of Emperor Lothair IV (106/25–35)
is spoiled by the clumsy insertion of a parenthesis (106/31–2).
A little later on, when Capgrave is trying to integrate English
material into his narrative as well, the passages taken over from
Martinus become spread out and some mistakes are made: the
odd pope is omitted, Alexander III (1159–81) for example,[1] and
two popes are dealt with twice, at different points in the
narrative.[2]

For the most part Capgrave takes over Martinus's narrative as
it stands; he shortens it and omits from it but generally does not
otherwise alter it. In some longer narrative incidents, however,
he fails to convey important points. For example, in the story
of Emperor Henry II as a child (97/5–31) Capgrave omits the
child's name and fails to make clear, as Martinus does, that
the grown-up child is the same person as Henry II. Again, in the
story of how Pope Gregory VII, suspecting that a certain bishop
was acting against the Holy Spirit, tested him by asking him to
say 'Gloria Patri et Filio et Spiritui Sancto', and discovered the
bishop's guilt because he was unable to utter 'et Spiritui Sancto',
Capgrave omits the circumstances of the test thereby obscuring
the connection between the inability to utter 'et Spiritui Sancto'
and guilt. This lack of concentration on over-all coherence is
revealed not only within a single (long) narrative incident but also
occasionally between incidents. For example, Capgrave fails to
make clear, as Martinus does, that the Hildebrand *whech was
pope aftir* (100/15) was the same person as Pope Gregory VII,
the account of whom begins at 100/21. Sometimes Capgrave
reorganizes the statements within a particular entry. In the notice
of the reign of Emperor Constantine IV his conflation of the
accounts of the fifth and sixth Councils of the Church gives rise to

---

[1] See Commentary, note to 111/25.
[2] See Commentary, note to 101/6–7.

over-simplification and confusion.[1] In the notice of Galen and
Ptolemy (53/1–8) Capgrave tries to impose a new order on a
confused model and the result is yet more confusion.[2] Elsewhere
the reorganization takes the form of simply altering the order of
the statements in an entry. In the account of Pope Siricius
(65/18–22) the statement about his summoning a Council of 350
(*recte* 315) bishops is moved to the beginning, presumably to give
the impression that his acts had the support of the corporate
Church. In the entry for Emperor Constantine the Great (61/20–
62/10) there is rather more drastic reordering. Capgrave's initial
statement about Constantine's conversion is taken from later in
Martinus's treatment and somewhat expanded, so that the power
and importance of the Faith are emphasized. Moreover, the
references to Constantine's building of churches (62/3–5) are
transferred from Martinus's account of Pope Sylvester I[3] and
put before the doubts expressed about Constantine's final faith-
fulness, so that the doubts seem ill founded. In these alterations
a moral purpose—to emphasize the power of the Faith and the
importance of sustained adherence to it—is evident. Such a
moral purpose emerges as a consistent principle of Capgrave's
treatment of both his major sources and is discussed further below.[4]

Since Capgrave's aim was to produce an abridged version
(*abbreuiacion*) of his sources he did not add very much to what he
took over from Martinus. The small additions that he did make
fall into two groups, (*a*) theological, and (*b*) explanatory.

(*a*) Of the theological additions the most numerous are in the
accounts of the various heretical beliefs held by a section of the
Church from time to time, those of Manes (59/18–20), Arius and
Donatus (61/32–62/2), Priscillian and Pelagius (66/24–8), Dioscorus (69/3–5), the Monothelites (76/18–19), and Joachim (109/2–
10).[5] Slightly less frequent are the expansions of the notices of
important Church Fathers and theological writers, Origen (54/22–
3), Ambrose (65/3), Augustine (66/3–9, 66/32–67/2), Rabanus
Maurus (84/29–32), and Hugh of St. Victor (107/1–3).[5] There
is nothing Anglophile about these expansions as Capgrave omits
Martinus's treatments of both Bede and Boniface.[6] On three

---

[1] See 77/7–15 and note in Commentary.
[2] See Commentary, note to 53/4–6.
[3] See Commentary, note to 62/3–5.   [4] See pp. lxxxvii–lxxxix.
[5] See also the notes to these lines in the Commentary.
[6] If included, the notice of Bede would have occurred after 78/6, and that of

occasions Capgrave adds details of works of which he evidently
had personal experience: Theodore's *Penitencial* (76/1–3), Odo
of Cluny's work *upon þe Sauter* (untraced), and a collection of his
sermons (91/4–6), and Hugh of St-Cher's *Concordantiae* (121/2).

(*b*) One of the explanatory additions, that concerning the law-
code of Justinian (71/23),[1] resembles the theological additions in
that the text has apparently been expanded from Capgrave's own
knowledge. Of the other two both seem to have been added for
the sake of clarity, one where the meaning might otherwise have
been obscure (72/25), and the other where Capgrave evidently
thought a reminder of what had gone before was called for
(73/27–8).[2]

For Part III, which focuses on the kings of England, the major
source is the St. Albans Chronicles of Thomas Walsingham.[3]
This source accounts for most of the material in the *Abbreuiacion
of Cronicles* from the end of the reign of Henry III (126/18–25)
to the end of the work in the reign of Henry V (249/29), but
Capgrave's text does not begin to follow Walsingham closely
until *þe xxiii ȝere* (132/6) of Edward I (1295). The St. Albans
Chronicles of Thomas Walsingham are the annalistic chronicles
written by Walsingham at St. Albans between 1376 and 1421/2.
Basically, there are two versions of Walsingham's chronicle,
a longer version and a shorter version,[4] but consultation of these
works is made difficult because neither has been printed as a

---

Boniface after 80/28. The omission of Bede, at least, may have been accidental
as Capgrave included a reference to him in the summary account of emperors
in *Solace* 58/32.

[1] See also the note to these lines in the Commentary.

[2] See also the notes to these lines in the Commentary.

[3] This source was first identified by C. L. Kingsford in his *English Historical
Literature in the Fifteenth Century* (Oxford, 1913), p. 39. Possibly Hingeston's
reference to Walsingham in his Glossary, s.v. *Chestiveris* (*sic*) provided a clue
which led Kingsford to his identification of Walsingham as a source. Kingsford
says that 'It [the *Abbreuiacion of Cronicles*] is derived very closely from Walsingham's *Historia Anglicana*' but he seems to have had only the later part of
Capgrave's work in mind. The source of the English material before 1272 is
still not known. Matthews, 'Martinus . . . ', in *Med. Lit.* (1959), p. 282, probably
misunderstood Kingsford, as he is in error in stating that when 'Capgrave
reaches William the Conqueror . . . he . . . moves to Walsingham as his major
source'.

[4] See V. H. Galbraith, *The St. Albans Chronicle 1406–1420* (Oxford, 1937),
pp. xxvii–lxxi. See also his earlier article 'Thomas Walsingham and the Saint
Albans Chronicle, 1272–1422', *EHR* xlvii (1932), 12–30.

whole and parts of the shorter version are still unprinted. The longer version, called the *Chronica Maiora*, can be pieced together from five volumes, viz.:

(1) 1272–1375 in the *Historia Anglicana* (RS 28/1), i. 7–320, with additions, ii. 360–83;[1]

(2) 1376–82 in the *Chronicon Angliae* (RS 64), pp. 68–354.[2]

(3) 1382–92 in the *Historia Anglicana*, ii. 70–212, with additions, ii. 395–406.

(4) 1393–1406 in the *Annales Ricardi II et Henrici IV* attributed to Trokelowe (RS 28/3), pp. 155–420.

(5) 1406–20 in *The St. Albans Chronicle 1406–1420*, ed. Galbraith, pp. 1–126.

The shorter version, called the *Short History*, which begins in 1327, can be partially pieced together as follows:

(1) 1328–70 in the *Chronicon Angliae*, pp. 1–68.

(2) 1382–8 in the *Chronicon Angliae*, pp. 355–87.

(3) 1392–1422 in the *Historia Anglicana*, ii. 212–346, with additions, ii. 411–24.

The text for 1327, 1370–82, and 1388–92 has never been printed.

One of the reasons why neither Walsingham's *Chronica Maiora* nor his *Short History* has been printed as a whole is the manner in which they have survived. Of the two most important manuscripts of Walsingham's chronicles, one, London, British Library Royal MS 13.E.ix, stops in 1392, and the other, Oxford, Bodleian Library MS Bodley 462, contains the *Short History* from 1327 to 1392 and then the *Chronica Maiora* from 1392 to 1420. Another manuscript, London, College of Arms MS Arundel 7, contains the *Chronica Maiora* from 1272 to 1392 and then the *Short History* from 1393 to 1422. These three manuscripts are the only ones to contain text for a long continuous run of years.

Ideally, an edition of the *Chronica Maiora* would be based on Royal MS 13.E.ix for 1272–1392 and on MS Bodley 462 for 1392–1420. Unfortunately, as the basis for his edition of the *Historia Anglicana*, Riley used MS Arundel 7, so his text of the

---

[1] For 1272–1307 the text of the *Chronica* attributed to William Rishanger (RS 28/2, pp. 1–230) is more or less the same.

[2] There is a translation of the entries for 1376–7 in *Archaeologia*, xxii (1829), 212–84.

Chronica Maiora covers only the period from 1272 to 1392 and
has to be supplemented by reference to Appendix B (which
contains additions from Royal MS 13.E.ix) in volume II of the
Historia Anglicana.[1] There is a better text of the period from
1376 to 1382, based on Bodleian Library MS Bodley 316 and
British Library MS Harley 3634, in the *Chronicon Angliae*.[2]
For the period 1392 to 1406 there is the text in the *Annales*
attributed to Trokelowe, printed from Cambridge, Corpus Christi
College MS 7(2).[3] The only part of the *Chronica Maiora* to be
printed from an 'ideal' base-manuscript is that for 1406–20
printed by Galbraith.

Again ideally, an edition of the *Short History* would be based on
MS Bodley 462 for 1327–92 and on Cambridge, Corpus Christi
College MSS 7(1) and 7(3) for 1392–1405 and 1393–1422 respectively. For the periods 1328 to 1370 and 1382 to 1388 we have
the text in the *Chronicon Angliae* printed from MS Bodley 316
and MS Harley 3634.[4] For the period 1392 to 1422 there is
Riley's text in the *Historia Anglicana*, based on MS Arundel 7,
which has to be supplemented by reference to Appendix D (which
contains additions from Corpus Christi College MSS 7(1)) in
volume II of the *Historia Anglicana*. No part of the *Short History*
has been printed from an 'ideal' base-manuscript.

In the *Abbreuiacion of Cronicles* Capgrave nowhere refers to
Walsingham's chronicles by name but the source alluded to in the
phrase *as it is wrytyn* (222/2–3) is Walsingham. For the period 1327
(where Walsingham's *Short History* begins) to 1417 (where the
Abbreuiacion of Cronicles breaks off) Capgrave could in theory have
followed either the *Chronica Maiora* or the *Short History*. In
fact he followed a version of the *Chronica Maiora* until 1376
(181/6) and a version of the *Short History* from 1376 (181/7)
to the end.[5] This statement can be confidently maintained even

[1] See also the Appendix to Galbraith, *St. Albans Chronicle*, pp. 127–31
(entries for 1300, 1306, 1327, 1329, 1330, 1333, 1338, 1343) and 134 (entries
for 1389, 1390).

[2] For 1376–7 see also the Appendix, pp. 391–401, where a text based on
Royal MS 13.D.i and MS Lambeth 160 is printed.

[3] For a few variants from MS Bodley 462 see the Appendix to Galbraith,
St. Albans Chronicle, pp. 134–5 (entries for 1399, 1404).

[4] For some additions from MS Bodley 462 see the Appendix to Galbraith,
St. Albans Chronicle, pp. 131–4 (entries for 1338, 1339, 1342, 1345).

[5] For an instance where this statement is probably verifiable from the wording
of the text (for 1402) see Commentary, note to 220/18–19.

though the *Short History* for 1370–82 is not in print; the amount that Capgrave takes over and the amount he leaves out from his source remains fairly constant, and the point where the proportional relationship changes from that between 'longer' source and derivative to that between 'shorter' source and derivative is fairly easily found. As will be seen the word 'version' is extremely important. The text of Walsingham used by Capgrave was, I believe, a good one, closer to that of the author than that of any of the surviving manuscripts.

For the period up to 1376 (181/6) Capgrave used a version of the *Chronica Maiora* akin to that preserved in Royal MS 13.E.ix. This observation is based on the use by Capgrave of material which appears in Royal MS 13.E.ix but does not appear, or does not appear in the same form, in MS Arundel 7; the most notable example is the long passage 155/8–159/20, but other examples occur at 136/8–9, 145/32–146/2, 154/16–22, 161/1–14, and 161/19–27.[1] Capgrave's manuscript of the *Chronica Maiora* was evidently quite closely akin to Royal 13.E.ix as he takes over an omission which occurs in it but which is not recorded from any other manuscript. At 159/8–12 he notes that Edward III *mad sex erles* and names five but then says that *þe sext is not now in mende*. Royal MS 13.E.ix also lacks the name of the sixth earl, which, however, is given in MS Arundel 7.[2] There is also an error evidently taken over by Capgrave from Walsingham and which occurs in Royal MS 13.E.ix; at 156/24–5 the birth of the Black Prince is wrongly placed in *June* rather than July. Although Capgrave took over the odd omission and error from a version of Walsingham's *Chronica Maiora* (up to 1376) akin to that in Royal MS 13.E.ix he also has the odd correct reading where Royal MS 13.E.ix is in error. At 181/2 the death of the Black Prince is correctly placed in the month *of Juni* whereas Royal MS 13.E.ix has *Julii*. Since the correct month is given in both Royal MS 13.D.i and MS Lambeth 160[3] it would seem probable that Capgrave got it from his manuscript of the *Chronica Maiora* (up to 1376). From this evidence it follows that he used a manuscript of the *Chronica Maiora* (up to 1376) akin to Royal MS 13.E.ix

---

[1] From the point of view of establishing the version used by Capgrave, Riley's choice of Arundel 7 as his base-manuscript followed by his decision to print variants from Royal MS 13.E.ix in an appendix proves advantageous.

[2] See further Commentary, note to 159/11–12.

[3] See Commentary, note to 181/2.

but antecedent to it in the line of descent from the author's version. This conclusion is confirmed by other evidence. At 171/1–2 the reading *þe son of Kyng Edward* is evidently taken from Walsingham but, while *filius regis Edwardi* occurs in the *Short History*, it does not occur in the *Chronica Maiora* as printed from MS Arundel 7 with variants from Royal MS 13.E.ix. The antecedent version of the *Chronica Maiora* (up to 1376) used by Capgrave (which, for convenience, I shall henceforth refer to as W) was evidently slightly fuller than that preserved in Royal MS 13.E.ix. At 164/21–3, where the equivalent entry in Walsingham ends *etc.*, Capgrave has an additional statement which presumably derives from W. Similarly, the additional elements at 179/21–4 and 180/7–10 also presumably derive from W.[1] No doubt W also contained the details of Edward III's claim to the French crown which are included by Capgrave (160/15–31) though they are lacking in Royal MS 13.E.ix and MS Arundel 7. It is hard to believe that the story of Jewet Metles at 159/21–7, the account of various apparitions at 172/30–173/7, and the account of Geoffrey Hardeby (170/21–5) were not also taken over from W. On the other hand, Capgrave may well have added himself the details of the history of the Augustinian order at 141/10–14, the section on the burial of Lionel of Clarence (176/25–7), which relates to the Austin friary at Clare, and the explanatory information about the constitutions of Pope Benedict XII (158/25–6).

For the period from 1376 to the end (1417) Capgrave used a version of Walsingham's *Short History*. It will be convenient to deal first with the first part of this period, from 1376 to 1392 (181/7–201/19). For these years the *Short History* is in print only for 1382 to 1388; the equivalent text in the *Abbreuiacion of Cronicles* runs from 186/28 to 194/24. Even within this relatively short space it is evident from one entry in particular, dealing with King Richard II's abortive attempt to raise forces against the nobles through the agency of Robert de Vere in 1388 (194/11–20), that Capgrave was using a version of the *Short History* which was fuller than that preserved in the surviving manuscripts and indeed which contained details not included in the best surviving manuscript (Royal 13.E.ix) of the *Chronica Maiora*.[2] This

---

[1] For details see Commentary, notes to 179/21, 21–2, 23–4, 180/7–8, 9–10.

[2] See Commentary, notes to 194/13, 14–15, 16, 17–18, 19–20. One detail not in the *Short History* is in the *Chronica Maiora*: see note to 194/12.

conclusion is corroborated by other evidence, for circumstantial details not in the *Chronica Maiora* as printed from Royal MS 13.E.ix and MS Arundel 7 are included by Capgrave at 182/16–19, 26–8, 183/27–30, 185/31, 195/22–8, and 198/27–30. Nevertheless, the version of Walsingham's *Short History* (from 1376 to 1392) used by Capgrave (which henceforth I shall refer to as X) must have been based on a manuscript of the *Chronica Maiora* akin to Royal MS 13.E.ix (rather than MS Arundel 7), as part of the paragraph reporting Richard II's first acts as king in the *Abbreuiacion of Cronicles* (182/1–6) derives from a passage in Walsingham preserved in Royal MS 13.E.ix but not in MS Arundel 7. Evidently X was compiled from a slightly fuller version of the *Chronica Maiora* antecedent to that contained in Royal MS 13.E.ix. From that fuller version X probably took over the material on which Capgrave based the four entries (in this part of the work) which lack any known source, those at 184/1–3, 186/26–7, 195/6–9, 195/29–196/2. In the main, however, X was a more or less drastic abbreviation of the *Chronica Maiora*; this is reflected, for example, in Capgrave's account of the Peasants' Revolt of 1381 (185/20–186/14), which is very much shorter than that in the *Chronica Maiora*, and there is some slight reordering of events. Occasionally X presumably drew together material dealing with separate aspects of the same event, and this is reflected in Capgrave's account of Edmund of Cambridge's expedition to Portugal (185/10–19). From the fact that the section of text at 199/1–15 is apparently misplaced in the sequence of events it seems reasonable to assume that the manuscript of X used by Capgrave may have had a leaf or sheet reversed at this point. Capgrave may well have added himself the comment relating to the chronological framework at 181/23–4, the announcement *The first pingis he ded* at 182/1, and the explanatory statement *and rich men schuld pay a subsidie to þe kyng* at 183/8–9. He was also presumably responsible for the addition of the connective *because* (183/5) which links two events merely juxtaposed in Walsingham.

For the period 1392 to 1417 the whole of the *Short History* is in print and the printed text is based (wholly or in part) on three manuscripts, Arundel 7, which has apparently been collated with Corpus Christi College 7(3), and Corpus Christi College 7(1); the equivalent text in the *Abbreuiacion of Cronicles* runs from 201/20 to 249/29. From Riley's edition of this part of the *Short*

History in the *Historia Anglicana* it is evident that the fullest surviving version is that contained in Corpus Christi College MS 7(1), since for the years it covers, 1392–1405, it contains many passages not in MS Arundel 7 or Corpus Christi College MS 7(3).[1] Capgrave must have used a version of the *Short History* (from 1392 to 1405) akin to that preserved in Corpus Christi College MS 7(1). Several passages in the relevant part of the *Abbreuiacion of Cronicles* (201/20–229/12), which cannot otherwise be accounted for (or can only be partially accounted for) from the *Short History*, can be accounted for (or more fully accounted for) by reference to this fuller version.[2] Nevertheless, even in these passages details occur which cannot be accounted for from Corpus Christi College MS 7(1).[3] One of these details was evidently omitted from Corpus Christi College MS 7(1) accidentally as a cross-reference to it is included.[4] It follows that there was a fuller version still of Walsingham's *Short History*, antecedent to Corpus Christi College MS 7(1), and that some such version (which, for convenience, I shall henceforth call Y) was the one used by Capgrave. The details which Capgrave took over from Y were no doubt in turn taken over from the *Chronica Maiora*, but only some of these details can be accounted for from the texts of the *Chronica Maiora* printed from the surviving manuscripts.[5] Moreover, there are other details (outside the passages specifically to be accounted for from the version contained in Corpus Christi College MS 7(1)) which occur in the text of the *Abbreuiacion of Cronicles* for 1392 to 1405, but which cannot be accounted for from the printed texts of the surviving manuscripts of either the *Chronica Maiora* or the *Short History*.[6] Capgrave presumably took these details from Y. He may have added himself the detail relating to Lynn at 217/17 and was probably also responsible for the error in the

[1] See Walsingham, *Historia Anglicana*, Appendix D. Riley refers to Corpus Christi College MS 7(3) as 'vii(5)'.

[2] These passages occur at 219/29–30, 220/24–9, 220/30–221/4, 222/12–16, 222/28–223/7, 223/17–28, 223/29–224/5, 224/17–21, 224/24–225/2, 225/3–23, 226/24–31, 227/1–3, 9–15, 16–31, 229/1–12. One of these passages, that at 224/24–225/2, is not in the *Chronica Maiora* as printed from the surviving manuscripts.

[3] See Commentary, notes to 221/1–4, 223/4–5, 17, 20–1, 26, 29, 224/26–7, 225/10, 227/2, 229/7–8.

[4] See Commentary, note to 220/26–7.

[5] See Commentary, notes to 223/4–5, 17, 225/10, 227/2.

[6] See Commentary, notes to 205/19–20, 208/23–5, 32, 209/1, 210/16–17, 213/9, 214/8–9, 218/5–6.

story of Henry IV's sword left at Great Berwick (Salop).[1] Possibly Capgrave used some other source to give the alternative theory regarding Richard II's death recorded at 217/7–9. On the face of it, some source other than Walsingham was apparently used for the short passage 220/21–3 concerning the chronological position of the Scottish incursion leading to the battle of Homildon Hill (dealt with at 220/1–3), but it is also possible that the passage was taken over from Y and that the other source referred to in *sum sey* (220/23) was one of Walsingham's sources rather than one of Capgrave's.

For the period 1405 to 1417 it is possible to collate Capgrave's text in the *Abbreuiacion of Chronicles* (229/13–249/29) with the printed text of the *Short History* only in so far as the latter work is available from MS Arundel 7 and Corpus Christi College MS 7(3); there is no manuscript with as full a version as that contained for 1392 to 1405 in Corpus Christi College MS 7(1). This factor is of crucial importance in any consideration of Capgrave's source version for this period, and was presumably overlooked by Galbraith when he pronounced a version of the *Chronica Maiora* such as that found in MS Bodley 462 to be the source of the later section of Capgrave's work.[2] Although four passages and a number of details from the *Abbreuiacion of Cronicles* which do not occur in the *Short History* can be accounted for from the *Chronica Maiora*[3] Capgrave's text agrees with the *Short History* in a number of significant details. In the passage (233/20–234/2) dealing with Alexander V, pope at Pisa (1409–10), Capgrave follows the *Short History* including details noted by Galbraith as additions from the *Short History* to the account in the *Chronica Maiora*.[4] At 235/16–17 Capgrave takes over the brief entry regarding the visitation of Oxford University from the *Short History*; the *Chronica Maiora* is incomplete at this point, containing only the heading for this entry, but no text. In the

[1] See Commentary, note to 222/12–16.

[2] *St. Albans Chronicle*, p. xvi.

[3] The four passages occur at 229/17–19, 230/12–26, 249/3–11, and 249/12–19. For the details see Commentary, notes to 230/1, 231/28–232/1, 232/6, 23–4, 25–6, 233/2, 8–11, 14–15, 16–17, 234/8, 235/13, 236/8, 238/18, 239/9, 240/1, 244/15, 245/5, 12–13, 246/3, 247/4, 7–8, 13, 14–15, 22, 23–4, 247/27–248/8, 248/18–23, 27–8.

[4] *St. Albans Chronicle*, p. 51, notes *a* and *c*. The words in Capgrave which correspond to the Latin in note *a* are *consentid all* (233/24), and in note *c* they are *in þe first day of his creacion* (233/28).

list of personages given at 236/8–10 Capgrave's text agrees with the *Short History* against the *Chronica Maiora* in omitting the earl of Warwick, in giving Oldcastle his title (*þe Lord Cobbam/ Dominus de Cobham*), and in mentioning the large number of armed men (*many/in numero copioso*); this agreement is in wording as well as in substance. The sentence *But . . . enmies* (236/12–14) is from the *Short History* and has no equivalent in the *Chronica Maiora*, and the detail *in a strong place* (236/14–15) is from *in locum quodam forti* in the *Short History*, but lacking in the *Chronica Maiora*. From the *Short History* also Capgrave took the name of the bishop of Norwich appointed in 1415, [*Jon*] *Wakeryng* (245/8–9). Even when Capgrave's version is fuller than that contained in the *Short History*, as in the passage at 232/12–16, it does not appear likely that he modelled his text on the very much longer version of the *Chronica Maiora*. Evidently Capgrave was following a version of the *Short History* for the period 1405–17 and equally evidently this version of the *Short History* was considerably fuller than any that has survived. Very probably it was a continuation of the version used for 1392 to 1405 and referred to above as Y; I shall henceforth refer to this fuller version for 1405 to 1417 as Z. This Z must have contained the passages and details noted above as lacking in the *Short History* (as it has survived) but preserved in the *Chronica Maiora*.[1] Z also probably included a number of details which Capgrave preserves but which are not included in the surviving texts of Walsingham (as printed).[2] Besides these details Capgrave has two passages in this section of the *Abbreuiacion of Cronicles* which are not preserved in Walsingham. One concerns a deterioration in Henry IV's physical appearance (229/13–16), and the other is Henry IV's death-bed confession to Friar John Tille (238/6–16). Despite Galbraith's admonition 'that the friar Tille story should be omitted from any future history of the reign of Henry IV',[3] it seems probable that Capgrave took it and the other passage over from Walsingham. Galbraith himself notes that there was a fuller version of the

[1] See above, p. lxxxiv and n. 3.
[2] For these details see Commentary, notes to 229/28–9, 231/21, 232/7–8, 10, 21, 235/2–4, 237/9, 241/18, 243/26, 246/4, 247/19–20, 248/1, 19, 249/13–15, 25.
[3] *St. Albans Chronicle*, p. xvi. The first passage is outside the scope of Galbraith's book (1406–20) and he was apparently unaware of it as an addition to Walsingham's account as it has come down to us.

'St. Albans Chronicle' than any which has survived.[1] In one respect at least such a fuller version has survived. At 248/10 Capgrave refers to *xii articles* in the treaty of 1416 between Henry V and Emperor Sigismund, and presumably this reference was taken over from Z. At this point therefore Z must have been based on a fuller version of the *Chronica Maiora* than that contained in MS Bodley 462 and printed by Galbraith. For this particular part of the narrative such a fuller version is evidently preserved in Bodleian Library MS Rawlinson B 152.[2] Besides being based on a fuller version of the *Chronica Maiora* than that contained in MS Bodley 462 Z must also have differed occasionally from the surviving printed versions in the ordering of events; this difference is presumably reflected by Capgrave in the occurrence of the entry at 229/30–230/4 after that at 229/26–9 and in the occurrence of the entry at 238/25–6 before that at 238/27–8. On one occasion Capgrave presumably reflects a reading in Z that was correct where the reading in MS Bodley 462 is in error,[3] though on another occasion Capgrave's text presumably reflects an error which is also in Z.[4] Capgrave probably added himself the comment *These be þe articules whech þei profered* (237/16–17) in order to clarify the narrative, and was probably also responsible for apparently making slight alterations in the text of one passage in order to make a new unit of narrative out of what were originally two separate items.[5] He may also have added the details relating to Lynn at 230/2–4.

From this survey of Capgrave's use of Walsingham's chronicles the following conclusions are evident. From 1295 (or perhaps earlier) to 1376 Capgrave followed a version of Walsingham's *Chronica Maiora* (called W) antecedent to and slightly fuller than that preserved in the best surviving manuscript. From 1376 to 1417 he followed a version of Walsingham's *Short History* (called X (1376–92), Y (1392–1405), Z (1405–17)) antecedent to and slightly fuller than that preserved in the best surviving manuscripts, and containing some details not preserved even in the *Chronica Maiora*,[6] to which, in one minor respect, Capgrave also

---

[1] *St. Albans Chronicle*, p. xviii. Cf. also p. 83, note *b*.
[2] See Galbraith, *St. Albans Chronicle*, p. 101, note *a*, also pp. xvii–xviii.
[3] See Commentary, note to 247/16.
[4] See Commentary, note to 238/22–4.
[5] See Commentary, note to 249/24.
[6] See above, p. lxxxi, n. 2, p. lxxxiii, n. 6, and p. lxxxv, n. 2.

provides a correction.[1] It follows from these conclusions[2] that Capgrave's *Abbreuiacion of Cronicles* is more important as a repository of information derived from Walsingham's chronicles than has previously been allowed. In particular, Capgrave preserves seven complete entries which are probably from Walsingham, those at 172/29–173/7 (1361), 184/1–3 (1380), 186/26–7 (1382), 195/6–9 and 195/29–196/2 (1388), 229/13–16 (1405), and 238/6–16 (1412), also some substantial additions to existing entries at 170/21–5 and 176/25–7. It may be noted that none of these substantial additions to Walsingham's testimony (as hitherto understood) is from the period (1392–1405) covered by the best surviving manuscript of the *Short History* (Corpus Christi College MS 7(1)). Very possibly Capgrave had just one manuscript of Walsingham's chronicles containing the *Chronica Maiora* to 1376 and the *Short History* from 1376 onwards; this manuscript may have had a leaf or sheet reversed in the entry for 1390.[3] In view of the fact that the *Abbreuiacion of Cronicles* ends incomplete in 1417 it would seem plausible to assume that the manuscript of Walsingham's chronicles used by Capgrave ended in 1417. This plausibility becomes probability when it is remembered that one of the Walsingham manuscripts (MS Rawlinson B 152) also 'ends imperfectly in 1417'.[4]

On the available evidence Capgrave added very little to what he took over from Martinus and Walsingham.[5] He did, however, make a number of minor alterations to his sources as he went along, and as the same pattern emerges from his use of both Martinus and Walsingham it will be appropriate to deal with these alterations of both major sources together.

The emergence of an over-riding moral purpose in Capgrave's alterations to one passage in Martinus has already been remarked.[6] This is not an isolated example. There are at least thirty instances of Capgrave making minor alterations or additions which either

[1] See above, p. lxxxvi and n. 3.

[2] In his edition of the *Historia Vitae et Regni Ricardi Secundi* (Pennsylvania, 1977), pp. 12–20, G. B. Stow has recently shown that the first portion of this text (c.1392) derives, as does Capgrave's *Abbreuiacion of Cronicles*, from a version of Walsingham's St. Albans Chronicles slightly different from any that survives. The evidence from Capgrave is, however, much fuller and more revealing in regard to the nature of the Walsingham version(s) which have not survived.

[3] See above, p. lxxxii.   [4] Galbraith, *St. Albans Chronicle*, p. xxvi.

[5] See above, pp. lxxvi–lxxvii, lxxxi, lxxxii, lxxxiii–lxxxiv, and lxxxvi.

[6] See above, p. lxxvi.

constitute direct moral comment or make the intended moral interpretation clear. By far the largest addition of this kind is the comment on the response of the Teutonic Knights to the king of Poland's request for help: *Behold what zelatouris þei were of oure feith! Her religion was ordeyned to defende þe feith, and now couetise stereth hem to distroye it* (235/2–4). But the same effect of moral condemnation is achieved elsewhere merely by the addition of an adverbial phrase: *and worthi* (261/26), *ful wel worthy* (249/19), *to grete harm of þis nacioun* (222/17), *ageyn þe lawe of God* (191/32), *wrongfully* (91/26, 189/29). Quite often moral judgement is indicated simply by adding an adjective. An opinion contrary to Christian teaching becomes *fals* (59/17), a heresy *wikkid* (61/27), the followers of the Ottoman sultan become *cursed* (204/19), the pupils of John Scottus Eriugena who murder him *malicious* (86/16), and a Roman prefect who imprisons the pope also becomes *fals* (100/22). The addition of approbatory epithets is less common: an English squire who undertook a punitive naval action against the French becomes *worthi* (223/23), and Archbishop Richard le Scrope of York, who is portrayed as a well-meaning rebel, earns from Capgrave the description *the good prest* (228/20).[1] Capgrave is much more concerned with the enormity and condemnation of evil. Martinus's unfavourable notice of Pope John XII, *Hic erat venator et totus lubricus, adeo quod etiam publice feminas tenebat* (431/13–14), is expanded by Capgrave to: *He was vicious of lyuyng, a hunter outeragious, a lecchour withouten schame; for he held women openly— and þat dyuers* (92/2–4). Not content with the fact that Sir John Oldcastle was *cursed . . . for contumacie* Capgrave adds that he was a *grete fautour of heretikes* (240/2–3). Heresy leads to evil deeds. Having subscribed to Arianism the king of the Vandals is said by Capgrave to have acted against the Church out *of malice* (69/31). Evil deeds lead to suffering. So by the addition of the connectives *perfor* or *so . . . þat* men's actions and their subsequent fate become cause and effect: Emperor Aurelian was struck by lightning because he persecuted Christians (addition of *perfor* 58/33); Emperor Carus was drowned for his wickedness (addition of *perfor* 59/27); two popes, because they got themselves elected

---

[1] On the posthumous cult of Archbishop Scrope see J. W. McKenna, 'Popular Canonization as Political Propaganda: The Cult of Archbishop Scrope', *Speculum*, xlv (1970), 608–23.

by dubious means, had short reigns (addition of *perfor* 98/15); Emperor Anastasius II was deposed because of his wickedness (addition of *so . . . pat* 80/24). Only once does Capgrave make a pleasant experience result from a good deed (other than where these are taken over as effect and cause): for putting Christianity before knightly chivalry Valentinian II is elevated to the empire (addition of *Therfor* 64/31). Men's deeds, whether bad or good, are subject to divine control and intervention. Henry III is not to be prevented from becoming emperor because, as Capgrave adds, *Goddis ordinauns wold not be broke* (97/30). On two occasions Capgrave adds that *God suffered* an emperor's death for wicked deeds (58/4, 65/6) and on another occasion Capgrave adds that it was *our Lord* who *mad . . . blynd* the would-be murderer of a pope (76/7). Again, this time where good deeds are concerned, Capgrave adds that it was *oure Lord* who was responsible for Valentinian II's elevation to the empire (64/31), and that it was *be pe grace of God* that a victory was won over the Turks (174/28–9); similarly Capgrave adds that an anti-heretical tract was miraculously corrected *aftir pe pleasauns of God* (68/27). Conversely, when something undesirable happens, it is specifically attributed to some godless influence: when Emperor Constans *was turned . . . to pe heresie of pe Arianes* Capgrave adds that he was so turned *be a fals prest* (62/21–2).

Underlying Capgrave's minor alterations and additions to include moral comment or indications of the intended moral interpretation is a rather simplistic 'black and white' moral outlook on human behaviour. This outlook is more directly indicated by some other minor alterations and additions made by Capgrave. A small example is afforded by a change of working in the process of translation and adaptation. According to Martinus, Berengar of Tours *asserebat* 'asserted' certain beliefs but Capgrave says that he *held pis heresie* (99/21), thereby putting Berengar firmly on the black side of the fence. There are three further, and more substantial, examples of this process. According to the *Abbreuiacion of Cronicles* Emperor Julian the Apostate *mad feith to a deuel* (63/18); by attributing this action to Julian, as Martinus does not, Capgrave puts him even further on the black side of the fence than Martinus does. Whereas in Walsingham the man who, having received the Host in church, *fro his mouth voyded it to his hand, bare it hom, and ete it with his oystres* (191/28–9), was a knight known only by a pseudonym (the Laurens de Sancto Martino mentioned by Capgrave at 191/29), and hence rather shadowy, in Capgrave the sacrilegious act is ascribed to a known Lollard, John Montague; by this means Capgrave fixes an obvious black mark firmly to the Lollards. Again with the Lollards, at 241/9 Capgrave makes Sir John Oldcastle's answer more incisively disrespectful than it is in Walsingham so that the reader's possible sympathy for Oldcastle is totally alienated and the Lollard leader is understood to be firmly on the black side of the fence. All these examples illustrate Capgrave's tendency to paint what is already black (or at least a darkish shade of grey) blacker still. Elsewhere he tends to heighten the contrast between white and black. When Capgrave reports (from Martinus) that the German king Conrad III subscribed to the second crusade he adds that Conrad did so *for to go to þe Holy Lond and fite ageyn þe enmies of Crist* (107/8–9). At 223/17–18 Capgrave makes the French rather than the Bretons the chief attackers on Plymouth, thereby concentrating attention on the conflict between the French and the English. In the account of the charges made against Roger Mortimer of Wigmore there is another instance of Capgrave shifting the responsibility for an action. Whereas Walsingham says that *ipse* [Mortimer] *et Regina abundabant* Capgrave says that *he* [Mortimer alone] *had consumed þe kyngis tresoure and þe qwenis liflod*, the words *and þe qwenis liflod* having no equivalent in Walsingham (156/20–1). In this way the queen is whitewashed and the blackness of Mortimer's reputation intensified.

Similar to Capgrave's tendency occasionally to heighten the contrast between white and black is his tendency occasionally to intensify dramatic or potentially dramatic situations.[1] Sometimes the dramatic possibilities of an incident are brought out simply by transposing material into direct speech, for example, at 139/16–19, where the barons demand a change in the king's policy, at 140/3–5, where the king demands the opening of St. Alban's tomb at Ely, and at 223/14–16, where the archbishop of Canterbury defends the clergy against suggestions that they should be stripped of their wealth—Walsingham says merely that the archbishop spoke *animose*. On one occasion conflict is heightened by the insertion of epithets where they do not occur in the source:

---

[1] Cf. Fredeman, 'Capgrave's . . . "Norbert" ', pp. 300–9.

Sir Robert Knollys, leader of an expedition to France which ended in dissension and failure, is described as *a elde werriour* in charge of *zonger lordis* (177/17), so that the cause of the dissension is suggested at the outset. Here dramatic tension is increased by the minimum alteration. On another occasion Capgrave alters the order of Walsingham's narrative with the effect of dramatizing a conflict. In the account of the 1376 parliament, at which the king *asked a gret summe of mony*, Sir Peter de la Mare is brought in much earlier than in Walsingham and the reported words of the Commons' forceful reply are specifically attributed to him, so that the conflict is effectively dramatized as a clash between two individuals.[1] In the account of the 1404 parliament at Coventry (225/24–226/23) all three methods of heightening dramatic conflict are employed together. The Speaker is brought in earlier and given a much more prominent role than in Walsingham and the disagreement between the lords temporal and spiritual is seen as a personal conflict between the Speaker and the archbishop, whose first speech is considerably expanded to give it even greater forcefulness.[2]

Finally, while dealing with Capgrave's use of his sources it is appropriate to make a few remarks on some stylistic traits which are illuminated by reference to the source. On the whole, Capgrave's English reflects little direct influence from the Latin he was translating and adapting. There are, however, instances of syntactic constructions which have obviously been rather closely modelled on the Latin original. For example, Capgrave twice takes over the Latin ablative absolute construction, *lyuyng Thomas Arundel* (230/31) from L *vivente Domino Thoma de Arundelia*, and *his fadir Philip lyuand* (248/19) from L *vivente patre suo Philippo*. And twice he takes over Latin constructions with *causa* (abl.), *cause of deuocion* (86/25–6) from L *devocionis causa*, and *for his cause* (239/12) from L *causa praedicti Johannis*. But such instances are rare. Examples of Capgrave varying the pattern of his original are less rare. For example, on five occasions Capgrave uses double-headed noun phrases where there is only a single noun in the Latin original: *with a leuene and pundir* (59/2) from L *fulmine*; *with gold and gemmes* (59/3) from L *gemmis*; *feith and treuth* (200/14) from L *devotionem*; *barettoures and riseris* (207/29)

[1] See further Commentary, note to 180/13–14.
[2] See further the notes to this passage in the Commentary.

from L *malefactores*; *her secte and her opiniones* (239/8) from L *sectam suam*. And on four occasions Capgrave uses double-headed verb phrases where there is only a single verb (or its equivalent) in the Latin original: *he endited and reported onto hem* (56/6–7) from L *ex ore ipsius*; *schuld consent and conferme* (136/21–2) from L *se ratum tenere*; *hem þat appeled and accused* (215/17–18) from L *appellantes*; *for to rise and distroye* (239/7) from L *ad insurgendum*. Once a double-headed verb phrase involving word-play is included as a straight addition to the source: when Henry Percy (Hotspur) is said to have been *percid or presed* to death (222/18) the play on the victim's name can hardly have come from the Latin original. But these instances of double-headed phrases which vary the pattern of the original are not particularly common either. And I have found only one instance of Capgrave apparently consciously trying to add stylistic flair to his translation of the Latin original. For Latin *Anglia semper fertilis ab aliis regionibus petere alimoniam coacta est* Capgrave has *Ynglond, þat was wone to fede oþir londis, was fayn to be fed with oþir londis* (168/7–8). Several rhetorical devices are employed here and can be seen to have been added through the adaptation of *semper fertilis* to *þat was wone to fede oþir londis*. There is *conversio* (*antistrophe*) in the repetition of *oþir londis* at the end of successive clauses, *adnominatio* (*polyptoton*) in the use of two forms based on the same root (*fede/fed*), *contrarium* (*antithesis*) in the opposition of *to fede* and *to be fed*, *compar* (*parison*) in the balancing of clauses with almost exactly the same number of syllables, *þat was wone to fede oþir londis* (9 syllables) with *was fayn to be fed with oþir londis* (10), and *alliteratio* in *fayn/fed*, *fayn* probably being chosen for its alliterating properties as it is rather weaker in sense than L *coacta*.[1] But this instance is exceptional. Indeed all the features discussed in this paragraph are unusual to a degree. The relative paucity of appropriate examples points to the conclusion that Capgrave sought to provide a straightforward English prose narrative (or series of narratives) free from the constraints of the Latin originals but as a general rule without any particular stylistic embellishments.[2]

[1] On rhetorical terminology see R. A. Lanham, *A Handlist of Rhetorical Terms* (Berkeley and Los Angeles, 1969) and L. A. Sonnino, *A Handbook to Sixteenth-Century Rhetoric* (London, 1968). I have preferred the Latin terms but the equivalent Greek terms are given in brackets.

[2] Cf. Fredeman, 'Capgrave's . . . "Augustine" ', pp. 304–9.

HISTORIOGRAPHICAL VALUE

Capgrave refers to his *Abbreuiacion of Cronicles* as *a schort rememberauns of elde stories* (7/13) wherein the reader may *se schortly touchid þe most famous þingis þat haue be do in þe world fro his beginnyng onto þe ȝere of oure Lord Crist a m cccc and xvii* (7/16–18). It is a universal chronicle the material of which *it plesed me as for a solace to gader* and to abridge from other works. In writing such a chronicle Capgrave was following in a long line of distinguished ecclesiastical writers, descending from Eusebius, whose *Chronicon* (or *Chronographia*) was translated into Latin by Jerome, through Sulpicius Severus (*Chronicorum libri II*), Prosper of Aquitaine (*Epitoma Chronicorum*), Fulgentius (*De Aetatibus Mundi*), Victor of Tunnuna (*Chronicon*), Cassiodorus (*Chronica*), Isidore of Seville (*Chronicon*), and Bede (*Chronica minora et maiora*) to the ninth century and beyond. Like many of his predecessors Capgrave seems to have regarded his work as a kind of chronological reference book, so that *whanne I loke upon hem* [the entries] *and haue a schort touch of þe writyng I can sone dilate þe circumstaunses* (7/13–15). It provided a framework for world history.

Universal history was essentially *historia sacra*, history seen as a continuation of the Bible, which was the most significant historical work ever written. Accordingly Capgrave's *Abbreuiacion of Cronicles* begins where the Bible begins, with the Creation. However, besides recording biblical events the early section (Part I) also includes notices concerning all parts of the world. From this universality of scope the work gradually narrows in range. After the birth of Christ the focus is West European (emperors and popes), then from 1216 English (kings of England). The transfer from West European to English focus is a little awkward as after 1066 the entries relating to England suddenly become quite long and then gradually become longer, so that from 1066 until 1216 the West European standpoint is steadily being ousted. Indeed, the narrower the range the fuller the treatment. As the *Abbreuiacion of Cronicles* progresses it imposes increasing strains on the philosophy of history underlying it.

Capgrave inherited his philosophy of history from St. Augustine, who argued that the shape of history was fixed before it began. In this providential view of history, in which history, prophecy, and the study of time were all one, there was little room for considering cause and effect in human terms.[1] By analogy with the six working days of Creation Augustine divided history into six ages,[2] the first ending with the Flood, the second with the death of Abraham, the third with the death of David, the fourth with the captivity of the Israelites in Babylon, and the fifth with the birth of Christ. The sixth age is that currently being experienced and will last until the second coming of Christ, to be followed, at the end of history, by the seventh age, a period of eternal rest. Augustine's scheme was first used as a framework device for a historical work by Isidore in his *Chronicon de sex aetatibus* and is still followed by Capgrave a thousand years after it was first promulgated. In the first five ages Capgrave incorporates the whole history of pre-classical and classical antiquity. The kingdom of Egypt began in the time of Serug (22/10 ff.), the kingdoms of the Assyrians and Sicyonians in the time of Nahor (22/29 ff.), the Argive kingdom in the time of Isaac (25/10 ff.). In the time of Othniel, the first judge of Israel,

regned at Attenes her v kyng, summe men cleped him Pandion, and summe Neptunus. And in þe cité of Tebes regned þanne Cadmus. Eke þe grete musician cleped Linus, he leued in þoo dayes.   (28/5–8)

Hercules is put in the time of Ehud (28/15 ff.). All through Part I of the *Abbreuiacion of Cronicles*, which deals with the first five ages, Capgrave stays fairly close to the chronological narrative derived from the Bible, adding in contemporary events from classical and pre-classical antiquity where appropriate. Up to the birth of Christ the human focus is on the Jews, the chosen people of God. After the birth of Christ the human focus shifts to Christians (who, as the new faithful, have taken over the function of the Jews as God's chosen people), specifically the Christians of the Roman empire. For Rome was seen as the last of the four great empires of Daniel's prophecy (Dan. 7: 2–27)—the others being Babylon, Persia, and Macedon—and the one under which Christianity prospered. As long as the Roman empire survived, in whatever transmuted form, the continuity of God's purpose in history remained manifest. The problems arise when *þe empire in maner sesed* (116/31)—in 1212 according to Capgrave—and the

---

[1] But Capgrave does sometimes indicate cause and effect when there is a moral in it: see above, pp. lxxxviii–lxxxix.

[2] *De Civitate Dei*, xxii. 30. Capgrave refers in passing to this notion when he says *al þe labour of þe world is figured in sex dayes* (8/21).

human focus shifts from the Christians of the Roman empire to the English. From the point of view of Capgrave's inherited philosophy of history there is no longer the continuity that is a prerequisite of medieval providential history. Moreover, consistency in moral outlook, which might have been a saving grace—for medieval Christian chronicles sometimes evaluated the deeds of pre-Christian pagans according to their moral worth—is also lost sight of. Capgrave condemns the Flemish seamen who, pretending to be allies of the English, took an English ship *be treson* (183/21), but apparently approves of Sir Oliver Ingham's deception and defeat of the Frenchmen who besieged Bordeaux (161/28–162/4). The development of this blatantly partisan approach can be illustrated from the use of the word *oure*. In Parts I and II, apart from authorial or editorial *we* and apart from quotations, *oure* is used only with the sense 'of us Christians' as in *oure Lord* (47/26 and *passim*), *oure Lady* (55/25–6 etc.), *oure feith* (23/15, 235/3), and *oure messe* (62/14). In Part III a new usage, which does not occur in Parts I and II, is found, in which *oure* means 'of us English', as in *oure kyng* (132/17, 162/28, 174/9), *oure Englischmen* (236/16), *oure armed men* (157/4), *oure archeres* (157/3–4), *oure side* (191/3, 246/4), *oure enmyes* (196/4), and *oure frendis* (183/21), this last instance coming in the passage mentioned above, in which the Flemish seamen pretend to be allies of the English. It is as if the English had become God's chosen people. Indeed, on at least three occasions Capgrave apparently supports the king of England against the pope.[1] By attempting to extend a universal chronicle by the addition of national history Capgrave merely exposes the cracks that the passage of time had opened in the philosophy underlying universal history. Already humanist historians were beginning to replace the theory of the six ages with a division between classical antiquity and the period that followed. Capgrave's *Abbreuiacion of Cronicles* is one of the last works in a long, already outmoded, tradition.[2] The fact that it is written in English rather than Latin merely confirms, by its very up-to-dateness in this respect, that it was, by contrast, anachronistic in its conception.

[1] See the passages at 118/23–9, 122/5–15, and 163/23–164/6.

[2] Though even in the second quarter of the eighteenth century some men still attempted to write a Universal History: see R. W. Southern, 'Hugh of St. Victor and the Idea of Historical Development', *TRHS*, ser. V, xxi (1971), 159–79, esp. 178–9.

The primary organizing principle of Capgrave's *Abbreuiacion of Cronicles* is the chronology. There are no chapters, as, for example, in Higden's *Polychronicon,* and it would have been contrary to the work's primary organizing principle to try to group together in one place narrative dealing with a single subject, as, for example, the treatment of the Lollards and Oldcastle. Each year is given a line (or more) so that in the early part of the work there are sometimes whole pages with just year numbers but no entries. As the author says,

If othir studious men þat haue more red þan I, or can fynde þat I fond not, or haue elde bokes whech make more expression of þoo stories þat fel fro þe creacion of Adam onto þe general flod þan I haue, þe velim lith bare saue þe noumbir, redy to receyue þat þei will set in.

(7/27–32)

The second organizing principle is kingship. Years are grouped according to the reigns of rulers, from the Israelite patriarchs, judges, kings, through the emperors of Persia, Macedon, Egypt to those of Rome, the holy Roman emperors, and finally to the kings of England. But this second organizing principle only goes so far; there is no evidence of any particular attempt to make a reign into an independent narrative unit. The only time Capgrave comes even remotely near to this is in the reign of King Henry IV, which happens to begin with Henry's speech claiming the crown (214/13–16) and which happens to end with his death-bed confession defending his right to the crown (238/12–16), so that the reign is sandwiched between these two dramatic incidents. However, it is probably largely accidental that the two incidents seem to provide a narrative frame for Henry IV's reign. All through the *Abbreuiacion of Cronicles* the focus is on events, *þe most famous þingis þat haue be do in þe world* (7/17), and these are recorded in a somewhat matter-of-fact way as they happened, without regard to larger matters such as how units of narrative are grouped together. For example, the statement of the author's date of birth (203/13–14) comes in the midst of an account of Richard II's economic and military problems in Ireland, which Capgrave must have broken in two in order to make the insertion. Sometimes Capgrave draws attention to an individual incident by playing on the meaning of words. On hearing how Eadric engineered the death of Edmund Ironside King Canute says, '*I schal sette þe hiest of ony lord in Ynglond*'. *So he ded smyte of his hed and sette it on þe hiest tour in Londoun* (98/33–5). And the death of William II from Walter Tyrrell's arrow during a hunting expedition is reported similarly: *as he wold a smet a hert, he smet þe kyng to þe hert* (104/12). By using word-play in this way Capgrave makes what is already a dramatic incident into a particularly memorable one which stands out at the expense of any over-all narrative coherence or development. He must have intended the organizing principle of chronology to be predominant. Events are recorded at the appropriate point in the time-sequence but relate to each other only through that time-sequence.

Capgrave's confidence and sense of security in the providential view of history which he inherited emerges from the tone he adopts when addressing the reader. Having explained the scope and chronological arrangement of the *Abbreuiacion of Cronicles* he says, *These reules had in mynde þe reder schal more parfitely vndirstand þis book* (8/6–7). And when he is about to explain the transference from the regnal years of the holy Roman emperors to those of the kings of England he prefaces his remarks with a magisterial *ȝe schal vndirstand þat . . .* (116/29).[1] He never shows the slightest concern at a reader's possible reaction to what he has written. Capgrave's confidence in the providential view of history also emerges from the very lack of comment on events such as the deposition of Richard II and the deception and execution of the Earl Marshal, Thomas Mowbray, and Archbishop Richard le Scrope of York in 1405. For the logic of events provides its own commentary. After the deposition of Richard II Henry IV is anointed with the rediscovered *holy oyle þat was take to Seynt Thomas of Cauntirbury be oure Lady* (214/28–9). After the execution of Richard le Scrope *the kyng . . . lost þe beuté of his face* (229/13) and *þe archbischop of Cauntirbury . . . fel in a tercian* (229/17–18). Although judgements are given only when the views of others are cited, as, for example, St. Bernard's on King Henry I (109/35–110/3), moral pointers, as already noted,[2] are sometimes added by Capgrave, and others are taken over from his sources. It was a characteristic of history written in the providential tradition that successes were attributable to God, as when the English defeat the French in a naval battle *by þe help of*

---

[1] This formula is also used at 8/20 and 79/10.
[2] See above, pp. lxxxvii–lxxxix.

God (162/18), and disasters were attributable to the devil, and before Capgrave's time this approach had already been adapted for propaganda purposes.[1] Capgrave, however, stays firmly within the constraints of the tradition, taking over from his sources even the most inane 'marvels', evidence, he no doubt believed, of God's providence in this world.

[1] As, for example, in the *Gesta Henrici Quinti*: see E. F. Jacob, *The Fifteenth Century* (Oxford, 1961), pp. 122 ff., and J. S. Roskell and F. Taylor, 'The Authorship and Purpose of the *Gesta Henrici Quinti*', *BJRL* lii (1970), 428–64, and liv (1971), 223–40.

SELECT BIBLIOGRAPHY

I. Biography and Bibliography

D. J. Brimson, OSA, 'John Capgrave, O.S.A.', *Tagastan*, ix (1946), 106–13.

E. Colledge, OSA, 'John Capgrave's Literary Vocation', *Analecta Augustiniana*, xl (1977), 185–95.

A. B. Emden, *A Biographical Register of the University of Cambridge* (Cambridge, 1963), s.n. *Capgrave, John.*

J. C. Fredeman, 'The Life of John Capgrave, O.E.S.A. (1393–1464)', *Augustiniana*, xxix (1979), 197–237.

P. J. Lucas, 'John Capgrave and the *Nova Legenda Anglie*: A Survey', *The Library*, V. xxv (1970), 1–10.

—— 'Sir Robert Kemp and the Holograph Manuscript containing Capgrave's *Life of St. Gilbert* and *Tretis*', *BMQ* xxxvi (1972), 80–3.

—— 'The Growth and Development of English Literary Patronage in the Later Middle Ages and Early Renaissance', *The Library*, VI. iv (1982), 219–48.

A. de Meijer, OESA, 'John Capgrave, O.E.S.A.', *Augustiniana*, v (1955), 400–40 (biography), and vii (1957), 118–48, 531–75 (bibliography). [de Meijer, cited by the appropriate page numbers]

F. Roth, OSA, *The English Austin Friars, 1249–1538*, vols. i–ii, Cassiacum vi–vii (New York, 1961–6), esp. i. 111–16, 413–21, 523–8. [Roth]

II. The Author and his Scriptorium

H. M. Bannister, 'Introductory Note' to Capgrave's *Solace*, ed. Mills (1911), pp. xi–xviii.

E. Colledge, 'The Capgrave "Autographs"', *TCBS*, VI. iii (1974), 137–48.

P. J. Lucas, 'John Capgrave, O.S.A. (1393–1464), Scribe and "Publisher"', *TCBS*, V. i (1969), 1–35.

—— Untitled review of C. L. Smetana's edition of *Norbert*, *MÆ* xlviii (1979), 316–19, esp. 316.

—— 'A Fifteenth-century Copyist at Work under Authorial Scrutiny: an Incident from John Capgrave's Scriptorium', *SB* xxxiv (1981), 66–95.

C. L. Smetana, in his edition of Capgrave's *Norbert* (1977), pp. 4–7.

III. Extant Works by Capgrave other than the *Abbreuiacion of Cronicles*

(1) *Life of St. Norbert* (before 1422, completed 1440). [*Norbert*]

MANUSCRIPT:

San Marino, California, USA, Henry E. Huntington Library, MS HM 55. Autograph, the presentation copy for John Wygenhale, O. Praem., abbot of the Premonstratensian abbey at West Dereham, Norfolk.

EDITION:
C. L. Smetana, OSA, *The Life of St. Norbert by John Capgrave, O.E.S.A.* (*1393–1464*), Pontifical Institute of Mediaeval Studies, Studies and Texts 40 (Toronto, 1977).

DISCUSSION:
E. Colledge, OSA, and C. Smetana, OSA, 'Capgrave's *Life of St. Norbert*: Diction, Dialect and Spelling', *MS* xxxiv (1972), 422–34.

J. C. Fredeman, 'John Capgrave's First English Composition, "The Life of St. Norbert"', *BJRULM* lvii (1975), 280–309.

W. Grauwen, O. Praem., 'Recente Studies over de Vita metrica Norberti door Capgrave (1393–1464)', *Analecta Praemonstratensia*, lv (1979), 111–15.

P. J. Lucas, Untitled review of Smetana's edition, *MÆ* xlviii (1979), 316–19.
—— 'On the Date of John Capgrave's *Life of St Norbert*', *The Library*, VI. iii (1981), 328–30.

(2) *Commentarius in Genesim* (1437–8)
MANUSCRIPT:
Oxford, Bodleian Library, MS Oriel College 32. Partly holograph, the presentation copy received by Humfrey duke of Gloucester.

Unprinted, except for the Dedicatory Preface in Hingeston, *De illustribus Henricis*, pp. 229–32, and (incomplete) in translation in Hingeston's *Illustrious Henries*, pp. 229–32.

(3) *Commentarius in Exodum* (1439–40)
MANUSCRIPT:
Oxford, Bodleian Library, MS Duke Humphrey b. 1. Revised by the author, the presentation copy given to Humphrey duke of Gloucester.

Unprinted, except for the Dedicatory Preface in:
P. J. Lucas and R. Dalton, 'Capgrave's Preface Dedicating his Commentary *In Exodum* to Humfrey Duke of Gloucester', *The Bodleian Library Record*, xi (1982), pp. 20–5, and (incomplete) in translation in Lucas, 'The Growth . . . of . . . Literary Patronage . . .' (cited above, p. xcix), pp. 236–7.

(4) *Life of St. Katharine of Alexandria* (before 1445). [*Katharine*]
MANUSCRIPTS:
London, British Library, Arundel MS 20, art. 1.
London, British Library, Arundel MS 168, art. 9.
London, British Library, Arundel MS 396, art. 1.
Oxford, Bodleian Library, MS Rawlinson poet. 118, art. 1.

EDITION:
C. Horstmann, *The Life of St. Katharine of Alexandria by John Capgrave*, with Forewords by F. J. Furnivall, EETS, OS, 100 (1893).

DISCUSSION:
J. C. Fredeman, 'Style and Characterization in John Capgrave's *Life of St. Katherine*', *BJRULM* lxii (1980), 346–87.

A. Kurvinen, 'The Source of Capgrave's *Life of St. Katharine of Alexandria*', *NM* lxi (1960), 268–324.

D. Pearsall, 'John Capgrave's *Life of St. Katharine* and Popular Romance Style', *M&H*, NS, vi (1975), 121–37.

T. Wolpers, *Die englische Heiligenlegende des Mittelalters* (Tübingen, 1964), pp. 330–42.

(5) *De illustribus Henricis* (completed 1446–7)

MANUSCRIPTS:

Cambridge, Corpus Christi College, MS 408. Autograph.

London, British Library, Cotton MS Tiberius A viii.

EDITION:

F. C. Hingeston, *Johannis Capgrave Liber De Illustribus Henricis*, RS 7 (London, 1858).

TRANSLATION:

F. C. Hingeston, *The Book of the Illustrious Henries, by John Capgrave* (London, 1858).

(6) *Life of St. Augustine* (before 1451). [*Augustine*]

MANUSCRIPT:

London, British Library, Add. MS 36704, art. 1. Holograph.

EDITION:

J. J. Munro, *John Capgrave's Lives of St. Augustine and St. Gilbert of Sempringham, And a Sermon*, EETS, OS, 140 (1910), pp. 1–60.

DISCUSSION:

R. Arbesmann, OSA, 'Jordanus of Saxony's *Vita S. Augustini* The Source for John Capgrave's *Life of St. Augustine*', *Traditio*, i (1943), 341–53.

—— 'The "Malleus" Metaphor in Medieval Characterization', *Traditio*, iii (1945), 389–92.

J. C. Fredeman, 'John Capgrave's "Life of St. Augustine"', *Augustiniana*, xxviii (1978), 288–309.

G. Sanderlin, 'John Capgrave Speaks up for the Hermits', *Speculum*, xviii (1943), 358–62.

(7) *The Solace of Pilgrimes* (c.1451). [*Solace*]

MANUSCRIPTS:

Oxford, Bodleian Library, MS Bodley 423, art. 5. Holograph, possibly the presentation copy made for Sir Thomas Tuddenham, lord of the manor of Oxburgh.

Oxford, All Souls College, MS XVII, fols. i–ii and pp. 221–4 (fragment).

Oxford, Balliol College, MS 190, fols. 116–19 (fragment).

EDITION:

C. A. Mills, *Ye Solace of Pilgrimes*, British and American Archaeological Society of Rome (London, 1911).

The text of the two fragments is printed by Hingeston, *Chronicle*, pp. 357–66.

DISCUSSION:

R. Beadle, 'The East Anglian "game-place": a possibility for further research', *REED Newsletter*, 1978:1, 2–4, suppl. by D. Galloway, *REED Newsletter*, 1979:1, 24–6.

P. J. Lucas, 'A Fifteenth-century Copyist at Work . . .' (cited above, p. xcix), pp. 66–95.

C. A. Mills, 'Ye Solace of Pilgrimes', *Journal of the British and American Archaeological Society of Rome*, IV. v (1912), 440–65.

G. B. Parkes, *The English Traveler to Italy*, i (Rome, 1954), 596–600.

(8) *Life of St. Gilbert* (1451). [*Gilbert*]

MANUSCRIPTS:

London, British Library, Add. MS 36704, art. 2. Holograph.

London, British Library, Cotton MS Vitellius D xv, art. 4 (burnt fragment).

EDITION:

J. J. Munro, *John Capgrave's Lives of St. Augustine and St. Gilbert of Sempringham, And a Sermon*, EETS, os, 140 (1910), pp. 61–142.

DISCUSSION:

J. C. Fredeman, 'John Capgrave's *Life of St. Gilbert of Sempringham*', *BJRULM* lv (1972), 112–45.

(9) *Tretis of tho Orderes þat be vndyr þe Reule of oure Fader Seynt Augustin* (written up and revised 1451 from a sermon of 1422). [*Tretis*]

MANUSCRIPT:

London, British Library, Add. MS 36704, art. 3. Holograph.

EDITION:

J. J. Munro, *John Capgrave's Lives of St. Augustine and St. Gilbert of Sempringham, And a Sermon*, EETS, os, 140 (1910), pp. 145–8.

(10) *Commentarius in Actus Apostolorum* (after 1457)

MANUSCRIPT:

Oxford, Balliol College, MS 189. Autograph, the presentation copy given to William Gray, bishop of Ely.

Unprinted, except for the Dedicatory Preface in Hingeston, *De illustribus Henricis*, pp. 221–4, and (in part only) in translation in Hingeston's *Illustrious Henries*, p. 228.

(11) *De Fidei Symbolis* (*c.*1462)

MANUSCRIPTS:

Oxford, Balliol College, MS 190. Revised by the author, the presentation copy given to William Gray, bishop of Ely.

Oxford, All Souls College, MS XVII. Revised by the author.

Unprinted, except for the Dedicatory Preface in Hingeston, *De illustribus Henricis*, pp. 213–17, and (in part only) in translation in Hingeston's *Illustrious Henries*, pp. 226–7.

IV. *Abbreuiacion of Cronicles*

(1) MANUSCRIPTS:

M: Cambridge, University Library MS Gg.4.12. Autograph, probably the presentation copy intended for King Edward IV. For a description see above, pp. xxix–xxxvii.

P: Cambridge, Corpus Christi College MS 167. For a description see above, pp. xxxvii–xxxix.

(2) EDITION:

F. C. Hingeston, *The Chronicle of England by John Capgrave*, RS 1 (London, 1858). [Hingeston]

(3) SELECTIONS:

H. Craik, *English Prose Selections* (London, 1893), i. 89–94.

W. Matthews, *Later Medieval English Prose* (London, 1962), pp. 28–34.

K. M. Warren, *A Treasury of English Literature: Twelfth Century to Age of Elizabeth* (London, 1908), pp. 133–4.

(4) DISCUSSION:

P. J. Lucas, 'Sense-Units and the Use of Punctuation-Markers in John Capgrave's *Chronicle*', *AL*, NS, ii (1971), 1–24.

—— 'Consistency and Correctness in the Orthographic Usage of John Capgrave's *Chronicle*', *SN* xlv (1973), 323–55.

—— 'John Capgrave's *Chronicle*, Additions, Antedatings, Postdatings and Corrections to *OED* and *MED*, A–L', *NM* lxxx (1979), 231–7.

—— 'Computer Assistance in the Editorial Expansion of Contractions in a Middle English Text', *ALLC Bulletin*, ix. 3 (1981), 9–10.

(5) LANGUAGE:

(i) Other texts emanating from Lynn on external evidence:

English Gilds, ed. T. Smith, L. T. Smith, and L. Brentano, EETS, OS, 40 (1870). Gild ordinances of Lynn, Lynn Bishop, W. Lynn, and N. Lynn.

The Book of Margery Kempe, ed. S. B. Meech with H. E. Allen, EETS 212 (1940).

The Promptorium Parvulorum, ed. A. L. Mayhew, EETS, ES, 102 (1908).

(ii) Modern studies of general importance:

E. J. Dobson, *English Pronunciation 1500–1700* (Oxford, 1968 edn.). [Dobson]

G. Forström, *The Verb 'To Be' in Middle English*, Lund Studies in English, xv (1948).

R. Jordan, *Handbuch der mittelenglischen Grammatik* (Heidelberg, 1968 edn.), also rev. and trans. E. J. Crook, Janua Linguarum, ser. pract. 218 (The Hague, 1974). [Jordan]

A. Kihlbom, *A Contribution to the Study of Fifteenth Century English* (Uppsala, 1926).

H. Kökeritz, *The Phonology of the Suffolk Dialect* (Uppsala, 1932).

R. Lass (ed.), *Approaches to English Historical Linguistics* (New York, 1969).

M. M. Long, *The English Strong Verb from Chaucer to Caxton* (Menasha, Wisconsin, 1944).

K. Luick, *Historische Grammatik der englischen Sprache* (Leipzig, 1914–29, repr. Oxford, 1964). [Luick]

D. W. Reed, *The History of Inflectional N in English Verbs before 1500*, Univ. of California Publ. in English, VII. iv (1950), 157–328.

J. F. Rettger, *The Development of Ablaut in the Strong Verbs of the East Midland Dialects of Middle English*, Language Dissertations xviii (1934).

M. L. Samuels, *Linguistic Evolution* (Cambridge, 1972).

H. C. Wyld, *A History of Modern Colloquial English* (Oxford, 1936 edn.).

(iii) Modern studies relevant to the language of the W. Norfolk area:

J. Bennett, 'The *Mary Magdalene* of Bishop's Lynn', *SP* lxxv (1978), 1–9.

R. A. Caldwell, 'The Scribe of the Chaucer MS, Cambridge University Library Gg 4. 27', *MLQ* v (1944), 33–44.

E. Colledge and C. L. Smetana, 'Capgrave's . . . *Norbert* . . .' (cited above, p. c), pp. 422–34.

N. Davis, 'A Scribal Problem in the Paston Letters', *E&GS* iv (1951–2), 31–64.

—— 'A Paston Hand', *RES*, NS, iii (1952), 209–21.

—— 'The Letters of William Paston', *Neophil.* xxxvii (1953), 36–41.

—— 'The Language of the Pastons', *PBA* xl (1954), 119–44.

—— 'Scribal Variation in Late Fifteenth-century English', in *Mélanges de Linguistique et de Philologie; Fernand Mossé in memoriam* (Paris, 1959), 95–103.

—— and G. S. Ivy, 'MS Walter Rye 38 and its French Grammar', *MÆ* xxxi (1962), 110–24.

W. Dibelius, 'John Capgrave und die englische Schriftsprache', *Anglia*, xxiii (1901), 153–94, 323–75, 427–72, and xxiv (1901), 211–63, 267–308.

M. Eccles, 'Ludus Coventriae: Lincoln or Norfolk?' MÆ xl (1971), 135–41.

P. J. Lucas, 'Consistency . . . in the Orthographic Usage of Capgrave's Chronicle' (cited above, p. ciii), pp. 323–55.

—— 'John Capgrave's Chronicle, Additions . . . to OED and MED, A–L' (cited above, p. ciii), pp. 231–7.

A. McIntosh, 'The Language of the Extant Versions of Havelok the Dane', MÆ xlv (1976), 36–49.

J. J. Munro, John Capgrave's Lives of . . . Augustine . . . Gilbert . . . And a Sermon, (cited above, pp. ci–cii), pp. xiv–xxi.

E. Schulz, Die Sprache der 'English Gilds' aus dem Jahre 1389 (Hildesheim, 1891).

M. C. Seymour, 'A Fifteenth-century East Anglian Scribe', MÆ xxxvii (1968), 166–73.

H. C. Wyld, 'South-eastern and South-east Midland Dialects in Middle English', E&S vi (1920), 112–45.

(6) SOURCES:

(i) Martinus Polonus (Martin of Troppau):

W. Matthews, 'Martinus Polonus and Some Later Chroniclers', in Medieval Literature and Civilization, Studies in Memory of G. N. Garmonsway, ed. D. A. Pearsall and R. A. Waldron (London, 1969), pp. 275–88.

L. Weiland (ed.), Martini Oppaviensis Chronicon Pontificum et Imperatorum, MGH, Scriptores xxii (Hanover, 1872), 377–475, continuations 476–82 and Scriptores xxiv (Hanover, 1878) 251–65.

L. Weiland, 'Zur Ausgabe der Chronik Martins von Troppau', Archiv der Gesellschaft für ältere deutsche Geschichtkunde, xii (1874), 1–79.

(ii) St. Albans Chronicles:

V. H. Galbraith (ed.), The St. Albans Chronicle 1406–1420 (Oxford, 1937).

—— 'Thomas Walsingham and the Saint Albans Chronicle, 1272–1422', EHR xlvii (1932), 12–30.

H. T. Riley (ed.), Chronica et Annales 1259–1307 (by William Rishanger), RS 28/2 (London, 1865).

—— (ed.), Chronica et Annales (1392–1406, by John de Trokelowe), RS 28/3 (London, 1865), pp. 153 ff.

—— (ed.), Historia Anglicana (by Thomas Walsingham) vols. i–ii, RS 28/1 (London, 1863–4).

E. M. Thompson (ed.), Chronicon Angliae (1328–88), RS 64 (London, 1874).

(iii) Other possible sources:

C. Babington and J. R. Lumby (eds.), *Polychronicon Ranulphi Higden* vols. i–ix, RS 41 (London, 1865-86).

F. W. D. Brie (ed.), *The Brut*, EETS, os, 131, 136 (1906–8).

A. Griscom (ed.), *The Historia Regum Britanniae of Geoffrey of Monmouth* (London, 1929); also L. Thorpe (tr.), *The History of the Kings of Britain* (Harmondsworth, 1966).

T. Mommsen (ed.), *Chronica Maiora Isidori Iunioris*, MGH auct. antiq. xi (Berlin, 1884), 394–488.

(7) HISTORIOGRAPHY:

V. H. Galbraith, *Historical Research in Medieval England* (London, 1951).

D. Hay, *Annalists and Historians* (London, 1977).

A. R. Humphreys, 'Shakespeare and the Tudor Perception of History', in *Shakespeare Celebrated*, ed. L. B. Wright (London, 1968).

M. Keen, 'Mediaeval Ideas of History', in *The Mediaeval World*, ed. D. Daiches and A. Thorlby (London, 1973).

R. W. Southern, 'Aspects of the European Tradition of Historical Writing', *TRHS*, ser. V, xx (1970), 173–96; xxi (1971), 159–79; xxii (1972), 159–80; xxiii (1973), 243–63.

J. Taylor, *The Universal Chronicle of Ranulf Higden* (Oxford, 1966).

J. W. Thompson, *A History of Historical Writing*, i (New York, 1942).

V. Works of Reference

C. R. Cheney, *Handbook of Dates*, Royal Historical Society Guides and Handbooks 4 (London, 1978 edn.).

R. Cleasby and G. Vigfusson, *An Icelandic Dictionary*, rev. Sir W. A. Craigie (Oxford, 1957).

G. E. C[okayne], *Complete Peerage*, rev. Hon. V. Gibbs and H. A. Doubleday (London, 1926).

F. L. Cross, *The Oxford Dictionary of the Christian Church* (London, 1974 edn.). [*ODCC*]

A. Dauzat and Ch. Rostaing, *Dictionnaire étymologique des noms de lieux en France* (Paris, 1963).

E. Dekkers, *Clavis Patrum Latinorum* [= *Sacris Erudiri*, iii (1961)], (Steenbrugge and The Hague, rev. edn. 1965).

J. Earle and C. Plummer, *Two of the Saxon Chronicles Parallel*, vols. i–ii (Oxford, 1892–9, repr. 1952).

E. Ekwall, *The Concise Oxford Dictionary of English Place-Names* (Oxford, 1960 edn.).

P. P. B. Gams, *Series Episcoporum Ecclesiae Catholicae* (Ratisbon, 1873, repr. Ganz, 1957).

F. Godefroy, *Dictionnaire de l'ancienne langue française* (Paris, 1881–1902).

F. Gregorovius, *History of the City of Rome in the Middle Ages*, tr. A. Hamilton, vols. i–viii (London, 1902–11).

J. G. Th. Graesse and F. Benedict, *Orbis Latinus*, rev. H. Plechl (Braunschweig, 1971).

W. A. Hinnebusch, op, *The Early English Friars Preachers* (Rome, 1951).

Dom D. Knowles, *The Religious Orders in England*, vols. i–ii (Cambridge, 1948–55).

——, C. N. L. Brooke, and V. London, *The Heads of Religious Houses England and Wales 940–1216* (Cambridge, 1972).

—— and R. N. Hadcock, *Medieval Religious Houses* (London, 1953).

R. E. Latham, *Dictionary of Medieval Latin from British Sources* (London, 1976–). [*DML*]

—— *Revised Medieval Latin Word-List* (London, 1965). [*RMLWL*]

H. E. L. Mellersh, *Chronology of the Ancient World 10,000 B.C. to A.D. 799* (London, 1976).

Sir F. M. Powicke and E. B. Fryde, *Handbook of British Chronology*, Royal Historical Society Guides and Handbooks 2 (London, 1961).

P. H. Reaney, *A Dictionary of British Surnames* (London, 1958). [Reaney]

S. Rossiter, *Rome and Environs*, Blue Guides (London, 1971).

F. Stegmüller, *Repertorium Biblicum Medii Aevi*, vols. i–v (Madrid, 1950–5).

S. H. Steinberg, *Historical Tables 58 BC–AD 1965* (London, 1966 edn.).

R. L. Storey, *Chronology of the Medieval World 800 to 1491* (London, 1973).

B. J. Whiting, *Proverbs, Sentences, and Proverbial Phrases From English Writings Mainly Before 1500* (Cambridge, Mass., and London, 1968). [Whiting]

G. Wissowa, *Paulys Real-Encyclopädie der Classischen Altertumswissenschaft* (Stuttgart, 1894–1972). [Pauly–Wissowa]

E. G. Withycombe, *The Oxford Dictionary of English Christian Names* (Oxford, 1977 edn.).

J. Wright, *The English Dialect Dictionary* (London, 1898–1905).

THE TEXT

ESTABLISHING THE TEXT

Because it is autograph M must be the base manuscript for the text. But P is important too because it is copied from an autograph (or holograph)—hence the corrections adopted from it. There are some problems for the editor in deciding whether a variant reading from P is a 'correction' or not. In a few cases there may be two 'authorial' readings. For example, for M's *knowyng* in *hauyng no knowyng of his deth* (222/29) P has *knowlech*, Capgrave's usual form of that noun in M which the P-scribe twice retains (94/26, 193/18) but which he often alters to *knowleg*: Capgrave's characteristic form here suggests that P got it from the exemplar *A but that in copying the text in M Capgrave altered *knowlech* to *knowyng*. For the purposes of establishing the text M must be assumed to have the author's final authority and M's readings are not therefore departed from in favour of P except where there seems to be good reason to do so. Such 'good reason' may be the requirements of sense, the requirements of form (Capgrave's norm rather than merely predominant practice), or preference for a fuller reading where M has an apparently shortened reading added as a correction. All these 'good reasons' can be illustrated from instances where P has the definite article against M's lack of it. At 78/3 P's *þe* is necessary because without it the sense would be different, or at best ambiguous; a similar instance occurs at 201/31. At 236/18 P's *þe* is necessary because Capgrave does not normally omit the definite article from a nominal group of this kind in this position; a similar instance occurs at 43/3. At 101/12 P's *son onto*, with presumed retention of Capgrave's characteristic *onto* against the P-scribe's more usual *vnto*, has been preferred to M's *son to* inserted suprascript where space was limited; a similar instance, with *þe*, occurs at 67/7. These instances relating to the use of the definite article have been chosen for the purposes of illustration because there are very many such instances where P has the definite article against M's lack of it and in most of them there is no 'good reason' to adopt P's reading. As a group the instances where P 'adds' the definite article illustrate in microcosm the kind of editorial problems this particular text predominantly raises *qua* text, problems relating to minor variations in the way things are said rather than to what is said.

EDITORIAL PROCEDURE

The aim has been to produce a reliable text in a form suitable for the modern reader, and to be as consistent as possible in the treatment of spelling and punctuation. The text followed is that of M, the autograph manuscript, which is a fair copy in the author's handwriting. The spelling of this manuscript has been reproduced, except for the correction of apparent errors. Among these errors are a good many that are apparent from variation between M and P. Emendations are indicated by textual footnotes, which give the forms in both manuscripts. Also recorded in the textual notes are alterations made by the original scribe of M (the author)—including suprascript letters; unless otherwise stated these authorial alterations are written in a shade of ink indistinguishable from that of the contiguous main body of the text. In addition the textual notes include all substantive errors and variants from P, except that the omission of dates (other than those incorporated within the text) from P is not noted. Annotations added in later hands (which are not part of, or modifications to, the text) have been ignored in both manuscripts.

In M there is no distinction in form between the letters *ȝ* and *z*, the graph *ȝ* serving for both; but where the letter is *z* it has been so printed. Similarly, there is no distinction in M between *þ* and *y*, the graph *y* serving for both; but where the letter is *þ* it has been so printed. It is often difficult to distinguish letters composed of minims (*i, m, n, u*) from each other—though *i* is frequently dotted it is not always so—but the only problem case is *comnaunt*, on which see below. There is a distinction in M, between *i* and *j*, *j* having a long descender which goes below the line, but this *j* is merely a calligraphic variant of *i*; *i* has been printed except where the letter has been presumed not to represent a vowel sound, when *j* has been used.

Abbreviations and contractions have been expanded without notice. Each contraction has been expanded in accordance with the full spelling of it most frequently employed in the word in which it occurs. When no instance of a word occurs in which a full spelling is written out, or when there is an equal number of different full spellings, then the contraction has been expanded in accordance with the full spelling of it most frequently employed after the letter which it follows—for example, in such cases, final *ę*, the mark of contraction for *-es/-is* has been expanded as *-es* after *l*, *n*, and *r*, but as *-is* after *g* and *t*. This procedure has been followed with one exception: the word *parson*(-), *person*(-), is never spelt in full, but when 'parson' is meant the contraction has been expanded to give *par-*, and when 'person' is meant the contraction has been expanded to give *per-*.

A particular difficulty arose with forms of *comenaunt* (= covenant), a difficulty which is at two levels: (*a*) when the manuscript has *cõnaũt* the contraction may be expanded so as to read either *comnaunt* or possibly *couinaunt*; (*b*) when the word is written more fully, since letters composed of the same number of minims are hard to distinguish with certainty and since *i* is not always dotted, it is again impossible to know whether *comnaunt* or *couinaunt* was intended. The former, *comnaunt*, has been preferred because it agrees more closely with the only form of the word whose spelling is indisputable (*comenaunt*). See also Commentary, note to *Poumfrecte*, 142/26–7.

Most contractions offer no further difficulty. But the interpretation of the strokes with which some letters are often furnished, usually when in final position, has proved difficult, since these strokes may be either marks of contraction, usually for *-e*, or calligraphic flourishes. The letters concerned are final *g*, final *h* (once), final *l*, usually *ll*, final *n*, final and (occasionally) medial *r*, and final *s*. The strokes can undoubtedly be both meaningful and meaningless: for example, where *r* is the letter concerned, the stroke is a meaningful one in *thr'* 'three' (155/5), and *cuntr'* 'country' (27/26, *etc.*, 21×), but a meaningless flourish in *labour'ed* (69/24), and *mor'ed* (68/15). After all the letters, where a large proportion of full spellings of a word clearly lends justification, the stroke has been treated as a mark of contraction and expanded accordingly; otherwise the stroke has been interpreted as an otiose flourish and so ignored. (For this purpose *þan'*, *whan'*, where the flourish has been ignored, are treated separately from *þann'*, *whann'*, which have been expanded as *þanne* and *whanne* respectively.) Very occasionally, after final *d*, *g*, and *l*, such an additional stroke may indicate *-es/is*, and has been so expanded in *among*is (37/29, *etc.*, 3×), *ell*is (139/18, *etc.*, 3×), and where the pl. or poss. pl. form is appropriate, as *marchaund*is (137/10), *annuell*es (231/7). (Cf. also textual note to *tretoures* (146/7).)

Another problem has been the treatment of final *-o(u)n*. Since *n* and *u* are usually indistinguishable, two minims surmounted by a nasal titulus may indicate *u* with a mark of contraction, giving *-oun*, or *n* with an otiose flourish (or even, in a few cases, *n* with a mark of contraction, giving *-one* or *-onne*). The former alternative, giving *-oun*, has been preferred.

The only diacritic introduced is an acute accent to mark an unaccented final *e* when it stands for etymological *i* or OF *é*, as in *Beuirlé, cité*.

Word-division has been regularized without notice and generally follows the usage of *OED*: words which stand divided in M, such as

be gat (19/31) have been joined (some collocations are hyphenated, as *corner-ston*, *in-as-mech*, *o-rowe*, *ouyr-homeli*), and many which are written without space, such as *hereschulȝe* (18/25), have been separated. Indications of word-division made by the original scribe of M (the author) are noticed in the textual notes, e.g. at 38/7.

Capital letters have been used as far as possible in accordance with the practice in modern historical works in English, but when (on a very few occasions) a capital letter is used in exceptional circumstances in a manuscript, especially M, it has been noticed in a textual note. Modern punctuation has been supplied, but this punctuation is never at variance with the revealed intention of that in M, to which it conforms as far as possible. Where the text runs over a column division (as it usually but not invariably does) the position of the division is marked in the text by a vertical stroke.

SOURCE REFERENCES

Below the textual notes references are given to the printed version of Capgrave's source when it is known. These references are to make comparison of Capgrave's text with the available version(s) of his source easier. Reference to a source does not mean that Capgrave worked with a version of the source identical to that in a modern printed edition. Nor should a source so referred to be assumed to account for every statement in the section of Capgrave's text for which it is given. Significant differences between Capgrave's text and a source version are noted in the Commentary, and the source references are intended to be used in conjunction with these notes. Comparative references (preceded by 'cf.') to very similar treatments of the same subject-matter are also occasionally given but such references are not to be taken as implying that the passage referred to was an actual source. All references to the 'St. Albans Chronicle' for the years 1376–82 and 1388–91 are comparative because Capgrave was evidently using a shorter version of that chronicle for those years but only the longer version is in print. Source versions and comparative material are cited by means of the following short titles:

Brut	*The Brut*, ed. F. W. D. Brie, EETS, os, 131, 136 (London, 1906–8).
Higden	R. Higden, *Polychronicon*, ed. C. Babington and J. R. Lumby, RS 41 (London, 1865–86).
Isidore	Isidore of Seville, *Chronica Maiora*, ed. T. Mommsen, MGH auct. antiq. xi (Berlin, 1894), pp. 394–488.

Martinus	Martinus Oppaviensis, *Chronicon Pontificum et Imperatorum*, ed. L. Weiland, MGH script. xxii (Hannover, 1872), pp. 377–475; *Continuations*, ibid., pp. 476–82, and script. xxiv (Hannover, 1878), pp. 251–65.
Murimuth	A. Murimuth, *Continuatio Chronicarum*, ed. E. M. Thompson, RS 93 (London, 1889).
Trokelowe	J. de Trokelowe (attrib.), *Annales Ricardi Secundi et Henrici Quarti* (1392–1406, by Thomas Walsingham), ed. H. T. Riley, RS 28/3 (London, 1865), pp. 153–420.
Walsingham, *Chron. Ang.*	T. Walsingham, *Chronicon Angliae* (1328–88) ed. E. M. Thompson, RS 64 (London, 1874).
Walsingham, *Chronicle*	T. Walsingham, *The St. Albans Chronicle 1406–1420*, ed. V. H. Galbraith (Oxford, 1937).
Walsingham, *Hist. Ang.*	T. Walsingham, *Historia Anglicana* (1272–1422), ed. H. T. Riley, RS 28/1 (London, 1863–4).

youre yer were mad ful trewly зet
be yer vicat be ye writeris eke
ye cronicles of euseby ierom ⁊
oyir haue grete dyuersite ⁊ non
but̄ß of зeres This is ye cause
Why I sette my noubris oꝛ be
also if зe memorie yat in yoo
зeres fro adam to ye flood of
noe sumtyme rene a hundred
зere or more Where ye noubir
stant here and no writing yin
vis sthal be myn excuse for soth
I cude non fynde not withstand
yat I soute with grete diligens
If oyir studios men yat haue
more rod yan I or can fynde yat
I fond not or haue elde bokes
which make more expression
of yoo stories yat fol fro ye cre
acion of adam on to ye genial
flod yan I haue. ye belim lith ba
re sane ye noubir redy to rety
ue yat yei will set in. whan ye
tyme of crist is come yin rene
to nouberes to gidir ye blak for
uith for ye age of ye world ye
rede for uith for ye annotacio
of crist Ther is also a noþ ying
for to note yat ye зeres of ye
inꝛes of isrl and of ye kinnis
of inda and of ye kinnis of perse

PLATE II

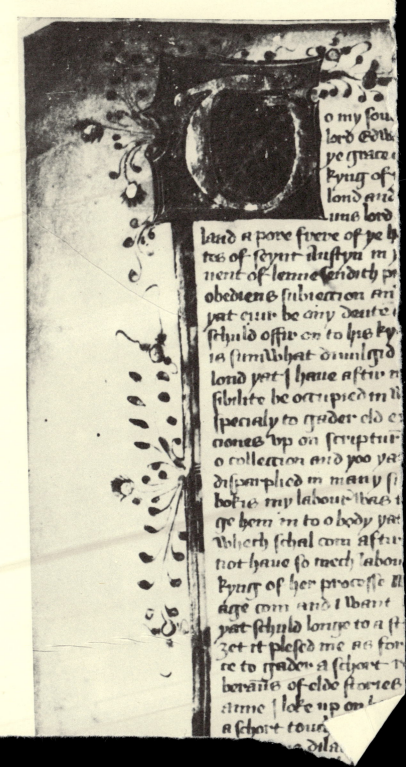

o my sou...
lord Edw...
ye grace...
kyng of...
lond and...
...une lord...
lind a pore frere of ye h...
tes of seynt austyn in...
nent of lenne sendith p...
obedient subieccion an...
yat euir be any dente...
schuld offir on to hir ky...
is sum what onmlitid...
lond yet I haue after m...
sibilite be occupied in li...
specialy to gader olde e...
nones vp on scriptur...
o colleccion and yoo ya...
disparplied in many f...
bokis my labour was...
ge hem in to o body yat...
Wherof schal com after...
not haue so mech labour...
kyng of her processe th...
age com and I want...
yat schuld longe to a st...
Zet it plesed me as for...
re to gader a schort...
berans of olde stories...
aime I loke vp on...
a schort touch...
...dila...

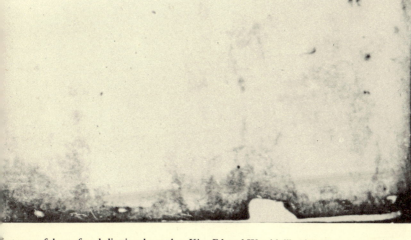

...irst page of the preface dedicating the work to King Edward IV, with illuminated ...ned an ornamental vine-stem border.

Cambridge University Library MS Gg.4.12, fol. 1ᵛ (actual size): the
initial *T* to which is attac

Dedicatory Preface

To my souereyn lord Edward, be þe grace of God kyng of Ynglond and of Frauns, lord of Yrland, a pore frere of þe Heremites of Seynt Austyn in þe conuent of Lenne sendith prayer, obediens, subjeccion and al þat euir be ony deuté a prest schuld offir onto his kyng. It is sumwhat diuulgid in þis lond þat I haue aftir my possibilité be occupied in wryting specialy to gader eld exposiciones vpon scripture into o colleccion, and þoo þat were disparplied in many sundry bokis my labour was to bringe hem into o body, þat þei whech schal com aftir schal not haue so mech labour in sekyng of her processe. Now is age com and I want ny al þat schuld longe to a studier, ȝet it plesed me as for a solace to gader a schort rememberauns of elde stories, þat whanne I loke upon hem and haue a schort touch of þe writyng I can sone dilate þe circumstaunses. This werk send I to ȝow where ȝe may turne and se schortly touchid þe most famous þingis þat haue be do in þe world fro his beginnyng onto þe ȝere of oure Lord Crist a m cccc and xvii. If ȝe merueyle whi þe ȝeres be set oute as on, too, thre, þis is þe cause: for þe elde bokes in her noumberes, | þouȝ þei were mad ful treuly, ȝet be þei viciat be þe writeres; eke þe cronicles of Euseby, Jerom and oþir haue grete dyuersité in noumbiris of ȝeres. This is þe cause whi I sette my noumbiris o-rowe. Also, if ȝe merueile þat in þoo ȝeres fro Adam to þe flood of Noe sumtyme renne a hundred ȝere or more where þe noumbir stant bare and no writing þerin, þis schal be myn excuse: forsoth I coude non fynde, notwithstand þat I soute with grete diligens. If othir studious men þat haue more red þan I, or can fynde þat I fond not, or haue elde bokes whech make more expression of þoo stories þat fel fro þe creacion of Adam onto þe general flod þan I haue, þe velim lith bare saue þe noumbir, redy to receyue þat þei will set in. Whan þe tyme of Crist is come þan renne to noumberes togidir—þe blak seruith for þe age of þe world, þe rede seruith for þe annotacion of Crist. Ther is also anoþir þing for to note, þat—þe ȝeres of þe juges of Israel and of þe

5
10
15
f. 1vb
21
25
30
35

kingis of Juda and of þe kingis of Perse onto þe tyme of grete
Alisaundre—euir þat ȝere where þe kyng is first set is þe last ȝere
of his regne; for swech is þe computacion of Ysidir. And fro
gret Alisaunder forth þat ȝere where þe king is sette first is þe
5　first ȝere of his regne; for þe newe cronicules vse þat forme.
These reules had in mynde þe reder schal more parfitely vndirstand þis book.

f. 2ra　　O myn benigne lord, receyue þis bok þouȝ it be simpil, and
lat þat gospel com in mynde where þe widow offered so litil and
10　had so mech þank.

　　Now wil I make ȝou pryuy what maner opinion I haue of
ȝoure persone in my pryuy meditaciones. I haue a trost in God
þat ȝoure entré into ȝoure heritage schal and must be fortunat for
many causes: first, for ȝe entered in þe sexti ȝere of Crist aftir
15　þat a m and cccc were complet. This noumbir of sex is amongis
writeres mech comendid, for þat same perfeccion þat longith
to sex whan he riseth be on, þe same longith to him whan he is
multiplied be ten. The noumbir of sex is applied to a sware ston
whech hath sex pleynes and viii corneres: wher-euyr þou ley him
20　or turne him, he lith ferme and stabill. Ȝe schal vndirstand þat
al þe labour of þe world is figured in sex dayes, for þe Sunday
betoknyth þe rest þat schal be in heuene. We pray God þat al
ȝoure laboure in þis world may rest on God, whech joyned
be þe corner-ston Crist þe to walles of Jewes and hethen into o
25　feith. This noumbir eke of sex is praysed for his particuler
noumberes, whech be on, too, and thre, and þese be cleped cote,
for in her reuoluing þei make him euyr hool: as sex sithe on is
sex, threes too is sex, twyes thre is sex. This consideracion may
ȝe haue in þis arsmetrik. Serue o God all þe daies of ȝoure lyue,
f. 2rb　whech daies, as is | seid, be comprehended in þe noumbir of
31　sex, and þere is sex sithis on. Make in ȝoure soule to ternaries,
on in feith, anoþir in loue: beleue in God—Fadir and Son and
Holy Gost; loue God in al ȝoure hert, al ȝoure soule, and al
ȝoure mynde. Make eke thre bynaries. As for þe first, þink þat
35　ȝe be mad of to natures, body and soule; loke þat ȝoure soule
haue euyr þe souereynté and þat þe bestial meuyng of þe body
oppresse not þe soule. The secunde bynarie is to þink þat þere
be to weyes in þis world, on to lyf, anoþir to deth. That wey þat
ledith to euyrlastyng lyf, þouȝ it be streite, kepe it. Tho men þat

24 þe (1)] *suprascript* M

PLATE III

Cambridge University Library MS Gg.4.12, fol. 2ᵛ (actual size): the end of the dedicatory preface, showing Capgrave's triquetra, with characteristic 'pendant', and his signature.

renne þe large weye, clepe hem ageyn be ȝoure power. The þird
bynarie is loue of God and loue of ȝoure neybour; for euene as it
is ȝoure deuté to loue God with drede, so is it ȝoure offise for to
se þat men loue ȝou with drede. The apostil, whan he spekith of
potestates, 'He bereth not his swerd', he seith, 'withouten cause'. 5
The Romaynes lawe was to spare hem þat asked grace and to
smyte down þe proude.

Ferþermore, ȝet fynde I a grete conueniens in ȝour tytil, þat ȝe
be cleped Edward þe Fourt. He þat entered be intrusion was
Herry þe Fourte. He þat entered be Goddis prouision is Edward 10
þe Fourt. The similitude of þe reparacioun is ful lich þe werk of
þe transgression, as þe Cherch singith | in a preface: 'Because f. 2ᵛᵃ
Adam trespased etyng þe frute of a tre, þerfor was Crist nayled
on a tre'. We trew loueres of þis lond desire þis of oure Lord
God, þat al þe erroure whech was browte in be Herry þe Fourte 15
may be redressed be Edward þe Fourte. This is þe desire of many
good men here in erde and, as I suppose, it is þe desire of þe
euirlasting hillis þat dwelle aboue.

God for his mercy fulfille þat he hath begunne, send oure Kyng
Edward good lyf and good gouernauns, and, aftir his labour, good 20
reward in þe blys of heuene. Amen.

ȝoure seruaunt Capgraue.

6 was] *suprascript with caret* (*in red*) M

PLATE IV

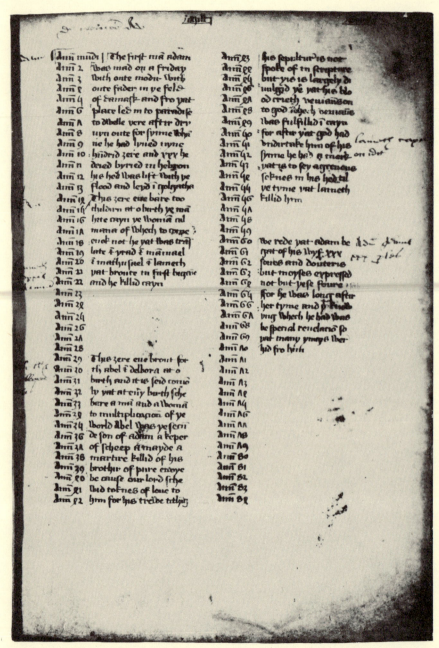

Cambridge University Library MS Gg.4.12, fol. 3ʳ (reduced): the first page of the *Abbreuiacion of Cronicles*, showing the annalistic lay-out with each year (Anno Mundi) enumerated and the arrangement by millennia (central heading) and the Augustinian six ages (right-hand heading).

PLATE V

E. 6

Cambridge, Corpus Christi College MS 167, p. 1 (reduced): the first page of the *Abbreuiacion of Cronicles* showing how the text is written straight out without dates or headings.

Anno Mundi 1. The first man Adam was mad on a Friday, f. 3ra
withoute modir, withoute fader, in þe feld of Damask, and fro
þat place led into paradise to dwelle þere, aftir dryuyn oute for
synne. Whanne he had lyued nyne hundrid ȝere and xxx, he
deied, byried in Hebron; his hed was lift with þe flood and leyd in 5
Golgatha.

Anno 2–14.

Anno 15. This ȝere Eue bare too childirn at o birth, þe man
hite Cayn, þe woman Calmana, of whech to come Enok—not
he þat was translate—and Yrad and Mammael and Mathusael 10
and Lameth, þat broute in first bigamie; and he killid Cayn.

Anno 16–29.

Anno 30. This ȝere Eue brout forth Abel and Delbora at o
birth, and it is seid comonly þat at euery birth sche bare a man
and a woman to multiplicacioun of þe world. Abel was þe secunde 15
son of Adam, a keper of scheep, a mayde, a martire, killid of his
brothir of pure envye because our Lord schewid toknes of loue
to him for his trewe tithing. | His sepulture is not spoke of in f. 3rb
scripture, but þis is largely diuulgid þere, þat his blood crieth
venjauns onto God, whech venjauns was fulfillid in Cayn, for, 20
aftir þat God had vndirtake him of his synne, he had a merk, þat
is to sey a greuous seknes in his hed, til þe tyme þat Lameth
killid him.

Anno 31–59.

Anno 60. We rede þat Adam begat of his wyf xxx sones and 25
douteris, but Moyses expressed not but þese foure and Seth;
for he was long aftir her tyme, and þat knowyng whech he had
was be special reuelacion, so þat many þingis were hid fro him.

Anno 61–99; Anno Mundi centesimo. f. 3va

Anno 101. We rede þat Adam in his first beginning named all 30
þe bestis and foules upon erde, and þat same name þat þei haue
in þe Hebrew tonge he gaue it to hem. Eke we rede þat he prophecied both of þe flood þat schuld distroye þe world, and eke of

18 tithing] tiching P   sepulture] sepulcure P   spoke of] touchyd P
26 and Seth] *in r.h. margin* M   28 reuelacion] reuelalion P

þe fire; therfor he wrote þese prophecies in too pileres, on of brasse, whech schuld not be distroyed with watir, anothir of tyl, whech schuld not brenne with fyre.

f. 3vb   Anno 102–129.

5   Anno 130. Of þis ȝere, a cxxx, be dyuers opiniones amongis þese croniculeres. Moises seith þat Adam begat Seth whanne he was of age a c wyntir and xxx. Alle othir cronicles sey þat whan Seth was bore Adam was of age cc and xxx. The cause of þis dyuersité is assigned be studious men þat Moises counted nowt þat hundred ȝere in whech Adam ded his penauns; for in þis secunde hundred ȝere Adam ded penauns for his sinne and so ded Eue. Anothir cause is assined of writeris, þat, aftir tyme Cayn had killid Abel his brothir, þanne Adam mad his avow þat he schuld neuir in al his lif comoun with Eue, and þis continens kept he a hundred ȝeres, whech ȝeres be not anoumbred of Moises. So, aftir þat hundred ȝere of continens, be an aungel he was warned þat he schuld vse the werk of generacioun to plesauns of God and multiplicacion of frute.

f. 4ra   Anno 131–199; Anno Mundi cc.

20   Anno 201. Thow it be soo þat þe book whech is clepid *þe Penauns of Adam* be cleped *Apocriphum*, whech is to sey 'whan þe mater is in doute' or ellis 'whan men knowe not who mad þe

f. 4rb book', ȝet in veri soth we rede þat he | ded penauns in a place fast be Ebron, for þere is ȝet a vale clepid þe vale of weping.

25   Anno 202–229.

Anno 230. This ȝere, aftir the trewer opinion, was Seth born, whech man was of so holy lyf þat his childirn were cleped þe sones of God, and þei kepte þat same reule onto þe seuene generacioun. In othir bokes, þat be not of so grete auctorité as is þe scripture, is told þat Adam schuld a sent Seth onto þe gates of paradys for þe oyle of mercy, and Michael gaue him þis answere, þat he must abyde v þousand and to hundred ȝere and þanne schuld he haue þat oyle.

f. 4^{va–vb}   Anno 231–299; Anno Mundi ccc°.

35   Anno 301. In þis tyme begunne men sore to multiplie, and Cayn at þoo daies, because he ded mech wrong and meynteyned hem þat ded wrong, mad a cyté and named it Enok aftir his son. This

---

5 amongis] amonis P   7 and] *om.* P   sey] seythe P   10 þis] the P   13 Abel his brothir] his brother Abell P   14–15 kept he] he kept P   21 cleped] *om.* P   27 of so holy] so holy of P   29 þe] *om.* P

Enok was fader to Yrad, and Yrad fader to Mammael, Mammael
fader to Matusael, Matusael fader to Lameth, whech Lameth
weddid to wyues: on of hem hite Ada, the othir hite Sella. Ada
sche broute forth Jabel; he was þe first fynder of tentis in whech
schepherdis restid in for to kepe her scheep. And his brothir be 5
þe same woman hite Jubal; he was fader to alle hem þat singe in
þe orgoun or in the crowde. Sella, his othir wif, sche broute forth
Tubal-cayn; he wroute first with hambir and stith in all þoo
werkis þat longyn to yrun or bras. The first son Jabel departed
þe flokkis of scheep fro þe flokkis of goot; and aftir her qualité 10
þei þat were of | o colour be hemselue, and þei þat were of too f. 5ra
or dyuers be hemselue; and, aftir her age, ȝeringis be hemselue,
and elder be hemselue. Jubal, his brothir, he was fynder of musik—
not of þe very instrumentis whech be vsed now, for þei were founde
long aftir—but þis man fond certeyn soundis acordyng, and to þis 15
entent, þat þe grete labour in schep-kepyng schuld haue sum
solace of musik; and, þat þis craft schuld not perch, he ded write
it in to pileres, on of marbil, anothir of tyl, for feer and for watir.
The othir man, Tubal-cayn, þat fond first smythis craft, he mad
first wepenes of batayle both inuasif and defensif, and he began 20
first grauing in metallis to plesauns of þe sith. And as it is seid,
þe forsaid Jubal proporcioned his musik aftir þe sound of Tubal
hamberes, for he ded make hem of dyuers proporciones, sum
heuyer, sum liter, aftir his delectacion. He set eke on fire many
trees, and þe metall þat was in þe fire, be hete of þe fire, malt, 25
and ran in certeyn | veynes of þe erde, and took þerof certeyn f. 5rb
figures. Vpon þis he mad certeyn moldes, and pored þe metal
new molten in hem, and so made figures aftir his fantasie. The
sistir of Tubal-cayn, cleped Noema, sche fond first spinning,
karding and weuing and swech labour as longith to making of cloth. 30
    Anno Mundi 302–424.   f. 5va
    Anno 425. This ȝere, whan Seth was of age to hundred and v,
he begat a son whech he clepid Enos. This Enos is noted þe
first þat prayed onto God. For Enos in oure langage soundith

---

2 Lameth (1)] Laneth P   8 wroute] worute P   11 þat (1)] t *suprascript
with caret* M   þei (2)] *om.* P   20 inuasif] iuasif P   began] begam P
22 proporcioned] proporcionyd P, perporcioned M   24 delectacion] delec|
tacion *over line division* M, declection P   33 he (2)] was P   34 onto] to P
soundith] loundyth P

32: cf. Isidore, 426/5.

'a resonable man'; for he droue oute be reson þat God was his
maker, and þerfor is it seid he was first þat called onto God.
Summe men suppose þat he mad certeyn orisones to þe prays-
ing of God; but þe Hebrewis sey þat he mad certeyn ymages
5 representing God, and þou3 he erred in swech liknesse, 3et he
excited many hertes to þe knowlech of God and encres of deuocioun.

f. 5ᵛᵇ   Anno 426–499; Anno Mundi d.

Anno 501. Men þat be studious meve þis questioun, whi men
f. 6ʳᵃ at þat tyme lyued so longe, and | þei asyne many resones. On is
11 þe godnes and þe clennes of complexion whech was newe goue
hem be God; for whan it was newly take, it had more vertu
because of þe 3iuer. Anothir cause is þat men lyued þat tyme with
more temperauns þan þei do now. The þirde cause may be cleped
15 þe goodnes of þoo metes whech þei ete, for þei ete noþing but
swech as growith frely on þe erde, neithir flesch, ne fisch, and be
þe flood,†whech cam for þe most part oute of þe salt se cleped þe
occean, þe erde was so apeired þat it bar neuir so good frutes
sithe. The fourte is of þe grete sciens whech Adam had and whech
20 he taute his issew, for he knew þe vertue of herbis and sedis bettir
þan euir ded ony erdeli man saue Crist, and he knew þe pryuy
werking of hem whech were most able to preserue men in longe
lyf. The v cause is of þe good aspecte of sterres þat was ouer hem
f. 6ʳᵇ at þoo dayes, whech aspecte profiteth | mech to þe length of lif to
25 man and to best, for þis is a comoun prouerbe at þe philisopheres,
þat þe bodies in erd be mech reuled aftir þe planetis aboue. The
sexte cause is of Goddis ordinacioun þat wold þo men schuld
lyue so longe for multiplicacion of her kynrod and eke for to
haue longe experiens of certeyn sciensis.

f. 6ᵛᵃ   Anno Mundi 502–624.

31   Anno 625. In þis 3ere Enos, whan he was of age a hundred
3ere and nynty, he begat a son whom he kleped Caynan, whech
f. 6ᵛᵇ Caynan was rich in pos|sessiones and ful sori at othir mennes
tribulaciones, and so soundith his name in þe Hebrew tong

---

5 God and þou3] þor P   13 3iuer] 3eu P   14 cause] is the cause P
15 for þei ete] *om.* P   16 as] þᵗ P   ne] nor P   17 þe (4)] *om.* P
18 so (1)] *om.* P   20 of] *om. over line division* P   22 were] wer kyng of
them whech wer P   in] *om.* P   24 profiteth] profith P   25 is] *om.* P
prouerbe] *in r.h. margin* M   34 tribulaciones] trobyllacions P

31–2: Isidore, 426/6.

'Lamentacion' or 'Possession'. Thus may men se þat at þoo dayes summe were richer þan summe, and redier eke to geue elmesse.

Anno Mundi 626–795.   f. 7^{ra–va}

Anno 796. In þis ȝere Caynan, whan he was of age a hundred ȝere and | seuenety, begat Malaleel, whos name is as mech to sei f. 7vb as 'A praiser of God' for he had litil othir delite in þis word but 6 in prayer and in praising of God. And here may men note þat þe kynrod of Cayn were euir bisi for to make armour and wepun, and þe kinrod of Seth bysi to plese and praise God.

Anno Mundi 797–929.   f. 8^{ra–va}

Anno 930. In þis ȝere deyed Adam and was biried in Ebron, 11 whech is a cité of Inde, and sumtyme it was cleped Arbe. The geavntes mad it vii ȝere before þat þe cité clepid Thanis was mad in Egipte; and it was cleped Arbe for þe birying of foure patriarkes, Adam, Abraham, Ysaac and Jacob. It was cleped sumtyme 15 Mambre aftir þe name of Abraam frend; and sumtyme it was cleped Cariath-arbe, 'þe cité of Arbe'.

Metodius seith here, þat, þe same ȝere þat Adam deyed, þe generaciones of Seth and Cayn were departed asundir. For Seth led his generacion onto þe est side of the world onto a grete 20 hille þat was rite ny onto paradise; and þere he dwellid. Cayn and his kynrod dwelled stille in þe same place where he had slayn his broþir, and þere he mad a cité whech he cleped Effrem, as Metodius seith.

Anno 931–959.   25

Anno 960. This ȝere Malaleel, whan he was of age | a hundred f. 8vb and sexti and v ȝere, begat Jareth, and Jareth soundith in oure tonge 'Coming-doun' and 'Coumforting'. Se now þat þe generacion of Seth was disposed to all vertues, summe to pray, sum to tithe, summe to offir, summe, as þis man was, to coumfort hem 30 þat were in seknes and distresse.

Anno 961–999.

Anno Mundi M°. In þis first þousand ȝere was þis world occupied with þese sex faderis and | patriarkes: Adam, Seth, Enos, f. 9ra

1 se] in r.h. margin M   2 þan] thant P   9 and praise] the prays of P   12 is] was P   13 þe cité] om. P   14 þe] they P   16 aftir þe name] after the tyme Mambre aftyr þe name P   21 þat] that P, þas M 22 dwelled] dewellyd P   29 pray] prayse P   30 tithe] teche P

4–5: cf. ibid. 427/7.
26–8: ibid. 427/8.

Caynan, Malaleel, and Jared. These sex and her childryn cam of þe stok of Seth, for þe kynrod of Cayn was more multiplied þan þis kynrod. So semeth it þat þe world had mech puple at þat same tyme.

f. 9^{rb–va}   Anno Mundi 1001–1121.

6   Anno 1122. This ȝere Jared, whan he was of age a hundred ȝere sexti and too, begat Ennok. This Ennok is þe seuene persone

f. 9vb   fro Adam and ȝet he is o-lyue, for he was translate be | God onto paradise and þere is he with Helie, whech too schul come and

10   preche ageyn þe errouris of Antecrist and be mad martires. This Ennok mad a book of prophecie whech the lawe acoundith among bokis þat be clepid *Apocripha*; of whech I haue mech wondir, for in þe epistil of Judas, whech is incorporate to þe Bible, þe same apostil makith mynde of þis book and seith þus, 'Of þis mater

15   prophecied þe vii fro Adam, and þus he seid, "Behold oure Lord schal come with his seyntis mani þousandis for to do rithful dome to alle men and to vndirtake wikkid men of here euele werkis in whech þei ded amys"'.

      Anno 1123–1141.

20   Anno 1142. This ȝere deied Seth aftir many good dedis. The dayes of his lyf were nyne hundred and xii ȝere.

f. 10^{ra–vb}   Anno Mundi 1143–1286.

      Anno 1287. In þis ȝere Ennok, whan he was of age sexti ȝere and v, begat Mathusalem, of whos dayes be many sundry opiniones.

25   Jerom, in his book *De Hebraicis Questionibus*, seith þus, 'Aftir þe bysi computacion of þe Hebrewis þis Mathusale schuld a leued xiiii ȝere aftir þe flood; for he was lxx ȝere of age or he begat Lameth, and Lameth was of age a hundred iiii score and viii or he begat Noe, so were þe ȝeres of Mathusale onto þe tyme þat

30   Noe was bore ccclv, and in þe sex hundred ȝere of Noe was þe flod; be þis computacioun he schuld a leued xiiii ȝere aftir þe

---

1 These] ese *over erasure* M   2 multiplied] P, multipied M   4 same] *om.* P   5 *the year numbers* 1101 *and* 1102 *miswritten as* 10101 *and* 10102 *respectively* M   7 sexti] & sexti P   This] *om.* P   8 onto] & onto P 9 he] *om. over line division* P   11 prophecie] prophesei P   16 come] *in r.h. margin* M   21 xii] *over erasure* M, xxx P   25 book] koke P   27 flood] folod *written over* for P   30 þe (1)] *om. over line division* P

6–7: Isidore, 427/9.
23–4: cf. ibid. 427/10.

flood'. But þere is erroure in þe noumbir; for þis is determyned
in certeyn, þat he deyid þe same ȝere before þat þe flood was.

Anno Mundi 1288–1339.   f. 11ʳᵃ

Anno 1340. This ȝere deyid Enos, aftir he had lyued nyne
hundred ȝere and v.   5

Anno Mundi 1341–1453.   f. 11ʳᵇ⁻ᵛᵃ

Anno 1454. This ȝere Mathusalem, whan he was of age a   f. 11ᵛᵇ
hundred foure score and vii ȝere, begat Lameth. And here is for
to note þat þere were too men of þis same name Lameth: on was
of þe kynrod of Cayn and he broute in first bigamie; the oþir   10
was of þe kynrod of Seth and he was fader to Noe.

Anno 1455–1496.   f. 12ʳᵃ

Anno 1497. This ȝere was Ennok translat into paradise, in
what maner we haue no writyng, but who he schal come is expressed, þat Helie and he schal come in saccis, and preche at   15
Jerusalem, and werk many wonderes, and be martired be Antecrist.

Anno Mundi 1498–1534.

Anno 1535. This ȝere deied Caynan, of age viii hundred nynty
ȝere and v.   20

Anno Mundi 1536–1639.   f. 12ʳᵇ ᵛᵇ

Anno 1640. In þis ȝere, as Methodius seith, began mech sinne
growe upon erde so foule and soo abhominable þat it is schame to
sey. Than went þe sones of God, whech were cleped þe kynrod of
Seth, and comouned with þe douteres of men, whech were Cayn   25
douteris, and þei begotin geauntis, and for þis and mech oþir
þing God was wroth with þese sinneres and purposed for to venge
him, as schal be told aftir.

Anno 1641–1651.

Anno 1652. This ȝere Lameth, whan he was a hundred ȝere   30
of age iiii score and viii, begat Noe. Noe was a just man and a
parfite, þe ten persone fro Adam, maker of þe schip, and deliuerid |
in þe same fro þe grete flood. This man was þe first þat reysid   f. 13ʳᵃ

1 is (2)] *suprascript* M   2 before þat] þe flood (*after* before) *expuncted*
M, þat *om*. P   9 þis] the P   14 maner] namys P   15 Helie] *in
r.h. margin* M   and he] *over erasure* M   in] *om*. P   16–17 and be martired
be Antecrist] *in darker ink* M   19–20 nynty ȝere] *long* r' *inserted on the line*
M, yer nynty P   23 soo] s P   abhominable] P, abhominabe M   it] *om*. P
27 purposed for] *om*. P   30 ȝere (2)] *om*. P   31 Noe (1)] none P   a (1)] of a P

7–8: cf. ibid. 428/12.
30–1: cf. ibid. 428/15.

up auter aftir þe flood and made offering to God. He lyued nyne
hundred ȝere and fourty.

ff. 13rb–14va   Anno Mundi 1653–1921.

Anno 1922. This ȝere deied Jareth; his age was nyne hundred
5 sexti and too ȝere.

ff. 14vb–15vb   Anno Mundi 1923–2141.

Anno 2142. In þis ȝere was Noe v hundred ȝere of age, and
þan began he for to gete childirn, as it schal be touchid aftirward.
And in þis same ȝere began he to make his schip, whech was of
10 grete quantité whan all maner beestis and foulis were in þe same—
of summe seuene and seuene, of summe too and to, and all her
mete for a ȝere. This arck, as Hugo seith de Sancto Victore, þat
mad a special book þerof, was in length half a myle and xl passes.

f. 16^{ra–rb}   Anno Mundi 2143–2241.

Secunda Etas

15

Anno 2242. In þis ȝere deyed Mathusale.
And in þis same ȝere was þe flood þat ouyrflew al þe world,
f. 16va for it was xv cubites | aboue þe hiest hillis; þis flood in party
cam fro þe grete se clepid þe occean, and in parti fro þe grete
20 wateres þat ar aboue.
In þis same tyme þe childirn of Noe took wyues and entended
onto generacion, of whos issew here schal be a declaracioun.
Sem, þe eldest son, he begat Arphaxat, and of Cham descendid
Chus; Japheth, he was fader to Gomer. So of þese thre sones
25 grew al mankynde in þis world, and be what order here schul ȝe
haue abreuiacioun.
Of Sem come v puples in special, of whech Elam was first,
and of him were cleped þe puple þat dwelle in Perse Elamites.
The secunde hite Assur, and of him þe Assirianes took her first
30 name. The þird was clepid Arphaxat, of whom come þei þat
dwelle in Chaldé. The fourt hite Ludi, and of him cam a puple
so clepid þanne. The v hite Aram, and he was fader to þat puple
f. 16vb þat dwelle in Surré; the hed cité is cle|pid Damask. These be þe
childir of Elam, son onto Sem: Vs, Vl, Geter, and Mer. Vs

2 ȝere and fourty] and fourty yere P   7 ȝere (1)] tyme P   15 Secunda
Etas] *in red* M, *om.* P   19 occean] occiam P   22 a] *om.* P   23 descendid]
in r.h. margin M   24 to] *om.* P   26 abreuiacioun] all breuiacioun P
27 first] st *suprascript* M   29 him] *in r.h. margin* M   31 cam]
come kame P   32 Aram] aratn P   33 þe] *in r.h. margin* M
34 onto] to P

inhabited þe cuntré cleped Traconides, of whech cuntré Job was a
dweller; for his book beginnit so, 'There was a man in the lond of
Vs'. Of Vl cam þei þat dwelle in Armenie. Of Gether cam a puple
þei clepid Carmenes. Of Mer cam þat puple þat dwelle in Ynde.
This is þe kinrod of Arphaxat: þe first Heber—of him com þe 5
puple Hebrewis; Jectan, Heber son, he brout forth a puple aftir
his name dwelling in Ynde; Sale, he was son to Jectan and of him
com þei þat be clepid Bactrianes. These be þe puples þat com of
þe stok of Sem, and þei inhabited mech of þe est side of þe world,
fro þe spring of þe sunne onto hem of Fenise. 10

Cam had iiii childirn: Chus—of him cam þe Ethiopes; Mesram
—of him com þei of Egipte; Futh—of him come þei of Libi and
eke þe Mauritanes, | for þe flood þat rennith by hem at þese f. 17ra
daies þei clepe it Futh; Canaan—of him come þei of Affrik and of
Phenice, and of him come all þe ten puples þat dwelled in þe 15
lond of Canane.

Japheth, he had vii childyrn: the first was Gomer—of him
cam þe Frensch puple; Magog—of him cam þei of Scithia and
eke þe Gothis; Medai—of him come þe Medis; Jone—of him
come þe Greces, for her see is ʒet clepid *Mare Ionicum*; Tubal— 20
of him come þe Spaynardis (þei were sumtyme cleped *Hiberi*), and
summe men sey of him come þei of Itayle; Mosok, he was fadir to
þe Capadoses, for ʒet is þere a cité amongis hem whech þei clepe
Mosaca; Tiras—of him come þe puple of Trace.

Anno Mundi 2243–2380.   f. 17rb

Anno 2381. Here is þe veri successioun of faderes fro Adam 26
onto Abraam: Adam, Seth, Enos, Caynan, Malaleel, Jared,
Enok, Mathusale, Lameth, Noe, Sem, Arphaxat, Caynan, Sale,
Heber, Phalech, Ragau, Saruch, Nachor, Thare, Abraam.

Anno Mundi 2382–2508.   ff. 17va–18ra

Anno 2509. In þis ʒere Sala begat Heber, and of þis Heber, 31
as auctouris sey, cam þe puple Hebrak, for Heber was neue onto
Sem. This puple is clepid sumtyme Israel, of Israel þat was son
onto Ysaac—his oþir name was Jacob. For þei sey þat he was

---

2 beginnit] begune P   lond] *in r.h. margin* M   4 Mer] more P
puple] *om.* P   6 Hebrewis] of Hebrews P   7 him] them P
8 be (1)] he P   9 stok of] *in r.h. margin* M   13 eke] eke of P   18 þei
of] the P   19 Medai] Media P   20 Ionicum] Ronicum P   29 Phalech]
Paleth P   Nachor] Nathore P   Thare] *om.* P   30 *on f. 17^{v} 1st digit
of year numbers* 2416–2499 *miswritten as* 1 (*i.e.* 1416 *etc.*) M   31 Heber
and of þis] *om.* P   32 for] fro P

named be þe aungell and al þe puple named aftir him; for þe
xii kynrodis cam oute of him. Aftir, whan þei were departed in
Roboam tyme, þan þei þat left aboute Jerusalem were clepid
þe puple of Juda, and þe oþir x tribus, þat dwelt in Samarie, kept
5 stille here elde name Israel.

f. 18^{rb–vb}   Anno Mundi 2510–2632.

Anno 2633. This ʒer Heber begat Phalegh whan he was of age a
hundred ʒere and xxiiii.

In þis tyme was þe Tour of Confusion mad be iii princes,
10 Nembrot, Jectan and Suffene. This Nembrot, whech was of þe
kynrod of Sem, herd sei þat þei þat come of þe kynrod of Cham
schul first regne amongis the puple; for Noe, aftir þe flood, begat a
son, and he was clepid Ionicus, whech prophecied swech þingis.
For þis cause þis same Nembrot forsook þe kynrod of Sem, went,
15 and dwellid among þe kynrod of Cham. For he was a man of
gret stature, in heith of x cubites. So was he chose kyng ouyr þe
kynrod of Cham. And sone aftir Jectan was mad kyng upon þe
f. 19ra   kynrod of Sem. Than þei þat were come of | Japhet, þei chose
Suffene to her kyng. Thus þese iii princes come togidir in þe
20 feld of Senar, and þere þei determined to make a tour. Thei
ded bake erde onto þe hardnes of ston, and þan had þei tow erde,
clepid bitumen; with þese too þei made þe Tour of Confusion,
so clepid because þere was þe first confusion of tongis.

f. 19^{rb–va}   Anno Mundi 2634–2762.

25   Anno 2763. Phalegh, whan he was a hundred ʒere old and xxx,
begat Ragau.

And in þis tyme began þe worchiping of fals ydolis, and in
þis maner. There were certeyn strong men and rich, makeres of
townes, edifieres of citées, in whos name, whan þei were ded, þe
30 puple edified ymages to her liknes, þat þei mite haue sum solace
of þo similitudes. But, whan þis erroure was brout in vse, þan, be
temptacioun of þe deuel, þei worchiped hem as goddis, and beleued þat þoo men whech were worchiped in þoo ymages were
f. 19vb   translate to heuene as goddis, and soo | spirites ʒoue answere

---

1–2 for þe xii kynrodis cam oute of him] *om.* P   3–4 þei þat left
aboute Jerusalem were clepid þe puple of Juda] they wer cleped the puple of
Juda wer left abowght Jerusalem P   9 Tour] cour P   11 of (3)] *om.* P
18 of Sem Than þei þat] f sem Than þei þat *over erasure* M   24 Anno
2642 *twice* M   Anno 2744 *twice* M   31 whan] *om.* P

25–6: cf. Isidore, 430/23.

in hem as reuelaciones whech þe puple supposed þei com fro heuene.

The Jewis sey þat Ismael mad first swech maumentis of erde, and compelled Ysaac, his brothir, to worchip þe same. The hethen men sey þat on Promotheus he mad first of erde ymages of men, 5 and of him cam al þat craft of maumentrie; and for þis cause þe poetes feyned þat he was þe first maker of men, for he mad first swech similitudes. The Grekis sey þat on Cicrops began þis ydolatrie with grauing ymages in olyue-tre, and Minerue was þe first þat he mad, whech is goddesse of cunnyng, for in hir 10 name was þe cité of Attenes mad; summe sey he mad first Jupitir and set him on a auter.

But þe treuhest opinion in þis mater rehersith Fulgens in his *Mithologiis*—he seith, 'There was a rich man in Egipte, whos name was Cyrophanes, whech had a son whom he loued | ouir- f. 20ra wel. This son deied in ȝong age, and, whan he was ded, he lete 16 make a ymage lich him and set it in his hous, þat he mite dayly haue a newe rememberauns. And þe seruauntis, for plesauns of her maistir, offered þerto garlondis and lite. And whan ony of hem had offended greuously þei fled to þe ymage and þere were 20 þei saf. This witnesseth þe poete where he seith, "Primos in orbe deos fecit inesse timor". Thus he meneth, "The first goddis þat were þei come in be dreed" '.

Anno Mundi 2764–2894. f. 20rb

Anno 2895. This ȝere was Sarugh bore, þe son of Ragau, whan 25 Ragau was of age a hundred ȝere and xxx.

And in þis same ȝere began þe kyngdam of þat puple whech þei clepe Scitas; this was þe secund regne, for þe first was of Assiriis—Thanaus was þe first kyng of þat lond. This puple sprang of Magog, whech was son onto Japhet. It was a grete lond 30 in space. On þe est | fro Ynde, and on þe north side, he was lyand f. 20va be þe grete fennes þat ly betwix þe flood Danubie and þe grete se onto þe ende of Germanie. It had mech voide folk; þerfor were here feldis bareyn for þe most part. Summe of hem were tilmen,

---

10 hir] ther P   16 whan] *om*. P   17 his] *in r.h. margin* M   20–1 were þei] ere þei *over erasure* M   23 in] *om*. P   27 kyngdam] kyndam P 32 se] *suprascript* M   32–3 Danubie and þe grete se onto] of Danubie a P

25–6: cf. ibid. 430/25.
27–9: cf. ibid. 430/26.

many leued be hunting, etyng blod and raw flesch both of beest
and of man. A rich lond men sei it is, but mech þerof is inhabitable.
For gold and gemmis be þere in habundauns, an for þe plenté
of grifes men dare not goo þertoo. These stones be þere in habun-
5 dauns: smaragdis, cristalis, and cianeus. He hath eke real flodis:
Ascor is on, anothir hite Fasiden, þe þirde Araxen.

ff. 20vb–21ra   Anno Mundi 2896–3034.

Anno 3035. In þis 3ere Sarugh, whan he was a hundred 3ere
old and xxxv, begat Nachor.

f. 21rb   And in þat same tyme began þe kyngdam of | Egipte. This
11 lond stant in þe south side of the world, where regned first xv
souereynes, cleped Dinastines, as mech to sey as 'hie potestates'—
þe first of hem hite Numeus. Than entered þat lond þei of Tebes
tyl xxxvi Dinastines had regned. Thanne regned þei cleped Dia-
15 politani—xviii of hem—and þei were clepid Pharaones. So þis
kyngdam dured onto þe tyme of Cambises, whech was son to
Cirus, king of Pers. The fadir of þis Cirus gaue his son þe kyngdam of Assirie, and cleped him Nabugodonosor, whos prince,
Oloferne, wan Egipte. And aftir þat tyme had Egipt his owne
20 kyngis onto þe tyme þat on Othus, cleped Artarxerses, kyng of
Perse, put owt Nectanabus and regned þere. So vndir iii kingis
of Perse was it gouerned onto þe tyme of grete Alisaundre. Thus
all þe kyngis of Egipt, fro þe first to þe last, Alisaundre, were
24 cccc and ix: summe of hem were clepid Dinastines, summe Pharao-
f. 21va   nes, summe | Lagidi, summe Tholomei.

Anno Mundi 3036–3113.

Anno 3114. In þis 3ere Nachor, whan he was of age seuenty and
nyne, begat a son cleped Thare, fader onto Abraham.

29   In his tyme began þe kyngdam of þe Assiriis and þe regne of
f. 21vb   Sciciniis. The kyngdam of þe Assiriis was in þe este, | vndir a

---

7 *the year numbers* 2908 *and* 2909 *miswritten as* 298 *and* 299 *respectively* M
the year number 3001 *miswritten as* 30001 M   11 world] *in r.h. margin* M
where] re *in darker ink* M, wherein P   12 Dinastines] da dinastines P
13 Than] than t P   14–15 Diapolitani . . . clepid] *om.* P   24 Dinastines]
Damastines P   24–5 Pharaones summe] *om.* P   26 *the year numbers* 3101
to 3108 *miswritten as* 30101 *etc.* M   29 his] thys P   29–30 þe Assiriis
. . . kyngdam of þe] *om.* P   29 of (2)] *suprascript* M

8–9: cf. Isidore, 430/27.
10: cf. ibid. 430/28.
27–8: ibid. 431/29.
29–30: cf. ibid. 431/30.

kyng cleped Belus Menpronides or Menprotides. It began in þe
xxv ȝere of Sarugh, whech was eldfader to Abraham, and it had
dominacioun ny of al Asie saue Ynde. For þe forseid Belus beganne
it, and Ninus, his sone, he set it in reule, and wan many londis
þerto, and mad þe grete cité of Nyniue aftir his name. Of þis 5
Belus summe sey cam al þis ydolatrie, for his son ded make an
ymage representing his fader, and þis ydol was moost general
amongis naciones; þerfor had he dyuers names: summe cleped
him Bel, summe Belzebul, summe Bel-phegor. The kyngdam of
þe Sciciniis was in þe west, in Europe, a grete part of Grecia, 10
fast by Archadie—þis lestid be xxx kyngis tyme onto þe tyme of
Zeucippe, þat regned in þe xxv ȝere of Hely þe preest.

    Anno 3115–3183.   f. 22ra

    Anno 3184. In þis ȝere Thare, whan he was lxx ȝere old, begat
Abraham, whech is clepid fader of oure feith, for, whan he was 15
redi to offer his child to God, he beleued verili þat God schulde
reise him ageyn to þe lif. He receyued first þe feith of þe Trinité
where he sey thre ymages and worchipid on.

    In þis tyme of Thare Zorastes lyued, whech was fynder of
wichcraft, of whom writith Eusebius þat þis Zorastes was Cham, 20
whech lyued onto þe dayes of Nynus. For þe same Ninus, as is |
seid before, mad þe cité of Niniue þe vii ȝere of Abraham age and f. 22rb
of his regne þe fourty ȝere and ix. And eke þat Ninus held bataile
with Cham, whech was cleped Zorastes, both killid him and brent
his bokes. This same Zorastes, desiring for to behald a god, gaf al 25
his entent to loke upon sterres, and with his craft he mad certeyn
sparkis fro þe eyer to appere upon him, and þis mad simple men
to studye, supposing þat he was a god. But at þe last þat same
familiar deuel whech he haunted moost with swech sparkis set
him on fire. Aftir his deth þe puple mad him a graue, as to þe 30
frend of God, with a chare of leuene and þundir led up onto
heuene.

    Of þis same man þus writith Seint Augustin in þe xxi book
De Ciuitate Dei: 'Zorastes, whan he was bore, low as no child
ded but he, and þis lawhing was no tokne of good, for it was 35

---

4 Ninus] minus P   10 Sciciniis] Saciniis P   14 lxx ȝere old] of
age lxx yere P   26 sterres] storis P   27 þis] thus P   29 moost]
myche P   33 þus] this P

14–15: ibid. 431/31.
19: cf. ibid. 431/32.

monstrows, þat is to seyn ageyn cours of kynde; for, þou he were
f. 22va fynder of wich|craft, ȝet was he killid in batayle of þe kyng of
Assiry, his name was Ninus'.

Anno Mundi 3185–3283.

5 **Etas Tercia**

Anno 3284. This ȝere Abraham, whan he was a hundred ȝere
of age, begat Ysaac be grete miracle, for his wif Sare had in age
nynety ȝere. This man is þe xi fro Noe, xx fro Adam, that beleued |
f. 22vb hertly in God and receyued þe Trinité to herborow; with oure
10 Lord God oftin he spak; he was blessid be þe handis of Melchisedech aftir his grete victorie. He begat a child in his age whom
he was redi to sle and offir to þe plesauns of God, had he not be
lettid be a aungell. In Chaldea was he bore, in Chanaan a pilgrime
ful rich was he and plesaunt to God. Whan he had lyued a hundred
15 ȝere and seuenety and v, þan deyed he, and byried be his childirn
in þe dobil graue þat he bout of Ephron, þe son of Ethe, fast by
þe cité of Cariath-arbe, þat is to sey Hebron.

Anno Mundi 3285–3321.

Anno 3322. In þese same dayes regned Melchisedech, of whom
20 we fynde many dyuers opiniones. Summe sey þat he was a aungell;
summe sey þat he was þe Holy Goost; summe sey þat he was Sem,
þe eldest child of Noe. But þe very treuth of him tellith þe apostil
f. 23ra in þe epistel whech | he wrote to þe Hebrewis. Thus he seith:
'His name is þe kyng of justise, and þan is he clepid kyng of
25 Salem, þat is to sey king of pes, withouten fadir, withouten modir,
withouten genelogie, neythir hauing beginning of dayes ne
ending, likned to þe Son of God, he dwellith a prest for euyr'.
The apostil menith not be þis þat Melchisedech had no fadir ne no
modir, but þat scripture spekith not of hem—and for he was
30 figure of Crist, þat had no fadir in erde. But sikir is þis, þat he
was kyng of Salem; not of Jerusalem, whech was sumtyme cleped
Salem, as Josephus seith, but of Salem in the lond of Canaan.

2 fynder] fyndus P   4 2 *in* Anno 3201 *written over* 1 M   5 Etas
Tercia] *in red* M, *om.* P   7 had] was P   10 Lord] *om.* P   13 Chaldea]
over erasure M   14 was he] he was P   15 ȝere and] *over erasure* M
16 bout] bowgthe P   19 same] *om.* P   Melchisedech] Meichisedech P
22 child] sone P   24 kyng (2)] the kyng P   25 Salem] Salrin P
26 genelogie neythir] ony genelogie neythe P   32 as Josephus seith but
of Salem] *om.* P

6–8: cf. Isidore, 432/34.

For it is a town fast by Scicopolin, where his paleis stood; in Seynt Jerom tyme men mith se þe ruyne of þe wall who grete a lord he was.

Anno 3323–3343.

Anno 3344. In þis ȝere Ysaac, of age sexti ȝere, begat Esau 5 and Jacob, twynnes. This Ysaac was bore of his modir Sare in þe cuntré cleped Geraris, betwix Cades and Seir, named of God befor his birth, circumcidid in the viii day, and offered in þe figure of oure Lord Jesu Crist.

In his daies began þe kyngdam of þe Argyues vndir her first 10 kyng, Yma|cho, whech was þe fader of Ysidis, and he regned f. 23ʳᵇ fifti ȝere. The secunde kyng was Phoroneus, whech mad þe lawes to þe Grekis, of whech lawes aftir schal we touche. And þis kyngdam dured fyue hundred wyntir and foure and fourty vndir xxiiii kyngis onto þe last ȝere of Delbora. 15

Anno Mundi 3345–3443. f. 23ᵛᵃ

Anno 3444. This ȝere Jacob, whan he was nynety ȝere of age and f. 23ᵛᵇ on, begat Joseph of fayre Rachel, þat was so longe bareyn.

And in þis tyme Foroneus, þe secunde kyng amongis þe Argyues, þe son of Ynachi, mad notabel lawes. He was þe first þat mad 20 causes to be pleted before juges, and þoo places in whech juges herd causes he cleped hem aftir his name 'forum', þat is to sey a hopen place or a market.

Aboute þis tyme eke Joseph was sold be his bretheren into þe lond of Egipt. 25

Anno 3445–3490. f. 24ʳᵃ

Anno 3491. This ȝere deied Jacob, brothir onto Esau, and, as his modir tawt him, his deceyuoure; for he receyued his fader blessing nowt knowyn to his fader, but plesauns onto God. This Jacob fadir was onto þe xii tribus of Israel. He sey þe ladder 30 þat touchid heuene, and aungellis clymyng up and down, and

---

2 ruyne] Ruleyng P   5–6 Ysaac of age sexti ȝere begat Esau and Jacob twynnes] begat Ysaac Esau and Jacobe twynese being of age syxti yere P 13 schal we] we schall P   17 nynety ȝere of age] of age nynty yere P 19 Foroneus] *initial* ff *over partially erased* ph, fo *in r.h. margin* M   21 and þoo places in whech juges] *om.* P   22 forum] *suprascript* M   27 ȝere] *om.* P   28 tawt] tawgthe P   29 knowyn] knowyng P

5–6: ibid. 432/35.
10–11: cf. ibid. 432/36.
12–13: cf. ibid. 432/37.
17–18: cf. ibid. 433/39.

oure Lord lenyng upon þe ladder. He deyd in Egipt, of age a
hundred ȝere fourti and seuene. There was he bawmed with
swete gummes, and aftir þe Joseph his son broute into þe lond of
Chanaan, and byryed where Abraham and Sare and Rebec be
5 byryid.

f. 24ʳᵇ   Anno Mundi 3492–3554.

Anno 3555. Here deyed Joseph, of age a hundred ȝere and ten.
He was byried in a place þei clepe it Bresith, and anoyntid with
swete gummys; his bones, as his comaundment was, were translat
10 aftir þe Moises, and broute into þe Holi Lond, and in Josue tyme
þe puple byried hem in Sichem. Sone aftir þe deth of Joseph
f. 24ᵛᵃ began þat wrecchid bondage of þe Hebrew | puple in Egipt, and
þat bondage lestid a hundred ȝere and fourty and foure.

In þis tyme lyued Athlans, þat fonde astronomie. The Mount
15 Athlans stant in þe occean beȝond Affrik, whech mount took his
name of þis king; for he was mech vsed to dwelle in þat hil for
most sikir consideracioun of sterris.

f. 24ᵛᵇ   Anno Mundi 3556–3609.

Anno 3610. In þis ȝere was Moyses bore, the son of Ambry,
20 whech Ambri was þe son of Cath, and Cath þe son of Leuy,
whech Leuy was son to Jacob; so was Moises þe vii man fro
Abraham. Aron was his brothir and Mari his sistir. Moises in
Egipt was bore and thre monthis hid, þan put in a uessel of
wykyris—fillid þe joyntis with tow erde, cleped bithumen—and
25 so put in þe watir. So was he take up be þe comaundment of
Pharao doutir, and þus norchid onto mannes age; therfor was his
name Moyses, þat is to sey 'Lift up fro þe watir'.

Whan he was growe to mannes age, he sey on of þe Egipcianes
do wrong to on of þe Hebrewis, he halp his brothir and killid
30 him of Egipte; wherfor he was fayn to fle into the lond of Madian
and þere dwelle with a preest, his name Jethro. þere he kept his
f. 25ʳᵃ schep and weddid on of his dowteres, whos name | was Sephora.
There appered God onto him with fire in a busch, and þe busch
onbrent, and mad him his messager to þe kyng of Egipte.

35   Anno 3611–3659.

9 was] om. P   18 in Anno Mundi tria Milia dc between Anno Mundi
the number 36 M   21 son to] the sone of P   31 his (1)] suprascript M
his name] om. P   35 Anno 3612 om. M

7: cf. Isidore, 433/42.

Anno 3660. In þis same tyme were letteris and writyng first
founde. For þe letteris of þe Hebrew tonge were first founde be
Moises, and þe letteris of þe Chaldé tonge were founde be Abraham; for þei acorde with þe Hebrew letteres both in nowmbir
and in sownd, but in þe maner of writing and schap of þe letteres 5
þei haue grete dyuersité. The letteris whech þe Egipcianes vse
were found be Ysis, qween of þe same lond, dowtir onto Ynachi,
king of Grece. The Latyn letteris a woman þat hite Carmentis
brout first into Itayle; sche was cleped Carmentis for sche vsed
many charmes.   10
    Anno Mundi 3661–3728.   f. 25ʳᵇ
    Anno 3729. In þis ȝere deyed Moises, and no man myte fynde
his graue. For be þe comaundment of God he went up to þe hil
of Phasga, | and þere oure Lord schewid him all þe Lond of f. 25�vᵃ
Behest, and saide onto him, 'Thou schal se þis lond, but þou schal 15
not entir it'. So deied he þere and was biried in þe vale. He lyued
here a c ȝere and xx. At his deth his eyne were not dym, ne no
toth falle fro his heed.
    Anno 3730–3755.
    Anno 3756. This ȝere deied Josue, þe son of Nun, seruaunt 20
onto Moises, born in Egipte, aftir þe deth of his maistir prince of
þe puple. This man sent his spies into þe cité of Jericho and wan
it with grete miracle. He spak with God seiand swech wordes
onto him, 'I schal preferre þe þis day befor al þe puple, and make
the leder to hem alle'. þis man led þe puple þorow þe water cleped 25
Jordan with dry feet. Many townes des|troyed he in þe cuntré f. 25ᵛᵇ
cleped Galgalis, whos dwelleres were blasphemeres of God.
At his comaundment þe sunne stood stille ageyn þe cours of
nature til he had vengid him on Goddis enmies. He disposed and
distribut þe Lond of Behest to þe puple. He lyued a hundred 30
ȝere and ten, byried in Tamnath-sare, his owne possession,
whech is in þe mount of Effraim.
    Anno 3757–3795.
    Anno 3796. This ȝere deied Othoniel, þe first juge of Israel,

2 þe (2)] *om.* P   first] *om.* P   9 Itayle] Ytayle P, ttayle M   13 co-
maundment] commundiment [P   14–18 and . . . heed] *in darker ink* M
30 distribut] distried but P   31 Tamnath-sare] Tamnasare P

12: cf. ibid. 434/54.
20: cf. ibid. 435/59.
34: cf. ibid. 435/61.

for aftir Josue was ded þe puple was gouerned be juges onto þe
tyme of Samuel. This Othoniel was broþir onto Caleph, and
gouerned þe puple ful vertuously xl ȝere, distroied her enmies,
killid þe kyng of Surré, his name was Cusan-rasathaim.

5   In his time regned at Attenes her v kyng, summe men cleped
him Pandion, and summe Neptunus. And in þe cité of Tebes
f. 26ra regned þanne Cadmus. Eke þe grete musician cle|ped Linus, he
leued in þoo dayes.

f. 26rb   Anno Mundi 3797–3865.

10   Anno 3866. In þis ȝere deied Ayoth, þe secunde juge of Israel,
þe son of Gera, þat used þe lift hand for þe rite, þat is to sey,
what grete dede of armes schuld be do, he ded it as weel with þe o
hand as with þe othir. He killid þe fat Kyng Eglon, and delyuered
Israel of her grete enmy.

15   In þis tyme regned Hercules, of whos strong dedis is grete
fame: the first is þat he destroied iii wilde bestis, whech were
clepid Arpie; the secunde, þat he flay a leon qwik oute of his
scyn; the þird, þat he mad þe centaures for to fle (centaures were
monstres, half best, half man); the iiii, þat he bare þe appeles of
20 gold fro Athlantis gardeyn, where a dragon was keper; the v is
bynding of Cerberus, þe hound of helle; the vi, ouircomyng of
f. 26va Diomede, the kyng of Trace; the vii, killyng | of þe grete serpent
cleped Ydras; the viii, distroyng of þat best þat chaunged himself
into so many liknes, his name was Thasis; the ix is þe gret victorie
25 of þe beste Achildes, þat blew oute fyre at his mowth; the x,
killing of Anthé, þe geaunt of Libi; the xi is killing of þe grete
boor in Archady; the xii, bering up of þe firmament whil Athlas
rested.

    Anno Mundi 3867–3915.

30   Anno 3916. This ȝere deied Delbora, a woman þat be the
auctorité of God gouerned Israel many ȝeres. The enmy of Israel
hite Cisara, whech had a gret hoost, and nyne hundred cartis dith

---

12 grete dede] dedese P   15 regned] d *suprascript* M   17 qwik]
all quyk P   19 iiii] *each digit surmounted by short stroke in red* M   27 firma-
ment] firmanente P   29 *the year numbers* 3904 *to* 3909 *miswritten as* 394
etc. M   30 þat] t *suprascript* M   32 had] *in r.h. margin* M

6–7: Isidore, 435/62.
7–8: ibid. 435/63.
10: cf. ibid. 435/65.
30: cf. ibid. 436/73.

with hokis of yrun þat oppressed and rent al þat cam before hem.
This woman, with a prince whech hite Barach, ouyrcam þis
Sisara, and pursewid him til he was fayn to fle to a womannes
hous þat hite Jael. Sche hid him and refrecchid him with milk
and broute him to rest, and whan he slepe, with a malle an a 5
nayle sche smet him in þe hed, and þus he joyned slep and deth
togidir.

Anno 3917–3934.

Anno 3935. In þis tyme regned Appollo, whech was | fynder of f. 26ᵛᵇ
medicines, and eke first maker of þe harp. But þat maner of myn- 10
stralsie was aftir more plenteuously conceyued be Mercurye,
as Ysider tellith in þe third book of *Ethimilogies*, where he seith
þus: 'Whanne Nylus þe grete ryuer had ouirflowe þe cuntré,
and aftir descendid into his costomable mesure, þan were left in
þe feldis many ded bestis, whos flesch þan was wasted and the 15
bones dryed. Thanne certeyn cenewes fast by þe bones, and dryed
with þe sunne, were left, and whan Mercury cam forby he smet þoo
stringis, and, party be þe bones, party be þe leddir, þere was a
gret sound. And aftir this liknes Mercury ded make an instrument,
whech he cleped a harp, and þis instrument took he to on hite 20
Orphé, whech was ful studiows in swech þingis, for with þis
melodye, as þe poetis sey, he mad tame wilde bestis, and stones
and trees were solaced be him'.

Anno 3936–3955.

Anno 3956. In þis ȝere deied Gedeon, þat was juge to þe puple 25
of Israel fourty wyntyr. This man receyued of God a meruelous
tokne; for first was a flees of wolle wette, and al þe erde drye,
þan was al | þe erde wette, and þe flees drie. Aftir þis tokne he f. 27ʳᵃ
went to bataile with trumpis, pottis, lampis, and fire, and be þe
puruyauns of God had þe uictorie. He was juge in Israel xl ȝere. 30

Aftir him Abimelech iii ȝere—vndir him was a parable mad þat
þe trees schuld chese hem a kyng.

Anno 3957–3980.

12 book] boke P, bood M   13 Nylus] Jubis P   15 feldis] foldyse P
and] in P   21 with] *suprascript* M   26 God] P, good M   28 erde
wette and þe] *om.* P   31 Aftir him] *om.* P   him (2)] *om.* P   a] *suprascript* M   33 Anno 3977 *om.* M

9–10: cf. ibid. 436/74.
25–6: cf. ibid. 437/77.

Anno 3981. This ȝere deied Thola, þat was her juge xxii ȝere. He was byried in Sanir, in þe movnt of Effraim.

Anno Mundi 3982–4002.

Anno 4003. This tyme was Jayr juge of Israel xxii ȝere. This f. 27rb man was a Galadite, whech had xxx sones, good rideres, | specialy 6 on asses, and þei were princes of xxx citées named aftir her names.

Anno 4004–4017.

Anno 4018. In þis tyme Esebon was juge in Israel seuene ȝere. 10 Summe men clepe him Abessem; he had xxx sones and xxx douteres.

In þis same tyme Alisaundre of Troye raueschid fayre Heleyne owt of Grece, for whech dede began þe sege of Troye.

Anno 4019–4033.

15 Anno 4034. In þis tyme was Abdon, or elles Labdon, a juge in Israel, and he had xl sones and xxx douteres.

In his tyme was Troye distroyed.

And in þis same tyme began þe annotacioun of Olimpias, as we rede: 'Olimpiade tercio, uel quarto'—þe þird Olimpiade, or þe 20 fourte'. And þus it began: the Grekes, whan þei had þe victory of þe Troianes, þei ordeyned þat euery fift ȝere þei schuld haue exercise of al maner games þat longyn to power or swiftnesse, and f. 27va þis sa|me playes were begunne in Macedonie, where þe hie hill Olimpe stant, of whech cam þis name, for þereaboute was 25 þe play.

Anno 4035–4043.

Anno 4044. This ȝere deied Samson, with deceyt of a woman, whech was þe juge of Israel xx ȝere. His strength passed all men; he rent a leon; he brak þe bondis þat he was bound with; þe 30 gates of a town and þe postis he bare hem away; and at þe last,

---

9 tyme] *om.* P   10 men] *om.* P   12 raueschid] Raueschid M   14 *the year number 4020 miswritten as* 40020 M   Anno 4021 *om.* M   15 a] *change to darker ink* M   in] of P   18 same] *om.* P   20 þus] thys P 21 þei (2)] þey P, *om.* M   22 swiftnesse] switnesse M, sustinesse P

1–2: cf. Isidore, 437/83.
4: ibid. 438/86.
9: cf. ibid. 438/92.
12–13: cf. ibid. 438/91.
15: cf. ibid. 438/94.
17: cf. ibid. 438/95.
27–8: cf. ibid. 439/98.

be stering of þe Holy Goost, he pullid down too postis where a
hous felle and oppressed him and mech oþir puple.

In þis same tyme Ascanius, the son of Eneas, in þe þird ȝere
aftir Troye was distroyed bigged a town, Alba, whech stod
upon þe flood whech had þe same name, but now it hite Tibir, 5
and þat same town is now a part of Rome.

Anno 4045–4083.   f. 27ᵛᵇ

Anno 4084. This ȝere deied Hely, þe preest of þe tabernacle,
þat was in Silo, vndir whom Samuel first was mad a ministir of
þe same tabernacle. This Heli, for his necligens, þat he corrected 10
not his sones of her insolens, fel down fro his chayer where he
sat in þe tabernacle, and þus punchid with temporal deth, scaped,
as we suppose, þe deth þat is euirlasting. In þe tyme of þis same
Hely was þe arke of God take be the Philisteis to her grete confusion. For whan it was sette in her temple, her god Dagon fel 15
down and was al tobroken; the puple eke was smet with greuous
sores, as þe first book of Kyngis makith mynde.

In þis same Hely tyme Brute, þat was of Eneas kyn, cam into
þis lond and called it Britayn aftir his name. Whan he deyid,
he departed his kyngdam to his thre sones: the first hite Loegrius, 20
and to him he gaf þe lond fro Douyr onto | Humbyr; the secund   f. 28ʳᵃ
son hite Albanactus, and to him gaue he al Scotlond onto Humbir;
the þird hite Camber, and to him gaue he all Walis. The first
cuntré was called in þoo dayes Loegria; the secunde Albania;
þe þird Cambria.   25

Anno Mundi 4085–4123.

Anno 4124. This ȝere deyed Samuel, whech gouerned Israel
xxii ȝere or þat tyme þat Saul was mad king, and aftir þat tyme
lyued Samuel xviii ȝere. This Samuel was bore in Ramatha,
noumbird amongis þe Nazareis, of whech religion Criste was, and 30
eke Jon Baptiste. His modir Anne was long bareyn, and whan
sche had child, sche mad þat canticle 'Exultauit cor meum in
Domino'. This Samuel anoynted too kyngis, Saul and Dauid,

---

4 biggid] byldyd P   Alba] *in r.h. margin* M   stod] *suprascript* M   12 þus]
thys P   19 lond] *suprascript* M   21 him] hym *twice* P   22 he] *suprascript and in r.h. margin* M   23 he] *om.* P   24 Loegria] *over erasure* M
25 þe] *om.* P

3–4: cf. ibid. 439/99.
8: ibid. 439/101.
27–9: cf. ibid. 439/104.

and sette hem on her setes. He askid reyn fro heuene, and God
sent it him. In grete age he deied, byried in Ramatha. In his tyme
he mad certeyn couentes of religious men, whech wer seyd prophetis; and þat prophecie was not elles but songis to þe worchip
5 of God.

In þis tyme lyued þe grete poete Omere, þat was at þe batail
of Troye, and þe first writer of þe same.

f. 28rb   Anno 4125–4163.

Etas Quarta

10   Anno 4164. Here deieth Dauid, þe son of Jesse. He was born
of þe tribe of Juda in þe cité of Bethlem, fayre in nature, wise in
prophecye, both kyng and prophete. Kyngis he ouyrcam with
uictorye; psalmes he sang with melodie; bestes he killid, and
Goly the grete geaunt. Euyr he dred God. Cristis natiuité, his
15 baptem, his passion, resurreccion, ascencion, his comyng to
þe dome, ful openly in his psalmes he teld. His fadir scheep
kepte he ful mekly; aftir þat xl ȝere was he kyng, first vii ȝere
in Hebron upon þe tribe of Juda, aftir xxxiii in Jerusalem upon
al Israel. In grete age he deied, byried at Bethlem, whech is cleped
20 þe cité of Dauid.

In þis tyme þe grete cyté Cartago was begunne of a woman þei
cleped Dido vii ȝere or Rome began.

Vndir þis Kyng Dauid prophecied þese too men: Nathan and
Gad.

f. 28va   Anno Mundi 4165–4203.

26   Anno 4204. This ȝere deied Salamon, þe son of Dauid and
Bersabe, whech was þe wyf of Vry. First was he cleped Ydida
and þan Salamon. Twyes was he anoynted king, be þe comaundment of Dauid, be Sadoch þe prest: ones at þe welle whech þei
30 calle Gion, and þan in þe Temple befor al þe puple. He asked of
God wisdam, and God sent it him so plenteuously þat þere was

---

1 hem] *change to darker ink* M   2 his] this P   8 Anno 4150
twice M   9 Etas Quarta] *in red* M, *om.* P   10 son] *om.* P   16 His]
change to darker ink M   30 Temple] Tenpulle P

6: cf. Isidore, 439/106.
10: cf. ibid. 439/107.
21–2: cf. ibid. 440/109.
23–4: cf. ibid. 440/110.
26: cf. ibid. 440/111.

neuyr before him so wis a man in Jerusalem; for he made prouerbis
and songis of ful meruelous sentens. He mad þe Temple of God
and arayed it with mech ricchesse. With plesauns of women he
was browt into ydolatrie, but at his last ende he repent him and
ded penauns.   5

Anno 4205–4220.

Anno 4221. Roboam, son to Salamon, he regned aftir his
fadir, and he forsoke þe councell of elde men and was counceled
be 3ong puple; þerfor þe ten tribus forsoke him an þere left with
him but too.   10

Anno 4222–4224.

Anno 4225. Here deied Abia, of whom is not mech writyng but
þat he regned but iii 3ere, saue þei sey þat Maacha, Absalon
doutir, was his modir.

Anno 4226–4264.   f. 28ᵛᵇ

Anno 4265. Here deied Asa, kyng of Juda, þat in his age had   16
sore feet, whech passioun oure bokys sey it was podegra, and þat
seknes þei sey comth of grete plenté of mete and mech rest. This
man | lyued rithfully, and distroyed mech abhominable lecchery   f. 29ʳᵃ
in Jerusalem. He drow his modir fro cursed gouernauns, for   20
sche was princesse in a ful abhominable place, whech þei cleped
Sacra Priapi; it is not neccessari to declare what it was, but þis
man distroyed hous and auter, ymage and al. He ouyrcam eke
Zaram, kyng of Ethiop, þat cam into his lond with grete power.

Anno 4266–4289.   25

Anno 4290. Josaphat deieth here, þe son of Asa, whech regned
in Jerusalem xxv 3ere. The name of his moder was Azuba. This
man folowid his fader steppes in seruise of God.

In his dayes prophecied Helie, Helize, and Miche, whos com-
endacioun sumwhat wil we touch. Helie lyueth 3et in paradise,   30
whom Antecrist schal martir in þe ende of þe world. He reysed
fro deth a man þei cleped Jonas. He fasted xl daies withoute

10 too] to tribus P   13 saue] *twice* P   19 man] *in r.h. margin* M
lyued] loued P   23 man] *suprascript* M   24 þat] t *suprascript* M
29 Helize] Helizie P   32 cleped] d *over erasure* M

7: cf. ibid. 440/113.
9–10: cf. ibid. 440/114.
12–13: cf. ibid. 440/117.
16: cf. ibid. 440/119.
26: cf. ibid. 441/121.
29: cf. ibid. 441/122.

mete or drynk. He sperd heuene fro reyn iii ȝere and sex monthis.
He asked fire fro heuene. He killid Baal prestis. In a cart al fire
was he bore up to paradise. Helize, whech was his disciple,
had dobil þe grace whech his maystir had. He went þorw þe
5 flood with drye feet; he lift þe ex and mad it flete in þe watir.

f. 29ʳᵇ He cured Naaman, þe prince of Surré, fro seknesse of | lepre.
He smet his couetous seruaunt with þe same seknes. In Samary
deied he, and þere was he byried.

     Anno 4291–4297.

10   Anno 4298. This ȝere deied Joram, whech regned in Jerusalem
viii ȝere.

     Anno 4299; Anno Mundi iiii Milia ccc.

     Anno 4301. And þis ȝere, Occhozie, þat regned but o ȝere.

     Anno 4302–4307.

15   Anno 4308. And þis ȝere regned Athalia, vii ȝere in þe tyme of
Joiada, þat was þe hy prest. For þe seid Athalia had killid al þe
kyngis blod, whech tyme Jozabeth, þe kyngis dowtir Joram, tok
Joas the son of Occhozie and hid him in a pryuy hous of the
Temple, and þere was he norchid be consent of þis prest Joiada.
20 This Joiada lyued a hundred ȝere and xx; we rede þat no prest
lyued so long aftir þe tyme of Moyses.

     In these dayes was Helie in a firy cart or chare lift up to para-
dise; and in his goyng he threw down his mantil onto Helise in
tokne þat the dobil spirite schuld rest upon him.

f. 29ᵛᵃ   Anno 4309–4347.

26   Anno 4348. Here deyeth Joas, þat was kyng in Jerusalem xl
ȝere; the name of his modir was Sebra, sche was bore in Bersabe.
This kyng wroute þat was plesauns to God, for he restored þe
Temple and many houses þat longid þerto; for, fro þe tyme þat
30 he was mad kyng onto þe xxiii ȝere of his regne, the prestes spent
þe offering and mad no reparacion, and þerfor the kyng comaundid
þat þe offering schuld be put in a comoun box and kept to restauracion of þe Temple.

---

3 was he] he was P   8 he (2)] P, *om.* M   16 Athalia] i *surmounted*
by short stroke in red M   19 Temple] *in r.h. margin* M

10–11: cf. Isidore, 441/123.
13: cf. ibid. 441/125.
15–16: cf. ibid. 441/127–8.
20–1: cf. ibid. 441/129.
22: cf. ibid. 441/126.
26–7: cf. ibid. 442/130.

Anno 4349–4374.

Anno 4375. Here deieth Amasias, þat regned in Jerusalem xxix 3ere. The name of his moder: Joaden, born in | Jerusalem. f. 29ᵛᵇ
Whan he was confermed in his regne, he mad dew inquisicion of all hem þat were consenting to his fader deth, an whan he had 5
hem, condempned hem to þe deth; but her issew he harmed not, for it is wrytyn in Moyses lawe, 'The child schal not bere þe wikkidnes of þe fader, ne þe fader þe wikkidnes of þe child, but euery man schal be ded in his owne sinne'.

In þis tyme Ligurgius, kyng of Lacedomy, mad certeyn lawes 10
and mad his citeceynes for to swere onto him þat þei schuld kepe þese lawes til þat he com ageyn fro his pilgrimage. This sworne and ratified be seles, he went into þe ylde of Crete, and þere dwelled, and died in exile.

In þese dayes a man þat hite Siluius Aduentinus, þe xiii kyng 15
of þat region cleped Latinorum, died, and was byried in a mount þat stant in Rome, and for his biryng þe mount hath his name, Mons Aduentinus. Whan men go owt at Seynt Paule gate, þei go vndir it, and leue it on þe left hand.

Anno Mundi 4376–4426. f. 30ʳᵃ

Anno 4427. Here deieth Ozias, þat was kyng of Jerusalem lii 21
3ere. This man repayred þe wallis of Jerusalem rownd aboute. And in his age, in a grete fest called þe Propiciacioun, he presumed for to do upon him þe prestis stole, and for to sense 25
þe auter. And anon he was smet with þe seknes of lepre, and be þe lawe departed fro þe puple and fro þe gouernauns, and dwelt in a hous separat fro men. Joathan, his son, he dwelled in þe paleys and gouerned þe puple, and aftir his fadir deth was anoynted.

Anno 4428–4442. 30

---

2 deieth] deyed P   3 in] *twice over column division* M   4 inquisicion] inquisi|cion *over line division* M, inquision P   6 condempned] *2nd* e *written above* o *which is expuncted* M   but her] bu ther P   8 wikkidnes (1)]] wikkidne P   15 Siluius] Silius P   17 name] *suprascript* M   18 at] t *suprascript* M   20 Anno 4378 *twice over column division* M   *the year numbers* 4408 *and* 4409 *miswritten as* 448 *and* 449 *respectively* M   22 rownd] d *suprascript with caret (in red)* M   23 And] d *suprascript with caret (in red)* M   called] d *suprascript* M   24 to (2)] P, *om.* M   28 and (2)] *suprascript* M

2–3: ibid. 442/134.
10: cf. ibid. 442/133.
21–2: ibid. 442/135.

Anno 4443. Here deieth Joathan, þat was kyng in Jerusalem xvi ʒere.

In his tyme were þoo too childirn bore, Remus and Romulus, beginneris of Rome. There was a mayden in Itaile consecrat to a
5 religion þei cleped Vescal—whech were bownde to perpetuel virginité. This mayde hite Rea, and so it happed þat sche was with childe be þe god Mars, as sche feyned. The tyme cam, and þese
f. 30ʳᵇ too | were born—sche was byried qwik, and þe childir leyd be þe side of Tibir, þat bestes schuld deuovr hem. Summe sey þat a
10 wolf norched hem, and so it is peyntid in Itaile; summe sey þat a scheperde, whos name was Fastulus, fond hem and bare hem hom to his wif Laurens, whech woman was cleped 'Wolf' in þat langage for hir leccherie.

Anno 4444–4458.

15 Anno 4459. Achaz deieth here, that regned in Jerusalem xvi ʒere. This man was of wikkid gouernauns, for he forsook God, and worcheped maumentrie, in-so-mech þat he offered his son to þe mavment whech þei clepe Tophet in þe vale of Hennon. Therfor suffered oure Lord God Rasin þe kyng of Surré to com to
20 Jerusalem and distroye þe lond and put the kyng undir grete tribute; and þis was do þe fourte ʒere of his regne.

Vndir þis king prophecied Ysaie in Jerusalem, a grete prophete, and a holy martir. For he tellith in his bok þe misteriis of þe Cherch, of Cristis incarnacion and passioun, as pleynly as þouʒ
25 he had be present. He sey oure Lord sitte in a hey sete, and seraphin herd he synge with a clere sound, 'Sanctus, Sanctus, Sanctus'.
f. 30ᵛᵃ His lippis were porgid with heuenly | fyre, and in Jerusalem at þe comaundment of þe kyng, Manasses, was his body cut asundir with a sawe of tre.

30 Anno 4460–4487.

Anno 4488. This ʒere deied Ezechie, þat regned in Jerusalem xxix ʒere, whech plesid God in his lyuyng. He repayred þe Temple and þe vesseles þat longe þerto. He distroyed þe serpent of bras

1 Joathan] Jaithan *with 1st* a *altered from* o P   4 was] *in r.h. margin* M
9 deuovr] v *suprascript* M   10 it] P, *om.* M   15 Achaz] Acham P
19 Surré] Surr P   22 in Jerusalem] *om.* P   24 þouʒ] thowth P

1–2: Isidore, 443/142.
3: ibid. 443/143.
15–16: ibid. 443/145.
22: cf. ibid. 443/144.
31–2: ibid. 443/148.

þat Moyses set up, for þe puple at þo dayes forsoke þe dew seruise
of God, and honovrid þat same serpent. The sunne at his prayer,
for a tokne þat he schuld haue lenger lif, went bakward in his
horologe x lines, þat is to sey, sum men wene, x houres. Fiftene
ȝere be þe graunt of God were lengthid of his lif.   5

   In his tyme, as in Achaz, prophecied Ysaie, whech coumforted
þe kyng in his seknes, and gaue him a playstir of figgis, and
aftirward told him þat Senacherib, kyng of þe Assiriis, in no wise
schulde noye him. For in a nyte sodeynly God smet þe oost of þe
Assiriis, þat in þe morownyng þere were founde dede foure score   10
þousand and fyue þousand; and whan | þe kyng on þe morow say   f. 30ᵛᵇ
þis pestilens, he fled into Nynyue.

   Anno Mundi 4489–4539.

   Anno 4540. Here deyeth Manasses, þat regned in Jerusalem lii
ȝere. He ded mech euel and displesauns to oure Lord: he edified   15
auteres onto fals goddis; he killid prophetes and seruauntes of
God, þat þe stretes of Jerusalem were ful of blood. And for þis
erroure God suffered him for to be take and led into Babilonie,
and aftir grete penauns and weping, he was restored to his regne,
and with grete deuocioun amendid his defautes.   20

   In þis tyme lyued Sibille, þat was cleped Samia. Auctouris sey
here þat þere were ten Sibilles: on was of Perse; the secunde of
Libie; þe þirde of Delphis, where Appollo is worchiped, whech
made verse put in Omer book; þe fourt was cleped Cimerea—
sche dwelled in Itaile; þe v was Erithea, þat dwelled in Babilonie;   25
þe sext was Samia, born in a ylde of þe same name; þe vii hite
Amalthea, that mad ix bookes to on cleped Tarqui|nius Priscus,   f. 31ʳᵃ
in whech bokes were wrytyn þe lawes of Rome; þe viii was born
fast be Troye—sche was cleped Elesponcia; þe ix was amongis þe
Frises; þe ten, most famous, was at Rome, called Tiburtina, for   30
sche prophecied mech of Crist.

   Anno 4541–4553.

4 horologe] h *altered from* b M   is] it MP   sum men] as sume P
6 Achaz] Acham P   8 þe] *om.* P   8–9 no wise schulde] *om.* P
15 and] d *suprascript* M   17 blood] bood P   26 a] the P
27 Amalthea] Amalthe P   bookes] s *suprascript* M   on] n *in red* M
28 whech] *final* h *suprascript* M   29 sche was cleped Elesponcia] *om.* P

6: ibid. 443/149.
14–15: cf. ibid. 444/151.
21: ibid. 444/154.

Anno 4554. Amon endith here, þat was kyng of Jerusalem xiii
ȝere, and he folowid his fadir Manasses in al euel and al onclennes
of ydolatrie; þerfor his owne seruauntis mordred him in his owne
hous. And aftir his deth þe puple of þe lond ros and killid all
5 þoo traitoures.

In þis tyme was edified a cité in þe lond of Trace whech þei
cleped Bizans; but aftirward Grete Constantin mad it more, and
called it Constantinople.

Anno 4555–4575.
10 Anno 4576. Josias makith an ende of his lif, whech regned in
Jerusalem xxii ȝere. This man kept þe weyes of Dauid and porged
þe lond of al ydolatrie, but in batayle he was smet with a arow
and so deied.

Anno 4577–4586.

f. 31rb   Anno 4587. Joachim, whech þat is cleped Jeconias, he reg|ned
16 in Jerusalem xi ȝere. This same man was led be Nabugodonosor
into Babiloni, and mani prisoneres with him, most specialy þe
best of þe lond, as Thobie and Mardoche, with many othir.

Than þe kyng of Babilon sette Sedechie kyng at Jerusalem to
20 gouerne þe puple and pay tribute ȝerly, whech Sedechi rebelled
ageyn þe kyng. And þerfor þe kyng cam ageyn to Jerusalem, and
took þis kyng, put oute his eyne, and led him into Babilonie, and
þus was þe cité and þe Temple distroyed. And vndir þis Captiuité prophecied Jeremie, Ezechiel and Daniel, of whom sum-
25 what wil we write:—

Jeremie was a prophete and a preest, born in Anatoth, halowid
in his modir wombe. He began to prophecie whil he was a child.
The ruine of þe cité he morned with woful songis, foure distincte
be þe ABC. Nabugodonosor drew him oute of þe lake, and sent
30 him into Egipt with othir prisoneres, where for his prophecye
f. 31va   his owne puple killid him with stones in a town | þei clepe Tafnes,
and byried in þe same place, where Pharao dwelled.

Ezechiel began to prophecye in þe xxx ȝere of his age and in

7 mad it *separated by thin stroke in red* M   15 whech] *final* h *inserted
on the line* M   17 Babiloni] *final* i *surmounted by short stroke in red* M
19 Sedechie] Sedochie P   24 Jeremie] Jeromie P   29 lake] *suprascript with caret (in red)* M

1–2: cf. Isidore, 444/155.
10–11: cf. ibid. 444/157.
15–16: cf. ibid. 445/160.

þe v ȝere of her Captiuité. He sey a glorious trone in þe firmament.
He receyued a book and ete it. He sey many sites in whech diuers
kyngis and puples for synne schuld be distroyed. He sei eke a
feld ful of drye bones, and whil he prophecied onto hem þe
senewis and veynes, flesch and scyn, entered onto hem, eke þe 5
spirit, þat þei stood upon her feet.

Daniel, þe son of Abda, prophecied þis same tyme, born in
Inde, and but ȝong led into Babilonie, a meruelous prophete.
For þe dremes of Nabugodonosor in þe grete ymage and þe
grete tre he expouned. And of þe foure wyndis fityng in þe se he 10
meruelously touchid, who þe foure bestes rising with þese foure
wyndis foutyn ech with othir. A elde man sei he sitting in majesté,
and aboute him | a þousand þousand of ministres.   f. 31ᵛᵇ

Anno Mundi 4588–4689.

Anno 4690. Here regneth Darius upon þe Medes, and Cirus 15
upon þe Perses, in whos first ȝere þe Captiuité of þe Jewis was
relesid be þe same Cirus, whech gaue Zorobabel and Jesu, þe
grete preest, leue for to go hom to Jerusalem and to edifye it.
Summe sey þat it was in þe first ȝere of Cirus, sum sey in þe þird,
and þis is cause of þe variauns: for þei had leue in þe first, but 20
þei were not redy til þe þird ȝere. (And here is for to noten þat
þere is grete variacioun amongis auctouris both of ȝeres and of
kyngis names, for many had dyuers names.) Eke þis Darius and
Cirus destroyed | Babilonie, and þere sesed þe name of þat regne. f. 32ʳᵃ

In þis same tyme fel þe story of Susanne.   25

And in þis same tyme lyued þoo vii first philisophres þat were
of so grete fame, whos names be þese: Thales, Pitacus, Solon,
Cylon, Piriandus, Cleobolus, and Bias.

Anno Mundi 4691–4736.

Etas Quinta   30

Anno 4737. Here regned Xerses, the v kyng of Perse, and he
regned þere xxiiii ȝere. This man was so leccherous þat he ded

4 ful] *om.* P   prophecied] propheseid P, pphecied M   9 in] *twice
over line division* M   13 him] *in r.h. margin in red* M   ministres] P,
minstres M   15 Darius] *suprascript* M   17 and] d *suprascript* M
18 go] *suprascript and caret in red* M   19 Summe] Sum men P   in þe
þird] that it was in the thyrd yere P   20 cause] the kause P
22 þere] *suprascript and caret in red* M   28 and] d *suprascript* M
30 Etas Quinta] *in red* M, *om.* P   32 regned] d *suprascript* M

15: cf. ibid. 446/170.
31–2: cf. ibid. 446/173.

crye openly, what man coude bryng in a new circumstauns of lecchery, he schuld haue a grete reward. And whan he had gadered a gret ost ageyn þe Grekis, on seyde, 'The Grekis schul not only be ouyrcome, but þei schal be pressed down with swech a multitude'.

5 Demoratus þe philisofer answerd, 'There is swech a multitude
f. 32ʳᵇ þat þei may not be gouerned, | and þerfor is it þe more to drede'.

In þis tyme lyued þese too poetes, Sophodes and Euripides, þat were cleped tragedies. Trajedi is as mech to sey as he þat writith eld stories with ditées heuy and sorowful.

10 Anno 4738–4776.

Anno 4777. Here regneth Artharxerses, þe vi kyng in Perse, whech is clepid *Nothus*—xl ȝere he regned þere; vndir whom Esdras repayred þe lawe þat was brent be hem of Chaldé, whech Esdras broute in new maner of wryting of letteres, þat were more
15 esy for to write and more esi for to pronounce, and þerfor was he called a swift writer. And it is not grete wondir þou þat Esdras mite with his rememberauns write bokes new ageyn, for we know þat þere be summe men þat can hold in her rememberauns mech þing.

20 Anno 4778–4797.
f. 32ᵛᵃ Anno 4798. In þis ȝere regneth Da|rius, þe vii kyng in Perse, and he regned xix ȝere. This man was son of Ydapsis, and on of þe vii gouernouris of Perse, whech was chosen be þe nyhyng of a hors. Vndir him was þe probleme purposit of þe strength of a
25 king, a woman, wyn, and treuth.

In þis tyme was Plato disciple to Socrates, in whos bokes was founde a gret part of þat gospel, 'In principio erat uerbum'. Whan he was take with soudioures and broute to Dionisie þe Tyraunt, he, seing so many aboute þe tiraunt, seide onto him,

---

2 lecchery] *in r.h. margin with carets* (*in red*) M 3 gret] grest P schul not only be] schuld note be only P 8 tragedies] es *suprascript* M 11 in] of P 12 he] *suprascript* M 13 brent] *in r.h. margin* M 14 of letteres] *suprascript* M 15 write and more esi for to] *om.* P 18–19 rememberauns mech þing] au*n*s mech þing *over erasure* M 21 In þis ȝere regneth Darius] In þis ȝere regneth da *over erasure* M 24 strength] th *suprascript* M

7–8: cf. Isidore, 446/174.
11–12: cf. ibid. 447/176.
12–13: cf. ibid. 447/177.
12–16: cf. Higden, iii. 248/7–8, 11–13.
21–2: cf. Isidore, 447/181.
26: cf. ibid. 447/182.

'What hast þou do þat þou nedist so many men?'. This Plato
mad many bokes and named hem aftir his maystires: Thimeus
is on; Phedron a oþir; þe þird, Gorgialis; þe iiii, Pitharas. And
þou3 men feyne mech þing of his deth, he was hald in so gret
reuerens þat þei had doute, whan he was ded, whethir þei schuld 5
anoumbir him among þe hie goddis or semigoddes.

Anno Mundi 4799-4837.

Anno 4838. Here endith Artarxerses, whos regne lested xl 3ere.
Summe | sey þat his name was Assuerus, to whom Ester was coupled.   f. 32ᵛᵇ

In þis tyme lyued Diogenes, þat seld himselue onto bondage, 10
and whan his maistir, þat boute him, profered him to on Veniedes
for to by him, Veniedes inqwired of þe philisophre what craft he
coude; and he answerd, 'I can', he seith, 'þou3 I be bond, be a
gouernour onto hem þat stande in gret fredam'. And whan
Veniades herd þis answere, he merueiled gretly, and seide, 'I 15
make the lord of my childirn—do with hem at þi plesauns'.
Kyng Alisaundre fond him sitting in a tunne euyr open to þe
sunne, and whan Alisaundre comaunde him to aske what he wold,
he prayed him for to remeue and stand no lenger in his lite.

Anno 4839-4863. 20

Anno 4864. Here is þe deth of Artarxerses, whech had regned
xxvi 3ere, in whech tyme Demostenes and Aristotoles floured in
philosophie.

Of Demostenes rede we þat whan Alisaundre cam to Attenes
in purpos to distroye þe cité, þis man was sette withoute þe gate 25
because he had be maistir onto þe kyng. This vndirstood Alisaundre, and at þe first site swore be Amon þe god þat whatsoeuyr
he desired, it schuld not be had. Than þe philisophre prayed him,
be þe vertu | of þe same Amon, þat he schul neuyr leue til he had   f. 33ʳᵃ
distroyed þe cité. And so þe kyng turnyd fro his purpose, seyng, 30
'Euyr is wisdam aboue power'.

Aristotel, at his age of xviii 3ere, was disciple to Plato, a man
of excellent wit and grete eloquens. He wrote all þe philosophi

2 his] hys his P   5 þei (1)] i *inserted on the line* M   8 endith]
over regneth *partially erased*, deieth *suprascript in red partially erased also* M
11 profered] P, pofered M   him (2)] *supplied, om.* MP   12 for] *om.* P
16 þi] thei P   18 him] *suprascript* M   21 deth] *over erasure* M
Artarxerses] Artraxerses P   had] *suprascript in red* M   22 and] *change
to darker ink* M   23 philosophie] philosphie P

8: cf. ibid. 448/183.
21–3: cf. ibid. 448/186–8.

and sette it in dew forme. Summe men seide þat he was þe son
of swech a spirit whech þei clepe incubus for þe lithnes of his
body an the sotilté of his witte.

Anno 4865–4867.

5   Anno 4868. Here deyed Xerses, þat was kyng iiii ȝere. He had
anothir name, Arsanius.

In þis tyme was Zenocrates in Attenis, whos chastité is mech
praised; for whan a faire strumpet was hired with a gret summe
þat sche schuld enclyne him to leccherie, boldly sche went to bed
10 and lay be him al nyte, and in þe morowning, whan þei þat hired
hir asked her mony ageyn, sche answerd þat hir comnaunt was to
ouircom a man and not a blok.

Anno 4869–4873.

Anno 4874. Here deyed Darius, whech was ouyrcom of Alisaundre.
15   Anno 4875–4878.

Anno 4879. Here deyed Grete Alisaundre, þat regned xii ȝere,
sex ȝere with Darie, and sex ȝere aftir his deth. (And here leue we
þe maner of countyng vsed befor, where we sette euyr the regner
in his last ȝere; fro þis tyme forward we wil set hem in her first
20 ȝere.) In þe sexte ȝere of Darie Alisaundre rejoysed þe kyngdam of
f. 33ʳᵇ Babilon, þat was þan, as we seid before, de|uolute to þe kyngdam
of Perse, and now to þe kyngdam of Macedonie. Thus was Alisaundre brout to þat empire, and sette mech good reule in euery
lond. He visited þe Temple in Jerusalem and relesed hem of her
25 tribute euery vii ȝere. He deyed in Babilonie, poisoned with venim.

Anno 4880. Here beginnith Ptholomeus for to regne, and he was
þe son of on Lagus, and he regned xl ȝere. And here is for to note,
whan Alisaundre deied, foure of his princes occupied al his
empire: this Ptholome, þe south, and dwelled in Egipte; Philippe,

---

1 it] *suprascript* M   þat] t *suprascript* M   5 deyed] *over* regneth
partially erased, dyeth *suprascript in red partially erased also* M, dieth P   þat
was kyng] *in r.h. margin* M   10 morowning] morowing P   11 was to]
in r.h. margin M   14 deyed] *over erasure, word suprascript in red erased also*
M   16 deyed] *over erasure, word suprascript in red erased also* M, deyeth P
þat regned] *suprascript* M   21 Babilon] *in r.h. margin* M   22 kyngdam]
kyndam P   25 poisoned] i *suprascript* M

5: cf. Isidore, 448/190.
7: cf. ibid. 448/191.
14: cf. ibid. 448/192.
16–17: cf. ibid. 449/195.
26–7: cf. ibid. 449/196.

Alisaundre brothir, he kept him in þe west; Antigonus, þe north;
and Seleucus þe est. But þis Ptholomeus, whech was cleped
Sother, he regned in Egipte, and in his secund ȝere began þe
kyngdam of Asie. First regned þere Antigonus xviii ȝere, and þan
regned Demetrius xvii ȝere, and þat same Demetrius resigned his 5
rite onto Seleucus, kyng of Surré, and so cesed þe kyngdam of
Asie. This same Seleucus mad iii grete citées: on hite Antioche;
þe othir hite Laodicia; þe þirde, Seleuce, aftir his name.

    Anno Mundi 4881–4918.   f. 33ᵛᵃ

    Anno 4920. Here beginnith þe regne of Ptholomeus Philadel- 10
phus, and he regned xxxviii ȝere.

    Vndir þis man þe lxx translatouris were in Egipte, and þei
translat þe lawe of God owt of Hebrew into Grek tonge. For grete
Alisaundre and his successouris studied gretly for to gader many
bokes into her tresoure, and specialy lawes and decrés to gouer- 15
nauns of puple. But þis man was most desirous in þis mater. For
he multiplied so bokes þat þere were founde in his librarie at
Alisaundre lxx þousand bokes. For he sent to Jerusalem onto
Eleazar þe bischop for to haue þe Elde Testament translate out of
Hebrew into Greke tonge. And þis Eleazar sent him lxx wel lerned 20
men, whech þe kyng put in sundri houses, and ech of hem translate be himselue. And þis miracle fel, þat whan her translacion
was broute togidir, þere was no discrepauns in sentens ne variauns
in wordes, be uertu, as we fynde, of þe Holy Goost.

    Anno 4921–4955.   25

    Anno 4956. Here regneth Ptholomeus Euergetes, cleped so for f. 33ᵛᵇ
he browt many ydoles oute of Surré and mad Egipte rich with
hem, for þei were of syluir and gold.

    In þis mannes tyme lyued Jesus, filius Sirac, þat mad a book
of þe Bible whech we clepe *Ecclesiasticus*, whech book, for þe 30
similitude of speche, summe men supposed it had be of Salamones
makyng. It is clepid *Ecclesiasticus*, þat is to sey 'Of þe Cherch',

---

   3 Egipte] *over erasure* M   his secund ȝere began] *over erasure* M   þe]
the P, *om.* M   6 rite] *in r.h. margin* M   9 Anno 4919 *om.* M
19 Ptholomeus] p *suprascript* M   23 togidir] togeders P   24 in wordes]
over erasure M   31 similitude] simlitude P

  10–11: cf. ibid. 449/200.
  12–13: cf. ibid. 449/201.
  26: cf. ibid. 450/204.
  29–30: cf. ibid. 450/205.

for þere is mech þing longing to þe obseruauns and prouidens of þe Cherch.

Anno 4957–4981.

Anno 4982. Ptholomeus Philopater, he regned vii ʒere. He had
5 þat name for he was fader of al wrecchidnes, for he left al þe good occupacion of knythod and vsed ydilnes, leccherie, insolens, manslawth—al nyte occupied with leccherie, al day in glotonye. He weddid his sistir, cleped Erudite; aftir he killid hir. Þan had he euyr chaunge of women. And for þis cursed lyf Antio-
10 chus Magnus tok him, and killid him, and all his strumpettis he hing hem on galowis.

Anno 4983–4988.

f. 34ʳᵃ Anno 4989. Ptholome, clepid Epiphanes, he regned in Alisaundre xxxiiii ʒere, and for he was but v ʒere old whan he began to regne,
15 þerfor þei of Alisaundre sent onto þe Romaynes for to help her ʒong kyng ageyn þe power of Grete Antiochus. And þan þe Romaynes sent too legatis onto þis Antiochus, þat he schuld go oute of Egipte and do no harm to her frendis. And whan þis child was growe onto age, he weddid þe doutir of þe same Anti-
20 ochus, whech hite Cleopatra.

In þis same tyme lyued þe eloquent man whech hite Plauctus, and for al his eloquens he was compelled for pouert for to dwelle with a baxter and grinde his corn at a qwerne, and whan he had leisere, þan wold he write tales of ful grete sentens.

25 Anno Mundi 4990–5022.

Anno 5023. Ptholomeus Philometor regned in Egipt xxxv ʒere.

And in his tyme lyued þat conquerour at Rome whom þei clepe Scipio Affricanus. He was cleped so for þe grete conquestes þat
f. 34ʳᵇ he | had on Cartage, whech cité stant in Affrik. It was he þat coun-
30 celed þe Senate þat Cartage schuld not be distroyed. For whan

---

4 Philopater] pater *over erasure* M   5 wrecchidnes] wrechidnese P, wrech|chidnes *over line division* M   9 þan] n *over erasure* M   10 Magnus] Mangnus P   13 Ptholome] *change to darker ink* M   21 Plauctus] Planctus P   22 dwelle] dwel *at line end* M, dwell P   26 Ptholomeus] Pthomeus P

4: cf. Isidore, 450/206.
4–11: cf. Higden, iv. 40/2–13.
13–14: cf. Isidore, 450/209.
13–20: cf. Higden, iv. 74/3–20.
26: cf. Isidore, 451/212.
27–8: cf. ibid. 451/214.

þe Romaynes left her werre with Cartage, þan be ydilnesse began
mech debate in þe cité, euele drautes in þe puple, comnauntes
broken, opyn extorsion, pryuy theft; þerfor wold þis man þat
Cartage schuld not be distroyed, þat drede schuld oppresse leccherie, and bisinesse schuld distroye auarice. This man was 5
byried in straunge lond, and this vers writin on his graue, 'O
onkynd cuntré, my bones schal þou not haue'.

In þis tyme þe Romaynes conqwerd a grete part of Grece.

And in þis same tyme Judas Machabeus and his bretherin
conqwered þe lond of Jude, killid her enmies, purged þe Temple, 10
and had victorie of ful many tyrauntis.

Anno 5024–5057.

Anno 5058. Ptholome, cleped Euergetes þe Secunde, regned
xxix ȝere.

Vndir his tyme deied þe noble poete Terrencius, þat wrote so 15
many trajedies, whose graue was wrytin with þese vers:—

> Natus in excelsis tectis Cartagenis alte,
> Romanis ducibus | bellica preda fui.   f. 34ᵛᵃ
> Descripsi mores hominum, iuuenumque senumque,
> Quid meretrix, quid leno dolis, quid fingat auarus.   20
> Hec quoque qui legit, sic, puto, cautus erit.

Thus þei mene in Englisch:—

> Born in the toures hy in þe cité of Cartage,
> To þe dukes of Rome pray of bataile was I.
> I haue descriued þe maneris of men both eld and ȝong,   25
> What gile in woman is, what feyning in couetise.
> He þat redith al þis, þe betyr he may be war.

Anno 5059–5085.

Anno 5086. Ptholome, cleped Sother or ellis Phiscon, regned
xvii ȝere first. This man weddid his owne sistir, and aftir, in þe 30

---

1 her] P, *om.* M   3 theft] P, therft M   6 this] *over erasure* M
15 Terrencius] *suprascript in red* M   16 with] *om.* P   20 meretrix]
meretix P   24 pray] prynce P   27 þe] *suprascript* M   war] *in r.h.*
margin M   29 Phiscon] Phiston P

8: cf. ibid. 450/210ᵃ.
9–11: cf. ibid. 450/210.
13–14: cf. ibid. 451/215.
15: cf. ibid. 451/214ᵃ.
29–30: cf. ibid. 451/217.

first day of þe wedding, he killid hir child, whech was eyir of þe
lond. In þe xvii ȝere of his regne his moder Cleopatra, be grete
power, mad him to fle fro his lond and dwelle in þe ylde of Cipre.
Whan he was þere he killid anothir child of his, and put it in a
5 forser, and sent it to his modir and his wif at her fest, þe same day
þat þe qween was bore.

 Anno Mundi 5087–5102.

 Anno 5103. Here þe Qween Cleopatra, aftir Ptholome was
f. 34ᵛᵇ exiled, mad hir | ȝonger son kyng, whech hite Ptholome Alisaun-
10 dre. This man grew onto swech cruelnes þat he killid his owne
moder; þerfor þe puple ros vpon him, exiled him, and called in his
broþir oute of Cipre to regne ageyn.

 Anno 5104–5112.

 Anno 5113. Ptholome Sother, or ellis Phiscon, regneth ageyn
15 viii ȝere.

 Anno 5114–5119.

 Anno 5120. Here regneth Ptholome Dionisius x ȝere.

 Anno 5121–5129.

 Anno 5130. Here regnith Cleopatra. This woman was doutir
20 onto þe forseid Dionisius. And here is diuersité in counting of
ȝeres, for sum sey þat hir regne began here, and summe sey þat
sche regned to ȝere be hirselue, and þanne vndir Julius v ȝere,
and vndir Octauian xv ȝere.

f. 35ʳᵃ Anno 5131–5149.

25 Anno 5150. Here goth þe regne of Egipt onto þe Romaynes;
for Julius Cesar conquered Egipt and put it vndir tribute. And
in þis same tyme was þis lond conquered be þe same Julius þorw
mediacioun of a lord þei cleped Androche, whech was broþir to
þe kyng, his name was Cassebelian.

30 Anno 5151–5156.

 Anno 5157. Octauian began to regne þe ȝere of the world v

---

2 Cleopatra] Clepatra P 5 wif] *suprascript* M 8 Cleopatra]
Clepatra P 14 Phiscon] Phiston P 17 Anno 5120] *twice* M
19 This] *change to darker ink* M 27 þe] thys P

8–10: cf. Isidore, 451/220.
14–15: cf. ibid. 452/223.
17: cf. ibid. 452/226.
19–23: cf. Higden, iv. 188/5–8.
25–6: cf. Isidore, 452/232.
27: cf. ibid. 453/233ᵇ.

PLATE VI

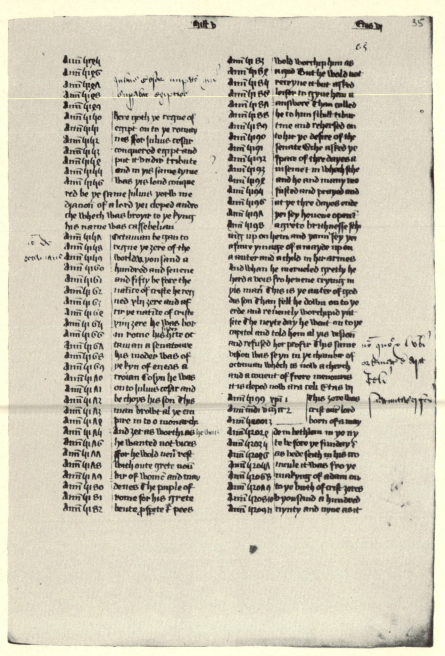

Cambridge University Library MS Gg.4.12, fol. 35ʳ (reduced): the page on which the birth of Christ is recorded. Anno Domini year numbers are given in red ink after the Anno Mundi numbers.

þousand a hundred and seuene and fifty; before the natiuité
of Criste he regned xlii ȝere, and aftir þe natiuité of Criste, xiiii
ȝere. He was bor in Rome—his fader hite Octauian, a senatoure;
his moder was of þe kyn of Eneas, a Troian. Cosyn he was onto
Julius Cesar and be choys his son. This man browt al þe empire 5
into o monarchi. And ȝet, as worthi as he was, he wanted not
vices; for he wold neuyr rest withoute grete noumbir of women
and maydenes.

The puple of Rome, for his grete beuté, prosperité, and pees, |
wold worchip him as a god. But he wold not receyue it, but asked f. 35ʳᵇ
leiser to gyue hem a answere. Than called he to him Sibille Tibur- 11
tine, and rehersed onto hir þe desire of the Senate. Sche asked
þe space of thre dayes auisement, in whech sche and he and many
mo fasted and prayed, and at þe thre dayes ende þei sey heuene
open and a grete brithnesse schining upon hem; and þanne sey 15
þei a faire ymage of a mayde upon a auter and a child in hir
armes. And whan he merueled gretly, he herd a vois fro heuene
crying in þis maner, 'This is þe auter of Goddis Son'. Than fell
he down onto þe erde, and reuerently worchipid þat site. The
nexte day he went onto þe Capitol, and told hem al þis visioun, 20
and refused her profir. This same vision was seyn in þe chambir of
Octauian, whech is now a cherch and a couent of Frere Menouris;
it is cleped now *Ara Celi*.

Anno 5158–5198.

Etas VI   25

Anno 5199; Cristi 1. This ȝere was Crist oure Lord born of a
mayde in Bethlem in þe nyte before þe Sunday, and as Bede seith
in his cronicule, it was fro þe makyng of Adam onto þe birth of
Crist ȝeres v þousand a hundred nynty and nyne, as it | is con- f. 35ᵛᵃ
teyned in þese vers:—   30

Vnum tolle datis ad milia quinque ducentis,
Nascente Domino tot Beda dat prothoplausto.

---

3 fader] *suprascript with caret* (*in red*) M   6 he was] *in r.h. margin* M
13 auisement] i *surmounted by short stroke in red* M   20 hem] hym P
22 Octauian] Octouian P   23 now] *om.* P   25 Etas VI] *in red* M,
om. P   27 nyte] nynte *or* nyute P

1–2: Martinus, 408/11.
2–23: ibid. 443/25–42.
26–7: ibid. 408/11–12.

This is þe sentens: 'Take on fro v þousand and to hundred; so many ȝeres be fro Adam onto Crist'.

Anno Mundi v Milia cc—Anno 5201–5209; 2–11.

Anno 5210; 12. This ȝere was Crist founde in þe Temple
5 amongis doctores.

And Tiberius was mad emperour þe xiiii ȝere of Crist, and he regned xxiii ȝere, xviii ȝere before þe passion, and v ȝere aftir.

In þis same tyme was Ouyde þe poete ded in exile.

And in þis same tyme Pilate was mad president of Jude.

10 Anno 5211–5217; 13–19.

Anno 5218; 20. In all þese ȝeres tyl Crist was xxx ȝere of age, þe gospell makith no gret declaracion of his dedis, but withoute ony doute he lyued a parfit lyf and ded many miracles, þou þei be not wrytin in bokis.

15 Anno 5219–5227; 21–29.

Anno 5228; 30. In þis ȝere was Crist oure Lord baptized, whan he was xxx ȝere old. And in þis same ȝere he turned watir into wyn.

And in þis same ȝere he chase his xii apostoles, of whech
20 Petir was first, born in Bethsaida, broþir onto Andrew, whom Crist mad prince to þe apostolis; sex and xxx ȝere aftir þe passioun of Crist he was martired at Rome vndir Nero.

Poule was not chose be Crist in his lyue, but aftir þe ascencioun |
f. 35ᵛᵇ with gret lite and ferful wordes turned to þe feith, whech in
25 honour is sette next Petir for his general labour in preching, and eke for þei both were ded for Crist in o cité and in o day.

Andrew was brothir onto Petir, þat was eke in Achay, and martired on a crosse.

Jacobus, brothir to Jon Euangelist, þe son of Zebede and Salome,
30 prechid in Spayne and deied in Jerusalem.

Jon þe Euangelist, his broþir, was exiled to Pathmos, wher he mad þe *Apocalips*, but he deied in Ephese, noþing founde in his graue but manna.

Thomas was he þat groped þe woundes of Crist; he was slayn
35 with a spere in Ynde.

3 5201] 52001 M   19 And] *om.* P   22 Nero] *suprascript* M
31 Pathmos] Pthmos P

4–5: cf. Higden, iv. 290.
6–9: Martinus, 444/12–22.
16–18: ibid. 408/41–2.

Philippe was eke of Bethsaide; in a cité of Frise, cleped Ieraple, he was put on þe cros.

Jacobus, þe son of Joseph, first bischop of Jerusalem, was þrowe þere fro þe pinacle of þe Temple and aftir smet with a fulleres bat.   5

Bartholomé prechid in þe region of Armenie, and þere in Albanie, her grete cité, he was both flayn and hedid.

Mathew, apostel and euangelist, mad his euangelie in Rome, aftir þat prechid in Macedonie, was slayn in Persida.

Simon, born in þe strete of Chana, prechid in Egipt, aftir   10 bischop of Jerusalem, and martired in þe same place.

Judas, whech is clepid Thadeus, was martired in Erico, a cité of Armeni.

Matheu was on of þe lxx disciples, and for Judas chosen. Anno 5229–5230; 31–32.   15

Anno 5231; 33. This ȝere was Crist ded for sauacion of man; for Cristus seith þat he was xxxiii ȝere old whan he deied and as mech more as was fro his birth onto Pase, and | be þat counting he   f. 36ʳᵃ deied in þe xxxiiii ȝere of his age.

Anno 5232–5233; 34–35.   20

Anno 5234; 36. Here seid Petir his first messe.

Anno 5235; 37.

Anno 5236; 38. Here is Gayus emperour. In þis ȝere Petir cam to Antioche, and Matheu writith his godspel.

Anno 5240–5253; 42–55. Here regneth Claudius, þat ȝaue   25 bataile onto þis lond, and killid þe kyng, clepid Gwynderyn. Than was Aruigarus, brothir to þe forseyd kyng, whech was acorded to Claudius in þis maner, þat he schuld wedde þe emperoures doutir and be kyng vndir Claudius; and at her wedding the emperour ded make a good town, and called it aftir his name   30 Kayerglau, þat is to seyn þe cyté of Gloucestir. This emperour Claudius was so obliuiows þat, sone aftir he had killid his wyf, he asked why sche cam not to soper.

1 eke] *om.* P   4 þe (2)] the *twice over line division* P   12 was] war P
Erico] Jerico P   21 seid] seith P   Petir] *om.* P   23 is] *suprascript* M
27 Aruigarus] Aruigarius P

21: ibid. 408/46.
23–4: ibid. 444/28 and 409/1–5.
25–6: ibid. 444/32–3.
26–31: cf. *Brut*, i. 35/7–28.
31–3: Martinus, 444/35.

In þis same tyme was Linus pope, whech ordeyned þat women schuld with lynand cure her heer.

Anno 5254–5267; 56–69. Nero regned aftir þis Claudius, of all men wrecchidhest, redy to al maner vices, vndir whom Petir and
5 Poule were martired, Petir in a place cleped Vaticanus, in þe weye
f. 36rb þat is called Aurea, and Poule in a strete | called Hostiense, in a place þat is cleped *Aput Aquas Saluias*, 'At þe Scipping Wateres'—for Poules hed scippid thries aftir it was fro þe body, and at euery scip þere sprang a welle, þerfor is þat place clepid
10 soo.

Anno 5268–5278; 70–80. Vespasian regned aftir Gabba, whech regned but ix monthis. He was sent be Nero to Palestyn for to withstand þe rebellion of Jewis, and þere þe knytis of þe hoost chose him to þe empire. But of homely kyn was he born, but
15 endewid he was with þe best maneres. Summe sey þat he was cured of a greuous sekenes of waspis in his nose, and cured be sith of þe vernicle; and þis cure excited him to venge Cristis deth. He deied of þe flux of blood, and whan deth cam he stood rite up and seide, 'It semeth a kyng for to stand and dey'.

20 Anno 5279–5281; 81–83. Titus regned iii ȝere. This man with his fader destroyed Jerusalem, and all þe precious þingis þat were þere brout hem to Rome, and sette hem in þe Temple of Pes. He was swech a louer of vertue þat he was cleped þe most delicious of all men. So liberal eke was he þat no man went fro
25 him withoute reward.

In þis tyme Cletus was pope xi ȝere, whech cursed al þoo þat
f. 36va lette ony pilgrime to go to Rome. He deyed a martyr, | and byried in Vaticano.

Anno 5282–5296; 84–98. Domician regned xv ȝere. This
30 man was brothir onto Titus. In his first ȝeres he was resonabely good; and in his last ȝeres al defiled witȝ vices, so fer-forth þat al þe godnes of þe fader and þe vertu of his brothir be his vices

---

4 wrecchidhest] wrecchidnes P   14 him] *in r.h. margin* M   15 was (1)]
in r.h. margin M   27 pilgrime] pilgrimage P   32 vices] P, vice M

1–2: Martinus, 409/41–2.
3: ibid. 444/47.
11–19: ibid. 445/14–19.
20–3: ibid. 445/21 and 15–17.
23–5: cf. Higden, iv. 458.
26–8: Martinus, 410/3–10.
29–51/5: ibid. 445/29–36.

was forgete. He killid many nobel senatoures, and comaunded
þat euery man schuld clepe him god, and þat his ymages schuld
not be mad but of gold or siluyr. He put Jon the Euangelist in a
boilyng tunne of oyle, and þanne exiled him. In his tyme Seynt
Denise was martired at Paris.   5

And in þe viii ȝere of his regne was Clement mad pope of Rome,
whech astat he kept ix ȝere, for in þe tyme of Trajane his body was
þrow into þe se, and aftir broute to Rome.

Anno 5297; 99. Nerua was emperour but o ȝere. This man
dampned al þat Domician ordeyned, and for þat cause Seynt Jon   10
Euangelist was delyueryd fro his exile and cam to Ephese.

Anno 5298–5316; 100–118. Trajane regned in Rome xix ȝere.
This man multiplied þat empire gretly; for he conquered Asie,
Babilonie, and mech of Ynde. This man killid ny þe þird part of
Cristen men, not be his owne malice, but be stering | of his   f. 36ᵛᵇ
councel. Vndir him was martired Seint Ignace, bischop of Anti- 16
oche, disciple to Jon Euangelist. This mannes hert, whan it was
open, þei founde þe name of Jesu writin þere with letteris of gold.
In þis tyme was Eustace, his wif, and her issew, martired for Crist.

And þis tyme lyued Plutarc þe philisophre, maistir onto Trajan, 20
þat wrot onto him a book, where he counceled him þat he schuld
sese fro þe persecucion of Cristen men; for, as he wrote, þere
coude be founde no defaute in hem but þat þei worchiped no
ydolis, and rysin erly in þe morowning, and songin ympnis
to on þei cleped Crist—and as it is seide, þe emperour fro þat 25
tyme was not so cruel.

In his tyme was Simon Cleophas, bischop of Jerusalem, martired and put on þe crosse.

And in þe first ȝere of Trajane was Anaclete pope, a Grek of
nacioun, ix ȝere. He ordeyned þat prestis schuld no berdis haue. 30
He is biried in Vaticano.

---

3 Euangelist] *in r.h. margin* M   in a] *in l.h. margin* M   4 his] thys P
19 Eustace] Eustate P   20 tyme] *in r.h. margin with carets (in red)* M
þe philisophre] *om.* P   24 morowning] morowinge P   25 Crist and]
separated by thin stroke in red M   27 his] thys P   29 Anaclete]
te *suprascript* M

6–8: ibid. 410/11, 21–5.
9–11: ibid. 446/1–2.
12–28: ibid. 446/3–24.
29–31: ibid. 410/30–3.

The x ȝere of Trajane was Euaristus pope, a Jew, bore in
Bethlem. He dyuyded þe titeles þat cardinalis haue, and he
ordeyned þat vii deknes schuld kepe a bischop whan he prechid, for
drede of enmyes of þe feith. He was pope x ȝere, byried in Vaticano.

5   Anno 5317–5337; 119–139. Adriane regned xxi ȝere. He
went to Jerusalem and punchid þere þe Jewis þat were rebelle,
f. 37ʳᵃ and repaired þe Temple, put oute Jewis, and put | in hethen
men, and sette þere his ymage as a god. He mad eke a precept þat
no Jew into Jerusalem schuld entre, but Cristen men he forbade
10   not þe entré. Vndir him was martired þe holy mayde Seraphia,
þat cam fro Antioche and dwelled with anoþir mayde þei cleped
Sabine. In þis tyme was a philisophre cleped Secundus, þat kept
silens al his lif and answerd euyr be writing.

And in þis time was Alisaundre pope, þat ordeyned haliwatir,
15   and þat wyn schuld be put in þe chalis and watir þerto. In þis
tyme lyued on Aquila, þat translate þe Eld Testament out of
Hebrev into Grek.

In þe x ȝere of Adrian was Sixte þe First mad pope. He ordeyned þat Sanctus schuld be sunge at sacri, and no man schuld
20   handel þe chales but ministeris of þe auter. He was hedid withoute
gate þat is cleped Appia, and biried in Vaticano.

In þe xix ȝere of Adrian was Thelophorus mad pope, whech
was first a ancorite. He ordeyned þere schul no man say masse
before þat he had seid þe ters, þat is to sey, 'Legem pone'. He
25   ordeyned þo iii masses on Cristmas morow. He deied a martir,
biried in Vaticano.

Anno 5338–5360; 140–162. Antoni þe Meke regned xxiii
ȝere with his sones; he was cleped so for he mad many men of
pité for to forgyve her det. And eke he was good to Cristen men,
f. 37ʳᵇ for he | suffered hem to dwelle in pes in her owne places, not for
31   to by ne selle with no oþir men.

4 enmyes] em|nyes *over line division* P   6 þere] *om.* P   7 Temple]
Tempull P, Tem *at line end* M   13 lif and] *separated by small hole in
vellum* M   14–15 And . . . þerto] *in l.h. margin, position for inclusion in text
indicated by signes de renvoi in red* M   16 þat] t *suprascript* M   21 gate]
the gate P   23 say] schuld sey P   24 he] *suprascript with caret* (*in red*) M

1–4: Martinus, 410/40–6.
5–13: ibid. 446/25–41.
14–17: ibid. 410/46–411/3.
18–21: ibid. 411/4–8.
22–6: ibid. 411/16–20.
27–53/8: ibid. 446/46–447/12.

In þis tyme was lyuyng þe gret leche cleped Galiene at Rome,
þat had first studied at Alisaundre and in Rodis. He mad many
bokis of þis craft, whos names be þese: *Almagest*, *Perspectif*,
Centilogie, and oþir. Summe sey þat Ptholome, kyng of Egipt,
mad þis *Almagest*—perauenture þis man mored it or set it in 5
oþir forme; and sum sey þat þe same Galiene hite Ptholome—
he was of mene stature, white of colour, sone wroth, litil eter,
swete of onde, his cloþing white.

In þe viii ȝere of Antoni was pope of Rome Yginius, born in
Atenes. He ordeyned þat euery child, both in baptem and con- 10
firmacion, schuld haue godfadir and godmodyr. He was biried in
þe cherch of Seynt Petir.

And aftir him was Pius, born in Itaile, in whos tyme Hermes
wrote a book þat Estern-day schuld euyr be solempnyzed on a
Sunday, for a aungell appered to þe same Hermes and comaunded 15
þe same. And Pollicarpe, þat was disciple to Seyn Jon Euangeliste,
cam onto Rome for to reforme all þe bischoppis of Asie to þe
same reule; for þei alle onto þat tyme were vsed, in the cerymonie
of Jewis, for to hald Pase-day euir in þe myd monthe, þat is to sey,
þe xv day. 20

Anno 5361–5379; 163–181. Marcus Antoni þe Trewe, with
Lucye his bro|thir, regned xix ȝere. In þis ȝere began at Rome to   f. 37va
regne to emperoures. This man was good in gouernauns and,
aftir his name, trew in his dedis, but for al þat was þere grete
persecucion ageyn Cristen men in his tyme. And in þese dayes was 25
þe good old man Pollicarp, disciple to Jon þe Euangelist, martired
for Crist, and xii worthi men with him of þe cité cleped Philadelphia—þis was in Asia. And in Frauns was killid Seynt Justus,
bischop of Mamert, and Seynt Forcius, bischop of Lugdunense,
with many oþir martires. In þis tyme lyued þe notable writer of 30
stories of þe Cherch whech þei cleped Egecippus. And in þis

2 Rodis] þᵉ Rodys P   4 Ptholome] Pthome P   5 mored]
ed *suprascript with caret* (*in red*) M   7 wroth] worth P   10 child]
suprascript with caret (*in red*) M   17 for] *om.* P   22 Lucye his brothir]
Lucye his bro|thir Lucy *over page division* M, Lucye hys brothir Lucy P
ȝere (2)] *in r.h. margin with carets* (*in red*) M   27 cleped] clepe d *separated
by small hole in vellum* M   29 Lugdunense] Lugdumense P

9–12: ibid. 411/26–9.
13–20: ibid. 411/33–43.
21–54/2: ibid. 447/15–27.

tyme leued Praxede, þat with hir sistir Potencian byryed many a martir.

In þe first ȝere of þis Antonie was pope at Rome Anicetus. He mad a statute in the Cherch þat þere schuld no bischop be con-
5 secrate but of iii bischoppes at þe leest. He was biried in the cymytery of Kalixt.

And in þe x ȝere of þis Antonie was Sother pope; he ordeyned þat þere schuld no nunne handel the corporas ne cast non encense in þe cherch. He ordeyned eke þat þere schuld no man use his wif
10 but if þei were first offered be here frendis and blessed be þe prest. He was byried in Vaticano.

f. 37ᵛᵇ In þe xix ȝere of | Antoni was Eleutheri pope of Rome, a Grek of nacioun. He receyued a letter fro þe kyng of Grete Britayn, cleped Lucius, þat he schuld sende summe prestes to þis lond to
15 baptize him and his puple. And þe pope sent hedir Fugan and Damian, whech performed þis dede. Summe cronicles sey þis was in ȝere of oure Lord 165.

Anno 5380–5397; 182–199. Helius Pertinax regned xviii ȝere. In his tyme lyued þe fourt translatour of the Bibil, cleped
20 Simachus. And Narciscus was bischop of Jerusalem, a man ful of uertue. Terculian eke, a grete writer, was þat tyme. And Origene taute þanne at Alisaundre, whos wryting passith al oþir. This Helius Pertinax was a wel agid man; rithful in al maner þing, neuyr took he giftes of man.

25 He regned but vi monthes, and al þe oþir tyme occupied Seuerus, whech was a man euyr redy to batayl, weel lerned in bokes, and liberal in giftis. He began þe v persecucion ageyn Cristen men and killid many martires: on of hem was called Leoncius, fader onto Origene—and þan was Origene left of ȝong
30 age, with his moder and vii bretherin, whech with his teching of gramer susteyned hem alle. Yreneus, a grete clerk, bischop of Lugdune, was martired þat tyme.

8 handel] handyll P, handeled *followed by* handel *expuncted* M   12 of Rome] P, *om.* M   13 Britayn] Brytaỹng P   18 *the year numbers* 5386 *and* 5387 *both written without* 53 *because of small hole in vellum* M   20 Narciscus] Nariscus P   26 redy] rydy *with 1st* y *surmounted by* e *in red* M   29 fader] *suprascript with caret (in red)* M

1–2: see p. 53.
3–6: Martinus, 411/44–412/2.
7–11: ibid. 412/7–12.
12–16: ibid. 412/15–19.
18–32: ibid. 447/45–448/5.

And in þis | tyme was Victor pope of Rome. He gadered a   f. 38ʳᵃ
councell in Alisaundre, þat stant in Palestin, and þere he mad a
lawe þat Pase-day schuld be on Sunday euyr betwix þe xiiii day
of þe month and þe xxi. He ordeyned þat euery man þat wold be
Cristen mite be baptized, for nede, in euery watir, flood, welle, or   5
strem, so þat he mad confession of þe feith. He was martired, and
byried in Vaticano.

Anno Mundi 5398–5404; 200–206. Antonius Carcalla regned
vii ȝere. He was clepid Carcalla for a certeyn maner of cloþing
þat he was first fynder. This man was defiled with all wikkidnes.   10
In his dayes was found þe v translacion of þe Elde Lawe, but who
mad it is in doute. This Antonie was so leccherous þat he weddid
his owne fader wyf. He held batail ageyn þe Perses, and þere he
deied, biried in Edissa.

In his tyme was Zepherine pope. He ordeyned þat eueri   15
Cristen man schuld receyue þe blessed sacrament on Pase-day.

Anno 5405; 207. Matrinus regned but o ȝere. Befor his empire
he was a prefecte of þe court, and for envye he lost his heed.

Anno 5406–5409; 208–211. Antonius Aurelius regned iiii
ȝere. In his tyme ros þe heresie of Sabelly. He was before a prest   20
of a temple cleped Eliogabelum. He left no memorie aftir him
but euel exaumple of hordam, leccherie, and sweche stinking
synne; therfor þe knytes | risin ageyn him, and killid him, and his   f. 38ʳᵇ
modir eke.

In þese dayes was Kalixtus pope, whech mad þe cherch of oure   25
Lady in Transtibir, where þe welles runne oyle and wyn on þat
day þat Crist was bore. He ordeyned eke þe fastyng on þe Ymbir-
dayes. He mad þe cymyteri Via Appia vndir þe chirch of Sebastian,
and þere was he biried aftir his martirdam.

Anno 5410–5422; 212–224. Alexander Mammeas regned xiii   30
ȝere; he was cleped Mammeas for it was his modir name. This
man gouerned knythod on þe best maner, and lawe he norched in þe

11 dayes] tyme P   17 Matrinus] Mairinus P   22 leccherie]
rie *suprascript* M   25 Kalixtus] balixtus P   28 Sebastian] Sebastian P

1–7: ibid. 412/29–37.
8–14: ibid. 448/11–14.
15–16: ibid. 412/38–40.
17–18: ibid. 448/15.
19–24: ibid. 448/16–18.
25–9: ibid. 412/49–413/2.
30–56/13: ibid. 448/19–31.

best wise; for Vulpinianus, a gret maker of lawes, was gretly norchid be him. He was killid in Mens at a grete trouble and rising of knytes.

In his tyme Origene was in his floures, and most honourable in þe Cherch in sciens, eloquens, and witte; for þan mad he bokes of
5 grete sentens. For he had, beside oþir writeres, vii maydenes and vii ȝong men þat wrytyn dyuers bokes whech he endited and reported onto hem, and þat of dyuers materes. For as Seynt Jerom seith, he red of his making sex þousand volumes, beside episteles and many oþir werkis. Ther went a prouerbe of him in þat lond:
f. 38va 'His doctrine was lich his lyf: vpon bed he lay neuyr; | hosen and
11 schon wered he nowt; he ete neuyr flesch, ne drank neuyr wyn'. With his writyng Mammea, þe emperour moder, was cristen; and sche mad hir son more esy and sesed mech his persecucion.

In þis tyme was Urbane pope viii ȝere. He conuertid Valerian,
15 þe spouse of Cicile, and baptized him and his brothir. In þis tyme began the Cherch to haue possession of lond and hous, but not so largely as it had in þe tyme of Siluestir. And with þis possession Vrban hered notaries to write treuly þe lyf of martires.

Anno 5423–5425; 225–227. Maximiane regned iii ȝere, a
20 grete enmy to Cristen men.

Anno 5426–5431; 228–233. Gordian regned vi ȝere, that had grete victorie up þe Perses and in his comyng hom was slayn be treson.

In þis tyme was Poncian pope, þat was exiled, and dyed a martir.

And þan was Cyriacus pope, but, for he resyned and went with
25 xi þousand maydnes, he is not put in þe cateloge of popes.

Next him was Anteros pope—he was a Grek.

And þan was Fabian pope, and he was chosen be a wite dowe lityng on his hed. He ordeyned þat euery ȝere on Schere or Maundé þursday þe pope schuld consecrate crisme. He dyuyded
30 Rome onto vii regiones, and to euery region preferred he a decun, to write treuly þe lyf of holy martires.

---

13 and (2)] P, *twice over line division* M   14 Valerian] Valarian P
22 Perses] *1st* e *altered from* i M   and] P, ad M   24 pope] *suprascript* M
resyned] P, resyne M   27 Fabian] Fabiam P   28 on (2)] n *over*
erasure M

1–13: see p. 55.
14–18: Martinus, 413/4–12.
19–20: ibid. 448/34–5.
21–2: ibid. 448/37–9.
23–5: ibid. 413/14–19.
26: ibid. 413/22.
27–31: ibid. 413/25–36.

Anno 5432–5438; 234–240. Philippicus, with his son Philip,
reg|ned vii зere. This was þe first Cristen emperour. And in þe   f. 38ᵛᵇ
first зere of his empire was euene a þousand зere sith þe cyté of
Rome was begunne. And for þis cause þei of Rome mad a ful
grete solempnité, whech lested iii dayes and iii nytes. This em-   5
perour was baptized of Seynt Ponciaun in þe cité cleped Prouynce.
And both þe fader and þe son were killid, þe fadir at Rome, þe
son at Veron. This son was so sobir of chere þat þere mite no
myrth make him lawh. These too emperoures in her deth beqwathe
al her ricchesse to þe Cherch and Seynt Sixte; for whech Seynt   10
Laurens aftirward was, in þe tyme of Decius, put to þe deth.

Anno 5439–5440; 241–242. Decius regned ii зere, a cursed
venjabil man onto Cristen men; for vndir him were killid so many
þat his tyme was clepid þe vii persecucioun.

In his tyme was Cornelius pope. He lifte up þe bones of Petir   15
and Paule fro þe place cleped catacumbis, and Seynt Lucy, a
widow, receyued þe bones of Paule and sette hem in hir possession
in þe strete cleped Hostiense. The bonis of Petir sette Cornely
in Vatican, þat was sumtyme Nero paleys.

Anno 5441–5442; 243–244. Gallus and Uolucianus regned ii   20
зere, and of her tyme is litil writing. In þese dayes lyued þat
famous clerk and martir cleped Cipriane, whech was bischop of
Cartage.

And in þis tyme was Lucius pope. He ordeyned þat too prestis
and iii deknes schuld euyr be present with a bischop. He deied a   25
martir vndir Valerian.

Anno 5443–5457; 245–259. Valeriane, with his son Galiene,   f. 39ʳᵃ
regned xv зere. This man held batayl in Jerusalem and Mesopotamy ageyn Sapor, kyng of Pers, and þat same Kyng Sapor ouyrcam him to a schameful seruyse, þat, as long as þe kyng of Pers   30
lyued, he schuld stand on his bak, and Valerian ly, and so schuld

---

6 Ponciaun] Poncan P   7 son] some P   7–8 þe son] *in r.h.*
margin M   8 so] P, *om.* M   mite] *suprascript* M   9 These] Thes P,
Theso M   11 aftirward] aftyrward P, aftirwar M   18 bonis] nis *over*
erasure M

1–11: ibid. 448/41–449/4.
12–14: ibid. 449/9–10.
15–19: ibid. 413/43–6.
20–3: ibid. 449/12–13.
24–6: ibid. 414/1–3.
27–58/12: ibid. 449/15–25.

he take his hors. This man spilt mech Cristen blod, for vndir him were martired Lucius, þe pope, and Cipriane, þe bischop.

Galiene in his beginning was just and good to þe comnaunté, aftir þat ful dissolute in many vices; therfor God suffered him to
5 be killid with deceyte of on Aurely, a duke.

Vndir þis same Valeriane were martired both Sixte and Laurens be on Decius, þat was no emperour, but a meyhir, and þerfor is he cleped Decius Minor. It is seid þat Seynt Sixte went fro Rome to Spayn and þens he browt to fayre ȝong men, Laurens and
10 Vincent, cosynes of blod, and vertuous of maneris. These too broute he onto Rome: Laurens abod stille þere, Vincent turned ageyn to Spayn, and was martired vndir Dioclecian.

In þe þird ȝere of Valerian was Steuene pope. He ordeined þat prestes and deknes schuld not were here vestimentis but in
15 þe cherch. He was killid at messe and lith befor þe auter in þe cherch of Seynt Sebastian.

f. 39ʳᵇ And in þe vi ȝere | of Valerian was Sixtus pope. He ordeyned þat messe schulde be said upon a auter. He was martired with many mo, and aftir him iii daies was Laurens rosted on a grate.

20 And in þe x ȝere of þis Valeriane was Dionise pope. He departed þe cité of Rome into diuerse parches, and ordeyned cherchis and cymeteries and prestis for to serue, made lawe eke þat euery preste schuld kepe his owne cure, and non medel with othir.

Anno 5458–5459; 260–261. Claudius regned to ȝere and mad
25 grete conquest upon þe Gothis, upon Macedonie, and a cuntré is clepit Illiricum; and whan he had ouyrcome mech of Almayn he deied, þei sei, of pestilens.

In his tyme was Euticianus pope, and before him Felix. Felix ordeyned þat messes schuld be songe up martires graues. Eutician
30 gadered þe bodies of martires, and mad auteres upon her graues. He was biried in Kalixte cymiteri.

Anno 5460–5464; 262–266. Aurelianus regned v ȝere. This man

---

2 martired] d *suprascript* M   10 too] P, *om.* M   28 his] this P
29 up] vpon P   30 mad] *in r.h. margin* M

1–12: see p. 57.
13–16: Martinus, 414/4–7.
17–19: ibid. 414/8–11.
20–3: ibid. 414/12–18.
24–7: ibid. 449/27–8.
28–31: ibid. 414/20–8.
32–59/6: ibid. 449/30–8.

mad gret persecucion onto Cristen men, and þerfor was he smet
with a leuene and þundir, but not ded. This man was þe first þat
arayed his diademe with gold and gemmes. He walled eke þe
cité with strenger walles. A cité þat stant in Frauns, whech hite
sumtyme Genabum, he restored it, and called it aftir his name 5
Aurelianense—we clepe it Orgliauns.

Anno 5465–5470; 267–272. Probus regned | vi ȝere. He ouyr- f. 39ᵛᵃ
cam in batayl too grete kyngis.

And in his tyme was Gayus pope, born in Dalmacie, cosyn to
Dioclecian. He ordeyned þat þe ordres schuld be þus disposed in 10
þe Cherch: þat he þat schuld be mad a bischop schuld first be a
benet, in whech is included too or iii offices, and þan a colet, and
þan subdiacone, diacone, and prest. He deied a martir, byried in þe
cymiteri of Kalixt. He ordeyned eke þat in euery grete cyté schuld be
a bischop, and þat alle grete causes schuld be determined at Rome. 15

In þis tyme began þe heresy of Manichees. Ther was a man in
Perse þat hite Manes, scharp of witte, whech ymaged a fals opinion
ageyn þe feith: he put too begynningis and þe feith but on; he
seid þe deuele was eterne, as God is; he seide þe body of oure
Lord Jesu Crist was no very body, and mech oþir þing. His 20
disciples þat he gadered cleped him Manicheus.

Anno 5471–5472; 273–274. Floriane regned ii ȝere. He deyed
with cuttyng of his veynes. He left noþing of his lyf þat was
worthi to be writin.

Anno 5473–5474; 275–276. Karus, with his too sones, Karine 25
and Numerian, regned too ȝere. This man was wikkid in al maner
þing; þerfor he was dronchin in a smal watir. And his childirn
sone aftir were killid. In his tyme were martired too glorious
seyntis, of whech on was a man, Crisantus, þe oþir a woman, Daria
was hyr name.   30

Anno 5475–5494; 277–296. Dioclecian and Maximian regned f. 39ᵛᵇ
xx ȝere. This Dioclecian was but of pore birth, but a grete enmy

---

3 arayed] rayed P   10 þat] om. P   13 a] P, om. M   17 ymaged]
ymagened P   26 regned] P, regne M   29 of] supplied, om. MP
30 was hyr name] P, om. over column division M

7–8: ibid. 449/41.
9–15: ibid. 414/30–9.
16–21: ibid. 449/41–4.
22–4: ibid. 449/45.
25–30: ibid. 450/1–2.
31–60/16: ibid. 450/3–20, 27–8.

to Cristen feith. For þis practik he vsed to destruccion of þe feith, þat all þe bokes he mite gete þat spoke of Crist he brent hem withoute dispensacion. And þis persecucion lestid x ȝere þorwoute þe world. This was þe first emperour þat wered gemmes
5 in his cloþing and in his hosen; for all þe princes before him were content to were purpil alone. He sent Maximiane into Frauns to fite ageyn a grete puple whech disobeyed þe lordchip of Rome. And in þat same jornay was Seynt Maurice martired, and with him a hool legioun, whech þei cleped Thebees. This
10 persecucioun of Dioclecian in þe est and Maximiane in þe west was of swech cruelté þat, withinne xxx dayes, xx þousand men and women were slayn for Crist, bokes brent, cherchis distroyed, prelatis killid. In þat persecucion were slayn Sebastian, Geruase, Prothase, Gorgony, Quintine, Grisogonus, Cosmas, Damiane,
15 Anastase, Agnes, Agas, Lucy, Katerine. And in Britayne þe more part of Cristen men were ny distroyed.

f. 40ra   In þis tyme, aftir þe deth of Gayus, was Marcelline mad po|pe, and for very dred he obeyed onto þe precept of Diocleciane, worchipid and encensed þe ydoles. But aftir þat he ded penauns,
20 and in þe councele desired þat þei schuld asine him more penauns. And þei sayde,

Thi maystir Petir denyed Crist, and so ded þou. Whech of þe apposteles was so bold for to gyue him penauns? Therfor do þiself what þou lest—we haue no power ouyr þe.

25 So he comaunded hem þat, aftir his deth, þei schuld not byry him. And streite he went to Dioclecian, and offered himself for a Cristen man, and lost his hed; xxx dayes lay his body onbiried, til Seynt Petir appered to Marcelle, þe pope, and bad him bery it be þe body of Seynt Petir.

30 Aftir him was Marcelle pope v ȝere. He ordeyned xv cardinales in Rome for to baptize men and byry hem. For he wold not obeye Maximiniane and thurifie, he sette hym in a cherch wech stant in a strete cleped Via Lata, and mad him in þe same cherch for

1 For] om. P   4 world] in r.h. margin M   5 cloþing] g altered from n M   10 Dioclecian] Dioclsian P   16 part of] suprascript M 20 and in . . . more penauns] om. P   22 Thi] The P   32 hym] over erasure M

1–16: see p. 59.
17–29: Martinus, 414/41–415/13.
30–61/2: ibid. 415/18–23.

to kepe bestes as in a stabil, and þere was he ded, byried in þe
cymiteri cleped Priscille.

Eusebius cam aftir him, a Grek; and þan Melchiades, born in
Affrik. He ordeyned þat no Cristen man schuld fast neythir
Sunday ne þursday, for þo to dayes were solemply fastid among 5
þe hethen men.

Anno 5495–5496; 297–298. Galerius regned too ʒere, with
Constantine and Lucinie. This Constantine conquered al Spayn,
and aftir þat cam into Britayn and compelled þe lond to pay her
old tribute to Rome, wedded here a mayden þei cle|ped Heleyn,   f. 40ʳᵇ
þe kyngis doutir of Colchester, and of þis woman and of him   11
cam Grete Constantine, þat ded mech for þe Cherch. Than deied
þis Constantyn in Britayn, and was byried at ʒork, and left his
son, Grete Constantin, þe empire of Frauns and of Spayn, with
oþir cuntrés.   15

In þis tyme was Maxencius chosen emperour at Rome, and
he grew to swech insolens and cruelté þat þe puple of Rome sent
for þis Constantine, and aftir he had killid Maxensius þei mad him
emperour.

Anno Mundi 5497–5527; Cristi 299–329. Constantine þe   20
Grete regned xxxi ʒere. He was first cruel onto Cristen men,
aftir was he smet with þe seknes of leper, and so be miracle baptized and cured be þe pope, Siluestir. And aftir his baptem he
gaf leue to alle Cristen men frely to bigge cherches, and openly
to here masses and prechyngis in þe name of oure Lord Jesu   25
Crist.

In his dayes began þe wikkid heresy of Arry—þe secte is
clepid Arrianes. And ageyn þat heresie were gadered in Grece,
at a cité cleped Nycene, thre hundred and xviii bischoppis in þe
presens of Constantine, and þere was Seint Nicholas | þe bischop.   f. 40ᵛᵃ
The Donatistes heresie eke began in þis tyme, be on þei called   31
Donat. The Arrianes seid þat Crist was lesse þan his fadir, not
only in his manhod, as we sey, but in his godhed, as we sey not.

---

4 þat] t *suprascript* M   10 here] ther P   17 þat] that P, þa M
18 Maxensius] Maxensiius P, Maxens *at line end* M   21 regned] d *supra-*
script M   24 bigge] byld P   28 Grece] ce *suprascript* M, Gece P
29 þe] *om.* P   32 Arrianes] Arriane P

3–6: ibid. 415/24–31.
7–19: ibid. 450/22–7.
20–62/10: ibid. 450/29–451/24.

The Donatistes sey þat þe trewe feith is nowhere but with hem, and þoo þat schuld come to her secte must be rebaptized.

This Constantin ded make þe cherch of þe Saluatour, and þe cherch of Petir and Poule, and þe cherch of Seynt Laurens, and
5 many oþir werkis. Summe sey of him þat he erred fro þe feith in his ende and was rebaptized of on Eusebie, bischop of Nichomedi, but þis opinion is not trew, for it was his son, þat hite Constans. For Seynt Gregorie in his *Register*, and Ambrose *Upon þe XIII Psalme*, and Ysidre in his cronicles, sey þat he deied a holy man;
10 and þe Grekis hold of him a solempne fest þe xxi day of May.

In þis mannes tyme was Siluestir pope xxxi ȝere and x monthes, born in Rome. He mad þis grete councel to be gadered at Nycene of ccc bischoppes and xviii, where þe crede was mad whech we sey in oure messe. This pope went down into þe erde a hundred
15 grecis and fifty, and bond a dragon þat had slayn þousandis with þe wynd of his mouth.

Anno 5528–5551; 330–353. Constantine, þis mannes son, with
f. 40ᵛᵇ his too bretherin, Constant and Constancius, regned xxiiii | ȝere. These iii were þe sones of Grete Constantine. First regned þe
20 eldest al alone, and whan he was ded be þe councell of his broþir Constans, þan regned þe same Constauns, and was turned be a fals prest to þe heresie of þe Ariures. He pursewid all þe Cristen bischoppis and prestis þorow þe world: summe he exiled, summe he put oute here rite eyne, and namely þe worthi man, Athanasius,
25 whech mad *Quicunque vult*, pursewed so feruently þat he durst not appere openly vii ȝere. And al þis persecucion was for on Arrian, whech deyed at Constantinople ful schamefully. For as he went to cherch with his clientis and mech pride, þere fell upon him a appetite for to go to a sege; and with his issew went
30 all þe guttis oute of his wombe down into þe gong, and þis was kept ful grete councell fro þe emperour, seyng þat he deyed in a cothe.

In þese dayes Lucius was pope, þat mad a lawe þat þere schuld no clerk answere to no cause but in þe Cherch. In his dayes lyued

---

2 þoo] *suprascript* M   3 and] in P   24 namely] ly *suprascript* M
Athanasius] Athasius MP   25 whech] *suprascript* M   26 openly]
ly *suprascript* M   28 with] *suprascript with caret (in red)* M

1–10: see p. 61.
11–16: Martinus, 415/32–48.
17–23: ibid. 452/9–12.
33–63/2: ibid. 416/13–19.

þese men: Athanasius, Pafnucius, Eusebius, Nicholaus, Hillarius, Victorius, Hillarion, Epiphanius, Johannes Crisostomus.

In þese dayes was Liberi pope. He was exiled be þe emperoure, and on Felix chosen, and þan Liberius | ageyn, and so began a scisme in þe Cherch—for vii ȝere þis Liberius kept Seynt Petir cherch and Seynt Laurens with fors of armes. So was Felix—for he seid þat þe emperour and þe pope were heretikes— martired, and on Eusebius sperd in a litil hous, in whech he deyed for hungir. In þis tyme was Donate, þe grete gramarion, þat taute Seyn Jerom gramer. And þe grete heremite Antoni lyued in þis tyme. The bones eke of Seynt Andrew and Luk were brout to Constantinople.

In þis tyme Julianus Apostata was mad a monk. For þis Em- perour Constauns killid þe broþir of Julian, and þerfor he fledde, for he cam of þe imperial blood—Grete Constantin broþir was his fader—and þus Juliane walkid dyuers prouinces, drawyng euir to nigromanceres and wicchis, inquiring diligently if euir he schuld be emperour. And at þe last he mad feith to a deuel þat he schuld forsake his cristendam, and whan he had do þis he told him þat within fewe dayes he schuld regne in þe empire.

Anno 5552–5554; 354–356. This Julian regned too ȝere and ten monthis. He was Apostata, as is seid before, and weel lerned in all þe seculer sciens, but he lefte þe study of diuinité and en- tended al to nigromancie and familiarité of spirites. He porsewid Cristen men ful greuously, pryued hem of her worchip, to þis entent, for to bringe hem to ydolatrie. Vndir him were many martires, specialy Paule and Jon, keperis of þe chaumbir of Constantin dowtir.

He gaue leue to þe Jewis to bygge a|geyn þe Temple at Jeru- salem, but þe erdeqwaues come so often þei were fayn to fle fro þe Temple and fro þe cité.

As he went to fite with þe Perses, whan he cam to Cesarie, þat stant in Capadoce, he þrette Basile, þe bischop, þat whan he cam

7 þat] t *suprascript* M   emperour] P, empour M   14 þe broþir *in r.h. margin* M of] *in l.h. margin* M   15 blood] blood of P   16 walkid] warked P   17 wicchis] is *suprascript* M   20 within] in *suprascript* M 29 bygge] byld P at] of P   30 fle] *suprascript with caret (in red)* M

3–9: ibid. 416/30–41.
9–20: ibid. 452/14–23.
21–64/7: ibid. 452/24–37.

ageyn victour, he schuld distroy þe cité. Vpon þis þe bischop
comaunded þe puple to prey God þat he schuld lette þe cursed
mannes appetite, and withinne fewe dayes a knite whech hite
Mercurie, þat Julianus had martired for Crist, at þe comaundyng
5 of oure Lady, ros oute of his graue and with his spere killid þis
Julian, and in his deyng he cried, 'þou hast ouyrcome, þou Galilé!'
—for so cleped he Crist, and no oþir name.

   Anno 5555; 357. Jouiniane regned but o ȝere. He was first a
knyte with þe kyng of Perse, cleped Sapor, and whan Julian was
10 ded he byried him worchipfully, and þan was he chosen emperour.
All þe biscoppis þat were exiled in Constans tyme he cleped hem
hom to her cherchis; among hem was Athanase, clepid hom to
Alisaundre. He sperd þe templis of ydolis and opened Cristen
cherchis. He was ded in a certeyn hous þat was new waschid with
15 lym and clos fro þe eyir, strangillid with þe hete.

   In þis tyme was Damasus pope, a excellent man in uersifying.
He ordeyned, at þe praier of Seint Jerom, þat in þe ende of euery
psalme þe Cherch schul sey, 'Gloria Patri'. He ordeyned þe maner
of singing in þe qwere, þat half schuld singe on þe o side, and half
20 on þe othir.

f. 41ᵛᵃ   In þis tyme was Josaphat, a kingis son, mad a hermyte be þe
exortacion of on Barlaam. In þis tyme Seint Ambrose, bischop of
Melan, mad many ympnes, whech be sunge in þe Cherch, and
be his preching mani of Itaile were conuerted to Crist. In þis
25 tyme lyued Basilius, bischop of Cesarea, and his brothir Grego
Nazanzene, Dindimus of Alisaundre, and Jerom at Bethlem,
Seint Martyn, and þe too Macharies, Ysidre, and many othir.

   Anno 5556-5566; 358-368. Valentinian, with his broþir
Valent, regned xi ȝere. He dwelt before with Juliane þe emperour,
30 whom Julian put in choys wheþir he wold forsake his knythod or
his cristendam, and he forsok his knythod. Therfor oure Lord
exalted him onto þe empire. He deied of þe flix of blood. He was

---

1 distroy] *suprascript with caret (in red)* M 2 comaunded] ed *suprascript with caret (in red)* M, comaunde P 4 Julianus] Julius MP
comaundyng] commaundiment P 8 Jouiniane] Jominiane P 12 clepid]
d *altered from* t M 15 strangillid] r *suprascript with caret (in red)* M
17 ende] ede P 32 flix] *inked over, or possibly written over erasure* M

1–7: see p. 63.
8–10: Martinus, 452/38–9.
16–27: ibid. 416/46–417/7.
28–65/3: ibid. 452/40–9.

trew of condicion, fayre of visage, sotill of witte, fayre-spokyn, but he spak but seldam. In his tyme was Ambrose mad bischop of Melan, þat wrot many notabel bokes and episteles.

Anno 5567–5570; 369–372. Valens, with Gracian and Ualentinian, regned iiii ȝere. This Valens was a Arrian, and ded mech 5 harm onto good Cristen men, but God suffered him to be killid in a batail whech he had with þe Gothis. He mad a lawe þat munkys schuld | fite and go to batayle, or ellis men schuld com- f. 41ᵛᵇ pelle hem with battis.

Anno 5571–5576; 373–378. Gracian, with his bretherin, 10 Valentinian and Theodosie, regned vi ȝere. This man was trewe in his feith and deuoute onto þe Cherch. For onto his tyme þe heresi of Arrianes was gretly meynteyned in Itaile. And he with good councel destroyed it finaly and broute þe cuntré to þe rith byleue. He was resonabily wel lettered, smal eter, mesured in 15 drynk, schort slepir, ouircomer of lustis, fulfillid with vertues at þe best.

In þis tyme was Ciricus pope. He gadered a councell at Constantinople of ccc and l biscoppis. He condempned þe heresi of Maniche, and exiled hem, and forbad all Cristen men her felau- 20 chip. He ordeyned eke þat non of hem schuld be receyued but to euyrlesting penauns.

In þis tyme Paula and Eustochium went oute of Rome to Bethlem to dwelle with Seint Jerom. In þis tyme a child was born at Emaus þat fro þe nowil upward had too bodies and too hedis, 25 and whan on ete, þe othir slept; be þe nethir part he had but to hepis and to leggis. Orosius was also in þis tyme, þat was messagere betwix Jerom and Augustin, whech mad a book onto Seynt Augustin—it is clepid *Ormesta Mundi*.

Anno 5577–5588; 379–390. Theodosius regned xii ȝere. In 30 his tyme fell a grete debate betwix Jewis and | hethen, whech f. 42ʳᵃ secte was of most perfeccioun, but þis man mad þis strif to cese,

---

7 a (1)] *om.* P   13 Arrianes] s *suprascript* M   16 slepir] slepis MP
25 nowil] *om.* P   upward] vpwad P   29 it is] *om.* P   de (*after* clepid)
expuncted M   31 his] this P   31–2 stat (*after* whech) *expuncted in red* M
32 secte] *suprascript in red* M   of most perfeccioun] *another* of *suprascript*
after most M, most of perfeccioun P

4–9: ibid. 452/50–453/4.
10–17: ibid. 453/5–10.
18–29: ibid. 417/15–33.
30–66/12: ibid. 453/11–18.

for he distroyed all þe temples of ydolis and put þe Jewis vndir
tribute.

In þis tyme was Augustin conuerted fro his erroure onto þe feith
be þe prayer of his modir, be þe preching of Seynt Ambrose, and
5 exortacion of Simpliciane. For as it may be gadered of cronicles,
he was bore in þe ȝere of oure Lord ccc and lx, and conuerted
in þe ȝere ccc and xc. He deied in cccc and xxx. He mad many
bokes, conuicte many herisies; for his grete labour is he cleped
þe flour of doctouris.

10 This Cristen emperour þat we speke of ouyrcam his enmies
more with orisen þan with swerd. He deied at Melan, and is
byried at Constantinople.

In þis tyme was Anastasius pope. He ordeyned þat þere schuld
no man be receyued to þe holy ordres of þe Cherch but he had his
15 membris of his body hole. He ordeyned eke þat whan þe Gospel
is red, euery man schuld stande.

Anno Mundi 5589-5601; 391-403. Archadius and Honorius
regned xiii ȝere. In his tyme was a bischop in a town þei cleped
Pire, his name was Donate, whech kyllid a grete dragoun with þe
20 breth of his mouth; viii ȝok of oxen myte scarsly drawe þe dragon
f. 42rb to þe place | þere he schuld be brent. In þis same tyme þe bodies
of Abacuch and Miche were founde and translat.

In þese dayes sprong þo too heresies, þe Priscilianistes and
Pelagianes. The first saide þat Criste was no veri man. The
25 secunde saide þat men may of her owne nature do good dedis,
withoute mediacion of þe grace of God. These heresies were
beten and knokked be þe myty hambir of God whech was called
Augustin, þat þei wasted oute of mennes soules.

In þese dayes Albericus, kyng of Gothis, entered Ytaile and
30 cam to Rome, wastid þe cyté with swerd and fire, ȝeuing first þis
precept: þere schuld man do no harm to no cherch ne to no persone þat fled to þe cherch. And whan þe cité brent, þei þat were
not of Cristen feith blasphemed Crist, and seide þat þis mischef
cam upon hem because þei had lefte þe seruyse of her olde goddis

---

6 þe] om. over line division P   7 ȝere] yere P, ȝe M   8 conuicte]
i surmounted by short stroke in red M   11 orisen] suprascript with caret
(in red) M   18 his] this P   25 þat] þan M, than P   27 knokked] d
suprascript M

1–12: see p. 65.
13–16: Martinus, 417/34–8.
17–67/2: ibid. 453/21–7.

and were turned to Crist; and þis blasphemie was cause þat
Augustin mad þat solemp book whech is cleped *De Ciuitate Dei.*

In þese dayes was Innocent pope, whech ordeyned þat men
schuld fast on Satyrday, for þat day lay Crist in þe sepulcre. He
mad a constitucion eke þat þe child whech was born of a Cristen 5
woman schuld be baptized—Pelagius seid þe reuers. He ordeyned
eke þe consecracion of þe oyle with whech men be anoynted at her
ende.

Anno 5602–5616; 404–418. Honorius, with Theodosie þe
ȝonger, regned xv ȝere. In þis tyme were gadered | ccc bischoppis f. 42ᵛᵃ
and xiii at Cartage ageyn þe heresi of Pelagius, þat deneyed 11
Cristis grace. And in þese dayes lyued Cirille, bischop of Alisaundre; and Seynt Jerom deyed at Bethlem þe ȝere of his age
foure score and on, whos soule appered onto Augustin at Ypon
with grete lite and swete sauour, with wordis eke of coumfort, 15
swech as Seint Augustin wold neuir write. This Honorius was
lich his fader in þe trewe religion of Crist. He deied at Rome,
biried by Seynt Petir cherch.

In þese dayes was Zozime pope, a Grek. He ordeyned þat no
bondeman schuld be mad a clerk, and þat þe pascale schuld be 20
blessed at Pase.

Aftir him was Bonefas pope. He comaunded þat þere schuld
no woman wasch þe corporas ne touche it.

And aftir him was pope Celestinus Iᵘˢ. He ordeyned prestis
schuld sei, 'Judica me, Deus', before messe. He sent Seint Patrik, 25
þe son of Concha, whech was Seynt Martin sistir, into Erlond
for her conuercion. He gadered þe grete councell at Ephese, in
whech was condempned Nestorius, þat seide þere be to persones in
oure Lord Jesu Crist.

Anno 5617–5643; 419–445. Theodosius þe Secunde regned 30

---

1 blasphemie] blasphemieng P　　　　7 of þe oyle] of the oyle P, of
oyle *suprascript with caret (in red)* M　　　whech] þᵉ whech P　　　at] a P
10 gadered] *last word on page,* dered *written below last full line* M　　　13 þe]
in the P　　　20 clerk] crerk P　　　24 Iᵘˢ] *nine-sign suprascript in red* M

3–8: ibid. 417/41–7.
9–18: ibid. 453/35–45.
19–21: ibid. 418/3–5.
22–3: ibid. 418/6–8.
24–9: ibid. 418/9–15.
30–68/11: ibid. 453/50–454/25.

xxvii 3ere with Valentiniane, his neue. In his tyme þe deuel

appered in Crete in þe liknes of Moises, promising | to þe Jewis
þat he schuld lede hem ouyr þe se to Jerusalem with drye feet.
And many of hem þat folowed him he killid; þei þat scaped were
5 turned to Crist and baptized. In þis same tyme was þe fest of þe
bondis of Seynt Petir begunne. And Totila in þese dayes, kyng
of Hungri, cam with mech puple to distroye þe empire of Rome,
but at þe prayer of Seint Leon, þe pope, he left his purpos. The
vii sleperis, þat had slept to hundred 3ere in þis emperoures time,
10 risen in testimoni of þe general resurreccion, whech many heretikes
þat tyme denyed.

In þese dayes was Sixtus pope—he was þe iii of þat name.
He bylid þe cherch of Seynt Mari Major. Oþir men write þat
on Johannes Patricius schul a mad þis cherch in tyme of Liberi
15 þe pope. Vphap þis pope mored it or arayed it, as he ded many
oþir. He is biried be þe bodi of Seynt Laurens, Via Tiburtina.

Aftir him was Leon pope xxi 3ere. He held þe grete councell
at Calcidony ageyn Euticen, þe heretik. It happed on a Pase-day
he hoselid a certeyn woman, and sche kissid his hand, aftir whech
20 kissing he had swech temptacion þat for vexacion he ded smyte of
þat hand. Þan was þere mech | grucching in þe puple whi he
sang no messe. Tho was he fayn to pray oure Lady Mary of
help, and sche appered onto him and restored his hand. He
wrote eke a epistel ageyn þe heretikes, Fabian and Euticen, and
25 leid þe lettir upon Seint Petir auter, prayng to Seynt Petir þat if
onyþing were wrong writin, Seint Petir schuld amend it, and aftir
iii dayes he fond it rased and amendid aftir þe plesauns of God.
He is byried in Seynt Petir cherch.

Anno 5644–5650; 446–452. Marcianus and Valentinus regned
30 vii 3ere. In his tyme on Theodoricus, kyng of Gothis, went into
Spayn with a gret hoost, and conqwered al þat lond. Aftir þat
he killid þis Marcian at Constantinople. In þis tyme was Seynt
Genofepha at Paris, a holy woman, whech had þis special grace,
þat whom sche anoynted with holy oyle he was hol.

9 time] *suprascript* M   15 þe] *om.* P   18 a] *om.* P   20 þat] t *suprascript* M   25 þe] e *suprascript* M   Petir (2)] *in r.h. margin* M
27 amendid] *final* d *altered from* t M, amendyt P   30 his] thys P

1–11: see p. 67.
12–16: Martinus, 418/18–24.
17–28: ibid. 418/25–419/13.
29–34: ibid. 454/28–31.

Anno 5651–5667; 453–469. Leo þe First regned xvii ȝere, in whech tyme mech of Egipte an al Alisaunder was infecte with þe heresi of on Dioscorus, þat held þis opinion, þat þere is but o nature in Crist—the feith is þat in oure Lord Jesu Crist is o persone and too natures; with þis same heresie was þis emperour 5 infect, and with oþir, in-so-mech þat all þe yma|ges whech mite f. 43rb be founde at Rome of ony seyntis he caried hem to Constantinople, and þere he brent hem. In his dayes þe body of Helize was translate to Alisaundre, and þe body of Mark onto Venys. And in þese dayes lyued Seint Mamert, þat ordeyned þe iii dayes of 10 Rogacion before Ascensioun. In þese daies lyued on Prosper, notarie onto Leon þe pope, a holy man, þat mad a grete book of þe lif contemplatif.

In þese dayes was Hillari pope. He ordeyned þere schuld no biscop asigne his successour. He is biried be Seint Laurens. 15

Aftir him was Simplicius pope. This man edified a cherch of oure Lady and Seint Viuiane, and þere lith he, with iiii þousand martires cclxx, beside women and childirn.

In þese dayes was Arthure kyng of Bretayn, þat with his manhod conqwered Flaunderes, Frauns, Norwey, and Denmark, and 20 aftir he was gretely woundid he went into an ylde cleped Auallone, and þere deyed. The olde Britones suppose þat he is o-lyue.

Anno 5668–5684; 470–486. Zenon regned xvii ȝere. This man mad many lawes, and among al bysinesse he laboured for to kille Leon, þe forseid emperour son. But þe moder hid þe child, 25 and presented on vnto þe emperour þat was lich þe child. And he ded him make a clerk, whech lyued so onto þe tyme of Justine þe·emperour. | In þat tyme was founde þe body of Seynt Barnabé f. 43va þe apostel, and with him þe gospel of Seint Mathew writin with his owne hand. In þis tyme þe kyng of Affrik was mad a Arriane, 30 and he of malice exiled ccc bischoppis, and sperd her cherchis, and sent hem into a ylde is cleped Sardinia.

1 *the year number* 5656 *miswritten as* 5655 M   12 man] *suprascript with caret (in red)* M   22 Britones] s *suprascript* M   25 son] *om.* P 28–9 was founde þe body of Seynt Barnabé þe apostel] was founde *suprascript* M, the body of Seynt Barnabe the apostell was founde P

1–13: ibid. 454/34–51.
14–15: ibid. 419/14–16.
16–18: ibid. 419/21–4.
19–22: ibid. 419/17–20.
23–32: ibid. 455/3–15.

In þis tyme was Felix pope. He ordeyned þat, whan a man was accused, he schuld haue auysement of answere, and þat his juges schuld not be suspecte.

Anno Mundi 5685–5710; 487–512. Anastasius regned xxvi
5 ȝere. In his tyme Transamunde, kyng of Wandalis, sperd all þe cherchis in Affrik þat were not consenting to Arrius. In þat same tyme a bischop at Cartage, whos name was Olimpius, in a bath as he blasphemed þe blessed Trinité, for he was a Ariane, sodeynly with iii firi dartis a aungel smet him to þe deth. A othir bischop
10 of þe same secte, his name was Barabas, he baptized a man in þis forme, 'Barabas baptizeth þe be þe Son, in þe name of þe Fadir and þe Holy Gost'; sodeynly þe watyr vanisched awey, and he
f. 43ᵛᵇ þat schuld | a be baptized went and was baptized as þe forme of þe sacrament requirith.

15 In þese dayes was Gelasius pope viii ȝere. He mad many orisones, and tractes, and ympnes, and mad þat comoun preface, *Dignum et justum est equum et salutare.*

Aftir him was þe secund Anastasius pope ii ȝere. He ordeyned þat euery clerk schuld treuly sey his seruyse and not leue it for no
20 cause.

Aftir him was Simacus pope xv ȝere. He ordeyned þat *Gloria in Excelsis* schuld be songe at messe, for he mad þis ympne, saue þe beginning, whech was mad be a aungell. In his tyme was a scisme betwix him and on Laurens, whech had eleccion of many.
25 Simachus kept þe paleys Lateranense, and Laurens kept Seynt Mari Major, but in a grete councell at Rauen, present þe kyng of Itaile, Theodorik, Simacus was confermed and Laurence rejecte. But aftirward þe pope gaue him a bischoprich, whech is clepid Micherius. In þis tyme was Boys exiled fro Rome to Pauye, and
30 þere mad he his bokes, as is supposed, for þis is sikir: þere is he byried. In þis tyme was Seynt Remigius.

---

2 auysement] auysnent P   11 in (*after 1st* þe) *expuncted* M   19 clerk] crerke P   21 þat] P, þa M   23 whech] *om.* P   a (1)] *supplied, om.* MP his] thys P   24 many] *in r.h. margin* M   28 aftirward] d *suprascript* M 29 was Boys] Boys was P   exiled] d *suprascript* M   30 supposed] d *suprascript* M

1–3: Martinus, 419/37–45.
4–14: ibid. 455/18–23.
15–17: ibid. 419/46–8.
18–20: ibid. 420/1–3.
21–31: ibid. 420/9–24.

Anno 5711–5719; 513–521. Justine was emperour ix ȝere.
He was ful bisi to destroye þe heresi of þe Arrianes; for þere he
was at Constantinople he sperd her cherchis and suffered hem
not to teche. Therfor was þe king of Itaile wroth, and wold a
killid þe bischoppis of Itaile | but þat he dred indignacion of the f. 44ʳᵃ
emperour. Therfor he sent þe pope and oþir worthy men onto 6
Justine, þat þe Arrianes schuld be restored to her cherchis, or
ellis he wold kille þe bischoppis of Ytaile. And whil þei were oute
he killid Boys and many oþir. And whan þe pope cam hom to
Itaile and broute þe kyng graunt of his will, ȝet he put þe pope 10
in prison, where he deyed, and withinne a litil tyme aftir þat þe
king deied sodeynly, whos soule a holy man sey whan it was put
in a boiling pot in helle.

In þis tyme was Hormisda pope. He mad a grete bem of siluyr
before Seynt Petir whech weyed a þousand pound and xl. 15

Aftir him was Jon pope, in whos tyme Frauns was conuerted.
He deied at Rauenne in prison, and biried is at Rome in Seint
Petir cherch.

Anno 5720–5757; 522–559. Justiniane þe First, he regned xxxviii
ȝere. This man was in a grete erroure, whech began in Antioche, 20
but he was conuerted and reformed to þe feith by Agapitus þe
pope. This emperour mad many lawes, both þe digest and þe
code, whech ar þe grounde of Cyuyle. He had a lord vndir him
þat kepte his batailes, his name was Besibarius. He ouyrcam hem
of Perse, and mech of Affrik he put vndir tribute. | Than cam f. 44ʳᵇ
he to Rome and fond it besegid. He distroyed þe sege and gat 26
him mech worchip, for he took þe kyng of Gothis and led him to
Constantinople to þe emperour.

In þis tyme leued a Cristen poete, Orator was his name. He
mad a solempne werk in vers upon þe book whech þei clepe *Actus* 30
Apostolorum. And Precian, þe gramarion, was in þis tyme. And
Cassiodre, a senatoure of Rauen, was at þis tyme, first a senatoure
and þanne a monk, whech mad a nobel werk upon þe Sauter,
folowyng mech þe steppes of Seynt Augustin.

---

4 was] *suprascript* M   17 is] *suprascript* M   19 he] *om.* P
30 vers] *om.* P

1–13: ibid. 455/29–42.
14–15: ibid. 420/25–9.
16–18: ibid. 420/30–5.
19–72/6: ibid. 455/50–456/20.

In þis tyme Jewis and Sarasines gadered togidir at Cesaré in Palestine killid þe most part of Cristen men in þat cyté. And whan þis cam to þe emperoures knowlech he vengid here blood with myty power. This Justiniane mad a meruelous and a costful
5 temple in Constantinople, whech was cleped Seint Sophie, and þere is he byried.

In his tyme was Felix þe IIII pope iiii ȝere. He ordeyned þat men schuld be anoynted with holy oyle or they deye.

Aftir him was Boneface þe Secunde ii ȝere. He ordeyned þat
10 clerkis schuld stand be hemself, and þe puple be hemself, in þe tyme of dyuyne seruyse.

f. 44ᵛᵃ And þan was Jon þe Secunde pope ii ȝere. In | his tyme lyued Maurus, þat was disciple to Seyn Benet.

And aftir him was þe first Agapitus i ȝere. He ordeyned þat
15 men schuld go on processioun on Sundayes.

Than was Siluery pope iii ȝere. And for he cursed a byschop þei clepid Anthemius for heresie, þerfor þe emperour, at instans of his wif, exiled and killid him in a ylde þei clepe Ponciane.

And þan was Vigilius pope xvii ȝere. He ordeyned þat auteres
20 schuld stand into þe est. In þat tyme was in Cicile a clerk þei clepid Theophilus, whech denyed Crist and took him to þe deuel, body and soule, but aftir he was take to mercy be mediacion of oure Lady.

And in þese dayes was Pelagius pope iiii ȝere. He ordeyned þat
25 heretikes and scismatikes schuld haue no priuilege of þe Cherch, but þei schuld be punchid be seculer power. In þis tyme was Seynt Brandane leuyng in Scotlond, and in þis tyme þe bones of Seynt Steuene were browt to Rome and leide be Laurens.

Anno 5758-5768; 560-570. Justiniane þe Secunde regned xi
30 ȝere. In þat tyme a lord clepid Narses, for fer of Sophie þe em-

2 whan] *suprascript with caret* (*in red*) M   10 clerkis] crerkis P
13 þat] t *suprascript* M   18 him] *suprascript* M   20 þei] i *suprascript* M
30 for] r *suprascript* M

1-6: see p. 71.
7-8: Martinus, 420/36-8.
9-11: ibid. 420/39-40.
12-13: ibid. 420/42-4.
14-15: ibid. 420/45-6.
16-18: ibid. 421/1-4.
19-23: ibid. 421/5-16.
24-7: ibid. 421/23-8.
29-73/10: ibid. 456/25-46.

peresse, fled to þe Longbardis (whech dwelled not þan in Itaile),
brout hem with fors into Itaile. Before þat tyme þe puple of
Longobardis dwelled in Panonie, and þis same Narses had dwelled
with þe kyng, whech hite Aburre, and aftir þat with his successour,
Rotharie, and | þere mad þei comnaunt who þe kingdam of   f. 44ᵛᵇ
Itaile myte come to her dominacion and be broute fro Justinian,   6
þat dwelt at Constantinople, and þus, be mediacion of Narses,
þe Longobardis were brout into Itaile, and dwelle þere onto þis
tyme. And so aftir Narses was go fro Justiniane he had neuir
rest, but euir vexid with bataile.   10

In his tyme was Jon þe þird pope, þat in his dayes was a grete
repayrer of cimiteries þere martires were biried. He mad in
Rome a cherch of Philip and Jacob, but he is biried at Seint Petir
cherch. He was pope xii 3ere.

Anno 5769-5775; 571-577. Tiberius þe Secund regned vii   15
3ere, a Cristen emperour, to pore men a veri fader, for þe tresoure
of his paleis he departed among þe pore; and whan þe emperesse
vndirtook him for his wasting of þe comoun good, he wold sey
onto hir, 'Dame, I beleue verili if we be bisi for to gete us tresoure
in heuene, God schal send us sufficiens in erde'. Happid aftir   20
þat he went by on of his places and sei in þe ground a tabel of
marbil, on whech was a crosse. He comaunded þe table schuld
be remeued, for it was not goodly, as he seyde, þat men schuld
trede on þe crosse. Whan þat was reysid þei fond a oþir lich it,
and þan þe þirde, and vndir þat þere fond þei a grete tresoure.   25

In his tyme was Benedictus þe First pope iiii 3ere. In his tyme
þe Longobardis conquerid al Itaile—befor þei had but Melan and
þe cuntré aboute—and aftir | þat conquest folowid a gret hungir.   f. 45ʳᵃ

Than was Pelagius þe Secund pope x 3ere. In his tyme fell
swech reynes þat þe watir of Tibir rose as hey as Rome wallis,   30
drenchid þe houses; dragones and serpentis cam down in þe

---

1 Longbardis] g altered from n M   2 hem] in r.h. margin M   5 þei]
i suprascript M   6 be] supplied, om. MP   8 dwelle þere] ther
dwelle They P   16 3ere] suprascript with carets (in red) M   Cristen]
Crsten P   17 whan] in r.h. margin M   18 him] in r.h. margin M
25 þere fond þei] þei in r.h. margin M, they found P   26 his (1)] þis P
29 his] this P   30 þat] t suprascript M

watir, and oþir bestes dede, of whech was swech a stynk þat it caused gret pestilens in Rome.

Anno 5776-5795; 578-597. Mauricius regned xx ȝere. He kepte þe trewe Cristen wey, and he was ful strong and wis in batayle.
5 He ouyrcam many puples in batail, þe Perses, þe Armenes, be a noble man þat was his werriour.

In his dayes was Gregorie mad pope, and he confermed þat eleccioun with his imperial letteris. In þe þirtene ȝere of Maurice Gregori sent Austin and his felaues to þe conuercion of þe Saxones,
10 whech were newe come into þe lond be strength, and had dryuyn oute be strength þe very eyeris into Walis. In þese dayes Gregorie, bischop of Antioche, and Thebea, bischop of Jerusalem, fond þe vnsowid cote of oure Lord Crist in Sephath, a litil fro Jerusalem.

15 Than fel a stauns betwix þe emperour and þe Pope Gregori, in-so-mech þat þe emperour seid mech euel of þe pope and seide
f. 45ʳᵇ he schud be ded. And þan was seyn oft-tyme at Rome | a man goyng in a monkis habite, with a naked swerd in his hand, and criyng loude þat Maurice schal be ded þis ȝere. And whan þe
20 emperour herd þis noyse he repent him of his trespas, and ded penauns, and prayed oure Lord þat þis sentens schuld be chaunged, but within few ȝeres on Focas, a knyte of his, killid him.

Anno Mundi 5796-5803; 598-605. Focas regned viii ȝere. This man, with sedicious knytis, was sublimat in þe empire, and
25 he, for more sikirnesse, killid þe emperour and many of his lordis. This man graunted Bonefas þe pope leue to consecrate þe temple cleped Pantheon to þe worchep of oure Lady and all seyntis.

In his tyme were iii popes: Sauinian—he ordeyned ringyng to þe seruise of God; and þan Bonefas þe III—he ordeyned white
30 past for þe sacrament; and þan Bonefas þe IIII—he consecrate Pantheon, and ordeyned þe fest of All-halow.

Anno 5804-5834; 606-636. Eraclius, with his son Constantin,

---

4 was] *suprascript* M   7 he] *suprascript with caret (in red)* M
11 strength] stren|th *over line division* M, strenght P   24 sublimat] t *suprascript with caret (in red)* M   28 Sauinian] *each* i *surmounted by short stroke in red* M   31 Pantheon] e *altered from* o M

1-2 see p. 73.
3-22: Martinus, 457/10-26.
23-7: ibid. 457/32-5.
28-31: ibid. 422/25-45.
32-75/17: ibid. 457/38-50.

regned xxxi ȝere. The þirde ȝere of his regne Cosdre, the kyng of
Perse, cam to Jerusalem and took þe Patriark Zacari, and þe
holy crosse, and ledde hem both into Perse. And in þe xii ȝere of
þis Eraclius þe same Eraclius went in|to Pers, and killid þe Kyng f. 45ᵛᵃ
Cosdre, and brout þe holy crosse ageyn to Jerusalem.   5

In þis tyme began þat cursed Machomet, þe prophete of þe
Sarasines. He was a wich, and he had eke þe falling euele, and
whan he fel so, he feyned þat Gabriel þe aungell appered þan onto
him, and for þe clernesse þat he sey he myte not stand, but fel
down as ded. He began first with þeft and was a prince of þeues.   10
Aftirward he wedded a lady and was a gret lord. His book, whech
þei clepe *Alcoran*, was mad be þe councell of a munk þat was
dampned at Rome for heresie and exiled fro þe cité, his name was
Sergius.

In þe tyme of þis emperour was ordeyned þat fest whech is   15
cleped Exaltacion of þe Cros; whan þe emperour broute hom þe
cros, it schuld be halowid of þe puple.

In his time were seuene popes:—

The first hite Deusdedit, iii ȝere. He kissid a mysel, and sodeynly
þe mysel was hol.   20

The secund was Bonefas þe Fifte, v ȝere. He ordeyned þat
robberis of cherchis schuld be cursed openly.

The þirde was Honorius Primus, xiii ȝere. He ordeyned þat euery
Satirday prestis schuld go with þe letanie to Seint Petir cherch.
This man mad þe cherch of Seynt Agnes, and þere he lith.   25

The fourte, Seuerinus, o ȝere—he was a grete gyuer of elmesse.
He is | biried in Seint Petir cherch.   f. 45ᵛᵇ

The fifte was Jon þe Fourt, ii ȝere. He took grete tresoure oute of
þe Cherch for redempcion of Cristen men whech Sarasines had
take.   30

---

2 Patriark] P, Patriack M   6 þat] the P   12 of] P, *om.* M
13–14 was Sergius] *in r.h. margin* M   15 þat] t *suprascript* M   17 it]
supplied, om. MP   schuld be halowid of] *over erasure* M   of] be P   18 time]
suprascript with caret (in red) M   26 Seuerinus o ȝere] was Severinus P
28 was] P, wan M

19–20: ibid. 422/46–8.
21–2: ibid. 422/49–50.
23–5: ibid. 423/3–14.
26–7: ibid. 423/15–17.
28–30: ibid. 423/18–20.

The sexte was Theodorus þe First—he was pope sex ȝere. He mad a book whech is cleped *Penitencial*, where confessoures may lerne what penauns þei schal gyue.

The vii pope hite Martin þe First. He began in þe last ȝere of
5 Eraclius, and kept þat office vi ȝere. A swier of þe emperoures had in comaundment to kille þis pope as he stod at messe in þe cherch of Seint Mari Major, but oure Lord mad him blynd, þat he myte not se þe pope. This pope was exiled for he condempned Paule, þe patriarke of Constantinople, for heresie.

10 Anno 5835–5861; 637–663. Constantin þe þird, with Yradone his broþir, regned þan xxvii ȝere. This Constantin was son onto Eraclius, and he was killid in Scicile for his wikkid lif. Mech of his lordchip was consumed be þe Sarasines, for he was not þe seruaunt of God. First killid he Martine, þe pope, and þan cam
15 he to Rome, and spoiled þe cité, and al þe precious þingis whech he fond þere he bare hem into Scicile. Many good Cristen prestis |
f. 46ʳᵃ and oþir he flagellid and aftir exiled for þei wold not consent to his heresie, whech þei clepid Monalechites, for þei held þat þere was but o nature in Crist.

20 And because he was odious to hem þat dwelled at Constanti-nople, þerfor he took his jornay onto Itaile, purposing to dryue þe Longobardis oute of þe cuntré. But whan he cam to þe cuntré cleped Beneuent, þe duke of þat cuntré, Grinnaldus, put him of with myty power, and hurt mech of his hoost. Than went he to
25 Rome and robbid it ageyn, and fro þens into Scicile, where his owne men killid him in a bath.

In þese dayes was Eugenius Primus pope iii ȝere, a holy man, beloued of all men.

And aftir him was Vitalianus xiiii ȝere. He ordeined song and
30 orgones in þe Cherch. He mad on Theodre, þat was a Grek, bischop of Cauntirbiri.

Aftir him was Deodatus iiii ȝere. He was of swech gentilnesse

---

10 Yradone] þradone P   13 Sarasines] *final* s *suprascript* M
27 ȝere] *suprascript with caret (in red)* M   30 was] s *suprascript with*
caret (in red) M   31 of] P, *om.* M

1–3: Martinus, 423/23–5.
4–9: ibid. 423/29–33.
10–26: ibid. 458/20–37.
27–8: ibid. 423/35–7.
29–31: ibid. 423/38–44.
32–77/3: ibid. 424/1–5.

þat no man asked him ony peticion and went awey desolat. In his tyme was þe body of Seynt Benet translate fro þe Mount of Cassine onto þe monasteri clepid Floriacense.

Than was Donus pope iiii ȝere. He mad þe fayre place betwix þe strete and þe dores of Seyn Petir cherch—þei clepe þat place 5 now *Paradisus Sancti Petri*.

Anno 5862–5878; 664–680. Constantinus IIII regned xvii ȝere. In his tyme þe sexte councell is hold at Constantinople of bischoppis to | hundred iiii score and viii ageyn Gregori, þe f. 46ʳᵇ patriark, whech meynteyned þe same heresi of Crist in whech his 10 fader and his ayle was infecte. An in þat councell was determined þat in þe persone of oure Lord Crist be not only to kyndis, but to willis. This emperour of good prouidens took trews with þe Arabes þat dwelled in Damasc, and with þe Bulgaris. He re-payred many cherches whech were distroied be heretikes. 15

In þe secunde ȝere of his regne was Agaton pope ii ȝere. He kissid eke a misel and mad him hool.

Aftir him was Leo IIᵘˢ pope x ȝere. He ordeyned þat þe prest schuld kis þe pax and þan send it to þe puple. He was eloquent both in þe Latyn tonge and in þe Grek. 20

Thanne was Benedictus IIᵘˢ pope i ȝere, whech repaired many cherches. And þan Johannes Vᵘˢ but o ȝere. And þan Zeno, not fully o ȝere.

Aftir him was Sergius ny x ȝere. He ordeyned þat *Agnus Dei* schuld be songen thries whil þe preste reseyued þe sacrament. 25 This man, be a special reuelacioun, fond in þe sacrarie of Seynt Petir cherch in a desolat place a forser of siluyr so old þat it loked lich no siluir, and whan he had ondo it he fond þere a grete porcion of oure Lordis crosse, arayed with gemmis.

Anno 5879–5888; 681–690. Justinianus Secundus regned x 30 ȝere. He | took trews with þe Sarasines for x ȝere, both be lond f. 46ᵛᵃ

---

13 þe] *om. over line division* P   17 hool] *in r.h. margin* M   18 IIᵘˢ] *nine-sign suprascript in red* M   21 IIᵘˢ] *nine-sign suprascript in red* M 22 Vᵘˢ] *nine-sign suprascript in red* M   26 in] *om.* P

4–6: ibid. 424/10–12.
7–15: ibid. 458/47–459/3.
16–17: ibid. 424/13–14.
18–20: ibid. 424/17–20.
21–3: ibid. 424/25–32.
24–9: ibid. 424/34–8.
30–78/6: ibid. 459/14–19.

and be se. This man with his wisdam and largenes encresed þe
empire, and broute it to mech worchip. He mad eke many lawes
and ded grete reuerens to þe Cherch. And in þe x ȝere of þis
empire on Leo Patricius ouyrcam him in batail, put oute his
5 eyne, and cut of his nose, and exiled him onto a place þei clepe
Tersone.

And in þis Justiniane tyme was at Rome a pope þei cleped
Leon, whech is not put in þe cathologe of popes, for he entired
nowt be eleccion but by fors of seculer hand.

10 Anno 5889–5891; 691–693. Leo þe Secund regned iii ȝere.
For on Tiberius put him fro þe empire, cut of his nose, and exiled
him to þe same place þere Justinian was.

And in þe first ȝere was Jon þe Sexte pope of Rome, whech was
a martire, and biried in catacumbis.

15 Anno 5892–5898; 694–700. Tiberius regned vii ȝere. In his
tyme Justiniane was in exile in Tersone, as we seid; he noysed
himself openly þat he schuld be emperour ageyn. Vpon þese
wordis þe puple þere ros ageyn him, and for loue of Tiberi
purposed for to kille him. And when he had aspied þis, he fled
20 to þe prince of Turkis, and weddid his sistir, and with þat princes
socour he conquered both Leon and Tibery, and killid hem,
f. 46ᵛᵇ and recured ageyn þe empire. | Aftir þat he venged him so vttirly
on his enmies þat, whan any drope of flewme fell fro his nose,
anon he comaunded of his enmies on schuld be slayn.

25 In þese dayes was pope Johannes VII ii ȝere, a cunnyng man and
a eloquent. He mad a oratori in Seint Petir cherch, of Moises-werk
depeynted, in worchip of oure Lady, where he lith byried.

Aftir him was on Sisinnius, but xx daies. And þan was Constantine pope vii ȝere.

30 Anno Mundi 5899–5904; 701–706. Justinian þe Secund regned
now ageyn vi ȝere. He was first pryuyd of his empire, and now,

1 largenes] s *suprascript* M   3 þe (2)] the P, *om.* M   7 at] a M, in P
16 in exile] exiled P   17 þat] þᵗ P, þa M   24 his] *suprascript* M
25 VII] þᵉ VII P   28 þan] than P, *om.* M   31 vi ȝere] *in r.h. margin* M

1–6: see p. 77.
7–9: Martinus, 424/43–8.
10–12: ibid. 459/21–2.
13–14: ibid. 425/4–6.
15–24: ibid. 459/25–30.
25–7: ibid. 425/7–10.
28–9: ibid. 425/11–13.
30–79/4: ibid. 459/31–4 and 425/14–17.

aftir þe resumpcion, he regned ageyn vi ȝere. For aftir þe tyme he
was so restored, he serued Criste deuoutly, and sent aftir Constantin þe pope to Constantinople, and þere was he oseled of his
hand.

In þat tyme Constantine was pope vii ȝere. He cursed Philip 5
þe emperour, for þe cause þat he distroyed ymages. And vndir
þis pope too kyngis of Ynglond went to Rome and were mad þere
munkis; and þis was aftir þe Brutes blood was oute of þe lond, for
þan was þe lond diuided into vii kyngdammes.

And ȝe schal vndirstand þat þis diuision began in þe first coming 10
of Saxones, whech was in þe ȝere of oure Lord 455. And here
we will expresse þe vii regiones, who þei were departed in þis
lond:—

The first kyngdam was in Kent, where þe first kyng was Hengist;
þe secund, Esk; þe þird, Occa; þe iiii, Emericus; þe v, Ethelbert— 15
he was baptized be Seint Austin, | bischop of Cauntirbiry.   f. 47ra

The secunde kyngdam was in Southsex, whech hath Kent on
þe est side; on þe south side, þe se; on þe west, Hamptschire;
on þe north, Suthrey. The first kyng was Elle, and þan his iii
sones; þe v was Athelwold, and he was conuerted be Byryn, 20
bischop of Dorsete.

The þird kyngdam was Estsex: on þe est side is þe se; on þe
west side, þe cuntré of London; on þe south side, Temse; on
þe north side, Suffolk. þe first kyng was Erkynwyn; þe secunde,
Neda; þe iii, Sibertus; þe iiii, Sebertus; þe v, Sigbertus—he was 25
conuerted be Melite, bischop of London.

The iiii kyngdam was Est-Ynglond, þat is to sey Norfolk and
Suffolk; on þe est side and north side is þe se; on þe west side,
Cambrigschire and Seint Edmund Fosse. The first kyng was
Offa; þe secund, Titilinus; þe iii, Rodwaldus; þe iiii, Erwaldus; 30
þe v, Sigebertus—he was conuerted be Felice, biscop of Donwich.

The v regne was Westsex, hauyng on þe est side Southsex, Temse
on þe north side, in þe west side and þe south þe se occean. þe

6 þat] om. P   15 þird] d suprascript M   26 conuerted] d suprascript M, conuerte P   28 Suffolk] l altered from r M   north side] the
north P   31 Donwich] wich over erasure M   33 north] over erasure M

5–8: ibid. 425/13, 18–20.

first kyng was Kredicus; þe secund, Kynricus; þe iii, Cheulingus; þe iiii, Chelricus; þe v, Helwolphus; þe vi, Kyngilis—he was conuerted and baptized be Seint Birine.

The sext kyngdam was cleped Merceorum, þe grettest cuntré
5 of all. On þe west side was þe watir þei clepe Dee, þat rennyth be Leicestir, and þe flood cleped Sabrine, þat rennith be Schrouysbyry onto Bristow; on þe south side, þe Temse; on þe north side, þe watir of Humbir. þe first kyng was Aella; þe ii, Cuda; þe iii,
f. 47rb Tynla; þe iiii, Ceorlus; þe v, Penda— | he was baptized be þe
10 handis of Fynian, bischop.

The vii kyngdam was Northumbirland; on þe este side and þe west side it hath þe se; on þe south side, þe flood of Humbir, whech goth up be þe herldam of Notingham and Derbi; on þe north side, þe Scotisch se. The first kyng was Ida; þe secunde, Aella; þe
15 third, Athelford; þe iiii, Edwyne—he was baptized be Pauline, bischop of 3ork.

Anno 5905; 707. Philip þe Secunde regned but o 3ere and sex monthis. This man distroyed in cherchis all ymages and pictures, and for þis cause þo ymages of oure Lady, þat Luce depeyntid,
20 þe Romaynes hid hem til he was ded, and for þat cause Constantyn þe pope cursed him, and so he deied.

Anno 5906-5908; 708-710. Anastasius Secundus regned iii 3ere. He took þe forseid Philip and put oute his eyne. But þis same Anastasius was so wikkid þat þe puple ros and mad a newe
25 emperour, was cleped Theodosius Tercius; and þei mad Anastacius a prest.

In þis tyme was Gregorius Secundus pope, and in þese dayes began Karolus Magnus his gret conquestis.

Anno 5909; 711. Theodosius Tercius regned but o 3ere, a
30 blessid man and a benigne, but on Leon put him oute with fors, and he paciently was mad a clerk and continued so in holy lyf.

Anno 5910-5934; 712-736. Leo Tercius, with Constantyn

---

5 clepe] cleped P   12 it hath] *twice* P   20 Constantyn] Constantyne
P, Costantyn M   24 ros] *suprascript with caret (in red)* M

17-21: Martinus, 459/38-40 and 425/18.
22-6: 459/41-3.
27-8: ibid. 425/21-34.
29-31: ibid. 459/44-5.
32-81/10: ibid. 459/46-460/2.

his son, regned xxv ȝere. In his tyme Sarasines come to Con|stan-   f. 47ᵛᵃ
tinople and beseged it too ȝere, and spoiled it, and bar awey mech
ricchesse.

In the same tyme Luidbrande, kyng of Lumbardis, hering
þat Sarasines had distroyed Sardini, where Seynt Augustin body   5
was leid whan it was broute fro Ypone, he sent þidir solempne
legates and boute þat body of þe Sarasines, and þei broute it to
Gene, where þe kyng met it with gret reuerens, and led it onto
Papie, and set it þere in a cherch of Seint Petir, whech he cleped
Celum Aureum.   10

In þis time was pope Zacharie x ȝere. He mad pes with þe
Longobardis, and þe bokes of *Dialoges* he translate fro Grew
into Latyn. To þis pope cam þe monkis of Cassinense, with on
Grete Charlys, desiring þat þe body of Seynt Benet schuld come
ageyn to her monasteri, whech þe munkis Floriacense had as   15
þei seide vntreuly bore fro hem. The pope graunted her entent,
but whan þei cam to þe bodi þei were smet with blyndnes and fer,
þat þei failed of here desire.

Anno 5935–5959; 737–761. Constantinus Vᵘˢ, þe son of
þe seid Leon, regned eke xxv ȝere. He was | a folower of his fader   f. 47ᵛᵇ
steppes all þe dayes of his lyf. He studied all in wichcraft, in   21
nigromancie. He was occupied in leccherie and glotonie, þat many
men, both in þe clergy and in þe lay-fe, be him were hurt
in her feith. He had consenting onto him a grete fautour to his
erroure, on Anastase, fals patriark of Constantinople. This   25
Constantin ded clepe a gret councel at Constantinople, in whech
he comaunded þat all þe ymages in þe Cherch schuld be pullid
down, both of Crist and of oure Lady and oþir seyntes, and in þis
mater he mad as gret persecucion as euyr ded Dioclecian.

In þis tyme was Stephanus II pope, whech for þe grete hate   30
and persecucion of Arstulf, kyng of Lumbardi, fled into Frauns,
and þere he anoynted Pipine kyng of Frauns. Thre myle þei
sey þe kyng went on fote, and led þe pope bridil þe same space,

---

2 it (1)] *suprascript* M   4 Luidbrande] Lyudbrand P   5 where]
over erasure M   Augustin] P, Aug|stin *over line division* M   12 translate]
P, transale M   14 Charlys] s *suprascript* M   16 had (*after* seide) *deleted
in red* M   21 all (1)] *om.* P   23 in þe (1)] of P   29 ded] *om.* P
32 and þere . . . Frauns] *om.* P

11–18: ibid. 425/48–426/7.
19–29: ibid. 460/14–25.
30–82/3: ibid. 426/13–18.

til he had broute him to his paleys. This pope, in the last ȝere
of his office, translate þe empire fro þe Grekis onto þe Frensch,
onto Grete Charlis.

In þese dayes was Paule pope. He ordeyned þat in Lenton all
5 þe dyuyne seruyse, saue completori, schuld be seyd befor non.
f. 48ʳᵃ He trans|late þe body of Seynt Pernel, and set on hir graue þe
titil þat Seint Petir mad, 'Of golden Pernel, oure best-beloued
doutir, þis is þe memorial'. This pope, with his trosti seruauntis
nowt many, vsed for to go o-nites to prisoneris and bedred folk,
10 and uisite hem with elmesse. He deied at Seint Paule and beried
at Seint Petir cherch.

Anno 5960–5964; 762–766. Leo þe IIII regned v ȝere. He
was a passing couetous man; whatsoeuyr he sey, he desired it.
So happed him com to a cherch, where he sey a precious crowne
15 ful of charbunculis. He took it fro þe cherch and were it on his
hed, and sone aftir he caute a feuyr and deied þerof.

In þis tyme Constantinus II^us was pope, þat entered þe office
with grete slaundre; þerfor God suffered oþir men to put oute his
eyne, and eke owt of þe Cherch.

20 Aftir him was Stephanus III^us pope. He called a councel of al
Itail and Fraunce, in whech he dampned al þat þe oþir pope had
doo, saue baptem and crisme, and he deposed all þoo persones
þat took ony orderes of him.

Than was Adrianus I^us pope xxiii ȝere, be whos menes and
25 prayeris þe Grete Charlis besegid þe Lumbardis in Papie, where
he took Desideri, þe kyng, and þe qwen, and sent hem prisoneris
into Frauns; and went forth to Rome, and fulfillid al þing þat
Pipine his fader had goue to Seynt Petir. He mored it eke with
his owne deuocioun, ȝiuing to þe Cherch þe ducheries of Spolet
f. 48ʳᵇ and Beneuentane. | He restored þe cherch of Seint Anastace at
31 þe Scipping Wateris—so be þei cleped for þe hed of Seint Paule

2 Frensch] Frensch tong MP   9 vsed] *suprascript with caret* (*in red*) M
17 II^us] IIus P, II M   19 eke] *in r.h. margin* M   20 III^us] *nine-
sign suprascript in red* M   24 I^us] *nine-sign suprascript in red* M   28 his
fader] *suprascript with caret* (*in red*) M   Petir] *in r.h. margin* M   31 of]
suprascript M

1–3: see p. 81.
4–11: Martinus, 426/19–26.
12–16: ibid. 461/13–14.
17–19: ibid. 426/30–2.
20–3: ibid. 426/33–6.
24–83/6: ibid. 426/37–51.

scippit thries aftir it was of, and þere be iii wellis. In þe same place
eke is þe chapel þat is cleped *Scala Celi.* He repaired eke þe
walles of Rome and mad þe dores of bras at Seynt Peteres.

In þis tyme lyued he þat is clepid Albinus, of Englisch nacioun,
whech was maistir onto Charles in al þe seculer sciens, and he 5
broute þe forme of study fro Rome onto Parys.

Anno 5965–5973; 767–775. Nicheforus regned in Constantinople ix ȝere. In his tyme þat empire wastid and went to nowt.

In þat tyme was Adriane stille pope at Rome; he repaired
many cherches both withinne þe walles and eke withoute. 10

Anno 5974–5975; 776–777. Michael regned to ȝere, a god man,
redy for to releue pore men, for all þo þat were depauperat and
spoiled be his predecessour he releuid with his owne good, and
all enmyes of þe feith he was euyr redy to distroye.

Anno 5976–5989; 778–791. Karolus þe First regned xiiii ȝere. 15
This man was kyng of Frauns or he was emperour, and be þe
instauns of Adriane, pope, he was cleped into Ytail and bese|gid þe f. 48ᵛᵃ
kyng of Lumbardie, took him, and sent him into Frauns, as is
seid before. Charles had in his tyme a myty felawchip, of whech
Rouland and Olyuere were captaynes, for þei kyllid many Sarasines 20
in Spayn, but at þe last þei were deceyued be fals treson of an
erle, þei clepid him Ganerion. This Charlis, as is writin, mad a
brigge ouyr þe Rene—summe men sey to—and þat was at Coleyn;
now is non. He had a berd, as þei sey, a fote long; in mete and in
drink he was ful temporat. His sones, anon as þei were of age, 25
were lerned to ride and to exercise hemself in dedis of armes.
His dowteres he sette ful bisily to þe occupacion of wolle. Whan
he cam to Rome he went on his feet and visit al þe cherchis,
kissid euery holi auter and euery relik.

Than visite he Jerusalem, and þere he had a glorious victorie 30
on Cristis enmies. þan cam he hom be Constantinople, where þe
emperour wold a goue him gold, siluir, and precious stones, but

3 Rome] *in r.h. margin* M   5 þe] the P, þese M   8 went] *in*
r.h. margin M   9 Adriane stille] P, Adriane *in r.h. margin after* stille *with-*
out carets to mark place of insertion M   at] of P   12 redy for to releue
pore men] *om.* P   15 Karolus] *change to darker ink* M   18 him (1)]
om. P   23 at] a P   32 emperour] P, empour M

7–8: ibid. 461/24–5.
9–10: ibid. 427/3–4.
11–14: ibid. 461/26–8.
15–84/9: ibid. 461/29–462/2.

he refused al, and desired noþing but relikes of Crist and of seyntes. Than fasted þei þat were with him, and prayed God þat þis donacioun schuld be acceptable to his magesté. There þe emperoure gaue him a part of Jesu crowne, þat flowred þere in here
5 site, and a nayle, with whech oure Lord was nayled to þe tre,
f. 48ᵛᵇ and a part of oure Lordis crosse, | þe sudarie of oure Lord, þe smok of oure Ladi, þe arme of Seynt Simeon—all þese relikes broute he to Acon, and set hem þere in a cherch of oure Lady whech he ded make.

10 In þis tyme deied Adrian, þe pope, and Leon þe IIII was pope aftir him xx ȝere. This pope, as he went on Ascencion Euen with þe letanie and procession, sodeynly com his enmies and took him be the body, led him to a place where þei put oute his eyne, cut oute his tunge, but oure blessed Lord gaf him both site and
15 speche. Tho went he to Charles, kyng of Frauns, and compleyned of þis wrong, and he receyued him with grete worchip, took venjauns on his enmies, and þere þe pope porged himself of certeyn crimes þat were purposed ageyn him.

Anno Mundi 5990-6014; 792-816. Lodwicus, with Lothari
20 his son, regned xxv ȝere. This was þe son of Gret Charlis, and he had to breþerin, on þat was regent of Teutonye, a othir þat was regent of Spayn. He had also iii sones, Lothari, Pipine, and Lodewik. The first mad he gouernour of al Itaile; the secund, kyng of Gyane; þe þirde mad he kyng to þe Bauaris and þe Germanes.
f. 49ʳᵃ In þis tyme þe lega|tis of Michael, emperour of Constantinople,
26 broute onto þis Lodewik þe bokes of Seyn Dyonise, whech he took with ful grete joye.

In þis tyme was Rabanus, a munk of Wiltens, a grete poete, and in diuinité ful wel lerned. He mad a book to þe same Lodewik
30 *Of Natures of al þing*, not only with litteral teching, but with many mysti exposiciones. And for his reward Lodewik mad him bischop of Mense.

In þis tyme was Stephanus IIIIᵘˢ pope iii ȝere. He went into Frauns onto þe Emperour Lodewik, and þere was he receyued

5 nayled] d *suprascript* M   17 on] of P   18 crimes] s *suprascript* M
19 *the year number* 6001 *miswritten as* 60001 M   23 secund] d *suprascript* M
26 onto] to *suprascript* M

1-9: see p. 83.
10-18: Martinus, 427/8-13.
19-32: ibid. 462/10-17.
33-85/2: ibid. 427/24-6.

ful gloriously. And be þe weye he boute many prisoneris and payed
her raunson.

Aftir him was Pascale vii ȝere, to whom Seint Cicile appered
and bad him take up þe bodies of Tiburce, Valerian, and Vrban,
and biry hem in hir cherch. This man repaired þe cherch of Seynt 5
Praxede, and set in monkis of Grece, and biried þere ii m bodies
of martires whech he gadered in dyuers places. He ded eke mech
cost in Seynt Sabyn cherch, for þat was his titel whan he was
cardinal.

Aftir him was Eugenius II^us pope iii ȝere, and þan Valentinus, 10
xl dayes.

Anno 6015-6024; 817-826. Lotharius Primus regned x ȝere.
In his dayes Sarasines destroyed þe cherchis of Petir and Paule
and ny al þe cuntré aboute Rome. Aftir þat, as þei went | hom to   f. 49^rh
Affrik, fro whens þei cam, þei were dronchin in þe depe see. 15
Now began þe eldest of þese thre breþerin to take upon him to
regne al alone. Vpon þis þe othir to breþerin rise ageyn him, and
þere was swech batail and swech morder of men, was neuyr swech
in al Frauns.

Anno 6025-6029; 827-831. Aftir þis þe same Lothari, with his 20
son Lodewik, regned v ȝer, and so in þe xv ȝere of his regne he
departed his lond betwix his sones, and took a munkis habite,
and deied so, and mad a holy ende. For his soule whan he was
ded was gret strif betwix angellis and deueles whech of hem
schuld haue it, in-so-mech þat þe monkis sey þe bodi be pullid 25
too and fro, but aftir deuoute prayer of hem þe deueles fled and
aungelis preuailed. In þe ix ȝere of his empire þe body of Seynt
Heleyn, Constantin modir, was translate fro Rome into Frauns.

And in þis tyme was Gregorius IIII^us pope xvi ȝere. He destroyed þe cherch of Seynt Martin in Montibus, and aftirward mad 30
it al newe. In þis tyme eke was a gret troubel amongis Cristen
men, for summe men of wikkid condicioun went oute of Rome
onto þe soudan, praying him þat he wold come þidir, and he cam

5 hir] ther P   21 regned v ȝer, and so] reg over erasure, ned . . . so in
r.h. margin M   21-2 he departed] om. P   26 fled] om. P

3-7: ibid. 427/27-33.
7-11: ibid. 427/34-8.
12-19: ibid. 462/37-41.
20-8: ibid. 462/47-52.
29-86/5: ibid. 427/39-48.
21294   G

with swech a multitude þat þe cité Leonyne was besegid and take,
and of Seynt Petir cherch þei mad a stabil; all Tussie eke was

f. 49va clene distroyed. Than at þe | prayer of þe pope, Marchio Gy
with þe Lumbardis, and Lodewic with þe Frenschmen, put
5 oute þe Sarasines with mech hurt onto Cristen men.

Anno 6030–6050; 832–852. Lodewic þe Secunde regned xxi
ȝere. In his tyme þe bodies of Seynt Vrbane and Tiburce were
translat and broute to þe cherch of Seint Germyn.

In þis tyme þe Danes aryued into Ynglond with too cursed
10 capteynes, Hingwar and Hubba. Thei distroyed þe cuntré and
killid þe glorious Kyng Edmund, first with schot of arowis, and
þan smet of his heed.

In þis tyme was Jon, clepid þe Scot, a excellent man in study of
scripture. He, at þe praier of þis kyng, translated þe bokis of Seynt
15 Dionise oute of Grew into Latyn. The same man, aftir þat, be
his malicious disciples was punchid to þe deth with poyntelis.

That same tyme was Sergius II^{us} pope. His name was before
Swynmouth; þerefor was ordeyned a statute of þe Cherch þat
fro þis tyme forward þe pope schuld chese him a new name.

20 In þis tyme þe vii regiones of Ynglond sesed, and þe lond was
f. 49vb broute into o monarchie, and þat was þe ȝere of | oure Lord
dccc and viii. þan began Egbrite for to regne, and he regned
xxxvii ȝere.

And in þe ȝere of oure Lord dccc and xlv regned Adelwolf,
25 Egbrite son; in þe xix ȝere of his regne went he to Rome, cause
of deuocion, and before Leon þe pope offered þat tribute whech is
cleped Rome-scot, of euery hous a peny. He was first a munk of
Wynchestir, and whan his fader was ded þe pope dispensid with
him, and made him wedde þe doutir of Charles (whech was clepid
30 Caluus), and be hir had he iiii sones: þe first, Ethelwold; þe
secund, Ethelbrite; þe þird, Ethelthrede; þe fourte, Alurede.

This Pope Leon mad for hem of Napeles—whan þei faute in
þe se ageyn þe Sarasines—þis orison, 'Deus, cuius dextera beatum

2 and] om. P   7 Tiburce] r altered from c M   21 Lord] d suprascript M   24 regned] in r.h. margin M   25 he] suprascript M
30 he] om. P

1–5: see p. 85.
6–16: Martinus, 463/1–15.
17–19: ibid. 428/1–2.
25–7: ibid. 428/5–7.
32–87/3: ibid. 428/17–22.

Petrum ambulantem', et cetera. And aftir tyme þat he made þe wallis of þe cité Leonine, þan made he þis orison, 'Deus, qui beato Petro collatis clauibus regni celestis'.

Aftir þis Leon, was pope of Rome on þat hite Jon, of Englisch nacion as sum sey, and sum sey sche was bore in Mens. Pope 5 sche was iii ȝere. The processe is told þus, þat in hir ȝong age sche went lich a man with a clerk to Attenes, and þere sche lerned þe Liberal Sciens, þat sche had þere no felaw. Aftir þis sche cam to Rome and red þere solemply, and was þere in swech opinion þat sche had grete maistires to hir scoleres. And whan þe popes sete 10 was vacaunt, for hir cunnyng and hir fame þei chose hir pope. So happed him þat led hir to Attenes be homely with hir, as he was wone to be, and God wold no lenger suffir þat erroure to be | secret, so fel sche with childe, and sche went onknowyng hir f. 50ra tyme fro Seynt Peteres onto Lateran. Hir cothis fel upon hir 15 betwix þe Collisé and Seynt Clement cherch, and þere sche deied, and þere was byryed. And at þis tyme þe pope goth not þat way.

Aftir hir deth was Benedictus IIIᵘˢ pope iii ȝere. He mad þe gate of Rome þat goth to Seynt Paules, and þat gate eke þat goth 20 to Seynt Laurens.

Than was Nicholaus Primus pope ix ȝere. Aftir Seynt Gregory þere was no swech many day. In his tyme Seint Cirille, a holy man amongis þe puple of Slauis, oute of þe se broute þe body of Seynt Clement onto Rome. 25

Anno 6051–6054; 853–856. Charlis þe Secund regned ny foure ȝere. He went to Rome and, with fauour of the pope, and giftis þat he gaue sundri lordis, was mad emperour. This þing herd his broþir Lodwik, and reisid a gret puple ageyn him, and faute with him, but he was stille emperour. This man, both in 30 Frauns and in Itaile, repayred many cherchis. In his tyme was not Flaundres so rich ne so grete-named as it is now, for it had no oþir gouernouris but þe fosteres of þe kyng of Frauns.

1 et cetera] om. P   tyme] þᵗ tyme P   2 þe] om. P   20 þat (2)]
t suprascript M   31 not] t suprascript M   31–2 not Flaundres] Flaundris
not P

4–18: ibid. 428/27–36.
19–21: ibid. 429/1–4.
22–5: ibid. 429/6–14.
26–33: ibid. 463/16–21.

In þese dayes was Adrianus II^us v ȝere. To þis man cam
Lotharie, þe kyng of Frauns (whom Nicholas had cursed, because
he held a mannes wif beside his qween) desiring of him absolucion.
And þe pope mad him and oþir to swere on þe sacrament wheþir
5　he was gilty or nowt, and þei swore fals, and were hoseled upon
f. 50rb　her oth, and in þe same ȝere, | as is seid, alle þei deied.

Than was Johannes VIII^us x ȝere. Vndir him was þe v councell
holdyn at Constantinoble of ccclxxx bischoppis, where Petir,
cardinal, was president, joyned with him Paule, bischop of Anti-
10　oche, and Eugeni, bischop of Hostiense.

Anno 6055–6066; 857–868. Charles þe þirde, whech is clepid
Grossus, regned xii ȝere. In his dayes was a gret hungir þorwoute
Ytaile. This man had Frauns and Germanie in pees, an in þe
secunde ȝere of his empire he was crowned of Jon, þe pope.

15　In þese dayes was a gret conflicte betwix Frenschmen and
Normannes, in whech v þousand Normannes were slayn. Than
þe Normannes, with help of Danes, distroyed Frauns and Lotharinge with fire and yrun, and many cités þei distroyed. Than
was mad pes on þis maner, þat þe kyng of þe Normannes schuld
20　be baptized, and þe king of Frauns schuld be his godfader; þan
schuld he wedde þe kyng of Frauns doutir, and he and his puple
schuld frely rejoyse all þe londe of þe oþir side of Seyne. The
first duke of Normandie was Robert; þe secund, William; þe
þirde, Richard; þe fourt, Richard; þe fifte, Robert Guychardy;
25　þe sexte, William, cleped *Notus*.

In þis tyme was pope Martinus II^us o ȝere and v month; and
f. 50va　þan Adrian þe þirde i ȝere; and þan Steuene | þe V vi ȝere; and
þan Formosus v ȝere, whech was disgraded be Jon þe pope fro
all þe ordres of þe Cherch onto lay astat, and aftir þat he was
30　restored be Martin þe pope, of whech mater was grete altercacion
in þe Cherch.

4 and] d *suprascript* M　　8 Constantinoble] Constantinople P, Con-
stantin|noble *over line division* M　　16 Normannes (1)] s *suprascript* M
17–18 and Lotharinge] *om.* P　19 Normannes] Normanes P, Normanne M
20 baptized] d *altered from* t M　　21 þe] P, *twice over line division*
M　he (2)] *om.* P　　24 Guychardy] Suychardy P

1–6: Martinus, 429/21–4.
7–10: ibid. 429/26–34.
11–25: ibid. 463/25–36.
26–31: ibid. 429/36–430/4.

Anno 6067–6078; 869–880. Arnulphus was emperour xii
ȝere. He fawte ageyn þe Normanndes, þat had destroyed Frauns,
Lotharinge, and Dardani, and dwellid þere. Aftir þat he fel in a
grete seknes, þat þere myte no medycyne help him, ne delyuer him
fro þe multitude of lys whech fret him onto þe deth. He had a 5
son, but he cam neuyr onto þe crowne; for here was ende of þat
empire þat longid to þe posterité of Charles.

In þis tyme were at Rome þese popes: Bonefacius þe Sexte,
xv dayes; Stephanus þe Sexte, o ȝere—he was a grete enmye to þe
Pope Formose. Than was Romanus iii monthes; and þan Theo- 10
dorus, ix dayes; and þan Johannes IXᵘˢ, ii ȝere—he was frend to
Formose; þan Benedictus IIIIᵘˢ, thre monthis; and þan Leo Vᵘˢ,
fourty dayes, for on Cristofer deposed him and was pope aftir him
—Cristofer was pope vii monthis, and he was eject fro þe Cherch,
and mad a munk.   15

Than was Sergius þe þirde vii ȝere, monthes foure. In his tyme
þe cherch of Lateranense fel down, and he mad it newe. This
Sergius was a dekne vndir þe Pope Formose, and þe Pope Formose |
put him oute of þe Cherch, and he fled into Frauns, but aftir, f. 50ᵛᵇ
he was made pope; and þan he comaunded þe body of þat same 20
Formose whech exiled him to be drawe out of þe graue and arayed
lich a bischop, and þan þe hed smet of, and þe body þrow into
Tibir. But fischeres fond þe body and brout it ageyn to Seint
Petir cherch, and þei seid certeyn ymages þat were þere ded
worchip to þe body.   25

In þis tyme regned Alured in Ynglond, þe fourt son of Adelwold.
He began to regne in þe ȝere of oure Lord dccclxxii. This man,
be þe councell of Seint Ned, mad an open scole of diuers sciens at
Oxenford. He had many batailes with Danes, and aftir many
conflictes, in whech he had þe wers, at þe last he ouyrcam hem, 30
and be his trety Godrus, her kyng, was baptized and went hom with
his puple. XXVIII ȝere he regned, and deied þe seruaunt of God.

1 Arnulphus] *change to narrower letter-strokes probably from use of thinner
quill* M   2 Normanndes] s *inserted on the line* M   5 þe (2)] *om.* P
12 IIIIᵘˢ] *nine-sign suprascript in red* M   13 deposed him] *suprascript with
caret (in red)* M   and was pope aftir him] *om.* P   16 ȝere] *suprascript* M
17 þe cherch] *suprascript with caret (in red)* M   20 þan] *suprascript with caret
(in red)* M   23 it] *suprascript with caret (in red)* M   29 had] mad P

1–7: ibid. 463/42–50.
8–15: ibid. 430/6–22.
16–25: ibid. 430/23–9.

Anno 6079–6084; 881–886. Lodewik þe þirde regned vi ȝere. At þis tyme þe empire went fro Frauns onto Ytaile, aftir þe prophecye whech was among þe Romanes: thei saide, because þe Frenchmen wold not socour hem ageyn þe Lumbardis, þei schuld
5 not be worthi to be clepid emperoures of Rome. And fro þis tyme forward summe regned in Itaile, and summe in Almayn, til þe tyme of Octo þe First. This Lodewik mad Berengarie, þat regned
f. 51ra þan in Itaile, for to fle þat lond, and whan he had con|quered, as he supposed, al Ytaile, sodeynly, at Verone, his enmyes took
10 him, put oute his eyne, and sette Berengari ageyn in his dignité.

In þis tyme was pope Anastasius IIIus ii ȝere; and þanne Lando, ii monthis; and þan Johannes Xus, xiii ȝere. He entered wrongfully into þat astate; þerfor knytis of an erle þei clepid Gy tok him, put him in prison, leyd a pelow on his mouth, and so strangild
15 him. Leo þe Sext was aftir him but v monthis.

Anno 6085–6088; 887–890. Berengarius Primus regned iiii ȝere. He was wise in dedis of armes, and had many batailes with þe Romanes. And in his tyme was þe abbey of Cloyne nobely foundid be on Wiliam, þat was þe first prince of Burgundie.
20 And in þis tyme was Stephanus VIIus pope ii ȝere.

Anno 6089–6095; 891–897. Conrardus, a Alemane, regned vii ȝere, but he is not anoumbered among þe emperoures because he regned not upon Itaile—þerfor wanted he þe benediccion imperial. Whan he deyed, he assigned to be his eyer Henry,
25 þe son of þe duke of Saxone.

In þis time was pope Leon þe VII thre ȝere; and þan Steuene þe VIII, oþir iii ȝere.

Anno 6096–6103; 898–905. Berengary þe Secunde regned

3 prophecye] prophecie P, pphecye M   thei] i *suprascript with caret* (*in red*) M, Thi P   14 so] *om.* P   19 foundid] found|did *over line division* P 20 was] s *suprascript* M   21 *the year numbers* 891 *to* 897 *miswritten as* 991 *etc. and deleted, correct numbers in r.h. margin* M   Conrardus] *change to narrower letter-strokes* M   26 time] *suprascript* M   28 *the year numbers* 898 *to* 905 *miswritten as* 998 *etc. and deleted, correct numbers in r.h. margin* M

1–10: Martinus, 463/52–464/3.
11–15: ibid. 430/30–46.
16–19: ibid. 464/4–5.
20: ibid. 430/48.
21–5: ibid. 464/6–9.
26–7: ibid. 431/1–3.
28–91/1: ibid. 464/10.

viii ȝere in Itaile, in whech tyme þe pope was Mar|tinus III^{us}, f. 51rb
iii ȝere; and aftir him Agapitus, vii ȝere. In þis tyme deied Odo,
abbot of Cloyne; and aftir him was abbot þere Adamarius;
and aftir him Majolus, a grete beginner of religioun. Of þis Ode
haue I sey dyuers werkes, on upon þe Sauter, and a gret book of 5
omelies.

In þese dayes regned in Inglond Edward, þe son onto Alured,
his oþir name was *Senior.* He mored his kyngdam in many
þingis, mad newe borowes, þoo þat were falle reysid hem ageyn.
He conqwered þe Scottis, þe Walschmen; þe kyngdammes of 10
Est-Ynglond, of Essex, and of Merce he took fro þe Danis. In his
dayes deied a nobil lady cleped Ethelfled, dowtir onto Edred,
kyng of Merce; sche bilid many townes: Bronbury, Tamworth,
Bronbrigge, Stafford, and Warwik. This same kyng is biried at
Wynchester.   15

Anno 6104–6121; 906–923. Henrius þe emperour regned in
Almayn xviii ȝere—in Alemane, and not in Itaile; þerfor is not he
acountid among þe emperoures. In þis tyme Spigreuus, duke of
Bem, was conuerted to þe feith, and lyued aftir þat a ful blessed
lif. Necenlaus, his son, folowid his fader steppes, and, for enuye, 20
his broþir killid him. And ccc | ȝer aftir his passion he appered to f. 51va
Kyng Herri, king of Danis, and told him þat he schuld deye in
þe same maner whech he deyed, praying him þat in þe honour of
Nycenlaus he schuld make a monasteri. The kyng, whan he was
awakid, called his seruauntis and inqwired what þis Nycenlaus 25
was. Thei answerd him, 'A prince of þe lond of Bem, wrongfully
slayn be his broþir'. And anon he ded make a monasteri of þe
Cistewis, and leide þe body þere.

Vndir þis tyme was Johannes XII pope xii ȝere. This man had
a fader þei cleped Albert, a myty man of good. He cleped þe men 30
þat myte moost doo in þe eleccion, gaue hem grete giftis, and
mad hem for to swere þat, whan Agapitus was ded, þei schuld

---

4 Ode] e *altered from* o M, Odo P   10 Walschmen] s *altered from* c M
12 Ethelfled] Ethelfeld P   13 Bronbury] Bronbrigg P   14 Bronbrigge]
Bronbury P   16 *the year numbers* 906 *to* 922 *miswritten as* 1006 *etc. and
deleted, correct numbers in r.h. margin* M   þe] *the twice over line division* P
21 ȝer] *supplied, om. over page division* M, *om.* P   his (2)] s *suprascript* M

1–6: ibid. 431/5–9.
16–28: ibid. 464/11–36.
29–92/7: ibid. 431/10–15.

promote his son Constantine on þat same astat. And so was he
pope, and called Johannes XII^{us}. He was vicious of lyuyng, a
hunter outeragious, a lecchour withouten schame; for he held
women openly—and þat dyuers—to grete slandir of þe Cherch.
5 For þis cause many of þe cardinales writyn onto Octo, prince of
þe Saxones, þat he schuld come and help to remeue þis erroure
and þis vileny of þe Cherch.

Anno 6122–6129; 924–931. Berengarius Tercius regned viii
ȝere.

10 In his tyme was pope Benedictus V. He entered into þat astate
f. 51vb be violens of þe Ro|manes, for Leon was chose before him, and
he þus broute in be violens. But þe Emperour Octo cam to Rome
and deposed þis Benedicte, and sette in Leo, þat was rithfully
chosen. He made a statute ageyn þe pride of Romanes þat þere
15 schuld no pope be intronized withoute consent of þe emperour.

In þis tyme regned Athelstane, þe son of Edward. He fawte
ageyn Anlaf, kyng of Erlond, and ageyn Constantyn, kyng of
Scottis, at Banborow, where, þorow þe prayeres of Seynt Ode,
a swerd fel fro heuene into his schaberk. He maried on of his
20 douteris onto þe Emperour Octo, and þat same emperour sent him
þe swerd whech Constantine fawt with—in þe handelyng þerof
was closed on of þoo iiii nayles þat were in Cristis handis and feet.
He sent him eke þe spere of Constantyn—þe hed þerof was in
Cristis side—and mech more oþir þing. In his tyme was Seynt
25 Birstane bischop of Wynchestir, þat euery day sang messe or
requiem. And on a tyme, as he walkid about a cymyteri seying his
dirige, and endid þus, 'Requiescant in pace', he herde oute of þe
erde innoumbred voises sey, 'Amen'. He regned xvi ȝere.

Anno 6130–6131; 932–933. Lotharius þe Secunde regned to
30 ȝere. In his tyme þe sunne appered lich blood, and withinne fewe
dayes aftir þat þere were grete batayles and many men dede.

Anno 6132–6142; 934–944. Berengary the Fourte, with Albert
f. 52ra his son, reg|ned xi ȝere. This Berengari was comorows to þe

2 XII^{us}] XIIus P, XII M   3 he] *suprascript* M   7 vileny]
velenly P   22 þoo iiii] þe iii P   25 Birstane] Bristane P   or] r *altered
from* f M, of P   27–8 oute of þe erde] *om.* P   29 regned] P, regne M

1–7: see p 91.
8–9: Martinus, 464/40.
10–15: ibid. 431/20–5.
29–31: ibid. 464/41–2.
32–93/5: ibid. 464/43–465/2.

puple, and he tok Lothari wif—sche hite Daluida—and put hir
in prison. But Octo þe emperour cam into Ytaile and tok þe
woman oute of prison and weddid hir, put Berengari fro þe
regne, and he was þe last þat regned in Ytaile born of þat cuntré.
Than went Octo to Rome and receyued þe imperial crowne.   5

In þese dayes regned in Ynglond Edmund, þe broþir of Athelstan, ix ӡere. He begat of his qwene, Elgiue, to sones, Edmunde
and Edgare. He recured fro þe Danes v citées: Lyncoln, and
Leicetir, Staunford, Notingham, and Derby. In þo dayes William
Longswerd, duk of Normandie, was killid be deceyte of Lodewik,   10
kyng of Frauns. Thanne þe cheueteynes of Normandie tok þe
kyng of Frauns in Rone and streited him so þere tyl he graunted
þat Richard, þe son of þe forsaid Wiliam, schuld frely holde al
Normandy. And fro þis tyme forward, in euery collocucion of
þe kyng and þe duk, it schuld be lefful to þe duke to be girt with   15
his swerd, and þe king neythir haue swerd ne knyf. This Edmund
was killid at a feste on Seyn Austyn day of a man þat he sey sitte
at mete. The kyng was bysy to pulle him fro þe bord, and þe oþir,
in his pulling, gorid þe kyng and scaped withoute harm.

Anno 6143–6154; 945–956. Octo þe First regned xii ӡere. He   20
was | þe first þat regned both in Itaile and in Alemayne; for fro   f. 52ʳᵇ
þis day forward þe empire hath be among þe Almanes. This
Octo, aftir he had regned many ӡeres in Almayne, þe cardinales of
Rome sent for him for þe insolens of Jon, þe pope, and he rod
þidir with his wyf, and whan he had mad pes þorwoute al Ytaile   25
he rod ageyn into Saxon, and þere he begat a child to be his
successour, lich him both in condicion and in name. Ofte in his
lyf went he to Rome and hom ageyn for to se good gouernauns in
þe Cherch, and in his last ende he mad a real monastery at Maydenborow in his owne cuntré, and þere is he biried.   30

In þis tyme was Johannes XIIIᵘˢ pope, whech was exiled be
Petir, meyhir of Rome. First was he prisoned in þe Castel of
Aungel, and þan exiled into Campanie; but aftir x monthes, be
þe help of Octo, emperour, he cam to Rome and took venjauns of
his enmies, and dured viii ӡere.   35

5 to] *suprascript* M   12 Rone] Rome P   22 day] *suprascript with
caret (in red)* M   29 his] P, *om.* M   31 XIIIᵘˢ] XIIIIus P

20–30: ibid. 465/5–21.
31–5: ibid. 431/26–31.

Aftir him was Benedictus VI but o ȝere, for he was strangeled in þe Castel Aungel.

In þis tyme was Edred kyng in Ingland, þe son of Adelstan, broþir to þe forseid Edmund. He regned viii ȝere.

5 And aftir him was Edwyn. He was crowned of Odo, archbischop of Cauntirbiry, at Kingeston, fast be London, but þe first day þat þe
f. 52ᵛᵃ king had | take his crowne, fel in onleful lecherie beside his wyf; aftir, whan Dunstan was bischop, and whan Dunstan vndirtook him of his sinne, he exiled Dunstane, but þe king was deposed within v ȝere.

10 Anno 6155–6174; 957–976. Octo þe Secund, with Octo his son, regned xx ȝere. This man, as he pursewid þe Grekis in Calabir, onwisely lost his knytes, and so he fled fro her handis. Than gadered he a host and besegid Benevent; whan he had take þe cité he took þe bones of Seynt Bartholomé and broute hem to
15 Rome, and leyd hem þere in a ylde þat is in Tibir, purposing to cary hem into his cuntré. But he deied sone, and þe tresor left þere. This man went with his qwen onto Rome and þere was he receyued of Benedict þe VII with mech joye, and crowned with his qween. Than cam ageyn him into Calabir many naciones,
20 in whech batail he was fayn to fle, and seid he was on of þe emperores men, and whan he was schippid þe schipmen supposed verily he was emperour, and seide in Grew þat þei wold lede him to Constantinople to þe emperour. This vndirstod he and seide onto hem þat in þe ilde of Scicile he had gret tresoure hid, prayng
f. 52ᵛᵇ hem þei wold | aryue þere and þei schuld haue part, and whan þei
26 cam to þe brynk he sey a bischop of his knowlech, and with his helpe þus he scaped.

In þis tyme was Donus pope i ȝere; and þan Bonefacius þe Sexte, iii ȝere; and þan Gilbert, a nygromancer, þat deied at
30 messe, for he was dymembered be his owne comaundment, for his sinne, in a chapel at Seint Cruce, þei clepe it Jerusalem.

In þese dayes was Edgare kyng in Inglond vii ȝere. He cleped Seynt Dunstan hom oute of exile. He mad a very vnité of all þe

---

1 but] *suprascript* M　　　2 Aungel] of Aungell P　　　5 Odo] *letter erased after final* o M　　　6 but] but aftir whan Dunstan was bischop MP
7–8 aftir whan Dunstan was bischop] *supplied from position specified in preceding note*　　25 part] *suprascript* M　　31 at] t *suprascript* M　　32 Edgare] Egare P　　　33 Dunstan] P, Dunstam M

1–2: Martinus, 431/21–33.
10–27: ibid. 465/22–40.
28–31: ibid. 431/34–432/3.

vii kyngdammes. He was cleped pesibel Edgare. In þe v ȝere of
his regne, Ethelwold, bischop of Wynchestir, put chanones seculer
—and ouyr seculer—oute of þe monasterie, and set in munkis.
This Edgare founded þese abeyes: Glasconbyry, Abyngdon,
Borow, Staunforth, and Thorney.   5
     Aftir him was his son kyng, whech is a martir, killid be þe
fraude of Alfrik, his stepmodir; but aftir þat sche ded penauns:
sche translate him onto Schaftisbyry; and too monasteries of
women ded sche make, on at Werwell, where sche lith, a oþir at
Ambrisbury, fast by Salisbury.   10
     Anno 6175–6193; 977–995. Octo þe þirde regned xix ȝere.
This man was crowned at Rome of Gregori þe V. He browt þe
body of Pauline, þe bischop, to Rome. He beseged on Crescens,
þat mad mech debate in Rome, specialy in elleccion | of þe pope. f. 53ra
He besegid him, as we saide, took him, and smet of his hed. He   15
began to make a paleys, and þe Romanes letted him, and aftir
mech vexacioun of hem he deied.
     Thus regned þese iii Octones, ech aftir oþir. And aftir her deth,
þe empire went no lenger be succession, but be eleccion. The
institucioun was mad þus, þat vii persones schul chese þe em-   20
perour: iii chaunceleris—bischop of Mense, chaunceler of Ger-
mani; bischop of Treuer, chaunceler of Frauns; bischop of
Coloyne, chaunceler of Ytaile—the markeys of Branburgense,
chambirleyn; the duke of Ostrych, marchale; the duke of Saxon,
berer of þe swerd; the kyng of Bem, butler.   25
     In þis tyme was Gregori þe V pope; and þan Jon þe XVII;
and þan Siluestir þe Secund, þat was a nygromancer, as we saide
before, and deied at Seint Cruce: ther is his hert; his bones ly
at Lataranense. His bones clater, as þei sei, and his graue swetith
before þe deth of a pope. In þis tyme lyued Fulbert, bischop of   30
Carnotense, þat mad þoo responses of oure Lady, *Stirps Jesse* and
Solem justicie, and þat ympne, *Chorus noue Jerusalem*.
     Anno 6194–6205; 996–1007. Herry þe First regned xii ȝere.

1 Edgare] Edgarie P   7 stepmodir] o *suprascript* M   8 him]
suprascript with caret (in red) M   13 Pauline] Paline P   beseged] seged P
14 þat] t *suprascript* M   27 þan] *om. over line division* P   31 responses]
Respones MP   Stirps] Stripis P

11–25: ibid. 466/1–19.
26–30: ibid. 432/13–39.
30–2: ibid. 466/25–6.
33–96/8: ibid. 466/27–35.

He is clepid 'I' for he was first of þe empire—þe othir Herry was
_{f. 53rb} neuyr crowned emperoure, and þe same reu|le is vndirstand of
þe Conrardis. This Herry had a wif þei cleped Chymegundis,
and þei both be on asent kept hem virgines al her lyf; þei ly both
5 byried in þe cherch cleped Banburgense, doyng many miracles.
He was befor þe empire duke of Bem, and for his manhod þei
chose him emperoure, and aftir many batailes he and his qwen
chose a solitari lif and mad a blessed ende.

In þis tyme was pope Johannes XII v monthis; and þanne Jo-
10 hannes XIII, v ȝere. In his tyme was Robert kyng of Frauns,
whech was so deuout þat, in euery grete feste, he wold be in
summe monasteri at euery seruise and stand himselue in a cope
of silk and gouerne þe qwer. So it happed þat he besegid a castel,
and þe feste of Seynt Aniane fel in þe same tyme: he left sege,
15 went to cherch, and as he kneled at *Agnus Dei* at messe þe castell
wallis fell down. He mad þat sequens, *Sancti Spiritus assit nobis
gratia.*

In Ynglond regned þis tyme Ethelthredus, þe broþir of Edward
Martir. He was so acomered with Danes þat he, be þe councel of
20 þe bischop of Cauntirbury, he acorded with hem to pay hem
ȝerly x þousand pound, and þe secund ȝere xvi þousaund, and so
þei reised him to xl þousand. In þe xxiiii ȝere of his regne he
wedded Emme, cleped 'þe broche of Normandie', þe doutir of
Richard þe Secund, duke of þe same. And þan sodeynly he sent
_{f. 53va} letteris pryuyly þat alle | þe Danes schuld be killid on o day, but
26 it availed not, for on þe nyte befor Seynt Bryce day þe Danes
destroyed Excetre, Wilton, Salesbury, Norwich, and Thetforth.
And sone aftir cam Swayn and Anlaf, to whom Vtred, duke of
Northumbirland, and all Lyndesey mad subjeccion, and receyued
30 him as her kyng. Ethelthredus fled into Normandye. Than sent
many of þe lond onto him and seid, if he wold be more gentil
onto hem þan he was before, he schuld be welkom. So cam he and
distroyed mech of Lyndisey, but he caute not Knowt, þat dwelt
þere. Than mad Swayn a grete comminacion to þe town of Seynt

---

2 neuyr] neur P   3 þei cleped] *om.* P   8 blessed] d *over erasure* M
ende] *om.* P   12 seruise] *in r.h. margin with carets* (*in red*) M   19 Danes]
s *suprascript* M   20 of Cauntirbury] *in r.h. margin with carets* (*in red*) M
30 her] hir P   34 comminacion] comminiacion P

1–8: see p. 95.
9–17: Martinus, 432/40–8.

Edmund, þat he schuld distroye it. Ferþermore he seid vilens
wordis ageyn þe seint, and sone aftir, in þe town of Gaynysborow,
Seint Edmund appered onto him and killid him with a spere.

Anno 6206–6207; 1008–1009. Imperium vacat ii annis.

Anno 6208–6227; 1010–1029. Conrardus Primus regned xx 5
ȝere. He loued pes aboue al þing, and þerfor he mad a lawe þat,
who þat brekith pes betwix ony princes, he schuld lese his hed.
Than was a erle in his lond þei clepid Lupold. He was accused to
þe emperour þat | he had broke þis statute, wherfor he fled into f. 53ᵛᵇ
wildirnesse, and lyued as a heremit with wif and childirn—no man 10
wist where he was. And happed aftirward þe kyng huntid in þe
same forest, lost his meny; nyte fell on, and for very nede was
loggid with þis heremite. And þat same nyte þe cuntesse had
childe, and a voys herd þe emperour þat þis same child schuld be
his successour. And þe emperour had scorne þat so pore a child 15
schul regne aftir him, comaunded his seruauntis to bere þe child
into þe wod, sle him, and bring him þe hert. Thei þoute of pité
þei myte not fulfille þis; þei leide þe child in þe leuys and broute
him þe hert of a hare. A duke þei cleped Herry fond þe child,
bare it to his hous, and because his wif was bareyn þei feyned it 20
was her. Whan þe child was growe þe emperour dyned with þis
duke, þe child stood before him, and he gan remembre þe face of
þat child whech he comaunded to be slayn, desired him of þe
duk, led him forth, sent him to þe emperesse with swech a lettir,
'þat day þat ȝe receyue þis child, ordeyn for him þat he be ded'. 25
So happed þe child for to slepe in a prestes hous be þe weye,
and þe prest red þe lettir, of pité he raced þe clause and chaungid
it into þis sentens, 'That day ȝe receyue þis child, in moost
goodly hast wedde him to oure doutir'. Whan þe emperour cam |
hom and sey þat Goddis ordinauns wold not be broke, took it f. 54ʳᵃ
more at ese, specialy whan he knewe what man was his fader. 31

In þese dayes of Herry and Conrard were at Rome þus many
popes: Benedictus VIII, Johannes XX, Benedictus IX—in his
tyme was mech scisme, and he appered to a holy man aftir his

2 Gaynysborow] Gy'a'nisboro *with* a *inserted suprascript with caret* P
4 1009] *supplied, om.* M   17 him (2)] *suprascript with caret (in red)* M
Thei] i *suprascript with caret (in red)* M   21 her] hir P   þe (1)] þis P
22 he *suprascript* M   gan] began P   30 be] *suprascript* M   it] *suprascript* M

4: ibid. 466/27.
5–31: ibid. 466/37–467/12.
32–98/18: ibid. 432/49–434/4.

deth in straunge liknesse, his hed and his tayl lych a asse, al þe
body lich a bere. Than was Sergius IIII, a man of good conuersacion; and þan Gregorius VI. In his tyme þe Cherch was spoiled,
pilgrimes robbed, þe offeringis of þe auter take with violens.
5 First þis man cursed hem þat vsed þese dedis. Aftir he distroyed
hem with strong hand. Therfor, whan he schuld deye, þe cardinales saide he was not worthi to be biried in Seynt Petir cherch,
for þe habundauns of blood whech he had spilt. And he answerd
ful sobirly, 'Put my body whan I am ded upon a bere, and set it
10 before Seint Petir dores, schette hem, and as ȝe se, so do'. Whan
it was set þere, sodeynly þere cam a wind and brast þe dores ope
with swech a violens þat þei stoyned on þe wall, and þan þei
biried him worchipfully. Than was Clement þe Secund; and þan
Damasus þe Secund. These to entered not wel, and þerfor þei
15 lyued not long, þe on but xix monthis, þe oþir xxiii daies. Than
was Leo X^{us} v ȝere, a holy man; than Victor II^{us}—he held a
councel at Florens, where he deposed many bischopis for symony
and fornicacion. Than was Stephanus IX.

In þis tyme was kyng in Inglond Edmunde, cleped Yrunside. |
f. 54rb He had many batayles, specialy with Knowt, and aftir many
21 conflictes þei wer acorded þat þei to schuld fite alone, and in her
strif Knowt aspied þe grete corage of Edmund, and seyd, 'Sese!'
and þan þus, 'Broþir myn Edmund', he seith, 'we wil no more fite;
lete us fro þis tyme lyue as breþerin. Half Denmark schal be þin,
25 half Inglond schall be myn'. And þus þei left bataile, and kissid,
and frendis for euyr. Alle þe puple þat was þere wept for joye.
But sone aftir was he slayn be þe councel of Edrede, þe duke, for
he mad his son for to hide him vndir a sege where þe king schuld
voide, and sodeynly with a scharp basulard he smet the kyng
30 among þe boweles and killid him. The duke cam to Knowt and
seide on þis wise, 'Heil, kyng alone!' And whan þe kyng had vndirstand þe maner of Edmundis deth, he seid onto þe duke, 'And I
schal sette þe hiest of ony lord in Ynglond'. So he ded smyte of
his hed and sette it on þe hiest tour in Londoun. This Edmund is
35 biried at Glascunbury.

3 þan] *om.* P   10 dores] dore M, dor P   13 Clement] t *supra-*
script M   16 X^{us}] *nine-sign suprascript in red* M   23 myn] *om.* P
he seith] seith he P   28 þe king] *in r.h. margin* M   34 hed] *suprascript*
with caret (in red) M

1–18: see p. 97.

Anno 6228–6230; 1030–1032. The empire voyde iii ȝere.

Anno 6231–6247; 1033–1049. Herry þe Secund regned xvii ȝere. In his tyme was founde at Rome a body of a geaunt, not roten; þe wownde þat he deyed of was foure feet of length. þe bodi of him was | as hy as ony wal; a lanterne at his hed brennyng f. 54ᵛᵃ was founde, þat myte not be qwenchid with lycour ne with wynd, 6 but anon as þei had mad a hole, þat þe eyre myte entre, þe lite was oute. Thei sey Turnus killid þis geaunt, for his epitafi was wretin þus:—

Filius Euandri Pallas, quem lancea Turni 10
Militis occidit more suo, iacet hic.

'The son of Euander, Pallas, whech þe spere of Turnus þe knyte killid on his maner, here he lith.'

In þis tyme was in Naples a ymage of marbil, with a sercle of bras, in whech was wrytyn þus:— 15

In þe kalendis of May, whan þe sunne schynyth in his uprysyng, I schal haue a hed of gold.

And, be wit of a Sarasine, þei merked þe schadow of his hed, þe same houre diggid þere, and founde mech gold.

In þis tyme was þere grete scisme in þe Cherch of Frauns 20 be on Berengarie, þat held þis heresie, þat þe sacrament of þe auter is not very Cristis body and his blood, but figure of his body and his blood. And agayn þis heresy Nicholas, þe pope, gadered a hundred bischoppis and xiii, and mad him to reuoke þis heresie, and þis reuocacion is put in þe book whech þei clepe *Decrees de* 25 *Consecratione*, distinctio ii, 'Ego Berengarius'.

In þes dayes were þese popes: Benedictus Xᵘˢ, x monthes; and Nicholaus IIᵘˢ, ii ȝere; and þan Alexander IIᵘˢ, xi ȝere.

In þis tyme regned in Ynglond Alured, þe | first-begote son of f. 54ᵛᵇ Ethelthrede. Than was a sly man duke of Kent, his name was 30 Godwyn. He had a fayre doutir, þei cleped hir Ydanie, and for he supposed þat þis king wold not wedde hir, he procured sotily

---

13 killid] *suprascript with caret (in red)* M   he] *om.* P   25 in] P, *om.* M
26 distinctio] *om.* P   27 þes] s *suprascript* M   32 þat] *om.* P   hir]
suprascript with caret (in red) M

1: Martinus, 466/37.
2–26: ibid. 467/14–33.
27–8: ibid. 434/6–11.

þe deth of þis man, þat he mite wedde hir to Edward, þe ȝonger
broþir, wheche aftir him schuld be kyng. Be þis maner he deceyued
þe puple: 'This king', he seith, 'is a Norman o þe moderes side,
and now hath he brout in Normannes with him to distroye this
5 Englisch puple'. So, be his councell, þei met þe Normannes at
Gildeforth, and bonde hem, killid euyr ix and saued þe x. The
kyng þei took, þut oute his eyne, and brout him to Hely, where he
deied within few dayes.

Than cam Edward into þis lond but with fewe persones, and
10 was crowned at Wynchestir on Pas-day. In þe xi ȝere of his regne
deyed his modir, Emme, þe duke doutir of Normandie. It is þe
same Edward þat lith at Westmester.

Anno 6248-6296; 1050-1098. Herry þe þird regned xlix ȝere.
In his tyme was mech hungir and pestilens ny þorwoute þe world.
15 In þat tyme Hildebrande, a cardinal, wheche was pope aftir, whil
he was a legate in Frauns, in a councell wheche was gadered ageyn
f. 55ra þe simonianes, saide onto a bischop þat entred | be symonie þat
he schuld sey, 'Gloria Patri et Filio et Spiritui Sancto'. He coude
neuir sey 'Spiritui Sancto' tyl he was deposed, and þan he seid it.
20 In his tyme were þese popes:—

Gregorius VIIus—he was a man of good conuersacion, and ȝet
a fals meyhir of Rome þei cleped Censius took him at messe on
Cristmesse morow and prisoned him. But þe Romanes distroyed
þe prison and delyuered him. He cursed þe Emperour Herry
25 for þe scisme he set in þe Cherch, and compelled him to com
barefoot in frost and snow and aske his absolucion.

Aftir him was Victor IIIus o ȝere; and þan Vrbanus IIus, xi
ȝere—in his dayes a duk þei cleped Beamunde recured þe sepulcur
of Crist. He held a councell at Claremount in wheche was ordeyned
30 þat mateyns and houres of oure Lady schuld be seid euery day,
and on Satirday hir hool seruyse. This pope gadered a councel in
Frauns, where many princes, þorw his stering, went into þe
Holi Lond, and be reuelacion þei fond þere Cristis spere; and

6 hem] *suprascript with caret (in red)* M   7 þei] i *suprascript* M
22 him] *in r.h. margin* M   23 prisoned] ed *suprascript with caret (in red)* M
26 barefoot] bar' M, bar P   32-3 into . . . reuelacion] into þe Holi Lond
in r.h. margin M, & be reuelacion into þe Holy Lond & P

13-19: Martinus, 467/34-46.
21-6: ibid. 434/23-9.
27-101/2: ibid. 434/39-435/8.

þere þei conqwered Acon, | Antioche, Tripolim, and ny al þe f. 55ʳᵇ
lond, and Jerusalem.

Aftir him was Paschasius xviii ȝere. In þis tyme entred Seynt
Bernard þe order of Sistewys vndir þe Abbot Steuene—he but
xii ȝere old. In þis tyme eke began þe order of Premonstracense.   5

Than was Gelasius þe Secund pope o ȝere; and þan Kalixtus IIᵘˢ,
v ȝere.

In þese dayes, þat is to sey þe ȝere of oure Lord mlxvi, William
Bastard, duke of Normandie, cam into Ynglond, and what rite
he had for to regne, here I wil write onto ȝou:—   10

Harald occupied þe crowne and had no rite þerto, for he was
son onto þat fals tretour Godwyn, whos doutir King Edward
weddid, þei clepid hir Ydani, of whom is seid, 'As a þorn bringith
forth a rose, so sprang Ydani of Godwyn'. This Godwyn killid
Edward broþir, and was tretour to Edward. So happed it on a   15
tyme he sat at mete with Kyng Edward, and þe kyng rehersid
onto him his eld treson and þe suspecion þat men had to him of
new treson. And þan Godwyn took a pece of bred in his hand,
and seid þus, 'Mi souereyn lord, if euyr I ment treson onto ȝou,
I pray God þat þis o mussel strangil me'. Thus he seid, and þus   20
it was. His son was Haraldus, whom Kyng Edward cleped before
his deth, and sent him into Normandye, to Duk William, for to
telle him þat þe kyng asined him his successour, both be testament, and eke as nexte of kyn. And þere þe same Harald swore
to Duke William þat he schuld be to him trew ligeman, and ded   25
or mad onto | him homage. The same feith mad he to Kyng   f. 55ᵛᵃ
Edward, but whan Edward was ded he took upon him þe regalie,
and was crowned kyng. Than went Duk William to Alisaunder,
þe pope, and expressed onto him þe rite whech he had to þe
crowne of Ynglond, and þe pope comaunded him on his blessing   30
þat he schuld porsewe his rite. Tho cam he into Inglond, and

6 þan] om. P   8 þe] þ altered from ȝ M   12 son onto] P, son
to suprascript with caret (in red) M   13 hir] om. P   Ydani] Ytani P
16 Kyng Edward] þe kyng P   23 asined] i surmounted by short stroke
in red M

3–5: ibid. 435/11–36.
6–7: ibid. 435/37–40.

londid at Hastingis, and ageyn him was Harald with grete power. It is told þat þere were certeyn knytes xx on Wiliam side þat swore þei schuld not leue til þei broke þe hoost and cam to Haraldis standard. And þou3 it were hard for to do, 3et it was doo. So had William þe victori, and rod forth to London, and at Westminster was he crowned in Cristmesse of Aldred, bischop of 3ork. This bataile was on Seynt Kalixte day, and in þe same feld where it was, he ded make a abbey—it is clepid at þis houre þe abbey of Batayle.

The secund 3ere of his regne William went into Normandy, and led with him þe bischop of Cauntirbyri, whos name was Stigand, and many oþir lordis. He mad leftenaunt of þis lond his owne broþir, bischop of Bathe, his name was Odo. And a litil before wyntir he cam ageyn with his wif, Maute, and in his comyng he distroyed Excetre, for þei rebelled. Sone aftir was þe qwene crowned. And þat 3ere he founded þe castel of Nothingam and þe castel of 3ork.

In þe v 3ere of William, Baldewyn, þe abbot of Bury, purchased of Alisaundre, þe pope, þe rite to singe as a bischop, and | þe pope gaue him a ryng and a superaltarie of porphiri-ston whech he had halowid and blessid.

In þis kyngis dayes was hald a councel at Wynchester, in þe presens of to cardinales, where Stigandus, archbischop of Cauntirbury, was deposed for iii causes: on was for he kepte þe chirch of Cauntirbury and þe cherch of Wynchestir both in his handis dyuers 3eres; a othir cause, for, lyuyng his predecessour Robert, he vsurped his office, in-so-mech þat he used þe palle; the þirde cause, for þe palle þat he took whan he was mad bischop he took of Benedicte, whech was a antepope, and stood acursed. Thus was he deposed and put in prison, and þere he seide he had not a peny in þe world; so was he susteyned at þe kyngis cost ful porely. But whan he was ded þei fonde a keye aboute his nek þat broute hem to mech tresore hid. Aftir he was deposed, Lamfrank was bischop of Cauntirbury, a monk and priour of Bek, born in Itaile, a gret clerk—and þat is schewid in many þinges, specialy in a book whech he mad ageyn Berengary. And at 3ork þe kyng mad a bischop, þei cleped him Thomas—he was born in Bayon. Ther was gret strif betwix Lamfrank and him for subjeccion, but at þe

f. 55vb

last þei were acorded þat þe archbischop of Ʒork owith subjeccion to him of Cauntirbury.

This Kyng William rod into Scotlond, and took homage þere of Malcolyn, þe kyng.

Whan he had regned xxii Ʒere he mad his testament, and be- 5
qwathe þe kyngdam of Ynglond to his son, clepid William Rede; and to Robert, clepid Curthose, þe duchi | of Normandie; and to f. 56ra
Herri, cleped Clerk, al his tresore; and so he deied, and is biried at Kame.

William þe Rede was crowned in þe Ʒere of oure Lord m 10
lxxxvi, and streit he rod to Wynchestir to departe his faderes tresore. Ther fond þei lx þousand pound, beside gret jewelis. Robert herd sey þat his fader was ded and cam into Inglond to chalenge þe crowne. He aryued at Hampton, and þan William, his broþir, sent onto him swech letteres: þat he knew wel it was 15
rite he schuld be kyng, and he kepte þe crowne to no oþir entent but to regne vndir him, knowyng wel þat he was worthier and elder; and, if it plesed him þat he myte regne þus vndir him, he wold gyue him euery Ʒere iii þousand mark; and who ouirlyued oþir to haue al. And so Duk Roberd went hom ageyn, bering rith 20
nowt with him but fayre promisses.

In þe x Ʒere of þis William was Ancelme mad bischop of Cauntirbury. He was eke born in Ytaile, and lerned at Bek vndir Lamfrank. Betwix him and þe kyng fell gret distauns, for fro þe tyme þat he was bischop myte he neuyr hold no sene, ne 25
vse no correccioun, for þe kyng reised so many tributes to make þe wallis of þe Tour of London and þe grete Halle at Westminster, and eke þe kyngis meny vsed mech raueyn.

In þis tyme Herbert Losinga, sumtyme abbot of Ramsey, but þanne bischop of Thetforth, sowyd a gret seed of symonie in 30
Ynglond, for he boute his benefice of þe Kyng William for a grete summe. But whan his Ʒong dayes were go, he went to Rome, and gat licens to remeue | his sete to Norwich, where þat he foundid a f. 56rb
worchipful monasteri of his owne gode, and a othir of þe order of Cloyne at þetforth. He was wone to sey, 'I entred euel, but with 35
þe grace of God I schal wel go owte'. And þat word of Jerom wold

---

1 acorded] *in r.h. margin with carets (in red)* M   3 William] Willam P
7 *another* clepid (*after* Robert) *expuncted in red* M   11 he] *om.* P   12 tresore]
om. P   22 William] Willam P   Ancelme] P, Ancel *at line end* M
25 bischop] kyng MP   29 Losinga] i *surmounted by short stroke in red* M
31 þe] *om.* P   34 at norwich (*after* gode) *expuncted in red* M

he ofte reherse, 'We erred whan we were ȝong; lete us amende it
in oure age'.

This William mad Westminster Halle, and whan he sei it
first, he seide it was not half mech inow.

5   In þe xiii ȝere of his regne he deyed on þis maner:—
He schuld hunte in þe Newe Forest and, in þe nyte before, he
lay in a parsonage and þere þei assayed her arowes. The kyng had
on in his hand, and þe parson stood before him with a new-
schaue crowne. The kyng took a arow, and threw it at þe prestis
10 crowne, and hurt him, and seid, 'This is a fayre site'. On Water
Tyrel stood beside, and asked þat arow for his fe, and þe nexte
day, as he wold a smet a hert, he smet þe kyng to þe hert.

Anno 6297–6311; 1099–1113. Herry þe Fourt regned xv ȝere.
He, anon as he was emperour, he took his fader and set him in
15 prison til he deyed.

In his tyme, whan Pascale þe pope was ded, þe Cherch chase on
Jon, þe popes chaunceler, and clepid him Gelasius. The emperour
was not consenting to þat eleccion, and þerfor þe emperour, with
f. 56va his clientis, chase | a Spaynard, his name was Burdine. Than
20 deied Gelase, for he was pope but o ȝere, and þe cardinales
chose Kalixt þe Secund. He, with his councell, cursed Herry
þe emperour, and þe Romanes took Burdine, and sette him on a
asse, þe taile in his hand—so rode he before þe pope to Rome. In
þis tyme Kalixt mad þe bischop of Compostel a archbiscop, for
25 reuerens of Seyn Jame.

This Herry, be þe rithful dome of God, deied withoute ony
eyer, for he was so cruel to his fadir.

In þese dayes regned in Inglond Herry þe First, whech was
named Herry Clerk, þe þird son of William Bastard. Summe men
30 writyn he began to regne in þe ȝere of oure Lord a m and a c.
He was crowned at Londoun of Maurice, bischop of London.
Than weddid þe kyng Maute, doutir to þe kyng of Scottis, whech
hite Malcolyn.

In his first ȝere cam his broþir, Robert Curthose, with his
35 wif, whech he had weddid in Scicile, for to chalenge þe crowne

<hr>

1 we] P, *om.* M   3 This] *in r.h. margin* M   William] *in l.h. margin* M
mad] *preceded at beginning of line by short word* (? he) *erased* M   14–15 in
prison] *in r.h. margin* M   20 þe] *om. over line division* P

<hr>

13–27: Martinus, 468/51–469/22 and 435/37–46.

of Inglond, whech he preferred before þe crowne of Jerusalem.
For þat was profered him, and he forsoke it; þerfor had he neuyr
prosperité aftir þat.

In þe xix ȝere of his regne was a grete bataile betwix him and
þe kyng of Frauns, Lodewik, where a knyte cleped William 5
Crisping on þe French side hitte Herry þe kyng on þe hed twyes,
and because þe basnet was strong and inpenetrabel þe strok
bent it to þe kyng hed, þat þe blood ran oute. The kyng smet him
ageyn with swech corage þat þei fell to grownd, both hors and
man.   10

Sone aftir þis bataile deied Maute, þe good qween, of whos
curtesie and | humilité, scilens, and oþir good maneris, þe Englisch f. 56ᵛᵇ
poetes at þo dayes mad ful notabel vers.

In þe ȝere of oure Lord a m cxx Kyng Herry cam hom ageyn
into Inglond, and in þe se too of þe kyngis sones, William and 15
Richard, and þe kyngis doutir, and his nece, and many worthi
folk, chaumbirleynes and butleres, and Richard, schreue of
Chestir—all þese were dronch in o schip, in noumbir a cxl, non
saued saue a boistous carl þat was among hem. Thei were grete
slaundered in þe synne of sodomye. The next day men fond on 20
þe brynkis mech tresore, but body was non founde.

Sone aftir þis þe King Herri wedded a new wif, doutyr to þe
duke of Lotharinge—þe wedding was at Wyndesore—sche hite,
as þei sei, Adelida. Of hir beuté was mech spech and mech wryting.

In þe xxiiii ȝere of Herry cam to þis lond Jon Cremense, a 25
cardinal; at gret cost of bischopis and abbottes, in þe natiuité of
oure Lady, he held a grete councell at Londoun, in whech was
determined þat prestes schuld in no wise haue no wyues, but he
was þat same day detect þat a strumpet was in his chaumbir.

In þis Herry dayes was his dowtir, Maute, wedded to Herri, 30
þe emperour, whech Herri, as we seide, was þe fourt emperour
þat was cleped Herry. Summe sey he deied befor þe secund wedding; sum sey he was mad a munk at Chestir. But who it be of þat,
his wif, þe emperesse, cam into Ynglond to hir fader, and broute
with hir þe hand of Seynt Jame þe apostil not corrupt, and þe 35
crowne imperial. And for joye of þis hand þe kyng foundid a

---

1 he] *suprascript* M   9 þat] t *suprascript* M   19 boistous] boistoys
M, boystois P   23 was] *suprascript with caret* (*in red*) M   24 Of]
change to darker ink M   29 þat same day detect] detect þᵗ same day P
32 secund] *in l.h. margin with carets* (*in red*) M   33 was mad] *in r.h. margin* M

f. 57ra nobil monasterie of munkys at Redyngis. And sone | aftir was þis
Maute, emperesse, weddid to Geffrey Plauntgenet, erl of Angoye.
Sone aftir þe kyng held a parlement at London, where he mad al
his lordis to swere þat, aftir his deth, þei schuld be trew lige to
5 þe emperesse his doutir, and to þe eyeris born of hir body. At
whech swering Steuene, erl of Boloyn, or of Blesens, as othir
wryte, was principal, and he mad þe forme and þe maner of
swering.

In the xxvii ȝere of þis kyng he mad þe knytes þorw þe lond to
10 cut her heer, for þei went with as long her as women. Sone
aftir appered onto þis kyng meruelous visiones. First, he sey in his
slep a gret multitude of plowmen, with swech instrumentis as þei
use, com ageyn him, as þouȝ þei wold kille him. Than sey he a
multitude of armed men with speres and dartis ageyn him. In
15 þe þird vision com prelatis with her crosses and croses sore
þretyng him. The kyng wook, ros, and took his swerd in his
hand, wenyng al had be soth. This same vision was schewid to a
leche, þei clepid him Grimbald, and he warned þe king, as
Daniel ded Nabugodonosor, to redeme his sinnes with elmesse.

20 Sone aftir þis he went into Normandy for to wite if his doutir
were with child, and, as he cam fro hunting, he desired gretly to
ete a lamprey, for þat mete loued he wel, and euyr it ded him
harme. This mete caused him a feuyr, of whech he deied. He
regned xxxv ȝere.

25 Anno 6312–6322; 1114–1124. Lotharius þe Fourt regned
xi ȝere. In his tyme was gret hungir þorw Itaile. In þe beginnyng
f. 57rb of | his empire he gadered a grete host, with archbischopis and
bischopis, and set Pope Innocent þe Secunde in his sete at
Lateranense, for on cleped þe son of Petir Leon had put þis
30 pope oute of Rome. Thus was he broute ageyn be þe Emperour
Lotharie, and þere he crowned þe emperour. (This Innocent was
pope xiii ȝere, and before him was Honorius þe Secund v ȝere.)
This Lotharie rod with þe pope into Naples ageyn on Roger,
þat vsurped to be lord of þat lond. He mad him to fle oute of þe
35 lond, and sette þere a gouernour þei cleped Raymund.

5 his] hir MP   9 þe (1)] om. P   12 with] suprascript with caret
(in red) M   swech] P, whech M   14 him] suprascript with caret (in red) M
15 croses] croyses P   sore] for P   19 ded] final d suprascript M   Nabugo-
donosor] Nabugodonesor P, Nabugodononosor M

25–107/3: Martinus, 469/23–31 and 435/48–436/20, also 469/11.

In þis tyme was at Paris a notable clerk þei clepid Hugo de
Sancto Victore, of þe Chanones ordre. He mad many fructuous
bokes, drawyn mech oute of Seynt Austen werkis.

Anno 6323–6337; 1125–1139. Conrard þe Secund regned xv
3ere. In his dayes deied a knyte, þei clepid him Jon of þe Tymes, 5
whech lyued, as þei sey, ccc 3ere lxi, for he was a werriour in þe
tyme of Gret Charles. This Conrard took þe caracte of þe cros
of Seint Bernard hand for to go to þe Holy Lond and fite ageyn
þe enmies of Crist. And in þis pilgrimage he had many felawys,
summe of Lotharinge, summe of Frauns, of Inglond, and of 10
Flaundres— | too hundred schippis were occupied with hem. f. 57ᵛᵃ
Whan þei cam in þe Holy Lond, þere met þe kyng of Frauns with
hem. Ther had þei many batailes, and wonne many townes, as
þe cronicle makith mencioun.

And in þis same tyme was Steuene kyng of Ynglond, neue to 15
þe King Herri, for he was his sisteris son. Anon as he herd sey
þe king was ded, he cam into Ynglond and chalenged þe crowne,
notwithstandyng his oth þat he had mad. He was crowned of
Wiliam, bischop of Cauntirbury, and had prosperité in his first
3eres, but in his last 3eres mech aduersité. For he, trosting in his 20
gret power, went ouyr into Frauns, for he purposed for to fite
with Gefrey Plauntgenet, dreding þat he schuld begete ony
child whech schuld forbarre him his rite. This Gefrey was war of
þis, and with myty power mad resistens, and droue þe Kyng
Steuene ageyn into Ynglond. And as summe men write, Herry 25
þe Secund was bore þat tyme. So grew this child and was norchid
til þe fifte 3ere of Steuene.

Than cam þe modir with hir child and with hir frendis—whech
were Robert, hir brothir, begoten of bast, þan erl of Gloucetir,
and Ranulf, erl of Chestir, and many mo—and besegid Kyng 30
Steuene in þe cyté of Lyncoln. That day þat þe kyng schuld fite
he herd masse and offered a candel, whech brak on peces in þe
offering. And sone aftir þe eleuacion, the lyne brak, and þe pix
fel on þe auter. These toknes men þoute were not gode. Thei
faute þat day, and | þe kyng was take, and led onto Bristow, þere f. 57ᵛᵇ
þe emperesse was, and kept in prison in þe castel many dayes. 36

1 In] *change to paler ink* M   6 sey] *suprascript* M   16 King . . .
was] *over erasure* M   18 had] *om.* P   22 with] wit *at line end* P
27 fifte] first P   34 Thei] i *inserted on the line* M

4–14: ibid. 469/35–44.

Many conflictes were betwix þe emperesse and þe kyng, but at
þe last þei were þus acorded, be consent of al þe lond, þat Kyng
Steuene schuld haue þe regal possession whil he lyued, and
aftir his deth Duk Herry schul entyr. This was promittet be all
5 þe lordis, and a solempne charter mad þeron.

In þis tyme were þese popes: Celestinus II, v monthes; Lucius
II, xi monthis; Eugenius III, viii ȝere; Anastasius IIII, o ȝere.
Than Adrianus II^{us}, a Englischman, iiii ȝere. As þe fame seith,
he was bore at Seint Albones, and natif to þe same monasteri.
10 He desired to be a munk þere, and þei refused him. So þe man
gaf him to lerning, and first was mad a bischop, þan a cardinal,
and legate into a nacion þei clepe Wormancie, where he conuertid
þe puple to God, and aftir was he mad pope. It was he þat graunted
Kyng Herri þe Secunde to go into Yrlond and turne hem to þe
15 feith, and to þat entent he mad him lord of þe lond, on þis condicion, þat euery hous schuld paye ȝerli a Petir-peny to Rome. This
pope eke graunted grete pryuylegis to þe hous of Seint Albones.

Steuene þe kyng deyed þe viii kalend of April, byried at Feuersam, whech hous he mad.

20 Anno 6338-6374; 1140-1176. Frederik þe First regned xxxvii
ȝere. He was crowned in þe cherch of Seint Petir at Rome, a
large man and bold, faire of tunge.

f. 58ra   In his tyme a kyng of þe Sarasines tok þe cyté cleped Edissa,
whech in þe first bok of Moises is clepid Arath. Alle þe Cristen
25 men whech were þere, he mad hem for to reneye her feith or
ellis to lese her hedis. This is þe same cité in whech Abgarus was
kyng, þat sent lettir onto oure Lord Criste þat he schuld come to
him for to cure him. And oure Lord sent him answere þat as now
he myte not come, but aftir his deth he schuld send him on of
30 his disciples, and he schulde cure him—and þat was Thade.
This kyng was not content with þat epistil of Crist onto þe tyme
þat Criste sent him his ymage, depeynted in a fayre lynand cloth.

In þis tyme was þe sepulcre of our Lord take, and þe holy crosse,
of þe soudan, and many oþir Cristen places.

---

1 betwix] *change to darker ink* M   26 was] s *suprascript* M   27 þat (1)]
& P   28 And] A *altered from* a M   as] *om.* P   31 content] *change
to darker ink* M

6–8: Martinus, 436/21–41.
20–109/10: ibid. 469/49–470/29.

In þis tyme was Abbot Joachim in Calabir, þat wrote many þingis vpon þe *Apocalipse*, but he erred in many þingis, first in a mater concernyng þe holy Trynyté, for þe Cherch hath determined his opinion fals in þe beginning of þe *Decretales, capitulo, Damp|namus*. And Maystir Pers þe Lumbard, þat mad *þe iiii Bokes of Sentens*, aftir bischop of Paris, mad mech þing ageyn þis Abbot Joachim. This same abbot mad also a oþir book, *De Seminibus Literarum*, where be gret craft he droue oute þe ȝere in whech þe Day of Dome schuld falle; but he failed foule, and erred in his counting.

f. 58ʳᵇ
6

10

In þis tyme regned in Ynglond Herry þe Secunde, son to Gefrey Plaungenet and Maute þe emperesse. Or þat he regned, he weddid a woman þat was qwen of Frauns, hir name was Helianore. There fel gret strif betwix þe kyng and hir, and þerfor þe qwen laboured to haue a dyuors betwix hir and hir husband, pretendyng þat sche was of his kyn, but hir principal cause was, as is seid, for sche desired gretly to be wyf to þe duke of Normandy. But in dede þe dyuors was had, and þe mariage mad, and be hir he was a grete lord, for sche was douter and eyir to þe duke of Gyan. So was he þan duk of Normandie, erl of Angoye and Cenoman, and duke of Gyan. All þese londes had he in possession whil Kyng Steuene lyued, and aftir his deth he cam into Ynglond and was crowned of Theobald, bischop þan of Cauntirbury.

15

20

And here, as we fynde wrytyn, we wil declare his genelogie. The fader of Gefrey Plauntgenet wedded a wyf only for beuté. He wist not fro whens sche cam, ne of what kynrod sche was. Seldom wold sche com to cherch, but neuyr abyde þe sacre. And whan þis was noted of hir husbond, he mad foure knytes on a day to hold hir stille al | þe masse, and so þei ded, but a lytil before þe sacri, as þei held hir be þe mantel, sche fley fro hem oute at a wyndowe, and to childir þat were on hir left hand sche bare with hir, oþir to þat were on þe rite hand sche left behynde hir. Kyng Richard of Ynglond was wone to telle þat it was no merueile þouȝ þei þat cam of swech kynrod ech of hem was contrari to oþir, for þei cam fro þe deuel, and to þe deuel schul goo. It is eke reported þat Seint Bernard schuld sey þe same of þis King Herry, noting

25

f. 58ᵛᵃ
30

35

4 fals] *in r.h. margin with carets (in red)* M   8 þe (1)] *om.* P   þe (2)] P, þei M   14 laboured] labored P, labour M   16 kyn] kyng P   21 in] i *surmounted by short stroke in red* M   24 his genelogie] *in r.h. margin with short horizontal strokes in red to indicate continuity of text* M   33 wone] w *almost erased* M

herby who þat Gefrey, þis mannes fader, ded gelde Gerard, þe
bischop Sagiense, and prophecying of þe grete wrong þat þis
man schuld do to Seynt Thomas. Ferþermore þis Gefrey Plauntgenet warned Herry, his sone, þat he schuld in no wise wedde
5 Helianore, þe qwen of Frauns, for he told him in very treuth þat,
whan he was steward of Frauns, and dwelled with þe kyng, he had
comounde with þe same qwen ofte-tyme. This Helianore had be
Kyng Herry sex childirn, iii sones: Herry, Rychard, and Jon;
and iii douteris: Maut—sche was weddid to þe duke of Saxone;
10 Helianore—and sche was weddid to þe kyng of Spayn; and Jone—
sche was weddid to þe kyng of Scicile.

In þe sext ȝere of his regne, as he cam fro Tollouse, he maried
his son of seuene ȝere old onto Margarete, thre ȝere old doutir to
þe kyng of Frauns.

15   In þe vii ȝere of Herry deied Theobald, bischop of Cauntirbury,
f. 58ᵛᵇ and Thomas, | þe kyngis chaunceler, entred into þat benefice.
Aftir þat fel gret strif betwix him and þe kyng for liberté of þe
Cherch, for whech first was þe bischop exiled and many wrongis
do to him and to his kyn. þan cam he hom ageyn and was killid,
20 as all þe nacion knowith, and þis was in þe ȝere of oure Lord a m
clxx:—

> Annus milenus centenus septuagenus
> Anglorum Primas corruit ense Thomas.

In þese dayes was Arthures body founde in þe cherchȝerd
25 at Glaskinbury in a hol hok, a crosse of led leyd to a ston, and þe
letteres hid betwyx þe ston and þe led. This was þe wryting, as
Giraldus seith, whech red it:—

> Here lith þe nobil Kyng Arthure, with his secunde wyf,
> Veneraca, in þe ylde cleped Auallone.

30 His bones, whan þei were founde, passed þe mesure of oþir men.
In xxxi ȝere of Herry cam into þis lond Eraclius, patriark of
Jerusalem, with letteris of þe Pope Lucius, and prayed þe kyng to
strength hem ageyn þe Sarasines. He excused him be þe werre
þat he had with Frauns; with his good, he seid, he wold help,
35 with his body he myte not. Than þe patriark seide, 'All þe
partes of þe world send us mony; we seke a prince, and not mony'.

10 Helianore] Helanor P   25 at Glaskinbury] *suprascript with caret* (*in
red*) M

The kyng folowid him onto Douer, and plesed him with fayre wordis. But þe patriark seide onto him on þis wise,

'Thou at þis tyme forsakest þe labour for þi Lord. Before þis tyme þou hast regned in gret joye; fro þis tyme schal þou regne in gret misery. To the kyng of Frauns hast þou be fals, Seynt Thomas hast þou killid, and now to forsake þe proteccion of all Cristen | men'.

f. 59ra

And whan þe patriark aspied þat þe kyng was wroth, for he wex pale for angir, he bowed his hed and his nek, and seide,

'Do with me as þou ded to Seynt Thomas. I had as lef be killid of þe in Inglond as of a Sarasine in Surré, for I holde þe wers þan ony Sarasine'.

The kyng seide, 'And all my men had o body and o mouth, þei durst not sey þat þou seist'. And he answerd, 'Thei folow þe pray, and not þe man'; and so þei departed.

Sone aftir, Crist appered in þe eyir, visibily hanging on þe crosse, at Dunstable, fro mydday tyl euen, be whech signe was vndirstand þat oure Lord was wroth with þoo men þat wold not venge his cause.

In þis tyme, þat is to sey þe ȝere of oure Lord 1172, was þe cherch of munkys in Norwich brent be þe malys of þe cité, as men sey, and þe cyté þerfor lost grete pryuylegis.

And þe nexte ȝere folowand was Mary, þe sistir of Seynt Thomas, mad abbes of Berkyng.

In þis tyme were þese popes:—

Lucius III, foure ȝere—in his tyme Maister Pers, called Commestor, mad þat book þat is clepid *Historia Scolastica*, where þe bybil is abreggid, and many oþir stories put in þerto.

Aftir him was Vrbanus Tercius o ȝere, for whan he herd Jerusalem was take he deied for heuynesse.

And þan was Gregorius VIII. He sent many bulles to Cristen princes to go to Jerusalem.

5

10

15

20

25

30

---

6 to] *suprascript* M   10 to] be P   17 be] P, *om.* M   20 Lord] *in r.h. margin* M   26 papa (*in paler ink*) *in l.h. margin beside this entry* M   29 him] *om.* P

26–8: Martinus, 437/25–7.
29–30: ibid. 437/28–9.
31–2: ibid. 437/31–2.

And þan was Clement þe þirde. He mad þe cloystir at Seynt
Laurens oute of þe Wallis, and the paleis Lateranense he mad
newe.

f. 59rb   Anno 6375–6382; 1177–1184. Herry þe V regned viii ȝere.
5   He was crowned in Rome, and þe same monthe went he into
Naples for to conqwere it, and in þe fourt ȝere of his regne he had
conclusion of his conquest.

In þis tyme was Celestinus III pope vi ȝere. He corowned þis
Herry.

10   And þan was Innocencius III xxiii ȝere. He mad þe gret hospital in Rome of Seynt Spirit, and renewyd þe cherch of Seynt
Sixte. He mad many decretales, many sermons, and a book whech
is clepid *Of the Wrecchid Kynde of Man*. In þis tyme þe Frenschmen took Constantinople, and þe Venecianes holp hem gretly.
15   The cuntré merueiled gretly for þe strength of þe wallis and for þe
prophecye þat was þerof, þat it schuld neuyr be take but be an
aungell; and happed so þat þei broke þe wal at a certeyn place
where an aungel was depeynted. In þis tyme was Almaricus
dampned, þat held many straunge heresies at Parise.

20   Anno 6383–6386; 1185–1188. Octo þe Fourte, of þe nacion of
Saxones, regned iiii ȝere, and he was corowned of Pope Innocent
in Seint Petir cherch; but he was not gretly honoured, for his
malicious condiciones. He faute with þe Romanes, and went into
Naples ageyn þe popes comaundment, and took awey þat kyngdam
25   fro Frederik, þat was kyng of Scicile. Therfor þe pope cursed
f. 59va   him. And in þe fourt ȝere | of his regne was Frederik þe Secund
chosen, and he rod into Almayn and ouyrcam þis Octo.

Anno 6387–6409; 1189–1211. Frederik þe Secunde was
crowned of Honory, þe pope, in Seint Petir cherch, and regned
30   xxiii ȝere. This man fro his ȝong age was be þe Cherch supported
and broute to þis dignité, and he, aftir his promocion, was ful

1 at] of P   5 crowned] d *suprascript* M   8 III] *in r.h. margin* M
15 cuntré] cunte P   16 but] *suprascript with caret* (*in red*) M   29 crowned]
r *suprascript in red* M

1–3: Martinus, 437/34–6.
4–7: ibid. 470/43–471/4.
8–9: ibid. 437/37–8.
10–19: ibid. 437/40–438/38.
20–7: ibid. 471/20–5.
28–113/3: ibid. 471/26–31.

onkind onto þe Cherch; þerfor þe same pope þat corowned him, considering his rebellioun, cursed him, and asoiled al his barones fro þat feith whech þei had mad to him.

In þese dayes began þe too ordres of Prechoures and of Menowres. The Prechoures order began Seynt Dominicus in 5 Tholous, þe ȝere of oure Lord a m cciii. The order of Menoures began Seint Fraunceys fast be þe cité of Assisé, whech couent is clepid Seynt Mary of Aungeles, iii ȝere aftir Dominic. The oþir too ordres, Heremites of Seint Austin, and heremites of þe Mount Carmele, were longe befor, but þei were not confermed of þe 10 Cherch tyl Honorius was pope. And in þe tyme of Innocent þis same ordir of Seynt Austyn had a place pry|uyleged be þat pope, f. 59ᵛᵇ or þe Prechoures were confermed. The place is biggid in þe worchip of Seynt Antony in þe cuntré cleped Ardyngnete, whech stant in þe prouynce of Senys. 15

In þese dayes deyed Kyng Herry þe Secunde, and whan he was ded, Richard, his broþir, was crowned of Baldewyn, bischop of Cauntirbyry, þe ix day of September, whech day is hald suspect of supersticious men; and onto þe Jewys it was not esy. For þan dwelled þei in þis reme, and at þe kyngis coronacion þei drew to 20 London in hope for to haue grace of þe kyng, þat þei schuld paye lesse tribute þan þei dede before. The kyng comaunded þat þere schuld no Jew com in þe chirch in tyme of his coronacion, ne in þe halle at tyme of mete. Summe of hem were malapert, and entred into þe halle, and happed a man to smyte a Jew and seid 25 onto him þat he brak þe kyngis comaundement. The puple þat stod þere, supposyng it was þe kyngis wil þat þe Jewis schuld be seruid soo, and with stonis and staffis soute þe Jewis þorw London, beet hem, and robbed hem, and be þis exaumple þus were þei serued þorwoute þe rem, and þus voyded þei þe rem. 30

The kyng, for he purposed to go to þe Holy Lond, and must make cheuesauns for mech mony, he sent aftir þe kyng of Scottis, and aftir he had do his homage he seld him þe castelles of Berwyk and Rokisborow for ten þousand mark. Than was þere at Dorham

---

5 The] *change to darker ink* M   in] P, *twice over line division* M   11 tyl] *over erasure* M   þis] þe P   13 þe (1)] *suprascript* M   were confermed] *in r.h. margin* M   17 ded] *in l.h. margin with carets (in red)* M   broþir] *om.* P   20 at] *suprascript* M   23 tyme] þe tyme P   24 at] in P 25 a man] *suprascript with caret (in red)* M

4–8: ibid. 438/38–45.

a bischop, a old man and rich: to him seld þe kyng þe prouince of
f. 60ra Dorham for his lyue for a gret summe | of good. And þan wold
þe kyng sumtyme in merth sei, 'I am a crafty werkman, for I can
make of a elde bischop a ȝong erl'.

5 In þe secund ȝere of his regne Philip, þe kyng of Frauns, and
he took her jornay into þe Holy Lond, Richard be lond, and Philip
be þe se, where þe kyng of Frauns in face schewid himself a lomb,
and in werk a leon. Thei cam both onto þe yld of Scicile, and to
þe cyté of Messane; Philip lay in þe cyté, and Richard in a hospital
10 withoute. On Cristmesse Day many of Richard men com into
towne to bye vitaile, and þe Frenschmen, coupled with a nacion
þei clepe Griphones, bet and killid many of Richard men.
The same day Richard leid sege to þe cité, and þei sperd þe
gates and kept þe wallis, but Richard power was so strong þat
15 þe kyng of Frauns asked him forgifnesse, and proferd grete
amendis; for he had a castel of tre, whech he cleped Mate-
grifon, to whech men myte make no resistens, and with þat same
he took þe cyté of Acon in þe Holy Lond—summe men clepe it
Acris.

20 Fro Cicile, as þei went in þe se, a grete wynd blew hem into
Ciper, where þat schip þat his modir was in and his wif was al
broke, and þei of þe cuntré cam and spoiled it, and treted þe
ladies onmanerly. Richard sent to þe kyng of þe ild þat amendis
schuld be mad, and he wold not, wherfor Richard pursewid
25 him fro town to town til he besegid him, and þe kyng graunted to
f. 60rb make amendis on þat condicion þat | Richard schuld not put him
in no fetteris of yrun. He graunted his peticion, but whan he had
him, he put him in fetteris of syluyr. So kepte he þe kyng, and
disposed al þe ylde at his plesauns.

30 In þe ȝere of oure Lord m cxciii was þe cité of Acris take—
sum men, as we seid, clepe it Acon, and in elde tyme was it cleped
Tholomaide—at whech takyng þe duk of Ostrich folowid þe
Kyng Richard, desiring for to haue part both of his worchip and
eke of swech tresoure as schuld be take. And who it happed,
35 wheþir be chaunce or elles of purpos, þe dukes standard was
trode vndirfote, whech vilony þe duke peisid ful heuyly, and
hom he went with his hoost, purposing in þis mater to be venged.

2 þan] *suprascript with caret* (*in red*) M   20 Fro] for P   30 Lord]
P, *om.* M   m cxciii] m cxiiii P   take] P, tale M   33 haue] *change to
darker ink* M   both] *om.* P   his] *om.* P   35 of] be P

The Kyng Richard had þere all þe worchip, and þei too, Philip
and Richard, departed þe tresore of þe cité, and eke þe prisoneres.
Philip sold his prisoneres, Richard hing his.

But as Kyng Richard cam homward, he was aspied be þe
duke of Ostrich men, and þe duke took him prisonere, and seld   5
him to þe Emperour Frederik for a hundred þousand marc and
xl þousand. Too bischoppis were leyd for him in plegge, and he
cam hom to purueye þis mony, and, as it is seid, þe jewelis of
cherchis were molten, chalis and crosses, gold and siluyr on ymages
feet, an al for to pay his raunson. The pope cursed þis duk of   10
Ostriche, and he, aftir mech sorow and tribulacion, deied so
acursed, but for al þat þe mony was payed.

Aftir þis doo, Kyng Richard sat at mete at West|minster, and   f. 60ᵛᵃ
tydynggis cam onto him þat Kyng Philip was entred into Normandie to take þat cuntré fro him. Than saide þe kyng, 'Treuly   15
and I schal neuyr turne my face fro him ward onto þe tyme þat I
mete with him'; and anon he mad breke þe wal of þe hous þat
he sat in, and streyt went he to þe se. There faute he with the kyng
and drof him oute of Normandie.

Aftirward, at besegyng of a castell—þe name is castel of Cha-   20
lomes—he was hit with a arblast, of whech wounde he deyed, and
in his testament he asigned his broþir son, whech hite Arthure,
for to be kyng aftir him. For Jon, his broþir, was so fals onto him,
and odious to þe puple, þat no man desired him. And because Jon
soute occasiones for to kil þis Arthure, þerfor þe modir of Arthure,   25
cleped Constauns, put hir son to dwelle with þe kyng of Frauns.
But Jon sowte him oute, and killid him, and took his sistir, Helianore, and put hir vndir þe kepyng of foure men, þat þere schuld
no frute growe of hir wombe.

Than pursewed he a dyuors betwix him and his wif, whech   30
was doutyr to þe erle of Gloucetir, because þei were cosynes in
þe þirde degré, and weddid a fayre lady, þei clepid hir Blanc,
doutyr to þe erle of Engelysyn.

Than felle in þis lond a gret strif for eleccion of þe bischop of
Cauntyrbyry, for summe of þe munkes chose þe supprioure of þe   35
same place, and summe chose þe bischop of Norwich aftir þe
kyngis wil. Whan þese e|lecciones cam to þe pope, he anulled   f. 60ᵛᵇ

6 to whom richard (*after* Frederik) *deleted in red* M   7 in] to P   8 it]
P, *om.* M   11 Ostriche] r *suprascript* M   12 þat] *in r.h. margin* M
18 he (2)] P, *om.* M   þe] *om.* P   34 eleccion] þe eleccion P

þe eleccion of þe bischop for insufficiens, and þe eleccion of þe supprioure for þe kyng hated hym, and so he assyned hem to Bischop Maystir Steuene Langdon; and whan þe kyng herd þat þe munkys consentid þerto, he banechid hem all oute of þe
5 monastery. For þis inobediens, and many myscheuous dedis whech he ded, in manslauth, gloteny, and lecchery, and specialy robbyng and spoilyng of monasteries, þe pope cursed þe kyng, and assoiled all his lichmen fro his obeychauns; the lond eke was enterdited ny seuene ȝere. And þan cam fro Rome a legate and
10 Steuene Langdon, and aftir þe kyngis repentauns and promisses, he assoiled him and losed þe enterdite.

The ende of þis kyng was lich his lif, for, as þei sey, he deyed of poyson at Swyneshede. He was caried ferþer o-lyue, but þere was he seruyd.
15 In þo dayes was founde a bok in Spayn in a town þei clepe it Tollete. A Jewe brak a bank of ston for to make more space to his vine, and fond þere a grete ston, in whech ston, whan it was broke, þei fond a book, with leues as þik as a bord, whech was wrytyn with Hebrew, Grew, and Latyn. As mech lettir was þerin as in a
20 sauter. The general sentens of þe bok was of þe tripartite world þat schuld be fro Adam to Antecrist. There he expressed þe propirté of men: what dyuers condicion þei schuld haue þat schuld leue in þe dyuers worldis. The first begynnyng of þe þirde world schuld be Crist; for it was wrytyn þus, 'In þe þird world
f. 61ʳᵃ schal | þe Son of God be bore of a mayde, Mari, and deye for þe
26 helth of man'. And whan þe Jew herd þis he was baptized, and all his hous.

Anno 6410–6413; 1212–1215. These iiii ȝere be þe last ȝeres of þe regne of Kyng Jon. And ȝe schal vndirstand þat fro þis
30 tyme forward oure annotacion schal be aftir þe regne of þe kyngis of Ynglond, for þe empire in maner sesed here, and on þis maner: for aftir þat tyme þat Frederik was deposed, þe eleccion was dyuyded, and þis diuision lastid many ȝeres. Summe of hem chose

2 to] to be P   6 ded] had do P   8 assoiled] d suprascript M
eke was] was eke P   10 Langdon] Langoun P   aftir] suprascript with
caret (in red) M   13 ferþer] 1st e altered from o M   16–17 for to
. . . vine] for to mak mor space to his vyne & for to mak mor space to hys vyne P
28 ȝere be þe last] om. P   29 And ȝe schal vndirstand] om. except for stand P

15–27: Martinus, 472/17–25.
31–117/3: ibid. 472/28–34, also 440/22–4.

PLATE VII

Cambridge University Library, MS Gg.4.12, fol. 61ʳ (reduced): the page on which the arrangement ceases to be by holy Roman emperor and begins according to the reigns of the kings of England. The right-hand heading indicating the Augustinian age is joined by another indicating the reigning English king—cf. Plate I.

þe kyng of Castel, in Spayn, and summe chose þe erl of Cornwayle, Richard, broþir to þe kyng of Ynglond, whech mad þe
abbey of Hayles, and þere is he byryed.

Anno 6414–6468; 1216–1270. Herry þe þird, kyng of Ynglond,
regned lv ȝere. Whan he was but ix ȝere old he was crowned at 5
Gloucetir be þe hand of Guallo, a legat sent into þis lond to make
pees in þis lond. For Lodewik, þe kyngis son of Frauns, was com
into þis lond at request of þe lordes in Kyng Jones tyme. And
what titil he had to þe crowne þei telle: for he weddid Arthure
sistir, whech Arthure was very eyir. This was þe cause whi 10
Herry was crow|ned at Gloucetir, for þei durst not go to London f. 61rb
for þe power of Lodewik. Eke in his crownyng þei sette on his hed
but a chapelet, þat þei schuld do no prejudise to the cherch of
Cauntirbyry, to whom longith to crowne þe kyng. Than mad þei
crye þorw þe reme þat no man in þat month folowyng schuld 15
go oute at his dore, ne no woman, but þei had a chapelet on
her hed.

In þe secund ȝere of þis Herry, Lodewik cam fro London and
besegid þe cyté of Lyncoln, for his councel gided him þat he
schuld haue þe principal townis in possession, and þan he schuld 20
conqwere sone þe lond. So he cam on þe south side, and þe
kyngis hoost on þe north side, and because þei had þe hill þei
put Lodewik to a gret rebuke, for he fled, and went onto London.
Sone aftir þat, be mediacion of þe legat Guallo, þe parties were
gadered in a wood fast be Kyngston upon Temse, and þere | 25
was a trety of pes, and, aftir mech þing rehersid, Lodewyk was f. 61va
bownde be his oth þat all þe londis whech þe kyng of Ynglond
had sumtyme in his possession, as Normandie, Gyan, and swech
oþir, schuld be restored ageyn to Kyng Herry, and þat he schuld
labour to his fader þat he schuld consent þerto. Thus were þei 30
acorded, and Lodewyk went hom into Frauns—the cité of London
lent him v m pound to his costis. In þat same ȝere was þe translacion of Seynt Swithine.

In þe þird ȝere of his regne he was crowned ageyn at Westmister of Steuene Langdon, bischop of Cauntirbyry, for certeyn 35
causes whech we rehersed before; and in þat same ȝere þe blake

6–7 to make pees in þis lond] om. P   8 into] to P   14 whom]
whon P   20 townis] i surmounted by short stroke in red M   26 aftir]
suprascript M   30 his] hir M, hyr P   34–5 Westmister] i surmounted
by short stroke in red M

munkys had her first chapetre at Oxeforth for reformacion of þe ordyr.

In his iiii ȝere was þe new cherch at Westminster begunne; and in þat same ȝere was þe translacion of Seynt Thomas.

5 In his v ȝere deyed Seint Dominic, and in þat same ȝere þe Frere Prechouris cam into Ynglond vndir proteccion of þe bischop of Wynchestir, his name was Petrus de Rupibus. There cam of hem in noumbir xiii, with here priour, clepid Gilbertus de Fraxineto. Her mansion was first at Oxenford in þe parch of 10 Seynt Edward; sith were þei remeued to þe place where they be now.

In þe sext ȝere Steuene, bischop of Cauntirbiry, held a councel at Osney, where a dekne was accused þat, for loue he had to a
f. 61vb ȝong woman, doutyr to a Jew, | he suffered hem to circumcide 15 him, and reneyed Crist and his baptem, and took þe sacrament of þe auter and broute it to þe Jewis, and for þese enormes was he brent. There was accused eke a carl þat procured men to nayle him on a crosse, for in his handis and feet were seyn þe woundes of þe nayles, and in his side a wound eke, and in his 20 fonnednesse he wold sey þat he was so arayed for sauacion of þe world. He was put in prison for euyr, and neuyr to haue oþir repast but bred and watir.

In his vii ȝere þe Pope Honorius sent down to þe kyng and þe parlement þat þei schuld graunt him þis liberté in þe Cherch of 25 Ynglond, þat he schuld gyue o benefice in euery cathedral cherch and in euery monasteri þat is wel endewid. It was answered in þis maner, þat þis mater myte not be sped withoute consent of þe patrones, and consent eke of þe general councell—so was þe mater fayre put o-side.

30 In þe x ȝere of Herry deyed þe Pope Honorius, þat was pope x ȝere and viii monthis. He mad grete reparacion in Rome, both in wallis and in cherchis. And aftir him was Gregorius IX xiiii ȝere; with him dwelled a Frere Prechour cleped Raymund. He was penytauncer vndir þe pope, and be his comaundment þe 35 frere gadered oute of many bokes þat book whech þei clepe

1 had] *in r.h. margin* M   8 here] her *twice* P   9 Fraxineto] i *sur-mounted by short stroke in red* M   of] f *suprascript*, of *also in l.h. margin* M
10 Edward] Eward P   12 Cauntirbiry] Cawnntrbiry P   held] d *supra-script* M   18 his] *supplied, om.* MP   20 sauacion] savicion P

30–119/2: Martinus, 439/1–21.

Decretales, and þe pope wrot to all Doctoures of Lawe þat þei
schuld in scole vse þis compilyng.

In þe xi ȝere of Herry deied Steuene Langdon, bischop of
Cauntirbury, þat was | a grete clerk in his dayes in making of f. 62ra
many bokes, specialy upon scripture; for his werk *Upon þe XII* 5
Prophetys haue I seyn.

In his xii ȝere cam into Ynglond þe archbischop of Burdews,
and many of þe best of Gyan and of Normandie, desiring of þe
kyng þat he schuld come into þat cuntré, and þei wold help him
with al her power. But þis mater was dilayed be on Fulco of 10
Borow, a justise, and þei went hom frustrat of her purpos.

In þe xiii ȝere of Herry fel a meruelous þing at London, for
euene as þe bischop was at masse at Seynt Poules þere fell a
þundir and a wedyr so dirk and so lowd þat men supposid þe
cherch schuld falle. Alle þat were þere runne awey for fere; with 15
þe bischop at þe auter abod no man but a dekyn. Ther was eke
swech stynk þat no man myte suffir it.

In þat same ȝere Richard, þe kyngis broþir, weddid þe Lady
Ysabelle, þat was wyf to Gilbert, herl of Gloucestir. That same
Gilbert was ryth affectuous onto þe Heremites of Seynt Austin, 20
for, as it is seid, he was aqweyntid with Doctour Gilis in Frauns,
and at his request Gylis was meued to make þat bok *Of Gouer-*
nauns of Princes. But neuyrþelasse he entitiled it to Philip, dauphin
of Frauns. It is saide among us comounly þat þis Gilbert grauntid
onto Gylis þat he schuld make a hous of oure ordre in Ynglond, 25
and because Gilbert deied or it was doo, Richard, his son, fulfillid
his fadir desire. For in þe ȝere of oure Lord 1230 Alisaunder þe
pope gaf us leue for to edi|fie couentis in þese places: Surek, f. 62rb
Clayanger, Clare, and Sidingborn, and oþir; but þei tok no place
but Clare and Wodous, which was þan clepid Bica or ellis Vilen- 30
tynge. Than had þis ordre leue for to entyr and bigge, but þei
biggid not gretly onto þe ȝere of oure Lord 1248.

In þe xvi ȝere of Herry fell a new contrauersie at Cauntirbury,
for summe chose þe priour of þe Trinité cherch, and summe
chose Maystir Jon Blundy. Whan þis eleccion cam to þe pope he 35
cassed it, and þan þe priour of þe Trinité resined his ryte, and þe

---

1 Decretales] *in r.h. margin with carets (in red)* M   17 þat] P, *om. over*
line division M   20 Austin *in r.h. margin with carets (in red)* M   22 and]
suprascript M   29 þei] þer M, ther P   33 contrauersie] contrauersi
P, contauersie M   35 Maystir] Mayster P, *repeated in the form* Maistir *over*
line division M

pope refused Maistir Jon Blundy because þe bischop of Wynchester wrot onto þe emperour for his promocioun. This cause
was alleggid ageyn him, þat he had too benefices with cure of
soule withoute leue of þe cort. Than were þe munkis at her lyberté
5 to haue a new eleccion, and þei chose Maistir Edmund Abyngdon,
a holy man, whech was þan tresorer of Salisbury.

In þe xviii ȝere of Herry deied Maistir Hewe Welle, bischop
of Lyncoln, and þei chose to her bischop Maistir Robert Grostede,
whech man we clepe in scole 'Lyncolniense'; for he wrot mech
10 þing upon philosophye—he mad eke a noble book þe clepe his
Dictes.

In þat same ȝere King Herry weddid Helianore, doutir to þe
erl of Prouince. The wedding was in þe fest of Fabian and Sebastian at Westminster.

15 In þe same ȝere þe Jewys of Norwych were conuicte before þe
kyng þat þei had stole a child, whos name was William, and
f 62ᵛᵃ þei | circumcided him, and kept him in secrete place many dayes,
and, as it is comonly said, at Norwich þei put him on a crosse, and
so he deyed.

20 In þe xix ȝere of þe kyng, at Wodstok, cam in a clerk, whech
feyned him a prophete, and sumtyme feyned him frentik, whech
had upon him to scharp knyues, with whech he had slayn þe
kyng had not a holy woman sent him warnyng. So was he taken
and sent to Couentré, þere drawen and hanged. Men sey þat he was
25 sent be on William Marys, þat was outelawed and dwelled in a ylde
betwix Cornwayle and Wales—þei þat dwelle þere clepe it Lundy.

In xxii ȝere of Herry was Edward þe First born in þe feste of
Seynt Bothulp, and he was baptized of Otho, legat, and confermed
be Seint Edmund, þan bischop of Cauntirbury. The modir of þis
30 Edward was Helianore, as we seide doutir to Raymund, erl of
Prouynce, whech had a othir doutyr, cleped Margarete—sche
was maried to þe kyng of Frauns.

In þis same ȝere Maystir Richard Maydeston, bischop of
Hertforth, resigned his bischoprich, and took þe habite of Frere
35 Menouris at Oxenforth.

And in þis tyme was Hewe a cardinal of þe order of Prechoures,

7 Welle bischop] *separated by thin stroke in red* M   9 whech man]
separated by thin stroke in red, final h *in* whech *inserted on the line* M
20 þe (1)] *om.* P

36–121/2: Martinus, 440/10–12.

þat postiled al þe Bible. He was eke þe first begynner of þe con-
cordauns, whech is a tabil onto þe Bibil.

In þe xxiiii ȝere of þis kyng þe legat Otho went oute of Ynglond,
and þouȝ he went straunge weyes, ȝet was he aspied of þe emperoures meny, take, and robbid of al þat he had gote in Ynglond,   5
and þerto put | in prison.   f. 62ᵛᵇ

In þe xxvi ȝere of Herry þe kyng gaf to Edward his son al þe
cuntré of Gascon.

And in þe same ȝere deyed Celestin þe Fourte, and Innocent
þe IIII was mad pope. This Innocent canonized Seynt Petir of   10
Melan.

In þe xxx ȝere of his regne he let make a new mony of gold,
whech we clepe now a ferþing of gold—þan þei clepid it a peny
of gold, for þis was þe cry þorw þe lond, þat no man refuse
a peny of gold, but take it in stede of XXd.   15

In þe xxxii ȝere was merkyd with þe tokne of þe holy crosse for to
go to Jerusalem, for þe pope wrote down to all þe foure orderes
þat all þe prechouris whech schuld sey sermones schuld excite
þe puple onto þis holy viage.

In þe next ȝere was þe kyng of Frauns take prisoner be þe   20
soudan and raunsond to a horibil summe. For, aftir tyme he had
wunne a grete cyté, he was bold and faute with þe soudan in þe
feld; heraudis seid þat þe soudan had but litil pupil, but in þe
myddis of þe batail come Sarasines innoumbirabel, and distroyed
þe kyngis host, and took him prisoner.   25

In þis same time risin in Frauns many þousand of carlis, pretending all þat þei were schippardes. The leder of hem seid he had a
reuelacion be oure Lord Jesu þat swech maner meny schuld haue
victori of þe Sarasines and wyn þe Holy Lond. The lordes were
aferd of swech maner puple so sodeynly up, and, with þe power   30
of hem þat were redy to þe viage of Jerusalem, faute with hem, and
distroyed hem, and whan her maistir was take he was aknowe
þat al his felauchip | was infect with heresie.   f. 63ʳᵃ

In þe 35 ȝere þe munkis of þe ordir of Sistewis entred her
monastery at Hayles, whech edified Richard, duk of Cornwaile,   35

---

2 onto] to P   6 þerto] other to P   13 clepid] d *altered from* t M
15 a peny] *in r.h. margin* M   16 ȝere] *suprascript* M   22 and] d *supra-*
script M   24 innoumbirabel] l *suprascript* M   26 time] *suprascript* M

9–11: ibid. 439/31–440/7.

þe kyngis broþir, and aftir chosen emperour. They entred in þe
assumpcioun of oure Lady.

　　In þe xxxvi ȝere of his regne deied Robert Grostede, born in
Suffolk, and bischop of Lincolne. He beqwathe al his bokes to
5 þe Frere Menoures of Oxenforth. He had be at Rome, and pleted
for þe rite of þe Cherch of Ynglond vndir þe Pope Innocent, for
þat same pope reised many new þingis of þis lond, and gaf þe
benefices withoute consent of þe kyng or patrones or ony oþir,
and þis same Bischop Robert wrot and seid ageyn þe pope, and at
10 Rome in his presens appeled fro him to þe hy Juge of heuene.
So cam he hom, and deied, and in his deth he appered to þe
pope, and smet him on þe side with þe pike of his crosse-staf,
and seid þus, 'Rise, wrech, and com to þe dom'. This wordis
herd þe cubiculeres, and þe strok was seyn in his side, for he deyed
15 anon aftir þat.

　　In þe xxxvii ȝere he put fro his office Simund Mountforth,
for he was seneschal of Burdews, and sent in his stede on
Steuene Longspere. This Symund was eke erle of Leycetir,
and whan he wist he schuld oute of his office, he dylyueryd to
20 þe Frenschmen thre good castelles, and he went and dwelled in
Frauns. On of þe casteles hite Frunsak; þe secund, Renauges; þe
þird, Reglan.

　　In þe xxxviii ȝere went Edward into Spayn and browt hom
Helianore, his wyf—sum sey sche was þe kyngis doutir of Castille,
f. 63ʳᵇ summe sey sche was his sistir. The kyng eke | took Edward a
26 chartor, seled with gold, in whech he relesid al þe rite þat he had
to Gian and Gascon. For he schewid þere þat Herry þe Secund
had goue him þo londis, and Richard and Jon had confermed þat
gift, and al his rite he relesid at þat mariage.

30 　　In xxxix ȝere was Seynt Clare canonized, whech was of þe
ordir of Seyn Fr`auceys and Seynt Damian. And in þat same ȝere
were biggid too couentis in Ynglond of Austines, on at Ludlow,
a othir at Leycetir.

　　And in þe next ȝere was a grete hungir. And þat ȝere was biggid
35 þe couent of Schrouysbury, of þe same ordir.

　　In þe same tyme Seynt Austen appered onto Alisaundre þe

pope with a grete hed and a lytil body; and þe pope inqwired whi he appered soo. Augustin seid, for his succession were not called to dwelle in cités and townes, as were þe Prechoures and þe Menoures. And anon þe pope mad a bulle, in whech we had leue to dwelle in citées, and gyue ensaumple of good lyf.   5

In xliiii ȝere was a grete hungir, þat men and bestis deied for defaut of mete.

In þe same ȝere was a parlement hald at Oxenforth, where þe kyng was swore þat he schuld kepe þe statutes were mad þere. On was þat he schuld exile all alienes, specialy his breþerin on þe   10
modir side, and eke Richard, his broþir, whech was chose emperour—noþing with worchip, for he payed to þe electoures grete summes of god for to haue her voyses. Ther were chose eke xxiiii lordis whech schuld gouerne þe kyngdam, and herto was þe kyng swore.   15

In þat same tyme þe munkis of | Norwich chose to her bischop   f. 63ᵛᵃ
a man þat hite Simon, because he lent hem ccc mark, of whech eleccion were mad þese vers:—

Trecente marce, Simon, si pontificent te,
Per numisma teres, fit Simon Simonis heres.   20

This is þe Englisch: 'Thre hundred mark, Simon, if þei make þe bischop. With mony þou tredis þi trace, so Simund Simon eyer he was'.

In þis tyme were condempned be þe Pope Alisaundre too cursed bokes. On seid þat all religious men, þou þei preche þe   25
word of God, if it be soo þat þei be of swech order as begge, þei schal neuyr be saued. The oþir seyde þat þe gospel whech Crist prechid bryngith no man to perfeccion, and þat same gospel schuld be avoided in þe ȝere of oure Lord m cclx, and þat same ȝere schuld beginne þe doctrine of Joachim, whech doctrine þe   30
maker of þe book clepid þe *Euyrlastyng Gospell*.

In þe ȝere of Herri 46 was conuencion mad betwix þe kyng of Frauns and him þat þe kyng of Frauns schuld haue Angoye, Rone, Cenomaine, and Picardie, so þat þe same kyng of Frauns schuld pay xxv þousand marc be ȝere, and many oþir comnauntis were   35

1 pope (2)] P, po *at line end* M   2 Augustin] Aug' *over erasure* M, Aug*us* P
seid] *in r.h. margin* M   11 his] *twice over line division* P   24 Alisaundre]
om. P   26 as] þat P

24–31: Martinus, 440/25–32.

betwix hem, so þe kyng of Ynglond schuld do homage to þe kyng of Frauns.

In þe xlvii ȝere of Herry was þe general chapeter of þe Pre-choures ordre at London, with gret cost and gret solempnité.

5   And in þat same ȝere þe grete debate betwix þe kyng and his barnes was compromitted to þe dom of þe kyng of Frauns, þat f. 63ᵛᵇ whatsoeuyr he dempt, þei schuld obserue. So mette þei all | at Amyas, and þere þe kyng of Frauns gaue sentens directly ageyn þe barnes. Than began mech werre and many batayles betwix 10 þe kyng and þe barnes. The first batail was at Northampton, where þe kyng beseged Simund Mountforth and his felauchip, and þe kyng brak þe wallis, and entred upon hem, and þere was take Simon Mountforth, þe ȝonger son to þe forsaid Symon, þat was erle of Leycetir. Ther were take with him Baldewyn Wade, Raf 15 Basset, Petir Mountforth, and ny a hundred knytes.

In þe xlix ȝere had þe kyng with þe lordes anothir batayle fast be Lews. On þe kyngis party was Richard, emperour of Almayn, and Prince Edward, but in þat batail þe kyng was take, and Ed-ward was plegge for his fader, and Richard, emperour, was 20 take in a mylle, and led to þe Tour of London. Than had þei þe þird bataile, at Euesham; þere was Simon taken, and scham-fully ded, for þei smet of first his hed, and þan his armes, and þan leggis, and so lay þe body lich a stok.

In þe l ȝere of þis kyng he besegid London, for þei were 25 with þe barnes ageyn þe king; ther þe kyng tok þe principalis of London and sette hem in prison at Wyndesore. So þe cyté was fayn to bye her liberté of þe kyng for xx m marc, and þan was Gilbert, erle of Gloucetir, acorded to þe kyng in þis maner, þat þe erle schuld ask þe kyng forgeuenesse of all trespas, and so 30 he ded ful mekly, and þe kyng took him to grace. Than was set a f. 64ʳᵃ peyne, if euyr he trespa|sed more he schuld pay to þe kyng x m marc.

In þe li ȝere Octobon, a legate, cam into Ynglond and mad ful good constituciones for pes of þe Cherch, and he confermed 35 þe constitucion mad before be Otho.

In þat ȝere Edward was merkid with þe holy crosse for to go to Surry with þe kyng of Frauns.

11 Simund Mountforth] Symountforth P   12 was] were M, wer P
13 Mountforth] Mountforth & his felawschip P   16 be] suprascript M
22 þan (1)] om. P

In þis same ȝere deied Clemens IIII. He was first a weddid
man, and a aduocat to þe kyng of Frauns, and aftir deth of his
wif, for his sobirnesse and good lyuyng, þei chose him pope.
It is seid of him þat he wold neuyr graunt pluralité of benefices.

In þe lii ȝere of Kyng Herri Kyng Lodewik of Frauns went 5
into þe Holy Lond; Prince Edward and Gilbert, erl of Gloucetir,
folowid him. Kyng Lodewik deyed þere, and mad a ful holy
ende. þan cam Charlys, his son, and continued þe deuocion of his
fader. Ther faute þei with þe Sarasines; and þat cuntré is passing
ful of drye sond, and þe Sarasines went up onto a hill and reised 10
þe sond for to blynde þe Cristen men, but God of heuene sent
his seruauntis swech a reyn þat þe dust greued hem not. Than
tretid þe Sarasines with þe Cristen men, þat þere schuld be pes
betwix hem, upon certeyn condiciones: þat all Cristen men whech
were prisoneres schuld frely go withoute raunson, and all Cristen 15
prestis or freris schuld frely go þorw þe lond, and preche þe
feithe, and baptize alle þat wold receyue it; eke þat alle cherchis
whech were used with Cristen men and all monasteriis schuld be
restored | to þe elde possessouris.   f. 64rb

In þe liii ȝere of þis kyng deied Herry, son to Richard, emperour of 20
Almayn. He deied at Viterb, but he was caried into Ynglond—his
hert was biried at Westmister, and his body at Hayles.

In þis same ȝere the Prince Edward, with his naue, cam into
þe ilde of Cipir, and þere was he weel receyued; þere he stored
him with vitaile and went to Acon, where Cristen men were 25
besegid of þe Sarasines—þei had grete coumfort of his comyng,
for had he not come þe cyté had be ȝoldyn.

In þis ȝere was Gregori þe X chose pope. He was with Edward
in his expedicioun, and þe cardinales gadered at Viterbe chose
him pope. He was pope iiii ȝere.   30

And in þis ȝere Richard, emperour of Almayn, deied in þis
maner. He was let blede for þe agw whech he had, and þat blod-
last smet him in a paralisé, and aftir þat he deyed, and lith at
Hailes.

2 aftir] *in r.h. margin* M   8 son] *suprascript* M   9 Ther] r *supra-*
script M   10 onto] to P   hill] dry hyll P   12 dust] *letter erased between*
u *and* s M   20 þe] *om.* P   21 Viterb] Vitreb P   25 Cristen] þe
Cristen P   men] *supplied, om.* MP   28 chose] *om.* P   31 ȝere] ȝer
twice P   33 a] P, *om.* M

1–4: Martinus, 441/3–12.
28–30: ibid. 442/25–8.

In þe liiii 3ere of Herry the soudon sent a sotil spie onto Edward
whil he was in Acon, pretending þat þe soudon wold a slayn him
for fauour whech he schewid to Cristen men. So was he homly
in Edward hous, and men begun to truste him. At þe last he said
5 he wold telle þe prince a pryuy councell whech schuld be to his
auayle. Thei to went into a chambir al be her one, and þe Sarasine
sperd þe dore, and þan took oute a knyf alayed with venym, and
smet þe prince twies. The prynce, so hurte, took þe knyf fro him,
and anon mad a ende of him. Thei þat stood withoute wondred
f. 64ᵛᵃ of noyse, þei broke up þe dore and founde þe prince | bledyng,
11 and þe Sarasin ded. Than were lechis broute onto him, and,
with myracle more þan with nature, he was mad hool.

In þat same 3ere certeyn men of Norwich brent þe monastery
and þe place of munkis, with whech dede þe kyng was gretly
15 offendid, for he kam to Norwich, and all þoo malefactores were
punchid with iii maner peynis, for þei were first drawe, þan
hange, and last brent.

In þe lv 3ere of his regne þis kyng deied in þe fest of Seint
Edmund, archbischop—his age was lx and vi—and was byried at
20 Westmister, whech werk he reisid and biggid oute of þe grownd.
The lordes gadered hem togidir and swore þei schuld be trewe
ligemen onto Edward þe prince, whech was þan in Acon, sumtyme cleped Tholomayda. The principal stereris to þis oth were
Gilbert of Gloucetir, erl, and Jon, count of Warenne. Tho þei
25 mad a new seal to þe kyng, new officeres, and new justises.

Anno 6469–6470; 1271–1272. These to 3ere ar betwix þe deth
of Herry and þe coronacion of Edward.

Anno 6471–6505; 1273–1307. Edward þe First began to regne
in þe 3ere of oure Lord 1273. For anon as he had tidyndis of his
30 fader deth he took his viage to Rome. There was he weel receyued
of þe pope. Than cam he down to Parys, an þere mad his omage
f. 64ᵛᵇ for þe londes whech he held of þe kyng of | Frauns. Fro þens he
went into Gyan ageyn a grete enmy of his, þei cleped him þe

3 he (2)] suprascript M   7 þan] om. P   9 wondred] þei wondred P
18 regne] rengne P   23 were] was ser' M, was ser P   27 Herry and
þe coronacion] P, h. & cor' M   Edward] inserted two lines above with a line in
red to indicate that it belongs after of M   28 Edward þe First] Edwardus P
29 tidyndis] 1st d altered from t M   31 pope] pope Honorius P   33 þei]
i inserted on the line in paler ink M

Gaske of Bierne. Edward folowid him at many a straunge passage.
Than cam he hom and was coroned at Westmister of Robert,
bischop of Cauntirbury, and with him was coroned Helianore,
doutir to þe kyng of Spayn.

Than sent he v sundri lordis into Gian to fite with þis Gascon 5
of Bierne, for he had accused the kyng of Ynglond befor þe kyng
of Frauns of treson. And þo v lordis profered for to fite with him
þat his accusacion was fals; and more, þei profered þat he schuld
chese with whech of hem he wold fite. Tho he forsok his apel
and put him in þe disposicion of þe kyng of Frauns. Than þe 10
kyng gaue þis dom, þat þis Gask schuld neuyr haue o fote of lond
in his possession til he was reconciled to þe kyng of Ynglond,
and in partie to stand to his justise.

In þat same tyme þe woundes þat were hurt in Surré broke
oute ageyn, of whech Edward was sore aferd, but with prayeris and 15
medicines he was sone holpen.

In þe þird ȝere of his regne, ther was a gret erdqwaue at London, Cauntirbury, and Wynchestir, and dede þere grete harm,
and specia|ly, a gret cherch of Seynt Michael (whech stood on a f. 65ra
hil fast by Glasconbury) þe erdqwaue þrew it fer awey, and left 20
þe ground pleyn.

In þe same tyme were þe Jewis inhibite þat þei schul no more
lende no siluer to no Cristen man, for it was aspied þat with her
vsure þei encresed hemselue to grete ricchesse and mad many a
Cristen man pore. Thei were also accused of clipping of mony, for 25
þe kyngis coyne þorwoute þe lond weied lesse þan it dede at his
makyng be þe þird part, and þerfor þere was in þis mater streith
inquisicion, and doutles þei were founde gilty, and summe of
þe goldsmythis. And for þis cause were hangid at London iii
goldsmythes—summe men þoute ouyr fewe, for many mo were 30
gilty, but of þe Jewis were hanged cc and xiii.

In þe same tyme was Innocent þe V pope but v monthis—
he was a Frere Prechour; and þan Adriane þe V, but o month
and x dayes—he was Octobone, þat was in Ynglond to make pes

---

1 Bierne] vierne P   11 o] no P   12 of] suprascript M   20 þrew it]
separated by thin stroke in red M   23 her] r suprascript M   28 þei]
suprascript M

17–21: ibid. 15/7–9.
22–31: ibid. 18/27–30.
32–128/2: Martinus, 442/41–443/23 and (Continuation) 476/13–14.

betwix þe king and þe barnes; than was Jon þe XXI viii monthis;
and þan Nicholas þe Fourt iiii ȝere.

   In þe iiii ȝere of Edward þis kyng went into Walis, and þer
soute he aftir Leulyn þe prins, and, for hillis and wodis, he coude
5 not cach him, and at þe last he smet down a gret wood and þan
caut him, and browt him to London. Aftir þat þe kyng and he
were þus acorded, þat Leulyne schuld be clepid prince of Walis,
and because a prince must haue summe lordis vndir his dominacioun, he assined him v baronies, þat schuld hald speciali of þe
f. 65ʳᵇ prince— | all oþir baronies schuld hald of þe kyng. Eke þei were
11 acorded, þe king and þe Prince Leulyne, þat þe prince schuld haue
Angliseye in ful possessioun, and at þe entré þerof he schuld paye
to þe kyng v m marc, and euery ȝere aftir in þe fest of Seint
Michael i m marc. Than weddid Leulyn þe doutir of Symund
15 Mountforth, erle of Leicetir, and called euyr aftir þe prince of
Wales.

   In þis tyme William, bischop of Norwich, aftir tyme þat he
had biggid þe cherch ageyn, desired þat þe kyng schuld com to þe
dedicacion. The king cam, and þe qween, and many oþir lordis
20 and ladies, and þere was gret solempnyté.

   In þe v ȝere Edward went into Frauns and took seson in his
wyues heritage, for hir modir was cuntesse of Pounteys. þere
entred he þat same counté, with al þe fauour þat þe kyng of Frauns
myte do, and þese lordchipis: Ageny, Lemouica, Petrigoricum,
25 Sanctone, and oþir.

   In þat ȝere mad he chaunge of his coyne, and distroyed al
þat was clipped. He ded make ferþingis and halfpenies, whech
were not used before; and þere was þe prophecye of Merlyn
fulfillid, þat seith, 'Dimidium rotundi erit', that is to sey, 'þere
30 schal be half of þe round'.

   In þe ix ȝere of Edward, Leulyne, prince of Walis, began to
rebelle, payed not his tribute, distroyed pore men. The kyng went
into þe marches, and with him þe bischop of Cauntirbury.

---

4 soute] P, sought *in later hand over erasure* M   5 at] *suprascript* M
6 þat] P, þan M   9 baronies] barones P   10 baronies] barones P
11 þe (3)] *suprascript* M   19 cam and þe qween] and þe quene cam P
22 Pounteys] eys *over erasure* M   23 counté] cuntre P

1-2: see p. 127.
6-16: Walsingham, *Hist Ang.* i. 17/5-29 and 18/22-6.
26-30: ibid. 19/23-8.
31-129/4: cf. ibid. 21/38-41.

Because Leulyne wold not come to þe kingis presens, þerfor þe
kyng sent þe bischop onto him, to trete him to pes. But he fond
him ontretable, for | whech cause þe bischop cursid him, and f. 65ᵛᵃ
so þe kyng left þat jornai for þat tyme.

In þe ten ȝere of his regne he entyred into Snowdon, and whil 5
þe kyng was þere thei faute togidir, þe Englischmen and þe
Walchmen—mech harm was do on both sides. So happed Edmund Mortimer for to ransake þe ded bodies, and amongis dyuers
hedis þat were þere he fond Leulyn hed, whech he brout to þe
kyng. þe kyng sent it to London, and mad it be set on þe Tour. 10

In þe nexte ȝere folowand, þe kyng took Dauy, Leulyne broþir,
and put him in prison; þan had he disposicion of al Wales at his
plesauns. Sone aftir he sette a parlement at Schrouisbury, and
þere was Dauy, Leulyne broþir, drawen, hangid, and quartered,
and his quarteres sent to dyuers places of Ynglond.   15

In þis tyme was Martyn þe Fourt pope; he was first a senatoure.
And in his first ȝere was take a fisch in þe se, lich a leon; it was
broute to þe popes presens, and many a man went þidir for to se it.
He had row her, lych a leon, feet and tayl in þe same similitude,
hed, eres, mouth, teeth, tunge, and all maner membris. Thei 20
seide þat fischid him þat in his takyng he mad a horibel and a
woful noyse.

Sone aftir þei þat were dwelleres of Scicile risen ageyn þe
Frenschmen, whech had þe gouernauns þere vndir Philip, kyng
of Frauns; þese same Sicicilianes—summe men clepe hem Panor- 25
mitanes—killid all þe Frenschmen, and women of þe same cuntré,
whech had conceyued of þe Frenschmen, þei slitte her wombes and
distroyed þe childyrn.

In þe xv ȝere | of þis kyng, aftir tyme þe kyng of Frauns was f. 65ᵛᵇ
slayn in batayle, whech he held ageyn Petir, kyng of Aragoyne, 30
þan þe kyngis son sent aftir Edward þat he schuld come and
helpe him to venge his fader deth. The cause of þe strif betwix
þese to kyngis was þat þe kyng of Frauns chalenged seruyse and
subjeccion of þis kyng of Aragon, and he deneyed it, and saide

4 so] *om.* P   5 entyred] entred P, entyr M   32–3 betwix þese] of þe P
33 þat] t *suprascript* M, that þat P

5–10: cf. ibid. 22/1–7, 23–40.
11–15: ibid. 24/31–25/9.
16–28: Martinus (Continuation), 477/7–478/9.

he aute non but to þe kyng of Spayn. Thus is Edward forth in his viage—God spede him.

In þat same ʒere a Frere Prechour, cleped Richard Cnapwelle, whas cleped be þe archbischop for to answere to certeyn simpil
5 opiniones whech he held, and whan he cam to answere, he coude not redily defende his part, wherfor his articules were condemp- ned. There was þe prouincial of þe ordre alegging for him her exempcion, who þei were immediatly vndir þe pope, wherfor he appeled fro þe bischop, but withinne few dayes þe mater was put
10 to silens.

In þese dayes were all þe Jewys of Ynglond, man, woman, and child, arestid, and put in prison onto þe tyme þei had payed þe kyng x m libras.

In þis tyme was pope Nicholace, of þe Menoures ordre, iiii
15 ʒere. He declared þe Frere Menoures reule at her instauns.

In þe xvi ʒere of Edward was a grete feyer at Boston, and sodeynly þe feyer and þe town was set on fyre. Men seide þat malicious men ded it, to þis entent, þat whil men were bysy to saue her housyng, theues schuld stele her good.
20 In þis same tyme þe vniuersité of Oxforth chose a chauncelere,
f. 66ra Maistir William Kyngeston. þei | sent onto þe bischop of Lincoln for his confirmacion; þe bischop seide it was his deuté to com himselue. Thei answerd þat þis was her elde priuylege, and þis wold þei kepe. The bischop was inflexibil, and þei were obdurat,
25 and so of malice þei left her redyng and her teching: many scoleres went away; þei þat abode were euel occupied. But at þe last þe bischop condescendid to her elde custome.

In þe xvii ʒere, in þe nyte of Seint Margarete, was swech reyn, þundir, and leuene, þat it distroyed al þe corn, for a buschel of
30 whete, þat was beforn but at iii pens, was aftir þis tempest worth IIs., and þis same derth lastid ny xl ʒere.

In þis ʒere Dame Jone Acris, the kyngis doutir, born in Acon in þe Holy Lond, was weddid onto Gilbert, herl of Gloucetir, whech was a ful holy woman, for sche was biried in þe Frere
35 Austines at Clare; and aftir hir biriing lii ʒere, at þe desire of

1 Thus] This P   18 entent] entend P   21 onto] P, on M   22 his (2)]
om. P   27 condescendid] final d altered from t M

14–15: cf. Walsingham, Hist. Ang. i. 28/13–18.
16–19: cf. ibid. 30/30–7.

Dame Ysabel of Borow, sche mad hir bare, and sche was found hol
in all membris: hir tetis, whan þei were pressid with handis, þe
flesch ros up ageyn; hir eyeledes, left up, fel down ageyn. The
cloþis þat were aboute hir, whech were dipped in wax and rosyn,
þoo were roten, but þe lynand cloth whech was next hir, þat was 5
dite with no craft, þat was found clene and hool.

In þe xx ȝere of þis kyng, be þe precept of Charles, broþir
to þe kyng of Frauns, þei of Normandie kepte þe se, and no
Englischman myte passe but þei toke him, and whan þei had take
him þei ledde | him to þe se-bank on þe Frensch side, and þere f. 66ʳᵇ
þei hing him. For þat same Charlis had mad galowis at euery 11
town on þe seside for þe same venjauns. Than þei of Ynglond
ordeyned grete schippis too hundred and xx, and manly went
into þe see, faut þere with Normanndes, and took of hem to
hundred—and xxviii schippis þei bored and drenchid hem. 15

In þe xxii ȝere was Celestinus þe Fifte pope take fro his hous,
for he was a ankir; and whan he was pope he ordeyned a statute
þat euery pope myte resigne if he wold, and anon as þe statute
was mad he resined, and went ageyn to his elde lyf. Than must
þei chese a new pope, and for þei myte not acorde, þei com- 20
promitted to þis man þat was pope þat he schuld chese iiii cardinales whech he wold; and as þe foure chose, þei all schuld assent.
Tho named he a cardinal hite Benedicte and oþir thre, and þe
oþir iii chose þat Benedict, and he was cleped Bonefacius VIII.
Al þis mater was do be þat Bonefacius for to make himselue pope. 25
For anon as he was entered, he annulled þat statute þat þe pope
schuld haue liberté to resigne. Therfor, þat man þat he deceyued
so for to be pope himselue, he prophecied þus of him, 'Thou hast
entered as a fox; þou hast lyued as a leon; þou schal deye as a
dogge'. His entering was sly, so sotily to promote him. His lif 30
was cruel, for too cardinalis, þat were of þe progenie of þe Columpnes, he put fro her dignité. And to þe kyng of Frauns he was
grete | enmye, for he wroute ageyn him al þat he myte, in-so-mech f. 66ᵛᵃ

---

1 hir] *suprascript* M   and sche was] *over erasure* M   3 hir eyeledes . . .
ageyn] *om.* P   5 þat] t *suprascript* M   was (2)] *om.* P   8 þe se] *separated by thin stroke in red* M   14 Normanndes] þe Normandes P   15 þei]
suprascript M   bored] bored hem P   22 and] *suprascript* M   23 Benedicte]
Benedite P   24 chose] *twice over line division* P   he] *om.* P   27 resigne]
1st e *suprascript over* i *expuncted* M

16–132/5: cf. ibid. 48/29–49/19.

he wolde a deposed him. Therfor, with power of þe kyng and of þe cardinales, þei toke þis pope, and sette him on a hors withoute sadill, and þe tayl in his hand, and so þei mad him ryde þorwoute Rome, and aftir þei infamynde him for hungir. This

5 same Boneface in his tyme mad þe sexte book of *Decretales*.

In þe xxiii ȝere the marchaundis of þis lond compleyned to þe kyng þat þe Normanntes spoiled hem, so þat þei myte kepe no market, wherfor þei praied þe kyng of sum remedye, and þe kyng anon sent Ser Herry Lacy, þan erl of Lyncoln, enbassiatour

10 onto þe kyng of Frauns. There was he long taried, and whilis he was þere too hundred schippis oute of Normandye sailed into Burdews, and ded al þe harm þei myte do onto Englichmen. Ther were þei laden, and com hom ageyn; in her comyng sexti Englisch schippis met with hem, and took schip, good, and man, saue þei

15 þat scaped in botys, and brout it into Ynglond.

Thei of Frauns were astoyned and wroth with þis dede, and mad her kyng to write into Ynglond to oure kyng, þat he schulde se þese schippis and þe godes be dylyuered onto þe owneris. The Kyng Edward wrot ageyn þat his court was his owne, and þerfor

20 he wold þe marchaundis of Frauns schuld com into Ynglond and make her compleynt, and here what schuld be aleggid ageyn of marchaundes here; and þe king schuld se justise schuld be had on |

f. 66ᵛᵇ both partyes. This answere plesed not þe French kyng, and þerfor he ded make somounis in a cyté of Gyan þat þe kyng of Ynglond

25 schuld apere before þe kyng of Frauns at Paris, upon a gret peyne. The kyng of Ynglond cam not, and þerfor þe Frenchmen ridyn into Gian, and occupied mech of þe kyngis londis.

That tyme was in þat cuntré Edmund, þe erle of Cornwaile, to whom Edward wrote, for he was his broþir, þat he schuld asaye

30 to trete þe kyng of Frauns to a resonabil mene. He coud not spede þat mater, and as he was homward þe to qweenes sent aftir him, purposing to fynde menys of pes. These too qweenes— on was þe wif to þe kyng of Frauns, þe oþir was to his fader, and now weddid to þis Edmund. But to þo comnauntis þat were

---

4 infamynde] P, infamyde M   6 xxiii] xxii MP   7 þei] i *supra-script in darker ink* M   9 Ser] for P   18 owneris] oweris P   24 somounis] somounes P, somonounis M   27 londis] P, lond M   30 coud] cou*n*de P   not] P, no M   31 to] *om. over line division* P   34 But] *change to darker ink and narrower letter strokes* M

1–5: see p. 131.
6–133/4: Walsingham, *Hist. Ang.* i. 43/13–48/3.

mad betwix Edmund and þe qweenes þe kyng of Frauns wold
not consent; wherfor Edward, with his naue, sailed streit into
Geround, and þere took he Borow, Bloys, Burdeus, and Bayon. þe
cuntré was glad of his comyng; þe capitanes were sent into Ynglond.

In þe xxiiii ȝere of his regne had Edward grete conflicte with 5
þe Scottis, for Jon, her kyng, wrote onto Edward þat he awte him
no subjeccion, but he was annexed and swore to the kyng of
Frauns. The kyng gadered his men, and first he took Berwik
fro þe Scottis. Than had þei a batail at Dunbarr, where þe kyng
took of þe Scottis part iii erles and vi barnes, and sent hem into 10
Ynglond. Than took he many casteles and strengthis so fer-forth
þat þe kyng of Scottis was compelled to | excuse him þat his   f. 67ra
rebellion was be councell of his barnes, in whech letter he mad
a newe obejauns to þe kyng, and all þe barnes of þe lond wrote
a lettir of þe same sentens.   15

Than sent Edward a lettir onto þe kyng of Frauns, in whech
he desired þat all Englischmen whech were prisoneres in Frauns
schuld be dylyuered, and þe Frenschmen þat were prisoneres in
Inglond schuld go hom to Frauns. The kyng of Frauns wrot
ageyn þat he wold graunt it, with þat condicioun, þat Jon, kyng 20
of Scottis, schuld be on of hem þat schuld be delyuered. To þat
peticioun þis was þe answere, þat he longed not to þe kyng of
Frauns, ne he was not takyn as a prisoner of Frauns, but as a
rebelle to þe kyng of Ynglond.

In þe 26 ȝere þe Kyng Edward weddid Margarete, þe sistir of 25
þe kyng of Frauns.

And in þat same tyme Pope Boneface wrote onto þe Kyng
Edward of þe kyngdam of Scotlond, exhorting him þat he schuld
cese of his werre, for it longid immediatly to þe Cherch of Rome,
in whech lettir swech suasiones were made: þat in þe letteris 30
of Herri, Edward fader, was conteyned þat Alisaunder, kyng of
Scottis, ded neuyr no seruise to Kyng Herry of dewté, but of
curtesi and of benyuolens; eke, whan þat same Alexander went
to þe coronacion of Herri, it was for gentilnes, and not of dewté.

6 wrote] *suprascript with caret (in red)* M   onto] on P   9 Dunbarr]
in r.h. margin M   12 was] *suprascript* M   21 schuld (1)] *om.* P

5–15: ibid. 52/21–30, 53/15–25, 55/40–56/21, 58/6–61/20.
16–24: cf. ibid. 73/43–74/5, 74/35–75/2.
25–6: ibid. 79/5–22.
27–134/11: ibid. 85/25–97/19.

So þe pope concluded þat he regned neuyr but be strength and violens ouyr þe kyng of Scotlond.

Edward wrot ageyn, and prayed him þat his holy faderhod schuld not beleue ouyr-sone swech feyned | suggestiones (for in treuth all þe kyngis of Ynglond, fro þe tyme of Arthure, whech was a Britoun, had dominacioun ouyr þe kyngdam of Scotlond), where he rehersed be rowe þe rite of Edgare, of Edward þe Martir, of Edmund Yrunside, William Conqwerour, Richard, and many mo. The barnes eke of þe lond writin letteris of the same sentens, and moreouyr þei saide who þei were swore with body and good to stand be þe kyng in his rite, whech oth þei wold not breke.

In þis same tyme þe kyng of Frauns appeled fro þe pope onto a general councell, puttyng upon þe pope þat he was both a heretik and a scismatik.

In þe xxviii ȝere was a Frere Prechour chose pope, and leuyd but o ȝere. Of him mad a writer too vers:—

Oro, nomen habe: 'Benedic', 'Benefac', 'Benedicte';
Aut rem peruerte: 'Malefac', 'Maledic', 'Maledicte'.

Thus is it in Englisch:—

I pray þe, haue þis name: 'Sey-wel', 'Do-wel', and 'Be-good';
Or ellis turne þi fame: 'Sey-euel', 'Do-euele', 'Be-cursed-and-wood'.

In þe xxxii ȝere þere was a man þei cleped Wyliam Waleys, þat was in Scotland, and reisid þe puple, and mad al þe cuntré rebel to Edward þe kyng. But he was take and broute onto London, hanged and draw and qwartered, his hed sette on London Brigge, his body dyuyded in iiii quarteres and sent to foure townes of Scotland.

In þis tyme, aftir Benedicte, was Clemens V[us] pope. He was before archbischop of Bordews. Moost besynesse he had to gader ricchesse, and make casteles and strengthis. He mad þe vii book

11 his] om. P   12 a] þe P   13 he] in r.h. margin M   17 Benedicte] P, Benedice M   18 Maledic] Meledic P   Maledicte] P, Maledice M   23 þe] om. P

1–11: see p. 133.
12–14: Walsingham, Hist. Ang. i. 100/32–7.
15–22: ibid. 104/36–41 and 107/1–2.
23–8: ibid. 107/15–108/3.
29–135/2: cf. ibid. 108/4–5.

of *Decretales*, but þei were not publisced til þe | tyme of Jon þe   f. 67ᵛᵃ
XXII. This Clement translate þe courte fro Rome to Auinioun.

In þe xxxiiii ȝere was a man in Scotlond þei cleped Robert
Brusse. He took upon him to be king of þe lond, and went to þe
abbey of Scone for to be crowned. Than þe cuntesse of Bowan 5
stal fro hir lord all his grete hors, and with swech men as sche
trostid cam to þat same abbey, and þere sche sette þe crowne
upon Robard hed. Sche was take aftir of Englischmen, and presentid to þe Kyng Edward. He comaunded sche schuld not be ded,
but þat þere schuld be mad a hous al of tymbir upon þe wallis 10
of Berwyk, and þere schuld sche be tyl sche deyed.

Aftir þis þe kyng dubbid his son knyte, and many oþir ȝong
men with him, and sent hem to Scotlond, and aftir hem folowid
Aymer of Valens, þe erl of Penbrok, Robert Giffard, Herry
Percy, and many oþir, and þei mad þat same Robert Brusse to 15
fle into þe ferþest yle of Scotlond.

In þe xxxv ȝere of his regne he deied, in þe translacion of
Seynt Thomas, and biried is at Westminster.

Anno 6506–6524; 1308–1326. Edward þe Secund regned xix
ȝere. He was crowned at Westminster þe sext kalend of March, 20
and his wif Ysabel, þe kingis doutyr of Frauns, be þe bischop of
Wynchestir, whech had special commission of þe bischop of
Cauntirbury for he was not in þis lond.

In the same tyme was grete tre|tyng betwix þe lordis for pes f. 67ᵛᵇ
of þe lond and for on Petir Gauerston, whech was exiled fro þe 25
lond in his fader tyme, and þis Edward had clepid him hom
ageyn—þerfor þe barnes þoute to lette þe kyngis coronacioun.
This aspied, þe kyng hite hem in good feith þat at þe next parlement he schuld fulfil here desire. Aftir þe coronacion of þe kyng
is wont þat certeyn officeres schul bere certeyn relikes of Seynt 30
Edward befor him into þe paleys, and he tok hem to oþir men,
þat is to seye, þe chalis of Seynt Edward, þe crosse, þe sceptir,
þe spores, and swech oþir, and þe corowne of Seynt Edward bare

---

8 Englischmen] men *suprascript with caret (in red)* M   18 is] *suprascript* M   Westminster] Westm' M   24 tyme] *suprascript* M   28 þat]
om. P   29 of] *supplied, om.* MP   30 certeyn (2)] P, certeynt M

3–11: ibid. 108/35–109/5.
12–16: ibid. 109/6–34.
17–18: ibid. 116/29–31 and 118/4–7.
19–23: ibid. 121/18–21, and cf. 119/5–8.
24–136/2: ibid. 121/21–40.

þat same Petir befor þe kyng, of whech þing ros grete indignacion, both in þe lordes and in þe clergy.

Not long aftir þis þe same Petir mad a gret torneament fast by Wallingford, where he had gadered many justeres alienes, and þei
5 bore down in justis many Englischmen, þat is to sey Thomas, erl of Lancastir, Humfrey of Herforth, Eymer of Penbrok, Johan Warenne, and many othir, for whech þe had gret indignacion.

In þis same 3ere Gilbert, erl of Gloucetir, wedded þe erle doutir of Wolinster, in Erland.

10 In þe same tyme, þe secund 3ere of Edward, þe lordes, considering þat þere was noþing do but aftir council of þis Petir, and he gadered mech ricchesse and euyr sent it ouyr þe se, þei cam to þe kyng desiryng þat þe gouernauns of þe reme schuld be directid
f. 68ra aftir þe council of his barnes. The kyng | mad difficulté, supposing
15 euyr þat þei wold purpose sum articule ageyn Petir, whech he loued. Vpon þis was sette a parlement at London, þat all men schuld come þedir whech were wone of dewté to be at þe parlement, where was grete instauns mad to þe kyng þat he schuld suffir þe barnes to purpos certeyn articules, whech schuld be
20 worchip to God, an profit to þe reme. The kyng graunted his consent, and swore whateuyr þei ordeyned he schuld consent and conferme. Than þe barones gadered onto here councell certeyn bischoppis, to make her party more strong.

In þe þird 3ere of his regne he held anoþir parlement at London,
25 aftir þe tyme he had mad þat oth to þe barnes; þan he renewid þe same oth befor all þe lordes. And þan þe bischop of Cauntyrbury, Maistir Robert Wynchilseye, with all his suffraganes, cursed all hem þat schuld lette þe entent of þe barones. Than in þe cherch of Seynt Poule at London, in þe presens of þe kyng and lordes
30 and comownes, were red certeyn articles, among whech was red þe Grete Charter, and oþir þingis, and þat he schuld conferme þat his fader comaunded, for to put alienes fro his court, and

---

7 þe] he MP   10 þe lordes] *in r.h. margin with carets* (*in red*) M
15 þat] *twice* P   16–18 at London . . . þe parlement] *om.* P   16 London]
Lond' M   17 whech] *suprascript* M   were] wher' M   25 he (1)] *change
to darker ink* M   26 þan] *om.* P   28 hem] hen P

1–2: see p. 135.
3–7: Walsingham, *Hist. Ang.* i. 122/10–18.
8–9: ibid. ii. 364/3–5.
10–23: ibid. i. 122/22–123/31.
24–137/3: ibid. 124/6–33.

þat all þing þat schuld be do schuld be aftir þe councel of þe
barnes, ne he schuld not begynne no werre withoute þe same
councell, and eke þat he schuld exile þe forseid Petir into Erlond.

Aftir þe parlement þe kyng was very sory for þe exile of Petir,
and comoned with his Pryuy Councell what remedy myte be had in   5
þis mater. They avised | him þat he schuld wedde þe sister of þe   f. 68rb
erl of Gloucestir, þat be swech mene he myte purchace þe loue
of many lordes. Than þe kyng sent for him into Erlond, and maried
him onto þis woman. Than was Petir prouder þan before. He
gadered gret good, and sent it to marchaundis handis. The kyng   10
wex so pore þat he had not to fynde his houshold. The qween
eke wrote to hir fader, kyng of Frauns, compleyned of grete
pouerté. So þe kyng, compellid on o party be nede, on þe oþir
party be instauns of þe lordes, compelled þis Petir for to swere
þat he schuld in hast go oute of þe lond, and neuyr his lyue dwelle   15
in no soile longing to þe kyng of Ynglond, and if he ded þe
contrari he schuld lese his hed. He went oute of þis lond into
Frauns, where þe kyng of Frauns comaunded al his officeres
þat if þei mite take him, þei schuld kepe him in hold, þat he com
no more in Ynglond. Fro þens þan went he into Flaundres; þere   20
was he not welkom. Mani places soute he, but at þe last he cam
ageyn to Ynglond. And whan þe king sey him, all othis and
comnauntes were forgoten, and he was welkom.

In þis same 3ere were brent at Parys be þe jugement of Philip,
kyng of Frauns, liiii men of þe ordir of Templaries, for þat same   25
3ere were þei condempned in þe councel at Vyenne. For þis
kyng of Frauns purposed to make on of his breþerin kyng of
Jerusalem, and þerfor, as it is seid, he procured þe distruccion of
Templaries, þat her go|dis schuld be goue to þe same kingdam.   f. 68va
It was deposed ageyn hem, þat whan on schuld be receyued   30
onto þat ordir, þei schuld go all to a pryuy place, and he schuld be
al naked, and þan on of þe felawis schuld rise and kisse him
behinde; and þan schuld þei clothe him, and gird him with a
girdill of canvace. Than schuld Crist crucified be broute before

---

1 schuld (2)] in l.h. margin M   9 He] P, om. M   10 to] suprascript M   19 him (2)] suprascript M   22 king] in r.h. margin M
27 breþerin] brethern P, beþerin M   28 is] suprascript M   29 þat]
t suprascript M   her] þoo MP   33 þan schuld þei clothe him and] om. P
34 crucified] ci suprascript M

4–23: ibid. 124/37–126/24.
24–138/6: ibid. 127/7–128/8.

him, and it schuld be seid onto him þat Crist is no god, but a
fals prophete, whech deceyued þe world, killid of Jewis for his
fals lyuyng. Than schuld þei þrow down þe crosse, and trede
it vndirfote, and þries spitte þeron. Than schuld þei schewe him a
5 hed of a ydol, to whech þei ded euery day ful grete honour. Thei
were eke infecte gretly with þe vice of sodomye.

   In þe v ȝere of Edward, whan Petir was come ageyn, þe qween
and all þe lordes were gretly meuyd, specialy Thomas of Lancastir
whech was son to Edmund, þe son of þe first Edward, and be
10 succession and heritage he cam to possession of v erldammes:
Lancastir, and Leycetir, and Ferreres; þan, aftir decese of Herry
Lacy, erl of Lyncoln and Salesbury, be mariage of his doutir he
entered into þo to erldames. And whan þis Herry schuld dye, he
cleped Thomas to him, and comaund him to stand with the rite of
15 þe reme, and þat he schuld be gouerned be þe councel of Gy, erl
of Warwik.

   Aftir his deth Thomas, at þe prayer of þe lordes, wrote to þe
kyng þat þis Petir schuld be avoyded, and rode to þe kyng, whech
f. 68vb   was þan at Newcastell. | Whan þe kyng herd sey þat þe lordes
20 com with swech strength he fled onto Tynmouth, and be þe se
led Petir to þe castell of Scarborow, and þere left him, comaunding
þe cuntré þat þei stuf þe castel with vitail and with men. But,
schort to seye, þe lordes took þis man, and he preyed hem of no
grace but on, þat he myte speke with þe kyng or he deied. Thei
25 wold a loggid him in a town fast by Warwic þei clepe Dodington,
but þe erl of Warwik cam with strength and led him to his castel.
And whan þei were in grete doute what þei schuld do with him—
wheþir þei schuld lede him to þe kyng or not—a grete-wittid
man sayd þus, 'Many day haue ȝe huntid, and failed of ȝoure game;
30 now haue ȝe caute ȝoure prai. If he scape ȝoure handis, ȝe gete
him not litely'. Sone was he led oute, and his hed smet of; he
called Gy of Warwik no oþir name but þe Blak Dog of Arderne,
and in Gyis lordchip his hed was bityn fro þe body. The careyn
was buried amongis þe Prechouris of Oxenforth; his tresore and
35 alle his jeweles þei sent to þe kyng.

14 him to stand] *in l.h. margin with carets (in red)* M   23 þe] *om.* P
þis man and he] man & he *in r.h. margin with carets (in red)* M, hym & he P
32 Dog] *in r.h. margin* M   33 hed] *in r.h. margin* M

1–6: see p. 137.
7–16: Walsingham, *Hist. Ang.* i. 128/31–130/20.
17–35: ibid. 131/11–133/17, 134/26–9.

This same ȝere Isabell þe qween broute forth Edward þe
þirde. Many Frensch lordis, þat were aboute hir, wold a clepid
him Philippe, aftir þe kyng of Frauns; þe Englisch lordes wold
haue him Edward. The kyng had so grete joye of þis child new
born þat his heuynesse for Petir cesed sone.   5

In þe vi ȝere of his regne were many fals tongis with þe kyng:
þei seid it was derogacioun to swech a state þat he schuld rite nowt
do withoute coun|cell; and so with swech suggestions þei en-   f. 69ra
cresed grete rancour betwix þe kyng and þe lordes.

Than was þere gadered a parlement at London, in whech þe   10
kyng mad a gret compleynt ageyn þe barones þat at Newcastell,
in despite of him, come þedir armed, and who þei pursewid Petir
his frend, and þerto killid him. The barnes answered ageyn þat
þei ded þat dede to Goddis worchip, for þei killid non but a fals
traitour banysched fro Ynglond and fro Frauns, and þei had   15
spent her good and her labour to profite of þe rem; 'and þe
kyng dryuyth oure materis withoute ony effect. But þese þingis
purposed we wil se amendid, or ellis we wil lyue and dey in þe
mater'.

Than þe qween, with certeyn prelatis, treted betwix þe kyng   20
and hem, þat þei schuld in Westminster Halle ask þe king forgifnesse of all her surfetis, and þe kyng schu'd take hem to grace
and graunt all her peticiones þat were resonable, and neuyr venge
þe deth of Petir Gauerstoun.

In þe vii ȝere deied Pope Clement, þat was sumtyme bischop   25
of Burdews; too ȝere was þe sete voyd, and þan was chose Johannes XXII.

The same ȝere cam þe kyng to Seynt Albones, and þere he
offered a cros, with grete relikes, and gaf hem a hundred mark to
makyng of her cherch, and þe profite of a maner tyl it was mad.   30
The Munday aftir Palme Sunday he tok his jornay to Hely, and
þere was he al þe Pase-tyme. As he loked aboute on dyuers

2 clepid] d *altered from* t M   4 joye] *suprascript with caret (in red)* M
14 worchip] plesauns P   21 and] and & P   24 Gauerstoun] Grauestoun
MP   25 In] *change to darker ink* M

1–5: ibid. 134/34–135/2.
6–9: ibid. 135/11–21.
10–19: ibid. 135/22–136/2.
20–4: ibid. 136/2–15.
25–7: ibid. 138/1–4.
28–140/11: ibid. 138/5–139/36.

þingis he fond þere wrytyng þat þe body of Seynt Albon schuld

be þere. He clepid þe bischop on|to him, and seide he wold wete in
certeyn where Seynt Albon was, 'for þei of Seynt Albone sey þei
haue him, and here at Hely þei sey þei haue him. Therfor we wil
5 se þe toumbe withinne, what relik is here of him'. Whan it was
ondo, þei founde a grete tabard of wrecchid cloth, and al ful of
fresch blood, as þouȝ it had be þe same day spilt. þan vndirstod
þei wel, þat same habite had Albone of his maistir, Amphibalus,
whan he went to þe Juge. Than sayde þe king, 'Now knowe we to
10 what þing we schal do worchip: to þe body at Seynt Albones, and
to þe cloth at Hely'.

Fro þens he went to Lyncoln, and þan to ȝork, and forth to
Berwik—ther was þe batayl of Stryuelyn, where Englischmen
were put to grete rebuk vndir Robert Brus, þe kyng of Scottis.
15 Ther were ded and take on þe Englisch part of lordes, barnes, and
knytes, cliiii.

This ȝere deied Philip, þe kyng of Frauns; and Lodewik, his
son, regned for him.

In þe viii ȝere of þe kyng was a parlement at London, where
20 was a gret ordinauns to chepe vitaile, and it auayled not. It was
ordeyned þat a oxe fed with gresse schuld be seld for XVIs.,
a fatte oxe for XXIIIIs., a fatte cow for XIIs., a good swyn, to
ȝere old, for XLd., a schep withouten wolle, XIIIId., a fat schep
with wolle, XXd., a fat goos, IId.ᵒᵇᵒˡᵒ, a capon, IId., a henne,
25 Id., iiii dowes, Id.; and if ony man seld for ony oþir pris, þe
vitail be forfete to þe kyng. That same ȝere fel swech a derth þat
vitaile coude not be founde. So þat statute was abrogat, and no
lenger kept.

Eke þat same ȝere þe king of Scottys | entered at Karlile, and
30 wasted all þe cuntré onto ȝork. And aftir þat þe kyng, Robert
Brus, sent his broþir Edward into Erland to occupie all þe londes
þere þat longin to the crowne of Ynglond.

---

2 wete in] *suprascript with caret* (*in red*) M   7 spilt] *in r.h. margin* M
13 Englischmen] men *suprascript with caret* (*in red*) M   22 a fatte cow
for XIIs.] *om.* P   24 a (1)] at P   25 for] *supplied, om.* MP   26 be]
in r.h. margin M   31 Erland] r *suprascript* M

1–11: see p. 139.
12–16: Walsingham, *Hist. Ang.* i. 139/37–141/26.
17–18: ibid. 143/16–17.
19–28: ibid. 144/1–16, 144/40–145/10, 145/28–31.
29–32: ibid. 144/25–39.

In þis ȝere were swech reynes in heruest þat baxsteres dryed
her corn in ouenes or þei myte grynde it, and þe bred þat was
mad þerof had no vertu, for as sone as men had ete þei hungered
ageyn, wherof fel mech mischef. Summe deied for hungir; þei
þat were put oute of houshold went into þe cuntré and robbid   5
pore men. So mech hungir grew in þe lond þat foure peniworth of
bred was not sufficient to fede a man o day.

In þis ȝere, aftir þe deth of Clement þe pope, þe sete was voyde
to ȝere, and þan þei chose Jon þe XXII, whech was before bischop
of Auynioun. This man was ful gracious to all men, and specialy   10
to þe order of þe Heremites of Seynt Augustin. For by his auctorité
þe kyng of Bem broute in þe same Heremites to dwelle at Pauye
with þe Chanones, and þere to kepe þe o side of þe qwer, and þe
Chanones þe oþir.

In þe ix ȝere of his regne Kyng Edward held his Estern at   15
Claringdoun, where a woman cam in rydyng as a jogulour, and
leyd a lettyr on þe kyngis bord. The sentens was þat þe kyng
norchid hem and avaunsed þat neuyr were in werre ne in distresse
for profite of þe lond, and þei þat had spent her good, and bled
her blod, wer in no reputacion, ne had no reward. The woman   20
was pursewid and ta|ken, compelled eke to telle be whos councell   f. 69ᵛᵇ
sche ded þis dede, and sche accused a certeyn knyte, whech cam
to þe kyng and avowid euery word, for whech constauns he was
gretly alowed and wel rewardid.

In þis same ȝere þei in þe north risin ageyn þe Scottis, for þe   25
kyng ne þe lordis holpe hem nowt, and whan þei were gadered,
for lak of vitaile þei robbed þe cuntré, and took awey ox, schep,
corn, mony, and þis robry continued ny foure ȝere.

In þat same tyme, at prayer of þe kyng, com into Ynglond to
legatis, on Gauceline, þe popes chaunceler, and Lucas de Flisco, to   30
reforme pees betwix Ynglond and Scotlond, with bulles of Jon
þe XXII, in whech he cursed þe kyng of Scottis for brekyng of his
treuth, whech he had mad to þe Englisch kyng. The oþir cause

6 peniworth] i *suprascript* M   11 Augustin] Austin P   31 betwix]
betwene P   33 oþir] *in r.h. margin with carets (in red)* M

1–7: ibid. 145/32–146/22.
8–10: ibid. 148/1–5.
15–24: ibid. 148/18–21, 149/21–150/7.
25–8: ibid. 150/13–31.
29–142/21: ibid. 150/32–151/37.

of her comyng was to sette pes betwix þe kyng and Thomas, erl
of Lancastir.

And as þe maner of Romanes is, þei ryde with grete solempnité
into þe north cuntré, for to make Lodewik Beamount bischop of
5 Dorham ageyn þe eleccioun of þe munkis, whech had chose a
othir. And þou3 þei were warned þat þei schuld not com þere,
3et þei ride til þei come ny at Derlyngton, and sodeynly oute of a
vale rise a gret puple, capteynes Gilbert of Mydilton and Walter
Selby; þei leid hand upon hem, and robbed hem of al her tresoure,
10 and Lodewik, whech þei entended to make bischop, þei led to a
town þei clepe Morpath, compellyng him to a grete raunson. In
f. 70ra þat affray eke was take Herry Be|amount, with al his hors and
tresoure, and led to þe castell of Mithforth, wher he was kept tyl he
had payed a grete summe of mony. The cardynales turned ageyn to
15 3ork, and whan þei were come þidir, thei cursed all þoo robberis
with horible sentens, and sent þe copies þorw þe rewme. So
were þei restored to þe most part of her losse, but not to all.
Than come þei to London, and þere asked þei of þe clergye VIIId.
of þe mark; þei were answerd þat þei gaue hem no councell for to
20 go so ferr north, but IIIId. of þe mark, whech was graunted before,
þat had þei.

In þe x 3ere þe kyng held a councell at London of þe harm
whech þe kyng of Scottis had do to him, at whech councell Thomas
of Lancastir cam not, wherfor he was named tretour in þe kyngis
25 hous. Than mad þe cardinales pees betwix þe king and Thomas,
but it lestid not longe. Sone aftir þis was a knyte taken at Poumfrecte, and presented to þe Erle Thomas, with letteris fro þe kyng
onto þe kyng of Scottis both of þe grete targe and þe pryuy
sel, þat þe king of Scottis schuld be sum trayn kille þis Thomas,
30 as he wold do plesauns to þe kyng of Ynglond, whech knyte þe
erle ded hange and drawe, because he was of his houshold before.

In þis same 3ere Gilbert of Mydilton was take be a trayne,
layd in yrunnes, and led to Londoun, and þere hanged and
drawen in þe site of þe cardinales whech he had robbed.

4 bischop (*after* bischop) *expuncted in red* M   9 Selby] Selvy P   11 Mor-
path] Norpath P   13 Mithforth] Muthford P   22 þe kyng held] of the
kyng was P   28 of (2)] *supplied, om.* MP   30 to] vnto P   of þe kyng (*after*
kyng) *expuncted in red* M   32 In] *change to darker ink* M   3ere] *in r.h. margin* M

1–21: see p. 141.
22–31: Walsingham, *Hist. Ang.* i. 150/8–12, 152/3–15.
32–4: ibid. 152/20–153/6.

In þis same ȝere Pope Jon puplischid þat | book whech þei f. 70ʳᵇ
clepe þe *Clementins*, mad be Clement, his predecessour. He
confermed eke þe fest of Crist, whech is cleped Corporis Cristi,
whech fest was mad before be þe Pope Vrbane.

In þis same ȝere þe kyng held his Cristmasse at Westminster, 5
where cam but fewe lordis, for þe debate þat was betwix hem and
þe kyng. Ther was a grete compleint of Scottis, for þei had distroyed þe cuntré onto ȝork on þe o side, and onto Lancastir on þe
oþir side, wherfor þe to legatis, with oþir bischoppis, prayed þe
kyng þat certeyn articles whech þe barnes desired schuld be 10
graunted, and þan schuld þe kyng be þe more strong ageyn þe
Scottis. The kyng graunted þat on Seynt Jon Baptiste day next
folowand, at Leycetir, schuld þis mater be concluded. The
legatis took her leue, as þouȝ þei had sped a grete mater, and turned
ageyn to þe court, but þe kyngis graunt was but a fraude. 15

The same ȝere, at Myhilmesse, ther was a parlement at London,
where was graunted þat euery good town of Ynglond schuld sende
þe kyng certeyn men to fite with þe Scottis—London, ii c armed
men, Cauntirbury, xl, and so forth—but whan þis hoost cam to
ȝork, for certeyn debate betwix hemself, þe hoost was departed, 20
and euery man cam hom.

In þat same ȝere Edward Brusse, broþir to þe kyng of Scottis,
whech was sent into Yrland to occupie þe Englisch lordschippis
þere—and he himself had crowned him kyng, of his owne auc-
torité—was slayn be þe kyngis frendis | þat were in Yrland. f. 70ᵛᵃ

In þe xi ȝere of his regne he held his Cristmasse at Beuirlé 26
with many lordes and prelatis, and þere was mad a prouision who
þis lond schuld be defensed ageyn þe cruelté of Scottis.

In þe same tyme a cursed man, cleped Petir of Spalding, whech
was keper of Berwyk, seld þe same town onto þe Scottis, and lete 30
hem entyr and kepe it, whech mater greuyd þe kyng sore. And
þanne he gadered a gret hoost, and beseged Berwik, and whil he

2 Clementins] Clementis P   7 a] P, *om.* M   10 barnes] s *suprascript* M   13 at] t *suprascript* M   27 prouision] prevision P   31 And]
change to darker ink M

1–4: ibid. 153/10–14.
5–15: ibid. 153/21–154/7.
16–21: ibid. 154/9–19.
22–5: ibid. 154/22–6.
26–8: ibid. 155/11–16.
29–144/10: ibid. 155/17–156/3.

was at þe sege, xx þousand of þe Scottis come in be anoþir weye,
purposing to take þe qwen, whech lay in þat cuntré. But sche was
warned, and fled to more sikir place. The king lay stille at þe
sege, and happed for to sey a word whech was confusion of þat
5 jornay: 'Treuly', he seide, 'whan we haue wonne þis town, we
wil make Ser Hewe Spenser keper of þe castell, and Roger
Tamary capteyn of þe town'. But whan Ser Thomas of Lancastir
herd þis, he withdrow him with al his power, wherfor þei cleped
him þere openly tretour. For sekirly, and he had abedyn, as þei
10 sey, þe town had be wonne.

In þis same tyme þei of Ʒork gadered x þousand men for to
fite with þe Scottis, whech lay þanne be þe flood cleped Swale,
and þere had þe Scottis victory. In that batail were killid many
men, among whech were many prestis and religious men, as was
15 seid. This cam to þe kyngis ere, and he left þe sege of Berwik,
f. 70ᵛᵇ purposing to mete with þe Scottis hom|ward, but he failed, for
þei went anoþir weye, leuyng cursed toknes of cruelnesse in euery
town, manslawth, brennyng, and robbing.

So was þe kyng fayn to take trews with hem for too Ʒere, and
20 þei were glad, for þei were rich be robbing, and wery of bataile.

In þat same Ʒere was grete moreyn of bestis, whech began in
Estsex, and aftir it spred þorw þe lond, it regned most in oxen,
and whan þe bestes were dede dogges wold not ete of þe flesch.

In þe xii Ʒere cam a Ʒong man to Oxenforth, and þere he prechid
25 openly þat he was son to Kyng Edward þe First, and very eyre of
Ynglond; eke he noysed þat þis Edward þe Secund was not þe kyngis
son, but a carter child, sotily broute in to þe qween. The meyhir
of Oxenforth took þis man and sent him to þe kyng, þat lay þan
at Norhampton, where he was hangged, and drawe, and qwartered.
30 In þis same Ʒere Scottis come euene to Ʒork walles, brent þe
subarbes, and took prisoner Ser Jon Bretayn, erl of Richemund,
notwithstandyng þe trews þat was take.

---

4 for] *om.* P   7 Lancastir] Lacaster P   9 him] *suprascript*
with caret (in red) M   he] þei P   10 sey] seyd P   16 to] for to P
20 be] of P   25 to Kyng] *separated by thin stroke in red* M   27 sotily]
om. P   30 to] P, *twice over line division* M

1–10: see p. 143.
11–20: Walsingham, *Hist. Ang.* i. 156/5–31.
21–3: ibid. 156/32–157/1.
24–29: ibid. 158/6–13.
30–2: ibid. 158/16–19.

And in þis same ȝere þe mysseles þorowoute Cristendam
were slaundered, þat þei had mad comnaunt with Sarasines
for to poison all Cristen men, to put venym in wellis, and all
maner vesseles þat long to mannes use, of whech malice many of
hem were conuicte, and brent, and many Jewis, þat gaue hem 5
councel and coumfort.

In þe xiii ȝere of Edward fell a grete distauns betwix many |
lordis, and þis was þe cause. There was a knyte þei cleped Ser f. 71ʳᵃ
William Brews, a gret wastour of good, whech had a baronye in
þe march of Wales, þei clepe it Gower Londis. He seld þis 10
baronie to dyuers lordis, and took his mony: first, to Humfrey
Bown, erl of Herford; next, seld he þe same to to lordes, both hite
Roger, and eke Mortimer—þe on was vncle an þe oþir cosin;
than was þere anoþir lord, þei cleped him Ser Jon Mounbray—he
had weddid þe doutyr of þis William Brews, whech was sole eyir 15
onto him, wherfor he chalenged þis lond be heritage; last of all, and
werst, Hugo Spenser þe ȝonger, he desired þese londes, and boute
hem, and because he was þe kyngis chambirleyn, þat sale was
moost alowed and appreued, in-so-mech þat he entered þe londis.

At þis dede þe oþir lordes had gret indignacion: þe erle of 20
Herforth, whech was þe first biere, compleyned onto Thomas of
Lancastir, and þei gadered many barones to lyue and deye on
þoo tretoures þat were about þe kyng, specialy on þe too Spenseris, þe fadir and þe son, for þei reuled þe kyng as þei wold, and
þere was no barn ne bischop schuld stand in þe kyngis grace but 25
if þei wolde. So Thomas of Lancastir gadered þe barnes togidir at
Schirborne, and þere were þei swore to pursewe þis conclusioun,
come hem lyf, or come hem deth. But aftirward alle went bak and
ȝold hem to þe kyng, saue Thomas of Lancastir and Hunfrey Boun;
alle þe | oþir barnes consented wel þat certeyn articules schuld f. 71ʳᵇ
be mad, and pursewid to be had, but þei fell sone fro her purpos. 31

In þis tyme was a knyte in Norfolk þei cleped Robert Walkfare;
he, with certeyn malefactoures, cam to Seynt Albones, and
robbed þe abbot chambir, and kept it as his in. He hatid þe abbot

---

1 in] *om.* P   11 baronie] i *surmounted by short stroke in red* M   13 an]
on MP   cosin] *suprascript with caret (in red)* M   14 him] hym P,
om. M   15 was] *in r.h. margin* M   19 in-so-mech] þat in so mech P
24 and (1)] P, *om.* M

1–6: ibid. 158/21–7.
7–31: ibid. 158/28–160/7.
32–146/2: ibid. ii. 364/32–365/3.

for he had deposed þe priour of Bynham and put him in prison
for euel gouernauns and wasting of þe godes of þe monastery.

In þe same tyme þe barnes were gadered at Seynt Albones,
and fro þens þei sent onto þe kyng þese v bischoppis, London,
5 Salisbury, Hely, and Herforth, and Chichestir, desiryng of þe
kyng þat Hugo Spenser þe elder and Hew þe ȝonger schuld be
banchid þe rewme as tretoures, and þat al þis rysing of þe barnes
schuld be pardoned, because þei ded it for þe comon profite.
The kyng answered þat þese too Spenseris had offered hemself
10 oftentyme to answere to her accuseris, and to make amendis to
ony forfet þat myte be seid ageyn hem, and it was no lawe þat
men schuld be condempned withoute answere. Ferþermore, on
of hem was ouyr þe se on þe kyngis message, þe oþir was in þe
see for defens of þe v portes. Whan þe barnes had þis answere,
15 þei cam down to Londoun with her hoost, and occupied þe
subarbes of þe cité. But, be mediacion of þe qween and prelates,
þe kyng was induced to condescend to her peticiones. And so in
f. 71ᵛᵃ Westmistir Halle Hewe þe elder, be þe crye | of Humfrey Bown,
was proclamed a tretour.

20 In þe same ȝere fel a case whech was cause of mech angir.
The qween went on pilgrimage to Cauntirbyry, purposing be þe
weye to rest in þe castell of Ledis—whech castell þe kyng had
goue in eschaunge for oþir londis to a knyte þei cleped Bartholomew Batilesmere, whil he was þe kyngis steward—where his
25 wif was, and his childyrn, and all his tresore, for he was with þe
barnes in her bysinesse. The qwenes puruyouris cam þedir, but
þei myte not entre. So þei herborowid hir in oþir place; þere
myte sche no logging haue. The qween, whan sche cam hom,
compleyned to þe kyng, and he with a grete multitude of puple,
30 specialy of Londoun, rod þidir. He asked entré, and þei denyed
it. At þe last þei ȝolde for defaut of vitaile. Thomas Colpepir,
keper of þe castell, was hange and drawe. The oþir men þat were
þere were slayn in dyuers maner. The women were sent to þe
Toure of London. The tresoure went to þe kyngis housholed.

1 for] P, fo M   6 ȝonger] *over erasure* M   7 tretoures] *final* rę
altered from r' M   þis] þese P   12 withoute] with P   25 childyrn
and all his] *om.* P   31 þei] i *suprascript in paler ink* M   32 drawe]
in r.h. margin M

1–2: see p. 145.
3–19: Walsingham, *Hist. Ang.* i. 160/25–161/27.
20–34: ibid. 161/34–162/26.

In þis same tyme Hewe Spenser the ȝonger cam onto þe kyng, be whos councell þe kyng sent writtis to all þe schryues in Ynglond, þat þei schuld ordeyne him sufficient puple to fite with þe barnes, whech conspired ageyn him.

In þe xiiii ȝere of þis kyng he gadered a grete hoost, purposing to be vengid on þe barnes. That herd þe too Mortimeres, and come | and ȝold hem to þe kyng, but þei fel not in swech grace as þei supposed, for þe kyng comaunded hem to þe Tour tyl þe tyme he schuld be auysed what he schuld do with hem. Than took þe kyng Ser Hewe Haudlé þe elder, and Ser Mauris Berklé, and sent hem to þe castell of Walyngforth. Oþir lordis he cacchid or caute with fayre wordes, and sent hem to dyuers holdis.

This herd þe erl of Herforth, and with his hoost rood into Gloucetirschire. Than Thomas Lancastir and he gadered a grete hoost, and cam to Burton upo Trent. The kyng wold a go ouyr þe watir þere, but þei letted him. Fro þens þei fled þe kyng, seyng his grete power, tyl þei cam at Borouhbrigge, and þere mette þei a grete strength comyng fro þe north ageyn hem: þe keper of Ȝork, Ser Symund Warde, and keper of Karlhill, Sere Andrew Herklé. There was Humfrey Bown slayn: as he rod ouyr þe brigge, on was beneth, and with a spere gored him. Ther was Ser Thomas of Lancastir take, and Ser Roger Clifforth, Ser Jon Mounbray, Ser Waryn of þe Ylde, and many mo, and broute to þe kyngis presens at Pountfreite, where he was with þe too Spenceres. The þird day aftir sat upon hem þese lordes, Hewe Spenser, erl of Wynchestir, Aymer, erl of Penbrok, John Wareyn, erl of Suthreye, Edmund, erl of Arundell, where Thomas was juged to drawyng, hanging, an hedyng. But þe kyng, of special grace, dispensid with him of þe too first | peynes. There wer slayn eke þat tyme Waryn of þe Ylde, Thomas Maudut, Herry Bradborne, William Williamson, William Cheny—þese were ded with Thomas. Aftir þat were slayn Roger Clifforth, Jon Mounbray, Goselyne of Muylla, Herry Tyes, Bartholomé Batlismere.

Than was þe kyng ful glad of þis chauns, and gadered a grete

4 ageyn] ageyne *twice* P   11–12 or caute] *om.* P   15 upo] vpon P
16 þens] þens thens *with* þens *deleted* P   25 hem] hym P   29 þe] *om.* P
31 Cheny] theny P

1–4: ibid. 162/30–6.
5–12: ibid. 163/10–33.
13–33: ibid. 163/34–165/34.
34–148/4: ibid. 166/1–21.

hoost for to goo into Scotlond, but whan he cam into þat lond þe
Scottis fled onto wodes and marices and oþir straunge places;
so fonde he þere no resistens ne no vitaile, wherfor he cam ageyn
into þis lond, and many of his puple deyed for hungir.

5 In þis ȝere deyed Philip, kyng of Fravnce.

In þe xv ȝere was take a man of þe houshold of Thomas Lancastir, whech was grete of his councell. Anon he was condempned
to be drawe, hangen, and qwartered. Thei þat were aboute þe
kyng prayed þat he myte haue his lif, and þe kyng, in gret angir,
10 said onto hem, 'Fals and fikil flatereres, for þe lyf of a fals knaue
ȝe make grete instauns, but for Thomas of Lancastir, my cosyn,
whech myte ha had lif and goue us good councell, wold ȝe neuyr
speke word'. And anon he comaunded execucion to be do on
þis man.

15 In þis same tyme cam embassiatouris fro þe king of Frauns,
cytyng þe kyng of Ynglond to come and do homage to þe new
Kyng Charles for þe londis of Gian. The embassiatoures in þis
mater were þe Lord Beouille and Ser Andrew of Florens, and |
f. 72rb þouȝ þei were counceled be Hewe Spenser and Robert Baldok,
20 chaunceler, þat þei schuld not notifie þis to þe kyng, ȝet þis
knyte Andrew Florens, because he was a notarie, he made upon this
a open instrument.

In þis same ȝere þe kyng of Scottis sent embassiatouris to þe
court of Rome, for to haue reles of þe curs and þe enterditing
25 whech þei were falle in for contumacye ageyn þe pope and
rebellyon ageyn þe kyng of Ynglond. And þere were þei so
answerd but be a simpil clerk of Ynglond, þat þei sped not in her
mater.

In þis same ȝere on Andrew Herclé, whech took Thomas of
30 Lancastir and broute him to þe kyng, and whom þe kyng had
rewarded gretly and mad erl of Carlyle, ros ageyn þe Spenseres,
and whanne he say it myte not avayle, þei were so wallid with þe
kyngis grace, he rebelled openly, and drow to þe Scottis, and

2 places] place *in l.h. margin with carets* (*in red*) M, place P   27 not]
om. P   33 drow] drow hym P

1–4: see p. 147.
5: Walsingham, *Hist. Ang.* i. 167/7.
6–14: ibid. 167/23–168/2.
15–22: ibid. 168/3–14.
23–8: ibid. 168/18–29.
29–149/6: ibid. 168/30–169/33.

fauoured her part ageyn þe kyng. Than was þere a nobil knyte
in þat cuntré, cleped Ser Antony Lucy. He, supposing to stande
þe bettir in þe kyngis grace, sodeynly fel upon þis tyraunt at
Karlhil, took him, put him in yrunnes, and brout him to London
to þe kyng, and þere was he schamefully deposed of all worchip, 5
and deed as a tretour.

In þis same ȝere Robert Brus, þe kyng of Scottis, wrote to
þe kyng of Ynglond þat trews schuld be had betwix both londis
for xiii ȝere, | and þis was grauntid.   f. 72va

In þe xvii ȝere of his regne he held a parlement at London, for 10
to wete if he schuld go into Frauns to do homage or nowt. And
þis was þe decré of þe parlement, þat þe king schuld not go, but
he schuld send solempne embassiatouris to proue if he myte be
excused so, or ellis for to dilaye þe mater til he myte come.

In þis same parlement was offered a peticion, both to þe   15
clergy, and to þe lay-fe, for þe raunson of Ser Jon of Bretayn,
erl of Richmund. And þis was þe answere, þat for þe kyng or þe
qween in swech maner men schuld be leyd to a certeyn contribucion, but for no oþir.

In þis parlement was arested Adam, bischop of Herforth, of   20
treson, and he stood and seid he schuld not answere in þis maner
but to þe bischop of Cauntirbyri, whech was his juge immediatly
vndir þe pope. At þis word alle þe bischoppes rise up, and
chalenged him as a membir of þe Cherch, and so was he comittid
to þe keping of þe bischop of Cauntirbury tyl þe tyme þat he   25
schuld answere to þoo objecciones þat schuld be aleggid ageyn
him. Not many dayes aftir, he was cyted to come before þe juges.
Ther went with him þe erchbischop, and oþir ten bischoppis,
with þe crosse of Cauntyrbury, and þere þei cursed all þoo þat
schuld ley ony hand in violens of þis Adam, bischop. This say þe 30
kyng, and mad a qwest for to be assigned, | and þei, dredyng more f. 72vb
þe kyng þan God, endited þe bischop of all þoo poyntes in whech
he was accused, and, as sad men supposed, not gilty. This plesid

3 grace] *suprascript with caret* (*in red*) M   4 Karlhil] Karhyll P
20 bischop] *change to darker ink* M   25 þat] *om.* P   31-2 more þe
kyng] þe kyng mor P

7-9: ibid. 169/37-170/1.
10-14: ibid. 171/18-28.
15-19: ibid. 171/29-37.
20-150/2: ibid. 171/38-173/1.

þe kyng wel, and comavnded all his temporal good to be achetid; his body was kept vndir tuycioun of þe bischop of Cauntirbiry.

In þis same parlement were chose too enbassiatoures, Edmunde of Wodstok, broþir to þe kyng, and eke erl of Kent, and with him
5 þe bischop of Dorham, to go into Frauns for to excuse þe kyng þat he cam not to make his homage. There were þei receyued worchipfully, but þei sped not for a certeyn offens whech a knyte of Ynglond had do ageyn þe plesauns of þe king of Frauns— þei cleped him Raf Basset. The Erl Edmund wold he schuld be
10 punchid aftir þe lawes of Frauns; þe bischop wold not consent þerto. So sent þei hom to þe King Edward to wite his will, and he sent letteris þat al þat euyr þe knyte had do was do in þe kyngis rite, wherfor he alowed al þat was doo.

In þese dayes Roger Mortimer þe ȝonger gaf swech a drynk to
15 þe keperis of þe Tour þat he scaped oute of all þe wardes, and met with a boot at his consent, and aftir in a schip seiled into Frauns, where he had frendis and leued merily. Roger, his vncil, deied þere in prison.

Many enbassiatouris were sent into Frauns to procure pees,
20 but it availed not. Than were þe Frenschmen in þis lond had in gret despite; þei þat dwelled with þe qween fled into Frauns.
f. 73ʳᵃ The lyflode of | þe qween was take fro hir; þei sent hir fro þe kyngis coferes what þei wold. In þat same tyme were sent to þe king of Frauns þese iii enbassiatouris, þe bischop of Wynchestir,
25 bischop of Norwich, and þe erle of Richemund, to trete of pes. Than þei þat were aboute þe kyng seyde þat it was conuenient þat þe qween schuld go, supposing þat þe mater schuld spede þe betir. Sche graunted to þis jornay ful mekly, and þei of þe kyngis councel sent hir to Frauns ful porely, but with o barne, Ser Jon
30 Krownwell, and iiii knytis. With þe mediacion of þe qween þus were þei acorded, þat þe Kyng Edward schuld gyue Edward, his sone, þe duchy of Gian and þe erldam of Pounte; and upon þis sent þe kyng his patent letteris, þat, if þe kyng wold com or sende, þei schuld com saf, and goo, to performe þis mater, and mech
35 oþir þing.

25 of (3)] for P   27 go] *suprascript with caret* (*in red*) M   34 saf] sefe P
35 oþir] othe P

1–2: see p. 149.
3–13: Walsingham, *Hist. Ang.* i. 173/15–174/11.
14–18: ibid. 174/27–40.
19–151/12: ibid. 175/1–18, 176/4–177/5.

And in þis mater were had many councellis þat þe king schuld go, but þe too Spenseres lettet þat, for þei durst not go to Frauns for her enmies þere, and þei durst not abide in Ynglond in þe kyngis absens for her enmies here. But þei counceled þe kyng þat þe kingis son schuld goo, and þat same councel turned oþirwise 5 þan þei supposed. Than mad þe kyng a chartor to þe prince, and enfeffed him in þe londes of Normannie and Gian, to him and to his eyres. But if it happed him to deye or his fader, þe londes schuld returne to his fader. And eke he wrote þat þe kyng of Frauns schuld not marie him, ne assigne | him no tutour. So went f. 73ʳᵇ he forth with certeyn lordes and mad homage to his vncle, king 11 of Frauns, and þan entered his londis.

In þe xviii ȝere of his regne Kyng Edward sent into Frauns to þe qween and þe prince þat þei schuld com hom. Thei sent hom many of her houshold, but þei abode stille. For þe qween wold not 15 com hom, as was seid, but sche myte bringge with hire all þoo þat were banchid oute of Ynglond, and specialy Ser Roger Mortimer. Than þe kyng, be þe councell of þese too Spenseres, mad crye in Londoun þat þe qween and hir sone, as rebelles, schuld be banchid. And þan procured he priuily be letteris writin 20 to Ser Jon of Bretayn, erl of Richemund, þat þe qween and þe prince schuld be slayn, but þis treson was bewreyed, and þe qween with þe prince fled onto þe erle of Hennow, and þere was sche reuerently receyued, and worchipfully.

In þat same tyme, be procuracion of þe qween, was mad a 25 mariage betwix Edward þe prince and Philip, doutir to þe erl of Hennow.

Sone aftir, þe qween cam into Ynglond with power of hir son Edward, xiiii ȝer old, and Edmund Wodstok, erl of Kent, and broþir to þe kyng, and many moo. Sche londed in þe hauene of 30 Herwich, and anon þere drow onto hir þe Erl Marchale, for sche londid on his ground, and þe erl of Leycetir, with many barones and knytes. There met hir eke certeyn bischoppis, Lincoln, Herforth, Dorham, and Hely. And William, bischop of Cauntir- 34 bury, sent | hir grete tresoure. f. 73ᵛᵃ

---

1 councellis] councell P　　3 in (2)] fo P　　7 enfeffed] P, enfessed M
19 as rebelles] *om.* P　　20 þan] *om. over line division* P　　26 to] *om.* P

13–24: ibid. 177/23–178/6, 179/13–26.
25–35: ibid. 179/38–180/20.

The kyng was at London whan sche entred, and axed of þe cyté help for to make resistens ageyn þe qween. Thei answerd þat þe qween and þe prince schuld be receyued as good zelatoris of þe rem. Oþir, þat were proued tretoures, schuld not be re-
5 ceyued þere. And as for hem of þe cité, þei wold kepe her old pryuylege þat þei schuld go no ferþer to fite but þat þei myte com hom þe same day.

This herd þe kyng, and stuffid þe Tour with vitaile and armour, and set þere his ȝonger son, Jon Eltham, and his nece, weddid to
10 Hew Spenser þe ȝonger. And he rod onto þe west partyes to reyse puple ageyn þe qween. He ded crye in London þat all men schuld rise and distroye þe qweenes power, but þei schuld saue þe lyues of hir and hir son and his broþir Edmund, 'and he þat bringith þe hed of Roger Mortimer to þe kyng schal haue a þousand
15 pound'. On þe qween side was cried, 'No man take þe valew of IIId. but if he pay, up peyn of lesing of a fynger, ne þe valew of VId., up peyn of lesing of his hand, ne þe valew of XIId., up peyn of his hed. And who bryng þe hed of Hew Spenser þe ȝonger' schuld haue ii þousand pound.

20 Thus fled þe kyng, first to Gloucestir, and þan to Strogoil. He sent Hugo Spenser þe fader to kepe the town and þe castel of Bristow, and þe kyng, with Hugo Spenser þe ȝonger, and on Robert Baldok, entered þe see.

The qween with hir hoost folowid euyr. And þei of London
f. 73ᵛᵇ in | þis tyme killid hem þat were not fauorable to þe qween: first,
26 a citeceyn þei cleped Jon Marchale, and þan Maystir Water Stapilton, bischop of Excetir, for he was noted for a grete enmye ageyn þe libertés of London. The qween jornayed forth to Gloucetir be Berklé, and þere sche restored þe castell to Ser
30 Thomas Berklé, þat was eir—whech Ser Hewe Spenser þe ȝonger had wrongfully kept fro him. Than cam þe qween to Bristow, and besegid it, and it was sone ȝoldyn onto hir, and in þe next day was Hewe Spenser þe elder hangid, in his owne cote-armour, upon þe comown galowis for theuys.

35 In þe xix ȝere were mad open cryes þorwoute þe reme þat þe kyng schuld com hom and take þe reule of his puple, on þat

1-7: Walsingham, *Hist. Ang.* i. 180/31–181/1.
8-19: ibid. 187/1–28.
20-3: ibid. 181/31–5.
24-34: ibid. 181/37–183/25.
35-153/6: ibid. 184/7–16.

condicioun, þat he schuld be reuled be his owne lawes. But because he wold not come, þerfor þe lordes of þe lond mad a councel at Herforth in Walis, in whech Edward, duk of Gyan, was mad keper of Ynglond be her comoun asent; þe bischop of Norwich chaunceler was mad þere, and þe bischop of Wynchestir 5 tresorer.

In þis mene tyme sent þe qween into Wales Herri, erl of Lancastir, and William, Lord Souch, and Maistir Reson Vphowel— for þei had londis þere, and were weel beloued—where, with helpe of Walschmen, þei took þe kyng, and Ser Hewe Spenser þe 10 ȝonger, and Robert Baldoc, and Simon Redyng, witȝ oþir mo. þis jornay was on Seynt Edmund day þe archbischop.

The king was broute onto Kenelworth, | where he lay al þat f. 74ra wyntir. The oþir thre were browt onto þe qween, and þei þat took hem were treuly payed too þousand pound. Hewe þe Spenser 15 was drawen at Herforth, and þan hanged of a galow þat was fifty fote in heith. In his cote-armour was writin, 'Quid gloriaris in malicia, qui potens es in iniquitate?'. Simon Reding was hangin on þe same trees ten fete lower. Robert Baldok was sent to London, and þere, in grete despite and miserie, deyed in Newgate. 20

The qween held a real Cristmasse aftir at Walingford, and þere were þese prelatis, archbischop of Cauntirburi, and of ȝork, bischop of Wynchestir, tresorer, bischop of Norwich, chaunceler, with oþir, bischop of Lyncoln, Hely, Couentré, and Herforth.

Sone aftir þe feest þei went to Londoun, and þere begunne a 25 parlement þe next day aftir þe ephiphanie, where was concluded be all þe lordes þat þe kyng was insufficient to gouerne þe puple, wherfor þei chose þe prince for to be kyng, and proclamed it openly in þe Halle at Westmister, and all þe puple consented þerto. Whan þe qween herd of þis, sche semed as sche schuld dey for 30 sorow, and þan Edward hir son mad his avow to God þat he schuld neuir take þe crowne withoute his fader consent.

---

8 into Wales *repeated after* Vphowel MP   11 Robert] on Robert P
15 treuly] r *suprascript* M   23 bischop (2)] b. MP   24 with] wit P
bischop] b. MP   27 was] *in r.h. margin* M   30 Whan] *change to darker ink* M   31 hir] hys P   32 withoute] oute *in l.h. margin with carets (in red)* M

7–20: ibid. 184/17–185/30.
21–4: ibid. 186/6–12.
25–154/7: ibid. 186/14–187/9.

Than, be þe decré of þe parlement, þei sent to þe kyng ii
bischoppis, ii herlis, to abbotes, iiii barones, and of euery schire
of Ynglond iii knytes, with burgeis of oþir townes, to notifie to
þe kyng the sentens of þe parlement, who þat he was deposed, and

f. 74rb his son Edward | chosen. Whan þe kyng herd þis he wept ful sore
6 þat his gouernauns had be swech þat his puple disobeyed him but
ȝet he þankid God specialy þat þei chose his son for to be her kyng.

Anno 6525–6574; 1327–1376. Edward þe þirde regned l ȝere.
In his first ȝere he wrote letterys to all þe schiris in Ynglond
10 þat his fader had resigned, and he was chose bi þe comenaunté
of þe reme for to be kyng. He was crowned in þe conuercion of
Seynt Paule at Westmister be þe handis of Walter, bischop of
Cauntirbury. In þat same tyme was assigned to þe qween, his
modir, a dowarye, þat men had no mende of swech asignament.
15 For þe kyng had ful scarcely þe þird part of his lyflod.

In þat same ȝere þe dwelleres of Bury risen ageyn þe monkys,
f. 74va and in þe mydday broke þe gates, robbed | þe place of joweles,
vestimentis, bokes, and speciali of dedis of maneres and of londes;
þei wold rith nowt restore ageyn onto þe tyme þat þe abbot had
20 graunted onto hem her peticiones, whech were ful onresonable.
In þe same ȝere þei of Seynt Albones rysyn in þe same maner
ageyn þe monastery.

That tyme þe old Edward was led pryuyli to many places,
but at þe last was he broute to þe castel of Berkley, and þere Ser
25 Thomas Berkley had þe kepyng of him o month and treted him
ful worchipfully, and Ser Jon Mauntrauers had þe keping of him
þe oþir month and treted him ful ongentyly. The qween sent
him plesaunt giftes and cloþis ful precious, but sche wold not se
him. Sche pretendid þat þe lordis wold not suffir hir. The old
30 Edward had euery month to his expensis a hundred marc.

In þis same ȝere was þis old Edward slayn with a hoot spete
put into his body, whech coude not be aspied whan he was ded,
for þei put a horn in his tewhel and þe spete þorw þe horn, þat

7 ȝet] t *suprascript* M   8 Edward] *change to darker ink and narrower*
letter strokes M   11 in] at P   20 were] *in r.h. margin* M   24 was
he] he was P   29 pretendid] *final* d *altered from* t M

1–7: see p. 153.
8–15: Walsingham, *Hist. Ang.* i. 187/14–188/13.
16–22: ibid. 188/14–21, and ii. 366/3–5.
23–30: ibid. i. 188/22–37.
31–155/7: ibid. 189/12–36.

þere schuld no brennyng appere outeward. This was be þe
ordenauns, as was seid, of Ser Jon Mauntrauers and Thomas
Gurnay, whech leyd | a gret dore upon him whil þei ded þis   f. 74ᵛᵇ
werk. And whan þis dede was doo þei fled both into straunge
cuntré, but Thomas Gurnay, thre ȝere aftir þat, was take in Marcyle   5
and sent into Ynglond, but þei þat broute him killid him in þe se
for dreed, þat he schuld not accuse persones of hier degré.

In þe secunde ȝere Simon, archbischop of Cauntirbury, held a
grete councel at Londoun, where was ordeyned þat Good Friday
and Soule-masse Day schuld be holy fro al maner seruyle werkis.   10
In þat same councel þei cursed all þo men þat killid Maistir Walter
Stapilton, bischop of Excetir, or leid ony handis of violens upon
him. In þat same councel was ordeyned þat þe concepcion of oure
Ladi schuld be a solempne fest.

That same tyme Kyng Edward went into Frauns to make his   15
homage to þe kyng of Frauns for þe duchy of Gian and þe erldam
of Pounte. He left Edmund his broþir, erle of Cornwaile, keper of
þe lond for þe mene tyme.

Whan he was come hom he held a parlement at Salesbury, where
he mad iii erles: Ser Jon Eltham, his ȝonger broþir, erl of Corn-   20
wayle; Ser Roger Mortimer, erl of March; and anoþir, erl of
Ormund.

In þe þird ȝere was a parlement at Wynchestir, where, be
procuracion of þe qween, Roger Mortimer was mad erl of Kent.
The kyngis vncle, Ser Edmund Woodstok, was hedid þere for   25
certeyn confessiones of himself and certeyn letteris found wyth
him, in whech þingis, as summe sayde, was conteyned no treson |
ne no cause for whech a man schuld deye. But þis was feyned on   f. 75ʳᵃ
him: that he and oþir moo had conspired to rere þe elde Kyng
Edward to his dignité—and þat was fals. Othir men were accused   30
of þe same, and þei were put in dyuers prisonis vndir pleggis.
Thus was þe erl ded for hem all, and he was þe lasse compleyned,
for his meny were of euel gouernauns, speciali in taking of vitail
and not paying.

5 Marcyle] r suprascript M   6 him (2)] suprascript M   11 same]
om. P   17 his] hir MP   31 in] into P   32 compleyned]
conpleyned P

8–14: ibid. ii. 366/31–367/3.
15–18: ibid. 367/5–7.
19–22: ibid. 367/13–18.
23–34: ibid. 367/38–368/15.

In þe iiii ȝere was a parlement at Notyngham, where Roger
Mortimer was take be nyte in þe qween chambir behinde a cor-
teyn. It is seid comouly þat þer is a weye fro þe hous of Lenton
onto þe castel of Notyngham vndir þe ground, and þis wey cam
5 þei in þat took him, of whech þe principales were too Vfforthis.
The qween was logged in þe castell, and þis Mortimer next hir,
and þe kyng forth in þe court. The keyes were in þe keping of
Mortimer. So þese knytes, whan þei were com into þe castell,
þei cleped up þe kyng, and told him who Mortimer had ymaged
10 his deth, þat he myte be kyng; þei told him eke who he mysused
his moder þe qween, and þan þei broke up þe dore and fond him
behinde þe curteyn, as we saide, and sent him to London, and
þere was he ded.

These causes were alleggid ageyn him: that he was gilty of old
15 Edwardes deth; the secund, þat Kyng Edward þat now is was
not sped ne worchipid at þe batayl of Stanpark, but he gaf fauour
f. 75ʳᵇ to þe Scottis and not to þe kyng; the þirde cause, þat | he receyued
of þe Scottis þat tyme xx þousand pound, and procured a wrecchid
mariage betwix þe kyngis son of Scotlond and þe kingis sistir of
20 Ynglond; the fourte, þat he had consumed þe kyngis tresoure and
þe qwenis liflod and þe tresoure þat Ser Hewe Spenser left, so þat
he was rich and oþir pore; the v cause, þat he had all þe wardes, all
þe mariages; and last of all, þat he was ouyr homeli with þe qween.

In þis same ȝere was þe Prince Edward born, þe xvii kalend of
25 June.

In þe v ȝere of Edward cam into Ynglond a man þei cleped
Edward de Baliol, pretending to haue rite to þe crowne of Scotlond. And anon drowe onto him Herry Bemount, Dauid, erl of
Asseles, Gilbert Vmfreuile, Richard Talbot, and many mor, for
30 þei had rite to grete possessiones in Scotlond, eydir be hemself,
or be her wyues. These all cam to þe kyng, and asked leue to
enter Scotlond, goyng þorw his lond. The king wold gyue hem
no leue, because Dauid, kyng of Scottis, had weddid his sistir.

6 Mortimer] Mortmer P   9 Mortimer] Mortmer P   14 alleggid]
al|leggid *over line division* M, all legged P   26 In þe v ȝere] 5 *in r.h.*
margin M   cleped] clepe P   27 pretending] & pretend P   28 onto]
to P   29 mor] *supplied, om.* MP

1–13: Walsingham, *Hist. Ang.* ii. 369/7–25.
14–23: ibid. 369/28–370/16.
24–5: ibid. 369/2–3.
26–157/9: ibid. 371/19–40.

Than gote þei schippis and took þe see aboute þe feste of
Seynt Laurens, and londed fast by þe Abbey Downfermelyn,
where þei fond grete resistens of Scottis, but a fewe of oure
archeres occupied þe Scottis til oure armed men were londed.
Sone aftir was þere a grete bataile in a place þei clepe Gledesmore, 5
where too þousand Englischmen had victorie ouyr xl þousand
Scottis. All men seide it was Goddis hande, and not man|nes f. 75ᵛᵃ
hand; for þe Scottis were so many—and Englisch so fewe—
þat ech of hem bar down oþir.

In þe sexte ȝere of þe kyng, Edward Baliol continued his werres 10
with þe Scottes, and aboute mydsomyr many worchipful men of
þis lond drow to him to help him, of her owne fre will, and at her
owne cost. The kyng, conseyuyng weel þat þe Scottis were euyr
ontrewe, and ful of treson, and þei toke neuyr no treus but to
make hem strong ageyn us, consideryng eke who þat þe mariage 15
and all þe pees was mad be Ser Roger Mortimer, him being vndir
ȝong age—all þis considered, he gadered a grete power for to go
onto Scotland.

In þe vii ȝere þe king went to Berwyk, and þe hoost al on fote,
where he fond many Scottis þat come to remeue þe sege of Berwik, 20
for þese forseyd lordis, aftir þei had crowned Edward Baliol at
Scone, þei cam streith and besegid þis Berwik. There had þe
kyng grete victorie, and þe Scottis grete vilonye; for þei fled all,
and þe king pursewid hem more þan v myle—viii erles were dede
of þe Scottis, a þousand and iii hundred of horsmen, and of 25
fotemen xxxv þousand. The leder of þe Scottis at þat tyme was
William Kech. In þis batayle wonne þe archeres of Ynglond
a perpetuel laude. In þis same tyme lay þe qween at Banborow.
Certeyn Scottis were sent to besege þat town, but whan þei herd
þat Berwik was take þei fled anon. 30

Than mad þe kyng þis sa|me Edward Baliol capteyn of Berwik f. 75ᵛᵇ
and keper of Scotlond, and he cam ageyn to Ynglond and visited

2 and londed] *in r.h. margin with carets (in red)* M　　16 being] *letter erased*
after e M　　17 power] hoost P　　18 onto] into P　　19 to] onto P
22 and] *om.* P　　Berwik] k *altered from* c M　　23 þei] i *inserted on the line*
in darker ink M　　24 pursewid] d *altered from* t M　　27 of Ynglond]
om. P

10–18: ibid. 372/5–17.
19–30: ibid. 373/2–26.
31–158/3: ibid. 373/31–43.

many pylgrimages. The same tyme þe prelatis of Scotlond fled
into Frauns, and summe to Rome, compleynyng of þis infortune,
sekyng socour and help, but þei founde non.

In þe viii ȝere þe king held a parlement at ȝork, and þere he
5 sent for þe kyng of Scottis, and he excused him þat he myte not
come for þe Scottis had leyd certeyn awayte upon him to his
grete hurt if he come. He sent þidir his enbassatouris, Ser Herry
Beamount and Ser William Mountagew, with oþir barones. But
in þat same ȝere, at þe fest of Geruase and Prothase, þe same
10 kyng of Scottis mad his homage onto þe kyng of Ynglond at
Newcastell upo Tyne.

In þat same ȝere was a parlement at London, but for because
tydyngis cam þat þe Scottis were rebelle, and had take Ser Richard
Talbot and vi knytis, þe kyng with his power mad him redy to go
15 to Scotland. And to þat entent þe clergy and þe puple graunted
him a grete summe of good. Thus went he to Scotlond, and
abood þere til wyntir-tyme, þat he myte go on þe hys, and þan
distroyed he þe lond euene onto Galowey. There delyuered he
Ser Herry Beamount, þat was besegid in a castel.

20 This ȝere were so grete wateres þat þei broke down walles in
Temse and oþir places, ouyrcured þe londis, and kyllid many bestes.

f. 76ra This ȝere deied Jon, þe xxii pope of | þat name, and was
byried at Avinion, and aftir him was mad pope an abbot of þe
Sistewes, and cleped Benedictus XII. He mad many constituciones
25 to religious men, for þe Chanones clepe here constituciones at
þis day Benedictines.

In þe ix ȝere þe kyng held his Cristmasse at Rokesborow, with
grete noumbyr of Englischmen, and þat same tyme was trews
take with Scottis tyl þe fest of Seynt Jon Baptiste. And þan was
30 hald a parlement at ȝork upon þe same mater, and it was concluded
þat þe king schuld jornay into Scotlond, and so he ded, but þe
Scottis feyned þat þei wold haue pees. And aftirward þe erle of

---

2 compleynyng] conpleynyng P   12 because] cawse P   16 him]
om. P   23 him] om. P   24 and] om. P   28 tyme] suprascript
with caret (in red) M   29 Baptiste] Batist P

1–3: see p. 157.
4–11: Walsingham, Hist. Ang. ii. 375/19–29.
12–19: ibid. 376/2–11, 22–9.
20–1: ibid. 376/31–4.
22–6: ibid. 376/38–377/10.
27–159/5: ibid. 377/17–37.

Asseles cam and asked for hem pees, but þe oþir lordis wold not
come; for whech cause, aftirward, was take þe Lord Moris at
Edenborow and browt to þe kingis prison. In þat same tyme Ser
Richard Talbot, whech was take prisoner in Scotlond, for ii m
mark was delyuered.   5

In þe x ȝere þe kyng, aftir þe deth of his broþir, Jon Eltham,
whech was erl of Cornwayle, mad Edward his sone duke of Cornwaile and erl of Chestir. And in þat same tyme he mad sex erles:
Herry of Lancastir þe ȝonger, erl of Derby; William Mountagew,
erl of Salesbury; and Hewe Awdlé, erl of Gloucetir; William   10
Clynton, erl of Huntyndoun; Robert Vfford, erl of Suffolk; and
þe sext is not now in mende.

This ȝere deyed Richard Walingforth, abbot of Seynt Albones,
a studious man in astronomie. Be his avis was mad þat grete
horologe, | þat standith þere, with many meruelous meuyngis of   f. 76rb
astronomye.   16

This ȝere was mad a statute þat no man schuld were no precious
cloth but swech as is woue in Ynglond except þe kyng, þe qween,
and her childyrn, and no man were no precious furre but swech as
is in Ynglond but if he myte spend a hundred pound.   20

In þis same tyme was at a litil town cleped Berwik, v myle fro
Walsyngham on þe west syde, a woman þei cleped Jewet Metles,
so cleped for sche ete no mete, but receyued þe sacrament on þe
Sunday, and þerby lyued al þe weke. Prestes asayed þat sche
schuld receyue a hoost not consecrat, but sche knewe it. Sche was   25
examined be þe officeres of þe Cherch and no defaute fond þei
in hir feith, ne no synne in hir conuersacion.

In þe xi ȝere of his regne Southamptoun was brent be þe
galeyes of þe kyng of Frauns, and þe same kyng of Frauns occupied mech lond in Gyan, þat longid to þe kyng of Ynglond, wher-   30
for the Kyng Edward wrote onto him letteris of grete humilité,
but he sped not. And whan þat was aspied, he gadered power,

5 was delyuered] *in r.h. margin* M   7 erl] duk P   8 in] *om.* P
13 deyed] ed *suprascript* M   14 man] *om.* P   17 were] *suprascript* M
19–20 swech as is in Ynglond but] *om.* P   21 tyme] *suprascript with caret* (*in
red*) M   at] *om.* P   22 a woman] *in r.h. margin* M   24 sche] *suprascript* M

6–12: ibid. 378/29–379/5.
13–16: ibid. 379/23–7.
17–20: ibid. 379/7–10.
28–160/3: ibid. i. 221/21–30.

þis same Edward, and cast him verili to chalenge þe crowne of Frauns. And upon þat purpos he held a parlement at Notingham, where was graunte a xv of þe puple, þe x peny of þe borowis.

And in þis parlement was ordeyned þat all þe cloth-makeris 5 of Flaundres þat wold dwelle in Ynglond schuld be wolkom. For iii 3ere before þat, was forbode þe passage of wollis, because þe f. 76ᵛᵃ pride of Flemingis schuld | be repressid, þat set more prys be wollesakkes þan be Englischmen.

In þe xii 3ere of his regne were here to cardinales, sent to reforme 10 pees betwix þe kyngis of Ynglond and of Frauns, and whan it was aspied þat þei were more fauourable to þe kyng of Frauns þan to þe kyng of Ynglond, þe archbischop roos up, and declared þat þei were not sufficient reformeres whech held with þe Frensch party.

Than rose þe noyse þorw þe lond þat þe kyng had rite to þe 15 crowne of Frauns be his modir. For Seynt Lodewik was þe rithfull kyng and eyre of Frauns. He had a son þei clepid Philippe, and þat Philip begat anoþir, þei cleped him Philip þe Fayre, whech Philip had iiii childyrn: Ysabell, moder to Kyng Edward, sche was eldest; þe secunde was Lodewik—he was kyng aftir his 20 fader; þe þird was Philip, and he had to dowteres—on was weddid to þe erl of Flaunderes, þe oþir to þe delfyn of Vienne, and both deied withoute issew. Thus deied þis Philip withoute issew, whech regned in Frauns aftir Lodewik. This same Lodewyk had to wyues: on was dowtir to þe duke of Borgayn—sche had no child— 25 anoþir was dowtir to þe kyng of Hungarie, of whom cam Jon, cleped Postumus. Than was þis þe ordre of kyngis. First regned Lodewik, þe eldest son, and aftir him Jon Postumus was treted as kyng—he deied withoute issew. Than regned Philip, þe secund f. 76ᵛᵇ broþir, whech had to douteris, as we saide, and neythir of | hem 30 had issew. He ded, þe þird broþir regned, cleped Charles, and because he had no child he mad a statute þat no woman schuld be eyer of Frauns, to forbarre þe rite of Kyng Edward, his sistiris son.

7 þat] t *suprascript with caret* M 9 xii] xi P were] wher P 11 of] *om. over line division* P 13 sufficient] cient *over erasure* M Frensch] *supplied, om.* MP 15 Lodewik] *in r.h. margin with carets (in red)* M 20 had] d *altered from* t M 30 ded] died P þird] d *suprascript* M 32 Edward] *final* d *suprascript* M

1–3: see p. 159.
4–8: Walsingham, *Hist. Ang.* i. 221/31–6.
9–13: ibid. 222/16–21.
14–32: ibid. 222/21–3, and cf. Murimuth, 100/7–101/1.

In þis same ȝere, in þe translacion of Seynt Thomas, the kyng
went ouyr þe se, and þe qween grete with childe, for to trete with
þe duk of Braban, and oþir lordis, to help him in his rite þat he
had to Frauns. He londid in þe port þei clepe Swyn, where þei of
Flaundres com onto hym and profered all her good seruyse. Fro 5
þens he went into Braban, where þe duke of Braban, his cosin,
met him with gret solempnyté. And whan þe duke of Bauaré
herd sey he was come, he cam nyher, so þat þei met fast be Coleyn.
Ther was gret wondir of þe emperoures men why þe kyng of
Ynglond kissid not his feet, and it was answerd be Englichmen 10
þat her kyng was anoynted, and had power ouyr lif and membris,
þerfor he schuld not do so mech subjeccioun as he þat is not
anoynted; 'eke, for he is a insulane, þerfor he doth no subjeccion
onto no man'.

In þis same ȝere þe qween had child at Anwerp, whom þei 15
cleped Leonell.

In þat same ȝere welowes bore roses rede and frech, and þat
was in Januarie.

In þe xiii ȝere of þis kyng þe kyng left þe qween at Anwerp,
with þe houshold, and he pryuyly cam to Londoun, and fond in 20
þe Tour iii of his childyrn, and iii seruauntis with hem. The
constable of þe Tour was þat tyme Matheus de la Bech. Anon þe
kyng sent | aftir þe chaunceler and tresorer and justises many, f. 77ʳᵃ
and set hem in prison. Than held he a parlement at London, and
sette þe puple at swech a tribut whech men had not herd of; for 25
men payed him þe v part of her goodes, and alle þe wolles he
took onto him.

In þis same tyme þe cyté of Bordews was besegid be þe power
of þe kyng of Frauns. Thei withinne sette ope þe gates and sette
on þe towres þe kyngis armes of Frauns. That aspied, þe Frensch- 30
men, wenyng þat þe cyté had be taken, com vnarmed withoute
reule, for to bribe þat þei myte. Ser Olyuere of Yngham was keper

5 and profered] in r.h. margin M   6 into] to P   7 him] with
hym P   13 he is a insulane] he is a in over erasure M   14 onto] on over
erasure M   27 onto] on om. over line division P   31 wenyng] & wenyng
with & deleted and expuncted in red M, & wenyng P

1–14: Walsingham, Hist. Ang. ii. 380/23–37, and i. 223/4–12.
15–16: ibid. i. 223/23–4.
17–18: ibid. 223/30–2.
19–27: ibid. 224/6–22, ii. 380/40–2.
28–162/4: ibid. i. 225/25–226/3.

of þe cité at þat tyme, and whan he sey þei were com in, fel upon
hem, and killid grete noumbir. Befor þis dede þe kyng had behote
hem to com and remeue þe sege, but whan he had letteris of
þis jornay, he sent hem letteris of gret plesauns and gret behestes.
5 In þe same ȝere þe qween had childe at Gaunt, þei cleped him
Jon.

In þe xiiii ȝere, whan þe kyng purposed him into Frauns, com
tydingis of þe conspiracioun of Frauns and Normannye, þat þei
had gadered ageyn hym too hundred schippis, and many galeies,
10 with xxv þousand of chose men. All þei had mad her oth to take
Edward þe kyng, and presente him to þe kyng of Frauns, eydir
lyuyng or ded. And all þese abydyn in þe hauene of Slus. And
þow þe kyng had redy to hundred schippis, ȝet sent he Ser Water
Burwage, bischop of Lincoln, into þe south cuntré to gete him mo.
f. 77ʳᵇ And þe king | went to ȝermoth, and þere mette his naue. Ser
16 Robert Morley, he gadered þe schippis of þe north and met with
þe kyng in þe se. There was gret batayle betwix þo to nauees,
but by þe help of God þe Englischmen had þe victory; for whan
þe Frenschmen felt þe gret hurt of arowes, many were ded, and
20 many scippid into þe se. There deied on þat side xxx þousand
men. Whan þis jornay was don, þere durst no man telle þe
kyng of Frauns tydyngis, saue a sage fool stood in his presens
on o day, and seid to þe king, 'þe Frenschmen þei be hardi,
and þe Englischmen be but cowardis'. The kyng inqwired whi
25 he seide so. 'Forsoth', he seith, 'for at þe last jornay þe Englischmen stood stille in her schippis, and durst not scip into þe se as þe
Frenschmen ded'. Be þis word þe kyng vndirstood þat his puple
was put to rebuk. In þis conflict oure kyng took too hundred
schippis, and in o schip of þe Normannes þei founde xl ded bodies.
30 Than þe kyng, with þe duke of Braban and þe erl of Hennow,
with þe strength of þe puple of Bruges, Gaunt, and Ypres,
entered into Frauns, and besegid þat cyté whech þei clepe Torneacense. Whill he lay at þe sege, þe erl of Hennow and Ser
Walter Mawny and Ser Reynald Cobham took mo þan ccc

4 þis] *suprascript* M   15 naue] *in r.h. margin* M   18 þe (1)] *om.* P
25 for] *om.* P   28 oure] þe P   31 puple] *over erasure* M   32 cyté
whech þei clepe] þᵉ cite cleped P

1–4: see p. 161.
5–6: Walsingham, *Hist. Ang.* i. 226/16–17.
7–29: ibid. 226/30–227/35.
30–163/6: ibid. 230/19–34.

townes in Frauns, grete and smale, and spoiled hem. The kyng
of Frauns lay but fast by, and durst not stere a foot, þow þat
he had redy a grete hoost. But he sent too cardinales for to haue
a trews, | for þe cause þat his puple deyed for hungir and þirst, f. 77ᵛᵃ
whech trews þe kyng of Ynglond accepted with þe bettir wil, 5
because mony cam not redily oute of Ynglond as was promised.

In þe xv ȝere þe pope put al Flaundres vndir interdict for because þei obeyed not þe kyng of Frauns. And þei answerd þat
þei knew weel þat þe kyng of Frauns occupied þe crowne onrithfully, þerfor þei wolde not obeye him. Than were sent too 10
cardinales, and trews was take for iii ȝere, tyl it myte be discussed
wheythir Edward had rite to þe corowne of Frauns or nowt.

In þis same ȝere the qween had child in þe Tour of London,
a dowtir þei cleped Blaunch. Sche deyed sone, and is byried at
Westminster.   15

In þe xvi ȝere þe emperour reuoked þe letteris þat he had mad
and turned to þe part of þe kyng of Frauns.

And in þat same ȝere þe kyng went into Litil Britayn for to
help Jon Mountforth, whech was very eyir þerof, ageyn Charles
de Bloys, and þere he wan many castelles and strengthis. Aftir, 20
he beseged þe town of Vanes, and wan it, and kept it.

In þe xvii ȝere deied Benedictus XII, and Clemens VI was pope
aftir him, whech was before archbischop of Rone. This pope gaue
þe benefices of Ynglond to þe cardinales þat were vacaunt, and
mad new tytiles þerto. That herd þe kyng, and withstood it, and 25
forbad in peyne of prisonment no man bryng no swech prouysiones
into his lond, and upon þis he wrote a solempne letter onto þe
pope, þat he schuld not | interrupt þe priuilege of þis lond, ne f. 77ᵛᵇ
pryue hem of her rite þat were patrones of cherches; 'for whan a
aliene hath cure of a puple, þat knowith not her tonge, þe goodes 30
of þe Cherch ar trewly gadered, but þe teching of soule is not had'.
Eke he wrote þat it was perel onto þe rem þat swech men schuld
be promoted here, þat were enmyes to þe lond, whech schuld

3 for] *twice over line division* P   4 a] *om.* P   8 not] not to P
10 were] was P   24 þat were vacaunt] *om.* P   25 þerto] ther P   29 a]
om. P   31 soule] the soule P

7–12: ibid. 227/36–228/4, 250/18–253/9.
13–15: ibid. 228/5–8.
16–17: ibid. 253/34–8.
18–21: ibid. 253/39–254/7.
22–164/6: ibid. 254/13–21, 255/21–258/31.

knowe al þe councel of þe lond, to confusion of þe same; and þe
clerkys of þis lond, þat were of gret letterure and of blessed lyf,
schuld be rejecte, and alienes accepted—þis schuld growe to
gret mischef of þe lond, for few men schuld haue appetite for to
5 lerne. Many oþir suasiones were þere in þat lettir ageyn þoo
prouisiones.

In þis same ȝere deied Herry Burwayche, bischop of Lyncoln,
and whan he was ded, he appered to on of his swyeres with a
bowe, arowes, and horn, in a schort grene cote, and seid onto him,
10 Thou knowist wel, whan I mad þis park I took many pore
mennes londes, and closed hem in. Therefor go I here, and
kepe þis park with ful mechil peyne. I pray þe, go to my
breþerin, Chanones of Lincoln, and prey hem þat þei restore
þe pore men to her lond, breke down þe heggis, make pleyn
15 þe dykes, and þan schal I haue rest.

Than, be þe comoun assent of þe chapeter of Lyncoln, þei sent a
chanon cleped William Bacheler, and he fulfillid all þis restoryng.

In þe xviii ȝer þe kyng sent Herry of Lancaster, erl of Derby,
with Hewe Spenser and Raf Stafford and þe bischop of Excetir, |
f. 78ʳᵃ with many oþir, for to trete with þe pope of þe rite þat he had to
21 þe crowne of Frauns, not as to a juge, but as to a councelour, and
because þe pope was a Frenschman þei found but litil coumfort
þere.

This ȝere was William Bateman mad bischop of Norwich,
25 whech was þe popes auditour before.

This ȝere þe kyng renewed þe Round Tabil at Wyndesore,
whech was first mad be Arthure. That aspied, þe kyng of Frauns
mad a Round Tabil in Frauns, to drawe þe knytehod of Almayn
fro þe kyng of Ynglond.

30 This ȝere Herry of Lancastir, in þe cuntré of Gyan, took a strong
cyté þei clepe Brigerak, and oþir strengthis and townes, in noumbyr
lvi.

2 of (3)] *om.* P   lyf] *in l.h. margin with carets (in red)* M   3 accepted]
in r.h. margin M   5 þere] þer P, *om.* M   13 þei] i *suprascript with
caret* M   18 ȝer] *in r.h. margin in red* M

1–6: see p. 163.
7–17: Walsingham, *Hist. Ang.* i. 254/37–255/18.
18–23: ibid. 261/2–9.
24–5: ibid. 262/16–18.
26–9: ibid. 263/1–18.
30–2: ibid. 265/11–19.

In þe xix ȝere þe kyng entered þe se, and no man wist whidir
he wold. Whan he was in þe se, a Frensch knite þei cleped N.
Harecort, whech was exiled oute of Frauns, mad þe kyng for to
londe on þe south side of Normannie, at a port þei clepe Hogges.
There took he Cane and many oþir townes, and had grete richesse   5
þere. And because Kyng Philip had brok all þe briggis þat led
into Frauns, þe kyng cam to Picardie, and distroyed þe cuntré,
and þan went þei ouir þe watir of Seyne, and þere þe erl of
Norhampton killid v hundred men þat letted hem to make þe
brigge ageyn. Than went þei ouir þe watir of Summe, and fond   10
a passage þat was neuir founde before. There killid þei to þousand
men þat wold lette here passage.

In þe xx ȝere þe Lord Spencer tok þe town of Crotey, where
were killid iiii hundred armed men. Than cam Philip, þe king of |
Frauns, and kept batail at Cressi with þe kyng of Ynglond, whech   f. 78ʳᵇ
is in Pountuey. There fawte þei þe xxvi day of August, where þe   16
king of Frauns was fayn to fle, and þe king of Bem, and þe
King Maioricarum; and þe duk of Lotharinge was ded þere—too
bischoppis, viii erles, too þousand knytes, and mech oþir puple
eythir slayn or put to flite. In þis same bataile þe kyng of Frauns   20
was wounded in þe þrote and in þe thi, and twies onhorsid be þe
kyng of Ynglond. For had he not fled on swift hors, he had be
take þere.

Fro þens Kyng Edward rood onto Kaleys þe ix day aftir þe
batail, and besegid þat town, for it was a cursed place, and cruel   25
onto Englischmen. This sege lastid a ȝere. The king of Frauns cam
þedir for to dissolue þe sege, but schamfully he fled with his
puple, and left his tentis and his vitaile behinde.

In þe same ȝere, þe xiii day of Octobir, was a grete bataile
betwix Englischmen and Scottis at Dorham, whech be þe councell   30
of þe kyng of Frauns was procured, for he supposed, whil þe king
was at Caleys, þe Scottis schuld haue but lytyl resistens, for
wantyng of puple. There was take þe kyng of Scottis, and William
Duglas, and many oþir lordis slayn. Thei þat had þis victorye

2 N.] om. P   4 þei] i suprascript M   8 went] t suprascript M
11 to] over erasure M   20 of] P, om. M   27 for] om. over line division P
33 and] d suprascript M

1–12: ibid. 267/15–268/2.
13–23: ibid. 268/2–269/7.
24–8: ibid. 269/9–15, 271/13–19.
29–166/3: ibid. 269/17–34.

were Ser Wylliam la Souch, archbiscop of ʒork, with his clergie,
Ser Gilbert Vmfreuyle, Herry Percy, Raf Neuyle, William
Dayncourt, and Herry Scroop.

In þat same ʒere þe Lord Dagworth, with foure score armed
f. 78ᵛᵃ men an a hundred archeres, held batail | with Charles de Bloys,
6 whech pretended to be duke of Bretayn, and þere had þe victori
ouyr v hundred armed men and viii þousand arbelasteres.

In þe xxi ʒere, whan Kyng Philip of Frauns was fled þus
kowardly fro þe sege of Caleys, þei of þe same town offered þe
10 town to Kyng Edward withoute ony poyntment. And he lay in
þe town a month, considering þe strong disposicion þerof.

Than, at instauns of þe pope, was take trews betwix þe to
kyngis for a ʒere. Aboute þe fest of Seynt Michael þe kyng took
þe se into Ynglond, and þere had he grete tempest and meruelous
15 wyndes, and þan he mad swech a compleynt onto oure Lady,
and seide, 'O blessed mayde, what menyth al þis? Euyr whan I
go to Frauns I haue fayre weddir, and whan I turne to Ynglond
intollerable tempestis'.

In þe xxii ʒere were grete reynes, whech dured fro þe Natiuité
20 of Seynt Jon Baptist onto Cristmasse. And aftir þat reyn, þere
folowid a grete pestilens, specialy in þe est side of þe world,
amongis þe Sarasines. So many deied þat þere left scarsly among
hem þe x man or þe x woman. Thei, seyng þis venjauns amongis
hem, purposed veryly to be Cristen. But whan þei wist þat þe
25 pestilens was among þe Cristen men, þan her good purpos sesed.

In þe xxiii ʒere was þe grete pestilens of puple. First it began in
þe north cuntré, þan in þe south, and so forth þorwoute þe reme.
f. 78ᵛᵇ Aftir þis | pestilens folowid a moreyn of bestis, whech had neuyr
be seyn. For, as it was supposed, þere left not in Inglond þe ten
30 part of the puple. Than cesed lordes rentis, prestis tithes; because
þere were so fewe tylmen, þe erde lay vntillid. So mech misery
was in þe lond þat þe prosperité whech was before was neuyr
recured.

7 arbelasteres] arbasteleres MP   12 trews] r *suprascript* M   16 and
seide] *om.* P   20 þat] t *suprascript with caret* M   28 folowid] d *suprascript* M

1–3: see p. 165.
4–7: Walsingham, *Hist. Ang.* i. 270/14–21.
8–18: ibid. 271/11–272/2.
19–25: ibid. 272/29–273/5.
26–33: ibid. 273/8–22.

In þis ȝere was a knyte of Frauns þei cleped Geffrey Charneys. He mad a comenaunt with þe capteyn of Caleys þat Caleys schuld be delyueryd onto him for a certeyn summe of mony. The capteyn, whech was a Januense, had take a grete part of þis summe. Whan þe kyng knew þis treson, pryuyly he went þidir. The French knyte 5 sent to þe capteyn to haue entré into þe castel; he was late in and þe brigge of tymbyr was drawe. And anon þe kyng gaf hem a saute, and took þe knyte and all þe felauchip, hing þe Januense, and mad a new capteyn.

In þe xxiiii ȝere þe kyng had a gret bataile with þe Spaynardis 10 in þe se a lytyl fro Wynchilissey, in whech batayle þere scaped but fewe of þe Spaynardis; xxx grete schippis were take of her part.

In þe xxv ȝere William Edyngton, bischop of Wynchestir, whech loued bettir þe kyngis profite þan þe puples, mad þe kyng 15 to make a new coyne, grotes, and pens of too pens, distroying all þe elde sterlyngis, whech were of gretter white, quantité for quantyté.

In þe xxvi ȝere deied Pope Clement in þe fest of Seynt Nicholas, f. 79ra and in his stede was chose Steuene, bischop of Hostiense, and 20 cleped Innocent þe Sext.

In þat same ȝer Haymo at þe Heth resyned þe bischoprich of Rouchestir frely, and þe pope gaf it to Maystir Jon Schepey, priour of þe same place.

In þat same tyme was gret derth of yrun, led, and bras, and oþir 25 metall.

And þat tyme þe duk of Seland weddid Duke Herry doutyr of Lancastir.

In þo same dayes Ser Raf Bentlé, keper of Britayn, in þe vigil of þe assumpcioun of oure Lady, faute with þe marchale of Frauns 30 fast be Mauron, betwix Reymes and Plumerel, wher were killid

2 þat] t superscript with caret (in red) M   8 all] om. P   16 grotes and pens of too pens] grotes .pens of too and .pens M, grotes pens of too and pens P   22 ȝer] suprascript with caret (in red) M   30 þe (1)] om. P

1–9: ibid. 273/24–274/16.
10–13: ibid. 274/27–275/9.
14–18: ibid. 275/30–276/3.
19–21: ibid. 276/28–9.
22–6: ibid. 276/30–5.
27–8: ibid. 277/1–2.
29–168/3: ibid. 276/15–25.

on þe Frensch side xiii lordis, of knytes a cl, swieres a hundred, of comoun puple without noumbir. Ther were take ix lordes, and of knytes and swieres a hundred and xl.

In þe xxvii зere was þere swech a droute in þe lond þat fro þe
5 monthe of March onto July fel not a drope of reyn on þe ground, and for þat cause þe gres and þe corn was euene dreid up. So Ynglond, þat was wone to fede oþir londis, was fayn to be fed with oþir londis.

The same зere Herry, erl of Derby, was made duke of Lancastir,
10 and þat same tyme Raf Stafford was mad erl of Stafford.

In þe xxviii зere was mad acord be þe kyngis of Frauns and Ynglond, and confermed with othis, but not with seles, vndir þis forme, þat þe kyng of Ynglond schuld haue pesibyly al his londes
f. 79ʳᵇ whech þe kyng of Frauns had vnritefully occupied, but he | must
15 first renounce all þe rite and þe chalenge whech he mad to þe crowne of Frauns. Vpon þis were sent solempne embassiatouris of þe kyngis party of Ynglond to þe court of Rome: Herry, duk of Lancastir; Richard, erl of Arundel; William, bischop of Norwich; and Gy Brian, knyte. But whan þei come þidir, with fraude of
20 þe courtesanes, whech were comensalis with þe pope, þe lordis were illuded. Anon as þe kyng herd þis he went into Frauns and began to distroye þe cuntré. Than cam tiding þat Scottis had take Berwik, and he cam hom ageyn and wan it.

In þis tyme þe dwelleres of Oxenforth gadered þe cuntré and
25 spoiled summe scoleres: summe fled, summe were slayn, but alle wer þei robbid and dryue fro þe town. Thanne was þe town put vndir interdict for a tyme, tyl þe tretys was mad þus, þat þei whech caused þe discord schuld be bounde, in greuous peynes, þat þei schuld no more do so, and eke þat þe chaunceler schuld
30 haue al þe gouernauns and all þe correccion.

In þe xxix зere deied Philip, þe kyng of Frauns, and aftir him Jon, his son, was kyng, whech was aftir prisoner in Ynglond. Anon as he was crowned he gaf Charles, his eldest son, þe duchie of

22 tiding] *at line end* M, tydyng*is* P   25 summe (2)] *suprascript* M summe (3)] and sume P   30 and] d *suprascript* M

1–3: see p. 167.
4–8: Walsingham, *Hist. Ang.* i. 277/19–23.
9–10: ibid. 277/28–30.
11–23: ibid. 277/33–278/16.
24–30: ibid. 278/21–34.
31–169/5: ibid. 279/11–280/4.

Gyan. For whech cause Kyng Edward was wroth, and gaf þe
same duchie to Edward þe prince as his riteful heritage, and he
anon gadered a host, and at þe natiuité of oure Lady sayled into
Gian, where he | took many townes; all þat were rebel ageyn him   f. 79ᵛᵃ
he prisoned or killid, and þere abod he al þat wyntir.   5

The kyng his fader had letteres into Ynglond þat Jon, kyng of
Frauns, had gadered a gret host at Seyn-Omeres to fite with
Edward, king of Ynglond. And anon þe kyng went to Caleys, and
with him his too sones, Leonell and Jon, and Herry, duk of Lancastir, with þese erles, Norhampton, March, and Stafford. This   10
aspied, þe kyng of Frauns distroyed all þe vitale of þe cuntré,
and pryuyly fled awey, and so Kyng Edward cam ageyn to Caleys.

This same ȝere Scottis took þe town of Berwik, but not þe
castell.

And in þis ȝere was graunted be þe parlement to þe kyng   15
of euery sak of wolle ls. for vi ȝere aftir.

And þis ȝere þe qwen had a son at Wodstok, þei cleped him
Thomas.

In þe xxx ȝere of Edward þe Scottis were fayn for to delyuer
þe town of Berwik frely. And þe same tyme Edward Baylol, kyng   20
of Scottis, resyned all þe rite of þe crowne of Scotlond to Kyng
Edward, at Rokisborow, be his patent letteris.

In þe same ȝere Prince Edward rod oute of Burdews be þe
cuntrés of Agenes, Peregor, Lymozin, Bery, and Saloigne; all
þat euyr mad resistens to him he took or killid, and þei þat receyued   25
him he suffered hem lyue vndir tribute. So, be þe weye, he tok
many Frensch lordes and many armed men. At þe last ende of
þat ȝere he met with þe king of Frauns fast be Peytris. The prince
had in his felauchip not passid iiii þousand, | and þe kyng of Frauns   f. 79ᵛᵇ
had iiii batayles. But, for al þat, þe Frensch fled, þe kyng was   30

---

1 Kyng] *om.* P   2 þe] *om.* P   4 where he] wher he P, where
he *twice over page division* M   6 Ynglond] d *suprascript* M   17 ȝere
þe] re þe *suprascript* M   19 Scottis] scot *over erasure* M   20 Edward]
om. P   23 rod] *preceding letter* (k *or* R) *erased* M   29 not] t *suprascript* M

6–12: ibid. 280/7–22.
13–14: ibid. 280/24–6.
15–16: ibid. 280/28–30.
17–18: ibid. 280/31–2.
19–22: ibid. 280/35–281/10.
23–170/5: ibid. 281/19–283/17.

take, and Philippe, his ʒonger son, James Borbon, and xi erles, þe
Bischop Senonense, with oþir lordis and knytis to þe noumbyr
of too þousand. There were killid too dukes, xix lordes, and
fyue þousand of men of armes, beside oþir puple. The prynce rood
5 streit to Burdews with his noble pray.

In þe xxxi ʒere of Kyng Edward þe prince cam into Ynglond
aboute þe feest of Pentecost, brynging with him Jon, þe kyng of
Frauns, and many oþir prisoneris. Whan he cam to London þere
was so mech prees of puple þat, whan he was at þe bregge at nyne
10 befor non, it was on aftir noon or he myte com to Westminster.

In þat same ʒere were sent to cardinales into Ynglond, to reforme
pes betwix þe to kingis. The þird cardinal cam only to visite and se
þe kyng of Frauns. And all þese iii abydyn here ny to ʒere.

In þis same ʒere was Dauid, kyng of Scottis, delyueryd oute of
15 prison, for he had be kept in þe castell of Odiham xi ʒere. His
raunson was a hundred þousand marc.

In þe xxxii ʒere fell a grete strif betwix on Armacan and þe iiii
orderes of freres. For þe same Armachan, archbischop of Yrland,
accused þe iiii orderes before þe pope þat þei lyued not aftir þe
20 writing of her reule. He wold eke a distroyed her pryuyleges, but
he preuailed not. In Oxenforth he held straunge opiniones, whech
f. 80ʳᵃ Wiclef meyntened aftirward more venemously, but at þat | tyme
was a frere Augustin, þei clepid him Geffrey Hardeby, aftirward
prouincial and confessour to þe prince, whech mad ageyn his
25 opinion a notable book we clepe De Euangelica Uita.

In þis ʒere Frere Jon Lyle, of þe Dominic ordre, mad a grete
compleynt of þe Lady Wake and hir councell, of many wrongis do
to him and to his cherch of Hely. And upon þis þe pope wrote to
þe bischop of Lincoln and oþir prelatis comaundyng hem þat þei
30 schuld curse all hem þat had do wrongis, and þoo þat were ded
and gilty in þis mater to digge hem oute of her graues and þrowe
hem out of saunctuarie. Mech manslauth fell in þis mater, for
þei þat broute þe bulles were killid for þe most part.

1 and (2)] P, & | and *over line division* M   6 ʒere] ʒer P, *om.* M
17 þe (1)] *om.* P   21 not] *in r.h. margin* M   22 at þat] *over erasure* M
25 opinion] opynyon P, opinon M   28 of Hely] *in l.h. margin* M   30 had]
om. P

1–5: see p. 169.
6–13: Walsingham, *Hist. Ang.* i. 283/23–284/3.
14–16: ibid. 284/12–16.
17–25: ibid. 285/12–23.
26–33: ibid. 285/25–286/6.

In þe xxxiii ȝere Jon Gaunt, erl of Richemund, þe son of Kyng
Edward, weddid Dam Blaunche, þe doutir of þe duk of Lancastir,
be whech mariage he was aftir mad duke of Lancastir.

In þis same tyme Jon, kyng of Frauns, prisoner at London,
profered to Kyng Edward all þoo londis þat Edward had ouyrrydyn 5
before, þat is to sey Flaundrys, Pycardye, Gyan, and oþir londis.
For whech graunt King Edward sent into Frauns, and þe councell
of Frauns wold not consent þertoo.

Than was þe kyng gretly mevyd, and rood into Frauns with þe
prince, þe duk of Lancastir, and many oþir lordes; he had in his 10
naue to lede him to Caleys xi hundred schippis. The iiii day of
October he entered into Frauns, and on Seynt Lucye day he cam
into Burgenye. There mette with him þe duk of Burgeyn, and pro-
fered him vii hundred þousand florenis, vn|dir þis condicion, þat f. 80ʳᵇ
he schuld do no hurt onto his cuntré. Thanne þe kyng went and 15
remeued to Reymes, and dwelled þere onto Seynt Gregory day.

In þis same tyme þei of Normannye londed at Wynchilsey,
and robbed þe town, and led awey many women. The cuntré
ryse to her defense, but al for nowt, for þei were go or þei cam.

In þis ȝere blod ran owt of þe toumbe of Thomas, duk of 20
Lancastir, at Poumfreit.

And in þe same ȝere þe kyng began þe newe edifiyng of Wyndesore, and mad Maystir William Wikham suruiour of þe same
werk, whech was aftir bischop of Wynchestir.

In þe xxxiiii ȝere þe Kyng Edward remeued fro þe heyer cuntré 25
of Frauns and cam down to Paris. There brent he þe subarbes
of þe cité be þe corage of iiii hundred knytes whech were
newly mad.

And in þe same tyme þei of Ynglond gadered a gret naue,
iiii score schippis, in whech were xiiii þousand men. Thei sailed, 30
and took þe ylde of Caus. And þan cam þe abbot of Cloyne and

---

4 þis] the P   14 vii] v over erasure M   15 and] suprascript M
19 ryse] y written over o M   26 he] in r.h. margin M   31 And þan
cam] over erasure M

1–3: ibid. 286/21–5; cf. Chron. Ang. 39/35–7.
4–16: Walsingham, Hist. Ang. i. 286/28–287/21.
17–19: ibid. 287/22–288/4.
20–1: ibid. 288/5–6.
22–4: ibid. 288/7–12.
25–8: ibid. 288/19–31.
29–172/18: ibid. 288/32–290/10.

þe Erl Tankeruyle, whech was steward of Frauns, and Bursigalde, constabil of þe same, and oþir lordis many onto Kyng Edward, and offered onto him a certeyn tretis and a forme of pes, whech wrytyng displesid gretly þe kyng, and he forbad hem his presens
5 onto þe tyme þei had mad anoþir forme. Then cam þei aftir to þe king, and broute him writing sumwhat aftir his plesauns. This was þe maner of þe oth þei swore:—

We, Charles, gouernour of Frauns, þe first-begotin son of
f. 80ᵛᵃ Jon, kyng of Frauns, vp|on þe holy sacrament swere here, and
10 on þe holy godspell, þat we schal kepe pees and concord whech is mad betwix þe kyngis, and make no contradiccion ageyn it.

The same oth mad þe Prince Edward and þe to kyngis and all þe lordes on both parties. And for more sikirnesse þe kyng of
15 Ynglond took pleggis, v dukes, vii erles, ix lordes, and many honourabil knytes. So was þe kyng of Frauns delyuered, and his raunson set at iii milliones of florenes, of whech too schuld weye a nobil.

In þe xxxv ʒere, in þe parlement at Westminster, before þe
20 Englisch lordis and þe Frensch was þis acord purposed and graunted, and all þei þat had not swore mad her othis þere before þe archbischop at messe.

This ʒere was Ser Jon Gaunt, erl of Richemund, mad duk of Lancastir be þe rite of his wif, whech was doutir to good Herry of
25 Lancastir, late ded.

In þis ʒere Prince Edward weddid Jone, þe cuntesse of Kent, whech was before departed fro þe erl of Salesbury, and weddid aftir to Ser Thomas Holland, knyte.

This ʒere was grete pestilens, speciali of men.
30 And þis same time fell many merueyles in dyuers londes. At Boloyne, on Corporis Cristi Day, appered a blody crosse in þe eyr fro morow til it was noon, and þan it fel into þe se. Anon aftir,

1 Tankeruyle] of Tankervyle P   2 constabil] *over erasure* M
3 certeyn] n *over erasure* M   tretis] *suprascript with caret (in red)* M   4 he]
om. P   6 king] *in r.h. margin* M   8 begotin son] gotin son *over
erasure* M   27 weddid] wedded P, weddir M   30 time] *suprascript* M
31 Corporis] Corpus P

1–18: see p. 171.
19–22: Walsingham, *Hist. Ang.* i. 294/23–295/2.
23–5: ibid. 295/22–5.
26–8: ibid. 296/7–9.
29: ibid. 296/10–11.

woluys cam oute of wodis and deuoured many men. In Burgundy
was a reyn all of blood. Both in Ynglond and in Frauns appered
too castellis in certeyn forestis and in desert places, out of whech
castellis | went too hoostis, on white, þe oþir blak, and sumtyme   f. 80ᵛᵇ
þe white had þe victorie whan þei faute, and sumtyme þe blak   5
had þe victorie, and sodeynly þe castell and þe hoostis vanysched
and were not seyn.

In þe xxxvi ȝere blew þe grete wynd oute of þe south-west,
fro euensong tyl mydnyte, þat blewe down many a hous, of whech
wynd þese vers were mad:-   10

> C ter erant mille decies sex vnus et ille
> Luce tua Maure vehemens fuit impetus aure.

This is þe Englisch:-

> A þousand iii hundred sexti and too
> Was *Maurus* wynd whech blew soo.   15

This ȝere a pound of wax was worth XVIIId.

In þis same ȝere, on Seynt Bris day, þe kyng was fifti wyntir
old. Therfor þe kyng mad þis ȝere his jubilé, losed prisoneres,
forgaf all forfetis.

And þis ȝere was ordeyned þat all plees at þe barre schuld be in   20
Englisch tunge, and in no oþir tunge.

And þis ȝere was Leonel mad duke of Clarens, and Edmund,
his broþir, erl of Cambrig.

It was ordeyned eke in þe parlement þat þe kyng schuld haue iii
ȝere folowand of a sak wolle XXVIs. VIIId.; and þat puruioures   25
schuld take no vitale but þei payed þerfor; and eke þat þere
schuld no men haue swech puruioures but þe kyng and þe qween
and dukes.

This ȝere Pope Innocent deied, and aftir him succedid Vrbanus
Quintus, whech mad a constitucion ageyn pluralités, but it availed   30
but litil; for clerkis plesed so lordes þat þe constitucion was not
admitted.

---

1 and] d *suprascript* M   9 euensong] even *at line end* P   11 sex]
supplied, om. MP   12 vehemens] s *over erasure* M   16 wax] *suprascript* M   18 þe] *suprascript* M   prisoneres] risoner *over erasure* M
21 and in no oþir tunge] *om.* P   25 þat] *om.* P   29 Innocent deied
and] nocent deied and *over erasure* M   30 Quintus] Quitus P

8–15: ibid. 296/19–26.
16: ibid. 296/27.
17–28: ibid. 297/31–298/5.
29–32: ibid. 298/6–10.

In þe xxxvii ȝere, in þe month of October, þe kyng held a
^{f. 81ra} parlement at London, fro whech mite no man | of power absent
him. There was forbode þat syluyr and gold schuld not be used in
knyues, ne girdelis, ne brochis, ne ringes, ne no oþir ornamentis,
5 but in swech persones þat myte spend x libras be ȝere, and eke þat
no man schuld were peloure or precious cloth but he myte spend be
ȝere a hundred pound. It was ordeyned eke þat þe comoun puple
schuld not use no precious mete ne drink.

In þis same tyme thre kingis came into þis lond to se oure kyng:
10 the kyng of Frauns, þe kyng of Cipir, þe kyng of Scottis. And whan
þei had be receyued worchippfully, too kyngis turned hom ageyn,
þe þird, þat is to sey of Frauns, fell seek, and deyed at London in
Saueye in þe next ȝere, whos exequies Kyng Edward ded holde
worchipfully in dyuers places. His body was caried at þe kyngis
15 cost onto Douer, and þan þe Frenschmen led him, and byried him
at Seint-Denys.

This ȝere a quarter whete was sold for XVs.

In þe xxxviii ȝere Charles de Bloys cam with a gret hoost into
Bretayn to fite with Jon Mountforth, duk of Bretayn, for þis
20 same pretendid to be duke of þe same, and þere was þe same
Charles slayn, and many of his men, in noumbir a þousand and
fyue hundred. Off Jon side deyed but vii men.

In þis same ȝere þe Lumbardes accused her felawes þat þei
had deceyued þe king in certeyn marchaundise. Than were þei
25 put in þe Tour, onto þe tyme þat þei contented þe kyng euene
aftir his plesauns.

In þis ȝere, in þe pleyn of Turkye, was a greuous batayle on
^{f. 81rb} Al-halow Day betwix Cristen men | and paynymes, where, be þe
grace of God, Cristen men had þe victory. On þe Cristen side were
30 slayn Jon, kyng of Hungarie, Seward, kyng of Gorganye, and þe
maistir of þe hospital in þe ylde of Rodis, and of þe puple v
þousand to hundred and x. On þe oþir side were killid fourty

---

22 hundred] *final* d *altered from* t M   24 marchaundise] archaundise *over erasure* M   25 contented] content M, contend P

1–8: Walsingham, *Hist. Ang.* i. 299/1–11.
9–16: ibid. 299/13–22.
17: ibid. 299/38–9.
18–22: ibid. 300/15–25.
23–6: ibid. 300/29–32.
27–175/4: ibid. 301/3–16.

þousand of myty men, and of oþir comowneres withoute noumbyr. The princes of þat side were þese: the soudan of Babilony; the kyng of Turkye; the Kyng Baldak; þe Kyng Belmaryn; þe kyng of Tartaré; þe king of Lettow; of whech iii were slayn.

In þe ȝere of Edward xxxix was born Edward, þe first-begote child of Prince Edward, and whan he was vii ȝere old he deyed. 5

In þe same ȝere þe grete cyté of Alisaundre was take be þe kyng of Cipir, but, for þei þat tok it were Cristen men and fewe, þei robbed þe cyté and fled with þe godes or þe soudan cam with his strength. This same kyng of Cipre was in Ynglond before þis 10 jornay, and had of Kyng Edward men, schippis, and mony.

In þe xl ȝere was born a child to Prins Edward at Burdews, whom þe kyng cleped Maioricarum left fro þe funt and cleped be his name Richard.

In þo same daies þe kyng of Frauns wrote letteris onto þe kyng 15 of Ynglond þat he schuld help him ageyn þe grete cumpanye of Englisch þat ouyrrydin Frauns. The kyng wrot onto hem þat þei schuld leue her ridyng, and go fro Frauns. Thei answerd þat þo londis whech þei had gote þei wold not forsake, and eke, in-as-mech as þei longed not to þe crowne of Ynglond, | þei were not bounde to his comaundment. Whan þe kyng had letteres of þis rebellion he 21 proclamed a viage into Frauns, gadered a gret puple, and purposed for to venge him patently, as þe answere was dyuulged. This aspied þe kyng of Frauns, and prayed þe kyng þat he schulde not performe þis jornay; for he was aferd, if þe kyng cam on þe o side 25 and þe cumpany on þe oþir side, þat it schuld be destruccion of his kyngdam. Whan Kyng Edward herd þe letteris he swore be þe blessed mayden Marie, 'þouȝ þei ouyrryde all þe regne of Frauns, þe kyng schal neuyr haue help of me'.

In þat same tyme Bertran Claykyn and Hew Caluyrlé, þat were 30 lederes of þis cumpany, left Frauns at reuerens of þe kyng, and went into Spayn with grete puple into lx þousand at comaundment

f. 81ᵛᵃ

4 Lettow] Lectow P   7 In] *change to darker ink* M   same ȝere] *over erasure* M   9 soudan] P, soudam M   17 hem] hym P   19 þei (2)] i *inserted on the line* M   27 herd] *suprascript* M   28 mayden] *over erasure* M   30 Bertran] Bertan P   32 at] t *suprascript* M

5–6: ibid. 301/17–22.
7–11: ibid. 301/26–302/4.
12–14: ibid. 302/15–20.
15–176/5: ibid. 302/21–303/16.

of þe pope ageyn Petir, kyng of Spayn, to pryue him of his lordchip. Whan Kyng Petir herd of her comyng he fled into Gascoyne
onto Prynce Edward, þat he myte recure his regne be his fauour.
In þe same tyme þei of Spayn chose hem a newe kyng, þat was
5 broþir to þe forseid Petir, and a bastard.

In þe xli ȝere was a greuous bataile in Spayn betwix þe Prince
Edward and Herry, þe wrong kyng of Spayn, where þe Englischmen had þe bettir. This batail was by þe town and þe watir of
Naȝar. The kyng of Spayn fled, for he myte not susteyne þe
10 tempest of arowes; vii þousand men of his were slayn þere, and
many mo dronchin in þe watyr. There were take þe erl of Dene,
f. 81vb and Bertram Cleykyn, þat | was his principal councelour. Aftir þis
victorie þe Kyng Petir was restored to his dignité, and þe prince
returned into Gyan. This kyng, aftir þe prince was go, be fals
15 deceyt of his enmyes, was killid at his mete. The prince eke
in þat viage was poysoned, for aftir þat tyme he had neuyr helth
of body.

In þe xlii ȝere, in þe month of March, þere appered betwix þe
north and þe west a sterre þei clepe comata, directing his bemes
20 rite onto Frauns.

And in þe same ȝere, in þe month of April, Sere Leonel, duk
of Clarens, with a chose felauchip, took his jornay onto Melan,
for to haue the duke doutir to his wif, and half þe lyflod of þat
duchy. Aftir þe tyme he had weddid þat lady he lyued not longe,
25 but deied in þat cuntré aboute þe natiuité of oure Lady. His body
was byried at Pauy, fast by þe toumbe of Seyn Austin; his hert was
broute to þe freres of Clare, and biried or kept in leed.

In þis ȝere þe Frenschmen broke þe pees and ouirridin þe kyngis
londes in Pounte, distroyed castellis and townes, and took many
30 prisoneres, putting all þe cause upon Englischmen.

In þe xliii ȝere þe kyng held a parlement at Wesminster, wher
was purposed what is best to doo ageyn þe rebellion of Frauns,
notwithstandyng her wryting and her othis. Ther it was concluded
þat þe kyng schuld chaleng his rite ageyn; vpon þis purpos he

4 kyng] *suprascript* M   25 cuntré] cunctre P   34 purpos] *om.* P

1–5: see p. 175.
6–17: Walsingham, *Hist. Ang.* i. 303/26–306/1.
18–20: ibid. 306/14–18.
21–7: ibid. 306/19–28.
28–30: ibid. 306/29–307/20.
31–177/7: ibid. 307/30–308/23.

sent his son Jon, duk of Lancastir, and Humfrey Bown, erl of
Herforth, into Frauns for to cleyme his rite. And whil þei taried at
Chalkhul, abydyng þe resistens of þe French part, þere cam oute
of Ynglond | þe erl of Warwik, Ser Thomas Belchaump, whech had   f. 82ʳᵃ
euyr grete worchip in batayle. The Frenschmen, þat had sette þe   5
day of batayle, whan þei sey þat nauy in þe se, wenyng þe kyng of
Ynglond had come, þei fled, leuyng mech of her stuf behynde hem.

In þis same tyme was Ser Herry Spenser, a grete werriour in
Ytaile, or þe tyme þat he was promoted, and Ser Jon Haukwod,
a meruelous man of armes, whech led in Itale a grete cumpany,   10
clepit þe White Felauchip—his dedis wold ask a special tretys.

In þe xliiii ȝere þe king borowed gret good of dyuers astatis,
pretending þat it schuld be spent in profite of þe reme, but it was
spent al oþirwyse. At þe fest of Seint Jon Baptist þe kyng gadered
a hoost of þe best men þat mite be chose, and sent hem into Frauns.   15
Amongis hem was þe Lord Graunson and þe Lord FitzWalter,
with oþir ȝonger lordis. And Ser Robert Knollis, as a elde werriour,
was assigned be þe kyng for to be her capteyn. Whan þei cam into
Frauns, as long as þei were gouerned be Knollis, þei had no rebuke.
Than was among hem a knyte þei clepid Ser Jon Monstreworth,   20
and he seid onto þe lordis þat it was schame onto hem þat þei
schuld be gouerned vndir swech a elde theef. Thus were þei
disparplied into dyuers cumpanies, and Ser Robert, with his mené,
went into Britayn to a castel of his owne. The lordis, þus departed,
were take summe, and summe slayn, be þe Frensch party, and   25
Ser Jon Monstreworth fled into Ynglond and accused Ser Robert
Knollis of treson, | for whech cause Ser Robert durst not se þe kyng   f. 82ʳᵇ
tyl he sent him mech tresoure, and þan he cam to his excuse.
The forseid Monstreworth aftir þat fled, and held with þe kyng
of Frauns.   30

In þis ȝere deyed Pope Vrban, and for him was chose Gregorius
XI.

In þis ȝere many cytées in Gyan felle fro þe obediens of Prince
Edward and held with Frauns, for greuous exacciones þat were

6 þe se] *separated by thin stroke in red* M   8 Ser] *om.* P   12 borowed]
P, borowred M   13 profite] r *suprascript* M   18 assigned] d *suprascript* M
20 hem] *suprascript* M   34 with Frauns] *in r.h. margin with carets (in red)* M

8–11: ibid. 309/2–11.
12–30: ibid. 309/33–311/9.
31–2: ibid. 311/10–22.
33–178/5: ibid. 311/24–312/13.

leyde upon hem, and specialy þe cité Lemouicense, whech cyté þe
prince distroyed onto þe ground. Aftir þat, with his wif, and
Richard, his son, þe prince cam into Ynglond, and resined al Gyan
and Gascon into his faderes hand, leuyng in þat same cuntré his too
5 breþerin, Jon, duke of Lancastir, and Edmund, erl of Cambrigge.

In þe xlv ȝere þe clergi and þe puple lent onto þe kyng fifty
þousand pound, whech was graunted for a subsidy, and late payed
ageyn. And to pay þis summe þe annual prestis were compelled,
and pore benefises, þat neuyr payed before.

10 In þis ȝere þe lordes asked þat þe bischoppis schuld be remeued
fro þe offises chaunceler, tresorer, and pryuy sel, and þat temporal
lordes schuld haue þo offises, and so was it fulfillid in dede, and
all þis was don for hate of þe clergie.

In þis same ȝere cam solempne messageris fro þe pope to trete
15 pes betwix þe to kyngis, but it availed not.

In þe xlvi ȝere þe kyng held a parlement at Wynchestir, to whech
parlement was somound foure bischoppis and foure abbotis and
f. 82ᵛᵃ no mo, and þis cause | was pretendid, þat þe citeceynes of London
and of Norwich and othir cytés had conspired ageyn þe kyng.

20 In þis ȝere þe duke of Lancastir and his broþir Edmund cam
oute of Gyan with þe too douteris of þe king of Spayn: þe duke of
Lancastir weddid þe elder—sche hite Constauns—and Edmund
weddid þe ȝonger—sche hite Ysabel.

In þis ȝere was a batail betwix Englischmen and Flemingis in
25 þe se, where þe Englischmen killid many Flemingis and took xxv
schippis laden with bay-salt.

In þat ȝere was Rochel besegid with Frenschmen, and þe kyng
sent þidir þe erl of Penbrok, Ser Jon Hastingis, for to remeue þe
sege, and sodeynly in þe port of Rochel met with him a grete naue
30 of Spaynardes, distroyed þe Englisch blod, brent all þe schippis,
and led þe forsaid lord into Spayn, and xx þousand mark, whech

2 þat] om. P   9 benefises] benefyces wer compelled P   12 þo] þe P
18 pretendid] *final* d *altered from* t M   27–8 ȝere . . . þidir] *over erasure* M
31 mark] rk *over erasure* M

1–5: see p. 177.
6–9: Walsingham, *Hist. Ang.* i. 312/34–313/2.
10–13: ibid. 313/3–6.
14–15: ibid. 313/7–12.
16–19: ibid. 313/13–21.
20–3: ibid. 313/22–6.
24–6: ibid. 313/35–8.
27–179/3: ibid. 314/5–25.

þe kyng had tak him to his viage. This infortune fel onto him on Missomyr Euen, whech is þe feest of Seynt Audré, as summe suppose for he was a gret enmie onto þe cherch of Hely.

In þe xlvii ȝere þe duk of Lancastir, with strong hand, rood into Frauns, and be Paris onto Borgoin, and took tributes of cités as 5 he went, euene aftir his plesauns; þei offered him good for dreed. þan went he be þe hillis of Aluerne, not Maluerne, where many of his deied for hungir, so was he compelled to turne ageyn to Bordeus. Ther was prefixed a bataile betwix him and þe duke of Angoye, but it turned to a treus til þe xx day of May—þe day of 10 batail was sette first þe | x day of April.   f. 82ᵛᵇ

The same ȝere þe kyng wrote to þe pope þat þe elecciones of cathedral cherchis schul be kept aftir þe eld custom of þe lond. And in þe parlement holden aftirward at London it was ordeyned þat þe cathedral cherchis schuld haue her dew eleccion, and þat 15 þe king schuld not write þe contrari to þe pope, but promote þe same eleccion.

In þe xlviii ȝere Ser Jon, duk of Lancastir, cam out of Gyan into Ynglond, and aftir he was go all þe cuntré turned Frensch, saue Burdews and Bayon.   20

In þis same ȝere was a grete treté at Bruges betwix þe councellis of þe too remes, for to make a fynal pes. For þis cause was sent Jon, duke of Lancastir, William Mountagew, erl of Salisbiry, Regnald Cobbam, and many oþir. For þe Frensch side was þe duke of Angoy, with many oþir lordes. Ther were eke of þe clergi 25 of Ynglond Simon Sudbyry, with many oþir prelatis. This trety lasted ny to ȝere, not withoute grete expenses, and no pes had. For al þat same tyme þe Frenschmen purueyed hem for to fite with Englischmen. So was þere graunted trews for o ȝere.

In þe xlix ȝere Ser Jon Mountforth, duk of Bretayn, rod with 30 þe kyngis son Edmund, erl of Cambrige, and þe erles of March, Warwic, and Stafforth, and þe Lord Spenser—all þese went into

5 and (2)] *change to darker ink* M   6 þei] *suprascript with caret* (*in red*) M
12 þat] *change to darker ink* M   15 cherchis] *in r.h. margin with carets* (*in red*) M   21 councellis] councel M, councell P   22 cause] *in r.h. margin* M   29 Englischmen] þe Ynglyschmen P

4–11: ibid. 315/16–316/10.
12–17: ibid. 316/19–34.
18–20: ibid. 317/5–10.
21–9: ibid. 317/31–318/16, 318/27–9.
30–180/6: ibid. 318/30–319/4.

Bretayn. Anon as þei were come, þe castell of Seint-Mathew, þe
castell of Orcey, and þe castell of Brest were ȝolde onto hem, and
þan beseged þei þe town of Kemperlé, where were all þe worþi
f. 83ʳᵃ men of þe lond, and þat had þei take, had not let|tyng be with
5 a messager þat cam fro Ynglond with þe kyngis letteris þat þei
schuld leue þe sege, and com hom ageyn.

In þis tyme was take þe ylde of Constantyn, with þe castel of
Seynt Sauyour, be a swyere þei clepid Thomas Karington, whom
Ser Jon Anyslé, knyte, apeched aftir of treson, and faut with him,
10 and killid him.

In þe fifti ȝere of Edward, whech was þe ȝere of oure Lord 1376,
was gadered a gret parlement at London, in whech was asked a
gret summe of mony to þe kyng, and it was answerd be Petir de
la Mar, knyte, and speker of þe parlement, þat þe kyng nedith not
15 for to haue þe godes of þe pore men if he were wysely and treuly
gided; and if it were so, þat þe kyng had so gret nede, he offered,
be asent of þe comownes, þat þei wold largely help him, up condicion þat certeyn officeres schuld be remeued, þat is to sey þe
chambirleyn, whech was þe Lord Latymer, and many oþir, and
20 new men were assigned in her place. But þis statute lest not fully
iii monthis. The comnaunté asked eke þat Dame Alis Pereres
schuld be remeued oute of þe kyngis hous as a woman malapert
and entirmeting in euery mater. This woman wolde sumtyme
sitte be þe juges on þe Bench, and sumtyme be þe doctoures in the
25 consistory, and plete with þe treuth, and ageyn þe treuth, be þe
kyngis auctorité, whech turned gretly onto his vileny and slaundir.
And be þe instauns of þis woman was þis Petir de la Mar con-
f. 83ʳᵇ dempned to perpetuel prison at Notyngham, but | within too ȝere
aftir he was delyueryd.

---

1 of Seint-Mathew] *over erasure* M   3 where were] *over erasure* M
4 with] *om.* P   5 kyngis] kygys P   7 was take] *in r.h. margin*
with carets (in red) M   7–8 with þe castel of Seynt Sauyour] *om.* P
8 Karington] i *surmounted by short stroke in red* M, Kyryngton P   9 knyte]
om. P   faut] fauncte P   15 for] *om.* P   16 nede] *in r.h. margin*
M   17 up] vpon P   20 were] *om.* P   21 comnaunté] comi-
naunte *with* i *expuncted* M   23 entirmeting] entirmēting M, entir-
mētyng P

1–6: see p. 179.
7–10: Walsingham, *Hist. Ang.* i. 319/7–12.
11–29: ibid. 320/7–321/5, 321/12–21, and *Chron. Ang.*, Appendix, 391/4–
392/12, 392/21–393/2.

In þe tyme of þis parlement deyed þe noble Prince Edward on þe Trinité Sunday, þe viii day of Juni. His deth bare awey al þe sikirnes of þis lond.

In þis parlement Richard, son onto þe forseid prince, was mad erl of Chestir, and sone aftir þat duke of Cornwayle, and not long 5 aftir prince of Walis.

In þis tyme on Jon Wiclef, maystir of Oxenforth, held many straunge opiniones: that þe Cherch of Rome is not hed of all Cherchis; that Petir had no more auctorité þan þe oþir aposteles, ne þe pope no more power þan anoþir prest; and þat temporal 10 lordes may take awey þe godes fro þe Cherch whan þe parsones trespasin; and þat þo reules mad be Augustin, Benet, and Fraunceys adde no more perfeccion ouyr þe gospel þan doth lym-whiting onto a wal; and þat bischoppis schuld haue no prisones; and many oþir þingis. Vpon þese materes þe pope sent a bulle to þe arch- 15 bischop of Cauntirbury and bischop of London, þat þei schuld areste þe same Wiclef, and make him to abjure þese seid opiniones, and so he ded, in þe presens of þe duk of Lancastir, but aftirward he erred in þese and in mo.

The same tyme þei of London wold a killid þe forseid duk, had 20 þei not be lettid be her bischop.

In þe on and fifty ȝere of his regne he deyed at Schene, and is biried at London, whech ȝere is acountid onto Richardis tyme and not to his. This King Edward was gracious and fortunat in pes, | deuoute onto þe Cherch, fortunat in batayle, neuyr steyned, saue f. 83va þat in his age he was gretly langaged with lecchery. 26

Anno 6575–6596; 1377–1398. In þe ȝere of grace a 1377 Richard of Burdews, þe son of Edward þe prince, was crowned at London þe sextene day of Jule be þe handis of Simon Sutbyry, archbiscop of Cauntirbury—þe ȝere of his age, xi. 30

---

4 onto] to P   5 þat] *om. over line division* P   8 of (2)] to P
10 and þat] That the P   12 Benet] or Benedict P   14 onto] on P
15–16 archbischop] archbyschop P, arbischog *with* ar *suprascript* M   16 bis-
chop] byschop P, *om.* M   17 him] *suprascript* M   seid] *om.* P   18 aftir-
ward] aftir þat P   24 in pes] *om.* P   27 a] *om.* P   28 þe (2)] *om.* P

1–6: Walsingham, *Hist. Ang.* i. 321/22–41; cf. *Chron. Ang.*, Appendix, 393/8–24.
7–21: cf. Walsingham, *Hist. Ang.* i. 324/8–325/29.
22–6: cf. ibid. 326/33–328/31.
27–30: cf. ibid. 332/21–337/10.

The first þingis he ded:—He mad pees betwix his vncle, Jon
of Gaunt, and þe cyté of London. In þe day of his coronacion he
mad iiii newe erles: Thomas Wodstok, þe ʒongest son of Kyng
Edward, erl of Bokyngam; Richard of Angolisme, erl of Huntyn-
5 don; Thomas Mounbray, erl of Notingam; Herry Percy, erle
of Northumbirlond.

In þis same ʒere þe Frenschmen took þe Ilde of Man, al saue
þe castel, whech Ser Hewe Tyrel manfully defended, but þei of
þe ylde were fayn to gyue þe Frenschmen a m marc þat þei schuld
10 not brenne her houses.

In þe same ʒere þei londed in Southsex, fast by a town cleped
f. 83ᵛᵇ Rotyng|dene, and ageyn hem went þe priour of Lews, and þere
was he take, and with him to knytes, Ser Jon Fallisle, and Ser
Thomas Cheyne, and a swyere, Jon Brokas.

15 In þe secund ʒere of Rychard deied Gregori þe XI, and for him
was chose Vrbane þe VI, whech was before bischop of Baré, and
ageyn him ros þe Cardinal Jubanense, þat procured certeyn
cardinales to chese him, notwithstanding þat he and al his party
had mad her obediens to þis Vrbane before. This cardinal cleped
20 himselue Clement, whech fled oute of Rome with his clientis.

In þis ʒere þe king of Nauern lete to Kyng Richard Cherborow,
in Normandie, for a certeyn pension to be payed euery ʒere, þat
he schuld haue esy londyng into þe ground of Frauns.

In þis ʒere þe kyng of Frauns asked of hem þat dwelled in
25 Litil Bretayn her castelles and her strengthis, and þei þat were his
rebelles he killid vilensly. This was þe cause þat þei of þe lond
desired gretly þat Ser Jon Mountforth schuld come hom ageyn, as
very eyer.

In þe þird ʒere of Richard Ser Hew Caluirlé and Ser Thomas

1 þingis] thyng P   5 erle] P, *om.* M   6 Northumbirlond] d *suprascript* M   8 defended] kept P   15 deied Gregori þe] d gregori þ
over erasure M   16 and] but P   17 him] *suprascript* M   18 and] d
suprascript M   19 her] *om.* P   24 dwelled] P, dwelle M   25 his]
in r.h. margin M   29 þird] d *suprascript* M   Richard] hys reyn P

1–6: cf. Walsingham, *Hist. Ang.* i. 330/4–331/3, ii. 383/15–384/5, and
   i. 338/3–12.
7–10: cf. ibid. 340/27–341/22.
11–14: cf. ibid. 342/8–14.
15–20: cf. ibid. 368/36–369/12, 381/15–382/9.
21–3: cf. ibid. 371/22–372/4.
24–8: cf. ibid. 389/18–24.
29–183/2: cf. ibid. 390/10–14, 20–4.

Percy were mad Amirelis of þe Se, and þei tok many schippes
and caused gret plenté of all maner marchaundise in þis lond.

In þis tyme þe Bischop Cassilense, a Erischman, was sent fro
þe pope to þe kyng, doyng him to wete þat þe kyng of Frauns was
acursed, because he ded crye þorw þe lond þat þere schul no man in 5
Frauns do obediens to Pope Vrbane, up peyne of lesing of his hed.

In þis ʒere was hold a parlement, where was ordeyned þat for
þis tyme þe como|nes schuld be spared, and rich men schuld pay f. 84ʳᵃ
a subsidie to þe kyng: euery duk, x marc; euery archbischop, x
marc; euery erl, vi marc; and euery bischop and euery abbot 10
mitred, vi marc, notwithstanding þat euery abbot mitred and polled
schuld pay for euery monkis hed XLd. There was no religious man,
ne woman, justise, schreue, knyt, swyere, parson, vicarie, simpil
prest, þat scaped þis tax, but ech of hem payed aftir his degré.

In þis same tyme þe fals Flemyngis took a barge of Fowey, 15
whech is in Cornwayle, and þe men þat were within schip þei
killid, saue o boy þat fled to on of þe Flemysch schippis and hid
him in þe horrok. The Flemingis com into Ynglond for to selle þe
marchaundise whech þei had take; þe boy herd Englischmen
speke and cryed for help. Anon as he was pulled up he told who 20
þei took þe schip be treson, pretendyng þat þei were oure frendis,
and þus killid all þe men saue him. So were þe Flemyngis take, and
sent to dyuers prisones.

In þis same ʒere Edmund Brounfeld, munk of Bury, entered þe
place of Bury be þe popes gift, and took upon him to be abbot of 25
þe place, wherfor þe kyng put him in þe Tour of London, and all
þo monkes þat fauoured him. But at þe last he was deliuered, on
þat condicion, þat he schuld not come at Bury, ne he schuld not
passe þe se. But he brak his oth, went to Rome, and þere was he
mad lystir of þe paleis, and comensale with þe pope. 30

1 Amirelis] Amyrall P   4 wete] knowe P   5 þe] his P   6 of (1)] P,
om. M   10 euery erl vi marc and] om. P   14 þat scaped þis tax] scaped
þat taske P   his] her P   15 Flemyngis] Flemnyngis P   16 and]
change to paler ink M   schip] the schip P   17 Flemysch] Flem-
myng P   22 So] Thanne P   24 þis] þe P   25 þe] suprascript in red and inked over in brown, with caret (in red) M   and] P, om. M
26 þe (3)] suprascript in red and inked over in brown M   27 þo] þe P
deliuered] deliuer over erasure M   29 he (2)] om. P

3–6: cf. ibid. 391/12–25.
7–14: cf. ibid. 392/24–393/4.
15–23: cf. ibid. 400/8–401/24.
24–30: cf. ibid. 414/6–418/11.

In þe iiii ȝere of Richard, þe eyer of þe Emperour Constantino-
politan and þe patriark | com and mad her obediens to Pope Vrban
þe Sexte, of whom he was crowned.

In þat same tyme was betwix þe bischop of Norwich, Herry
5 Spenser, and Thomas de la Mar, abbot of Seynt Alboun, a ple, in
whech ple þe abbot opteyned þat þere schuld no priour longing to
Seynt Alboun, in þe dyosise of Norwich, be compelled for to
gadere þe dymes to þe king.

In þis ȝere Ser Thomas Wodstok, herl of Bokyngham, þe
10 kyngis vncil, Hugo Caluirlé, Robert Knollis, Thomas Percy,
William Wyndesore, proued knytes, tok þe se to help Ser Jon
Mountforth, duke of Bretayn. Thei myte not lond þere for þe
multitude of galeies whech þe king of Frauns had hired. Therfor
þei turned agayn to Caleis and riden be lond þorw Frauns, where
15 þei brent and killid withoute ony resistens.

In þat same tyme deyed þe king of Frauns, and beqwath þe
crowne to his ȝonger broþir, duk of Burgon, for whech cause þe
elder broþir, duke of Angoye, reysid batayle ageyn his broþir,
profitable to hem þat were in Britayn. But ȝet, be fauour of þe
20 lordis, þis ȝonger broþir was crowned, a child but x ȝere old. In
his begynnyng was grete trouble in þe lond for greuous taxes þat
were reysid of þe puple. The lordis were fayn to fle, and eke þe
Januensis were killyd, where þei myte be get. For þoo xxv galeies
receyued euery day seuene hundred and fifty pound; and þis
25 payment lastid fro þe beginning of May onto þe last ende of
August. Thus was þe mony of þe | regne consumed.

In þis ȝere, at þe fest of Seynt Martyn, was a parlement at
Norhampton, where was reysid a greuous taske, whech mad mech
troubyl in þis lond. For euery religious man and euery religious
30 woman was compelled for to pay a nobil; and seculer prestis
payed as mech; eke euery man and woman þat were weddid payed
XIId. for her hed.

2 Pope] P, *om.* M   5 a ple] *suprascript* M   6 ple] *om.* P   7 of]
in P   8 dymes] d *altered from* t M   10 Hugo] Hewe P   15 þei] i
suprascript with caret M   withoute] oute *suprascript* M   18 reysid] rered P
broþir (2)] brothyr P, boþir M   19 þe] *om.* P   24 day] *in r.h. margin* M
28 taske] tax P   30 compelled] *change to darker ink for* lled M

4–8: cf. Walsingham, *Hist. Ang.* ii. 389/15–391/36, 391/38–392/22.
9–15: cf. ibid. i. 434/24–435/23.
16–26: cf. ibid. 440/34–446/19.
27–32: cf. ibid. 449/1–30.

In þe v ȝere of Richard Jon Wiclef resumed þe eld dampned
opinion of Berengari, þat seide, aftir þe consecracion of Cristis
body, bred remayned as it was before. Mani foul errouris multiplied Wiclef, more þan Berengari: that Crist was þere, as he is in
oþir places, but sumwhat more specialy; that þis bred was no 5
bettir þan oþir bred, saue only for þe prestis blessing; and, if
Cristis bodi was þere, it was possible to a man forbreke Cristis
nek. He seid eke it was lasse synne to worchip a tode þan þe
sacrament, 'for þe tode hath lyf, and þe sacrament non'.

In þis ȝere Edmund Langlé, erl of Cambrigge, and vnkil to 10
þe king, with William Beucham, Mathew Gurnay, and many oþir
expert in bataile, went into Portingale to help þe kyng ageyn
þe hethen Spaynardis. And aftir þei had dwelled þere too ȝere,
þe Spaynardis were weri of hem, and were acorded to þe kyng
of Portingale, and þei of Portingale were eke wery of hem, for 15
ryueling and oppression. Thus cam þe erl hom on|to Ynglond   f. 84ᵛᵇ
with his wyf, þe ȝonger douter of Kyng Petir, kyng of Castile in
Spayn; and a son of his, first begotyn in Ynglond, was weddid
þere to þe kyngis dowtir of Portingale.

In þis ȝere, in þe monthe of May, þe comones risen ageyn þe 20
kyng and þe lordes, and in her wodnes þei kyllid þe bischop of
Cauntirbiry, Simon Sudbury, chaunceler, and Ser Robert Hales,
tresorer, whech was priour of Seynt Jones. Her duke was Wat
Tyler, a proude knaue and malapert. Anoþir capteyn was þere fast
be Bury, þei cleped Jon Wraw, a preest. He heded þe abbot of 25
Bury, and fast be Bury he killid þe principal justise, Jon Caundisch.
There was with him anoþir malefactour, Robert Westbrom, whech
named himself kyng. There smet þei of þe prioris heed, with oþir
munkis and seculeris. Fast be Norwich rose anoþir wrech, cleped
Jak Lister; he smet of þe hed of þat nobyl knyte, Ser Robert Salle. 30
At Hely þei killid a man of cort þei clepid Edmund Galon. For her
entent was to kille all þe men þat lerned ony lawe, and in hate of
hem þei brent her place at London, clepid Tempil-barre. Eke þe

1 of Richard] *om.* P   3–4 multiplied] P, multipled M   8 a tode]
suprascript M   13 dwelled] be P   16 onto Ynglond] *om.* P   21 þei] i
inserted on the line in paler ink M   24 Tyler] r *suprascript* M   25 a]
suprascript M   30 Jaf] Jek M, Jake P   31 clepid] called P

1–9: cf. ibid. 450/9–25.
10–19: cf. ibid. 453/1–35, and ii. 82/21–83/27.
20–186/15: cf. ibid. i. 453/36–484/17, and ii. 1/1–15/16.

duke of Lancastir place, cleped Sauey, and þe hous of Seynt Jones
at Clerkenwelle þei lete brenne vii dayes. At Seynt Albones mad
þei gret destruccioun in housing, brenning dedis and chartoris;
all clausures of wodis þei distroyed, bokis and rolles of cortis and
5   obligaciones þei rent and brent. But sone aftir, þis sedicious man,

f. 85ʳᵃ Wat Tiler, was killid at | London be þe handis of William Wal-
worth, meir of London. Than was Jon Straw taken, and befor
his deth he mad þis confession openly:—

When we were on þe Blakheth and sent aftir þe kyng, if
10   he had come onto vs, we schuld a killid all þe lordes and
gentilmen þat cam with him, and led him with us to make þe
puple to suppose þat he were auctour of oure rising, aftir þat
to sle þe kyng, and þan ech of us schuld haue þe reule in
dyuers places of Ynglond and make lawes aftir oure owne
15   fantasies.

In þis same ȝere cam into Ynglond þe kyng of Bem sistir,
Anne, for to be maried to þe king.

In þe sexte ȝere of Richard was þis mariage performed with
gret solempnité and justis of pes.

20   And in þe same ȝere Edmund Mortimer, erl of March, deied
in Yrland, whan he had caused in þat lond ful grete pes.

And in þat same tyme Jon Wraw, prest, leder of riseris at Mildnale, was hang and drawe be auctorité of þe parlement at London.

In þe xii day of June, in þe ix houre, was a gret erdqwaue in
25   Ynglond.

In þis same ȝere Vrbane þe pope ordeyned þat þe vigile of
natiuité of oure Lady schuld be fastid.

In þe seuenet ȝere, in þe month of March, in þe parlement at
London Ser Herry Spenser, bischop of Norwich, was markyd with
30   þe cros ageyn þe scismatikes of Frauns and of Flaundres, with grete

---

7 Jon] Jac P   15 fantasies] fantasy P   21 ful] full P, *om.* M
22 And] P, *om.* M   tyme] *suprascript* M   22–3 at Mildnale] *om.* P
24 gret erdqwaue in] *over erasure* M   26 same] sam P, *om.* M   ȝere]
suprascript M   27 natiuité] þe natiuite P

1–15: see p. 185.
16–17: cf. Walsingham, *Hist. Ang.* ii. 46/1–34.
18–19: cf. ibid. 47/36–48/9.
20–1: cf. ibid. 49/13–16.
22–3: cf. ibid. 63/1–9.
24–5: cf. ibid. 67/1–4.
28–187/9: Walsingham, *Chron. Ang.* 355/19–356/14; cf. *Hist. Ang.* ii.
    71/33–80/8, 84/11–99/24.

auctorité of Vrbane þe Sexte, and aboute myd May he went into
Flaundres with myty hand, and with a saute he took Grauening,
and aftir þat Dunkirk, Neuport, and | many oþir. And in þe viii   f. 85ʳᵇ
kalende of Juli he faute with xxx þousand scismatikes, he hauyng
but v þousand, where he killid seuene þousand of Frenschmen,   5
Fleminges, and Britones, and of his hoost were ded but seuene men.
Than beseged he þe town of Ypris, and þere was he deceyued and
rebuked be þe couetise of too knytes, Ser William Elman, and Ser
Thomas Tryuet.

In þis tyme þe kyng of Frauns besegid þe town of Burburgh, in   10
whech were þat tyme þe Lord Bemound, Thomas Triuet, William
Elman, and William Faringdoun, knytes, and aftir many sawtes,
whech availed not, þe kyng profered hem þis issew, þat þei, with her
seruauntis and her hors and swech tresore as þei wold cary oute of
þe town, schuld passe frely, up condicion þat þei schuld streite go   15
to Ynglond, and to þis profir þei obeyid, and cam hom to Yngland.
In þe same forme þe kyng of Frauns acordid with þe bischop, and
he cam hom fro Grauenyng, but first he distroyed þe town.

In þis same tyme was ordeyned be þe kyng of Frauns a grete
nauy to lette hem þat were sent be þe kyng of Ynglond to help þe   20
bischop of Norwich. And þei of Dertemouthe and Portesmouthe
distroyed all þat hoost saue ix men. Than þe vyntage of Ynglond
took a othir felauchip, where þei hadde a þousand tunne wyn and
v hundred.

In þe viii ȝere of Richard, þe duke of Lancastir sailed into Frauns,   25
and þere mad a trews betwix both londis for half a ȝere.

And in the | same ȝere, befor Lenton, þe same duke, with   f. 85ᵛᵃ
Thomas, erl of Bokyngam, his brothir, and with a gret noumbyr,
went into Scotlond. That aspied of Scottis, þei fled ouyr þe se,
and summe hidde hem in forestis. So þe Englisch host was fayn   30
to com hom ageyn, compelled for cold and hungir.

---

3 many] may P   þe] P, *om.* M   6 men] P, *om.* M   9 Thomas]
Thonas P   11 William] and William P   15 streite] streyt P, streight
with ght *in later hand over erasure* M   19 þis] the P   21 Dertemouthe]
Dortesmouth P   22 þat] the P   28 and] *suprascript* M   29 Scottis]
þe Scottis P   30 host] *suprascript* M   31 to] *om.* P

10–18: Walsingham, *Chron. Ang.* 356/16–357/12; cf. *Hist. Ang.* ii. 100/15–
    103/42.
19–24: cf. Walsingham, *Hist. Ang.* ii. 106/14–32.
25–6: Walsingham, *Chron. Ang.* 358/10–15.
27–31: ibid. 358/24–359/2.

In þis ȝere, in þe xx day of August, in þe fest of Seynt Oswyn
þe kyng, at Newcastell upon Tyne a wryte hew on a tre whech
schuld long to a schip, and at euery strook he smet ran owte blood
as it had be a beste. He beþout him of þe festful day and left his
5　werk. His felaw stood beside, hauyng no reuerens to þis myracle,
took þe ax, and smet, and anon blod ran owte. He fel for fer, and
cryed mercy, and al þe town merueylid and gaf worchip to God.
The tre was bore to Tynmowth in token of þis myracle.

In þe ix ȝere of þis kyng, Jon Wyclef, þe orgon of þe deuel, þe
10　enmy of þe Cherch, þe confusion of men, þe ydol of heresie, þe
merour of ypocrisie, þe norcher of scisme, be þe rithful dome of
God was smet with a horibil paralsie þorwoute his body. And þis
venjauns fel upon him on Seynt Thomas day, in Cristmasse, but
he deyed not til Seynt Siluestir day. And worþily was he smet on
15　Seynt Thomas day, ageyn whom he had gretely ofendid, letting
men of þat pilgrimage; and conueniently deied he in Siluestir fest,
ageyn whom he had venemously berkid for dotacion of þe Cherch.

f. 85ᵛᵇ　In þis ȝere | Pope Urbane degraded þese cardinales, Ser Adam
Eston, monk of Norwych, of þe title of Seint Cecile, and þe
20　cardinal of Venice, cardinal of Jene, whech were worchipful men
and Professoures of Diuinité. Oþir iii cardinalis were men of
gret birth and good condicion. The vii was Cardinal Reatinense,
a Doctour of Lawe, on whom þe pope put defaute of al þe conspiracion þat he schuld fauour þe kyng of Cicile ageyn þe pope.
25　For þe pope had promised many þingis to þis king, and noþing
fulfillid. But aftir þis þe kyng besegid þe pope in a town þei clepe
Lucery, where þe pope was compelled to make pes with him,
and so with grete difficulté he fled.

In þis same ȝere fel a contrauersie betwix þe kyng and þe duke
30　of Lancastir, in-so-mech þat summe of þe kyngis hous had con-

---

1 in (1)] om. P　　　2 Tyne] tyme P　　　wryte] wright in later hand over
erasure M, wryȝt P　　　4 his] om. P　　　8 token] worschyp & token P
10–11 heresie þe merour of] om. P　　　11 þe (2)] om. P　　dome] hand P
14 worþily] ryȝtfully P　　16 he] in r.h. margin M　　19 Eston] om. P
20 Venice cardinal of] om. P　　worchipful] worschipschipfull P　　21 Diuinité]
Dinite P　　22 gret] good P　　27 Lucery] Luceri or Luceme P

1–8: Walsingham, Chron. Ang. 360/27–361/15; cf. Hist. Ang. ii. 116/27–
117/17.
9–17: Walsingham, Chron. Ang. 362/19–32.
18–28: ibid. 363/9–364/3; cf. Hist. Ang. ii. 121/4–125/22.
29–189/3: Walsingham, Chron. Ang. 364/6–14; cf. Hist. Ang. ii. 126/7–29.

spired þe dukes deth. That aspied, þe duke vitailed þe castel of
Pountfract and kept him þere, but sone aftirward, be mene of þe
kingis modir, þere was procured pes betwix hem.

In þis same ȝere, at þe feste of Seynt Martyn, was a parlement
at London, where Ser Robert Ver, erl of Oxforth, was mad 5
markeis of Dulyn in Erlond, and Ser Thomas Wodstok, erl of
Bokyngham, was mad duke of Gloucetir; his broþir Edmund, erl
of Cambrige, was mad duke of Ȝork; Michael at þe Pool, þan
chaunceler, was mad erle of Suffolk, and graunted of þe kyngis
cophir ȝerly a þousand mark. 10

In þe ten ȝere þe kyng of Armeny cam onto Ynglond to trete
of pes betwix Frauns and Ynglond, but it avay|led neythir partye, f. 86ʳᵃ
for al þe avail turned onto himself; for, beside a þousand pound
þat þe king gaue him in a smal schip of gold, he mad him letteris
patent to receyue euery ȝere a þousand mark. He was put oute of 15
his lond, as he seide, be þe Sarasines, and vndir þat pretens he
gadered mech good of kingis and lordis.

In þis same ȝere þe duke of Lancastir took his viage into Spayn
to chalenge his rite þat longid onto him because of his wif,
Constauns, whech was elder dowtir and eyir to þe king of Spayn, 20
Petir. And because þat þe Spaynardis were scismatikes, þe Pope
Vrban graunted euery man in þat viage plener remission of synne
þat wold go with þe duke or gyue ony good to his viage. As he went
toward Spayn he took þe castel of Brest in Bretayne, and delyueryd it fro þe malice of Frenschmen, whech had layd þere a sege. 25
Fro þens he sayled into þe port of Groyne. Of þis viage we wil
sey more aftir.

In þis same ȝere þe duke of Ostrich, enmy to þe Pope Vurbane,
troubled wrongfully þe pilgrimes þat went to Rome, and constreyned hem to pay grete tribute, to þis entent, þat men schuld not 30

2 Pountfract] Pounctfract P   sone] P, om. M   aftirward] aftir P   4 þis]
thys þis P   5 Oxforth] Oxenforth P   6 Ser] P, om. M   7 broþir]
brothyr P, boþir M   8 was mad] om. P   9 was mad] om. P
10 mark] pownd P   11 onto] into P   13 onto] to P   16–17 he
seide . . . kingis] over erasure M   17 and] in l.h. margin M   20 þe]
suprascript M   26 he] om. P   into] to P   27 more] more largely P
28 þis] þe P   29 to] in r.h. margin M   and] P, om. M   30 hem]
suprascript M

4–10: Walsingham, Chron. Ang. 367/9–22.
11–17: ibid. 367/27–368/5; cf. Hist. Ang. ii. 142/1–12.
18–27: Walsingham, Chron. Ang. 368/23–369/9.
28–190/4: ibid. 369/20–370/10.

desire to go to Rome. And for his puple ros ageyn him in þis
cause, allegging þat it was gret hurt onto hem, he gadered a strength
and kyllid many of hem; but þei left not her rebellion, for þei
risen ageyn and killid þe duke and many oþir lordis.

5   This ȝere come tydannes þat þe kyng of Frauns wold besege
f. 86ʳᵇ Caleys, wherfor þe king | sent þidir Herry Percy þe ȝonger, whom
þe Scottis clepid Herry Hatspor. Anon as he cam þidir he had
a gret jornay upon þe Picardis, and brout fro þem a gret pray.
So was þe kyng of Frauns purpos lettid for þat tyme.

10   In þese dayes was it noysed þat þe kyng of Frauns was comyng
to distroye Ynglond, with xv dukes, xxvi erlis, a c knytes, a c m
men, schippis a mcc. He lay at Slus fro þe kalendis of August to
þe vigile of All Seyntis, and neuyr had wynd. Than had he wynd
tyl he was in þe myd se, and þoo turned it contrari, and brak many
15   of his schippis or þei cam to londe. Thus was he frustrat of his
entent, and Ynglond delyueret fro daunger. In þis mene tyme þei
of Londoun were so aferd as þou þe kyng of Frauns had be at her
wallis, þei broke down þe houses þat were ny þe wallis, and sette
up gunnes, and mech aray þei made, and al for nowt.

20   In þis tyme Michael at þe Pool was accused be þe parlement of
certeyn poyntis of treson, and deposed fro his office of chaunceler,
but it plesed not þe kyng, for he restored him aftir þat to þe same
office. And þan conspired þis Mychael the deth of þe duke of
Gloucetir, and of oþir lordis, whech schuld a deied at a soper in
25   London, had not þei be warned be Richard Exston, þan meyhir
of London.

In þe eleuene ȝere of Richard, the erl of Arundel, Richard, and
þe erl of Notingham, Thomas, went to þe se for to seke oute þe

---

4 oþir] *om.* P   5 þat] t *suprascript* M   9 þe kyng of Frauns
purpos] þe purpos of the kyng of Frauns P   10 þese dayes was it] þe same
tyme it was P   11 Ynglond] all Ynglond P   a (1)] P, *om.* M   12 a mcc]
& cc P   Slus] P, Sclus *with* sc *in later hand over erasure* M   15 frustrat] P,
frustat M   15–16 of his entent] of his entend P, *om.* M   16 daunger]
grete drede P   tyme] whyle P   17 so] as (*before* so) *expuncted in red* M,
om. P   þe kyng of] P, *om.* M   19 gunnes] s *over erasure* M   nowt] nougᵗ
with ugᵗ *in later hand over erasure* M, nouth P   20 tyme] P, ty *at line end* M
at þe] de la P   22 restored] d *suprascript* M   24 a deied] *over erasure* M

1–4: see p. 189.
5–9: Walsingham, *Chron. Ang.* 370/12–23.
10–19: ibid. 370/24–371/3, 371/32–372/8, 373/17–27.
20–6: ibid. 372/19–373/5.
27–191/12: ibid. 374/32–375/36; cf. *Hist. Ang.* ii. 153/14–156/19.

þeues, and in þe vigil of þe anunciacion of oure Lady | þei had   f. 86ᵛᵃ
a gret jornay with a naue of Frenschmen, Flemyngis, Normannes,
and Spaynardis. The victori fell on oure side, for in þat viage þei
took a hundred schippis, in whech þei had nyneten þousand
tunnes of wyn. Than remeued þei þe sege of Breste, þat was newly   5
layd, and þere took þei too castellis of tymbyr, whech þe Frenschmen had reysid to destruccion of Breste. The on þei brent, þe
othir left þei in þe castell with þe Englisch dwelleres. This grete
viage was not comendid in þe kyngis hous, for þe duk of Erlond,
Robert Ver, and þe erl of Suffolk, Michael de la Pool, and Symon   10
Burlé, and Richard Sturry, enformed þe kyng þat it was grete
wrong to robbe so good marchauntis.

In þat tyme a frere Carme, cleped Maystir Dys, whech went
with þe duke of Lancastir into Spayn, for reuerens of his lord
procured gret graces of þe cort, amongis whech graces he had   15
power for to receyue men, þat þei schuld be chapuleynis of þe
pope, with all þe libertés þat long þerto. Many men boute þese
graces and mysused hem; amongis whech was a frere Augustyn
þei clepid Petir Patteshul, for, aftir he had þat liberté, he felle in
þe secte of Wiclefistis, and grew to so gret malice þat he sette   20
letteris on Poules dore slaundiring his order and his breþerin on
þe moost malicious wise. At þis mater þe hodid men had grete
joy—hodid men were cleped þanne þoo Lolardis þat wold neuyr
auale her hood in presens of the sacrament; of whech at þat tyme |
þese were þe principales: William Neuyle, Lodewic Clifforth, Jon   f. 86ᵛᵇ
Clambowh, Richard Sturry, Thomas Latymer, and, werst of all,   26
Jon Mountagu, for he reseyued þe sacrament in þe cherch, and
fro his mouth voyded it to his hand, bare it hom, and ete it with his
oystres. Summe write þat Laurens de Sancto Martino ded þis ded,
and of Jon Mountagu þei sei he was a gret distroyer of ymages.   30
In þis ȝere Robert Ver, whom þe kyng had mad duke of Erland,
ros in so grete pride of hert þat, ageyn þe lawe of God, he refused his

6 castellis] castell P   7 destruccion] þe distruccion P   þei brent] brent
þei P   8 dwelleres] men that dwelled ther P   10 and (2)] om. P
11 Richard] P, Rich' M   13 Carme] Carmelite P   17 þerto] in r.h.
margin M   20 so] suprascript M   22 wise] maner P   26 Richard]
Ric' M, Ryc' P   and werst of all] om. P   27 Mountagu] Mounagew P
28 fro his mouth] om. P   30 Jon] P, J. M

13–30: Walsingham, Chron. Ang. 376/25–378/10; cf. Hist. Ang. ii. 157/
  10–159/21, and see note to 191/27–9 in Commentary.
31–192/20: Walsingham, Chron. Ang. 378/12–379/10.

wif, a fayre woman and good, and eke born of grete blood, for
Kyng Edward dowtir was hir modyr. The woman whech he weddid
aftir þis rejeccion cam oute of Bem, a sadeler doutir, hir name was
Lancecrone. The kyng gaf fauour to þis mater, but þe lordes were
5 wroth with it, specialy þe duke of Gloucestir, vncle of þe forseid
Ysabel, þat þoute sumtyme to set remedy in þis mater. This was
not onknowe to Robert Ver, and þerfor be sotil ymaginacion he
þoute for to distroye þe duke of Gloucetir. Now was Pase-day
go—at whech tyme þis Duke Robert had behestid he schuld a
10 be in Erland—for whech cause, and þat þe lordes among hem
schuld not gruch, þe kyng led him into Wales fer fro his enmyes,
whech were þe duke of Gloucetir, þe erles of Arundel, Warwyc,
Derby, and Notyngham, and oþir; for þese were þe lordis þat þe
kyng hated moost at þe instigacion of Michael at þe Pool, Robert
15 Tresilian, justice, Alisaundre Neuyle, bischop of Ȝork, þis Robert
f. 87ʳᵃ Ver, and oþir many. Thus þe | kyng taried with þe duke and
Michael in Walis tyl, as he supposed, þe lordes conjecture was
sesed, and þan cam he home with him onto þe castel of Notyngham. Thidir cleped he to councel all swech men whech were not
20 weel-wyllid to þe duke of Gloucetir and his felauchip.

In þe xii ȝere the kyng, abyding at Notyngham, wrot to þe
scryues of Ynglond þat no knytes ne burgeys schuld be sent onto
þe parlement but swech as þe kyng wold chese. And to þis peticion
was answerd ful scharply þat þe usage had be þat þe comones
25 schuld chese þe knytes and þese burgeises, and þat it was ful hard
to put hem fro her liberté.

Than were þese justises cleped before þe kyng: Robert Tresilian,
principal justise, and Robert Belknap, cheef for þe Bench, with his
felawes, Jon of Holt, Roger Fulþorp, William of Borow, knytis
30 and justises. These were charged before þe kyng, upon her feith
and ligauns, to answere to swech poyntis as schuld be layde before

8 to] P, *om.* M   10 and] P, *om.* M   11 into Wales fer fro] to Wales
and fro *over erasures* M   13 Notyngham] P, Bokyngham M   14 þe (1)]
om. P   at þe] de la P   15–16 þis Robert Ver] P, *om.* M   16 oþir
many] many othyr P   kyng] duke P   duke] kyng P   and (2)] *suprascript*
M   18 home] P, *om.* M   22 onto] to P   23 wold] schuld P
24 answerd] *over erasure* M   ful] P, *om.* M   25 þese] the P   28 Belknap]
Belkap P   28–9 with his felawes] *om.* P   29 of (1)] *om.* P   of (2)] *om.* P
knytis] knȝtes P

1–20: see p. 191.
21–193/17: Walsingham, *Chron. Ang.* 379/18–382/28.

hem. The first was if it were derogacioun to þe regalie þat þe
duke of Gloucetir, with his felauchip, schuld purchace a commission of þe kyng, ageyn þe kyngis wil, as it was seid, to make in-
quisicioun upon þe defautes of Michael de la Pool. Thei answered
al þat it was derogacioun to þe regalie. The secund point was 5
what þei were worthi þat purchased swech a commission. Thei
answered, þei were worthi to lese her hedis but if þe king wold
gyue hem grace. The þird was answered þat all þei þat stered þe
kyng to þat | conclusion were worthi þat same peyne. Many oþir   f. 87ʳᵇ
articles were purposed þere, upon whech þe duke of Gloucetir 10
and oþir lordis were endited. And þe forseid justises seled al þis
with her seles, and Jon Lokton, serjaunt, Alexander of Ʒork,
Robert of Dulyn, archbiscoppis, eke þe bischop of Dorham,
bischop of Chestir, Robert Ver, duk of Erlond, Michael de la Pol,
erl of Suffolk, Jon Ripon, clerk, Jon Blake, swyere. And aftir þis 15
endytment þe kyng sent onto þe most powerful of þe lond þat
þei schuld strength him in his rite.

The tydingis of þis endytment cam to þe knowlech of þe duke of
Gloucetir, and he clepid to him þe bischop of London and many
othir lordes, and þere, befor þe bischop, he swore on þe holy gospel 20
þat it was neuyr his purpos, ne his wil, for to purpos noþing ageyn
þe welfare of þe kyng, saue þat he coude not loke meryly on þe
duke of Yrland, whech had so horribyly disparaged a lady þat was
ny cosyn to þe kyng and to him.

And whan þe bischop had mad þis report to þe king, and his 25
hert in maner was stered to beneuolens to his vncil and þe oþir
lordis, Michael de la Pool, þat stod beside, dreding þat, if þe duke
were reconciled onto þe king, it wold bring him onto grete schame,
anon began to reproue þe grete rebellion of the duke and þe sotil

9 þat (1)] *in r.h. margin* M   11 justises] justise P   12 Alexander]
Alex' M, Alysaundr P   13 of (1)] *om.* P   archbiscoppis] archbyschop P
eke þe] P, *om.* M   14 Robert] P, R M   Michael] Michaell P, M. M
16 endytment] P, endyment M   onto] P, vnto *with* vn *in later hand over
erasure* M   powerful] power MP   þe (3)] thys P   17 strength him in
his] rength him in hi *over erasure* M   rite] right *in later hand over erasure* M,
ryӡte P   21 wil] *in r.h. margin* M   23–4 þat was ny] *over erasure* M
26 in maner was stered] was stered in maner P   stered] *suprascript with caret*
(*in red*) M   28 onto (1)] to P   him onto] hem to P   29 to] P, *om. over
line division* M

18–24: ibid. 382/28–383/3.
25–194/7: ibid. 383/3–12; cf. *Hist. Ang.* ii. 162/34–163/9.

ymaginaciones ageyn þe kyngis seruauntis. To him þe bischop
answerd,

> Hold þi pees, þou Michael! It becomth þe rite euel to sey
> swech wordis, þou þat art dampned for þi falshed, booth be
> 5 þe lordes and be þe parlement.

f. 87ᵛᵃ At þis word þe kyng was so wroth | þat he comaunded þe bischop
to voyde fro his presens.

The bischop told all þis to þe duke of Gloucetir, and he told it
to his felawes, and sone aftir þei all were gadered with her powere
10 in a wood fast by London cleped Haryngey.

Whan þe kyng wyst þat þei were þere he dred mech þat gaderyng,
and with his councel took avisament what myte best be do in þis
mater. Than sent he þe duke of Erlond into Lancastirschere and
Chestirschere to gadir him puple, with whech puple he myte make
15 resistens ageyn þese lordes. That cam onto þe lordis eres, and þei,
with anoþir puple, rood up to Oxenforth; þere met þei with þis
duke of Erlond, and in fayre maner turned al þe puple hom ageyn
to her cuntré. Robert Ver fled anon as he say þese lordes. This
puple, or þei went, submitted hem to þe duke of Gloucetir, and
20 delyueryd him King Richard baner, whech Robert Ver broute hem.

Than cam þese v lordis, with her host, to Londoun, and leid
hem aboute London lich as þei schuld besege it. The kyng lay
þann in þe Tour. And þei of London sent þe keyis of þe cité to
þese lordes, seying þat þei were wolkom.

25 Than sent þe kyng for hem into þe Tour, þat þei schuld come
and telle þe cause why þei had rered swech a power. The duke of
Gloucetir had þe wordis:—

> Souereyn Lord, 3e schal vndirstand þat we be, and schul
> be, onto 3ou as trew ligemen as ony be in 3oure lond. But þe

---

3 þi] þei P   4 be] of P   9 and] *om.* P   aftir] P, *om.* M   all]
om. P   10 Haryngey] Haryngey Park P, Harnasey *with* nasey *in later hand
over erasure* M   13–14 and Chestirschere] *om.* P   14 with whech
puple] þat P   15 onto] to P   16 anoþir] all her P   þis] þe P
19 Gloucetir] u *suprascript* M   20 him] *suprascript* M   broute] brou3t
P, broûte M   21 with her host] *om.* P   22 schuld] wold P   23 þann]
om. P   28 be] be onto yow P

1–7: see p. 193.
8–10: Walsingham, *Chron. Ang.* 383/12–32.
11–20: ibid. 384/1–385/33; cf. *Hist. Ang.* ii. 164/15–169/13.
21–4: Walsingham, *Chron. Ang.* 386/32–387/17.
25–195/5: cf. Walsingham, *Hist. Ang.* ii. 171/28–172/30.

cause of oure commocyon is þat certeyn malefactoris, whech
be euyr hid vndir ȝour | proteccioun, be not correct aftir þe   f. 87ᵛᵇ
desire of ȝoure lordis and ȝoure comounes.

Than þe kyng graunted hem to set a parlement, in whech all
þese þingis schuld be correcte.   5
Whan þis was graunted Michael de la Pool took a schip in
Humbir, and sailed into Frauns, and þere he deyed. Robert Ver
sailed into Midelborow, and cam neuyr hom. Alexaundir Neuyle
deied at Dunbar, in Scotlond.

At þe parlement þese men were condempned to dyuers prisones: 10
Simon Burlé, William Helman, Nicholas Dagworth, Jon Golofir,
knytis of þe kyngis hous, Jon Clifforth, prest, Nicholas Slake,
clerk, were condempned to þe castell of Notingam; Jon Beuchamp,
steward of þe kyngis hous, Thomas Tryuet, Jon Salesbury, knytes,
Jon Lincoln, clerk, were assined to Douyr; James Benerles, knyte,   15
Richard Mutforth, clerk, were sent onto Bristow. Alle þese folowing
were swore þat þei schuld not com in þe kingis hous tyl þei had leue
be þe parlement: Jon Fordam, bischop of Doram, Frer Thomas
Russoc, of þe Dominices, bischop of Chestir, and confessour to
þe kyng, þe Lordis Souch, Louel, Burnel, Beuchamp, Camuse, and   20
Clifforth, and þese ladies, þe Lady Moyne, þe Lady Powningis,
and þe Lady Moleyns. This Thomas Russok was sent to no prison,
but cleped before þe juges and condempned gilty to þese euel
lederis of þe kyng in his ȝong age, and because he was a bischop,
and men had not herd þat ony bischop schuld be in prison, þerfor   25
þe court voyded, and he stood stille at þe barre. Sone aftir cam
a knyte and | bad þe bischop go to his in; for aftir þat he was   f. 88ʳᵃ
exiled into Yrlond.

In þis parlement þe lordes desired of þe kyng to make his
sacramental oth byfore þe puple, because þe oth whech he had   30
mad before was in his childhod. And so ded þe kyng, and all

8 into] vnto P   10 dyuers] certeyn P   15 James] s *suprascript* M
Benerles] Beverle P   16 were sent] wer sent P, *om.* M   onto] to P
17 þei (2)] i *inserted on the line in darker ink* M   18 be] of P   20 þe (2)]
þese P   20–1 Souch Louel Burnel Beuchamp Camuse and Clifforth] Lord
Souch Lord Lovel Lord Burnel Lord Beucham Lord Camuse Lord Clyfford P
21 þe (1)] *om.* P   þe (2)] *om.* P   22 and þe] *om.* P   25 in] *suprascript* M

10–16: cf. ibid. 173/9–19.
16–22: cf. ibid. 172/35–173/9.

þe lordis and states of þe parlement mad her new othis to be
trewe ligemen to her kyng.

Aftir þe feste of Pentecost, þe erl of Arundel, Richard, was mad
Amyrel of þe Se, and iiii score schippis of oure enmyes he took or
5　brent, and fewe men were lefte o-lyue þat were in hem. Than took
he þese yles: Bas, Vs, Ré, Lemustre, Rochel, Olun, and Olorum,
where þe lawes of þe se were mad.

Aftir þe fest of natiuité of oure Lady was a parlement at Cambrige, in whech parlement were mad many statutes: of seruauntis
10　heres; of open beggeres, þat þei schuld not begge but in þe townes
where þei dwelle; of bering of armour, not withouten grete cause;
of pleyes, that non schuld be used but schotyng; and þe stapil
schuld be remeued fro Mydilborow to Caleys; and þat no prest
schuld purchace no benefice at Rome withoute leue of þe kyng.

15　In þis tyme Ser Thomas Tryuet, in þe kyngis presens, betwix
Bernwelle and Cambrige, with a falle fro his hors brake his
bowelis and deyid.

In þe xiii ȝere of þis king, þe kyng sodeynly cleped his houshold
togidir, and inqwired of hem what age he was of, and sum saide
20　xx, sum saide xxii. Than saide the kyng,

f. 88ʳᵇ
　　Sith I am of sufficient age, it is not wel þat my condicioun |
　　schuld be wers þan oþir þat dwelle in my lond. I am, as ȝe
　　sey, of sufficient age to gouerne my lordis and my puple.
　　Before þis tyme I haue lyued vndir gouernaunce; now wil
25　　I take þe gouernauns upon me.

And anon he comaundid þe chaunceler to resigne þe sel, and
forth anon he took þe sel to Ser William Wikkam, bischop of
Wynchestir, and mad all newe officeres. The duke of Gloucetir

---

2 her] þe P　　　6 Bas Vs Re Lemustre Rochel Olun and Olorum]
þe yle of Bas þe yle of Vs þe yle Lemuster þe yles Olym and Olorum P
8 natiuité] þe natiuite P　　　9 many] om. P　　　10 heres] hyr P
12 pleyes] playes with a in later hand over erasure M　　　12–14 and þe stapil
. . . þe kyng] om. P　　　18 sodeynly cleped] cleped sodenly P　　　19 of (2)] om. P
20 saide (1)] om. P　　　22 wers] worss with orss in later hand over erasure M,
werr P　　　as] om. P

3–7: cf. Walsingham, *Hist. Ang.* ii. 175/5–13.
8–14: cf. ibid. 177/2–11.
15–17: cf. ibid. 177/16–20.
18–197/2: cf. ibid. 181/10–182/3.

and þe erl of Warwyk he remeued fro his councell, and pulled in othir þat plesed bettir his yȝe.

In þis same tyme flatereres þat were aboute þe king told þe kyng þat þe duke of Gloucetir had gadered a gret hoost to destruccioun of þe kyng and his frendis. The kyng sent aftir þe duke, and þere 5 was prouyd fals al þat euir was seyd. And whan þe duke began to declare his innocens, to confusion and schame of hem þat stood in þe kyngis presens, þe kyng prayed þe duke for al þe loue þat was betwix hem þat he schuld hold his pes.

In þis same ȝere, at þe fest of Seynt Jon Baptiste, was take a 10 trews betwix Frauns and Ynglond, and both kyngis swore þat it schuld be kept iii ȝere.

In þis tyme were many miracules do at Hely and Bridlington, and fast by Wymundam, at a crosse whech þei clepe West Wade.

This ȝere deyed Mychael at þe Pool in þe cyté of Paris.   15

And þis same ȝere Vrbane þe pope ordeyned þat þe jubilé schuld be broute fro l ȝere onto xxxiii, aftir Cristis age.

In þis tyme þe disciples | of Wiclef grew in so grete erroure þat f. 88ᵛᵃ her prestis tok upon hem for to sacre prestis. Thei saide þat 'euery prest hath as grete power as þe pope'. All þis erroure began 20 first in þe diocyse of Salesbury. Thei prechid openly ageyn pilgrimage, and specialy Walsingham, and þe rode of north dore. The bischoppis of þis lond saide rite nowt to þis mater, but kepte hem in her houses, and opened no mouth to berk ageyn þese erroneous doggis.   25

In þis ȝere deyid Pope Vrbane, and aftir him was intronized Bonifacius þe IX.

In þe beginning of Nouembir, þis ȝere, Ser Jon, duke of

1 and (1)] *change to darker ink* M   3 þis] þe P   flatereres] flateres P
11 betwix] betwene P   12 iii] for iii P   14 and] *change to darker ink* M
17 be] *in r.h. margin with carets* (*in red*) M   onto] to P   18 Wiclef]
Wichelse P   19 upon] on *suprascript* M   for] *om.* P   20 All] And P
22 north dore] nordor P   23 rite nowt] right noȝt *with* ght noȝt *in later hand*
over erasure M, ryȝt nowt P   to] onto P   28 þis ȝere] *om.* P

3–9: cf. ibid. 182/6–13.
10–12: cf. ibid. 182/19–20.
13–14: cf. ibid. 183/30–185/29, 189/10–26.
15: cf. ibid. 187/21–7.
16–17: cf. ibid. 187/31–188/3.
18–25: cf. ibid. 188/13–34.
26–7: cf. ibid. 193/1–12.
28–198/20: cf. ibid. 193/14–194/32.

Lancastir, þat had be in Gyan and Spayn iii ȝere, cam hom, saued
fro many pereles. For many of his men in Spayn, for hungir and
cold and pouerté, fled fro him onto þe Frensch party, whech were
hired into Spayn to help his enmy, þe kyng of Castill. And þe
5 Frenschmen receyued hem as her breþerin, and refreschid hem in
al goodly maner. The duke, whan he had aspied þe miseri of his
hoost, with wepyng teres he cried to God, prayng him of his
coumfort. And oure Lord, þat neuyr forsakith hem þat be desolat,
sent him redy coumfort; for his aduersarie, þe kyng of Castile,
10 towchid only be oure Lord, sent onto him embassiatouris for to
trete for pes. Than were þei þus acordid, þat þe son of þe kyng of
Castile schuld wedde þe douter of þe duke and Dame Cunstauns,
whech Cunstauns was doutir to King Petir of Spayn; and þe
f. 88ᵛᵇ childirn of hem ii schuld be eyeres of Spayn; | and if þere come no
15 frute of hem too, þan schuld þe heritage remayne to þe duke son
of ȝork, whech duke was broþir to þe duke of Lancastir, and had
weddid þe ȝonger doutir of þat same Petir, kyng of Spayne. These
comnauntis were confermed with writing, and a gret summe of
gold goue to þe duke, and letteris mad for to receyue his lyue, and
20 his duchesse lyue, euery ȝere x m pound.

In þis same ȝere Jon Hasting, erl of Penbrok, in justing in þe
presens of þe kyng, was wounded to þe deth. He þat smet him hite
Ser Jon Seint Jon. It was seid of þat kynrod þat, fro þat tyme
of Eymer of Valauns, whech was on of þe juges þat sat on þe deth
25 of Thomas of Lancastir, onto þis Jon, þat þere was neuir erl of
Penbrok þat say his fader.

And þis same ȝere was Thomas of Lancastir canonized, for it
was seid of him comounly þat he schuld neuyr be canonized
onto þe tyme þat all þe juges þat sat upon him were ded, and al
30 her issew.

1 Lancastir] Lacastir P   Spayn] in Spayn P   2 For] *om.* P   3 onto]
on P   6 al] *change to darker ink* M   8 forsakith] forsoke P   10 onto]
to P   11 for] *om.* P   12 Cunstauns] Constauns P, Custauns M   14 ii]
(*? in later hand*) *over erasure* M   17 same] *om.* P   19 goue] gove P,
geuĕ *with 1st* e (*over erasure*) *and nasal titulus both in later hand* M   22 presens]
pres *altered from* ju M   þe (2)] *om.* P   hite] was P   24 of (1)] þat P
26 say] sey P, saw *with* w *in later hand over erasure* M   28 of him] of hym
P, *om.* M   29 upon] on P

1–20: see p. 197.
21–6: cf. Walsingham, *Hist Ang.* ii. 195/19–31.
27–30: cf. ibid. 195/32–3.

In þe xiiii ȝere of Richard Bonifacius þe IX ordeyned þat þe
fest of þe visitacioun of oure Lady schuld be saide of all Christen
men.

In þis ȝere fel gret distauns betwix þe kyng and þe cité of London,
for þei wold not lende him a þousand pound. And þe kyng pryued 5
hem of her libertés, and ordeyned þat þei schuld no meyhir haue,
but a wardeyne, whech was first Edmund Dalyngbrig, and aftir
him Baldewyn Radyngton. Than payed þei grete good to haue
her liberté ageyn.

This ȝere þe kyng of Frauns fel in a frenesi, and þe cause was, | 10
as it is saide, for an ontrew bataile whech he rered ageyn þe duke of f. 89ra
Bretayn. And all his lyf, as long as þe wedir was hote, his seknes
cesed neuyr; in wyntir and in cold it greued not mech.

In þis same ȝere deyed Robert Ver in Louayn, sumtyme duke
of Erlond, now desolat and pore.   15

And in þis ȝere Ser Adam, munk of Norwich, and cardinal, þat
was deposed by Vrbane þe pope, now was restored be Bonifas,
his successour. It is seid comounly þat þis Urbane was a very
tiraunt, and þis Cardinal Adam lettid him mech of his wrong
desire, and for þis cause and non oþir he deposed þis Adam and 20
put him in prison, for þis was his open confession whan he
schuld deye. At instauns of þis Cardinal Adam, þe Pope Bonifas
mad a declaracion upon þe plener remission þat is graunted
men be certeyn indulgens, þat þis remission is not verily had,
þouȝ a man be schryue in many pereles, til his last ende at 25
his deth.

In þis ȝere Ser Herri, erl of Derby, sailed into Prus, where, with
help of þe marchale of Prus and of a kyng þat hite Witot, he
ouyrcam þe kyng of Lettow, and mad him for to fle. Thre of his
dukes he took, and foure dukes he killid, with many lordis, and 30
knytis and swieres mo þan thre hundred.

1 In þe xiiii] *over erasure* M   ȝere] *suprascript* M   of Richard] P, *om.* M
Bonifacius] *change to darker ink* M   3 men] P, *om.* M   8 Radyngton]
dadyngtoun P   11 whech] þat P   13 and in] *twice* P   21 in] P,
om. M   22 þe] þis P   Bonifas] *om.* P   25 pereles] perelles P, *pe*rereles M

1–3: cf. ibid. 207/17–21.
4–9: cf. ibid. 207/30–211/22.
10–13: cf. ibid. 212/3–10.
14–15: cf. ibid. 212/11–14.
16–26: cf. ibid. 197/11–26.
27–31: cf. ibid. 197/28–198/3.

In þis ʒere þe kyng of Frauns sent worchipful men into Ynglond
for to haue a perpetuel pes, and, þat it schuld be þe more ferme
and stabil, it was desired þat þe kyngis schuld speke togider in sum
f. 89rb place ny be Caleys. This was graunted, | and þerfor King Richard
5 sent to all þe abbeyes of þis lond to puruey him grete hors and to
lende him mony to þis jornay. Thei þat were messageres saide
it was conuenient þat religious men with her goodes schuld help
to swech tretis of pes. The hors þat were asked of abeyes schuld
be in pris xx libras. The lone þat was asked was no lesse þan l mark.
10 In þese dayes was proclamacion, be consent of þe kyng, þat
eueri benefised man þat was in þe cort of Rome schuld be at hom
in þe fest of Seynt Nicholace. This cry stoyned gretly þe court,
and caused þat þe pope sent an abbot to the kyng, brynging swech
message. First, he comendid þe kyng of his feith and treuth, þat
15 he held euyr with þe Cherch ageyn þe antipope, whech antipope
was gretly supported be þe kyngis of Frauns and of Spayne.
Than saide he þat þe pope merueyled mech of certeyn statutes
whech were mad in þis lond ageyn þe liberté of þe Cherch, and
for þe pope supposed þat it was not þe kyngis wil, þerfor he sent
20 his messager to stere þe king þat swech statutes schuld be abrogat
whech be ageyn þe liberté of Holy Cherch, specialy þese too:
Quare impedit, and *Premuniri facias*. Also he notified onto þe
kyng þat 'þe antipope and þe kyng of Frauns be þus acordid, þat
þe seid kyng of Frauns, with help of þe duke of Burgony and oþir,
25 schul set þe antipope in þe sete at Rome, and þe same antipope
f. 89va schal make þe kyng of Frauns emperour, and oþir dukes he | schal
endewe in þe lordchippis of Itaile'. Also he enformed þe king what
perel schuld falle if þe antipope and þe kyng were þus acorded,
and þe kyng of Frauns emperour—he schuld be þat wey chalenge
30 þe dominion of Ynglond. 'Therfor þe pope counceleth þe king þat
he schal make no pes with þe kyng of Frauns but on þis condicion,
þat þe king of Frauns schal fauour þe opinion of þe trewe pope,
and suffir non of his puple to fite ageyn him.'

2 for] P, *om.* M   þat] *om.* P   4 be] *om.* P   6 þis] *suprascript
with caret (in red)* M   9 in] of P   þat] that P, *om.* M   was (2)] P, *om.* M
12 Nicholace] ace *over erasure* M   This] *change to darker ink* M   14 his]
om. P   17 mech] sor P   20 stere] excite P   22 Quare] Quar P
onto] to P   27 endewe] mak gret lordes and endewe hem P   28 and
þe kyng] *om.* P   32 of (1)] *suprascript* M

1–9: cf. Walsingham, *Hist. Ang.* ii. 198/32–199/32.
10–201/5: cf. ibid. 199/34–202/10.

These and many oþir þingis were put in delay til þe next
parlement, whech was at Halowmesse, and, as for promociones of
hem þat dwelled at Rome, it wold not be graunted; but, for fauour
of þe pope, þei graunted him his prouysiones til þe nexte parlement.
Othir materes were put in avisament.   5

In þe xv ȝere of þis kyng the duke of Lancastir sailed into
Frauns to trete with þe king of Frauns of þis final pes. And he and
þe bischop of Dorham were led fro Caleys onto þe cité Ambianense,
with a þousand hors of Englischmen, at þe costis of þe kyng of
Frauns. Whan þe treti was do, þei come hom ageyn, and browt   10
with hem treus for o ȝere, þat in þis tyme men myte be auysed
wheþir it was more neccesary to haue werre or pes. And for þis
mater was gadered a councel at Staumforth, where was no more
do but þat þei consented to þis truse.

In þis ȝere was þe duke of Gloucetir sent into Erlond for re-   15
formacion of þe cuntré, of whech | cuntré þe king had mad him f. 89ᵛᵇ
duke. And anon as he was absent his enmyes in þe kyngis hous
cried on þe kyng to clepe him ageyn. It was perel, as þei seide,
þat he schuld go for making of rebelles in þat wilde lond.

In þe xvi ȝere of þis kyng was a parlement at Wynchestir sone 20
aftir Cristmasse, where was graunted a gret summe of good for
þe expensis of þe Dukes Lancastir and Gloucetir, þat schuld
go into Frauns.

In þis same ȝere þe kyng of Frauns daunsed in his halle with iiii
knites, and was arayed lich a wodwous, hauing a streyt cote dippid 25
in rosyn and pich; and sodeynly, with touching of a torch, þe cote
was on fire, and he had brent, had not a lady rysen and pulled him
oute of þe dauns. It was seide þat þis was þe ymaginacion of his
brothir, whech desired to be kyng.

In þis ȝere þe bank and þe chauncelry was translate fro London 30
to ȝork, summe sayd for hate þat þe lordes had to London, summe

---

7 final] i *surmounted by short stroke in red* M   8 Ambianense] Ambianensis P   11 treus] r *suprascript* M   12 was] wer P   14 consented]
d *suprascript* M   19 þat he schuld go] P, *om.* M   24 þis] þe P
31 þe] P, *om.* M

6–14: cf. ibid. 205/26–206/26.
15–19: cf. ibid. 211/24–212/2.
20–3: ibid. 212/17–22; cf. Trokelowe, 155/12–16.
24–9: Walsingham, *Hist. Ang.* ii. 212/23–36.
30–202/2: ibid. 213/3–8.

said for fauour of ȝork, for þe archbischop of þat se was chaunceler.
But þis nouelté lastid not longe, for it went sone to London ageyn.
In þis same ȝere Ser Albré de Ver was mad erl of Oxenforth.

In þis ȝere Ser William Scrop boute þe Ylde of Eubony, with
5 þe crowne, of Ser William Mountagw, erl of Salesbury, for he
þat is lord of þis yle may were a crowne. This yle stant betwix
Ynglond and Yrlond, þe name is now þe Ile of Man.

In þis ȝere þe town of Cherborgh turned ageyn to þe kyng of |
f. 90ᵃ Nauern, for it was laid to wedde for certeyn ȝeris to Kyng Richard
10 for ii m pound.

In þe xvii ȝere of Richard, in þe octaue of Seynt Hillari, was
a parlement at London, where fel a gret strif betwix þe duke of
Lancastir and þe erl of Arundel. He bare þe erl on hand þat he
ros with a gret meny ageyn þe pes, in Chestirschere, in his castel
15 cleped Holt, to meynten also certeyn rebelles. The erl said 'Nay'
herto, and so, be menes, was had pes.

Aboute þe fest of Seynt Jon Baptiste þe same duke of Lancastir
cam ageyn fro Frauns, bringing with him treus for foure ȝere,
and consent of þe Frensch kyng þat all Scottis, where-euyr þei
20 dwelt, schuld be browt onto þe obechauns of þe king of Ynglond,
as þei owe of rite.

In þe same tyme þat þe duke was in Frauns deyed his wif, Dam
Constauns, doutir to Petir, kyng of Spayn, a woman ful blessed and
deuoute. Sone aftir deied Mari, cuntesse of Derby. And sone aftir þat
25 deied Qwen Anne, buried at Westminster. Eke þis ȝere deyed Dame
Ysabell, duchesse of ȝork, doutir to Kyng Petir of Spayn; and Ser
Jon Haukwod, þe nobil knyte, moost named in manhod and werre.

1 þe] *suprascript* M   3 Albré de] Albred P   9 for it] whech P
to Kyng Richard] *om.* P   11 In] *change to darker ink* M   of Richard]
of Rychard P, *om.* M   15 to meynten also certeyn rebelles] *om.* P
16 herto and so be menes was had pes] þerto and aftir mich strif wer found
menes of pes P   17 same] *om.* P   19 where-euyr] wher so ever P   þei]
i *suprascript in paler ink* M   20 onto] to *suprascript* M   21 owe] auȝte P
23 ful blessed] *separated by thin stroke* M   24 deuoute] full devowte P
25 þis] in þe sam P   Dame] *om.* P   27 Haukwod] P, Hakwod M   þe] þat P

1–2: see p. 201.
3: Walsingham, *Hist. Ang.* ii. 213/9–10.
4–7: ibid. 213/18–23.
8–10: ibid. 214/1–4.
11–16: ibid. 214/11–24; cf. Trokelowe, 166/7–26.
17–21: Walsingham, *Hist. Ang.* ii. 214/25–9.
22–6: ibid. 214/30–215/7.
26–7: ibid. 215/9–10; cf. Trokelowe, 171/20–6.

In þe month of Auguste was it proclamed þorowoute Ynglond þat all Erischmen be at hom in her owne lond in þe fest of natiuité of oure Lady, in peyne of lesyng of her hed. For it was proued be experiens þat þere were com to Ynglond so many Erischmen þat þe Erich cuntré, whech longeth to þe king of Ynglond, was so 5 voyded fro his dwelleris þat þe wilde Erisch were com in and had dominacioun of al þat | cuntré. And moreouyr it was noted þat f. 90rb in Kyng Edward tyme þe þirde, whan he had set þere his bank, his juges, and his chekyr, he receyued euery ʒere xxx m pound, and now þe Kyng Richard was fayn to paye ʒerly, to defens of þe 10 same cuntré, xxx m mark.

In þis ʒere, in þe xxi day of Aprile, was þat frere bore whech mad þese annotaciones.

And in þe same ʒere Kyng Richard went into Erland with þe duke of Gloucetir and erles March, Notingham, and Ruthland. 15 Many of þe Erisch lordis wold ha lettid his comyng, but her power was ouyr weyk. Ther was he fro þe natiuité of oure Lady onto Esterne. And in þat same tyme were sent onto him be þe clergi of þis lond þe archbischop of ʒork and þe bischop of London, prayng him þat he wold come hom ageyn to oppresse þe malice of 20 Lollardis; for þei laboured sore to take away all þe possessiones of þe Cherch, and aftir to distroye all þe lawes þat were mad to fauour of þe Cherch. Whan þe kyng herd þis he hastid him in al goodly maner to com hom ageyn.

In þe xviii ʒere þe kyng held his parlement at Dulyn, and þidir 25 com all þo lordes þat had mad subjeccion onto him.

And in þis same tyme Edmund, duke of ʒork, keper of Ynglond, held a parlement at London, to whech parlement cam þe duke of Gloucetir fro Yrland, expressing þe kyngis costis in Yrlond, and his legacion was so acceptabil þat þe clergy graunted him a dyme | and f. 90va þe lay-fe a fiftene. 31

2 natiuité] þe natiuite P   3 For] P, om. M   10 to (2)] for P 12 in] om. P   whech] þat P   18 same] P, om. over line division M   19 þis lond] Ynglond P   21 sore] for P   22 aftir] aftir þat P 23 fauour] þe fauour P   26 þat] t suprascript M   onto] to P   27 þis] þe P

1–11: Walsingham, Hist. Ang. ii. 215/11–25. 14–24: ibid. 215/26–216/9; cf. Trokelowe, 172/27–173/18. 25–6: Walsingham, Hist. Ang. ii. 216/10–14. 27–31: ibid. 216/15–23.

In þis tyme þe Lolardis set up scrowis at Westminster and at Poules, with abhominable accusaciones of hem þat long to þe Cherch, whech sounded in destruccioun of þe sacramentis and of states of þe Cherch. The meynteyneres of þe puple þat were so 5 infect were þese: Richard Storry, Lodewyk Clifforth, Thomas Latymer, Jon Mountagw—þei were principal instructoures of heretikes. The kyng, whan he had conceyued þe malice of þese men, he cleped hem to his presens, and snybbed hem, forbad hem eke þei schuld no more meynten no swech materes. Of Richard 10 Story he took a hooth, for he swore on a book þat he schulde neuyr meynten no swech opiniones. And aftir þis hooth þe kyng saide, 'And I swere here onto þe, if euyr þou breke þin ooth, þou schal deye a foul deth'. Thei þat were gilty in þis mater withdrow gretly her oterauns of malys.

15 In þis ȝere a ymage upon a crosse appered in þe eyir aboue þe stepil cleped Laudunense in Frauns, and þis apparicion lastid half a houre, þat all men mite se it.

And in þe same ȝere a hethen prince, cleped Morettus, with his cursed puple iii hundred þousand and 1 þousand, faut ageyn þe 20 maistir of Rodis, and þorw þe myte of oure Lord he lost of his puple a hundred þousand. Than asayed he to fite in schippis, and þere eke was he put to grete rebuke. And in þe same tyme þe emperour of Constantinople killid a gret part of his host, whech f. 90ᵛᵇ had besegid þe same | cyté.

25 In þis ȝere William, archbischop of Cauntirbury, hauyng no consideracion what costis þe cherchis in his prouynce had bore paying a subsidi to þe kyng euery ȝere, ȝet gat he bulles fro þe court to haue IIIId. of þe pound, both of exempt and not exempt. Many þat loued pes payed; and summe mad apeel in þis mater. 30 But þe ende of al þis strif was þe deth of þis William, whech folowed sone.

---

2 with] wit *at line end* P   3–4 whech . . . Cherch] *om.* P   4 meyn-
teyneres] maynteneris P, meyteyneres M   5 Storry] *2nd* r *suprascript* M
6 þei] þese P   10 þat] an oth þat P   13 Thei] *change to darker ink*
M   16 þis] *om.* P   25 archbischop] P, arbischop *with* ar *suprascript*
M   27 paying] *om.* P

1–14: Walsingham, *Hist. Ang.* ii. 216/24–217/9.
15–17: ibid. 217/10–13.
18–24: ibid. 217/14–25.
25–31: ibid. 217/33–218/13.

In þis ȝere in þe month of Nouembir Kyng Richard sent aftir þe body of Robert Ver, and beried it at Coln, and þere was he and þe archbischop of Cauntirbury.

In þe xix ȝere þe duke of Lancastir, whom þe kyng had mad duke of Gyan, cam hom to Ynglond, compelled be þe king, no 5 consideracion had at þe costis whech he mad þere to gete him pees and frendchip. He cam hom at þe fest of Cristis natiuité onto þe king, haldyng þat fest at Langlé. He was receyued in chere outeward as a frend, but not in hert, as he supposed; wherfor he took leue of þe kyng, and rood onto Lyncoln, where Katerine Swyn- 10 forth dwelled þat tyme. And sone aftir he weddid þe same woman, ageyn þe opinion of many men. Of þis woman cam many childirn, whech were aftir legittimat—so semeth it þat þei were bore befor þis mariage.

In þis ȝere þe pope wrote speciali to þe kyng for þese Lolardis, 15 tretoures to God and to þe kyng. In his letteris he prayed þe kyng þat he schuld be redy to punche al þoo whom þe bischoppis declared for heretikes. Othir bulles sent he, in whech was conteyned | þat all maner religious men þat dwelt fro her ordir, vndir f. 91ra pretens of swech graces as þei clepe *capellanis honoris*, þat þei 20 schuld be compelled to kepe her religion. This plesed wel þe iiii ordres of mendinauntis, for þei pulled hom many a man þat was of ful euel reule.

In þis tyme þe kyngis of Frauns and of Ynglond mette togidir fast by Caleys, and þere picchid her tentis, and before ony trety 25 both kyngis were swore for hem and all her frendis þat, viii dayes befor þis trety, and viii dayes aftir, þere schuld no man o neithir side harme oþir be no maner ne no weye.

In þe xvi day of Octobir þe kyng of Ynglond rood fro Caleys onto Gynes, and with him þe duke of Barry, þat was sent to Kaleys 30

2 Coln] toln P   4 whom] *change to darker ink* M   5 to] into P
8 haldyng] ȳg *with* g *altered from* n M   9 wherfor] *change to darker ink* M
13 aftir] aftirward P   17 þat] *om.* P   19 maner] maner of P   21 be]
in r.h. margin M   22 mendinauntis] mendevauntes P   þei] i *inserted on
the line* M   23 of ful euel reule] full evel rewlyd P   24 Frauns] Ynglond
P   of Ynglond] Fravns P   togidir] *om.* P   29 þe (1)] *om.* P   30 onto
Gynes] *om.* P

1–3: ibid. 219/1–11.
4–14: ibid. 219/15–27.
15–23: ibid. 219/28–39.
24–8: ibid. 220/1–27.
29–206/11: ibid. 220/28–221/5; cf. Trokelowe, 189/11–191/23.

to receyue þe kingis oth. In þe morow þe kyngis met in þe feld, and þese Frensch lordes rood with þe kyng of Ynglond: þe duke of Barry, þe duke of Burgonie, þe Duke Aurelianense, þe duke of Borboun, the Erl Sancer, vicount de Meleyn, þe bischop of
5 Velamensse, and þe Lord Bussy. And on þe oþir part, with þe kyng of Frauns, rood þe duke of Lancastir, þe duke of Gloucetir, þe erl of Derby, erl of Ruthland, erl of Notingham, and erl of Northumbirlond. In þis feld þese to kyngis had her trety, and in þat place where þei tretid þei were acorded þat a chapel schuld
10 be mad at þe costis of hem both, and it schuld be cleped *Nostre Domine de Pace.*

　　In þe fest of Symund and Jude þei were swore to kepe certeyn
_{f. 91rb} articules whech were purposed | and wrytin, and aftir þat þe kyng of Yngland praied þe king of Frauns to dyner þe next day.
15 Helianore, þe doutir to þe king of Frauns was browt to Kyng Richard tent, and þere hir fader gaue hir to þe same kyng. He þankid his fader, and kissid þe mayde, and comendid hir to þe duchesses of Lancastir and Gloucetir, and cuntesses of Huntyngdon and Stafforth, and oþir ladies, for to lede hir to Kaleys.
20 Sche was ful scarsly viii ȝere of age, but sche broute oute of Frauns xii chares ful of ladies and domicelles. Thus went þe kyngis to mete. The kyng of Frauns sat on þe rite hand, and all þe corses of mete were seruid aftir þe gise of his cuntré, al in o disch. The kyng of Ynglond was serued in many dischis aftir his vse. Aftir
25 mete þe kyng of Ynglond led þe kyng of Frauns on his weye, kissid him, and toke his leue. In þis receyuing Richard spent iii c m mark.

　　This ȝere deyed Maistir William Courtné, and in his stede Thomas Arundel was bischop of Cauntirbury.
30　　In þe xx ȝere of Richard was a parlement at London, where þe duke of Lancastir purchased a legittimacion for þe childyrn þat

---

2 þese] þe P　　　3 Aurelianense] P, Aurialenense M　　þe (3)] *om.* P
5 Velamensse] relaniensse P　　　　　7 erl of (2)] þe erle P　　and] *om.* P
10 þe] *om.* P　　13 aftir] P, afir M　　14 þe (2)] in þe P　　18 duchesses]
final s *suprascript* M　　Gloucetir] of Gloucetir P　　cuntesses] cuntesse P
19 Stafforth] of Stafforth P　　for] *om.* P　　Kaleys] Cayles P　　　　26 his]
hys P, *om.* M　　26–7 In . . . mark] *om.* P　　31 for] fro P

1–11: see p. 205.
12–27: Walsingham, *Hist. Ang.* ii. 221/6–222/5.
28–9: ibid. 222/9–11.
30–207/3: ibid. 222/15–23.

he had begotin of Dame Katerine Swynforth. And in þis parlement Ser Thomas Beuforth, on of þoo childirn, was mad erl of
Somirsete.

In þis same tyme þe kyng, ageyn all þe othis þat he had mad,
cleped ageyn oute of Yrlond þoo justises whech were exiled be þe 5
parlement and be his consent.

In þis tyme eke risen tydingis in þis lond þat þe kyng was chose
emperour, for whech cause þe kyng mad mo | gaderingis and mo f. 91ᵛᵃ
taliages þan euyr he ded before. þere was no cyté, no town, no
prelate, lord, knyte, or marchaunt, but þei mote lende þe kyng 10
mony.

In þis same ȝere, whan men supposed all pes and rest to be had,
sodeynly þe kyng brak out with pryuy malice, whech he had longe
born, and ded his officeres arestin at Plasché, in Essex, his vncil,
þe duke of Gloucetir, and streite sent him to Caleys. The erl of 15
Warwik, þe same day þat he had dyned with þe kyng and þe kyng
had hite him his good lordchip, was arestid and put in prison.
The erl of Arundel was arested and sent to þe Ilde of Wite. And
þat þere schuld be no grucching in the puple for þis maner doyng,
he ded proclame þorow þe rem þat it was not for eld treson, but 20
for newe. And sone aftir, at Notingham, all þese lordes were
endited. These were þe lordis assined be þe kyng þat schuld accuse
hem in þe next parlement: Ser Edward, erl of Ruthland, Ser
Thomas Mounbray, Erl Marchale, Ser Thomas Holland, erl of
Kent, Ser Jon Holland, erl of Huntingdon, Ser Thomas Beuforth, 25
erl of Somirsete, Ser Jon Mountagew, erl of Salesbury, Thomas,
Lord Spenser, and William Scrop, chaumbyrleyn.

In þis tyme þe kyng, because he dred conspiracion of puple,
sent into Chestirschire for barettoures and riseris, þat þei schuld
com and haue þe kepyng of his body.   30

---

2 Beuforth] Beufor *over erasure* M   þoo] þe P   5 þoo justises]
separated by thin stroke in red M   7 in þis lond] *om.* P   9–10 no
town no prelate lord] ne no town ne prelate lord ne P   10 mote] mvst P
14 in Essex] *om.* P   19–20 doyng he] *separated by thin stroke in red* M
22 endited] *final* d *altered from* t M   29 barettoures] barrettoures P,
barectoures M   30 his] þe kyngis P

4–6: ibid. 222/26–9.
7–11: ibid. 222/30–223/3; cf. Trokelowe, 199/15–200/3.
12–27: Walsingham, *Hist. Ang.* ii. 223/4–224/2; cf. Trokelowe, 201/18–
    207/28.
28–30: Walsingham, *Hist. Ang.* ii. 224/5–7; cf. Trokelowe, 208/5–9.

At þe natiuité of oure Lady was a parlement at London, and
f. 91ᵛᵇ þider cam many lordis with gret aray. In | þat parlement þe
grettest spekeris were iii proud coueytous men, Jon Bussy, William
Bagot, and Thomas Grene. These iii, with grete clamour, cried
5 þat swech chartouris of pardon whech were graunted before
schuld be reuoced. And to þis mater both þe clergy and þe lay-fe
consented, hauyng no consideracion whi it was don. The Archbischop Thomas took leue to be absent o day, praying þe kyng þat
þere schuld noþing be concluded in his absens. And notwith-
10 standing þat þe kyng hite him þis, he was exiled þe next day,
þat, up peyn of his hed, he schuld not abide in þe lond lenger
þan viii wekis. And in þis mene tyme þe king sent pryuily to
þe court þat Roger Walden, tresorer, schuld obteyne þe benefice, but within a litil tyme he was accused of certeyn crym, and
15 refused.

In þe day of Seint Mathew was Richard Arundel condempned
to be ded as a tretour, saue þe king pardoned him of all oþir
circumstauns saue lesyng of his hed. He myte not be excused
be his chartour þat was graunted him. Whan he cam to þe place
20 þere he schuld deye, he chaunged no chere, but took þe swerd fro
him þat schuld smyte, and felt if it were scharp, and seyde, 'It is
scharp inow. Do þi dede. I forgyue þe my deth'. With o strok his
hed went of, and a frere Augustin, cleped Fekenham, Maystir of
Diuinité, bare it hom in his lap. His oþir breþerin bare hom þe
25 body onto þe couent.

f. 92ʳᵃ   Aftir his deth þe king was tormented with dredful dremes, | þat
he myte not slepe. Eke he þoute euyr þat a schadow of a man
walkid before him. Moreouyr þis greuid him, þat þe comoun puple
talked þat he was a martir, and þat his hed was growe ageyn to
30 his bodi. For þese causes, in þe tent day aftir his sepulture, at
þe x houre at euen, þe kyng sent certeyn dukes and erles to delue
up þe body, and make a frere for to go betwyx þe hed and þe body,
and with þis dede þe kyng was more qwiet, but, for al þis, he

3 proud] proûd M, *om.* P   12 þis] þe P   20 chaunged] d *over*
erasure M   21 It] þus it P   22 Do þi dede I forgyue þe my deth]
I forgyf þe my deth do they dede P   dede] *final* e *altered from* i M
23 Augustin] Austyn P   23–4 Maystir of Diuinité] P, *om.* M   32 betwyx]
x *suprascript* M   33 qwiet] qwieted P

1–15: Walsingham, *Hist. Ang.* ii. 224/8–36; cf. Trokelowe, 209/9–213/33.
16–25: Walsingham, *Hist. Ang.* ii. 224/37–225/27.
26–209/2: ibid. 225/28–226/10; cf. Trokelowe, 218/13–219/23.

comaunded þe wax aboute his graue, and clothis, and oþir aray,
for to be take away, and to leue þe graue desolate.

Aftyr his deth was þe erl of Warwik arested, and qwan þei inqwired of him what was his entent for to gader so mech puple to
ride with þe duke of Gloucetir, þe man, seing who Arundel was 5
ded, and he endited of treson, was aknowe, as þei seid. For whech
confession þe king gaue him lif, and exiled him to prison in þe Ylde
of Man.

Aftir þis, because men þoute it was not to þe kyngis worchip
þat his vncil schuld be slayn openly, for fauour of þe puple, whech 10
loued him, for þis cause þe kyng comaunded þe Erl Marchale þat
he schuld be pryuyly slayn. So be þat mannes seruauntis he
was slayn at Caleys, oppressed betwix to fedir-beddis.

Than mad þe king do crye þat þis parlement schuld be jorned
tyl aftir Cristmasse, and þan ended at Schrouesbury.   15

In þe xxi ȝere of Richard, in þat same parlement þe kyng procured ful sotilly þat, be þe consent of all þe statis of þe parlement,
þat þe power | of certeyn peticiones, whech were porrect in þe f. 92ro
parlement, mite be determined be certeyn persones vii or viii
aftir þe parlement was do. This graunted, þe kyng put in his 20
stile 'Prince of Chestir', and þan mad he certeyn dukes: þe erl of
Derby, duke of Herforth; Erl Marchale, duke of Norfolk; Erl
Rutland, duke of Albemarle; erl of Kent, duke of Suthrey;
erl of Huntingdon, duke of Excetir; þe cuntesse of Norfolk,
duchesse of þe same; þe erl of Somirsete, markeis of Northfolk; 25
þe Lord Spencer, erl of Gloucetir; þe Lord Neuile, erl of West-
morlond; Ser William Scrop, erl of Wiltschere; Ser Thomas
Percy, erl of Wicestir; and to þese lordes gaue he mech of þe
liflod of þe duke of Gloucetir, erl of Warwik, and erl of Arundel.
He purchased eke bullis of þe pope, whech confermed al þat was 30

1 wax] x *over erasure* M   2 to leue þe graue] þᵉ grave to be left P
3–4 þei inqwired] *in l.h. margin with carets* (*in red*) M, þey inqwred P   4 for]
om. P   6 endited] entited P   9 to] *supplied, om.* MP   13 at]
P, a M   15 þan] *om. over line division* P   22 Erl (1)] þe erle of P
of (2)] *om.* P   23 Albemarle erl of Kent duke of] *om.* P   24–5 þe
cuntesse . . . þe same] *om.* P   26 Neuile] Novill P   29 erl (1)] of þe
erle P   erl (2)] þe erle P

3–8: Walsingham, *Hist. Ang.* ii. 226/11–22.
9–15: ibid. 226/23–32.
16–210/2: ibid. 226/33–227/31.

do in þe parlement, and grete censuris were þere ageyn all þat schuld breke hem.

In þis ȝere þe kyng exiled þe duke of Norfolk, and set grete peynes þat no man schuld pray for him. And þis was do þat same
5 day tweluemonth in whech first day þe duke of Gloucetir was suffocat at Caleys.

In þis ȝere þe kyng translate Jon, bischop of Lincoln, onto þe cherch of Chestir, and þe cherch of Lincoln gaue he to Herry Beuforth, on of þe childirn of þe duke of Lancastir and Katerine
10 Swynforth. Jon, þat was bischop of Lincoln, wold not admitte þis translacion, but went to Cauntirbyry, to Crist Cherch, and þere deied amongis þe munkis.

f. 92ᵛᵃ   In þis tyme cam a messanger fro þe | pope, Petrus de Bosco, Bischop Aquitense, for to pray þe king þat he schuld suffir his
15 ligemen to haue prouisiones of þe popes hand, and to distroye þat writ *Quare impedit*. But because þe patrones wold not consent þerto, þerfor þe king honoured him with grete giftis, and sent him hom ageyn.

In þis tyme was founde a gret summe of mony at Rome in a
20 rotin wal, whech was þe tresoure of Heleyn, Constantyn modir, for in þe serkil was writin hir name, and euery pes þerof was worth XXs. With þis mony þe pope ded renewe þe Capitol and þe Castell Aungel.

In þe xxii ȝere, in þe fest of circumcision, a depe watir in Bed-
25 forthschire, þat rennyth betwix Snelleston and Harleswode, sodeynly stood stille, and departed him into oþir place, and þe ryuer þat was wete before stood drye iii myle o length, þat men myte go ouyr. This merueyle betokned, men seide, gret dyuysion þat schuld falle in þe puple.

30   In þat tyme Roger Mortimer, erl of March, was deceyued be þe Erischmen and slayn. Whan þe kyng knew it, he purposed

7 of Lincoln] *in r.h. margin with carets (in red)* M   onto] to P   8 to] onto
P   16 Quare] Quar P   22 þe Capitol and] *om.* P   23 Aungel] of
Aungell P   27 was] stood P   28–9 This . . . puple] *om.* P

1–2: see p. 209.
3–6: Walsingham, *Hist. Ang.* ii. 228/6–11.
7–12: ibid. 228/12–19.
13–18: ibid. 228/31–7.
19–23: ibid. 228/38–229/3.
24–9: ibid. 229/7–14; cf. Trokelowe, 229/14–22.
30–211/3: Walsingham, *Hist. Ang.* ii. 229/15–25; cf. Trokelowe, 229/23–
230/12.

for to venge his deth and make a jornay into Yrlond, upon whech
he purueyed mech þing of his ligis, and payed rite not, so þat ny
all men hated him.

In þis tyme deied Jon, duke of Lancastir, and was byried at
Seyn Paules, in London. Aftir his deth þe kyng, þat had exiled 5
Herry, his son, for x ȝere, now he exiled him for euyr, forbedyng
all his receyuoures þat þei schul | gader no mony to profite of her f. 92ᵛᵇ
lord, notwithstanding he had graunted hem patentis befor, þat
þei schuld gader a certeyn summe for her lordis redempcion, þat
he mite with his good purchace þe kyngis grace. 10

In þis same tyme þe kyng borowid more good of dyuers men,
and bond him be patent letteris to pay hem at certeyn dayes, whech
he neuyr payed. Than sent he to all þe schreues þat þei schuld make
þe puple to swere newly ageyn þat þei schuld be trewe to þe kyng.
And þo men þat were counted rich were bore on hande þat þei had 15
consented to þe tretoures þat were ded, and so were þei compelled
to pay grete summes. Euery persone, of what degré he was, if
þei were accused þat þei had seid ony word in derogacion of
þe kyng, þere was no mercy but payment or prison. And þis
mad þe puple to hate þe kyng, and caused gret murmour in the 20
puple.

Aboute þe fest of Pentcost þe kyng went into Yrland, with his
Chestirreres, and with þe Dukes Awlmarre and Excetir, þe eyeres
eke of Gloucetir and Herforth, certeyn bischoppis, and þe abbot
of Westminster, þat he myte make a parlement whan he wold. 25

In þis tyme, whil he was in Yrlond, þe duke of Lancastir,
Herry, beryng heuyly his exile and eke priuacioun of his heritage,
and considering who euel-beloued þe kyng was of his lychmen,
þinking þat now was tyme for to entir, cam into þe se with Thomas,
bischop of Cauntyrbury, and þe son and eyer of þe erl of Herforth, 30
whech had with him at þat tyme but | xv speres. Thus Herry kept f. 93ʳᵃ

1 into] to *suprascript* M   7 schul] schuld P, schal M   9 for]
ofor P   15 had] wer P   18 þat] P, *om*. M   þei (2)] *inserted on the
line* M   20 murmour] *1st* r *suprascript* M   23–4 þe eyeres eke] &
eyres P   26 In] *change to paler ink* M   28 and considering] consideryng eke P   þe] *suprascript* M   29 se] *suprascript* M   30 bischop]
archbyschop P   þe erl] *over erasure* M   31 at] t *suprascript* M

4–10: Walsingham, *Hist. Ang.* ii. 230/6–13.
11–21: ibid. 230/19–231/31.
22–5: ibid. 231/32–232/4.
26–212/2: ibid. 232/13–27; cf. Trokelowe, 240/24–242/25.

him in þe se, appering now in o cost, now in a othir, lokyng euyr if
ony resistens schuld be mad to lette him of his londing.

Whan Ser Edmund, duke of Ʒork, herd þese tydyngis þat
Duke Herri was in þe se, because he was þe kyngis vncil, and eke
5 keper of þe rem in þe kyngis absens, he cleped onto him Ser
Edmund Stafford, bischop of Chestir, and chaunceler at þat tyme,
and þe tresorer, William Scrop, erl of Wiltschere, and þese knytes
of þe kyngis councel, Jon Bussy, William Bagot, Thomas Grene,
and Jon Russel. They þus gadered he asked councell what was best
10 to do in þis mater, and what resistens mite be had ageyn Duke
Herry. They seyde it was best to go to Seynt Albonis, and gader þe
cuntré, and with þat strength mete with þe duke. But her councel
was nowt, for, whan þe puple was gadered, þei seide þei knew nowt
of Duke Herry but as of a good lord and a trewe, and a man whech
15 had suffered mech wrong, wherfor þei wold not let him to come
and receyue his dew heritage. Than þe tresorer and þese iiii
knytes lefte þe duke of Ʒork, and fled to þe castell of Bristow.

And þe duke of Lancastir londid at Rauenesporne, fast be
Grymisby, in þe translacion of Seynt Martyn, no man makyng
20 resistens. To him cam anon Herry, erl of Northhumbirlond, and
Herry Percy, his son, and Raf Neuyle, erl of Westmorland, and so
many mo þat within fewe dayes þe noumbir of fytyng men cam
onto lx þousand. Than was her comon councel at þe first to
f. 93ʳᵇ destroye | Kyng Richardis euel councel. So cam þei to Bristow,
25 and took alle þat were þere, and smet of her hedis, saue William
Bagot, for, er þei cam, he was fled to Chestir and so sailed into
Erland.

When Kyng Richard herd in Erlond of þe coming of Herry,
anon he took þe se with þe dukes of Awmarle, Excetir, and Sotherey,
30 and Bischoppis London, Lincoln, and Carlil, þat he schuld mete

---

1 þe] *suprascript* M   appering] *om.* P   6 chaunceler] *over erasure* M
9 and] *om.* P   10 þis] *suprascript* M   12 þat] þe P   But her]
separated by thin stroke M   14 a (2)] *om.* P   19 no man makyng]
withowte P   21 and (1)] *om.* P   23 onto] to P   to] *suprascript*
M   25 took alle þat were þere and] all þat were þer þei P   saue] save of
P   26 er þei cam he was fled to] þei cam he fled vnto P   sailed] *om.* P
29 dukes] s *suprascript* M   of Awmarle] Awlmarle P   30 and (1)] *om.* P

1–2: see p. 211.
3–17: Walsingham, *Hist. Ang.* ii. 232/28–233/6; cf. Trokelowe, 234/10–
244/12.
18–27: Walsingham, *Hist. Ang.* ii. 233/6–21.
28–213/13: ibid. 233/22–234/10.

þe duke with strong hand or he had gadered ony power. Whan he
was com to Ynglond, and herd telle what power Duke Herry had
with him, and vndirstood who many heuy hertis he had in þe
puple, he left all his puple and soute pryuy places, where he myte
best dwelle, for þe duke of Lancastir euyr folowid him. At þe 5
last he was founde in þe castell of Conweye, and þere desired he to
speke with Thomas Arundel, bischop of Cauntirbiri, and þe erl of
Northumbirland. To hem seid he þat he wold resigne his regaly,
and all þat longe þerto, saue þe carectis of his soule, so þat his lif
schuld be graunted him, and sufficient liflod to him and viii 10
persones. Thei graunted his peticioun, and broute him forth to þe
castel of Flynt, where þe duk and he had but a smal talkyng, and
þan rydyn to þe castell of Chestir.

In þe xx day of August, þe xlvii fro þe tyme þat þe duke entered
into Ynglond, þe kyng ȝald him to þe duke, and all his tresore, his 15
ornamentis, and his hors cam to þe dukes hand. The lordis and all
þe host þat cam with þe king were robbid be northen men and
Walschmen withoute | mercy. Fro þat place was þe king led to   f. 93ᵛᵃ
London to þe Tour.

And in þis tyme were sent writtis þorowoute þe lond þat þe 20
parlement schuld be at London at Myhilmesse, to whech parlement all men were cited whech of custome schuld be þere, and þese
writtis were sent vndir þe name of Kyng Richard. Whan þis tyme
was come, euene on Mihelmesse Day, þe kyng in þe Tour, with
good wil, as it semed, and mery chere, red þe act of his cessacion 25
before þese lordis and oþir men present: arsbischop of Cauntirbury,
Thomas Arundel; þe oþir, of Ȝork, Richard Scrop; Jon, bischop
of Herforth; Herry, duke of Lancastir; Herry, erl of Northumbirland; Raf, erl of Westmorland; Hew, Lord Burnel; Thomas,
Lord Berklé; abbot of Westminster; priour of Cauntirbyry; 30
Lordis Ros, Wilbey, and Bergeueny; William þirnyng, and Jon

  1 hand] *suprascript* M   2 to] into P   3 he] hymself P   4 he (1)]
P, *om.* M   all his puple] as hys retenew P   7 bischop] archebyschop
P   and] and with P   8 he (1)] *suprascript* M   9 longe] longeth P
his (2)] *om.* P   10 to him] *om.* P   13 to] forth to P   14 xlvii]
xlvii day P   16 hand] handis P   17 be] with P   and] and with P
26-7 arsbischop of Cauntirbury Thomas Arundel] Thomas Arundel archbyschop
of Cauntirbury P   27 þe oþir of Ȝork Richard Scrop] Richard Scrop archbyschop of Ȝork P   31 and (2)] *om.* P

14-19: ibid. 234/10-17.
20-214/7: ibid. 234/18-235/13; cf. Trokelowe, 251/27-258/3.

Markam, justises; Thomas Stoke, and Jon Burbage, Doctoures
of Canon; Thomas Erpyngham, and Thomas Grey, knites;
William Ferby, and Dyonise Lopham, notaries—before all þese
red he his resignacion and assoyled all his ligemen fro þe treuth
5 and þe oth whech þei had mad to him. And þis renunciacion
was openly red in Westminster Halle, and euery state singulerly
inqwyred who þei likid þis, and þei saide all þei consented þertoo.
Anno 6597–6610; 1399–1412. In þe ȝere of oure Lord 1399, in

f. 93ᵛᵇ   þe fest of Seyn Jerom, aftir þis renun|ciacion, þe kyngis sete þo
10 voyde, þe forseid Herry, duke of Lancastir, ros in þe parlement and
stood up þat men myte se him, blessed him with þe merk of þe
crosse, and saide swech wordes:—

In Dei nomine, Amen. I, Herry Lancastir, chalenge þe
corown with al þe membris þat long þerto as for descense of
15 þe real blod of Kyng Herry, be whech rite God hath graunted
me for to entir with help of my kynred.

And whan all þe states of þe parlement had consented to his
chaleng, þe arschbischop of Cauntirbiry took him be þe rite hand,
and sette him in þe kyngis se. Than was it proclamed þat a new
20 parlement schuld begynne þe next Munday aftir, and on Seint
Edward day folowing schuld þe king be corowned, and þis was
fulfillid in dede.

This Herry had þat tyme sex childyrn be Dam Mary, doutir to
þe erl of Herforth: þe eldest son hite Herry; þe secunde, Thomas;
25 þe þirde, Jon; þe fourte, Humfrey; to douteris had he eke—on of
hem was weddid into Denemarc.

Thus was he crowned on Seynt Edward day and anoynted with
þat holy oyle þat was take to Seynt Thomas of Cauntirbury be
oure Lady, and he left it in Frauns. This oyle was closed in a egel of
30 gold and þat egil put in a crowet of ston, and be reuelacion Herry,
þe first duke of Lancastir fond it, and brout it hom to Ynglond, |

1 and] om. P   2 and] om. P   3 and] om. P   5 þei] i suprascript M   renunciacion] resignacion P   9 renunciacion] renunciacion on P
10–11 and stood up] om. P   15 þe] om. P   be] of P   21 þis] al P
31 brout] u altered from v M

1–7: see p. 213.
8–22: Walsingham, Hist. Ang. ii. 237/12–238/5.
23–6: ibid. 238/20–5; cf. Trokelowe, 287/18–26.
27–215/10: Walsingham, Hist. Ang. ii. 239/3–240/9; cf. Trokelowe,
297/13–300/29.

and gaue it to þe Prince Edward, to þis effect, þat aftir his faderes   f. 94ʳᵃ
deces he schuld be anoynted with þe same. And aftir þe princes
deth it was left in þe kyngis tresory, and neuyr man tok kep þerto
til, a litil before þat þe king exiled þe Bischop Thomas, þis relik was
found, and certeyn writing þeron, as Thomas of Cauntirbury left 5
it. Than was Kyng Richard glad, and desired of þe bischop to be
anoynted new, but he wold not. But for al þat þe kyng bare it with
him into Yrland, and whan he was take in his coming ageyn, he
dylyuered it to Tomas Arundel, and soo was Herry crowned
with þe same.   10

In þis parlement þe kyng, with consent of alle þe hous, mad his
son Herri prince of Walis and duke of Cornwaile, and eke erl of
Chestir, and aftir þat duke of Gian.

In þat parlement þe kyng gaue to þe erl of Northumbirlond þe
Yle of Man, with þis addicion, þat he schuld bere before þe kyng 15
þe same swerd with whech he cam into Inglond. He gaue eke to
þe erl of Westmorland þe erldam of Richmund. And ageyn hem
þat appeled and accused þe duke of Gloucetir þis sentens was
pronounsed:—

    The lordis of þis present parlement decerne and deme þat þe 20
    Duke Awmarle, and duke of Suthrey, and eke of Excetir,
    schul lese her names, her honour, and her dignité, and þe
    markeis of Dorcete and þe erle of Gloucetir schul lese þe same
    for hem and her eyeris. And all þe castell and maneris, whech
    were þe dukes of Gloucetir, þei schul lese withoute ony gra|ce, f. 94ʳᵇ
    and all þe godes þat þei had sith þat tyme þat he was arested 26
    þei schuld forgo. Tho þat þei had befor þat tyme þei schuld
    haue stille, but þei schuld gyue no lyueries, as oþir lordis
    doo. And if euyr it may be knowe þat þei make ony gadering
    in coumfort of Richard, sumtyme kyng, þei to be punchid as 30
    tretoures.

  1 þe] *om.* P   2 deces] deth P   4 þat þe king] Kyng Richard P
5 of Cauntirbury] *in r.h. margin with short strokes in red to indicate continuity of
text* M   9 Herry] Kyng Herry P   crowned] anoynted P   11 hous]
lordes P   11–12 mad his son Herri] *in l.h. margin with carets (in red)* M
12 Cornwaile] Cornwayle P, Corwaile M   and eke] *om.* P   15 with]
wit *at line end* P   16 into] P, to M   21 Awmarle and duke] *om.* P
eke] duke P   23 and] *om.* P

11–13: Walsingham, *Hist. Ang.* ii. 240/10–13.
14–31: ibid. 241/1–39.

In þe secund ȝere of þis kyng þe erlis of Kent, Salesbury, and
Huntingdon, onkende onto þe kyng, risin ageyn him—vnkynde
were þei, for þe puple wold haue hem ded, and þe king spared hem.
These men, þus gadered, purposed to falle on þe kyng sodeynly at
5 Wyndesore vndir þe colour of mummeres in Cristmasse tyme. The
kyng was warned of þis, and fled to London. These men knew
not þat, but cam to Wyndesore with iiii hundred armed men,
purposing to kille þe king and his progenie, and restore Richard
ageyn onto þe crowne. Whan þei cam to Windesore, and þus were
10 deceyued, þei fled to a town where þe qween lay, fast by Radyngis,
and þere before þe qwenes houshold he blessed him, þis erl of
Kent. 'O benedicite', he seide,

who may þis bee, þat Herry of Lancastir fled fro my presens,
he þat is so worþi man of armes? Therfor, frendis, know
15 þis, þat Herry of Lancastir hath take þe Tour at London,
and oure very kyng, Richard, hath brokyn prison, and hath
gadered a hundred þousand fytyng men.

So gladed he þe qween with lyes, and rod forth to Walyngforth,
f. 94ᵛᵃ and fro | Walingforth to Abyngdon, warnyng all men be þe weye
20 þat þei schuld make hem redy to help Kyng Richard. Thus cam he
to Cicetir late at euen. The men of þe town had suspecion to hem,
þat her tydyngis were lyes (as it was in dede), risen, and kept þe
entrés of þe innes, þat non of hem mite passe. There faute þei in
þe town fro midnyte onto ix of clok in þe morow. But þe town
25 drow hem oute of the abbey and smet of many of her hedis. The
erl of Salesbury was ded þere, and worthi, for he was a gret
fauorer of Lollardis, a despiser of sacramentis, for he wold not be
confessed whan he schuld deie.

The erl of Huntingdon herd of þis, and fled into Esex, and
30 as often as he assaied to take þe se, so often was he bore of
with þe wynde. Than was he take be þe comones, and led to

---

1 Salesbury] of Salysbury P   4 purposed to] *separated by thin stroke* M
8 Richard] Kyng Rychard P   9 onto] to P   Whan] *change to darker ink*
M   12 O benedicite he seide] he seide *in r.h. margin* M, and seyd O benedicite P   13 fled] d *suprascript with caret (in red)* M   14 worþi] manly a P
15 Lancastir] Lacaster P   18 lyes] hys lyes P   19 Walingforth] þens P
24 clok] þe cloke P   morow] mornyng P

1–28: Walsingham, *Hist. Ang.* ii. 243/16–244/39.
29–217/5: ibid. 245/1–25.

Chelmisforth, and þan to Plasché, and his hed smet of in þe same place where he arestid þe duke of Gloucetir. In þe same tyme Ser Thomas Spencer, whech was cleped erle of Gloucetir, was take and heded at Bristow, and many oþir were so ded be þe comownes.

This cam to Kyng Richardis ere in þe castel of Poumfreit, and as sum men sey, he peyned himself and deyed for hungir. Summe othir seide þat he was kept fro mete and drink whil a knyte rode to London and cam ageyn. His body aftir his deth was caried to London, and at Seynt Paules had his | dyrige and his masse, þe   f. 94ᵛᵇ
kyng þere present. Than was þe body sent fro London onto 11
Langlé, for to be beried among þe Frere Prechoures. At þe byriyng was þe bischop of Chestir, þe abbot of Seynt Albones, and þe abbot of Waltham, and fewe othir.

In þat same ȝere þe schippis of Lenne, whech fischid at Aberden, 15
took certeyn schippis of Scotland, with her amyrel, Ser Robert Logon, knyte, and broute hem home to Lenne.

In þis ȝere began þe rebellion of Walis ageyn þe kyng, vndir a capteyn cleped Howeyn Glendor, whech Howeyn was first a prentise of cort, and þan a swyere in þe kingis hous, but for a dis- 20
cord þat fel betwix him and Ser Reynald Grey Riffyn for certeyn lond, first he faut with þe tenauntis of þe same lord, and because þe kyng pursewid him for brekyng of þe pes, he fled into Walis, and whan þe kyng folowid him þidir, he fled into þe hillis of Snowdon, and þe kyngis labour was frustrate. 25

In þis same ȝere cam þe emperour of Constantinople into Inglond for to haue sum socour ageyn þe Turkis. The Kyng Herry met him on þe Blakeheth on Seint Thomas day þe apostil, and led him to London, and þere had he good hostel at þe kyngis cost, and aftir went he ageyn with large giftis. 30

1 Chelmisforth] Chelm|forth *over line division* P   3 whech was] *separated by thin stroke in red as final* h *in* whech *inserted on the line* M   7 as] *suprascript with caret (in red)* M   sum men] sume P   11 onto] to P   15 þat] þe P   17 home] P, *om. over line division* M   18 In] *change to darker ink* M   19 Howeyn (2)] h *altered from* o M   20 for] *suprascript* M   22 þe (1)] *om.* P   24 whan] *om.* P   þe (1)] P, þei M   into] to P   26 into] to P   30 went he] he went P   large giftis] grete gyftis and large P

6–14: ibid. 245/32–246/11.
15–17: ibid. 246/14–17.
18–25: ibid. 246/23–38.
26–30: ibid. 247/4–10.

In þe þird ȝere of þis Herry was a parlement at London, wher
was mad a statute ageyn Lolardis, þat where-euyr þei were founde
preching her euel doctrine, þei schuld be take and presentid to þe
bischop, and if þei meyntened her opiniones, þei schuld be com-
f. 95ra mitted to seculer hand, and thei | schuld brenne hem and her
6 bokes. This statute was practized in a prest þat sone aftir was
brent in Smythfeld.

In þis ȝere þe kyng of Lettow killid Bassan, þe son of þe gret
soudan, Balthasardan. And because he had so grete victori,
10 ageyn þe opinion of many men, þerfor he was cristened, and lx
þousand with him of his secte. This herd þe emperour of Constantinople, þat was ȝet in Inglond, and with mery hert went hom
ageyn.

In þis ȝere Qween Ysabell was sent hom onto hir fader into
15 Frauns, not fully xii ȝere of age.

In þis same ȝere Howeyn Glendor ded mech harm upon þe
borderes of Ynglond.

And in þe same tyme was layd in þe kyngis bed a hirun with iii
braunchis, mad so scharp þat, where-euyr þe kyng had turned him,
20 it schuld sle him, but, as God wold, it was aspied, and so he skaped
þat perel.

In this same ȝere of þis man appered a sterre, whech þei clepe
comata, betwix þe west and þe north, in þe monthe of March, with
a hie bem, whech bem bowed into þe north. It betokened, as men
25 seid, þe blod þat schuld be spilt at Schrouisbyry.

Aboute þe fest of Pentecost, þat same ȝere, certeyn men, whech
had conspired þe kyngis deth, noised in þe puple þat Kyng Richard
was o-lyue and schuld sone come and rewarde hem gretly þat held
with his part. But þis langage sesid mech aftir tyme þat a prest,
30 on of þe first noyseres, was take at Ware. This prest had mad a rolle

4 meyntened] mayntened P, meynten M   8 Lettow] Lectow P   14 hom]
home ageyne P   16 Howeyn] Hewen P   20 sle him] in r.h. margin M
22 In this same] over erasure M   this] þe P   appered] change to darker ink M
28 held] hold P   30 Ware] in r.h. margin M

1–7: Walsingham, Hist. Ang. ii. 247/14–22.
8–13: ibid. 247/23–9.
14–15: ibid. 248/6–9.
16–17: ibid. 248/10–11.
18–21: ibid. 248/12–20.
22–5: ibid. 248/21–6.
26–219/10: ibid. 248/32–249/30; cf. Trokelowe, 339/3–340/8.

aftir his owne conseite, and writen in | certeyn mennes names, f. 95ʳᵇ
whech he knew neuyr, making þe puple beleue þat all þese wold
rise to help Kyng Richard. And whan þe men were broute before
him, and he knew not many of hem, and officeres inquired whi he
was so bold for to bille hem, he answered because þei were mad 5
rich be King Richard he supposed verily þei schuld meynteyne
his cause. The prest for his labour was hang and drawe. So was
a chanon, priour o Lawne, whech mite ha lyued but for his tunge.
So were certeyn religious men, and specialy of þe Menoures
order, endited of treson and hangen. 10

In þis same tyme Howeyn Glendor, with a multitude of Walschmen, entered into Herforthscire, kyllyng and brennyng as he
was vsed. And ageyn him rod Edmund Mortimer, with all þe
strength of þe cuntré, but be treson Edmund was take and his
part ouirthrowe. And aftir þe batayle ful schamefully þe Walsch 15
women cutte of mennes membris, and put hem in her mouthis
þat were ded, and many oþir inconuenientis ded þei þat same tyme.

In þis ȝere þe kingis doutir was led to Coleyn, and þere þe
emperour son weddid hir.

Sone aftir assumpcion of oure Lady þe kyng rod into Walis 20
for to venge him on his enmye Glendor, and þere, for diuersité
of reyn and cold and snow his host was ny lost. In þe vigile of
natiuité of oure Lady þe kyng had picchid his tent in a fayre pleyne,
but þere blew sodeynly so mech wynd, | and so impetous, with a f. 95ᵛᵃ
gret reyn, þat þe kyngis tent was felled, and a spere cast so violently 25
þat, and þe king had not be armed, he had be ded of þe strok. There
were many þat supposed þis was do be nigromancy, and be compellyng of spirites.

In þis tyme deyed Ser Edmund Langlé, and was byried at
Langlé be his wyf, doutir onto Kyng Petir of Spayn. 30

2 neuyr] ne uyr *separated by small hole in vellum* M   4 him] hyme P,
om. M   5 hem] P, *om.* M   16 hem in] *in r.h. margin* M   Fy *in r.h.*
margin in red M   17 oþir] mo P   same] P, *om.* M   18 doutir . . .
þere] *over erasure* M   20 assumpcion] þe assumpcion P   21 for (1)] *om.*
P   23 natiuité] þe natiuite P   picchid] *1st i surmounted by short stroke in*
red M   24 but] P, *om.* M   25 was felled] *in l.h. margin with carets (in*
red) M   27 þat supposed] supposed þat M, men supposed P   was] *om.* P
be (2)] *om.* P   30 onto] to P

11–17: Walsingham, *Hist. Ang.* ii. 250/11–23.
18–19: ibid. 250/24–8.
20–8: ibid. 250/29–251/16; cf. Trokelowe, 343/3–344/6.
29–30: Walsingham, *Hist. Ang.* ii. 411/25–412/3.

In þis ȝere was a gret batail at Humeldon Hil betwix Englischmen and Scottis, wher þe Erl Duglas was capteyn, and wounded þere, and taken, and of lordis and knytes foure score taken and slayn.

In þat same tyme þe Lolardis set up schamful conclusiones:
5 that þe vii sacramentis ar ded toknes in þat forme whech þe Cherch vsith; that maydenhod and prestod be not appreued of God, but þe state of wedlok is þe most parfit degré; ne þere schal no man ne woman be saued but if he be weddid, or ellis be in wil to be weddid—for þei distroye þe holy sed of whech
10 schuld grow þe secund Trinité; 'Item, if a man and a woman desire to be weddid, þat desire is veri matrimonie; the Cherch is þe sinagog of Sathanas; þe sacrament of þe auter is þe tour of Antecrist; Item, childirn newly bore nede not be baptized'. These conclusiones and many mo Lodewik Clifford broute to þe
15 archbischop, whech saide þat he had susteyned þese of simpilnesse and not of malice. He brout him also names of certeyn men whech susteyned þe same conclusiones.

f. 95ᵛᵇ   In þe fourt ȝere of þis king was | a parlement at London, to no oþir entent but for to haue siluyr both of þe clergi and eke of þe
20 lay-fe.

In þat same tyme þe Scottis, supposing þat all þe lordis had be into Walis with þe kyng, come into Ynglond, as is seid before, for sum sey it was þis ȝere.

In þis same ȝere þe embassatouris come oute of Bretayn, and
25 broute hom þe new qwen onto Wynchestir, whidir þe kyng rod with lordes and ladies, and þere was þe mariage mad þe vii day of Februari, and in þe xxvi day of þe same was sche corowned at London. Sche was before weddid to Ser Jon Mounteforth, duke of Bretayn, be whom sche bare childirn.

30   In þis tyme cam oute a bulle fro þe court whech reuokid all þe graces þat had be grauntid many ȝeres before, of whech ros

1 Hil] om. P   betwix] betwene P   3 and (2)] om. P   7 þe (2)]
om. P   8 if] om. P   13 newly bore] P, om. M   not be baptized] no
baptem P   19 entent] P, en at line end M   for] om. P   22 be into]
w (after be) expuncted M   Ynglond] þis lond P   is] it is P   23 for] om. P
27 Februari] Febravary P   28 was] s suprascript M

1–3: Walsingham, Hist. Ang. ii. 251/17–252/28.
4–17: ibid. 252/29–253/29.
18–20: ibid. 254/8–11.
24–9: ibid. 254/12–20, and 412/5–15; cf. Trokelowe, 350/15–24.
30–221/4: Walsingham, Hist. Ang. ii. 412/17–35.

mech slaundir and obloqui ageyn þe Cherch, for þei seide pleynly
þat it was no more trost to þe pope writing þan to a dogge tail,
for as ofte as he wold gader mony, so oftyn wold he anullen eld
graces and graunt newe.

In þis somyr eke, fast by þe townes of Bedforth and Bikilliswade, 5
appered certeyn men of dyuers colouris, renning oute of wodes and
fytyng horibily. This was seyne on morownyngis and at mydday,
and whan men folowid to loke what it was, þei coude se rite nawt.

In þat same tyme Ser Herry Percy þe ȝonger began to rebelle
ageyn þe king, and to him drew Ser Thomas Percy, erl of Wyscetir, 10
vncil onto þe same Herry. This man had þe prince in gouernauns,
whech sodeynly lefte þe princes hous, and drow to his neue. | And f. 96ra
þat her rebellion schuld be more excusabil þei writyn to þe cuntré
aboute þat þei wold not withdrawe her legauns fro þe king, but
þe cause whi þei strengthid hem þus was for þei wold go to þe 15
king for to enforme him þat bettir gouernauns schuld be had in
þe rem, and þei durst not go withoute strong hand; for, as þei
seid, þe taskes þat were gadered of þe puple, to her grete hurt,
were spent neythir to worchip of God, ne profite of þe lond. Whan
þe kyng had þis relacion he wrote and seide he had ful grete 20
wondir þat þei wold noyse him so; for he knew no cause why, but
þat þei mite come to his presens as safly as euyr þei ded. Eke he
wrote þat mech of þe good þat was gadered was sent to here handis
for tuycion of þe marches. But al þis meued hem nowt, for, with
her hoost, þei remeued streith onto Schrouisbury, abyding þere 25
þe help of Howeyn Glendor oute of Wales.

Whan þe kyng vndirstod her malys, in al hast he þoute to mete
with hem er þei wer fully gadered; for þe erl of Northumbirlond
was not ȝet come onto hem. Thei þat were with Herri Percy
noysed þorw þe cuntré þat þe Kyng Richard was ȝet o-lyue and 30
amongis hem, and for his rite þei were þus gaderid. The kyng rod
to Schrouysbury, where þis Herry Percy had beseged þe toun, but

2 tail] tayle waggyng P   5 eke] evene P   8 se rite nawt]
separated by thin strokes M   11 vncil] P, vncik M   12 neue] in r.h.
margin M   13 þei] i suprascript with caret M   15 was] supplied, om. MP
18 taskes] taxes P   20 he (1)] om. P   24 tuycion] i surmounted by short
stroke in red M, tuicoun P   29 onto] to P   30 Richard] Rich' in r.h.
margin M   31 rod] suprascript M

5–8: ibid. 254/21–7.
9–26: ibid. 254/28–256/3.
27–222/11: ibid. 256/3–257/17.

whan he say þe kyngis standard he lefte þe sege, and turned
sodeynly ageyn þe kyng. In þe ost of Herry Percy were, as it is
f. 96rb wrytyn, xiiii þousand men. The kyng, | whan he sey þe feld so
disposed, seide onto his men wordis of gret coumfort, and mad
5 hem hardi in his quarel.

Than sent þe kyng þe abbot of Schrouisbury, with þe pryuy sel,
onto Herry Percy, desiring þat he schuld com and ask grace, and
spare, þat þer be no blod spilt. Herri was sumwhat mevid with
þis message, and sent to þe king his vnkil, Thomas Percy, and
10 whan þe king, wit3 grete meknesse, had promised þe forseid Herri
his good and lordchip, þis Thomas told his neue al þe reuers.

Than þe kyng comaunded þei schuld bring him his swerd,
in whech he trostid mech; and þei seide it was left in a toun
beside, whech þei clepid Berwik. Whan þe kyng herd 'Berwik'
15 he was gretly astoyned, and seide, 'Forsoth, it hath be oftyn told
me þat in Berwik I schuld be in grete perel. But fite mote we nede'.

So faute þei, to grete harm of þis nacion, and Herri Percy,
aftir þe propirté of his name, percid or presed, in so fer þat he
was ded, and no man wist of whom. Thei fled þat myte fle. þe
20 Erl Duglas was take þere, þe erl of Wissetir, cause of al þe sorow,
Ser Richard Vernon, þe barne of Kynderton, and many oþir.
On þat side were ded þe most part of knytis and swieres of Chestirschire onto þe noumbir of to hundred, and mech of þe puple, of
whech we haue now no noumbir. This batail was on a Satirday, in
25 þe vigil of Mari Magdelen. The next Munday folowand were
heded at Schrouisbury þe erl of Wissetir, þe barn of Kyndirtoun,
and Ser Richard Vernon.

f. 96va And sone aftir, þe erl of Northum|birland cam with myty hand
to help Herry his son, hauyng no knowyng of his deth. Ther met

---

1 standard] dard *in r.h. margin* M   2 it] P, *om.* M   4 onto] to P
9 and . . . king] *over erasure* M   11 and] *supplied, om.* MP   14 whech
þei clepid] þey clepe it P   16 þat] t *suprascript* M   18 name] *suprascript with caret (in red)* M   20 þe erl of Wissetir . . . sorow] *om.* P
21 Ser Richard Vernon þe barne of Kynderton] þe barn of Kindirtoun Ser
Rychard Vernon P   22 were] was P   23 of (3)] *suprascript* M   24 now]
om. P   a] *om.* P   25 next] *om.* P   29 knowyng] knowlech P

1–11: see p. 221.
12–16: Walsingham, *Hist. Ang.* ii. 413/24–5; cf. Trokelowe, 365/14–26, and
    see note in Commentary.
17–27: Walsingham, *Hist. Ang.* ii. 257/18–258/29.
28–223/7: ibid. 258/30–259/12, and 415/6–7; cf. Trokelowe, 371/4–372/26.

with him þe erl of Westmorland and Robert Watirton, and mad
him turne ageyn, and took a castell of his and kept it. Whan þe
kyng had mad al pes at Schrouesbury he rod streyte to ȝork, and
be letteris sent aftir þe erl, in whech he hite him he mite and schuld
com harmles. He cam to þe kyng with fewe men þe nexte day   5
aftir Seynt Laurens. He was not gretly rebuked, but assigned to
certeyn places of his as for a tyme.

  Fro þe north þe king purposed to ride into Walis, but his letting
was þat he failed mony; and þerfor certeyn knytes counceled
þe kyng þat þe bischoppis whech were aboute him schuld be   10
pryued of hors and harneys and tresoure, and þis schuld be goue
to hem þat laboured with þe kyng. This herd þe bischop of
Cauntirbury, and seide,

      Treuly, þere is no knyte with þe kyng þat beginne ones for
      to spoile ony broþir of myn, but he schal for his spoilyng   15
      haue as good knokkis as euyr had Englischman.

  In þe fifte ȝere of þis kyng þe Frenschmen, with þe Bretones,
come to þe town of Plummouthe, brent it, and robbed it—þe
capteyn of hem was a Briton, þe called him lord of Castel. And
whan þei cam hom to Bretayn a elde man of þe same lond met   20
with hem, and seyde onto hem, 'Bewar of þe tayle. Trost verily
þe Englisch|men wil not leue þis mater þus'. And sone aftir, þei   f. 96ᵛᵇ
of Bretayn repented here dede; for a worthi swiere cleped William
Wilforth gadered a nauy and went into Bretayn, and took þere xl
schippis grete and smale, where þei fond yrun, oyle, talow, and a   25
þousand tunnes of wyn de Rochel. The good þei took, þe schippis
brent þei. Than londed þei at Pennarch, and brent sex myle
aboute, and Seint-Mathew town, and iii myle aboute.

  In þese dayes certeyn pilgrymes of Ynglond cam fro Jerusalem,
and erred in her wey, and lay in a forest be nyte, aboue in trees,   30

---

1 him] *om.* P   4 and schuld] *om.* P   7 as] *om.* P   11 harneys]
barnes P   12 bischop] archbischop P   14 for] *om.* P   15 for
his spoilyng] *om.* P   16 Englischman] ony Englyschman P   17 þe (1)]
change to darker ink and narrower letter strokes M   Bretones] Britones *with* e
suprascript above i; i *presumably intended for expunction* M   20 Bretayn]
Britayn *with* e *suprascript above* i M   22-3 þei of] *supplied, om.* MP   25 talow]
and talowe P   28 and Seint-Mathew ... aboute] *om.* P   29 cam fro] *over
erasure* M   29-30 Jerusalem and] *in r.h. margin* M   30 erred] *in l.h. margin* M

  8-16: Walsingham, *Hist. Ang.* ii. 259/13-25.
  17-28: ibid. 259/30-260/7, and 415/14-22; cf. Trokelowe, 375/1-376/12.
  29-224/5: Walsingham, *Hist. Ang.* ii. 415/25-416/16.

for fer of bestis; in þe morown þei cam to a hermites hous, whech man refrecchid hem and bad hem þank God, not only for þei had scaped þe perel of bestis, but for þei were not at hom at þe bataile of Schrouisbury, whech schuld falle in hast, as he
5 saide.

Aftir þe octaue of ephiphanie was a parlement at London, and þere was þe erl of Northumbirlond restored to his londis. Ther eke was graunted swech a task as had neuyr be herd, upon condicion þat þere schuld no memorial wryting be left of it.
10 In þis same tyme þe Frenschmen cam to þe Ylde of Wite askyng tribute of þe dwelleres to þe sustenauns of Qwen Ysabell. And þei of Wyte answered þat Kyng Richard was ded, and þe qwen pesabely sent hom, wherfor þei wold non pay; if þei cam for to fite þei schuld be welkom, and þei schuld gyue hem leue to entyr
15 þe lond, and reste hem iii dayes befor þe batayle. The Frenschmen

f. 97ra herd þis answere, and sayled | fro þat cuntré.

In þat 3ere a Bryton cleped lord of Castel londid at Dortmouth with grete pride, and of hem of whom he had ful gret indignacion—þat is to sey, þe rural puple—was he slayn. In þat jornay,
20 whech was þe xv day of April, were takyn thre lordis and xxti knytes.

In þis 3ere was þe translacion of Seynt Jon, priour of Bridlyngton.

In þis tyme þe cuntesse of Oxenforth, þe moder of Robert Ver,
25 whech was exiled, and ded in Louan, made hir seruauntis to noyse in þe cuntré þat Kyng Richard lyued and schuld sone come with myty hand for to regne ageyn. Eke sche ded make hertis of siluyr, and gaue hem aboute, and drow many hertis to hir conclusion. Many men were illuded be þese tydyngis, specialy þe abbot of
30 Colchestir, and þe abbot of Seynt Osithes. The cuntesse was put

6 ephiphanie] þe epiphanye P   8 eke was] was eke P   10 to] onto P   11 Qwen] þe Qwene P   13 non] not P   14–15 entyr þe lond and] om. P   18 grete pride and of] rete . . . of in darker ink M   19 þe] om. P   22–3 In . . . Bridlyngton] in darker ink M   24 þe (2)] change to darker ink M   25 ded] deyed P   Louan] in r.h. margin M   to] om. P   27–8 Eke . . . conclusion] om. P

1–5: see p. 223.
6–9: Walsingham, Hist. Ang. ii. 260/18–31.
10–16: ibid. 260/32–261/9.
17–21: ibid. 261/10–26, also 416/23–417/2.
22–3: ibid. 262/8–13.
24–225/2: ibid. 262/25–263/23, and 417/36–418/5, also Chronicle, 135/20–30.

in prison, and all hir godes acheted. The clerk þat wrot þese billis
was hanged and drawen.

Aftir, in þe fest of Seynt Jon Baptist, þe erl of Northumbirland
cam to Poumfreite, to þe kyng, with all his alye, and þere was
qwenchid mech suspecioun, for men dempt þei wold be riseris 5
ageyn þe kyng.

And with him cam Ser William Clifforth, knyte, with whom þe
kyng was offendid because he had kept Berwik ageyn þe kyngis
plesauns. But he purchased þe kyngis grace because he browt with
him on Serle, þat was pryuy with Kyng Richard. Whan þat Serle 10
was com, al men desired to knowe in what maner þe duke of
Gloucetir was ded. He confessed ve|rily al þe maner, and seid he f. 97ʳᵇ
was worthi to dey, for he was on of þe principal tormentouris
of þe duke of Gloucetir. And whan men inqwyred of him why he
noysed in þe puple þat Kyng Richard was lyuand, he seide he ded 15
it in despite of King Herry, for to drawe mennis hertis fro him.
He seide eke þat whan he was in þe kyngis hous of Frauns ful wel
at ese, and herd sei þat Kyng Richard lyued in Scotlond, he went
þidir to proue þe treuth, and fond veryly it was not soth. þan
cam he onto Berwik, onto William Clifford, for to seke socour, 20
and þus was he led to þe kyng. Than was he condempned to be
drawe þorowoute the good townes of Ynglond, and aftir to be
hangen and quartered at London.

In þis ȝere was a gret parlement at Couentré, in whech þe kyng
asked a grete summe of þe puple, and þe speker of þe parlement 25
answered þat swech summes myte not be rered so ofte in þe puple
but if þe Cherch schuld be put fro her temporaltés. This answere
was goue be Ser Jon Chene, knyte, speker of þe parlement.
And no wondir þouȝ he was enmy to þe Cherch; for he had
befor þat tyme take þe ordir of subdiacoun, and withoute dis- 30
pensacioun aspired to þe order of wedlak, and eke þe degré of
knythod.

1 and] *suprascript* M   2 was] *suprascript* M   10 þat (2)] *om.* P   13 was
on] *separated by small hole in vellum* M   15 noysed] naysed P   16 fro]
twice over line division P   17 þat] *om.* P   of Frauns] *in r.h. margin* M
18 sei] sey P, seid M   20 onto (2)] to P   for] *om.* P   21 Than] Thus P
29 And] *change to darker ink* M   30 þat tyme] P, *om.* M   þe] *om.* P
31 þe (2)] to þe P

3–23: Walsingham, *Hist. Ang.* ii. 263/24–264/29, and 418/7–9; cf. Trokelowe,
    390/22–391/3.
24–226/23: Walsingham, *Hist. Ang.* ii. 264/30–267/19.

The archbiscop ros and seide,

Now se I weel whidir þi malice walkith. Thou, renegate and
apostata of þin ordyr, woldist put þe Cherch al vndirfote, but
whil þis hed stant on þis body þou schal neuyr haue þi entent.

_{f. 97va} Remembir þe wel þat, at euery task, | þe Cherch haue payed
6   as mech as þe lay-fe. And all ȝoure besinesse is for to gadere
to make ȝoureselue rich. But know þis for a treuth, þat lond
schal neuir endure in prosperité þat despiseth Holy Cherch.

And þan ros þe archbischop, and kneled before þe kyng, and
10 prayed him he wold remembir him of þe oth þat he had mad in his
coronacion þat he schuld meynten þe Cherch and alle þe ministeres
þerof in al her libertées. Than þe kyng comaunded þe archbischop
to take his sete, behesting him þat he schuld leue þe Cherch in as
good astate as he fond it.

15 Than said þe archbischop to þe knytes,

Ȝe haue stered þe kyng to enchete all þe temporaltés þat
longyn to þe Frensch monkis in al þe lond, and þouȝ þe
valew of hem com to many þousandis, þe kyng is not amendid
þerby half a mark be ȝere; for ȝe amongis ȝou haue it, and
20   dispende it at ȝoure plesauns. And moreouyr, I sey ȝou myn
hed schal rather bowe onto þe swerd þan Holy Cherch schuld
lese ony part of his rite.

Thus sesed þe fals chalenge of þe enmyes to þe Cherch.

In þe same parlement þe archbischop, as he went in þe strete,
25 happed to mete þe prest beryng þe sacrament to a seke man, for
þere was grete pestilens in þe town at þat tyme. The archbischop
and oþir many ded reuerens to þe sacrament, as it was her deuté.
Many of þe puple in þe strete turned her bakkes and avaled not her
hodes, ne ded no maner reuerens. This was told onto þe kyng, and
_{f. 97vb} he ded in þis mater | dew correccion, for many of hem were of his
31 hous.

---

3 apostata] þou postata P   5 haue] hath P   6 lay-fe And]
separated by small hole in vellum M   for] *om.* P   9 þan ros þe archbischop and] þe archbyschope P   10 had] P, *om.* M   bischop]
byschop P   14 astate] state P   20 ȝou] to ȝow P   12 archbischop]
29 maner] maner of P   26 at] *om.* P

1–23: see p. 225.
24–31: Walsingham, *Hist. Ang.* ii. 419/2–38.

In þis ȝere þe se ros so hye betwix Caleys and Kent þat it drenchid many townys in Kent and Flaundris, Hollond, and Selond.

This ȝere deyed William Wikam, bischop of Wynchestir, þat foundid to nobil collegis, on at Wynchestir, anoþir at Oxenforth. 5 And in þe first day of Octobir deyed Pope Boneface þe IX, and in his stede was chosen þe bischop of Bononie, cleped Innocent þe VII.

In þe sexte ȝere of þis kyng, in þe fest of Cristis natiuité, certeyn men let make keyis of many dores in þe castell of Wynde- 10 sore, þere entered þei be nyte, and took þe eyres of March, and led hem owte. Summe sey her purpos was to lede hem into Wales, þat, be þe power of Glendor, thei myte rejoyse þe crowne as þe rite eyeres of Ynglond. But þei were pursewed, and summe were slayn, and summe fled; þe smyth þat mad þe keyes lost his hed. 15

In þis ȝere Thomas Mounbray, Erl Marchale, cam onto Maistir Richard Scrop, archbischop of ȝork, and mad confederacion þat þei schuld help to amende þe insolens in þe reme. Eke Thomas, Lord Bardolf, went onto þe erle of Northumbirlond for þe same cause. Thei cleped onto hem þe cité of ȝork and mech of þe 20 cuntré, and set up certeyn articles in cherch-dores, expressing what was her entent:—

First, þei desired þat þe puple of þe reme schuld haue fre elleccion of knytes of þe parlement aftir þe eld forme; the secunde, þat þer schuld be a remedie ageyns fals sugges|tiones, f. 98ra be which many men were disherid of her londis; the þirde, 26 þat þere schuld be ordeyned a remedye ageyn þese greuous taskes, and ageyn þe grete extorciones, and eke oppressing of marchauntis.

Whan þe puple had red þese articules, þei drow fast onto þe 30 bischop.

7 stede] *in r.h. margin with carets (in red)* M   13–14 þe rite] *separated by thin stroke in red* M, *very* P   14 were (2)] *om.* P   17 archbischop] archbyschop P, arbischop *with* ar *suprascript* M   confederacion] consederacion P 18 in þe reme] of þe renge of Ynglond P   19 onto] to P   21 cherchdores] þe cherch dores P   26 which] with P   27 þere] *om.* P   28 oppressing] oppression P   30 onto] to P

1–3: ibid. 267/30–268/2, and 420/14–18; cf. Trokelowe, 394/21–7.
4–5: Walsingham, *Hist. Ang.* ii. 268/3–8.
6–8: ibid. 268/10–12.
9–15: ibid. 268/14–18, and 420/33–421/6.
16–31: ibid. 268/33–269/19, and 422/8–35.

This herd, þe erl of Westmorland, þat was þat tyme with Lord Jon, þe kingis þird son, in þe cuntré fast by, gadered a grete felauchip, entendyng for to distroye þe archbischoppis power, but, whan he had aspied þe archbischoppis party strenger þan his, he sent onto him, and inqwyred why þis puple was gadered; and þe archbischop answered ageyn, for non oþir entent but for þei wold purpos certeyn materes to þe kyng, to whom þei durst not go withoute grete puple. Tho sent he him þe articules before rehersid.

And whan þe kingis son and þe erl had red hem, þai praised hem, and desired þat þei schul com speke togidir with fewer folk. The archbischop cam onto hem, and þere had þe erl of Westmorland þese wordis:—

Ser bischop, it is best, sithe ȝoure desire and oure is al on, þat þe puple vndirstande it, þat þei nede not þus to labour; wherfor we desire þat sum special man schal be sent in ȝoure name to comaunde euery man go hom to his labour, saue þei þat schul wayte upon ȝou.

This was do in dede, and as þe bischoppis men voided þe oþir party encresed. The good prest, bischop of ȝork, vndirstod neuir þe deceyte onto þe tyme þat þe seid erle arested him, and þe Erl Mar|chale was arested eke in þe same place, and behote hem þei schuld be saued harmles, but þis behest was not kept. Of þis fals behest not kept profecied Jon Bridlington vndir þese vers:—

Pacem tractabunt, set fraudem subter arabunt.
Pro nulla marca saluabitur ille ierarcha.

This is þe sentens:—

Pes schul þei tretyn; gile undir þat schul þei betyn.
For no maner mark schal be saued þat blessed ierark.

f. 98ʳᵇ (line 21 marginal)

---

3 archbischoppis] archbyschopp P, arbischoppis *with* ar *suprascript* M
4 þe archbischoppis party] þat þe same power was P 8 he] *om.* P
13 þese] sweche P 15 it] *suprascript* M 17 go] to go P 19 bischoppis]
archbyschoppes P 20 bischop] archbyschop P 24 not kept] *om.* P
Jon] P, *om.* M

1–30: Walsingham, *Hist. Ang.* ii. 269/20–270/30; cf. Trokelowe, 405/26–407/14.

In þis tyme was þe kyng in þe march of Walis, with many þousand, for to fite with Glendor. But whan he herd of þis mater, anon he cam to Ʒork, and þei of þe cité com oute with ropes aboute her nek, barefoot, crying mercy.

On þe Moneday in Pentecost weke, whil þe archbischop of Cauntirburi was at dyner with þe kyng, and long taried in talkyng, the erl of Arundel, and Ser Thomas Beuforth, and William Gascoyne, justise, be a commission, condempned þe bischop and þe erl to þe deth, and, þat þere schuld no prayer be mad for hem, led anon forth into þe feld, and þere were her hedis smet of. In þe place where þe bischop deied were many myracles and mech pilgrimage tyl þe tyme þat þe kyng forbade it, up peyne of deth.

The kyng aftir þat tyme lost þe beuté of his face, for, as þe comoun opinion went, fro þat tyme onto his deth he was a lepir, and euyr fowler and fowler; for in his deth, as þei recorded þat sey him, he was so contracte þat his body was scarse a cubite of length.

Whan þe archbischop of Cauntirbury | herd of þis dede, he took swech heuynesse þat he fel in a tercian, þat continued many dayes, and þerfor in al hast he was caried hom.

Aftir þis, whan þe kyng had punchid þe cyté of Ʒork to þe vtterest, he rod for to pursewe þe erl of Northumbirlond and Ser Thomas Bardolf, and þei fled to Berwik, and aftirward into Scotlond. The king pursewid hem, and took Berwik fro þe keperis, and many oþir casteles þat longid to þe erle. Aftir, he went into Wales, and þere lost he al his labour.

Tho called he a councel at Wycetir, to se what puruyauns myte be mad for mony to þe kyng, and þe archbischop of Cauntirbiry asked in þis mater deliberacioun, for þe lond was so pilled þat euery man was wery.

In þis Ʒere were sent embassiatouris fro þe kyng of Denmark for to haue þe kyngis dowtir, Philip, to be joyned in wedlok to her

5

10

15

f. 98ᵛᵃ

20

25

30

6 talkyng] her talkyng P   8 bischop] archbischop P   9 erl] Erl
Marchale P   12 up] *suprascript* M   15 fowler (2)] fowle P   16 of]
om. P   18 þat(2)] whech P   22 Bardolf] Bradollf P   to] *suprascript in red*
M   aftirward] aftir P   23 took] k *suprascript* M   24 Aftir] Aftir
þat P   25 he] *om.* P   26 called] d *suprascript* M   31 her] þat P

1-12: Walsingham, *Hist. Ang.* ii. 423/21-424/36, and 270/31-271/2.
17-19: Trokelowe, 411/15-21.
20-5: Walsingham, *Hist. Ang.* ii. 271/11-16 and 271/23-38.
26-9: ibid. 272/3-6.
30-230/4: ibid. 271/17-19; Trokelowe, 419/33-420/5.

kyng. The kyng broute hir to Lenne, for to take schip þere, and
in þat town he lay nyne daies—þe kyng, too qwenes, thre sones
of þe kyng, Herri, Thomas, and Vmfrey, and many oþir lordis and
ladies.

5　　In þis tyme a hundred schippis and xl sailed oute of Frauns into
Wales, for to help Howen Glendor. Thei cam into Mylforth Haue;
but al her hors were ded or þei cam þere for defaute of fresch
watir. Eke þe Lord Berklé and Herry Pay brent xv of hem in þe
same hauene; and, at anoþir jornay, þe Lord Berklé and Ser
10　Thomas Swynborn and Herry Pay took xiiii schippis of hem, in

f. 98vb　whech þei took þe steward of Fra|unce, with oþir vii capteynes.

In þis same tyme a strong þeef and loksmyth, whan he was
juged to þe deth be William Cokayn, he seide he schuld availe
þe kyng mech god if he mite lyue a day or too. Than appeled he
15　certeyn worthi men, and specialy abbotes, of treson, amongis
whech þe abbot of Ramsey was principal. A certeyn day was set
at Huntyngdon where þei appered alle, but first cam in þe abbot of
Ramsey, and befor him on of his monkis, he folowyng as a secundary. The juge saide to þe thef, 'What man is þis?' of þe monk
20　þat went first. The thef saide,

This is þe abbot of Ramsey; ful often hath he sent me with
gold into Wales, to meynten þat tretour Glendor in his
rebellion ageyn þe king.

Tho seid þe juge onto hem, þat þei schuld lede him to his deth as a
25　fals thef, and a fals accuser. Thus was þe abbot excused, and many
oþir worthi men, at þe noumbir of fifty.

This ȝere þe erle of Arundel weddid þe kyngis doutir of Portingale with grete solempnité.

In þe vii ȝere of þis kyng deied on Roger Walden, euir in-
30　fortunat. For fro grete pouerté Kyng Richard mad him first
tresorer, and þan bischop of Cauntirburi, lyuyng Thomas Arundel,

---

1 The kyng] They P　　　2 kyng] P, om. M　　　12 loksmyth] a lok-
smythe P　　　17 first cam] st cam over erasure M　　　18 him] change to
darker ink M　　　25 fals thef] þe expuncted after fals M　　　26 men, at
þe] n at þ over erasure in darker ink M　　　31 bischop] archbyschop P

1–4: see p. 229.
5–11: Walsingham, Hist. Ang. ii. 272/7–19; cf. Trokelowe, 415/5–24.
12–26: Trokelowe, 415/29–416/36.
27–8: Walsingham, Hist. Ang. ii. 272/22–4.
29–231/2: ibid. 272/29–273/1.

and fro þat honour was he put, and þan was he bischop of London, and put fro þat within o ʒere.

In þis tyme þe pope cursed openly all þoo þat consented to þe deth of Richard Scrop, archbischop of ʒork.

In þis ʒere eke was þe puple gretly oppresid with taskes, and ⁵ knites|-mete, and mech oþir þing. Eke prestis annueleris payed f. 99ʳᵃ nobles to þe king, and all religious, if þei had swech annuellis.

In þis ʒere þe Scottis ledde þe kyngis son of Scotlond into Fravns, to lerne þat tonge, and eke curtesie. And men of Cley, in Northfolk, took þe schip in whech was þis child, with a bischop, ¹⁰ and þe erle of Orkeney, and led hem to London to þe kyng.

In þis ʒere deied Innocent þe VII, and þe cardinalis swore solempne othis if ony of hem were chosen he schuld frely resine his dignité, upon þis condicion, þat þe antipope schuld resigne, and þan, be þe auctorité of both colleges, swech on schuld be chose, ¹⁵ be whom vnité schuld be had in þe Cherch. Than, in þe xxx day of Nouembir þei chosen on cleped Aungel, and him named þei Gregorius XII, and mad him for to swere and write þat he schuld kepe þis ordinauns.

In þis ʒere eke deied Herry Spenser, bischop of Norwich, and ²⁰ in his place was chose Alisaundre Totyngton, priour of þe same place.

In þe viii ʒere of þis kyng þe Pope Gregory, whan he was redy to ride onto þe cité þere þe vnité schuld be had, sodeynly, be stering of þe deuele, þe kyng of Napeles cam and leid sege at ²⁵ Seint Laurens gate. The pope with þe cardinales fled into Castell Aungel, and prayed Paule of þe Vrcines þat he schuld help in þis nede. Than was þere on Nicholas of þe Columpnes be whos

---

2 within] and al within P   3 tyme] same tyme P   4 Richard] Maystir Richard P   5 ʒere eke] eke *over erasure* M, same ʒer P   gretly] full gretly P   7 annuellis] anuell P   10 þis] þe P   12 Innocent . . . cardinalis] cent . . . cardinalis *over erasure* M   15 þe] *om.* P   16 day] *suprascript with caret (in red)* M   17 þei (2)] *in r.h. margin* M   18 XII] XI P   for to swere] to swer P, for swere M   20 eke] *om.* P   21 Alisaundre] *om.* P   24 redy] P, rydy M   25 stering] þe steryng P   26 cardinales] cardinall P

3–4: ibid. 273/3–4.
5–7: ibid. 273/5–14.
8–11: ibid. 273/21–7.
12–19: ibid. 274/15–275/9.
20–2: ibid. 274/7–11.
23–232/4: ibid. 276/23–34; cf. *Chronicle*, 21/11–33.

consent þe kyng of Naples brak þe wal and entered þe cité, and
þan þis Paule of þe Vrcines faute with his host, and killid of hem
f. 99ʳᵇ and took into a vii þousand. Tho fled þe king | into Naples, and be
þis mene was þe vnité of þe Cherch lettid.

5 In þis ȝere, at þe feste of þe assumpcion of oure Lady, deied
Ser Robert Knollis, whech man was ful victorious in many
batailes, and gretly famed in Frauns and Spayn and Bretayn and
many oþir cuntrées. He mad eke the brigge ouyr þe watir of
Medewey, fast by Rouchestir, and ded gret cost at þe Car-
10 melites of Londoun, where he is biried, and mad a colege at
Pountfrait.

In þis ȝere þe prince leide a sege to þe castell of Abrustwith, in
Wales, and streytid hem so, þat were in þe castel, þat þei promised
him to ȝelde þe castel at a certeyn day. But it avayled not, for
15 Glendor cam, and put new men in þe castell, and avoided al
hem þat consented be ony menis onto þe prince.

In þe ix ȝere of þis kyng was a gret wyntir, þat dured both
Decembir, Januari, Februari, and March, þat þe most part of
smale birdis were ded.

20 And þat same ȝere, in þe parlement tyme at London, the erl
of Northumbirlond and Ser Thomas Bardolf cam oute of Scotlond
ageyn to Ynglond, and whan þei cam ny þe town of Thrisk,
þere met þei þe schryue of Euerwik Ser Thomas Rokby, Alexander Lownde, Petir de la Hay, and Robert Helys, with many
25 othir. There faute þei, and þe erles side had þe betir part first,
but finaly þe erl was killid, and þe lord hurt and aftir ded, and
her hedis aftir þat born aboute London. The bischop of Bangor
was take þere, but because he was not armed he had his lyf.
f. 99ᵛᵃ Than was þere mech accusacion in þe north of hem þat | fauoured
30 þese lordis, for whech cause þe kyng rod to ȝork, and ded gret
execucion in þis mater, both in mennis deth, and enchetyng of her
godes.

2 killid of hem] kylled of hem P, killid of hem killid M   3 a] *om.* P   Tho]
þan P   5 þe feste of þe] *om.* P   7 and (2)] *om.* P   8 eke] *om.* P
13 þat (1)] þat þey þat P   þat (2)] *om.* P   16 onto] to P   17 þat] þa P
23–4 Alexander] and Alysaundr P   31 enchetyng] acheting P

1–4: see p. 231.
5–11: Walsingham, *Hist. Ang.* ii. 277/1–9: cf. *Chronicle*, 22/1–10.
12–16: Walsingham, *Hist. Ang.* ii. 277/22–5, *Chronicle*, 22/21–27/9.
17–19: Walsingham, *Hist. Ang.* ii. 277/28–32.
20–32: ibid. 277/33–279/5, *Chronicle*, 27/20–29/17.

In þis ʒere, þe nest day aftir Mari Magdalen, was a gret councel
at London of all prelates, exempt and not exempt, for to withdrawe
her obediens fro þe Pope Gregori, for he wold not kepe his promisse
and his oth. And upon þis þei stered þe kyng to write letteris to
þe pope þat he schuld kepe his promisse. A cardinal of Bordews 5
eke cam into þis lond to excite þe kyng and the prelatis þat þei
schuld withdrawe her obediens fro þe pope, whech was perjure.
And to þis conclusioun consentid þe king of Frauns, writyng to
princes and lordis þat þei schuld help to þis vnité; for it was
schame, he seid, to þe Cristen feith þat, for þe pride of to prestis, 10
so mech blod schuld be spilt. It was eke determined, as he wrote, be
þe vniuersités of Parise, Bononie, Aurelianense, Mounte-pesulane,
and Tholosane, þat no kyng ne prince ne prelate myte obeye ony of
þese too but if he were a fautour of scisme and of heresie. Sextene
cardinales eke were fled fro þe popes, and held þe same opinion. 15

Vpon þis, sone aftir þe ephiphani, was gadered a councel at
Paules at London, and þere were chosen certeyn prelates for to
go to þe councel of Pise, of whech Maystir Robert Alum, bischop
of Salisbury, was principal.

In þe xi ʒere of þis kyng began þe councell of Pise, for þer 20
were þe cardinales of both collegis, both of Gregori and Benedict,
and a gret noum|byr of prelatis, all sette on þis holy conclusion f. 99ᵛᵇ
to reforme vnité in Holy Cherch. Aftir þei had cleped þe Holy
Goost þei consentid all and chosen o person, whech þei clepid
Alisaunder þe Fift. Gregorie and Benet were not þere, but 25
grucchid ful sore ageyn þis eleccion. This Alisaundre graunted to
þe prioury of Seynt Bartholomé, in Smythfeld, plener remission
in þe first day of his creacion to all þoo þat visited þis place on

5 kepe] *change to darker ink* M   promisse] promys and hys oth P
10 feith] *in r.h. margin with carets (in red)* M   11 so mech blod schuld
be spilt] schuld be spylt so mech blood P   be (2)] *over erasure* M   16 was]
in r.h. margin M   17 prelates] s *suprascript* M   for] *om.* P   18 Robert]
om. P   Alum bischop] *separated by thin stroke in red* M   20 xi ʒere] *separated
by thin stroke in red* M   26 þis] þe P   27 Bartholomé] Bartholomes P
27–8 plener remission in þe first day of his creacion] in þe fyrst day of hys
creacion plener remission P   28 þoo] *om.* P   visited] visite P   place]
suprascript M

1–15: Walsingham, *Hist. Ang.* ii. 279/6–12, 279/25–280/8, *Chronicle*, 29/28–
    30/6, 31/1–44/13.
16–19: Walsingham, *Hist. Ang.* ii. 280/9–13, *Chronicle*, 44/16–21.
20–234/2: Walsingham, *Hist. Ang.* ii. 281/29–282/8; cf. *Chronicle*, 50/32–
    51/13.

Maundé þursday, Good Friday, Satirday folowand, and þe anunciacioun of oure Lady.

In þis ȝere was a parlement at London in tyme of Lenton, where a smyth was appechid for heresie. He held þis conclusion, 5 þat þe sacrament of þe auter is not Cristes body, but a þing withoute soule, wers þan a tode or a ereyne, whech haue lyf. And whan he wold not renouns his opinion, he was take to þe seculer hand, for to be sperd in a tunne in Smythfeld, and to be brent. The Prince Herry had pité on þe man, and counceled him to 10 forsake þis fals opinion, but he wold not, wherfor he was put in þe tunne; and whan þe fer brent, he cried horribily. þe prince comaunded to withdrawe þe fire, cam to him, and behite him grete þingis, but it wold not be, wherfor he suffered him to be brent into asches.

15 In þis ȝere eke was brent þe town of Seynt-Omeris, with þe abbey, for þe duke of Burgoyn had leyd þere all his apparament, with whech he þoute to besege Caleys, amongis whech was a horribile ordinauns, smale barellis filt ful of serpentis and venemous f. 100ʳᵃ bestes, whech he þoute for | to þrow into Caleys be engynes, 20 þat, whan þe barelles broke, þe corupt venym schuld infecte hem of þe town. All þis gere was brent be a ȝong man þat bewreyid it to þe soudyoures of Caleys, and þei gaue him grete good to sette þis town o-fire.

Alisaundir, þe pope new chose, deied in þe councell of Pise, 25 and aftir him was chose Balthasar, bischop of Bonony, with concent of all þe cardinales.

In þe xii ȝere of þis kyng þe kyng of Crakow, touchid with þe Holy Gost, was baptized in þe name of þe Trinité. Alle þei þat were Sarasines laboured eythir to peruerte him or elles to distroye 30 him; þerfor he disposed him to gete help of Cristen men, and supposed þat þe heres of Pruse schuld best help him. Thei,

1 þe] in þe P   3 tyme] þe tyme P   6 haue] hathe P   12–13 cam to him and behite him grete þingis] cam to him and behite him grete M, cam a behyte grete þynges to hym P   20 barelles] barel P   corupt] t *suprascript* M   21 brent] *in r.h. margin with carets* (*in red*) M   30 him (2)] *suprascript* M   gete] grete P   31 schuld best help] best schuld help P   him] hym P, *om.* M

1–2: see p. 233.
3–14: Walsingham, *Hist. Ang.* ii. 282/11–33; cf. *Chronicle*, 51/17–52/28.
15–23: Walsingham, *Hist. Ang.* ii. 283/31–284/12.
24–6: ibid. 284/13–16.
27–235/7: ibid. 284/17–285/5; cf. *Chronicle*, 58/5–31.

seing þat his frendis were turned fro him, set upon him on þe
oþir side, only to distroye him. Behold what zelatouris þei were of
oure feith! Her religion was ordeyned to defende þe feith, and
now couetise stereth hem to distroye it. The kyng, þat was newly
Cristis child, þoute it was best first for to fite ageyn þese religious 5
renegatis. He faute with hem, and put hem to flite, and conqwered
al þe cuntré, suffiring hem to use her eld lawes and customes.

In þis tyme Jon Prendirgest, knyte, and William Longe kepte
þe se so weel þat no Englischman had harm. But many of þe
kyngis hous had envye with him, þat he was compelled to take 10
Westminster, and þere so streytid þat he dwelled in þe porch of
þe cherch, both nyte and day. William Longe kept stille þe se
on|to þe tyme þat þe chaunceler sent for him, and hite him he f. 100ʳᵇ
schuld no harm haue, but whan he had him, he sent him to þe
Tour.   15

In þis ȝere þe archbischop of Cauntirbury wold visite þe
vniuersité of Oxenforth, but þei wold not obey it.

In þis ȝere began a gret debate betwix þe duke of Burgundy and
þe Duke Aurelianense for because þat þe first had killid þe fader
of þe secunde. With þe Duke Aurelianense was þe kyng of Nauerne 20
and Aragone, dukes of Berry and Britanny, with al Gascon and
Gyan, þe erles of Huys and Armanak, with many othir. With þe
duke of Burgeyn was þe kyng of Frauns, and for he sey his party
was not strong, he sent enbassatouris to þe kyng of Ynglond, þat
he schuld help, promitting him his doutir to be weddid to þe 25
prince, and mech gold and tresore with hire.

This kyng of Ynglond gaue hem þis answore. He þoute þe
titil of þis bataile not leful because the ȝong man was stered of
nature to venge his fader deth, and it was a febil cause to fite in

1 set upon him] *om.* P   2 side only] *separated by thin stroke in red as* e
in side *inserted on the line* M   4 The] *change to darker ink* M   5 for]
om. P   6 and (2)] *om.* P   10 him] hem P   he] Jon P   13 þe
tyme þat] þe tyme tha P, *om.* M   13–14 and hite . . . had him] *om.* P
14 whan] *in r.h. margin* M   19 Duke Aurelianense] *of expuncted after* Duke
M   for because þat] becawse P   20 of Nauerne] *in r.h. margin with
carets (in red)* M   21–2 and Britanny with al Gascon and Gyan] Brytayne
and all Gyan and Gascon P   22 with] and P   25 help] lp *over
erasure* M   26 and (1)] *om.* P   27 This] The P   28 not] t *suprascript* M

8–15: Walsingham, *Hist. Ang.* ii. 285/10–24; cf. *Chronicle,* 59/3–24.
16–17: Walsingham, *Hist. Ang.* ii. 285/25–6.
18–236/7: ibid. 285/27–286/14; cf. *Chronicle,* 59/28–60/15.

swech degré þere morder schuld be meynteyned; wherfor he
counceled þei schuld plese þe ȝong man with swete letteris and
fayre behestis, and offer onto him amendment aftir her power;
if he wold not be plesed, so withdrawe hem onto more sikir
5 place, where he mite not noye hem; and if þei ded al þis and
offered þese leful menes, and it availed not, þan had þe kyng of
Ynglond sum colour for to fite and to help his frendis.

And sone aftir þe kyng sent þis meny to him with lordis, þe
f. 100ᵛᵃ erl of Arundel, | þe erle of Kym, þe Lord Cobbam, Ser Jon
10 Oldcastel, with many men of armes, and archeres. Thei were
receyued be þe duke of Burgundi ful worchipfully, and waged
sufficiently. But whan þei had taried longe in Parys, vitaile began
to wax dere, and specialy flesch, wherfor þei seid þei wold go gete
sum vitaile among her enmies. This Duke Aurelianense lay in a
15 strong place, fast be a town þei clepe Seyn-Clo. This perseyued
oure Englischmen, and wold ha take þe town but þe brigge was
broken. Ther bikird þei, and on þe Frensch side, whech was with
þe Duke Aurelianense, many were dronchin and killid a m and
ccc. Many were taken and broute to Paris, and þere began a strif
20 betwix hem of Paris and Englischmen, for þei of Paris wold haue
hem ded as tretoures, and þe oþir parti had graunted hem lyf,
so þat þei payed raunson. Than þei of Paris payed her raunson,
and þan killed hem.

In þe xiii ȝere of þis kyng þis Duke Aurelianense, seing þis
25 fray mad be Englischmen had astoyned al his host, wrot onto
þe kyng of Ynglond, both he and his frendis, in þis maner:—

Jon, þe son of þe kyng of Frauns, duke of Biturie and
Aluerne; Charlis, Duke Aurelianense and Valens, Erl Blesens
and Bellemount, and Lord Concionat; Jon, Duke Burbon,
30 erl of Claremount and of Forestis, lord of Belleiocy; Jon,

---

1 he] þei P   2 þei] þat þei P   3 onto] to P   6 þan] n over
erasure M   8 And] om. P   10 men] other men P   11 ful] om. P
12 sufficiently] P, sufficienly M   14 sum] om. P   18 þe] P, om. M
and (1)] suprascript M   and (2)] P, om. M   22 her] the P   23 þan]
om. P   24–5 seing þis fray] perceyvyng thys grete affray P   27 þe
son of] son to P   of þe] separated by thin stroke in red M   28 Erl] supplied, om. M, & P

1–7: see p. 235.
8–23: Walsingham, Hist. Ang. ii. 286/15–287/10; cf. Chronicle, 60/16–61/22.
24–237/7: Walsingham, Hist. Ang. ii. 287/12–35.

Erl Alenconye, and Armenak, and lord de Pertica and Filgeriarum—we notifie to all men þat we send oure special
legates to trete and to acorde with þat worchipfull | Prince   f. 100ᵛᵇ
Herry, be þe grace of God king of Ynglond, and with all his
sones, of þe restitucion and þe real induccioun of þe duchy   5
of Gian (whech longith to him of heritage, as it is seide),
whech restitucion schal be mad be us.

Whan þis procuracie was come to þe kyng, þese articules were
offered of þe lordis: first, þat her bodies and her goodes schuld
be redy to his seruyse; secunde, þat her childyrn schuld be maried   10
be his disposicioun; the þird, þat her castellis, townes, and
tresoris schuld be his; the fourt, þat all her frendys in þe clergy
or in þe lay-fe schul be his frendis; the v, þat all þe londis in
Gyan and Gascon þat long to him be heritage schul be delyuered
him, and eke þoo þat þei haue in possession, and moreouyr þo   15
þat be in oþir handis, þei schul help to gete hem. These be þe
articules whech þei profered.

These articules folowand desired þei of þe kyng: þat þe kyng
and his successouris schal help þe Duke Aurelianense ageyn
þe duke of Burgeyn; the secund, þat þei schuld recure all þe   20
harmes whech were do to hem be þe same duke; the þirde, of
restitucion to her frendis and her seruauntis; the fourt, þat he
schal gyue assistens that pes may be had betwix þe to remes,
Ynglond and Frauns.

Sone aftir, in þe fest of assumpcion of oure Lady sent þe kyng   25
his son Thomas, duke of Clarens, and Edward, duke of 3ork,
Thomas, erl of Dorcet, with mech strength onto þe Duke Aurelianense ageyn þe duke of Burgundye, and 3et was not þe erl of
Arundel and his retenew | com hom. And of þis sodeyn chaunge   f. 101ʳᵃ
men had mech merueyle, þat in so schort tyme þe kyng schuld   30
fauour to contraries. Thei þat were sent londyd in Normandie,
and þere abiden long tyme, for þe Duke Aurelianense cam not as

1 Alenconye] Alentonie P   lord] *supplied, om.* MP   1–2 Filgeriarum]
silgenarum P   2 to] vnto P   5 þe (2)] *om.* P   10 secunde]
the secund P   11 castellis] castell P   12 in] both in P   14 dely-
uered] *final* d *altered from* t M   20 schuld] schal P   23 may] schal P
þe to remes] these to remes P, þe remes M   25 assumpcion] þe assumpcion P   þe kyng] *in r.h. margin with carets* (*in red*) M   27 onto]
to P   30 schort] h *suprascript with caret* (*in red*) M

8–24: ibid. 287/36–288/20; cf. *Chronicle*, 63/34–64/29.
25–238/4: Walsingham, *Hist. Ang.* ii. 288/22–289/3.

comenaunt was; wherfor þei brent townes, and took castelles, and ded mech harm. Sone aftir þei cam and spak togidir, þe Dukes Aurelianense and Clarense, and be her councell þe Englisch hoost went into Gian, and dwelt þere al þe wyntir.

5   In þe xiiii ȝere þis kyng deied, þe xx day of March, whan he had regned xiii ȝere and a half. At his deth, as was reported of ful sad men, certeyn lordes stered his confessour, Frere Jon Tille, Doctour of Diuinité, þat he schuld induce þe kyng to repent him and do penauns, in special for iii þingis: on, for þe deth on Kyng
10 Richard; the oþir, for þe deth of þe Archbischop Scrop; þe þird, for þe wrong titil of þe crowne. And his answere was þis:—

For þe to first poyntis, I wrote onto þe pope þe veri treuth of my consciens, and he sent me a bulle with absolucion and penauns assigned, whech I haue fulfillid. And as for þe þird
15 poynt, it is hard to sette remedy, for my childirn wil not suffir þat þe regalie go owte of oure lynage.

In þe ȝere of þe world 6611, and of our Lord Jesu 1413, was Herry þe V corowned at Westminster on Passion Sunday. And aftir his coronacion he was euene turned onto anoþir man, and
20 all his mocions inclined to vertu.

f. 101ʳᵇ   6612; 1414. In þe ȝere folowand he held a parlement at Lon|don, in whech parlement he asked no subsidy of no man, and þat was grete plesauns to þe puple; for þere was no parlement many day but sum subsidie was graunted.

25   In þis same ȝere a grete part of Norwich was brent, and a fayre couent of þe Prechoures ordir.

Eke in þis ȝere Thomas, duke of Clarens, cam hom fro Gian, and þe king held a solempne terment for his fader at Cauntirbury.

In a councell at London þis ȝere was ordeyned þat þe festes of
30 Seynt George and Seynt Dunstan schuld be dobbil festes.

2 Dukes] P, Duke M   8 induce] indute P   9 in special for] of P
12 to] om. P   13 absolucion] change to darker ink M   14 fulfillid] do P
And as] om. P   17 ȝere of þe] om. over line division with ȝer added in r.h.
margin P   24 graunted] d suprascript M   27 Eke] change to paler ink M

1–4: see p. 237.
5–6: Walsingham, Hist. Ang. ii. 289/16–21.
17–20: ibid. 290/3–19; cf. Chronicle, 69/8–26.
21–4: Walsingham, Hist. Ang. ii. 290/20–1; cf. Chronicle, 69/28–30, and see note in Commentary.
25–6: Walsingham, Hist. Ang. ii. 290/26–9.
27–8: ibid. 290/22–5, 290/30–2.
29–30: ibid. 290/33–7.

Alexaundir, bischop of Norwich, deied þis ȝere, and aftir him was Maistir Richard Courtnei bischop, a ful able man to þat degré.

In þis same tyme þe Lollardis, þat condempned þe teching of þe prophetis, þe gospel, and þe aposteles, set up billis on þe cherch-dores, in whech billes was conteyned þat a hundred þousand were redy for to rise and distroye all hem þat wold not consent to her secte and her opiniones. Thei trosted mech on þe witte and on þe power of a certeyn knyte þei cleped Ser Jon Oldcastell. He was cleped Cobbam, for he had weddid a woman ny of þat lordis kyn. A strong man in bataile he was, but a grete heretik, and a gret enmye to þe Cherch. For his cause þe arch-bischop gadered a councel at London, for he sent oute prestis for to preche whech were not admitted be non ordinarie, and he was present at her sermones, and alle þei þat seide ageyn his prestis was he redy to smite with his swerd.

For þese causes and many mo, because he was a knyte of þe kyngis houshold, þe archbischop compleyned of him to þe kyng. Aftir mech labour to his amendement, þe kyng wrot to þe arch-bischop þat he schuld somoun him to appere and answere. The knyte lay þat tyme in his castell, cleped Coulyng. The messager þat was sent was warned þat he schuld not entir his castell but if he had leue. Than entered onto þe castell on Jon Butler, þat was vscher of þe kyngis chambir, and he asked þe knite wheþir þe somnour schuld come to him or he schuld sende him þe lettir. The knyte refused both.

Than was þe somownes set on þe monasteri dores in Rouchestir,

---

1 Alexaundir bischop of Norwich deied þis ȝere] Thys tyme deyed Alisaundr byschop of Norwych P   him] *suprascript with caret* (*in red*) M   2 Courtnei bischop] *separated by thin stroke in red as* ei *in* Courtnei *inserted on the line in darker ink* M   4 teching] preching M, prechyng P   5 þe (2)] of the P and þe] *separated by small hole in vellum* M   billis] bullys P   6 billes] bullys P   7 for] *om.* P   and] to P   8 opiniones] opinyoun P   9 Jon] *capital* J *written over small* j M   10 had] *om.* P   14 admitted] *final* d *suprascript* M   15 þei] *om.* P   17 mo] oder P   because] & becawse P   a] *om.* P   18 houshold] hous P   23 if] *om.* P   entered] P, enter M   onto] into P   25 sende] sent P   27 Than] Tho P   set on] sent on M, sent to P

1–3: ibid. 290/38–291/3.
4–16: ibid. 291/4–25; cf. *Chronicle*, 70/15–71/8.
17–26: Walsingham, *Hist. Ang.* ii. 291/31–292/17.
27–240/21: ibid. 292/18–294/15; cf. *Chronicle*, 72/6–74/4.

but iii mile fro him. And at a day assined þe archbischop in þe castell of Ledis cursed him for contumacie and grete fautour of heretikes. Aftir þis, on a Satirday, aftyr þe fest of Seint Matheu apostil and euangelist, þe archbischop sat in Paules chapeter-

5 hous, and with him Herry of Wynchestir and Richard of London bischoppis, and Ser Robert Morlé at comaundment of þe kyng (þan keper of þe Towre) broute þis knyte Oldcastell onto þe presens of þese bischoppis.

There þe bischop rehersed þat for contumacie he stood acursed,
10 and if he wold mekely submitte him to þe Cherch he wold asoile him. Oldcastel stood and wold not aske it, but took oute of his bosom a bille endented, and whan he had red it, took it to þe bischoppis. Than seid þe archbischop,

f. 101ᵛᵇ   Lo, Ser Jon, here be many good þingis in ȝoure bille, |
16   but ȝe must answere to oþir þingis þat be put on ȝou, touch-
       ing þe sacrament of þe auter, and þe power of þe Cherch,
       and mech oþir þing.

He seide to þis þat he wold gyue no oþir answere þan was writin in his bille. Than þe archbischop took him certeyn articules in
20 a bille, to whech he assigned him þat he schuld answere on þe Moneday folowand.

And whan þe day was come, þe archbischop inqwired of him if he wold be assoiled aftir þe forme of þe Cherch. He seid 'Nay'; he loked aftir no absolucion but of God. And of þe sacrament of
25 þe auter he seid þus:—

       Euene as Crist, whil he went here, was God and man—þe
       manhod mite men se, but not þe godhed—so in þis sacrament
       is Cristis bodi and bred—þe bred may men se, but not
       Cristis body.

30 He seid more, þat 'þe determinacion of þe Cherch and þe doctoures, þat sei þe reuers, ar pleynly ageyn Holy Scripture'.

---

1 iii] *each digit surmounted by short stroke in red* M   a] P, *om.* M   2 cursed him] denownsed hym acursed P   contumacie] contu macie *separated by small hole in vellum* M   10 submitte] P, submᵗ|te *over line division* M
11 wold not aske it] P, wold non aske *followed by* it *suprascript almost erased* M
15 on] vnto P   16 and (1)] *om.* P   20 þe] *suprascript* M   22 whan]
in r.h. margin M   27 se] soe P

1–21: see p. 239.
22–241/11: Walsingham, *Hist. Ang.* ii. 294/16–295/22.

For þe sacrament of penauns he seide þat what man þat is in greuous synne and coude not rise fro his synne, 'it is ful neccessarie þat he haue a wise preest to telle him þe maner of his amendment, but þat a man schuld be schriue to his propir prest, or to a othir preest, it is no nede, for contricion withoute confessioun purgith 5 al synne'. For worchipyng of þe crosse he seide þat body þat hing on þe crosse schuld be worchipid, and noþing but he. And whan þei asked him what worchip he wold do to þe ymage on þe crosse, he seide he wold wipe it, and kepe it clene. Than þei asked him what he seid of þe pope. He seid 'þe pope is Antecrist; bischoppis 10 be his | membris, and freris be his tayl'.   f. 102ra

The archbischop sey no oþir amendment in þis man, condempned him for a heretik, and left him to seculer hand. And þan went he to þe kyng, and told him al þe processe, praying þe kyng to graunt him lif xl dayes, þat he mite do penauns. But þis 15 indulgens turned onto gret mischef, for within þoo xl dayes he brak oute of þe Tour, and sent letteris onto his secte. For al þat tyme, fro his euasion about Myhilmesse onto þe ephiphanie, he mad him strong to distroye þe kyng and many oþir. And þei þat were gadered to go with him, if þei mad question to what entent 20 þei schuld rise, þis answere had þei: 'It skil ʒou not, so ʒe haue good wagis and treuly payed'.

The king kept Cristmasse at Eltham, and Cobbam, with his retenew, had þoute to fulfille his entent. The kyng was warned of þis mater be certeyn men þat had consciens and were of councel 25 with Cobbam, and sodeynly þe kyng remeued onto Westminster. The Lolardis were warned þat þei schuld gader in Seint Gilis Feld, for þere schuld come to hem oute of London 1 þousand, as was behite hem. But þe king was war of al þis, and comaunded London gates to be sperd and kept. He sent owte eke men of 30 armes be dyuers weyes, whech apposed hem þat cam rennyng in hast whedir þei schuld, and þei seide to Cobham. Thus were take and slayn þousandis. The kyng was in þe feld sone aftir mydnyte. This aspied Cobbam; he fled, and many with him.

---

1 þat (1)] þus þat P   2 it] *written twice over line division with* 1st *instance* *expuncted* M   7 whan] *om.* P   8 on] of P   14 þan went he to] went to P   16 onto] to P   within þoo] with the P   26 onto] to P 29 behite] *change to darker ink* M

12–22: ibid. 295/35–297/16.
23–242/5: ibid. 297/26–299/22.

f. 102ʳᵇ Many of his were take, and | hang and drawe and brent. On was
þere of Dunstable, a special scoler of þis secte, þei cleped him
William Morlé. Oldcastell had behote him þat he schuld be a
knyte; and, in proue of þat beheste, þei fond with him too stedis,
5 and gilt sporis in his bosum.

In þis ȝere þe kyng foundid thre houses of religion fast be his
place, whech þei clepe Schene: on, of þe monkis of Charterhous;
anothir, cleped Celestines: thei kepe Seint Benet reule *ad litteram*,
as þei sey—thei are constreyned for to be recluses for euyr. The
10 þird is of Seynt Bride ordir: þei haue Seynt Austyn reule, with
certeyn additamentis, and þei clepe it now 'the reule of oure
Sauiour'. Thei haue noþing, propir peny ne halfpeny, ne touche
no mony. The noumbir of hem is sistiris lx, prestis xiii, dekenes
iiii, lewed men viii; whech acordith to þe noumbir of xiii aposteles
15 and lxxii discipules. Thei were no lynand, but wolland. Thei
haue o cherch, þe women aboue, þe men be þe ground. Aftir
her profession no man may license hem but þe pope. This religion
must haue sufficient dotacion. Before þe fest of Al Seintis þei
must counte þat þei haue sufficiently for þe nest ȝere, and al þe
20 remanent þei schul gyue in elmesse. On of þe xiii prestis schal
þei chese to her confessour, and to him schal þei alle obeye.
No seculer man ne woman schal entyr þe nunnes cloystir.

6613; 1415. In þe þird ȝere of þis kyng were chosen worchipful
men to go to þe councell at Constauns: þese bischoppis, Salesburi,
f. 102ᵛᵃ Herforth, | and Bathe, þe abbot of Westminster, and þe priour
26 of Wircetir, with othir clerkis; with hem eke went þe erle of
Warwik. Ther were gadered þe collegis of Gregori and Petir de
Luna. Gregori resined his rite up condicion Petir schuld do þe
same. He was in Aragony. Jon, þat was at Rome mad, was loth
30 to resine, but be þe emperour he was induct þat he schuld do it.
Mech joye was mad, euery man supposing þat þis mater schuld
haue good ende. But þis Jon be nyte fled with þe duke of Ostrich

1 and (1)] *om.* P   4 þat] t *suprascript with caret* M   8 kepe]
kept P   9 are] be eke P   for to be recluses] to recluse P   11 certeyn]
othyr P   oure] Seynt P   13 is] *suprascript* M   xiii] xiiii MP   17 man]
twice over line division P   20-1 schal þei] they schuld P   25 and (2)] *om.* P
26 eke] *om.* P   28 up] vpon P   29 mad] *suprascript* M   32 of
Ostrich] *in r.h. central margin and separated from* fast *adjacent word in column
b by thin stroke in red* M

1-5: see p. 241.
6-22: Walsingham, *Hist. Ang.* ii. 300/28-301/35.
23-243/10: ibid. 302/12-303/24.

into a cité of his, and sent letteris to þe emperour þat he fled for
no oþir cause but for þe eyer at Constance was not heilsom to
him. And whan he was sent for, to com to þe councel, he disgised
him, and fled with þe duke. That sey þe emperour, and rood into
Ostrich, and took þe duke and him eke. Jon was broute to þe 5
councell in þe same aray þei toke him in, schort cloþis, lich a
malandryn. There was he robbed of mech good whech he had
gadered. This was noysed in Ynglond, and a gret summe of
mony, whech was gadered for him in a hucch at Poules, was
take oute and spent in bettir vse.   10

In þis tyme, aftir many tretis betwix þis lond and Frauns,
and noþing þat þei profered was acording to reson, þe kyng mad
redy his schippis at Southampton to spede him to his conquest.
And þere were thre notabill men þat had conspired his deth.
On was Herry Scrop, on whom þe kyng trostid moost, and be 15
whos councell al þing was doo. Sobir was þe man in word and
chere, and vndir þat ypocrisie had | he a ful venemous hert. He f. 102ᵛᵇ
had a felawe consentyng onto him, Richard, erl of Cambrig,
and Thomas Grey, a knyte of þe north. But er þei broute aboute
her conclusion þei were detecte, condempned be her peres, 20
and ded.

In þis tyme þe Lolardis risin ageyn. Wenyng verily þat eithir
þe kyng was ded or sailed ouyr þe se, thei coumforted hem ech
to oþir, and seide, 'Now is þe prince of prestis goo, and oure vttir
enmy'. Her leder, whech had hid him longe tyme fast by Maluerne, 25
ros fro his den, and sent letteris to þe Lord Bergeueni þat he
wold be wrechid first upon him. And he, as a wise man, sent
aftir his frendis and his tenauntis and mad a host of a sex þousand
men. That aspied Oldcastell and fled—no man coude cacch him.
Ther took he a preest of þe secte and oþir seruauntis of his, whom 30
þe Lord Bergeueni streytid so þat þei told wher Oldcastell was
hid. þere founde þei his armour and his mony. Thei fond þere

---

4 That sey þe emperour] That sey þe emperour þat he fled P   14 men]
in r.h. margin M   17 a] *om.* P   18 onto] to P   24 and seide] *om.* P
24–5 vttir enmy] *separated by thin stroke in red* M   26 Bergeueni] ueni *in*
r.h. margin M   27 he] *suprascript with caret (in red)* M   28 tenauntis
and] tenauns P   31 Bergeueni] Bergeu' *over erasure* M   32 þei] *supra-*
script M   Thei fond þere] Ther fownd þey P

11–21: ibid. 304/41–306/18.
22–244/4: ibid. 306/26–307/17; cf. *Chronicle*, 88/15–89/21.

a baner, costfully depeynted with a host and a chalis. They fond
eke baneres depeynted with Crist ful of woundis, þe spere and
þe nayles. Al þese þingis were mad for to make simpil folk to
suppose þat he was a trew zelator of þe feith.

5   The kyng with his nauy took þe se, and londid at Kidkaus,
with a þousand schippis and fyue hundred. He entered þe lond
on a Wednesday, whech was þe vigil of assumpcioun of oure Lady,
and on þe Satirday aftir he leyde sege to þe town of Hareflw,
he be lond, þe schippis be þe watir. And þis sege lested til þe
f. 103ᵛᵃ Sunday befor Myhilmesse. In þe | Tewisday befor þat Sunday þe
11 lordes þat were keperes of þe town sent oute a man onto þe duke
of Clarense, praying him enterly þat þei myte trete with þe kyng,
and þat he schuld make his gunneres to sese, for it was to hem
intollerabil. The names of hem were þese: þe Lord Gaucort,
15 þe Lord Stuteuyle, þe Lord Boteuyle, and þe Lord Clere. The
duke of Clarens spak for hem to þe kyng, and þe kyng sent to
hem þe erle of Dorset and Ser Thomas Erpingham to knowe her
desire. Thei prayed þe kyng mekely þat he schuld ses of his schot
onto Sunday, and if þe kyng of Frauns cam not be þat tyme, þei
20 schuld delyuer him þe town. Thei profered him eke þat, if he
wold gyue hem leue and saue-conduct to ride to þe king of Frauns,
þei schuld ley plegges xxii knytes with þe best of þe town. So
þe Lord Hakevile and xii persones had leue to ride þorw þe host.
And on þe Wednesday, erly, cam oute of þe town þe lordes, xxii
25 knytes, swieres, and burgeys of þe town. And ageyn hem þe
kyng sent a solempne procession of prelatis and prestis and þe
sacrament, and aftir folowand lordis, knytes, and þe puple. Whan
þei had mad a solempne oth, þei went to mete into þe kyngis
tent, but þei sey not þe kyng. Aftir mete þei were comaunded for
30 to go with certeyn lordes þat schuld kepe hem. On þe Sunday

---

1 with] *suprascript with caret (in red)* M   1–2 a host . . . depeynted
with] *om.* P   3 for] *om.* P   to (2)] *om.* P   5 his] *in r.h. margin with
carets (in red)* M   6 a þousand] *over erasure* M   lond] d *suprascript* M
7 on] n *over erasure* M   8 aftir] folowyng P   9 þe (2)] *om.* P   til]
to P   10 þat] *om.* P   11 onto] to P   12–13 trete with þe kyng and
þat he schuld] *om.* P   14 Gaucort] Gaûcort MP   15 þe Lord Boteuyle]
om. P   19 if] *om.* P   20 Thei] i *inserted on the line in paler ink* M
þat] *om.* P   25 swieres and burgeys] and þe best P   28 þei (1)] i *suprascript with caret* M   29 þei (1)] i *suprascript* M   for] *om.* P

1–4: see p. 243.
5–245/5: Walsingham, *Hist. Ang.* ii. 307/29–309/21; cf. *Chronicle*, 89/33–
92/18.

com þe messageres ageyn withoute ony help of kyng or of daufyn.
Therfor þei þat were in þe town submitted hem onto þe kyng, and
þei þat were with þe kyng, sent be þe Frensch kyng to keping of þe
town, remayned as pri|soneres. The kyng mad capteyn of þe f. 103rb
town his vncle, Ser Thomas, erle of Dorset. 5

In þis sege many men deied of cold in nytes, and frute etyng,
eke of stynk of careynes. He deied þere, Maistir Richard Courtney,
bischop of Norwich, in whos place þe monkes chosen Jon Wakeryng. Ther deyed eke Mychael at þe Pool. The duke of Clarense,
þe erle of March, þe Erle Arundel, and þe Erle Marchale took 10
gret seknes þere.

The kyng, aftir þis conquest, purposed to go to Caleys, with
footmen for þe most part; for al his hoost was not acoundid passing
viii þousand, so many were left seek at Harflew. Merueile it was
þat he, with so fewe, durst go þorw all þe þik wodis in þat cuntré. 15
For þe Frensch parti in al þis tyme had mad an hoost of a hundred
þousand and fourty þousand. Vitailes were kept fro hem, þat
xviii dayes þei had walnotes for bred, and flech had þei sum, but
her drynk was watir.

So in þe xxiiii day of Octobir þe hostis met not a myle asundir. 20
The kyng coumforted gretly his men þat þei schuld trost in God,
for her cause was rithful. The Frensch part stod on þe hill, and
we in þe vale. Betwix hem was a lond new heried, where was
euel fotyng. Schort for to sey, þe feld fel onto þe kyng, and þe
French party lost it, for al her noumbyr and her pride. Ther were 25
ded þe duke of Lanson, þe duke of Braban, þe duke of Bauer,
v erles, þe constable eke of Frauns, and a hundred lordes, knites
and swieris iiii þousand sexti and ix—þe comon puple was not
noumbered. These were take: þe duke of | Aurelianense, þe f. 103va

2 onto] to P   5 his vncle Ser Thomas] Ser Thomas hys vnkyl P
Thomas] s *suprascript* M   7 eke of stynk of careynes] and stynke and careyn P
9 at þe] de la P   10 Arundel] *in r.h. margin* M   12 þis] þe P   15 with
so fewe] wold with so or P   þe] þo P   16 in al þis tyme had] had in all
thys tyme P   of] *suprascript* M   17 þousand (1)] d *suprascript* M   kept]
so kepte P   18 xviii] in xviii P   þei (2)] i *suprascript* M   24 Schort] h
suprascript M   onto] to P   25 were] *om. over line division* P   26 of (3)]
om. P   27 eke] *om.* P   28 and (1)] d *suprascript* M   29 These were
take] *om.* P   of Aurelianense] Aurelianenser P

6–11: Walsingham, *Hist. Ang.* ii. 309/22–38.
12–19: ibid. 309/40–310/21; cf. *Chronicle*, 93/1–21.
20–246/6: Walsingham, *Hist. Ang.* ii. 310/31–313/31; cf. *Chronicle*, 93/31–
   97/7.

duke of Burbon, þe erles of Ew, and Vendone, Arthure, þe dukis broþir of Bretayn, whech cleymeth to be erle of Richemund, and a knyte þei cleped Brucegald, marchale of Frauns, and oþir were take þere of cote-armour into a vii hundred. On oure side were
5 ded Edward, duke of Ʒork, þe erle of Suthfolk, iiii knytes, a swiere, Dauy Gamme, of þe comones xxviii.

In þe tyme of þe bataile þe brigauntis of þe Frensch side took þe kyngis cariage and led it awey, in whech þei fonde þe kyngis crowne; þei mad þe bellis to rynge and men for to synge *Te*
10 *Deum laudamus*, telling verily þat þe kyng was ded. But within fewe houres aftir, her joye was chaunged.

The king rood to Caleis and ouyr þe se to Douer, and in þe xxiii day of Nouembir cam to London, and þere was receyued in þe best maner.

15 6614; 1416. In his iiii Ʒere was a gret batail betwix þe erl of Dorcet and þe erle of Armenak, in whech batayle þere perchid many on both sides; for þis Armenak fell upon hem sodeynly, and þei were not auised. In þe tyme of þe bataile al her cariage was stole be þe Frenschmen; so mote þei nedis go hom on fote.
20 Thei laboured al þe þursday, and on Friday, in þe morownyng, þei sey þe Frenschmen on þe hillis comyng downward. Than sent to þe erl of Dorcet þis message þe Erl Armenak: 'Now art þou so streytid þat þe se is on þin o side and we on þe oþir. Therfor, be my councell, Ʒeld þe, for ellis schalt þou deye'. The
f. 103ᵛᵇ erl | of Dorcet sent þis answere ageyn: 'It was neuyr þe maner of
26 Englischmen to Ʒelde hem whan þei myte fite'. So faute þei, and þouƷ þe Englisch host had no mo men but xv hundred, Ʒet

2 broþir] *1st* r *suprascript* M   whech] þat P   erle] *over erasure* M
3 cleped] clepe P   of] f *inserted on the line* M   4 of] and of P   cote-armour] cote armour *separated by thin stroke in red* M   a] and P   7 þe (1)] *om.* P   8 and] *om.* P   it] *suprascript with caret (in red)* M   9 þe] *om.* P   12 king] *suprascript with caret (in red)* M   12–13 Caleis . . . cam to] *om.* P   13 cam to] *separated by thin stoke in red* M   and þere] wher he P   15–16 þe erl of Dorcet and þe erle of Armenak] þe Erle Armenak and þe erle of Dorcet P   18 þe (1)] *om.* P   22 to þe erl of Dorcet þis message þe Erl Armenak] þe Erle Armanak to þe erle of Dorcet þis message P   to] *suprascript* M   24 schalt] schall P   26 hem] *om.* P   So faute þei] So fauƷt they P, *om.* M   27 host] men P   men] *om.* P

1–6: see p. 245.
7–11: Walsingham, *Hist. Ang.* ii. 313/32–41.
12–14: ibid. 314/1–13.
15–247/2: ibid. 314/38–315/30.

had þei þe bettir of xv þousand, God and good prayeris hem helpyng.

In þis tyme was it defendid þat galey-halfpenies schuld not be used, for iii of hem were ful scarsly worth a peny.

In þis ȝere, in þe seuene day of May, cam þe Emperor Sigemund 5 to London, and was loggid in þe kyngis paleys at Westminster— the kyng lay at Lambhithe. The emperour offered a ymage of Seynt George at Wyndesore, mad of þure gold. There, on Seynt Georges day, was he mad broþir of knites of þe garter, and þere receyued þe kingis lyueri, whech he wered on solempne daies al 10 his lyue.

At þe fest of Ascencion cam þe duke of Holland, with gret aray of schippis and vitaile, to speke with þe emperour and þe kyng. His doutir was weddid to þe ȝonger son of þe kyng of Frauns, whech was now eyer aftir þe daufyn was ded. 15

In þe xviii kalend of Julii were þe moost horribil þunderes and litynnyngis þat euyr ony man herd.

Al þis somyr men supposed þat þe emperour schuld a sette pes betwix Inglond and Frauns, but þe Frensch kyng and his councell was euyr founde dobil; for, whil þis trety was in hand, þe 20 Frenschmen had gadered a gret nauy, with karikis and galeyes, for to take Harflew. And for þat cause þe kyng sent his broþir, Jon, duke of Bedford, with certeyn men | of Ser Herry Percy,   f. 104ᵃ whech Herry þe kyng had boute oute of prison fro Scotlond, and with þis help þei took and distroyed þe most part of þat 25 nauy.

Sone aftir þat þe emperour went oute of Ynglond, and in his

---

1 prayeris] prayer P   3 In] *change to darker ink* M   8 There] And þer P   9 knites of] *om.* P   þere] *om.* P   12 Ascencion] the Ascencion P   14 kyng His] dukes P   18 men supposed] *separated by thin stroke* M   a] *om.* P   22 for (1)] *om.* P   for þat cause] therfor P   25 distroyed] ed *in r.h. margin* M   27 þat] thys P

3–4: ibid. 315/35–6; *Chronicle*, 99/37–9.

5–11: Walsingham, *Hist. Ang.* ii. 315/37–316/7; *Chronicle*, 100/1–18.

12–15: Walsingham, *Hist. Ang.* ii. 316/8–10; *Chronicle*, 100/19–24.

16–17: Walsingham, *Hist. Ang.* ii. 316/11–15; cf. *Chronicle*, 100/25–31.

18–26: Walsingham, *Hist. Ang.* ii. 316/16–27; cf. *Chronicle*, 100/32–101/18.

27–248/16: Walsingham, *Hist. Ang.* ii. 316/28–40; *Chronicle*, 101/23–102/6.

goyng he mad his seruauntis for to þrowe billis be þe wey, in whech was writyn swech sentens:—

> Farewel, with glorious victory,
> Blessid Inglond ful of melody.
> 5 Thou may be cleped of angel nature,
> Thou seruist God so with bysy cure.
> We leue with þe þis praising,
> Whech we schul euir sey and sing.

Many conuenciones were mad betwix þe emperour and þe kyng, 10 and al her succession dyuyded in xii articles, whech were ageyn þe ordinauns of oure book, for we þink þat it myte be cleped rather *Abbreuiacion of Cronicles* þan a book. The kyng, þat men schuld knowe wel þat he was redy to haue pes with þe kyng of Frauns, saylid ouyr þe se with þe emperour to Caleys. There aspied þe 15 emperour þat þe proferes on þe French side were but fraude and sotilté; þerfor he left hem as þei were.

Than mad þe kyng a vnyté betwix þe duke of Burgayn and þe emperour. The cause of her debate was þis. The duke of Borgayn, long before þe same tyme, his fadir Philip lyuand, was 20 take prisoner be þe Turkes, and þe emperour boute him ageyn for a grete summe, whech summe he swore treuly to pay to þe emperour, whech was þan but kyng of Hungari. In þis mater þe kyng mad þe duke to take dayes and be bound, and forthwith f. 104rb þe duke ded homage to | þe emperour. The emperour fro Caleys 25 went to Dordraute, and with him went þe duke of Gloucetir and oþir, where þei took leue of þe emperour and cam hom ageyn.

In þis tyme on Benedict Wolleman, a citeceyn of London, a gret Lollard, whech had set up billes of grete erroure, was takyn, hanged, and drawe on Myhilmasse Day.

30 Aftir þat, in þe parlement, whech was hold at London, on

6 so with] with so P   9 þe emperour] hym P   11 rather] *final* r *suprascript* M   13 haue pes] *separated by thin stroke in red* M   with þe kyng of Frauns] *om.* P   17–18 þe duke of Burgayn and þe emperour] the emperour and þe duk of Burgoyne P   19 Philip] *om.* P   21 summe (2)] *om.* P   to (2)] *om.* P   23 forthwith] *1st* h *suprascript* M   24 to] onto P   25 went (2)] *om.* P   25–6 and oþir] *suprascript* M   30 on] of P

1–16: see p. 247.
17–26: Walsingham, *Hist. Ang.* ii. 316/40–317/6; *Chronicle*, 102/7–27.
27–9: Walsingham, *Hist. Ang.* ii. 317/7–9; cf. *Chronicle*, 102/28–31.
30–249/2: Walsingham, *Hist. Ang.* ii. 317/10–13.

Seint Luce day, Thomas Beuforth, erle of Dorcete, was mad duke
of Exetir.

This ȝere deied þe kyng of Aragoyne, whech was a gret letter
of þe vnion of Holy Cherch, meyntenyng þe antepope, Petir de
Luna. And notwithstanding þe emperour in his owne persone 5
exhorted him to þis vnité, and he hite þe emperour þat he schuld
withdrawe his obediens fro þat same Petir, al availed not, for he
deied sone aftir, and his sone meynteyned þe same erroure.
Eke þat same Petir, obdurat in malice, charged all his cardinales
þat aftir his deth thei schuld chese a newe pope of her owne 10
college.

In þe same ȝere iii beggeres stole iii childyr at Lenne, and of on
þei put oute his eyne, þe oþir þei broke his bak, and þe þirde þei
cut of his handis and his feet, þat men schul of pité gyue hem
good. Long aftir, þe fadir of on of hem, whech was a marchaund, 15
cam to London, and þe child knew him, and cryed loude, 'This
is my fader'. The fadir tok his child fro þe beggeres, and mad hem
to be arested. The childirn told all þe processe, and þe beggeris
were hangen, ful wel worthy.

6615. In þe v ȝere of þis kyng he held his Cristmasse at Kenel- f. 104ᵛᵃ
worth, where was leyd a gret avayte on þe kyng to his destruccion 21
be a swiere of þat Oldcastell. And in euery in of Seint Albone, in
Reding, and in Norhampton, were founde billes of gret malyce
ageyn God and þe kyng.

In þis tyme was þe councell gadered at Basili, where was 25
determined in her first act þat he þat were chose in þat councel
schuld be preferred for fadir of all þe Cherch, ferþermore, þat
of euery nacion schuld be chosen sex prelatis, whech schuld be in
þe conclaue with þe cardinales, and haue voys in þe same eleccion.

---

1 Beuforth] Benforþe P   5 notwithstanding] withstandyng P   8 meyn-
teyned] mayntened P, meyteyned M   10 pope] *suprascript* M   12 þe]
þis P   ȝere] *suprascript with caret (in red)* M   iii (2)] *each digit surmounted by
short stroke in red* M   13 þe (1)] of þe P   þe (2)] of þe P   14 his (1 *and
2*)] *om.* P   19 ful] *suprascript* M   21 a] P, *om.* M   avayte] wayȝt P
22 of (2)] *suprascript* M   23 in] *om.* P   24 þe] ageyne þe P

3–11: Walsingham, *Chronicle*, 103/5–16.
12–19: ibid. 103/17–27.
20–4: Walsingham, *Hist. Ang.* ii. 317/21–8.
25–9: ibid. 317/29–318/17.

COMMENTARY

THESE notes are intended for use in conjunction with the Textual Notes, the Source References, the Glossary, and the Glossarial Index. No attempt is made to provide a historical commentary.

Dedicatory Preface

7/1 For an illustration of the initial illuminated *T* see Plate II, and for a description see above, Introd., p. xxxv.

7/2–3 On the Order of St. Augustine see above, Introd., p. xxiii.

7/6–11 Presumably a reference to C's commentaries on the books of the Bible; so Colledge, 'Literary Vocation', p. 189. See further Introd., pp. xix–xxix, esp. xxiv.

7/11 *Now is age com*: in 1462 C was 69.

7/18 *a m cccc & xvii*: *a* here and in many similar instances is undoubtedly the indefinite article rather than an abbreviation for *anno*, as is shown by collocations such as *of age a c wyntir and xxx* 12/7. Cf. also 8/15. The roman numerals were no doubt read aloud in English. For the construction *a vii pousand* see note to 232/3.

7/34 ff. Evidently C's mind was still occupied with the fundamental problem of chronology when and after he was engaged upon his final revision. Galbraith notes the same point about Higden in 'An Autograph MS of Ranulph Higden's *Polychronicon*', *HLQ* xxiii (1959), 10.

8/9–10 *pat gospel . . .*: Luke 21: 1–4.

8/14–15 In fact Edward IV was proclaimed king on 4 Mar. 1461. But according to the contemporary calendar 1461 did not begin until 25 Mar. 1461; hence C's reference to 1460.

8/15 *a m and cccc*: cf. note to 7/18.

8/15–18 The *perfeccion* of 7 and 60 referred to here is not mathematical. In medieval mathematical usage a 'perfect' number seems to have been one which was the sum of a series of consecutive natural numbers beginning with 1: see *OED*, *Perfect a.* 8, quot. 1422, *tene . . . contenyth in hymsylfe foure nombres . . . one and two, and thre and foure*. Thus, while 7 is a 'perfect' number, being the sum of (and the next item in) the series 1, 2, and 4, 60 is not. The common feature that links the two numbers is apparently that of completeness. In particular each is used as an indefinite large number: for 7 see *OED*, *Seven a.* 1d; for 60 see S. I. Tucker, 'Sixty as an Indefinite Number in Middle English', *RES* xxv (1949), 152–3. The special significance of Seven is well known (for examples see *OED*, s.v. 6). The use of Sixty probably relates to the system of reckoning in dozens whereby it was half of a 'long hundred' of 120; but in addition, because it was composed of 6 and 10 (which are 'circular' numbers because when multiplied by themselves the resulting number contains the original number: i.e. 36 contains 6, and 100 contains 10), 60 also conveyed the notion of numerical circularity, which may be relevant here. Cf. also B. Smalley, *The Study of the Bible in the Middle Ages* (Oxford, 1952 edn.), p. 5.

8/21 *al þe labour of þe world is figured in sex dayes* . . .: an allusion to the Augustinian six ages of history, on which see above, Introd., pp. xciii–xciv.

8/25–8 There are several difficulties in this numerological passage. (1) *OED, Particular* a. 4, does not help by wrongly explaining *particuler noumberes* as factors (in which case the list would be incomplete since 6 is not included). The *particuler noumberes* of a number N are the consecutive natural numbers of which it is the sum; i.e. for 6 they are 1, 2, and 3. An aliquot part (*cote*) of a number N is a number which can be divided into N an exact number of times; for 6 the aliquot parts are 1, 2, and 3. Part of what C is saying is that Six is a remarkable number because its constituent numbers are the same as its aliquot parts; indeed it is the only number of which this is true. (2) The precise sense of *reuoluing*, which etymologically ought to mean something like 'turning back', can only be deduced from the context. (*OED* does not record *Revolve* or *Revolution* as mathematical terms, though *Involve* v. 8 'multiply into itself' is recorded from 1673 and *Evolution* 4b 'extraction of a root' (the opposite of *Involution*) from 1706.) Apparently C is trying to define an aliquot part with special reference to Six. In the equations at the end of the passage the third term is in each case 6 and the second terms are the aliquot parts 1, 2, 3. The first terms are the exact numbers which must be divided into Six to give the aliquot parts. Thus *in her reuoluing* means 'when multiplied by the appropriate exact number'. C appears to be defining an aliquot part by describing how to convert it back to the original integer. It was necessary for him to state his arithmetic in this way so that he could fit the ensuing precepts into the scheme. The passage may be translated: 'This number six is also commended because of its constituent numbers, which are one, two, and three; each of these is also called an aliquot part, because when they are multiplied by the appropriate exact number they give the original integer: thus, six times one is six, three times two is six, and twice three is six'.

8/33–4 Possibly an allusion to the metaphysical notion of the vital, sensitive and rational principles in human beings. Cf. *OED, Soul* sb. 5(c).

9/5 Rom. 13:4.

9/6–7 An allusion to Virgil, *Aeneid*, vi. 853: 'parcere subiectis et debellare superbos'.

9/8–16 Earlier C dedicated his *De illust. Hen.* to Henry VI, 'cujus ministeriis . . . me totum obtuli' (p. 125). Now C dedicates the *Abbreuiacion of Cronicles* to Edward IV. For this apparent volte-face, which spans fifteen years, C has been much criticized, most forcefully by Furnivall in his 'Forewords' to *Katharine*, p. xv. But flattery in dedications was characteristic of the period, and the dedications of both works are consistent in calling for *good gouernauns*. See further my 'English Literary Patronage', pp. 228–9.

9/12–14 Probably an allusion to Venantius Fortunatus's hymn *Pange lingua . . .*, line 6, 'Ipse lignum tunc notavit, damna ligni ut solveret'. Cf. *Piers Plowman*, B, xviii. 140.

9/18 *hillis*: evidently a figurative use, but an unusual one. Cf. *MED hille* n. 3.

9/21 *Amen* is followed by C's characteristic triquetra mark with pendant: see Plate III and above, Introd., p. xxxiv.

Abbreuiacion of Cronicles

11/1 *Anno Mundi I.* Throughout M all the AM year numbers are written consecutively at the left of the column, but, in this edition, only those years to which events are assigned are given separately, while the years in between are grouped together, as *Anno 2–14*. Centuries are written in roman (rather than arabic) numerals, but no special notice is given to them.

11/9 and 11/13 Cain and Abel did not each have a twin sister in the Bible. Jubilees, iv. 1, 8 says that Adam and Eve also had daughters, named 'Awan and 'Azura, but the only reference I have found to the notion that Cain and Abel each had a twin sister is in Islamic literature where, according to the typical post-Koranic Cain and Abel legend, each brother had a twin sister, their names being Aqlīma and Labūdā.

11/11 *Lameth*: so written here and elsewhere with *t* rather than *c*, though the letters are not easily distinguished. Cf. note to 36/5.

11/19–20 Gen. 4: 10.

11/30–2 Gen. 2: 19–20.

12/6 *Moises*: Gen. 5: 3.

12/7 *a c wyntir and xxx*: cf. note to 2/3.
   Alle othir cronicles: these include Isidore, 426/4.

13/32 *Anno 425*: 435 in Isidore, but 425 in MS *T*.

14/2 *he was first þat called onto God*: Gen. 4: 26.

15/5–6 *Anno 796*: 795 in Isidore.

15/18 *Metodius*: presumably an allusion to Methodius's lost commentary on Genesis.

15/23 Ephrath is apparently identified with Bethlehem in Gen. 35: 19.

16/9–10 An allusion to the medieval belief that before Doomsday Antichrist would come with a vast army to devastate the world, kill Enoch and Elijah and then succumb before Christ. See also 17/15–17, 33/31.

16/10–12 1 Enoch.

16/14–18 Jude 14–15.

16/21 Seth lived 912 years according to Gen. 5: 8. Presumably *A had *nyne hundred and xxx* in error and this was corrected in M but retained in P.

16/25–17/1 The original of this quotation is Jerome's commentary to Gen. 5: 25 in PL xxiii. 946–7.

17/7–8 *a hundred foure score and vii ȝere*: Isidore, against Gen. 5: 25, puts Methuselah's age at 167.

17/22 *Methodius*: as 15/18.

17/24–6 Gen. 6: 1–7.

17/30–1 *Anno 1652*: 1642 in Isidore.

17/33–18/1 Gen. 8: 20.

19/2–3 Job 1: 1.

19/19–20 *Jone . . . Mare Ionicum*. According to C's *Solace* (3/13–14), where *Jone* 'Javan' is called *Janus*, 'othir cronicles calle him *Ionicus*', and this alternative name is presumably the source of the spurious link between Javan and the Ionian Sea. Cf. note to 20/13.

19/21 *Hiberi*: i.e. *Ibēri*, L for 'Spaniards'.

19/26 ff. On biblical pedigrees see H. Bradley, 'The "Cædmonian" Genesis', *E & S* vi (1920), 16–17.

19/32–3 *neue onto Sem*. The meaning of *neue* offers slight difficulty. Eber was in fact Shem's great-grandson (Gen. 10: 21–4), but *neue* is recorded with neither of the senses 'great-grandson' or 'descendant' by *OED*, *Neve*[1]. The second is preferred in the Glossary and sense-transference is assumed from L *nepos*, which can mean 'descendant', also 'grandson', but not 'great-grandson' specifically.

19/33–4 God himself named Jacob Israel in Gen. 35: 10. Possibly this naming of Jacob has been confused with the naming of Ishmael by the angel of the Lord in Gen. 16: 11.

20/13 *Ionicus*: Javan, Noah's grandson—he was Noah's *son* in the sense of 'male descendant', though strictly the word *begat* requires an immediate son. See note to 19/19–20.

20/25–6 *Anno 2763*: 2773 in Isidore.

21/14–23 This passage is taken from the *Mitologiarum libri III* of Fulgentius Mythographus: see R. Helm (ed.), *Fabii Planciadis Fulgentii Opera* (Leipzig, 1898), pp. 15–17. It is clearer in Fulgentius than in C's abridged version that the servants made offerings to the idol *timoris potius effectu quam amoris affectu*.

21/19 *garlondis and lite*: *coronas . . . aut flores . . . aut odoramenta* and *florum atque turis . . . munuscula* in Fulgentius.

21/21–2 Fulgentius quotes the text correctly: *Primus in orbe deos fecit timor*. It is from the first line of Petronius, *Fragment XXVII* (Müller); see the Loeb Library edn. (tr. M. Heseltine), p. 340.

21/25–6 *Anno 2895*: 2905 in Isidore.

a hundred ȝere and xxx: 132 in Isidore (32 in Gen. 6: 20).

22/8–9 *a hundred ȝere old and xxxv*: 130 in Isidore (30 in Gen. 11: 22).

22/10 ff. This account of ancient Egypt offers some difficulties.
Than (13) to be historically correct would have to mean 'beginning
with the ninth dynasty'.
xxxvi (14) is perhaps erron. for *xvi*.
Dinastines (14) from L *dynastēs* evidently means 'rulers' (22/12, 24).
When used with roman numbers it ought to refer to dynasties, but the
close parallel in construction between *regned . . . xv souereynes, cleped
Dinastines* and *xxxvi Dinastines . . . regned* effectively forbids emendation
of the latter instance. (Following Hingeston *OED*, *Dynasty* 2, and *MED*,
dinastie, erron. quote this instance of *Dinastines* as *dinasties* and *ODEE*
evidently takes it to be the first instance of *dynasty* in English. If Trevisa's
un-Anglicized forms (quoted by *MED*) are disregarded the word *dynasty*
is apparently not recorded before the seventeenth century.)
Diapolitani (14–15) is prob. erron. for *Diospolitani*, formed on *Diospolis*,
the Roman name for Thebes. C was apparently unaware that *þei of
Tebes* (13) and these *Diapolitani* were from the same place.
xviii of hem (15) should mean that the *Diapolitani* were the Eighteenth
Dynasty, who, under Amosis (1555 BC), reunited Egypt under their rule
by driving out the Hyksos from the north. But, instead, the text says
that there were eighteen ruling *Diapolitani*.

22/21–2 *iii kingis of Perse*: Cambyses is one, Artaxerxes III another, but
the identity of the third is not clear—perhaps Cyrus, who seems to have
been confused with Nebuchadnezzar, king of Babylon? (The statement
in *AL*, NS ii (1971), 10, that the third king was Holophernes is incorrect.)

22/25 *Lagidi* and *Tholomei* were the same.

23/17–18 Gen. 18: 1–15.

23/20–1 *of whom writith Eusebius . . .*: see PL xxvii. 111 and note c.

23/21–2 *as is seid before*: see above, 4–5.

23/34–24/3 Augustine, *De Civitate Dei*, xxi. 14.

24/24–7 Heb. 7: 2–3.

24/30–25/3 This passage, including the reference to Josephus, is based
on Jerome, *Epistola 73*, §7. See CSEL lv. 20–1, or PL xxii. 680.

24/32 *as Josephus seith*: *Jewish Antiquities*, I. x. 2 (ed. Thackeray, iv.
88–9).

25/11 *Ysidis*: an incorrect Anglicization of the L gen. of *Isis*, with whom
Io, daughter of Inachus, has been identified. In order to distract Hera's
attention from his attachment to Io Zeus changed her into a heifer. In
this form, after many wanderings, she came to Egypt where she was
eventually worshipped as Isis. See also 27/7.

25/13 *of whech lawes aftir schal we touche*: see below, 19–23.

25/17–18 *Anno 3444*: 3434 in Isidore.
nynety ʒere of age and on: 90 in Isidore.

25/30–26/1 Gen. 28: 10–15.

26/7 *Anno 3555*: 3544 in Isidore.

26/10–11 Josh. 24: 32.

26/15 *þe occean beʒond Affrik*: i.e. the Atlantic Ocean.

26/16 *king*: Atlas was king of Mauritania.

26/18 note C began to write *Anno 3600*, using arabic figures, but changed to the L form half-way through writing *3600*.

27/7–8 Inachus was founder-king of Argos (25/10–11), but the term *Argivi* 'inhabitants of Argos' was widely used of the Greeks in general. Hence, probably, he is here erroneously styled *king of Grece*. C has apparently failed to connect the three occurrences of this personage, here and at 25/11, 20.

27/12 *Anno 3729*: 3728 in Isidore, but 3729 in MS *M*.

27/13 *went up to*: ascended (Deut. 3: 27). *OED, Up* adv.[1] 26, does not record this sense for *up to*, but the usual sense 'as far as' (as at 194/16) is evidently incorrect here. Emendation to *up onto* (as at 125/10), though it would make the sense clearer, is probably unnecessary.

27/15–16 Deut. 34: 4.

27/20 *Anno 3756*: 3755 in Isidore, but 3756 in MSS *YM*.

27/24–5 Cf. Josh. 3: 7.

27/34 *Anno 3796*: 3795 in Isidore.

28/2 *broþir onto Caleph*: *recte* nephew. Kenaz, Caleb's younger brother, was Othniel's father. The error could easily have arisen from the L of the Vulgate: *Othoniel videlicet filium Cenez, fratrem Caleb minorem* (Judg. 3: 9); cf. the version in the AV, which is apparently ambiguous.

28/10 *Anno 3866*: 3875 in Isidore.

28/12 *schuld*: the latest reference given by *OED, Shall* B. 12, for this use—'had to'—is 1400. See Glossary for further instances.

28/17 *flay*: this form of the p.t. of the verb 'flay' is apparently unique. It is not recorded by *OED, Flay* v., or *MED, flen* v. (2). It is recorded by Rettger, *Ablaut Patterns*, p. 152, but only here. The unique form could be avoided by emendation to *flayed*, but in view of possible mental assimilation to other p.t. forms like *lay* (from *lie*), this is difficult to justify.

28/30 *Anno 3916*: 3915 in Isidore, but 3916 in MS *V*.

29/13–23 Isidore, *Etymologiarum libri xx*, ed. Lindsay, III. xxi. 8–9.

29/13 P's *Jubis* is prob. the result of a misreading of **nilus* in the exemplar (**A*).

29/25 *Anno 3956*: 3955 in Isidore.

29/26 *God*: the spelling with -*oo*- is never otherwise used for 'God'; *God* occurs 117×. *God* 'good' occurs 2×, against *good* 84×, *gode* 2×. The error here is probably due to misapprehension (by the copyist) of the sense in the context *receyued of God* as 'received of good a . . .'.

29/31–2 Judg. 9: 8–15.

30/1–2 *xxii ȝere*: 23 in Isidore.

30/9 *Anno 4018*: 4016 in Isidore.

30/12 Perhaps *raueschid* occurred at the beginning of the line in *A and C inadvertently substituted a capital *R* in his copy. Cf. 169/23 and Textual Note.

30/15 *Anno 4034*: 4024 in Isidore.

30/18 *Olimpias*: apparently pl. of *Olimpiade* 30/19 (2nd). C probably transferred L nom. sg. *Olimpias* (acc. -*adem*) into English without integrating it properly into the grammar of his sentence. *Olimpiade*, though unobjectionable, may also be a straight transfer of the L form (30/19 (1st)) into English. Alternatively, *Olimpias* might be emended to *Olimpiades*.

31/5 The Tiber is said originally to have been called *Albula*.

31/17 1 Sam. 5: 6.

31/32–3 1 Sam 2: 1.

32/29–30 1 Kgs. 1: 33–40.

33/12 *Anno 4225*: 4224 in Isidore.
    Abia is the Greek form of Abijah, son of Jeroboam I the first king of Israel. This Abijah, who died early, is easily confused with his contemporary Abijam, son of Rehoboam the first king of Judah, and confusion must have occurred here, since Maacah was mother of Abijam (1 Kgs. 15: 2). Alternatively *Abia* may be erroneous for *Abiã* which would give *Abiam* 'Abijam'.

33/31–34/3 *reysed fro deth*, 1 Kgs. 17: 17 ff.; *fasted*, 19: 8–9; *sperd heuene fro reyn*, 17: 1 ff.; *asked fire*, 18: 36 ff.; *killid prestis*, 18: 40; *was bore up*, 2 Kgs. 2: 11.

34/3–8 *dobil þe grace*, 2 Kgs. 2: 9–10; *went þorw þe flood*, 2: 14; *lift þe ex*, 6: 5–7; *cured Naaman*, 5: 14; *smet his seruaunt*, 5: 27; *deied*, 13: 20.

34/8 *was he byried*: this reading seems preferable as more characteristic of C's general usage—cf. 61/1.

34/17 *whech tyme* 'at which time'. For the construction cf. 54/21, 32, 96/18, 132/28.

34/20 *a hundred ȝere and xx*: 130 in Isidore.

34/26 *Anno 4348*: 4346 in Isidore.

35/7–9 Deut. 24: 16.

36/3–13 Cf. the similar account in *Solace*, 4/26–5/11.

36/5 *Vescal*: definitely with *c* rather than *t*—cf. note to 11/11. The use of the adj. form as a sb. for the name of the cult is not recorded by *OED*, *Vestal*, and presumably arises from a misunderstanding of the L source. But the construction is clumsy and *whech* (followed by the pl. vb. *were*) requires an antecedent such as 'Vestal virgins'.

36/12 *Wolf*: the wolf is well known for its rapacity rather than its *leccherie*. Perhaps the L word *aviditas* occurred in the source and C mistook its emphasis.

36/33–37/1 *þe serpent of bras þat Moyses set up*: see Num. 21: 9.

37/14–15 *Anno 4540*: 4543 in Isidore.
   lii ȝere: 55 in Isidore.

37/24 The fourth Sibyl was *Cumaea* or *Cymaea* 'of Cumae' in Aeolia (Asia Minor) but has apparently been confused with the seventh Sibyl, here called *Amalthea*, who was of Cumae in Campania (Italy). There may also be confusion with the *Cimmerii*, a people who lived in darkness in caves by the coast of Campania.

37/25 The home of Sibyl *Erithea* was Erythrae (Ionia), not the Babylonian region, though she apparently wandered to various countries. The error may be due to confusion of Erythrae with Erech (near Babylon).

38/1–2 *Anno 4554*: 4555 in Isidore.
   xiii ȝere: 12 in Isidore. In fact Amon reigned for two years.

38/10–11 *Anno 4576*: 4587 in Isidore.

38/15–16 *Anno 4587*: 4598 in Isidore.

38/28–9 The reference is to the *Lamentations (of Jeremiah)*. In the Vulgate this contains four chapters (plus ch. v, which is separated off as Jeremiah's prayer) and each verse is, as it were, spoken by a letter of the alphabet.

39/9 ff. *þe grete ymage*, Dan. 2: 31 ff.; *þe grete tre*, 4: 10 ff.; *þe foure wyndis*, 7: 2 ff.; the *elde man . . . in majesté*, 7: 9–10.

39/15 *Anno 4690*: 4713 in Isidore.
   regneth: this use of the historic pr. tense and seven other similar instances between here and 49/25 (being all eight occurrences in the text) show signs of confusion. Confirmation that there was uncertainty comes from the fact that the instance of *regneth* at 40/21 is over an erasure. The confusion arose out of transferring from a system of recording each personage by the date of his death to a system of recording each ruler by the date when his reign began: see 42/17–20. Before 42/17–20 *regneth* means 'ceased to reign'; after 42/17–20 it means 'reigned' or 'began to reign'.

39/30 *Etas Quinta*: Isidore puts the beginning of the fifth age between 4609 and 4679.

39/31–2 *Anno 4737*: 4733 in Isidore.
   xxiiii ȝere: 20 in Isidore.

40/7 *Sophodes*: definitely so written.

40/8–9 C appears to have confused the writer's work, *tragedy*, with the writer, *tragedian*. *OED, Tragedy* 4, records this sense only in this instance; *Tragedian*, s.v., is first recorded in Chaucer. On the medieval conception of tragedy see J. W. Cunliffe, *Early English Classical Tragedies* (Oxford, 1912), pp. ix–xiv. *MED dite* n. 1(c) glosses *ditées* as 'dramas' but this gloss has been arrived at through a misunderstanding of the word *tragedy* in ME (see *OED*, s.v., 1a). It is unlikely that ME *dité* ever meant 'drama'.

40/11–12 *Anno 4777*: 4773 in Isidore.

Nothus: this appellation applies to Darius II in Isidore, who calls Artaxerxes I *Longimanus*.

40/21 *Anno 4798*: 4792 in Isidore. The column of text in M carries straight on from *mech þing* at the end of one line to *In þis ȝere* at the beginning of the next line, with no break in the vertical red line between the column of dates and the written text (on this red line see my 'Punctuation-Markers', p. 7). Nevertheless *In þis ȝere* clearly relates to the date *Anno 4798* by which it stands. For further evidence of the general confusion in the format of the text in M at this stage see Textual Notes to 41/8, 21, 42/5, 42/14, 16. On the reason for the confusion see note to 39/15.

40/22–4 *þe vii gouernouris* were the seven conspirators who united to kill Smerdis, usurper of the Persian throne after the death of Cambyses. Darius I was one of these and was subsequently made king by agreement because his horse neighed before that of any of the other six. This story has here been erroneously transferred to Darius II.

40/27 John 1: 1.

40/28–41/1 This anecdote about Plato corresponds most closely to one recorded by A. S. Riginos only from John of Salisbury: see her *Platonica: The Anecdotes concerning the Life and Writings of Plato* (Leiden, 1976), pp. 82–3, Anecdote 28.

41/3–6 Presumably a reference to Plato's reported Apollonian nature at his death, also recorded by John of Salisbury: Riginos, *Platonica*, pp. 25–7, Anecdote 7.

41/8 *Anno 4838*: 4832 in Isidore. The lack of visible break in the continuity of the text and the vertical red line on its left is as described in the note to 40/21. Cf. 45/29 and note. That *Here* relates to *Anno 4838* is made clear by the presence of a full paragraph mark before *Anno*, an unusual place for the mark to occur in this part of M: see my 'Punctuation-Markers', p. 6 and n. 29.

41/13 The pp. form *bond*, which occurs only here (see Introd., p. lxii), against *bound(e)* and *bownde* elsewhere, is perhaps *boud* (for *boūd*) with the nasal titulus erroneously omitted.

41/24–31 C tells a slightly different version of this story in *Solace*, ch. xii.

42/5 *Anno 4868*: 4862 in Isidore.

42/5–6 Artaxerxes III (41/21) was succeeded on the Persian throne by Darius III (42/14). Arsanes, son of the former and father of the latter, was not king and was not called Xerxes. He has presumably been confused with Xerxes II who reigned for less than a year (425 BC) between Artaxerxes I and Darius II.

42/14 *Anno 4874*: 4868 in Isidore, but 4874 in MS *Y*.

42/16–17 *Anno 4879*: 4873 in Isidore.
  sex . . . sex: 7 and 5 in Isidore.

42/17–20 Here C departs from the practice used by Isidore.

42/21 *as we seid before*: see 39/23–4.

42/22 If not an error for *kyngdam* P's *kyndam* postdates the latest instances of *Kindom* and *kinedom* recorded by *OED* and *MED* respectively.

43/12–13 The reference is to the Septuagint.

43/30–1 The similarity is that between the titles *Ecclesiastes* and *Ecclesiasticus*.

44/4 *vii ȝere*: *annis xvii* in Higden, and sim. Isidore.

44/14 *xxxiiii ȝere*: *viginti quatuor annis* in Higden (and sim. Isidore), but the number varies in some manuscripts.

44/19–20 *he weddid þe doutir of þe same Antiochus*: in Higden Antiochus marries Ptolemy's daughter.

44/22 *dwelle*: the spelling *dwel* never otherwise occurs, against *dwelle* (19×), *dwell'* (4×). The likelihood of error over the line division seems great enough to warrant the emendation; *dwel\le* over a line division occurs once.

45/13–46/17 This account of the later Ptolemies in Egypt is slightly confused. The Ptolemy whose reign was interrupted, and who was the son of Cleopatra (46/2), was Ptolemy IX *Soter II* or *Lathyrus*, not *Physcon* (as 45/30 *first* and 46/11–15). The length of (i) Ptolemy IX's initial reign (11 years) and (ii) his exile in Cyprus (18 years) appear to be interchanged, *xvii ȝere* (45/20) being ascribed to (i) and 11 years (*Anno 5103* to *Anno 5113*) to (ii). Ptolemy VII (145 BC) and Ptolemy XI *Alexander II* (81–80 BC) have been omitted.

45/15–16 Terence was, of course, a comedy-writer in the second century BC.; *trajedies* should perhaps be corrected to *comedies*.

45/29 *Anno 5086*: the lack of visible break in the continuity of the text in M and the vertical red line on its left is as described in the note to 40/21. Cf. 41/8 and note. Yet the entry beginning *Ptholome . . .* beside *Anno 5086* obviously relates to that date.

46/17 *x ȝere*: 30 in Isidore.

46/21 *and summe sey*: so Higden.

46/27 *þis lond*: Britain.

47/26 From now on in M AD year numbers are written in red after the AM numbers. In this edition the AD numbers follow the AM numbers after a semicolon.

47/27-8 See Introd., p. lxxii.

48/6 Though it refers to AD 14, the entry is part of that beginning at AD 12.

48/27 *eke in Achay*: *eke* refers back to Paul in the previous paragraph. According to a late and unreliable tradition Andrew was martyred in Patras in AD 60.

49/10-11 *Simon . . . bischop of Jerusalem*: Simon the apostle has apparently been identified with Simeon—see Index, s.n. *Simon Cleophas*.

49/21 P's *seith* may be the original reading as the two following entries are in the present tense, *is* (49/23), *regneth* (49/25).

49/23 *In þis ȝere*: as there is no visible break in M in the continuity of the text this entry could belong at either AD 38 or AD 39, by which date it stands. In C's source (Martinus 409) Peter's arrival at Antioch is assigned to AD 38, and this assignation has been followed, though the writing of Matthew is assigned to AD 40 (ibid.).

49/25 *Anno 5240–5253; 42–55*. From now on the material is arranged under the reigns of the Roman and holy Roman emperors and, after fol. 60, of the kings of England. In this edition the years of each reign are grouped together at the beginning of the account of the reign, since the material relates to the whole reign rather than just the first year. For the later period see note to 116/28.

49/26-31 This account of the British resistance to Claudius's invasion is probably taken from *Brut*, ch. xxxix—but cf. Geoffrey of Monmouth's *Historia Regum Britanniae*, iv. 13–15; apparently *Gwynderyn* corresponds to the real Togodumnus and *Aruigarus* to the real Caratacus. C's names for the British chiefs differ from those found in *Brut* (*Gynder* and *Armoger*) and in Geoffrey's *Historia* (*Guiderius* and *Arvirargus*); C's *Aruigarus* [sic] apparently possesses features which belong to both *Armoger* and *Arvirargus*.

49/31 *Kayerglau*: derived from the Celtic name for Gloucester, as OW *Caer Gloiu* 'bright fort'.

50/16 *waspis in his nose*: (?) irascibility. Cf. the proverb *The wasp got him by the nose* 'he was infuriated' (*OED, Wasp* sb. 2b). Whiting does not record the expression but cf. W50-2. This item is lacking in Martinus.

51/3-4 *in a boilyng tunne of oyle*: lacking in Martinus.

51/5 The erron. view that St. Dionysius was sent to Paris by Pope Clement I about AD 90 seems to have originated in the eighth century.

51/20 *Plutarc*: Martinus has *Plinius*, apparently correctly—the actions here attributed to Plutarch are applicable to Pliny the Younger, though both lived under Trajan.

51/29 Anacletus was pope before Clement (51/6) and is probably identical with Cletus at 50/26 where he is mentioned in the correct chronological position.

52/1 *a Jew*: Martinus has *nacione Grecus ex patre Iudeo*.

52/15–17 The item concerning *Aquila* is lacking in Martinus.

53/4–6 C has evidently confused Galen and Ptolemy. Ptolemy, the astronomer, who has also been confused with the Ptolemies who ruled Egypt, was the author of the *Almagest*, etc. The content of these lines is lacking in Martinus.

53/18–20 Lacking in Martinus.

53/22 *In þis ȝere*: *ȝere*, added in the margin in M, is perhaps a mistake for *wey*, which would make better sense.

53/28–9 St. Justus was bishop of Vienne (*Viennensis episcopus* in Martinus) where the cathedral was dedicated to St. Mauritius. This apparent error of *Mamert* for some form of *Mauritius* does not occur in Martinus even in any of the variant readings given by Weiland.

   Forcius: this erron. form (for Pothinus) is cited by Weiland as a variant occurring only in his MSS 2, 8, and 10 of Martinus.

54/1 *with hir sistir Potencian*: taken from Martinus 411/39 where both sisters are mentioned together.

54/8 *handel*: presumably *handel* (rather than *handeled*) was expuncted in error in M.

54/16 *Summe cronicles*: e.g. Bede, *Hist. Eccl.* i. 4, Geoffrey of Monmouth, *Hist. Reg. Brit.* iv. 19, *Brut*, ch. 44 (p. 38). The names of the missionaries, not given by Bede, are variously given as Fuganus and Dimianus (Martinus 412/18, but Damianus is cited as a variant from Weiland's MSS 8 and 9), Faganus and Duvianus (Geoffrey), Pagan and Elibrayne (*Brut*). The year is given by Bede and *Brut* as 156 and should perhaps be so emended here.

54/18 The omission of Commodus (180–92) from the series of emperors and the assignation of his initial date to Pertinax causes an error in the chronology of eleven years. This error is progressively reduced, to ten years at the time of Macrinus (217–18), eight years at the time of Decius (249–51), seven years at the time of Constantine the Great (306–37), six years at the time of Jovian (363–4), and one year at the time of Theodosius I (378–95).

54/19 *þe fourt translatour*: after the Septuagint, Aquila, and Theodotion.

54/22–3 *whos wryting passith al opir*: lacking in Martinus.

54/30 *vii bretheren*: Martinus reads 6 except for MS 1, with which the present text agrees.

54/31–2 *a grete clerk, bischop of Lugdune*: lacking in Martinus.

55/9–10 *He was clepid . . .*: this explanation of the name *Carcalla* is lacking in Martinus.

55/13 *Perses*: Martinus has *Partos* 'Parthians'.

55/17–18 *Befor . . . court*: lacking in Martinus.

55/19 *Antonius Aurelius*: for Martinus's *Antoninus II*, the variant *Anthonius* occurring only in MS 3.

55/20-1 This item concerning Heliogabalus's previous occupation, from which he took his name, is lacking in Martinus. Heliogabalus was the name of the deity who was worshipped in the temple.

55/26-8 *where þe welles . . . Ymbir-dayes*: lacking in Martinus.

55/28 *vndir þe chirch of Sebastian*: lacking in Martinus.

55/30-1 The name *Mammeas* and the sentence explaining it are lacking in Martinus.

56/4 *witte* corresponds to *vita*, rendered as *lyf* at 56/10, in Martinus.

56/10 *His doctrine . . .*, i.e. he practised what he preached.

56/13 *and sche mad hir son more esy . . .*: lacking in Martinus which by contrast has *ob hoc* (Mammea's conversion to Christianity) *a filio occiditur*.

56/15 *and his brothir*: *cum fratre suo Tyburcio* cited as an addition in MSS 1 and 6 of Martinus.

56/16-17 *but not so largely . . .*: lacking in Martinus.

56/17 *with þis possession*: apparently 'by using this wealth', but *OED* cites no instances of *Possession*, sb., meaning 'wealth' when sg. Emendation to *þis possessiones* would avoid this difficulty and also accord more closely to the L of C's source—*predia . . ., de quibus . . . Urbanus . . . notariis, qui gesta martirum conscribebant, sumptus deputabat*—but it is impossible to be sure that C did not mean what he actually wrote.

56/27-31 C's text follows the fuller AC rather than the B recension of Martinus.

57/1 *Philippicus*: *Philippus* in Martinus.

57/6 As Provence is a territory and not a city there is manifestly an error here. C's source, which reads *in Nicia civitate Provincie*, supplies the missing information that the city is Nice.

57/10-11 *for whech . . .*: an allusion to the story that when requested to produce the treasures of the Church St. Laurence brought the poor and the sick, whereupon he was roasted on a gridiron. Martinus records only the request.

57/12-14 C's account is a considerable exaggeration of what is in Martinus: *Iste in omnibus malus fuit . . . et septimam dedit persecucionem christianis*.

57/16-17 *a widow*: lacking in Martinus.

57/21 *of her tyme is litil writing*: presumably C's addition referring to Martinus. Cf. *Solace*, 54/28-31.

58/2 *þe bischop*: lacking in Martinus.

58/4-5 *God suffered him to be*: lacking in Martinus.

58/9-10 Saints Laurence (d. 258) and Vincent (d. 304) were not in fact related.

58/15–16 *and lith . . .*: lacking in Martinus. Cf. *Solace*, II. iii, *in þe same cherch* [San Sebastiano] *be þat dore þat goth to Rome lith Seint Steuene þe pope a-for an auter* (68/16–17), from which it is clear that the tomb was not before *þe* altar.

58/19 *iii daies*: lacking in Martinus.

rosted on a grate: lacking in Martinus, which merely says that Laurence followed Sixtus in martyrdom.

58/27 *þei sei*: presumably C's addition referring to Martinus.

58/29 *graues* corresponds to *reliquias*, cited as a variant from recension A, rather than *memorias* in Weiland's text of Martinus.

58/30 *and mad auteres upon her graues*: lacking in Martinus.

58/33 *þerfor*: the connection of these events as cause and effect is only implicit in Martinus.

59/5 *he restored it*: lacking in Martinus.

59/6 *we clepe it Orgliauns*: presumably C's addition.

59/12 *too or iii offices*: *hostiarius* 'door-keeper', *lector* 'reader', and *exorcista* (Martinus).

59/17–20 Expanded from Martinus, which lacks reference to the devil's eternity and Christ's non-incarnation. C also presumably adds the clear contrast between the *fals* heresy and the correct view of *þe feith*.

59/25 *Karus*: *Clarus* in Martinus.

59/27 *þerfor*: the connection of these events as cause and effect is only implicit in Martinus.

59/28–30 *In his tyme were martired . . .*: lacking in Martinus.

59/29 *of whech on*: the addition of *of* seems to be necessary. I have found no parallel for *which one*, meaning 'one of which', as the subject of a relative clause.

59/29–30 *þe opir a woman, Daria was hyr name*: for the construction cf. 71/29.

60/1–3 *For þis practik . . . withoute dispensacion*: expanded from Martinus's *divinis libris adustis*. Cf. *Solace*, 55/17–18.

60/11 *xx þousand*: so also *Solace*, 55/21. Martinus has *22 milia*.

61/9–11 Martinus lacks any reference to the renewed payment of tribute and for *þe kyngis doutir of Colchester* has *filiam regis Britannie*. C may have used *Brut*, ch. xlv (p. 39), to supplement Martinus. Cf. *Solace*, 55/25.

61/12 *þat ded mech for þe Cherch*: lacking in Martinus. Cf. *Solace*, 55/28–9.

61/20–62/10 On the organization of this entry see Introd., p. lxxvi.

61/27 *wikkid*: lacking in Martinus.

61/32–62/2 These summaries of the Arian and Donatist heresies are lacking in Martinus.

62/3–5 Reference to the churches of SS. Peter and Paul and of St. Laurence, etc., is apparently taken from Martinus 415/35–42, where Pope Sylvester I is credited with building them; he is also credited with building *Salvatoris nostri ecclesiam*.

62/8–10 For *Seynt Gregorie . . . May*: cf. *Solace*, 55/31–4.

62/8–9 Upon *þe XIII Psalme*: *super psalmum 14* in Martinus.

62/11 *xxxi ʒere*: *annis 23* in Martinus.

62/13–14 *where þe crede was mad . . .*: lacking in Martinus.

62/21–2 *be a fals prest*: lacking in Martinus.

62/22–3 *þe Cristen bischoppis and prestis*: merely *christianos* in Martinus.

62/23–32 No source for this passage is known.

62/24 *Athanasius*. This emended reading seems justified in view of the correct spelling with medial *-ana-* at 63/1 and 64/12.

62/33 *Lucius*: *Iulius* correctly in Martinus.

63/1 This Eusebius is the famous bishop of Caesarea, who wrote the *Ecclesiastical History*, as is clear from Martinus.

63/5 *vii ʒere*: *6 annis* in Martinus.

63/8 *hous*: presumably 'room'. The example at 64/14 (Martinus 452/38 ff.) is similar. Cf. 135/10 'dwelling'. Martinus lacks this anecdote about Eusebius.

63/18 *he mad feith to a deuel* corresponds to Martinus's *cui . . . demon apparuisset*.

63/22 *ten monthis*: *mensibus 8* in Martinus. Cf. *Solace*, 56/5: *uiii monthis*.

63/23–4 *entended al to . . .*: lacking in Martinus and probably repeated from 63/16–17.

64/5 *ros oute of his graue and with his spere*: lacking in Martinus.

64/7 *for so . . .*: this explanation is lacking in Martinus.

64/11–15 *All þe biscoppis . . .*: I have found no source for this passage.

64/14–15 Cf. *Solace*, 56/16–19.

64/23 *mad many ympnes, whech be sunge in þe Cherch*: perhaps adapted from *ritum canendi antiphonas in ecclesia instituit* (Martinus, 417/11; cf. 453/11).

64/26 *at Bethlem*: lacking here in Martinus. Cf. note to 65/23–4. Martinus notes that Jerome was at Bethlehem at 417/36.

64/27 *Ysidre*: at this date (second half of fourth century AD) only St. Isidore of Pelusium (died *c.*450) would be appropriate. Martinus has simply *Ysidorus*. But Isidore of Seville is not mentioned at an appropriate point in the chronological scheme anywhere else, so this reference is probably intended for him. Martinus includes him in the reign of Heraclius (457/50–458/2).

64/31 *Therfor oure Lord*: the connection of these events as cause and effect and the divine intervention are lacking in Martinus.

65/3 *þat wrot . . .*: lacking in Martinus.

65/6 *God suffered him to be*: this divine intervention is lacking in Martinus.

65/18–22 On the organization of this entry see Introd., p. lxxvi.

65/19 *of ccc and l biscoppis*: *cum 315 episcopis* in Martinus.

65/23–4 *went . . . to Bethlem*: *Iherosolimam adiit* in Martinus. Cf. note to 64/26.

65/25 *Emaus* is probably the village in which our Lord made his resurrection appearance to two of the disciples (Luke 24: 13 ff.). This probability is increased by the fact that Martinus reports the additional information that after one of the Siamese twins died the other, still attached, lived for three days, the same period as that between our Lord's death and resurrection. An alternative identification would be the Emmaus of 1 Macc. 3: 40.

65/27–8 *messagere betwix Jerom and Augustin*: merely *Augustini discipulus* in Martinus.

65/29 *Ormesta Mundi*: Martinus summarizes the contents but does not give the title of the book.

65/30 *xii ʒere*: *annis 11* in Martinus. Cf. *Solace*, 57/3: *xi ʒere*.

65/31–66/2 *whech secte . . . vndir tribute*: merely *Hic destruxit templa ydolorum* in Martinus.

66/3–9 This paragraph about Augustine is expanded from Martinus's *Augustinus cum esset Manicheus ad fidem convertitur*.

66/18 *his*, i.e. Arcadius's, as is clear from the fact that it was his reign (as emperor of the East) not Honorius's which lasted thirteen years. Sim. 68/30.

66/24–8 These summaries of the Priscillianist and Pelagian heresies and the statement that they were refuted by Augustine are lacking at this point in Martinus. For the summary of Pelagius's teaching cf. Martinus 417/47–9.

66/27–8 The metaphor of St. Augustine as a hammer against heretics was a common one in medieval writings: see R. Arbesmann, osa, 'The "Malleus" Metaphor in Medieval Characterization', *Traditio*, iii (1945), 389–92. C had previously used it in his *Augustine* at 52/10.

66/32–67/2 This explanation of how Augustine came to write *De Civitate Dei* is lacking in Martinus. It occurs also in *Solace*, 57/5–8.

67/14–16 *foure score and on*: *91* in Martinus, *lxxxxi* in *Solace*, 57/12. The account of how Jerome's spirit appeared to Augustine is lacking in Martinus.

67/26 *Concha*: (*filium*) *Conthes* in Martinus, except Weiland's MS 1, which has *Conches*.

68/6 *Totila*: *Attila* in Martinus, except for recension A, which has *Totila*.

68/10 *þe general resurreccion*: the rising again of all men at the Last Day.

68/13 *bylid*. This form of the p.t. of 'build' (OE *byldan*) no doubt arose from analogous association with verbs like 'fill' (OE *fyllan*). In ME the p.t. form *filt* subsumed the root *fil-*+p.t. ending *-t*. ME p.t. *bilt* was presumably understood similarly, albeit erroneously, and this misunderstanding led to a hyper-correct p.t. form *bil-*+*-ed*. At 91/13 P has *bylded* where M has *bilid*.

68/13–15 *Oþir men write . . . arayed it, as*: lacking in Martinus. For what *oþir men write* see *Solace*, II. vii (pp. 84–5), though C does not cite the 'surname' *Patricius* there. Presumably *Vphap þis pope mored it or arayed it* is C's speculatory addition.

68/14 *Johannes Patricius*: apparently C has erron. taken *patricius* as part of John's name. An alternative reading would be *on Johannes, patricius, schul . . .*, but this has a macaronic quality uncharacteristic of C's style. Cf. 78/4.

68/26–7 *aftir iii dayes*: *in fine 40 dierum* in Martinus.

68/27 *aftir þe pleasauns of God*: lacking in Martinus.

68/30 See note to 66/18.

68/32 *he killid þis Marcian*: Martinus does not credit Theodoric with Marcian's murder.

68/33–4 *a holy woman . . .*: these details about St. Geneviève's *special grace* are lacking in Martinus.

69/3–5 *þat held þis opinion . . .*: this explanation of the heretical beliefs of Dioscorus is lacking in Martinus.

69/6 *in-so-mech þat*: the connection between heresy and desecration of statues as cause and effect is lacking in Martinus.

69/12–13 *þat mad a grete book . . .*: merely *doctrina . . . claruit* in Martinus. Cf. *Solace*, 57/23. Presumably the reference is to *De Vocatione Omnium Gentium*, Prosper's best-known work.

69/16–17 *of our Lady and*: the dedication to our Lady is lacking in Martinus.

69/18 *cclxx*: 257 in Martinus.

69/21 *cleped Auallone*: lacking in the text of Martinus, but cited as an addition from MS 9 (*scilicet Analonie*).

69/31 *of malice*: lacking in Martinus.

70/5 *Wandalis*: the form with initial *W-* is from Martinus. It is also used by Trevisa where it is perhaps preserved from OE (cf. *Wendel-sǽ* 'Mediterranean'), but the usual form in the ME period and subsequently is with *V-* from L *Vandalus*. Possibly *W* stands for /v/ as in *dowe* 'dove' and *nowil* 'navel'.

70/6 *þat were not consenting to Arrius*: this explanatory statement, lacking in Martinus, was possibly added by C.

70/15 *viii ʒere*: *annis 4, mensibus 8* in Martinus.

70/23 *be a aungell*. In all other appropriate contexts (12/16, 24/13, 20, 53/15, 70/9, 112/16–18) C precedes *aungel(l)* with an indefinite article and presumably it was omitted here by mistake. Omission of *a* before a word beginning with that letter is easily explained.

70/29–31 *to Pauye . . .*: Martinus says that Boethius was exiled by the king of Italy, *ibique libros . . . edidit*. C appears to be supplying the information about Pavia.

71/8 *bischoppis*: *christianos* in Martinus.

71/20 *in a . . . erroure, whech began in Antioch*: *errore Heuticetis* in Martinus.

71/23 *whech ar þe grounde of Cyuyle*: lacking in Martinus.

71/24 *Besibarius*: *Belisarius* in Martinus.

71/26 The phrase *distroyed þe sege*, like *dissolue þe sege* 165/27, is based on L *dissolvere obsidionem*. One of the senses of L *dissolvere* is 'to destroy'. *MED, destroien* v. 9(c), records only one other instance of the phrase, slightly earlier than this one.

71/29 *Orator*: *Arator* in Martinus.

71/33–4 *whech mad . . .*: this information concerning Cassiodorus's *Expositio Psalmorum* is lacking in Martinus.

72/16 *iii ʒere*: *anno 1, mensibus 5, diebus 11* in Martinus.

72/25 *schuld haue no priuilege of þe Cherch*: lacking in Martinus and presumably added by C by way of explanation.

72/29 *Justiniane*: *Iustinus* in Martinus.

73/4 *Aburre*: *Albura* in Martinus.

73/9 *he*: Justin.

73/15 *Tiberius*: *Liberius* erron. in Martinus.

73/27–8 *befor þei had but . . .*: this explanatory parenthesis is lacking in Martinus and was presumably added by C, no doubt recalling Martinus 456/31–2.

74/6 *werriour*: apparently 'commander', as indicated by the source, Martinus 457/12—*per prefectum suum*—though this sense is not recorded by *OED, Warrior*.

74/8 *In þe þirtene ʒere*: *Anno 14* in Martinus.

74/10–11 *and had dryuyn oute . . . þe . . . eyeris into Walis*: lacking in Martinus. Cf. *Brut*, i, 54/32–3.

74/11 *strength*: the emendation is supported by the fact that on all twenty-two other occasions when the word occurs in M it is spelt with *-g-*.

74/11-14 This incident concerning the discovery of our Lord's coat is lacking in Martinus.

74/25 *for more sikirnesse*: lacking in Martinus.

74/27 This statement, taken over from Martinus, would be more accurate if *martires* were read for *seyntis*. When Boniface IV consecrated the original Roman temple as a Christian church in 609 it was dedicated to *Santa Maria ad Martyres* in allusion to the martyrs' bones—twenty-eight wagon-loads of them, according to tradition—which were brought from the catacombs.

74/29-30 *white past*: tr. L *nitidus pannus* (Martinus 422/30). Presumably unleavened bread is meant.

75/6 *cursed*: lacking in Martinus. Cf. *Solace*, 58/19.

75/11 Martinus lacks any account of Mahomet's marriage.

75/11-14 *His book . . .*: Martinus has merely *A quodam eciam monacho nomine Sergio apostata ad decipiendum populum informabatur.*

75/16 *Exaltacion of þe Cros*: 14 Sept.

75/25 *lith*: the sense 'died' is fixed by the source, which has *requiescit*. Honorius *sepultus est in ecclesia sancti Petri* (Martinus 423/13-14).

75/29-30 *for redempcion of Cristen men . . .*: closer to the variant reading of Martinus cited by Weiland from MS 9, *multos captivos redemit.*

76/2-3 *where confessoures may lerne . . .*: this description of the use of the *Penitencial* is lacking in Martinus.

76/6-7 *in þe cherch of Seint Mari Major*: lacking in Martinus.

76/7-8 *but oure Lord mad him blynd, þat . . .*: Martinus has merely *cecus effectus est*. God's intervention and the explanation of its consequences are presumably C's additions.

76/18-19 The Monothelite heresy is not specified in Martinus, nor are any of its tenets stated there. Cf. *Solace*, 58/22.

77/4 *iiii ȝere*: *anno I* in Martinus.

77/7-15 This entry shows considerable reorganization of what is in Martinus. Martinus deals with events as they occur here except that he refers to the fifth Council which is *contra Gregorium patriarcham*. After stating that Constantine *restauravit ecclesias* he moves on to the sixth Council, which dealt with the Monothelite heresy. C has conflated the two councils and dealt with both in the position accorded by Martinus to the fifth. Cf. *Solace*, 58/26-8.

77/8-9 *of bischoppis to hundred iiii score and viii*: *289 episcoporum* in Martinus. The same number is given in *Solace*, 58/27: *cc bischoppis iiii score and ix.*

77/18 *x ȝere*: *mensibus 10* in Martinus.

77/22 *Zeno*: *Cono* correctly in Martinus.

78/4 *Leo Patricius*: see note to 68/14.

78/4–5 *put oute his eyne, and cut of his nose*: *eumque naso et lingua privatum* in Martinus. Cf. *Solace*, 58/31–2: *priuyd both of his nase and eke of his tunge.*

78/20 *sistir*: *recte* 'daughter'.

79/7 The two kings were Coenred of Mercia and Offa of the East Saxons. Their names are given by Martinus as Coheret and Opha.

80/2 *Helwolphus*: for Ceolwulf. Initial *C-* is presumably lacking; the error may be C's or it may have existed in his source. In his Dedicatory Preface to the *Commentarius in Exodum*, written by another scribe under C's supervision, the same name is spelt with initial *Th* in *regi Theowulpho* 'for King Ceolwulf' (of Northumbria, d. 764): see Lucas and Dalton, 'Preface', p. 21, line 30.

80/5 *clepe*. Retention of the pr.t. form seems justified in view of the following *rennyth*.

80/17 *þe Secunde*: *secundus* occurs in Martinus only as a variant added in MSS 3, 6, 8, and 11.

80/19–20 *and for þis cause . . . he was ded*: lacking in Martinus.

80/22 *Secundus* occurs in Martinus only as a variant added in MSS 3, 6, and 9.

80/24 *so . . . þat*: Anastasius's wickedness is not given as the *cause* of his deposition in Martinus.

   þe puple: Martinus has *exercitus* so the sense of *puple* must be 'army'.

81/4 *Luidbrande*: *Lupandus* in Martinus.

81/9–10 This church was named after its former gilded vault, mentioned by Dante, *Paradiso*, x. 128, in connection with Boethius's burial there. The name *Celum Aureum* is lacking in Martinus.

81/28 *and of oure Lady*: not mentioned specifically in Martinus.

82/2 The manuscript reading *translate þe empire fro þe Grekis onto þe Frensch tong* is evidently erron.: Martinus reads *imperium a Grecis transtulit in Germanos*. Although *OED, Tongue* sb. 9, records the sense 'nation' it does so only 'in biblical use', a category into which the use of *tong* here will not fit. When copying this passage in *A Capgrave presumably had in mind the (here inappropriate) sense 'transferred from one language to another' for *translate* and this led him to make the incongruous addition of *tong*, which is taken over in both M and P. For constructions similar to that which C, as copyist, must have erron. had in mind here see 43/13 and 43/20.

82/5 *saue completori*: lacking in Martinus.

82/8 *þis is þe memorial*: these words are lacking in Martinus.

82/19 *and eke owt of*: and also to put *him* outside the limits of.

82/31–83/1 *so be þei cleped*: lacking here in Martinus, but no doubt recalled from 50/7–10.

83/1–2 Martinus lacks here any reference to S Maria Scala Coeli. Presumably it was added by C from personal knowledge: see *Solace*, II. iii (70/6–8).

83/4 *Albinus*: taken over from Martinus who also gives the correct form *Alcuinus* as an alternative.

83/19–20 Martinus lacks any reference to a *myty felawchip* and does not mention Oliver by name.

83/22 *Ganerion*: *Ganelon* in Martinus.

83/22–4 Martinus says *Colonie trans Renum duos pontes construxit.* Apparently C passed through Cologne, probably on his way to or from Rome *c.*1450, hence the hesitation: *as is writin, summe men sey to.*

83/28, 30 *visit(e)*: on these p.t. forms see Introd., p. liv, §21.

84/20–2 Charlemagne (d. 814) had intended to partition his empire between his three sons but Charles (d. 813) and Pepin (king of Italy, 781–810) died before him leaving Louis the Pious as sole successor.

84/28 *of Wiltens*: *Vuldensis* in Martinus, with *Waldensis* cited as a variant from MS 5.

84/29–32 Martinus lacks any reference to Rabanus's *De Universo* or Rabanus receiving the bishopric of Mainz as a reward.

84/33 *iii ȝere*: *mensibus 7* in Martinus. The error is perhaps taken over from the previous Pope Stephen (Martinus 426/33).

85/6 *ii m bodies*: Martinus has *innumera corpora* but *circa duo milia* is cited as a variant from MSS 5, 9, and 11.

85/7–9 *He ded eke mech cost in Seynt Sabyn cherch . . .*: attributed to Eugenius II in Martinus.

86/3 *Marchio Gy*: *Guido marchio* in Martinus. L *marchio* designates a foreign title approximately rendered by 'marquis'. C appears to have misunderstood the term as a Christian name.

86/9–10 Ingwar and Ubba the *too cursed capteynes* are not mentioned in Martinus.

86/11 *first with schot of arowis*: lacking in Martinus.

86/16 *malicious*: lacking in Martinus.

87/1 *et cetera*: Martinus completes the verse with the words *in fluctibus.*

87/3 *regni celestis*: lacking in Martinus.

87/17 The emphasis is on *þis*: even at the time of writing . . . .

87/26–7 *ny foure ȝere*: Martinus has *anno 1 et mensibus 9*, except for MS 1 which has *anno 5*, etc.

88/2 *Frauns* is erron. for Lotharingia: see Index, s.n. *Lotharie*. Martinus does not say here what country *Lotharie* was *kyng of*.

88/8 *ccclxxx bischoppis*: *383* in Martinus, except for MS 6 which has *380*.

88/16 *Normannes*: M has *normãnes*. Owing to the difficulty of distinguishing *n* and *u* M's reading could be interpreted as *Normaunes*. That this possibility is incorrect is shown by M's form *normã|nes* 191/2 split over a line division. Similarly *Normanndes* 89/2, etc., and *Normanntes* 132/7.

88/24 Richard III, fifth duke of Normandy (1027), has been omitted, as evidently in some manuscripts of Martinus.

89/11 *ix dayes*: *diebus 20* in Martinus.

89/12 *thre monthis*: *annis 3, mensibus 2* in Martinus.
  Leo V^{us}: *Leo VI* wrongly in Martinus.

89/31 The reference is to the Treaty of Wedmore (878).

90/1 This *Lodewik* must be taken as Louis III, but he may have been confused with Lewis III (the Child), German king (899–911), who is not mentioned separately.

90/4–5 *þei schuld not be worthi . . .*: lacking in Martinus and presumably added by C for clarity and emphasis.

90/12 *ii monthis*: *mensibus 6* in Martinus.

90/15 *Leo þe Sext*: *Leo VII* erron. in Martinus.
  v monthis: *mensibus 6* in Martinus.

90/18–19 Cluny abbey was founded by William of Aquitaine, who did not rule Burgundy. The error is taken over from Martinus. The notion that William was *þe firste prince* presumably corresponds to a reading, such as the variant cited from MS 1 of Martinus, which says that Cluny was founded *a [Guillelmo] primo*.

90/26 Pope John XI (931–5) is omitted before *Leon þe VII*.
  Leon þe VII: *Leo VIII* erron. in Martinus.

90/28 Berengary 'II' and 'III' (92/8) are the same person as Berengarius I (90/16), i.e. Berengar of Friuli who was king of Italy for thirty-six years, for the last nine of which he was also emperor. There is some general confusion in the chronology of this period partly because the imperial seat changed hands between the rulers of Burgundy, France, Germany, Italy, and the Lombard principalities. Arnulf (89/1), German king (887–99), was crowned emperor in 896, but his successors in Germany Lewis III (90/1 n.), [Conrad I (90/21), and Henry I (91/16) were not emperors. (The empire then passed to Germany under Otto I.) C (following Martinus) has imposed a single chronological scheme on the kings of Germany and Italy as if they were all emperors; consequently there is some distortion.

91/1 *viii ȝere*: *annis 9* in Martinus.

91/2 *vii ȝere*: *annis 8* in Martinus.

91/4–6 *Of þis Ode haue I sey . . .*: lacking in Martinus and presumably C's personal experience. No work by Odo *upon þe Sauter* seems to have survived. Five of his sermons are printed in PL cxxxiii. 709–52.

91/12–13 Æthelflæd was daughter of King Alfred (not *Edred*) who would not normally be described as merely king of Mercia. It is more likely that *Edred* is Ethelred, Æthelflæd's husband; consequently, for historical accuracy, *wif* should be understood for *dowtir*.

91/13 *bilid*: see note to 68/13.

91/18 *Spigreuus*: *Spitigneus* in Martinus.

91/20 *Necenlaus*: *Wenceslaus* in Martinus.

91/21 *And ccc ʒer aftir his passion*: since the passage does not make good sense as it stands in M and P (which has a point after *ccc*), there must be an omission. The word *ʒer* has been supplied in accordance with C's source for this passage: *post 300 annos passionis sue* (Martinus 464/29). The form *ʒer* (rather than the much commoner *ʒere*) has been adopted because it has the same final letter as the following word—this identity of final letter in the two words may partially account for the omission. Cf. 170/6.

91/21–2 *to . . . Herri*: *Erico* in Martinus. Eric IV of Denmark was eventually killed by his brother, Duke Abel, after four years of fighting.

91/26 *wrongfully*: lacking in Martinus.

91/29 *xii ʒere*: *annis 7* in Martinus.

92/1 *Constantine*: *Octavianum* correctly in Martinus.

92/2–4 C expands a little on Martinus's moral condemnation of Pope John XII. For Martinus's *venator* C has *a hunter outeragious*. Martinus's *publice feminas tenebat* C precedes with *a lecchour withouten schame*, and adds *and þat dyuers*.

92/8–9 *viii ʒere*: *annis 7* in Martinus.

92/14 *He*: Leo.

92/19–20 *on of his douteris*: Eadgyth, daughter of Edward the Elder, and sister (not daughter) of Athelstan, married Otto in 930.

92/28 *He* refers to Athelstan.

93/1 *Daluida*: erron. from Martinus's *Adaluida*.

93/4 *and he was þe last . . .*: this explanatory statement is lacking in Martinus, though easily enough deduced from 463/55–464/1, 464/6–7, 464/12–14, and 465/5.

94/2 *þe Castel Aungel*. In view of 93/32–3 P's reading, with *of*, may come from *A, but it is impossible to be sure as readings without *of* occur at 210/23 and 231/26–7.

94/3 Edred was in fact half-brother of Athelstan.

94/6–8 The clause *whan Dunstan was bischop* is inexplicable in the manuscript reading and the word *aftir*, preceding it, is also difficult; presumably both were misplaced. The passage refers to the famous scene after Edwy (Eadwig) left his coronation feast (Nov. 955, or possibly Jan. 956) to consort with two noble ladies (who subsequently became his wife and mother-in-law). Dunstan, then abbot of Glastonbury, and others apparently sought out Edwy and forced the reluctant monarch to return to the celebrations. Later, Dunstan, who became bishop of Worcester in 957, was apparently exiled, possibly through the influence that the queen and her mother may have exercised on the king. This exile may have arisen out of a row between Edwy and Dunstan. See further Stenton, *AS England*, pp. 365–6. To make good sense the words *aftir, whan Dunstan was bischop* must belong with *and whan Dunstan vndirtook . . .*, and the passage has been emended accordingly.

94/7 *his wyf*: i.e. his wife-to-be.

94/28 This fictitious Pope Donus has been taken over from Martinus.

94/28 *iii ʒere*: *mense 1, diebus 12* in Martinus.

and þan Gilbert: later Pope Sylvester II (95/27–30). C's papal chronology seems to have become disorientated here. In Martinus *Bonifacius VII* is followed by *Benedictus VII*, in whose entry *Gilbertus* is first mentioned, then *Iohannes XIV, XV*, and *XVI*, none of whom are mentioned by C. Possibly C was confused by the fact that Boniface VII reigned twice, first in 974, secondly in 984–5, though this fact is not given by Martinus.

94/29 *þat deied at messe . . .*: these details are taken from Martinus's entry for Sylvester II (432/22–39).

94/33 *a very vnité*: Edgar became king of all England in 959.

95/27–8 *as we saide before*: see 94/29–31.

95/31 *responses of oure Lady*: merely *laudabilia* in Martinus.

95/31–2 The words *Solem justicie* begin the versicle and *Stirps Jesse* the response to it from the responsory *De Beata Virgine* written for the feast of the Nativity of the Virgin by Fulbert of Chartres. For the full text see PL cxli. 345. For the text of the Easter hymn *Chorus noue Jerusalem* see PL cxli. 352. On Fulbert's literary achievements see F. J. E. Raby, *A History of Christian–Latin Poetry . . .* (Oxford, 1953 edn.), i. 258 ff.

96/3 *Chymegundis*: *Cunegundis* in Martinus, with *Kemegundis* cited as a variant from MS 1.

96/5 i.e. miracles were performed at their tomb. Cf. 229/10–11.

96/6 *duke of Bem*: *dux Bavarorum* correctly in Martinus.

96/9 *Johannes XII*: *Iohannes XVIII* in Martinus, *recte* XVII.

96/9–10 *Johannes XIII*: *Iohannes XIX* in Martinus, *recte* XVIII.

96/10 *of Frauns*: lacking in Martinus.

96/16–17 For the full text of this sequence see PL cxli. 942.

97/4 note The word *Imperium* is written immediately after *6207*, and consequently the AD year number *1009* is omitted.

97/20–1 C omits the important fact that the child was called Henry (after the duke who adopted him).

97/30 *sey þat Goddis ordinauns wold not be broke*: all this for *obstupuit* in Martinus.

97/31 C fails to make clear that Conrad's son-in-law is the future Emperor Henry II (159/1).

98/2–3 Sergius IV appears in his rightful place, before Benedict VIII, in Martinus.

98/12 *þei stoyned*: *þei* must refer to the doors and the sense of *stoyned* is 'crashed' or 'shattered'. The former is supported by Martinus's *cum magno fragore*, the latter perhaps by *OED, Stony*, v. 5 (only citation from *Promptorium Parvulorum*, ed. Mayhew, p. 467, s.v. *Stonyyn* (2nd)). *OED, Stoyne*, cites this instance, apparently taking it with passive sense, 'were stunned', *þei* referring to the cardinals, but this interpretation is awkward, makes inferior sense, and is not faithful to the source.

98/14 *þerfor*: lacking in Martinus.

99/12 Pallas, son of Evander in Roman legend, appears to have been confused with Pallas, a giant in Greek mythology.

99/14 *in Naples*: *in Apulia* in Martinus. Sim. 106/33.

99/21 *held þis heresie*: merely *asserebat* in Martinus.

99/23 *Nicholas, þe pope*: Berengar recanted at Rome in 1059 during the reign of Nicholas II. However, instead of Nicholas the text of Martinus has *Leo* (467/30), i.e. Leo IX (1049–54), who presided over the council in Rome at which Berengar was excommunicated and at the end of whose reign Berengar recanted at Tours. *Nicholaus* is cited as a variant from MS 8.

99/27 *x monthes*: *mensibus 9* in Martinus.

99/31 *Ydanie*: for 'Edith'. *Eden* is a diminutive of *Ede* (OE *Eadu*) which seems to have been associated with *Edith* (OE *Eadgyth*).

100/21 *he was a man of good conuersacion*: lacking in Martinus.

100/22 *fals*: lacking in Martinus.
   Censius is described as *prefecti filius* in Martinus.

100/26 *barefoot*: that the sense is 'with bare feet' is confirmed by Martinus's *veniens nudis pedibus*. Emendation of M *bare* does seem to be necessary. Although *MED, bar* adj. 1(d), cites one instance with the sense 'barefoot', *alle freres, shodde and bare* (*Romaunt of the Rose* 7461 rhyming with *square*), the presence of the antonym *shodde* and the necessity of rhyme almost certainly make this usage exceptional.

100/28 *Beamunde*: *Boamundus* correctly in Martinus.

101/3 *Paschasius*: *Paschalis* correctly in Martinus.

101/5 *xii ȝere old*: *22* in Martinus.
   began þe order of Premonstracense: under St. Norbert. See C's *Norbert*.

101/6–7 These popes, Gelasius II and Callistus II, are dealt with again at 104/16–25.

101/14 The rose was a symbol of perfection. See, for example, P. Dronke, *Medieval Latin and the Rise of the European Love-Lyric* (London, 1969 edn.), pp. 186 ff., and P. M. Kean, *Pearl, An Interpretation* (London, 1967), pp. 169–72.

101/15 *Edward broþir*: see Index, s.n. *Alured*[2].

101/16 *Kyng Edward*: in view of P's *þe kyng* possibly the reading in *A was *þe Kyng Edward*.

102/36 *a book*: Lanfranc's *De Sacramento Corporis et Sanguinis Christi* (*c*.1070).

104/1–2 *Erravimus juvenes, emendemur senes*: Jerome, *Liber tertius aduersus libros Rufini*, PL xxiii. 464.

104/22–3 *on a asse*: *in camelo* in Martinus.

104/24–5 Compostela, properly Santiago [i.e. 'St. James'] de Compostela, is traditionally supposed to be the burial place of St. James the Great.

104/34–5 *his wif*: Sibyl, daughter of the count of Conversana.

105/18 The two words *dronch in* are separated by a line division. Since this is the only example of *dronch* in this text, or apparently anywhere else (see *MED dronchen*), beside *dronchin* four times, there may well be a copying error here, in which case we should read *dronchin in*, as at 59/27, 85/15, 176/11. On pp.'s with and without final *n* see Introd., p. lv, §28.

105/19 *boistous*: in M *boistoys* and P *boystois*, both presumably reflecting a similar reading in *A, the spelling of the first syllable probably influenced that of the second. Elsewhere C spells *boistous*, *boystous*, e.g. *Solace*, p. 77, and *Norbert*, line 380, rhyming with *meruelous* and *corious*. Cf. *boystoyse* with second *y* suprascript in *Ayenbite* 103/24, on which see Wallenberg, *Vocabulary of the 'Ayenbite'*, p. 39.

106/29 *þe son of Petir Leon*: *Petrus Petri Leonis filius* in the account of Pope Innocent II in Martinus 436/8. Only *Petrus Leonis* (without his son) is mentioned in Martinus's account of Emperor Lothair IV. For another account by C of this schism in the Church see his *Norbert*, 3529–88.

106/33 *Naples*: see note to 99/14.

107/1–3 Martinus has merely *Hiis temporibus Hugo de Sancto Victore Parisius claret*.

107/7–8 St. Bernard preached the Second Crusade in 1146.

107/8 *for to go* . . .: merely implicit in Martinus.

107/13 *and wonne many townes*: lacking in Martinus, except by implication.

107/14 *þe cronicle*: Martinus.

108/6 *v monthes*: *mensibus 6* in Martinus.

108/8 *Adrianus II*[us]: *Adrianus IV* correctly in Martinus.

108/23–4 Presumably an allusion to a tradition that Edessa was built on the site where Noah's ark ran aground in the mountainous region of Ararat (Gen. 8: 4).

108/28–32 This expansion of the story of Abgar is not from Martinus. Martinus's source is Eusebius, *Hist. Eccl.* i. 13, but this account too lacks the detail of Abgar asking for Christ's picture (108/31–2).

109/2–10 *but he erred* . . .: lacking in Martinus, and presumably C's addition, some of it no doubt taken from Martinus 438/21–3, where the condemnations of Joachim of Fiore and Amalric (112/18) are dealt with together.

109/14 *þe kyng*: Louis VII of France.

110/24–30 This paragraph seems to be based on Giraldus Cambrensis, *De Principis Instructione* (RS 21/8), distinctio i, pp. 127–8. The inscription (110/28–9) cited by C from Giraldis reads in L: *Hic jacet sepultus inclitus rex Arthurus cum Wenneuereia vxore sua secunda in insula Auallonia.*

110/28–9 *Veneraca*: perhaps for *Gwenhwyvach* (with initial *V* for *W*), the name of Guinevere's sister, used erroneously for *Gwenhwyfar* 'Guinevere'.

111/14–15 The patriarch's message is more clearly spelt out in Giraldus Cambrensis, *De Principis Instructione* (RS 21/8), p. 211: *Putas igitur quod te diligant, qui opes tuas, et non opera, curant? Praedam, non hominem, sequitur ista turba; potestatem utique venerantur, non personam.* 'Do you think that those who care about your wealth and not your works really love you? That lot follow the spoil and not the man; in fact they respect your power and not your person.'

111/25 *þese popes*: Alexander III (1159–81) is omitted, though included by Martinus.

111/26 note This feature is not henceforth recorded in the Textual Notes. Other examples occur in the margins of M beside the entries in the text corresponding to 111/29, 31, 112/1, 8, 10, 118/30, 32, 122/36, 125/1, 134/15, 29, 139/25, 158/22, 163/22, 167/19, 173/29, 177/31, 182/15, 197/26.

111/27 For the text of the *Historia* see PL cxcviii. 1053–1722. See also B. Smalley, *The Study of the Bible in the Middle Ages* (Oxford, 1951 edn.), ch. v.

112/10 *xxiii ȝere*: *annis 18, mensibus 4 et diebus 23* in Martinus.

112/30 *xxiii ȝere*: *33 annis* in Martinus.

113/6 *þe ȝere of oure Lord a m cciii*: Martinus gives the year as 1198.

113/8 *Seynt Mary of Aungeles*: *Sancta Maria de Porciuncula* in Martinus. In medieval times what is now the Cappella della Porziuncola was the church of Santa Maria degli Angeli.

iii ȝere aftir Dominic: i.e. 1206, the date also given by Martinus. Martinus, however, indicates that St. Francis began his Order eight years after St. Dominic began his.

113/9 When applied to the Carmelites the word *heremites* has a rather different sense from when it is used of the Augustinians. The Carmelite order was founded in *c.*1154 by St. Berthold but claimed continuity with hermits settled on Mt. Carmel in earlier times. The Augustinian friars were called Hermits mainly to distinguish them from the Augustinian Canons.

113/17 Richard I was the son, not the brother, of Henry II. The error probably arose from confusion of Richard's elder brother, Henry, with their father, Henry II. This other Henry (1155–83) was in fact styled *rex Anglorum* after 1170, but he failed to live long enough to succeed his father.

115/6 *þe Emperour Frederik*: erron. for Henry VI. Frederick I died in 1190, three years before the capture of Acre.

115/8 *as it is seid*. With *it* included from P the construction is exactly paralleled by that at 137/28.

115/31–2 King John and Isabel of Gloucester were both great-grandchildren of Henry I.

115/35 *þe supprioure*: named Reginald.

116/28 *Anno 6410–6413; 1212–1215*. From now on the material is arranged under the reigns of the kings of England and is set out as explained in the note to 49/25. The AD dates at the head of each page are henceforth calculated in accordance with the number of regnal years attributed to the king concerned. These dates may therefore not synchronize with the true dates of events: for example, Henry III's full coronation (17 May 1220) is attributed to his third regnal year (Oct. 1218 to Oct. 1219), so the date given at the head of the page (117) is one year behindhand (1219).

116/32–3 *þe eleccion was dyuyded*: this situation in fact arose in 1198 after the death of Frederick Barbarossa's successor, Henry VI, in 1197. Two German kings were elected: Philip, duke of Swabia, Henry VI's brother, and Otto, duke of Saxony, later Otto IV.

117/2–3 *whech mad . . .*: these details about Richard of Cornwall are lacking in Martinus. Cf. 121/35–122/1, 125/33–4.

117/9–10 Louis married Blanche of Castile, granddaughter of Henry II by the latter's daughter Eleanor (who married Alphonso VIII of Castile). This Blanche has been confused with her cousin Eleanor, sister of Arthur of Brittany.

117/26 *a trety of pes*: the reference is to the Treaty of Lambeth (1217).

118/9–11 The first house of the Dominicans in Oxford was in Jury Lane, partly in St. Edward's, partly in St. Aldate's parish, in the angle between Blue Boar Lane and St. Aldate's and behind the present town hall. (St. Edward's parish was absorbed into St. Aldate's parish *c.*1450.) The second site (*where they be now*), to which the friars removed in 1245 and where they remained until the Dissolution, was outside the walls of St. Ebbe's parish, in the area south of Littlegate Street, roughly marked out by Albion Place, Cambridge Street, Speedwell Street, and the river

Thames. See Hinnebusch, *Early English Friars Preachers*, pp. 3–15, esp. maps on pp. 5 and 13.

118/17 ff. For comment on such stigmata and comparable material see H. Thurston sj, *The Physical Phenomena of Mysticism* (London, 1952 edn.), p. 37 and n. 2.

119/5–6 *Upon þe XII Prophetys*: this work is unprinted.

119/27 The year 1230 is an error for 1250. The date 1250 is usually assigned by chroniclers to the permission given by Henry III to the Augustinian Hermits in 1249 to settle in England (Roth, i. 18). Pope Alexander IV's action took place in 1255 when he exhorted the Augustinian Hermits to reorganize themselves (Roth, i. 21).

119/28–9 *Surek*: this place has not been identified with certainty. For the suggestion Surrex, Essex, see Roth, i. 342, no. 43 and n. 817.

   Clayanger: the same place as *Clæighangra*, ASC (C) 1016. See Roth, i. 264–5, no. 12 and n. 606.

   Clare: see Roth, i. 259–64, no. 11.

   Sidingborn: see Roth, i. 329–30, no. 37.

119/30 *Wodous*: see Roth, i. 358–60, no. 49, also *Victoria Co. Hist.*, *Shropshire*, ii (1973), 97–8. For a possible explanation of *Bica* as relating to the Picard family see Roth, and L. C. Perfect, 'The Austin Friary of Woodhouse', *Trans. Shropshire Archaeol. Soc.* lvi (1959), 140–4, esp. 140.

119/33 ff. This contest for the see of Canterbury was *new* in relation to the previous one (115/34 ff.). Before the elections of the prior, John of Sittingbourne, and John Blund, Ralph Nevill, bishop of Chichester, was postulated for Canterbury, and the criticism of Blund in 120/2–4 would have been more appropriate if levelled against him.

121/1 *postiled al þe Bible*: the reference is to Hugh of St.-Cher's *Postillae*, exegetical notes according to the literal and spiritual senses.

121/2 *whech is a tabil . . .*: this explanation is lacking in Martinus. The reference is to Hugh of St.-Cher's *Concordantiae Sancti Jacobi*, the first concordance to the Bible (*c*.1230–40).

121/10–11 This St. Peter was of Verona (so Martinus), not Milan. How the error came to be made cannot be determined on the evidence available: in his edition of Martinus Weiland cites no variants for *Veronensem* from the manuscripts he used.

121/20 *þe kyng of Frauns*: Louis IX.

122/7 *þingis*: i.e. subsidies. Since *OED*, *Thing* sb.¹, does not record any sense such as 'levy', there is no external support for taking the instance of the word here as having the sense 'subsidies' though that notion is what is indicated. Possibly, however, C did understand *þing* in the sense 'levy': cf. 211/2, 231/6.

122/31 St. Francis had his headquarters at the church of S. Damiano (just below Assisi) to which the foundation house of the Poor Clares was attached. It was appropriate that St. Francis's name should be linked with that of St. Peter Damian since the latter also advocated strict monastic discipline.

122/32 *Ludlow*: see Roth, i. 296–8, no. 24, also *Victoria Co. Hist., Shopshire*, ii (1973), 95–6.

122/33 *Leycetir*: see Roth, i. 280–3, no. 21.

122/35 *þe couent of Schrouysbury*: see Roth, i. 331–5, no. 39 also *Victoria Co. Hist., Shropshire*, ii (1973), 96–7.

122/36–123/4 For details of this vision see R. Arbesmann OSA and W. Hümpfner OSA, *Jordani de Saxonia Liber Vitasfratrum*, Cassiacum i (New York, 1943), I. xiv. 80 ff., and pp. 450–1, n. 9.

123/4 *a bulle*: *Licet ecclesiae catholicae* of 9 April 1256.

123/20 *teres*: (properly *teris*, pr.t.) to rhyme with *heres*.

123/31 The 'Eternal Evangel' was proclaimed in 1254 by the Spiritual Franciscan, Gerard of Borgo San Donnino, as superseding the Old and New Testaments.

124/12–13 That emendation of *were* to *was* and exclusion of P's *& his felawschip* (no doubt repeated from 124/11) is correct is shown by the reference back to the younger Simon in the words *with him* (124/14).

125/1 Urban IV (1261–4) has been omitted from the series of popes.

125/4 *It is seid . . .*: lacking in Martinus.

125/8 Charles of Anjou was Louis IX's brother. Louis's son was Philip III of France.

125/28–9 *He was with Edward . . .*: lacking in Martinus.

125/33 For *paralisé* preceded by the indefinite article cf. 188/12.

126/1–12 Matthews, 'Martinus . . .' in *Med. Lit.* (1969), p. 282, claims that this passage derives from 'the very last entry in Martinus's chronicle', i.e. 475/2–12, found by Weiland in only two manuscripts. But C's version of the story is much fuller.

126/18 *þe lv ȝere*: *annus . . . quinquagesimus septimus* in Walsingham, *Hist. Ang.*

126/19 *his age was lx and vi*: lacking in Walsingham, *Hist. Ang.*

126/22–3 *Acon, sumtyme cleped Tholomayda*: *Terra Sancta* in Walsingham, *Hist. Ang.*

126/24 *Jon, count of Warenne*: lacking in Walsingham, *Hist. Ang.*, where the only other person mentioned by name, apart from Gilbert, earl of Gloucester, is Robert Kilwardby, archbishop of Canterbury.

126/25 *a new seal . . . and new justises*: lacking in Walsingham, *Hist. Ang.*

126/26–7 *These to ȝere . . .*: lacking in Walsingham, *Hist. Ang.*

126/28–9 *Edward þe First . . . þe ȝere of oure Lord 1273*: lacking in Walsingham, *Hist. Ang.*

126/31 At first sight P's reading *þe Pope Honorius* may appear preferable. But Honorius III died in 1227, as recorded at 118/30 and Honorius IV did not become pope until 1285. The omission of *Honorius* in M may have been a conscious correction of the reading in *A which would have been copied unthinkingly in P.

127/4 *doutir to þe kyng of Spayn*: lacking in Walsingham, *Hist. Ang.*

127/9 *apel* 'accusation', wrongly glossed by *MED*, *ap(p)el* n. 1(b), 'challenge to trial by combat'.

127/17–21 *at London . . . left þe ground pleyn*: merely *in partibus Australibus Angliae, et Occidentalibus* in Walsingham, *Hist. Ang.*

127/34 *x dayes*: *diebus 9* in Martinus.

Octobone: Martinus does not give this name here (cf. 124/33) but it is given by Walsingham, *Hist. Ang.* i. 16/5.

128/1 John XXI is the last pope to be listed in Martinus's *Chronicon* but further popes are listed in the Continuations. The Continuation printed at the end of Martinus's text in MGH, Script. xxii, is referred to as Martinus (Continuation) and the Continuations printed separately in MGH, Script. xxiv, are referred to by the numbers they are given there, e.g. Martinus (Continuation III).

128/2 *Nicholas þe Fourt*: *Nycolaus III* in Martinus (Continuation and Continuation III).

iiii ȝere: *annis 2, mensibus 8, diebus 28* in Martinus (Continuation) but *annis 3, mensibus 9* in Martinus (Continuation III).

128/6 If M's *þan* were accepted it would be the only instance in the text of *þan* used substantively to mean 'that time'.

128/22 *Pounteys*: this spelling should probably be *Pounteyf*, but, since there is no way of showing that C was not himself responsible for the error, emendation cannot be justified; P also has *Pounteys*. The L for *Ponthieu* was *Pontivus pagus* and the spelling *Pountyff* occurs in Walsingham, *Hist. Ang.* i. 306. Cf. note to 165/16.

128/28–30 C appears not to have understood why Merlin's prophecy was invoked as relevant to this new coinage (1279–80). Before the monetary reform the smallest coin was a penny; a halfpenny was half of such a penny when cut in two. Edward I now introduced round halfpennies (and farthings). The Latin text of Merlin's prophecy should read *Dimidium rotundum erit* (so Walsingham, *Hist. Ang.*) 'the half shall be round', i.e. instead of being semicircular the halfpenny was now to be round. C's *half of þe round* would have to refer to the older, now superseded, semicircular halfpenny.

129/16–28 This passage is lacking in Martinus (Continuations I–IV).

129/20 *tunge*: lacking in the text of Martinus (Continuation) but *linguam* is added in MSS 1 and 3.

129/24–5 *whech had þe gouernauns þere vndir . . .*: apparently expanded from a reference in Martinus (Continuation) to an earlier statement about the French king.

130/2 ff. On this dispute between Knapwell and Archbishop Pecham and the support given to Knapwell by his provincial William Hothum see Hinnebusch, *Early English Friars Preachers*, pp. 352–6.

130/14 Pope Honorius IV (1285–7) has been omitted. He is the last pope dealt with in the printed text of Martinus (Continuation).

130/15 *He declared þe Frere Menoures reule*: correctly attributed to Nicholas III in Martinus (Continuation III) 254/22–6.

130/20–7 On this episode see H. Rashdall, *The Universities of Europe in the Middle Ages*, eds. F. M. Powicke and A. B. Emden (London, 1936), iii. 123, n. 3. On Kyngescote (here misnamed *Kyngeston*) see Emden, *BRUO*, s.n.

131/22 *as þe foure*: 'as they four' as is clear from P's *as þei iiii*.

132/4 *infamynde*. M's *infamyde* is the sole instance cited in *MED* under *infamen* v. (1) where it is derived from *enfaminen* (OF *enfaminer*). As is clear from P's *infamynde* a nasal titulus has been omitted in M over the *y*.

132/4–5 *This same Boneface . . . mad þe sexte book of Decretales*: lacking in Walsingham, *Hist. Ang.*, but mentioned in Martinus (Continuation III) 254/39–40.

132/28 *þe erle of Cornwaile*: lacking in Walsingham, *Hist. Ang.*

132/31 ff. *þe to qweenes*: Jeanne of Navarre, queen to Philip IV, and Marie de Brabant, queen dowager of France, widow of Philip III.

132/34 *now weddid to þis Edmund*: prob. a misunderstanding of Walsingham's *praesentibus Edmundo, germano Regis Angliae, et uxore sua Blanka, Regina Navariae, matre Reginae Franciae . . . .* Blanche of Navarre was Jeanne's mother, not to be confused with her mother-in-law, Marie, the queen dowager. Edmund of Almaine was divorced or separated from his wife Margaret (née Clare) in 1293/4 but I have found no confirmation that he married again.

133/3 *Bayon*: *Risuncium* in Walsingham, *Hist. Ang.*

133/3–4 *þe cuntré . . . into Ynglond*: lacking in Walsingham, *Hist. Ang.*

133/14 *obejauns*: otherwise spelt *obe(y)chauns* (2 ×). In this reading *j* must be for *g* and indicate voicing of /tʃ/ to /dӡ/ (Introd., p. liv, §23). Alternatively the word may be read *obeiauns* (so *OED*, *Obeyance*).

134/17–22 This verse about Pope Benedict XI, apparently deriving from Walsingham, *Hist. Ang.*, has become corrupted. For C's *Oro* 'I pray' Walsingham has *A re* 'from the truth', and *rem* of line 2 refers back to *re* of line 1. Also C has the order of *Maledic* and *Malefac* reversed. C's translation of *rem peruerte* is thus remote from its true meaning, and the translation as a whole has suffered from forcing the sense to obtain the rhymes *name/fame* and *good/wood*. *Benedicte* 'Bless you' is a pun on the vocative of the pope's name *Benedictus*; *Maledicte* means 'Curse you'.

134/26 *on London Brigge*: merely *in loco eminenti* in Walsingham, *Hist. Ang.*

134/30–135/2 *Moost besynesse . . . Auinioun*: lacking in Walsingham, *Hist. Ang.*, but cf. Martinus (Continuation IV) 262/26–30.

135/6–7 *with swech men as sche trostid*: lacking in Walsingham, *Hist. Ang.*

135/19 C begins Edward II's reign in 1308, the year of his coronation. Consequently the numbers for the years of his reign (136/10, 24, etc.) are one behind those given by Walsingham in *Hist. Ang.*; but see further note to 138/7.

135/19–20 *Edward þe Secund regned xix 3ere*: lacking in Walsingham, *Hist. Ang.*

135/25–7 *whech was exiled . . . and þis Edward had clepid him hom ageyn*: lacking at this point in Walsingham, *Hist. Ang.*, but see i. 119/32–120/1.

136/3 *gret*: lacking in Walsingham, *Hist. Ang.*

136/7 *þe* 'they': the emendation is supported by Walsingham, *Hist. Ang.*

136/8–9 The wedding referred to here must be that of 1308 between Elizabeth, sister and coheiress of Gilbert Clare, earl of Gloucester (d. 1314) and John de Burgh (d. 1313), son and heir of Richard de Burgh, earl of Ulster (1271–1326). For the form *Wolinster* see Dobson, §431, n. 5.

136/15–16 *whech he loued*: lacking in Walsingham, *Hist. Ang.*

136/16 *at London*: lacking in Walsingham, *Hist. Ang.*

136/17 *whech were*: originally M had just *wher'*, but *whech* was added suprascript. Since *wher'* was probably a conflation of *whech wer'*, the emendation of the remaining *wher'* to C's usual *were* seems justified. The usual form of the p.t. sg. is *was* (2004×), though there is one instance of *whas* (130/4): Introd., p. lxvi.

136/20 *to God*: *Ecclesiae Anglicanae* in Walsingham, *Hist. Ang.*

136/23 *to make her party more strong*: lacking in Walsingham, *Hist. Ang.*

137/27 *on of his breperin*: *unum de filiis suis* in Walsingham, *Hist. Ang.*

137/29 *her godis*. If retained *þoo* would have to be interpreted as the pl. of the definite article, a usage not otherwise recorded in this text, nor by *OED*, *Tho* 4, after 1300; and even when taken as 'the', the sense is not good. Possibly C's draft had *þer* 'their', a form not found in this text, and at the copy stage, i.e. in *A, he 'corrected' it to *þoo* instead of the much more appropriate *her*. Cf. the isolated single instance of *þem* beside *hem* (362×): Introd., p. lx.

137/34 *Crist crucified*: merely *crux* in Walsingham, *Hist. Ang.*

138/1 *Crist is no god*: *crucifixus non est Christus* in Walsingham, *Hist. Ang.*

138/2 *whech deceyued þe world*: lacking in Walsingham, *Hist. Ang.*

138/7 *þe v 3ere*: as no fourth year is specified C is here following the numbering in Walsingham, *Hist, Ang.*; cf. note to 135/19.

138/33–4 *The careyn was buried amongis þe Prechouris of Oxenforth*. Walsingham, *Hist. Ang.*, says the body was brought (*delatum*) and kept (*conservatum*) there for two years then buried at Langley: see *Hist. Ang.* i. 133, n. 1.

139/3 *Philippe, aftir þe kyng of Frauns*: Philip IV (1285–1314). The name 'Philip' is not given in Walsingham, *Hist. Ang.*

139/7–8 *þei seid it was derogacioun . . . þat he schuld rite nowt do withoute councell*: not stated in Walsingham, *Hist. Ang.*

139/14 *to Goddis worchip*: *potius Regis gratiam et amorem promeruisse* in Walsingham, *Hist. Ang.*

139/16–19 The use of direct speech is not taken over from Walsingham, *Hist. Ang.*

139/23 *þat were resonable*: lacking in Walsingham, *Hist. Ang.*

139/24 *Gauerstoun*: corrected in accordance with the only other occurrence of the surname (at 135/25) and with Walsingham's usual form *Gaverstone*; the surname is not given here in *Hist. Ang.* The misplacement of the *r* may be due to association with the word 'grave(stone)' in the phrase *þe deth of Petir Gauerstoun*.

139/26–7 *Johannes XXII*: merely *Johannes* in Walsingham *Hist. Ang.*

139/31 *Munday aftir Palme Sunday*: 1 April 1314.

140/4–5 *Therfor we wil se . . . what relik is here of him*: these words do not occur in direct speech attributed to the king in Walsingham, *Hist. Ang.*

140/20 *a gret ordinauns to chepe vitaile* renders loosely L *ad tractandum de . . . alleviatione pretii rerum venialium* (*Hist. Ang.* i. 144). *Chepe* is taken here as an adj. As such it is the first recorded instance of the word in English. (*OED, Cheap* a., states that it is 'not found before 16th c.', citing the first instance from 1509 Hawes, and *MED* does not cite the adj.) This interpretation seems best. However, *chepe* has previously been taken as a verb: by *OED, Cheap* v. 5, glossed as 'To fix the price of, set a price on, value', with citations also from 1483 *Cath. Angl.* (cited more fully by *MED, chepen* v. 1(a)) and from 1570 Levins, both being English–Latin glossaries. *OED*'s gloss 'set a price on' is justified only in the sense 'assess the value of (for buying and selling)', and 'fix the price of' is not justified at all. The Latin equivalents are (*Cath. Angl.*) *taxare* 'assess value of', (*com*)*mercari* 'trade', *nundinari* 'trade, purchase, sell', *negociari* 'engage in business', and (Levins) *licitari* 'bid (for)', *appreciare* 'assess value of, purchase'. In these instances (*Cath. Angl.* and Levins) *cheap* v. belongs in the other categories listed by *OED*; this view is confirmed by *MED* where the instance from *Cath. Angl.* is cited under the first sense 'engage in bargaining', i.e. 'barter'. In view of these considerations C's *chepe* as a verb with the sense 'fix the price of' would be an isolated instance. Since there is no support for this meaning it is surely more sensible to take *chepe* here as an adj. antedating the previously known first recorded instance by less than fifty years. In fact *OED*'s sense 2 'that is good value for money', first recorded 1611, would be even more appropriate than 'inexpensive' and is quite possible in view of the origin of *cheap* adj. as a shortening of *good cheap* 'a good bargain'. *OED*'s error may have arisen partly from Hingeston's glossary, s.v. CHEPE (p. 388).

140/25 Since *Sell* v. is not recorded by *OED* in the sense 'sell for (a price)' emendation seems to be necessary.

141/6–7 *So mech hungir grew . . . not sufficient to fede a man o day*: lacking in Walsingham, *Hist. Ang.*

141/10–14 *This man . . .*: no source for this passage is known. Pope John XXII is the last pope listed in Martinus (Continuations III and IV).

141/11–14 On this event of 1327 see Roth, i. 41, and ref.

141/16 *Claringdoun, where*: according to Walsingham, *Hist. Ang.*, this event took place at Westminster at Whitsun.

142/5–6 *whech had chose a othir*: lacking in Walsingham, *Hist. Ang.*

142/11 *compellyng him to a grete raunson* 'constraining him to pay a large sum for his release'. The construction, which does not occur before the fifteenth century and even then *MED* quotes only two examples (s.v. *compellen* v. 1(b); see also *OED, Compel* v. 1b), is based on L *compellere ad* (used in *Hist. Ang.*).

142/16–17 *So were þei restored . . . not to all*: not stated in Walsingham, *Hist. Ang.*

142/26–7 The expansion of the contraction at the end of the first element of the name *Poumfrecte* causes difficulty since it is never spelt in full. For M *poũ*- the spelling *Poum*- has been preferred, for M *poũt*- the spelling *Pount*-. The local pronunciation of Pontefract is /pumfrɪt/.

142/28 Unless *of* were supplied, thus giving *letteris . . . of þe grete targe and þe pryuy sel*, *targe* and *sel* would have to be taken as parallel and equivalent in sense to *letteris*. Such a sense is perhaps just possible for *pryuy sel* (*OED, Privy Seal* 2; see also *Seal* sb.[2] 1e) but is not recorded for *targe* (*OED, Targe* sb.[1] 2). Since it is difficult to make sense of the passage without emendation *of* has been added in order to avoid this difficulty; the emended reading is also much more acceptable syntactically.

143/2 *þe Clementins*: *Septimum Librum Decretalium* in Walsingham, *Hist. Ang.*

þe Clement, his predecessour: merely *a praedecessore suo* in Walsingham, *Hist. Ang.*

143/5 *In þis same ȝere*: at this point in Walsingham, *Hist. Ang.*, the account of the following year, the eleventh of the reign, begins.

143/7 Inclusion of the indefinite article from P seems justified in view of the usage at 139/11, 170/26–7, and also 166/15.

143/23–4 *whech was sent . . . þere*: *qui Hiberniam infestaverat* in Walsingham, *Hist. Ang.*, but cf. above, 140/30–2.

143/26 *þe xi ȝere*: *annus . . . duodecimus* in Walsingham, *Hist. Ang.*

144/16 *homward*: on *their* way home. Cf. 132/31.

144/24 *þe xii ȝere*: *annus . . . tertius decimus* in Walsingham, *Hist. Ang.* 157/19–20.

144/27–8 *The meyhir of Oxenforth*: *cives Oxonienses* in Walsingham, *Hist. Ang.*

144/32 *notwithstandyng þe trews þat was take*: lacking in Walsingham, *Hist. Ang.*

145/7 *þe xiii ȝere*: *annus . . . quartus decimus* in Walsingham, *Hist. Ang.*

145/7–8 *fell a grete distauns . . . þe cause*: not stated in Walsingham, *Hist. Ang.*

145/11 *Humfrey*: M *hũfrey* and three times elsewhere. The full spellings *Humfrey* and *Hunfrey* occur once each, and *Humfrey* has been preferred as the more obviously recognizable where expansion of the contraction was required.

145/13 Emendation of MP's *on* to *an* 'and' seems to be necessary. The construction *þe on was vncle on þe oþir* would be possible, if *cosyn* was added as an afterthought, as arguably in M, but P's reading *. . . þe oþer cosyn* is against this suggestion. The emended reading is supported by L *avunculus atque nepos* in Walsingham, *Hist. Ang.*

145/21 *whech was þe first biere*: lacking in Walsingham, *Hist. Ang.*

147/5 *þe xiiii ȝere*: *annus . . . quintus-decimus* in Walsingham, *Hist. Ang.*

147/27 *Edmund, erl of Arundell*: the only Earl Edmund cited in Walsingham, *Hist. Ang.*, was *Comes Cantiae*. Both Edmunds were present at the trial (McKisack, *Fourteenth Century*, p. 67, n. 1).

147/33 *Muylla* corresponds to *Inuylla* in Walsingham, *Hist. Ang.*; cf. *dEyvile* in Trokelowe, *Annales* (RS 28/3), p. 124. For the surname (from Déville, Seine-Inférieure) and the various spellings of it (employed mostly to distinguish it from *devil*) see Reaney, s.n. *Davall*.

148/2 *oþir straunge places*: the emendation of *place* to *places* pl. is supported by L *loca tuta* in Walsingham, *Hist. Ang.*

148/6 *þe xv ȝere*: *annus . . . sextus-decimus* in Walsingham, *Hist. Ang.* 167/19–20.

149/10 *þe xvii ȝere*: this year number agrees with that in Walsingham, *Hist. Ang.* 171/14–15. C has no entry assigned to the sixteenth year.

149/18–19 *leyd to a . . . contribucion*. This phrase is probably based upon OF *mettre à contribution* (cf. *OED*, *Contribution* 1b), but is not included in A. A. Prins's *French Influence in English Phrasing* (Leiden, 1952).

149/29 *with þe crosse of Cauntyrbury*: merely *erectis crucibus* in Walsingham, *Hist. Ang.*

149/31 i.e. had a tribunal set up.

149/33 *and, as sad men supposed, not gilty*: lacking in Walsingham, *Hist. Ang.*

150/3–4 *Edmunde of Wodstok*: not named at this point in Walsingham, *Hist. Ang.*

150/5 *bischop of Dorham*: *Archiepiscopus Dublinensis* (Alexander de Bicknor 1317–49) correctly in Walsingham, *Hist. Ang.*

150/15–16 *met with a boot at his consent*: this is explained more fully in Walsingham, *Hist. Ang.*: *quamdam cymbam reperiens, a quodam coadjutore sibi praeparatam, illam intravit*. Thus the phrase *at his consent* must mean 'by (pre-arranged) agreement (with another)': see Introd., p. lxviii.

151/7 *Normannie*: erron. for Poitou. Walsingham, *Hist. Ang.*, lacks the error.

151/10 The precise sense of *tutour* is unclear: it may mean 'tutor' as well as, or rather than, 'guardian'. Walsingham, *Hist. Ang.* has *tutorem aut curatorem* 'guardian or tutor'.

151/13 *þe xviii ʒere*: in Walsingham, *Hist. Ang.*, this year begins at the position equivalent to 150/19.

151/18 *be þe councell of þese too Spenseres*: lacking in Walsingham, *Hist. Ang.*

151/25 *be procuracion of þe qween*: lacking in Walsingham, *Hist. Ang.*

151/34 *Dorham*: *Dublinensi* in Walsingham, *Hist. Ang.*; see above, note to 150/5.

William: but the archbishop of Canterbury at this time was Walter Reynolds, and the Christian name is given correctly in Walsingham, *Hist. Ang.* Possibly the manuscript copy (of the source) used by C had *W.* or some such abbreviation which C expanded incorrectly.

152/35 *þe xix ʒere*: in Walsingham, *Hist. Ang.*, this year begins at the position equivalent to 151/25.

153/8 *Reson Vphowel*: the first name is lacking in Walsingham, *Hist. Ang.*

153/17–18 *Quid gloriaris in malicia, qui potens es in iniquitate?*: Ps. 52: 1 (Vulgate 51: 3). The second part of this verse (*qui potens . . .*) is lacking in Walsingham, *Hist. Ang.*, where it is stated that most of the psalm, from *Quid gloriaris* to *Ego autem sicut oliva* (v. 8, Vulgate 10), was written on his *cote-armour*.

153/21 In Walsingham, *Hist. Ang.*, the account of Edward II's twenty-first regnal year begins at this point.

154/1–2 *ii bischoppis*: *tres Episcopi* in Walsingham, *Hist. Ang.*

154/8 *Edward þe þirde regned l ʒere*: lacking in Walsingham, *Hist. Ang.*

154/14 *þat men had no mende of swech asignament*: lacking in Walsingham, *Hist. Ang.*, which says merely that the grant was *talis et tanta, quod Regi filio regni pars tertia vix remansit*.

155/17 *Edmund*: the name is lacking in Walsingham, *Hist. Ang.*

155/23–4 *be procuracion of þe qween, Roger Mortimer was mad erl of Kent*: *procurante Regina et Rogero de Mortuo Mari, Comes* (?erron. for *Comite*)

Canciae . . . in Walsingham, *Hist. Ang.* Mortimer was created earl of Kent in 1328.

156/3–13 This circumstantial detail about how Mortimer was discovered is lacking in Walsingham, *Hist. Ang.*

156/20–1 *and þe qwenis liflod*: lacking in Walsingham, *Hist. Ang.*, which on the contrary says that *ipse et Regina abundabant.*

156/24–5 In Walsingham, *Hist. Ang.*, this event occurs before the Nottingham parliament and disgrace of Roger Mortimer.

þe *xvii kalend of June*: for *June* read *Juli.* The error is taken over from Walsingham.

157/5 *Gledesmore*: the name is taken over from Walsingham, *Hist. Ang.*, but the reference is evidently to the battle of Dupplin Moor on 11 Aug. 1332.

157/9 *ech* . . . *oþir*, i.e. they (the Scots) knocked each other over.

157/16–17 *vndir ʒong age*: Edward III was fifteen at the time of the Treaty of Northampton (1328).

157/21–2 *for þese forseyd lordis* . . . *besegid þis Berwik*: lacking in Walsingham, *Hist. Ang.*, except for an earlier mention of Baliol's coronation (372/23–5). In fact the Scots came *to remeue þe sege* (157/20).

157/31 *capteyn of Berwik*: lacking in Walsingham, *Hist. Ang.*

158/25–6 *for þe Chanones clepe here constituciones at þis day Benedictines*: lacking in Walsingham, *Hist. Ang.*

159/4 *whech was take prisoner in Scotlond*: merely implicit in Walsingham, *Hist. Ang.*

159/11–12 *and þe sext is not now in mende*: presumably C's own addition. Walsingham, *Hist. Ang.* ii. 379/1–5, also lacks the sixth new earl. He was in fact William de Bohun, earl of Northampton, listed correctly in *Hist. Ang.* i. 197/36–198/1.

159/13 *Richard Walingforth*: on whom see J. D. North, *Richard of Wallingford* (Oxford, 1976).

159/21–7 No source for this passage is known: see Introd., p. lxxxi.

160/1–2 *and cast him verili to chalenge þe crowne of Frauns*: merely *mare transire disposuit* in Walsingham, *Hist. Ang.*

160/9 *to cardinales*: the number is not specified in Walsingham, *Hist. Ang.*

160/15–32 These details of Edward III's claim to the French crown are lacking in Walsingham, *Hist. Ang.* (cf. ii. 380/27–31), but occur in comparable form in Murimuth.

161/13–14 *eke* . . . *he doth no subjeccion onto no man*: lacking in Walsingham, *Hist. Ang.*

161/23 The Chancellor was Robert Stratford (bishop of Chichester, 1337–62), the Treasurer Roger Northburgh (see Index, s.n. *Couentré*). Both were dismissed 1 Dec. 1340.

161/25 *whech men had not herd of*: lacking in Walsingham, *Hist. Ang.*

162/13–14 *Ser Water Burwage*: Burghersh's Christian name was Henry, as correctly at 164/7. The error is apparently taken over from Walsingham, *Hist. Ang.* Possibly Burghersh was confused with Sir Walter Manny.

163/12 *wheythir*: beside *whethir* (1 ×) and *wheþir* (6 ×). Since þ is always written with a y-form M's spelling could be interpreted as *wheþthir*, showing a compromise between the use of þ and *th*. There is no parallel for such a compromise spelling, whereas the form adopted is supported by the occurrence of *wheithir* in *Augustine* 15/2. Phonologically the spelling is presumably a Northern form showing lengthening in a disyllabic word, or it is simply influenced by (*n*)*eythir*. P has *wheder*.

163/24 *þat were vacaunt*: qualifying *benefices*, as is clear in Walsingham, *Hist. Ang.* The clumsy word-order is not taken over from the L. Perhaps the words were an addition incorporated in the wrong place; P lacks them.

164/18 *In þe xviii ȝer*: in Walsingham, *Hist. Ang.*, this entry belongs to the previous year.

164/21–3 *and because þe pope was a Frenschman þei found but litil coumfort þere*: lacking in Walsingham, *Hist. Ang.*, where the entry on the subject of 164/18–23 ends *etc.*

164/27 *whech was first mad be Arthure*: lacking in Walsingham, *Hist. Ang.*

164/30–2 In Walsingham, *Hist. Ang.*, this entry occurs under the following year.

165/1 *In þe xix ȝere*: in Walsingham, *Hist. Ang.*, this entry occurs under the following year.

165/2–3 *N. Harecort*: Geoffrey of Harcourt's Christian name is not given in Walsingham, *Hist. Ang.*, which has *cujusdam militis de Harecourte*. Presumably C put down *n.*, for *nomen*, L for 'name', in his original draft and mistook it as Harcourt's initial when making his copy; P lacks it.

165/16 *Pountuey*: this spelling has been preferred to *Pountney* because it accords more closely with L *Pontivus* (*pagus*); P has *Pounttyuey*. Cf. note to 128/22.

165/29 *þe xiii day of Octobir*: *in Vigilia Sancti Lucae Evangelistae* in Walsingham, *Hist. Ang.*, so for C's *xiii* read *xvii*.

166/6 *whech pretended to be duke of Bretayn*: lacking in Walsingham, *Hist. Ang.*

166/7 *v hundred armed men*: *mille quingentos armatorum* in Walsingham, *Hist. Ang.*

166/13 *for a ȝere*: lacking in Walsingham, *Hist. Ang.*

166/14–15 *and meruelous wyndes*: lacking in Walsingham, *Hist. Ang.*

166/30 *Than cesed lordes rentis, prestis tithes*: merely *redditus perierunt* in Walsingham, *Hist. Ang.*

167/8–9 *hing þe Januense, and mad a new capteyn*: lacking in Walsingham, *Hist. Ang.*

167/11–12 *þere scaped but fewe*: *omnes . . . perierunt* in Walsingham, *Hist. Ang.*

167/12 *xxx . . . schippis*: *viginti sex naves* in Walsingham, *Hist. Ang.*

167/16 *grotes, and pens of too pens.* As it stands the reading in M and P suggests that the new coinage consisted of three units: groats (4*d.*), half-groats (*pens of too* [*pens*] = 2*d.*), and pennies. But according to Walsingham, *Hist. Ang.*, there were only two units: *grossum et dimidium grossum*; this is historically accurate—see C. Oman, *The Coinage of England* (Oxford, 1931, repr. London, 1967), pp. 175–7—though the penny (as well as the noble) was reduced in weight. Moreover, the expression *pens of too* as it stands in M is unparalleled in *OED, Penny*. With the emendation adopted in the text, the sense is that the new coinage comprised two units; and the idiomatic reading *pens of too pens* is allowed (*OED, Penny* 3). The points before each occurrence of *pens* in M probably support this interpretation. Points are usually closer to the preceding than the following word, unlike here, and the position in the clause of the second point, between *and* and *pens* is unique in M— in this case, therefore, it is probably not a punctuation-marker. These unusual features suggest that the points were intended to indicate that *and* should precede the first, not the second, point, thus coming before the first rather than the second occurrence of *pens*.

167/16–17 *distroying all þe elde sterlyngis*: lacking in Walsingham, *Hist. Ang.*

167/17–18 'heavier, weighing equal amounts (in value) of the old and the new coinage side by side'.

167/19 *in þe fest of Seynt Nicholas*: lacking in Walsingham, *Hist. Ang.*

168/1 *knytes a cl*: *milites . . . centum quadraginta* in Walsingham, *Hist. Ang.*

168/22–3 *Than cam tiding . . . wan it*: lacking in Walsingham, *Hist. Ang.*; cf. 169/13–14 and 169/19–20.

168/31 C puts the death of Philip VI in 1355 but he in fact died in 1350.

169/6 *had letteres into Ynglond*: merely *audivit* in Walsingham, *Hist. Ang.*

169/20 *Baylol*: in all three other occurrences the word is spelt *Baliol*.

169/29 *not passid iiii þousand*: *mille nongentis* in Walsingham, *Hist. Ang.*

169/30 *iiii batayles*: *septem millibus* in Walsingham, *Hist. Ang.*

170/7 *aboute þe feest of Pentecost*: *vicesimo quarto die mensis* [*Maii*] in Walsingham, *Hist. Ang.*, i.e. four days before Whitsun in 1357.

170/10 *on aftir noon*: merely *post meridiem* in Walsingham, *Hist. Ang.*

170/15 *xi ȝere*: *decem annis* in Walsingham, *Hist. Ang.*

170/21-5 *In Oxenforth* . . .: lacking in Walsingham, *Hist. Ang.* See further Introd., p. lxxxi.

170/23-4 On Hardeby see K. Walsh, *The 'De Vita Evangelica' of Geoffrey Hardeby O.E.S.A. (c.1320-c.1385)* (Rome, 1972) [= *Analecta Augustiniana*, xxxiii (1970), 151-261, and xxxiv (1971), 5-83]. The prince whom Hardeby is said to have confessed *aftirward* here was probably Richard II when Prince of Wales (created 20 Nov. 1376) rather than Edward the Black Prince: so R. L. Poole in *DNB*, s.n. *Hardeby, Geoffrey*, endorsed by Walsh, *Vita Evangelica*, p. 20.

170/26 *of þe Dominic ordre*: lacking in Walsingham, *Hist. Ang.*

171/1-2 *þe son of Kyng Edward*: *filius regis Edwardi* in Walsingham *Chron. Ang.*, but lacking in *Hist. Ang.*

171/3 *be whech mariage he was aftir mad duke of Lancastir*: lacking in Walsingham, *Hist. Ang.*

171/11-12 *The iiii day of October*: *quarto die mensis Novembris* in Walsingham, *Hist. Ang.*

171/16 *onto Seynt Gregory day*: *ad quintum diem post festum Sancti Gregorii Papae* in Walsingham, *Hist. Ang.*, but cf. ibid. 288/22-3, where the word *post* has probably been omitted (see *Chron. Ang.* 41/38).

171/24 *whech was aftir bischop of Wynchestir*: lacking in Walsingham, *Hist. Ang.*

171/25-6 *remeued fro þe heyer cuntré of Frauns and cam down to Paris*: merely *se convertit Parisius* in Walsingham, *Hist. Ang.*

172/15 *vii erles*: in Walsingham, *Hist. Ang.*, eight earls are listed, but in *Chron. Ang.* 44/1-2, only seven.

172/17-18 *of whech too schuld weye a nobil*: lacking in Walsingham, *Hist. Ang.*

172/24 *good Herry*: merely *Ducis* in Walsingham, *Hist. Ang.*

172/30-173/7 No source for this passage is known: see Introd., p. lxxxi.

173/9 *fro euensong tyl mydnyte*: lacking in Walsingham, *Hist. Ang.*

173/9-15 *of whech wynd . . . whech blew soo*: lacking in Walsingham, *Hist. Ang.*

173/11 This line does not scan regularly with or without *sex*.

173/23 *his broþir*: lacking in Walsingham, *Hist. Ang.*

173/30-2 *whech mad a constitucion . . . not admitted*: lacking in Walsingham, *Hist. Ang.*

174/15 *and þan þe Frenschmen led him*: lacking in Walsingham, *Hist. Ang.*

174/19-20 *duk of Bretayn . . . þe same*: lacking in Walsingham, *Hist. Ang.*

174/24 *in certeyn marchaundise*: the use of *in* perhaps owes something to the construction in Walsingham, *Hist. Ang.*, *sunt accusati . . . de magna infelicitate in mercimoniis suis facta Regi.* But cf. 199/25 where *in* is used for L *propter.*

174/25 Emendation of M's *content* is suggested by P's *contend* and supported by *finem fecissent* 'had paid a fine' in Walsingham, *Hist. Ang. OED, Content* v., and *MED, contenten* v., record *content* as a pp. but not as p.t.

174/28-9 *be þe grace of God*: lacking in Walsingham, *Hist. Ang.*

175/5 *first-begote*: not stated in Walsingham, *Hist. Ang.*

175/10-11 *This same kyng . . . and mony*: lacking in Walsingham, *Hist. Ang.*

175/21-3 *he proclamed a viage into Frauns . . . as þe answere was dyuulged*: merely *paravit se ad transfretandum* in Walsingham, *Hist. Ang.*

175/25-6 *if þe kyng cam on þe o side, and þe cumpany on þe oþir side*: lacking in Walsingham, *Hist. Ang.*

175/30-1 *and Hew Caluyrlé, þat were lederes of þis cumpany*: lacking in Walsingham, *Hist. Ang.*

176/8-9 *This batail was by þe town and þe watir of Naȝar*: lacking in Walsingham, *Hist. Ang.*

176/19 *a sterre þei clepe comata*: merely *stella comata* in Walsingham, *Hist. Ang.* Cf. 218/22-3 and note.

176/22-3 Actually Clarence married Violante, niece (not daughter) of Bernabo Visconti of Milan. In Walsingham, *Hist. Ang.*, he is described as *dominus Mediolani*.

176/25-7 *His body was byried at Pauy . . . his hert . . . kept in leed*: lacking in Walsingham, *Hist. Ang.* See further Introd., p. lxxxi.

176/33 *notwithstandyng her wryting and her othis*: lacking in Walsingham, *Hist. Ang.*

177/6-7 *wenyng þe kyng of Ynglond had come*: lacking in Walsingham, *Hist. Ang.*

177/8 *Ser Herry Spenser*: merely *Dominus de Spencer* in Walsingham, *Hist. Ang.*, where he is reported as fighting on the side of the Holy See against the Milanese.

177/11 *þe White Felauchip*: perhaps *La Compagnia della Rosa*. On Hawkwood see G. Temple-Leader and G. Marcotti, *Giovanni Acuto* (Florence, 1889).

177/15 *and sent hem into Frauns*: not specifically stated in Walsingham, *Hist. Ang.*

177/17 *with oþir ȝonger lordis*: *plures, tam armigeri quam milites, nobiles et valentes* in Walsingham, *Hist. Ang.* Later they are referred to as *dictos Dominos juvenes.*

177/17 *as a elde werriour*: merely *virum providum* in Walsingham, *Hist. Ang.* Later Knollys is called *Vispilionem Veterem* by Menstreworth but that is taken over as *elde theef* (177/22).

177/28 *he* (2nd), i.e. the king.

178/10-13 Those removed were William Wykeham, bishop of Winchester,

Chancellor, Thomas Brantingham, bishop of Exeter, Treasurer, and Peter Lacy, canon of Lichfield and Dublin, Keeper of the Privy Seal. Those installed were Sir Robert Thorp CJCP, Chancellor, Richard Scrope, lord of Bolton, Treasurer, and Nicholas Carew, Keeper of the Privy Seal.

178/20 *Edmund*: not named in Walsingham, *Hist. Ang.*

178/20–1 *cam oute of Gyan*: merely *in Angliam redierunt* in Walsingham, *Hist. Ang.*

178/28 *þe erl of Penbrok, Ser Jon Hastingis*: merely *Comes de Penbrok* in Walsingham, *Hist. Ang.*

179/2 *Missomyr Euen*: in *Vigilia Nativitatis Sancti Johannis Baptistae* in Walsingham, *Hist. Ang.*; both are 23 June.

179/4 *with strong hand*: see Glossary. The sense is confirmed by Walsingham's *cum ingenti exercitu*. Similarly 213/1 and cf. *withoute strong hand* 221/17. Cf. *OED, Strong hand*.

179/7 *not Maluerne*: lacking in Walsingham, *Hist. Ang.*

179/12 *wrote*: *misit ambassiatores* in Walsingham, *Hist. Ang.*

179/14 *at London*: lacking in Walsingham, *Hist. Ang.*

179/18 *Ser Jon, duk of Lancastir*: merely *Dux Lancastriae* in Walsingham, *Hist. Ang.*

179/21–9 This episode is attributed to the following year (1375) in Walsingham, *Hist. Ang.*

179/21 *at Bruges*: lacking in Walsingham, *Hist. Ang.*

179/21–2 *þe councellis of*: lacking in Walsingham, *Hist. Ang.*

179/23–4 *William Mountagew . . . and many oþir*: lacking in Walsingham, *Hist. Ang.*

180/7–8 *was take . . . be*: not stated in Walsingham, *Hist. Ang.*

180/9–10 *and faut with him, and killid him*: lacking in Walsingham, *Hist. Ang.*

180/11–181/26 An alternative version of Walsingham's St. Albans Chronicle for this passage is printed in *Chron. Ang.*, Appendix, 391–401, to which reference is occasionally made.

180/12 *at London*: *Londiniis* in Walsingham, *Chron. Ang.*, Appendix, 391/4, but *apud Westmonasterium* in *Hist. Ang.*

180/13–14 *þe Petir . . . of þe parlement*: Sir Peter de la Mare is not mentioned at this point in Walsingham, *Hist. Ang.*, or *Chron. Ang.*, Appendix. He is mentioned by Walsingham at the point of the narrative corresponding to 180/27; according to *Chron. Ang.*, Appendix, 392/23–4, *in hoc parliamento* Sir Peter *omnia quae erant demandanda pro parte communium Angliae proponebat*.

181/2 *þe viii day of Juni*: this date is correct. Walsingham, *Chron. Ang.*, Appendix, 393/11, has *sexto idus Junii*, but in *Hist. Ang.* it is *Octavo die Julii*.

181/7–21 This entry occurs under the following year (1377) in Walsingham, *Hist. Ang.*, but not in *Chron. Ang.*, Appendix.

181/23 *at London*: *apud Westmonasterium* in Walsingham, *Hist. Ang.*

181/23–4 *whech ʒere is acountid . . . not to his*: lacking in Walsingham, *Hist. Ang.*

181/24–5 A better reading would be: *gracious and deuoute onto þe Cherch, fortunat in pes and in batayle, neuyr steyned*, . . .

181/26 *langaged*: this form probably shows voicing of /tʃ/ to /dʒ/ such as occurred in words like PresE *knowledge*. It is the only instance of such a form quoted by *MED*, *languishen* v. *OED*, *Languish* v., cites the form *language* from the sixteenth century but does not give a reference for it.

181/29 *Simon Sutbyry*: not named at this point in Walsingham, *Hist. Ang.*

181/30 *þe ʒere of his age, xi*: not stated in Walsingham, *Hist. Ang.*

182/1 *The first þingis he ded*: lacking in Walsingham, *Hist. Ang.*

182/3–4 *þe ʒongest son of King Edward*: *avunculum suum*, i.e. Richard II's uncle, in Walsingham, *Hist. Ang.*

182/7 *þe Ilde of Man*: *insulam . . . de Wyght* in Walsingham, *Hist. Ang.*

182/11 *in Southsex*: not explicitly stated in Walsingham, *Hist. Ang.*

182/16 *Vrbane þe VI*: the name of the new pope is not given in Walsingham, *Hist. Ang.*

182/17 *Jubanense*: *Ambianensis Episcopus* in Walsingham, *Hist. Ang.* In fact Robert of Savoy, the future Pope Clement VII of Avignon, although from Geneva, was bishop of Cambrai before he became a cardinal in 1371.

182/18–19 *notwithstanding . . . before*: lacking in Walsingham, *Hist. Ang.*

182/19–20 *cleped himselue Clement*: lacking in Walsingham, *Hist. Ang.*

182/22 *in Normandie*: lacking in Walsingham, *Hist. Ang.*
for a certeyn pension to be payed euery ʒere: lacking in Walsingham, *Hist. Ang.*

182/22–3 *þat he schuld haue esy londyng into þe ground of Frauns*: merely *ad commodum tam Regis quam regni Angliae* in Walsingham, *Hist. Ang.*

182/26–8 *This was þe cause . . .*: lacking in Walsingham, *Hist. Ang.*; cf. i. 403/17–21.

183/2 *and caused gret plenté of all maner marchaundise in þis lond*: lacking in Walsingham, *Hist. Ang.*

183/5 *because*: lacking in Walsingham, *Hist. Ang.*

183/6 *up peyne of lesing of*: for other instances of this construction see 152/16–18.

183/8–9 *and rich men schuld pay a subsidie to þe kyng*: merely implicit in Walsingham, *Hist. Ang.*

183/18 *horrok*: recorded by *MED, hurrok,* only here and in *Patience* 185 and *Cleanness* 419, where the sense appears to be different—see J. J. Anderson (ed.), *Patience* (Manchester, 1969), note to line 185. *OED, Hurrock,* gives only the MnE sense current in Orkney and Shetland dialect: 'the part of a boat between the sternmost seat and the stern'. But, for this instance, the sense 'hold' is confirmed by Walsingham's *descendensque in sentinam ibidem latuit,* in *Hist. Ang.,* the *sentina* being the part of the ship below deck where the bilge-water collected. For this sense the word *thurrok* (*OED, Thurrock*) would also be appropriate; perhaps the two words became partially identified through the collocation *th'hurrock.* There is no doubt about the form: P also has *hurrok.*

183/18–19 *for to selle þe marchaundise whech þei had take*: lacking in Walsingham, *Hist. Ang.*

183/27–30 *But at þe last . . .*: lacking in Walsingham, *Hist. Ang.*; cf. i. 428/18–430/6.

184/1–3 No source for this passage is known: see Introd., p. lxxxii. The reference is apparently to the submission made by Emperor John V Palaeologus to Urban V in 1369, but the patriarch did not show.

184/4–8 In Walsingham, *Hist. Ang.,* the dispute to which this entry apparently refers is between the bishop of Norwich and the prior of Wymondham, a cell of St. Albans.

184/11–12 *Ser Jon Mountforth*: not named at this point in Walsingham, *Hist. Ang.*

184/16–20 C has got the facts wrong here despite their being accurately reported in Walsingham, *Hist. Ang.* When Charles V died in 1380 he was succeeded by his son Charles VI, a minor. The duke of Burgundy was not the new king but Philip the Bold, Charles V's youngest brother, and he was appointed the young king's guardian. Louis of Anjou objected because he was the eldest of the young king's uncles. Either C misunderstood his source or he was using a textually corrupt version of it.

184/16–17 *beqwath þe crowne to*: this should read 'appointed as guardian to the young king during his minority'.

184/20 *þis ȝonger broþir was crowned*: this should read 'this younger brother was preferred and the king crowned'.

184/27 The 1380 Northampton parliament assembled on 5 Nov., six days before the feast-day of St. Martin of Tours. C's *at* corresponds to Walsingham's *circa* in *Hist. Ang.*

184/32 *for her hed*: 'per head'. *OED, Head* sb. 7b, gives the use of the word for enumeration from 1535, but *OED*'s first citation is antedated, as well as by the present instance, by the use at 183/12; *MED* does not cite the usage. Walsingham, *Hist. Ang.,* has *ex singulis capitibus.*

185/3–4 *Mani foul errouris . . . more þan Berengari*: lacking in Walsingham, *Hist. Ang.*

185/30 *Jak*: since neither *MED*, *jak(ke* n.(1), nor *OED*, *Jack* sb.¹, record a form with *-e-* M's reading can hardly stand. Of the two alternative alterations *Jak* has been preferred to *Jef*, which is historically accurate, because Walsingham gives his first name as *Johannes*.

185/31 *a man of cort þei clepid Edmund Galon*: lacking in Walsingham, *Hist. Ang.*

186/18 *sexte*: *quintus* in Walsingham, *Hist. Ang.* ii. 46/39.

186/26–7 No source for this passage has been found: see Introd., p. lxxxii.

186/28 *In þe seuenet 3ere*: merely implied in Walsingham, *Chron. Ang.* In *Hist. Ang.* ii. 83/34 it is *annus . . . sextus*.

in þe month of March: His diebus Quadragesimalibus in Walsingham, *Chron. Ang.*

187/3 *Neuport*: in Walsingham, *Hist. Ang.*, but lacking in *Chron. Ang.*

187/3–4 *in þe viii kalende of Juli*: *octavo Kalendas Junii* in Walsingham, *Hist. Ang.* ii. 93/32, lacking in *Chron. Ang.*

187/18 *but first he distroyed þe town*: *villam destruit solo tenus* in Walsingham, *Hist. Ang.*, but lacking in *Chron. Ang.*

187/22 *þe vyntage of Ynglond* corresponds to Walsingham's *navigium Anglicanum*. Thus the sense required for *vyntage* is 'fleet', but with this sense the origin of the word is difficult to account for. *OED* cites this example, together with a similar use from *Brut*, as the only two instances of *Vintage* sb. in the sense 'produce of the vine' from the fifteenth century. (If these two instances are disregarded the first citation of the word would be 1523.) The passage from *Brut* (ii. 372/11) reads *þay . . . sette þe cuntre yn pees & rest tylle þe vyntage were redy to sayle*: here too the sense 'fleet' seems best. In an effort to explain the present usage *OED*'s editors were reduced to special pleading: 'Quot. 1460 refers to the capture of large supplies of wine from the French.' It seems doubtful whether these two fifteenth-century instances of *vyntage* belong where *OED* puts them. Possibly the word is based on OF *vint* 'twenty', i.e. 'small fleet', but there is no authority for this in OF. Despite this problem the sense 'fleet' seems clear. Translate: 'At that time the English fleet captured another (French) naval force (*octo naves*, according to Walsingham).'

187/25 *In þe viii 3ere*: *annus . . . septimus* in Walsingham, *Hist. Ang.* ii. 110/6, not stated in *Chron. Ang.*

188/4 *as it had be a beste*: *tanquam de pecude* in Walsingham, *Hist. Ang.*, but lacking in *Chron. Ang.*

188/6 *took þe ax*: lacking in Walsingham.

188/9 *In þe ix 3ere*: *annus . . . octavus* in Walsingham, *Hist. Ang.* ii. 119/24–5, not stated in *Chron. Ang.*

188/12 *paralsie*: M paralsie, so also P. This spelling, unrecorded by *OED*, *Paralysie*, is a blend of ME *paralisie* and the reduced form *palsie*. Emendation to *palsie* is a possibility but seems unnecessary.

188/13 *in Cristmasse*: lacking in Walsingham.

188/15–16 *letting men of þat pilgrimage*: lacking in Walsingham.

188/19 *of þe title of Seint Cecile*: *de Anglia* in Walsingham.

188/22 *[of] good condicion*: *valentes* in Walsingham, *Hist. Ang.*, but lacking in *Chron. Ang.*

189/3 *þere was procured pes betwix hem*: *inter eosdem pacem et concordiam reformasset* in Walsingham, *Hist. Ang.*, merely *discordia est sopita* in *Chron. Ang.*

189/4 The 1384 Westminster parliament assembled on 12 Nov., the feast-day of Pope St. Martin I. But on the two other occasions when a feast of St. Martin is mentioned (184/27 and note, 212/19) the reference is to St. Martin of Tours (feast-day 11 Nov.) and the reference here may well be to him also.

189/11 *In þe ten ʒere*: *annus . . . nonus* in Walsingham, *Hist. Ang.* 142/2, not stated in *Chron. Ang.*

189/13 *for al þe avail turned onto himself*: *quid profecerit ejus adventus, ipse solus sensit* in Walsingham, *Hist. Ang.*, but lacking in *Chron. Ang.*

189/26–7 *Of þis viage we wil sey more aftir*: see 197/28 ff. The statement is lacking in Walsingham, but would be appropriate, if unnecessary, in *Hist. Ang.* In *Chron. Ang.* the narrative of the episode is completed.

189/29 *wrongfully*: lacking in Walsingham.

190/10–19 The ordering of elements in this passage is different from Walsingham's.

190/11 *with xv dukes*: *cum duodecim ducibus* in Walsingham, *Chron. Ang.*, lacking in *Hist. Ang.*

190/11–12 *a c knytes, a c m men*: lacking in Walsingham.

190/12 *schippes a mcc*: *[cum] tribus millibus navium* in Walsingham, *Chron. Ang.*, lacking in *Hist. Ang.*

190/22–3 *he restored him aftir þat to þe same office*: *non multo post rex infirmaret quicquid in parliamento contra ipsum statutum fuit* in Walsingham, *Chron. Ang.*

190/27 *In þe eleuene ʒere*: *annus . . . decimus* in Walsingham, *Hist. Ang.* ii. 153/11–12.

190/28–191/1 *for to seke oute þe þeues*: lacking in Walsingham. The event to which it refers, the theft of arms by some would-be recruits, occurs in *Hist. Ang.* but is lacking in *Chron. Ang.*

191/10 *Robert Ver*: not named at this point in Walsingham.

191/11 *and Richard Sturry*: *cum Ricardo Styry* in Walsingham, *Hist. Ang.*, but lacking in *Chron. Ang.*

191/13 *Maystir*: *Walterus* correctly in Walsingham.

191/13–14 *whech went with þe duke of Lancastir into Spayn*: *cum eo, in Hispaniam tendenti, minime profectus est, sed domi remanserat* in Walsingham, *Hist. Ang.*, not mentioned at all in *Chron. Ang.*

191/17 *with all þe libertés þat long þerto*: lacking in Walsingham.

191/24 The phrase *in presens of* is used only of persons and thus implies the real presence of Christ in the consecrated host.

191/27–9 The *Summe* of *Summe write* in 191/29 presumably refers to Walsingham, who attributes the sacrilegious act to 'Laurencius de Sancto Martino', not Montague. In *Hist. Ang.* the incident is reported under 1381 (i. 450–1).

191/31 *whom þe kyng had mad duke of Erland*: lacking at this point in Walsingham, but see *Chron. Ang.* 372/10–12.

191/32 *ageyn þe lawe of God*: lacking in Walsingham.

192/2 *Kyng Edward dowtir*: Isabella (of Woodstock) who married Enguerrand de Coucy. She is named by Walsingham at this point. Their daughter Philippa, who is not named by Walsingham, is wrongly given her mother's name at 192/6. Cf. note to 193/24.

192/8 *Pase-day*: 7 Apr. 1387.

192/13 *Notyngham*: M's *Bokyngham* must be an error since the earl of Buckingham, Thomas of Woodstock, has already been mentioned in his capacity as duke of Gloucester.

192/21 *In þe xii ȝere*: there is no annual break at this point in Walsingham.

193/14 For *Chestir* read *Chichestir*, and similarly at 195/19; the error is taken over from Walsingham. Cf. note to 212/6.

193/17 *his rite*: i.e. to act in the way that he wished.

193/24 Philippa de Coucy was niece of Thomas of Woodstock, duke of Gloucester, and cousin of Richard II. Cf. note to 192/2.

194/4 *for þi falshed*: lacking in Walsingham.

194/4–5 *booth be þe lordes and be þe parlement*: [*damnatus*] *in retroacto Parliamento* in Walsingham, *Hist. Ang.*, but lacking in *Chron. Ang.*

194/10 *fast by London*: lacking in Walsingham.
  Haryngey: the restoration of the form from P is supported by Walsingham. Harringay is the older form, from which the development of Hornsey is difficult to explain.

194/12 *with his councel*: *convocatis familiaribus suis* in Walsingham, *Hist. Ang.*

194/13 *Lancastirschere and*: lacking in Walsingham.

194/14–15 *with whech puple he myte make resistens ageyn þese lordes*: lacking in Walsingham.

194/16 *to Oxenforth*: lacking in Walsingham.

194/17–18 *and fayre maner . . . cuntré*: lacking in Walsingham, where, on the contrary, the commander of the force is slain.

194/19–20 *and delyueryd . . . broute hem*: lacking in Walsingham.

194/21–2 *and leid hem aboute London lich as þei schuld besege it*: *se in campis . . . distincti pulchre per bellicas acies monstraverunt* in Walsingham, *Chron. Ang.*

194/23–4 *þei of London sent þe keyis . . . seying þat þei were wolkom*: *major Londoniarum . . . hospitia intra civitatem ac omnia necessaria bona . . . promisit* in Walsingham, *Chron. Ang.*

194/25–195/5 C's version differs considerably from Walsingham's in *Hist. Ang.* In particular the speech attributed to the duke of Gloucester is lacking.

195/6–9 No source for this passage is known: see Introd., p. lxxxii.

195/10 *dyuers prisones*: there is no mention of specific prisons, Nottingham, Dover, Bristol, in Walsingham, *Hist. Ang.*, and the list of persons arrested is therefore given as a whole, not divided according to destination.

195/11 *Jon Golofir*: lacking in Walsingham, *Hist. Ang.*

195/12 *of þe kyngis hous*: lacking in Walsingham, *Hist. Ang.*
    Jon Clifforth: *Ricardum Clifford* correctly in Walsingham, *Hist. Ang.*

195/19 *Chestir*: see note to 193/14.

195/20–1 *Louel*: merely *miles* in Walsingham, *Hist. Ang.*
    Beuchamp: *Bemond* correctly in Walsingham, *Hist. Ang.* Lord John Beauchamp has already been mentioned (195/13).
    Camuse: lacking in Walsingham, *Hist. Ang.*
    Clifforth: as *Louel*.

195/22–8 No source for this passage is known: see Introd., p. lxxxii.

195/29–196/2 No source for this passage is known: see Introd., p. lxxxii.

196/3 *Pentecost*: 17 May 1388.

196/3–4 *was mad Amyrel of þe Se*: lacking in Walsingham, *Hist. Ang.*

196/5 *and fewe men . . . in hem*: lacking in Walsingham, *Hist. Ang.*

196/10–11 *þat þei schuld not begge but . . . where þei dwelle*: lacking in Walsingham, *Hist. Ang.*

196/11 *not withouten grete cause*: lacking in Walsingham, *Hist. Ang.*

196/18 *þe xiii ȝere*: *annus . . . duodecimus* in Walsingham, *Hist. Ang.* 179/23–4.

196/19–20 *sum saide xx, sum saide xxii*: *Responsum est, quod jam viginti annos peregisset* in Walsingham, *Hist. Ang.*

197/2 *yȝe*: an isolated spelling, also in *Norbert* 762. My earlier reading of this word as *yze* 'eyes' ('Orthographic Usage', p. 336) is now corrected.

197/14 *at a crosse whech þei clepe West Wade*: merely *apud quandam crucem erectam in via publica* in Walsingham, *Hist. Ang.*

197/17 *fro l ȝere*: lacking in Walsingham, *Hist. Ang.*

197/22 The *north dore* is that of St. Paul's Cathedral, London, as is clear from Walsingham, *Hist. Ang.*

198/21–30 In Walsingham, *Hist. Ang.*, these events are assigned to the thirteenth year of Richard II (1390).

198/21–2 *in þe presens of þe kyng*: lacking in Walsingham, *Hist. Ang.*

198/27–30 *for it was seid of him comounly . . . issew*: lacking in Walsingham, *Hist. Ang.*

199/1–15 In terms of the chronology in Walsingham, *Hist. Ang.*, this section is misplaced and should occur after 201/14. Strictly the passage 201/15–19 should go between 199/9 and 199/10. See Introd., p. lxxxii.

199/7 *Edmund*: *Edwardum* correctly in Walsingham, *Hist. Ang.*

199/16 *munk of Norwich*: lacking in Walsingham, *Hist. Ang.*

199/18 *his successoure*: lacking at this point in Walsingham, *Hist. Ang.*

199/21 *him in*: the Textual Note may be misleading. What is in M is *h* followed by four minims. All that may be omitted is the nasal titulus for the final *m* of *him*.

199/29 *and mad him for to fle*: lacking in Walsingham, *Hist. Ang.*

199/29–30 *Thre of his dukes he took, and foure dukes he killid*: *captis quatuor Ducibus, et tribus peremptis* in Walsingham, *Hist. Ang.*

200/9 *xx libras*: *viginti quatuor marcarum* in Walsingham, *Hist. Ang.*

200/15–16 *whech antipope was gretly supported be þe kyngis of Frauns and of Spayne*: lacking in Walsingham, *Hist. Ang.*

201/15–19 See above, note to 199/1–15.

201/17–19 *And anon as he was absent . . . in þat wilde lond*: merely *sed praevaluit þenes Regem malignorum consilium, quod tamen, proh dolor! commodum impedivit* in Walsingham, *Hist. Ang.*

201/20 *In þe xvi ȝere*: in Trokelowe, but lacking in Walsingham, *Hist. Ang.*

202/8 M's spelling *Cherborgh* is unusual and P's *Cherborow* would be more characteristic of C's general usage.

202/14 *with a gret meny*: closer to Trokelowe's *multo milite* than Walsingham's *cum armata manu* in *Hist. Ang.*

202/19–20 *where-euyr þei dwelt*: lacking in Walsingham and Trokelowe.

202/24 *Mari*: the name is not given in Walsingham, *Hist. Ang.*, nor in Trokelowe.

202/26 *doutir to Kyng Petir of Spayn*: lacking in Walsingham, *Hist. Ang.*, and Trokelowe.

202/27 *moost named in manhood and werre*: presumably adapted from Trokelowe's *famosus . . . post subactas armis et potenti virtute civitates*, etc.

203/3–4 *it was proued be experiens*: merely *dicebatur* in Walsingham.

203/18 *Esterne*: 11 Apr. 1395.

203/18–19 *of þis lond*: *regni Angliae* in Trokelowe, lacking in Walsingham, *Hist. Ang.*

204/19 *cursed*: lacking in Walsingham and Trokelowe.

205/4 *In þe xix ȝere*: in Trokelowe, 187/15, but lacking in Walsingham, *Hist. Ang.*

205/12–14 *Of þis woman . . .*: lacking in Walsingham and Trokelowe.

205/19–20 *þat dwelt . . . capellanis honoris*: merely *qui capellanas obtinuerant* in Walsingham, *Hist. Ang.*, and Trokelowe. *Capellanis honoris* are 'chaplaincies of honour'; *capellanis* was presumably taken over with the ending of the abl. pl. because governed in a L source by the L equivalent of C's *vndir pretens of*.

205/27 *viii dayes aftir*: *septem dies sequentes* in Walsingham, *Hist. Ang.*, and Trokelowe.

205/30 *to Kaleys*: in Trokelowe but lacking in Walsingham, *Hist. Ang.*

206/13 *whech were purposed and wrytin*: Trokelowe has *qui redacti sunt in scripta*, but this clause is lacking in Walsingham, *Hist. Ang.*

206/15 *Helianore*: this erroneous name is not given in Walsingham, *Hist. Ang.*, nor in Trokelowe.

206/24 *in many dischis*: lacking in Walsingham, *Hist. Ang.*, and Trokelowe.

206/30 *In þe xx ȝere*: lacking in Walsingham, *Hist. Ang.*, and Trokelowe.

207/9–10 *no . . . lord, knyte, or marchaunt*: merely *nullus civis notatus locuples* in Walsingham, *Hist. Ang.*, and *nullus civis, nullus omnino notatus dives* in Trokelowe.

207/12 *when men supposed all pes and rest to be had*: *cum . . . regnum . . . summa videtur pace gavisurum* in Walsingham, *Hist. Ang.*, but perhaps closer to Trokelowe's *cum . . . videbatur Anglia in summa pace quiescere*.

207/13–14 *pryuy malice, whech he had longe born*: merely *astutia cuncta* in Walsingham, *Hist. Ang.*, *astutia, levitate, et insolentia* in Trokelowe.

207/14 *ded his officeres arestin*: merely *capit* in Walsingham, *Hist. Ang.*, but justified as a summary of the much longer account in Trokelowe. The use of the construction with causative *ded* may have something to do with the use of the inf. in *-n* (*arestin*). The only other instance of causative *do* in the text occurs in the formulaic phrase *doyng him to wete* 183/4.

207/28 *he dred conspiracion of puple*: merely *sibi metuens* in Walsingham, *Hist. Ang.*

207/29 *barettoures and riseris*: merely *malefactores* in Walsingham, *Hist. Ang.*, and Trokelowe.

207/30 *haue þe kepyng of his body*: perhaps closer to Trokelowe's *ad vallandum latus suum* than Walsingham's *noctium vigilias dierumque servarent, et dividerent, circa illum* in *Hist. Ang.*

208/4 *Thomas Grene*: *Henricus Grene* correctly in Walsingham, *Hist. Ang.*, but Trokelowe has *Thomas Grene* (209/22). So also at 212/8.

208/11 *up peyn of his hed*: lacking in Walsingham, *Hist. Ang.*, and Trokelowe.

208/12 *viii wekis*: *sex hebdomadas* in Walsingham, *Hist. Ang.*, and Trokelowe.

208/14 *he was accused of certeyn crym*: *reprobatus est* in Trokelowe, but lacking in Walsingham, *Hist. Ang.*

208/22 *I forgyue þe my deth*: lacking in Walsingham, *Hist. Ang.*, and Trokelowe.

208/23–5 *and a frere Augustin . . .*: C's version of Arundel's burial is fuller than those in Walsingham, *Hist. Ang.*, and Trokelowe (218/8–10). Walsingham has *cujus corpus, cum capite, inter Augustinenses Londiniis est humatum*. The name *Fekenham* is not given by either Walsingham or Trokelowe. Roth (i. 256, no 643) suggests tentatively that he was John Feckenham, a member of the Ludlow house licensed as a confessor for the diocese of Hereford in 1355 (see also Roth, i. 180, no. 423), adding that 'his membership of OESA is not beyond doubt'. If C's *Fekenham* was not an Augustinian he could have been Thomas Feckenham, OP, who took a D.Th. at Cambridge in 1396 (Emden, *BRUC*, pp. 222 and 675).

208/26–7 *þat he myte not slepe*: *dormire non ausus sine vigilibus* in Trokelowe, but lacking in Walsingham, *Hist. Ang.*

208/32 *and make a frere for to go betwyx þe hed and þe body*: lacking in Walsingham, *Hist. Ang.*, and Trokelowe.

209/1 *þe wax aboute his graue*: lacking in Walsingham, *Hist. Ang.*, and Trokelowe.

   clothis: *panni* in Trokelowe, but lacking in Walsingham, *Hist. Ang.*

209/10 *for fauour of þe puple*: 'because of the support for him amongst the people', tr. L *propter favorem populi*.

209/12 *be þat mannes seruauntis*: not stated explicitly in Walsingham, *Hist. Ang.*, or Trokelowe.

209/25 For *markeis of Northfolk* read *markeis of þe same*. John Beaufort, earl of Somerset, was created marquis of Somerset (not Norfolk) 29 Sept. 1397. Since P agrees with M the error is almost certainly C's own and no doubt arose from a misapprehension of the source; Walsingham, *Hist. Ang.*, has *Comitissam de Norfolke Ducissam Northfolchiae, Comitem de Somersete Marchionem ibidem*. C presumably took *ibidem* to refer back to *Northfolchiae* rather than *Somersete*.

210/14 *Aquitense*: *Aquensis* correctly in Walsingham, *Hist. Ang.*, and Trokelowe (228/8).

210/16–17 *because þe patrones wold not consent þerto*: lacking in Walsingham, *Hist. Ang.*, and in Trokelowe.

210/17–18 *and sent him hom ageyn*: not stated explicitly in Walsingham, *Hist. Ang.*, or Trokelowe.

210/24–5 *a depe watir in Bedforthschire . . . betwix Snelleston and Harleswode*: the location of this river is uncertain. Walsingham puts it *prope Bed(e)fordiam* and for *Harleswode* Trokelowe has *Harleslowe*. One possibility is the R. Granta running between Harston (earlier 'Herleston') and Shelford (Cambs).

210/26 *into opir place*: *ad alia loca* in Trokelowe, but lacking in Walsingham, *Hist. Ang.*

210/28 *men seide*: *ut putatur* in Trokelowe, but lacking in Walsingham *Hist. Ang.*

210/30 *Roger Mortimer*: the surname is not given either in Walsingham, *Hist. Ang.*, or in Trokelowe.

   was deceyued: *subito circumventus* in Trokelowe, but lacking in Walsingham, *Hist. Ang.*

211/22 *Pentcost*: 18 May 1399.

211/26 *whil he was in Yrlond*: *cum Rex ageret in Hibernia* in Trokelowe but not explicitly stated in Walsingham, *Hist. Ang.*

211/30 *þe erl of Herforth*: clearly erroneous since Henry was himself earl of Hereford by his marriage to Mary Bohun. For *Herforth* read *Arundel*, following Walsingham, *Hist. Ang.*, and Trokelowe.

212/6 Chester was not a separate diocese at this time but incorporated within the see of Lichfield and Coventry, though the title 'bishop of Chester' remained in use unofficially. Walsingham, *Hist. Ang.*, and Trokelowe both have *Episcopo Cicestrensi*, but Edmund Stafford was bishop of Exeter (1395–1419), not Chichester (or Coventry).

212/8 *Thomas Grene*: as 208/4.

212/10–11 *what resistens mite be had ageyn Duke Herry*: *quomodo resistere possent . . . Duci* in Trokelowe, but lacking in Walsingham, *Hist. Ang.*

212/13–16 *þei knew nowt . . . heritage*: not stated in these terms in either Walsingham, *Hist. Ang.*, or Trokelowe.

212/18–19 *Rauenesporne, fast be Grymisby*: merely *Raveneshere* (erron.) in Walsingham, *Hist. Ang.*, and Trokelowe.

213/9 *and all þat longe þerto, saue þe carectis of his soule*: lacking in Walsingham, *Hist. Ang.*, and Trokelowe. The phrase *saue þe carectis of his soule* is presumably a reference to the fact that his hereditary right to be king was ineradicable and sacred: see J. Taylor, 'Richard II's Views on Kingship', *Proc. Leeds Philosoph. & Lit. Soc.* (Lit. and Hist. Section), XIV. v (1971), 189–205, esp. pp. 194–5 and notes 17–20 (with refs).

213/18 *withoute mercy*: lacking in Walsingham, *Hist. Ang.*

213/20 ff. A much longer account of Richard II's abdication and Henry IV's accession is given by C in *De ill. Hen.*, pp. 102–8.

213/26 *before þese lordis and opir men present*: not stated explicitly in Walsingham, *Hist. Ang.*; cf. Trokelowe, 254/4–6.

213/31–214/2 Only the initials, not the first names, of all these men from *William Pirnyng* to *Thomas Grey*, except *Jon Burbage*, are given in Walsingham, *Hist. Ang.*, but the first names are all given in Trokelowe.

214/8–9 *in þe fest of Seyn Jerom*: lacking in Walsingham, *Hist. Ang.*, and Trokelowe.

214/18 *arschbischop*: the only time (out of a possible 1374 instances) that MnE *ch* is spelt *sch—archbisc(h)op*(-) itself occurs 49 ×. Possibly this isolated spelling is a mistake arising from confusion between *ch* in *arch-* and *sch* in *-bischop*. See also Introd., p. liii, §20, and p. lvi, §32.

214/23 *Dam Mary*: lacking in Walsingham, *Hist. Ang.* Trokelowe has *Domina* followed by a space in which the name *Maria* is lacking.

214/25–6 *on of hem was weddid into Denemarc*: see 229/20–230/1 and note. C's own observation of the event probably accounts for the addition.

214/29 *and he left it in Frauns*: not stated explicitly in either Walsingham, *Hist. Ang.*, or Trokelowe.

214/29–30 It is difficult to know whether C was right in thinking that the eagle-shaped flask of gold went inside the *crowet of ston*, if indeed this was feasible. Walsingham, *Hist. Ang.*, has *aquila aurea et ampulla lapidea*. But Trokelowe is less clear. Our Lady appeared to Becket *habens in pectore istam aquilam auream, et in manu tenens istam parvam ampullam lapideam*. Having received both the *aquila* and the *ampulla crystallina* he put them *in quodam vase plumbeo*. However, Richard II's searchers found *aquilam, continentem ampullam*; perhaps *aquilam* and *ampullam* became interchanged here? This confusion makes the interpretation of *crowet of ston* difficult: 'small crystal bowl' is perhaps least exceptionable.

214/31 *and brout it hom to Ynglond*: from Walsingham, *Hist. Ang.*, and Trokelowe it is not clear whether Henry of Lancaster or Prince Edward brought the container of oil back to England. Both sources say that Prince Edward *posuit in Turri Londiniarum unguentem*.

215/17–18 *hem þat appeled and accused*: *appellantes* in Walsingham, *Hist. Ang.*, and Trokelowe.

216/26 *and worthi*: lacking in Walsingham, *Hist. Ang.*, and Trokelowe.

217/4–5 *be þe comownes*: not stated explicitly either in Walsingham, *Hist. Ang.*, or Trokelowe.

217/7–9 *Summe othir seide . . . ageyn*: lacking in Walsingham, *Hist. Ang.*, and Trokelowe. Cf. *Brut*, ii. 360, ch. ccxliii.

217/10 *his dyrige and his masse*: merely *exequiae* in Walsingham, *Hist. Ang.*

217/15–17 The fact that this passage is from Walsingham invalidates Fredeman's claim, in her 'Life', p. 199, that it shows C's familiarity with Lynn.

217/17 *and broute hem home to Lenne*: lacking in Walsingham, *Hist. Ang.*, and Trokelowe.

218/2 *a statute ageyn Lolardis*: called *De heretico comburendo*.

218/5–6 *and thei schuld brenne hem and her bokes*: lacking in Walsingham, *Hist. Ang.*, and Trokelowe.

218/6 *a prest*: William Sawtry. Fredeman, 'Life', p. 206, notes that he came from Lynn.

218/22–3 *a sterre, whech þei clepe comata*: merely *cometa* in Walsingham, *Hist. Ang.*, and Trokelowe. Cf. *Brut*, ii. 363/19–22, ch. ccxliii. Cf. also 176/19 and note.

218/25 *at Schrouisbyry*: merely *circa partes Walliae et Northumbriae* in Walsingham, *Hist. Ang.*, and Trokelowe. Cf. *Brut*. ii. 363/19–24, ch. ccxliii.

218/26 *Pentecost*: 14 May 1402.

218/27 *þe puple*: *multos* in Trokelowe, but lacking in Walsingham, *Hist. Ang.*

219/7 *for his labour*: lacking in Walsingham, *Hist. Ang.*, and Trokelowe.

219/18–19 *þe emperour son*: Ludwig, son of Ruprecht, king of the Romans and count palatine of the Rhine.

219/24 *so mech wynd, and so impetous*: *tanti ventorum turbines* in Trokelowe, merely *venti* in Walsingham, *Hist. Ang.*

220/1 *Humeldon Hil*: *Halweden Hil* in Walsingham, *Hist. Ang.*, lacking in Trokelowe.

220/9 *þei*: priests and virgins. The sense is clearer in Walsingham, *Hist. Ang.*: by failing to reproduce children who would become capable of eternal salvation unmarried persons exposed themselves to the possibility of damnation.

220/18–19 *to no oþir entent but*: presumably C's own deduction from the account in Walsingham, *Hist. Ang.* He could hardly have made the deduction with justification if he had seen the longer account in Trokelowe, 349/17–350/8.

220/21–3 This passage has no known source: see Introd., p. lxxxiv.
   as is seid before: see 220/1–3.

220/26–7 *and þere was þe mariage mad þe vii day of Februari*: in Trokelowe, but lacking in Walsingham, *Hist. Ang.* The omission from *Hist. Ang.* was evidently accidental as the reference back *mensis ejusdem* (ii. 412/10–11) shows.

221/1–4 *for þei seide . . . newe*: lacking in Walsingham, *Hist. Ang.*

221/2 *it was no more trost to þe pope writing þan to a dogge tail*: cited by Whiting, D336, but he gives no other examples.

221/18 *to her grete hurt*: lacking in Walsingham, *Hist. Ang.*, and Trokelowe.

221/19 *were spent neythir to worchip of God, ne profite of þe lond*: *convertebantur . . . in usus indebitos, et inutiliter consumebantur* in Walsingham, *Hist. Ang.*, and sim. in Trokelowe (362/3–5).

222/4-5 *seide onto his men . . . quarel*: probably based on Walsingham, *Hist. Ang.* ii. 414/10-12, though the position in the narrative is different.

222/6 *þe pryuy sel*: Thomas Langley, dean of York.

222/7-8 *desiring þat . . . spilt*: . . . *offerrent . . . pacem et perdonationem, si disisteret ab inceptis* in Walsingham, *Hist. Ang.*, and sim. Trokelowe (366/20-4).

222/12-16 This incident, concerning the sword left at Great Berwick (Salop) and its ominous associations, is rightly attributed in Walsingham, *Hist. Ang.*, and Trokelowe to Henry Percy. C was presumably confused by the use on its own of the name *Henricus*, the king's name also, to designate the younger Percy.

222/17 *to grete harm of þis nacion*: lacking in Walsingham, *Hist. Ang.*, and Trokelowe.

222/18 *aftir þe propirté . . . in so fer þat*: lacking in Walsingham, *Hist. Ang.*, and Trokelowe.

223/2 *took*: the subject is Northumberland.

223/4-5 *in whech he hite him he mite and schuld com harmles*: *in quibus sibi repromisit indemnitatem* in Trokelowe, but lacking in Walsingham, *Hist. Ang.*

223/11 *and harneys*: lacking in Walsingham, *Hist. Ang.*, and Trokelowe.

223/12-13 *þe bischop of Cauntirbury*: *Dominus* followed by a space left for the name in Walsingham, *Hist. Ang.*, *Archipraesul* in Trokelowe (373/24).

223/14-16 This speech does not occur as such in Walsingham, *Hist. Ang.*, or Trokelowe.

223/17 *þe Frenschmen, with þe Bretones*: *Britones Armorici, sociatis sibi Gallicis* in Trokelowe, merely *Britones Armorici* in Walsingham, *Hist. Ang.* C is presumably responsible for making the French rather than the Bretons the protagonists.

223/20-1 *met with hem, and*: lacking in Walsingham, *Hist. Ang.*, and Trokelowe.

223/21 *Bewar of þe tayle* 'Be on guard against retaliation in kind', taking *tayle* in the sense 'reckoning' (*OED, Tail* sb.[2] 4b). However, this sense apparently does not accord with the Latin of Walsingham, *Hist. Ang., cavere de cauda* 'to be on guard against the tail', unless *cauda* was (incorrectly?) taken in the sense 'conclusion' (*DML*, s.v., 5). The use of *cauda* here probably relates to the French joke about the English, like scorpions, having tails: e.g. *Anglici, qui a Gallicis caudati dicuntur in improperium* [*DML, caudare*, b, quot. *c*.1370]. See also Whiting, E109. Thus *cavere de cauda* must be taken to mean 'Be on guard against the [sting in the English] tail'. Even so there does not seem to be adequate justification for transferring this sense to C's English; *OED, Tail* sb.[1], does not record any sense to which such a use of *tail* would be similar.

223/23 *a worthi swiere*: *scutifer* in Walsingham, *Hist. Ang.*, but lacking in Trokelowe. C may have added the commendation.

223/26 *The good þei took*: lacking in Walsingham, *Hist. Ang.*, and Trokelowe.

223/29 ff. As is clear in Walsingham, *Hist. Ang.*, this incident took place abroad before the Battle of Shrewsbury, but the pilgrims were not able to verify the foreign hermit's prophecy until they reached home.

223/29 *fro Jerusalem*: merely *in transmarinis partibus* in Walsingham, *Hist. Ang.*

224/15 *iii dayes*: *sex horarum* in Walsingham, *Hist. Ang.*, and sim. ɪɪɪ Trokelowe.

224/24–225/2 This episode, concerning Robert de Vere's mother, is lacking in Trokelowe.

224/26–7 *with myty hand*: lacking in Walsingham, *Hist. Ang.*

225/10 *þat was pryuy with Kyng Richard*: *Regis quondam Ricardi familiarem* in Trokelowe, but lacking in Walsingham, *Hist. Ang.*

225/18 *herd sei*: as at 20/11, 103/13, 107/16, 161/8. M's *herd seid* would be unique.

225/24–226/23 This passage differs from the corresponding passage in Walsingham, *Hist. Ang.* In particular the Speaker has been given a much more prominent role and the disagreement between the lords temporal and spiritual is seen as a personal conflict between the Speaker and the archbishop. See further the following notes and Introd., p. xci.

225/27 ff. *This answere . . . parlement*: Cheyne is not mentioned in *Hist. Ang.* until after the archbishop's first speech. In Trokelowe he is not mentioned at all.

225/29 *And no wondir . . . Cherch*: lacking in Walsingham, *Hist. Ang.*

225/31 *to þe order of wedlak*: lacking in Walsingham, *Hist. Ang.*

226/2–8 *Thou, renegate and apostata . . . vndirfote*: lacking in Walsingham, *Hist. Ang.*

Remembir þe wel . . . treuth: lacking in Walsingham, *Hist. Ang.*

þat despiseth Holy Cherch: *quod vacavit a precibus et devotione* in Walsingham, *Hist. Ang.*

226/28–9 Failure to lower the hood as a sign of respect was regarded as a mark of Lollardy: see 191/23–4.

227/2 *many townys*: *multae mansiones* in Trokelowe, but lacking in Walsingham, *Hist. Ang.*

227/5 *anoþir* [college] *at Oxenforth*: New College, Oxford.

228/2 *þird*: lacking in Walsingham, *Hist. Ang.*, and Trokelowe.

228/14–18 This speech accords more closely with Trokelowe than Walsingham, *Hist. Ang.*

228/17–18 *saue þei þat schul wayte upon ȝou*: lacking in Walsingham, *Hist. Ang.*, and Trokelowe.

228/20 *good prest*: lacking in Walsingham: *Hist. Ang.*, and Trokelowe.

228/21–2 *and þe Erl Marchale*: in Trokelowe, but lacking in Walsingham, *Hist. Ang.*

228/26 'They will negotiate for peace but in reality will set down in writing deceitful terms.' On John see M. Amassian, 'A Verse Life of John of Bridlington', *NM* lxxi (1970), 136–45, and refs.

228/29 *gile . . .* 'under cover of that (negotiating for peace) they will promote deceit'.

229/5 *þe Moneday in Pentecost weke*: 8 June 1405.

229/5–6 Formally only *þe archbischop . . . was . . . long taried* but clearly the king was too. Some such consideration may account for P's *in her talkyng* but to give the required sense unequivocally it would be preferable to read *þei were long taried in talkyng*.

229/7–8 *William Gascoyne*: a space is left for his name in Walsingham, *Hist. Ang.*, and it is not given in Trokelowe.

229/8–9 *þe bischop*: of York.
  þe erl: Earl Marshal.

229/13–16 No source for this passage is known: see Introd., p. lxxxv.

229/28–9 *for þe lond was so pilled þat euery man was wery*: lacking in Walsingham, *Hist. Ang.*, and Trokelowe.

230/1 *The kyng broute hir to Lenne, for to take schip þere*: in Trokelowe, but lacking in Walsingham, *Hist. Ang.* C saw this event with his own eyes (*De ill. Hen.*, p. 109). See also 214/25–6 and note.

230/1–4 *and in þat town . . .*: lacking in Walsingham, *Hist. Ang.*, and Trokelowe.

230/11 *vii capteynes*: *septem capitanei* in Trokelowe, but *octo* in Walsingham, *Hist. Ang.*

230/29 *In þe vii ȝere*: in Trokelowe 417/21, but lacking in Walsingham, *Hist. Ang.*

230/31 *lyuyng Thomas Arundel*: the syntax reflects L *vivente Domino Thoma de Arundelia*.

231/21 *Alisaundre Totyngton*: Walsingham, *Hist. Ang.*, gives only the first name, but the name is not given at all in *Chronicle*.

231/24 *þe cité þere þe vnité schuld be had*: Savona.

231/28–232/1 *Than was þere . . . þe cité*: in Walsingham, *Chronicle*, but lacking in *Hist. Ang.*

232/3 *a vii þousand*: the use of the indefinite article may have been suggested by the L construction with the genitive, *septem milia*. For other similar instances see 243/28, 246/4. Cf. 175/32.

232/6 *whech man was ful victorious*: *miles invictissimus* in Walsingham, *Chronicle*, but lacking in *Hist. Ang.*

232/7–8 *and many oþir cuntrées*: lacking in Walsingham.

232/10 *where he is biried*: lacking in Walsingham.

232/12–16 This incident is all too briefly and incorrectly (saying the Prince of Wales *cepit* Aberystwyth) dealt with in Walsingham, *Hist. Ang.*, while the account of it in *Chronicle* is out of all proportion to that here.

232/21 *oute of Scotlond*: not stated explicitly in Walsingham.

232/23 L *Euerwika* was an alternative for *Eboracum*.

232/23–4 *Ser Thomas Rokby . . . Robert Helys*: these names are given in Walsingham, *Chronicle*, but not in *Hist. Ang.*

232/25–6 *and þe erles side . . . hurt*: in Walsingham, *Chronicle*, but lacking in *Hist. Ang.*

233/2 *all prelates, exempt and not exempt*: in Walsingham, *Chronicle*, but not in *Hist. Ang.*

233/8–11 *writyng to princes . . . spilt*: in Walsingham, *Chronicle*, but lacking in *Hist. Ang.*

233/14–15 *Sextene . . .*: in Walsingham, *Chronicle*, but lacking in *Hist. Ang.*

233/16 The meeting to select representatives for the Council of Pisa was held in January of the tenth year of Henry IV's reign (see Walsingham, *Chronicle*, p. 44), but C moves on directly from the ninth year to the eleventh.

233/16–17 *at Paules*: in Walsingham, *Chronicle*, but lacking in *Hist. Ang.*

233/20 *In þe xi ȝere*: in Walsingham, *Chronicle*, but lacking in *Hist. Ang.*

234/3 *In þis ȝere*: *Hoc anno* in Walsingham, *Chronicle*, but lacking in *Hist. Ang.*

234/8 *and to be brent*: *incendio* in Walsingham, *Chronicle*, but lacking in *Hist. Ang.*

234/27 *In þe xii ȝere*: in Walsingham, *Chronicle*, but lacking in *Hist. Ang.*

235/2–4 *Behold . . . distroye it*: lacking in Walsingham. See Introd., p. lxxxviii.

235/8 *In þis tyme*: *Hoc tempore* in Walsingham, *Chronicle*, but lacking in *Hist. Ang.*

235/10 *him*: John Prendergast.

235/13 *þe chaunceler*: *ammirallius, qui pro tunc fuit regni cancellarius* in Walsingham, *Chronicle*, but merely *Admiralius* in *Hist. Ang.* Sir Thomas Beaufort (see Index, s.n. *Beuforth*) was both Admiral of the Fleet and Chancellor at this time.

235/18 *In þis ȝere*: *Eo tempore* in Walsingham, *Chronicle*, but lacking in *Hist. Ang.*

235/20–1 *was þe kyng of Nauerne and Aragone*: properly this should read *were þe kyngis of Nauerne and Aragone*.

236/8 *And sone aftir*: *Non multo post* in Walsingham, *Chronicle*, but lacking in *Hist. Ang.*

236/24 *In þe xiii ȝere of þis kyng*: in Walsingham, *Chronicle*, 61/24–5, but lacking in *Hist. Ang.*

237/1 The words *and Armenak* are included by mistake. See Walsingham, *Chronicle*, p. 62, n. 2.

237/8 Perhaps influenced by the notion that a person rather than a thing was more likely to have *come to þe kyng*, *OED*, *Procuracy*, cites *procuracie* as the only example of the 'rare' sense 'deputy, proxy, legate' (1b), i.e. makes a special category for the use of the word here, but the sense 'document delegating authority to negotiate' (2), recorded from 1425, is perfectly acceptable. Walsingham has: *Postquam legati suum Procuratorium exhibuissent* . . . 'When the delegates had made known their authority to negotiate . . .'.

237/9 *and her goodes*: lacking in Walsingham.

237/16–17 *These be þe articules* . . .: lacking in Walsingham.

237/18–24 In Walsingham, *Chronicle*, the French lords make five demands of the king of England, in *Hist. Ang.* four, as here. C's second demand, however, *þat þei . . . recure all . . . harmes*, is also the second in *Chronicle* but is lacking in *Hist. Ang.*, which has in its place the third demand in *Chronicle*, not included by C.

238/6–16 No source for this passage is known: see Introd., p. lxxxv.

238/7 According to D. Knowles, *The Religious Orders in England*, ii. 145, Henry IV's confessor during his later years was Stephen Patrington, O.Carm.

238/17 For this last part of the work C has abandoned his practice in M of writing the years of a king's reign consecutively down the left-hand side of the column where the account of the reign begins. Instead, the year is numbered (AM and AD) in the margin beside the beginning of the account of it in the text. In this edition these year numbers are incorporated in the text.

238/18 *at Westminster*: *apud Westmonasterium* in Walsingham, *Chronicle*, but lacking in *Hist. Ang.*

  Passion Sunday: Palm Sunday was on 9 Apr. in 1413.

238/22–4 On the contrary the new king *subsidium petiit et accepit*. Presumably C's manuscript of the St. Albans Chronicle contained some such erroneous reading as *subsidium non petiit* and C added the enthusiastic comment.

238/25–6 In Walsingham this whole incident concerning the fire at Norwich occurs after the return of the duke of Clarence. The fact that the passage is from Walsingham invalidates Fredeman's claim, in her

'Life', p. 209, that it reflects C's presence in Norwich at the time; cf. Introd., p. xxiv. Sim. 239/1-3.

239/9 *of a certeyn knyte*: *cuiusdam militis* in Walsingham, *Chronicle*, but merely *cujusdam* in *Hist. Ang.*

239/12 *For his cause*: the Latinate construction presumably results from slavish adaptation of L *causa praedicti Johannis* (Walsingham, *Hist. Ang.*).

239/27 *set*: the emendation, primarily on grounds of sense, is supported by Walsingham's *per edictum . . . affigendum*.

240/1 *but iii mile fro him*: *sibi vicine distantis a dicto castro sui nisi per tria miliaria anglicana* in Walsingham, *Chronicle*, but merely *sibi vicinae* in *Hist. Ang.*

240/2-3 *and grete fautour of heretikes*: lacking in Walsingham.

240/11 *wold not aske it*: tr. *absolucionem . . . petere noluit* in Walsingham.

241/4 *schuld*: the earliest reference given by *OED*, *Shall* B.22b, for this use—in a noun clause containing a statement relating to the necessity, justice, propriety, etc., of something contemplated as future—is 1527. Cf. 103/16, 150/27 (1st), 200/7, 209/10.

241/9 C makes Oldcastle's answer more incisively disrespectful than in Walsingham, who has *respondit, verbis expressis, quod illum honorem solum faceret sibi quod bene mundaret eam et poneret in bona custodia*.

241/18 *about Myhilmesse*: lacking in Walsingham.

241/18-19 *he mad him strong*: see Glossary and cf. *OED*, *Strong* a. 6d.

242/7 The first of these foundations was 'the House of Jesus of Bethlehem of Sheen'.

242/9-12 Syon House, Middlesex. From the form *Bride* it would appear that C has confused St. Bridget of Sweden, foundress of the Brigittine Order, with St. Bride or Brigid of Ireland. The L name of the Brigittines was *Ordo Sanctissimi Salvatoris*—hence the name of their rule.

242/13 *prestis xiii*: since both M and P have *xiiii* it was probably the reading in *A. That it is erroneous is shown by *þe xiii prestis* of 242/20 and confirmed by the arithmetic of 242/13-15. Walsingham has *sacerdotes tresdecim*.

242/20 *schal*: the latest reference given by *OED*, *Shall* B.3a, for this use—'have to', 'must needs'—is 1440.

243/1 *a cité of his*: (?) Fribourg.

243/4 *þe emperour*: see Index, s.n. *Sigemund*.

243/22-3 *Wenyng verily þat eithir þe kyng was ded or sailed ouyr þe se*: merely *regem . . . post iter arreptum transmarinum* in Walsingham, *Chronicle*, and lacking entirely, apart from *regem*, in *Hist. Ang.*

243/26 *ros fro his den*: lacking in Walsingham.

243/28 *sex þousand*: *quinque milium* in Walsingham.

243/29 *fled—no man coude cacch him*: *latebras requisivit* in Walsingham the sense of which seems to be required by 243/31–2.

244/2 *Crist*: *crux Christi* in Walsingham.

244/15 *þe Lord Boteuyle*: in Walsingham, *Chronicle*, but lacking in *Hist. Ang.* *Boteuyle* is probably identical with *Stuteuyle*: see Walsingham, *Chronicle*, p. 90, n. 4.

245/5 *his vncle*: *avunculum suum* in Walsingham, *Chronicle*, but lacking in *Hist. Ang.*

245/8–9 *Jon Wakeryng*: *Dominus   Wakeringge* (with a space left for the Christian name) in Walsingham, *Hist. Ang.*, lacking in *Chronicle*.

245/12–13 *to go . . . with footmen for þe most part*: *pedestrem viam arripere* in Walsingham, *Chronicle*, but *pedestrem* lacking in *Hist. Ang.*

246/3 *marchale of Frauns*: *qui eciam fuit maresallus dicti regni* in Walsingham, *Chronicle*, but lacking in *Hist. Ang.*

246/4 *of cote-armour*: lacking in Walsingham.

246/21–2 *Than . . . Armenak*: the word order is contorted. Only the position of *sent* seems to be attributable to the L word-order in Walsingham.

247/4 *for iii of hem were ful scarsly worth a peny*: *quia . . . tres eorum non equaverunt pondus unius denarij* in Walsingham, *Chronicle*, but lacking in *Hist. Ang.*

247/5 *Sigemund*: the name is lacking here in Walsingham.

247/7–8 *The emperour offered . . . gold*: in Walsingham, *Chronicle*, but lacking in *Hist. Ang.*

247/13 *of schippis and vitaile*: *navium nec non et victualium* in Walsingham, *Chronicle*, but lacking in *Hist. Ang.*

247/14–15 *His doutir . . .*: in Walsingham, *Chronicle*, but lacking in *Hist. Ang.*

247/16 *In þe xviii kalend of Julii*: 14 June. This date is correct. Walsingham, *Chronicle*, has *octavo kalendas Julij in festo sancte Trinitatis*: *octavo* should be emended to *xviii*, as suggested by Galbraith. Walsingham, *Hist. Ang.*, has merely *In festo Trinitatis*.

247/19–20 *þe Frensch kyng and his councell was euyr founde dobil*: merely *tergiversantibus Gallis* in Walsingham.

247/22 *for to take Harflew*: *que villam de Harefleu quoquomodo . . . infestaret* in Walsingham, *Chronicle*, but lacking in *Hist. Ang.*

247/23–4 *of Ser Herry Percy . . . Scotlond*: in Walsingham, *Chronicle*, but lacking in *Hist. Ang.*

247/27–248/8 In Walsingham, *Chronicle*, but lacking in *Hist. Ang.*

248/1 *he mad his seruauntis for to prowe billis be þe wey*: merely *sparsis cartulis* in Walsingham, *Chronicle*.

248/3–8 These verses are adapted from L prose.

248/10 *al her succession dyuyded in xii articles*: lacking in Walsingham, *Chronicle*, but see p. 101, note *a*. See also Introd., p. lxxxvi.

248/10–12 *whech were ageyn . . . þan a book*: merely *prout habetur in alia cronica* in Walsingham, *Chronicle*.

248/12 *Abbreuiacion*: first recorded with the sense 'abridgement' here by *OED*, *Abbreviation*, and *MED*, *ab(b)reviacioun*. *Abbreviatio* was not widely used in ME literature, except by the chronicler as opposed to the historian. 'Conciseness' became increasingly acceptable during the fifteenth century—see A. C. Spearing, *Criticism and Medieval Poetry* (London, 1964), pp. 50 and 123–31 and refs. For an earlier example of an abridged chronicle cf. the *Historia Aurea abbreviata* of John of Tynemouth, on which see V. H. Galbraith, 'The *Historia Aurea* of John, Vicar of Tynemouth, and the Sources of the St. Albans Chronicle (1327–77)', in *Essays in History presented to R. L. Poole*, ed. H. W. C. Davis (Oxford, 1927), pp. 379–98, esp. pp. 387–9.

248/18–23 *The cause . . . forthwith*: in Walsingham, *Chronicle*, except as indicated in the next note, but lacking in *Hist. Ang.*

248/19 *long before þe same tyme*: lacking in Walsingham.
   his fadir Philip lyuand: the syntax reflects L *vivente patre suo Philippo* (Walsingham, *Chronicle*).

248/27–8 *a gret Lollard*: *lollardus* in Walsingham, *Chronicle*, but lacking in *Hist. Ang.*

249/3–11 This paragraph is lacking in Walsingham, *Hist. Ang.*

249/3 *whech was a gret letter*: *cuius mors . . . impedivit* in Walsingham, *Chronicle*.

249/12–19 This paragraph is lacking in Walsingham, *Hist. Ang.*, though present in *Chronicle*. As noted in my 'Orthographic Usage' (1973), p. 324, n. 7, the fact that the passage is from Walsingham invalidates the claim that it shows C's familiarity with Lynn; nevertheless the claim is repeated by Fredeman, 'Life' (1979), p. 199.

249/13–15 *þei cut of his handis . . . good*: lacking in Walsingham, *Chronicle*.

249/18 *The childirn told all þe processe*: [the beggars] *confessi facinus* in Walsingham, *Chronicle*.

249/19 *ful wel worthy*: lacking in Walsingham.

249/20 This last column of text in M is not rubricated. Hence the absence of an AD date.

249/24 *ageyn God and þe kyng*: *contra status ecclesie* in Walsingham. C has apparently changed the wording in order to forge a (spurious) link between the conspiracy against the king and the distribution of Lollard tracts.

249/25 *Basili*: erron. for Constance. The error does not occur in Walsingham, *Hist. Ang.*, or *Chronicle*.

SELECT GLOSSARY

Scope. For this glossary the words have been selected from a complete *index verborum* of the text made with the aid of a computer. The primary aim is to explain words, senses, and (to some extent) spellings no longer familiar. Thus senses current today are not usually recorded, unless as comparative material beside unfamiliar uses. Spellings (even of commonplace words) which might check a modern reader are included, as also are instances of set phrases in which some common words occur, but words are not usually glossed when they lack complete familiarity only because of either habitual or small differences between Capgrave's spelling practice and that of today: for example, *sch* regularly stands for modern *sh*, *e* as a root vowel often for modern *ea*, *ee*. Plural forms of nouns which are identical with the singular headword except for the addition of *-es*/*-is*/*-ys*/*-s* are not entered, nor are references given to them, unless the sense in the plural is different. Forms of possible morphological interest are sometimes given.

References. These are selective: the numbers refer to page and line. Since the text is rather long it is desirable to try to illustrate the distribution of words and senses within it. To this end one reference is sometimes supplied (where possible) from the Dedication, from Parts I–II, and from Part III (Introd., p. lxxi). (Exceptionally, and rarely, more citations are given: see, for example, *soudan*.) Generally reference is to the first occurrence but occasionally a later instance has been preferred as better illustrating the sense or use of a word. Where round brackets enclose letters which indicate small variations in spelling or inflexional form reference is usually made to whichever of the variants occurs first. References to a form emended from that in M are printed in italics. When a reference is followed by 'n.', the relevant note in the Commentary should also be consulted.

Order. In the alphabetical arrangement ʒ follows *g*, but þ is treated as *th*; *y* (representing a vowel) is treated as *i*; *u* and *v*, when representing a vowel, come in the position of modern *u*, when a consonant in that of *v*; *k* as an occasional variant of more frequent *c* comes in the position of *c*— otherwise *k* comes in its usual alphabetical position. Words which appear in variant spellings or inflexional forms are usually given under the variant most commonly used in this text, though this general practice may be overridden by the rule that words subject to inflexion (or similar paradigmatic alteration) are set out according to the usual fixed order: e.g. for verbs (which are affected most), inf., pr.t., sg. (1, 2, 3 pers.), and pl., etc. As far as possible phrases are given under the word which is considered most likely to check the reader. The sign ∼ represents the headword in any of its forms.

Abbreviations. Those employed are in common use.

a (= *haue*) see **ha.**

abbey *n.* monastery 90/18, 117/3.

ABC *n.* poem of which successive verses begin with letters of (Hebrew) alphabet in order 38/29 n.

abedyn see **abyde.**

abhominable *adj.* loathsome 17/23, 204/2.

abyde *v.* wait 12/32; wait for 109/27. *pr.p.* **abyding, -yng** remaining in residence 192/21; waiting for 177/3. *p.t. sg.* **abo(o)d** marked time 158/17; stayed behind 58/11, 119/16; stayed 169/5. *p.t. pl.* **abydyn, abode, abiden** waited 162/12; waited expectantly 237/32; stayed behind 130/26; stayed 170/13. *pp.* **abedyn** stayed 144/9.

abjure *v.* renounce on oath 181/17.

aboute *adv.* nearby 73/28, 221/14; in every direction 223/28; to all 224/28; *rownd* ~ all the way round 35/22.

abreggid *pp.* abridged 111/28.

abreuiacioun *n.* summary 18/26. Cf. *Index*, s.n. **Abbreuiacion.**

abrogat *pp.* annulled 140/27.

achetid *pp.* made to revert to the crown 150/1.

acomered *pp.* harassed (w. *with* 'by') 96/19.

acord *n.* treaty 168/11.

acorde *v.* agree 131/20; come to an agreement 237/3. *pr.p.* **acordyng** harmonizing (with each other) 13/15. *p.t.* **acorded, -id** came to an agreement 187/17; agreed 96/20. *pp.* **acorded** brought to an agreement 108/2, 150/31; reconciled (w. *to* 'with') 49/28, 124/28; agreed on terms 117/31; agreed 98/2, 206/9.

acoundith *pr. 3 sg.* considers 16/11. *pp.* **acoundid** reckoned by counting 245/13; **acountid** included 91/18; credited 181/23.

act *n.* decree 249/26.

addicion *n.* additional provision 215/15.

additamentis *n. pl.* additions 242/11.

admitte *v.* consent to 210/10. *pp.* **admitted** accepted 239/14; approved 173/32.

aduocat *n.* royal law-officer 125/2.

aferd *pp.* frightened 121/30.

affectuous *adj.* well disposed 119/20.

affray *n.* attack 142/12.

aftir *prep.* in obedience to 170/19; in compliance with 14/26, 136/12; in harmony with 13/22; according to 12/26, 150/10; in conformity with 116/30; as appropriate to 197/17; in a manner proportionate to 7/6; in a manner befitting 53/24; *sent* ~ sent for 79/2, 129/31; *loked* ~ sought for 240/24.

age *n.* lifetime 23/22; age at death 197/17; *had in* ~ was aged 24/7.

ageyn *adv.* back 9/1, 35/12, 131/19, **agayn** 184/14; in reply 132/21.

ageyn *prep.* against 16/10, 120/3; contrary to 24/1, 142/5.

ageyns *prep.* against 227/25.

agw *n.* fever 125/32.

ayle *n.* grandfather 77/11.

aknowe *pp.* in *was* ~ confessed 121/32.

al *adv.* completely, entirely 31/16, 126/6.

alayed *pp.* coated 126/7.

alegging *pr.p.* claiming 130/7. *pp.* **aleggid** brought as charges 132/21.

Alemane *n.* German 90/21. See also *Index*, s.n. **Almayn.**

alye *n.* kindred 225/4.

alienes *adj. pl.* foreign 136/4.

all *adj.* every 55/10, 124/29.

alowed *p.t.* sanctioned 150/13. *pp.* ~ praised 141/24; approved of 145/19.

also *adv.* in this way 202/15.

amende *v.* rectify, correct 104/1, 227/18. *p.t.* **amendid** made amends for 37/20. *pp.* **amendid** rectified 139/18; made richer 226/18.

amend(e)ment *n.* moral improvement 239/19; atonement 241/3; reparation 236/3.

amyrel *n.* fleet commander 217/16; (phr.) ~ *of þe Se* naval commander-in-chief 196/4.

amys *adv.* in *ded* ~ acted wrongly 16/18.

among *prep.* in the course of 69/24.

amongis *prep.* among 8/15, 12/5, 129/8.

an *conj.* and 22/3 (adversative), 69/2, 126/31.

and *conj.* if 144/9.

ankir *n.* recluse 131/17.

annexed *pp.* in duty bound 133/7.

annotacio(u)n *n.* chronological reckoning 30/18; chronological notation 116/30; ~ *of Crist* notation of AD dates in sequence 7/34. *pl.* **annotaciones** historical records 203/13.

annual *adj.* in ~ *prestis* priests appointed to perform anniversary memorial services 178/8.

annueleris *adj. pl.* in *prestis* ~ priests who celebrate anniversary memorial masses for the dead 231/6.

annuellis *n. pl.* endowed incomes for celebration of anniversary memorial masses for the dead 231/7.

anoynted *p.t.* sanctified 68/34. *pp.* ~, **-id** embalmed 26/8; given extreme unction 67/7.

anon *adv.* immediately 35/25, 123/4. ~ *as* (conj. phr.) as soon as 83/25, 126/29.

anoumbir *v.* include 41/6. *pp.* **anoumb(e)red** counted 12/15; included 90/22.

answere, -swore *n.* decision 235/27; right to defence 146/12.

answere *v.* defend oneself (w. *to* 'against') 62/34, 130/5; be answerable legally 149/21; ~ *to* justify 130/4. *p.t.* in *answered ageyn* replied 139/13.

antipope, ante- *n.* pope chosen in opposition to the one canonically elected 102/29, 200/15.

anullen *v.* revoke 221/3. *p.t.* **anulled** set aside 115/37.

apeched *p.t.* charged (w. *of* 'with') 180/9. *pp.* **appechid** (w. *for* 'with') 234/4.

ape(e)l *n.* accusation 127/9 n.; *mad* ~ lodged an appeal 204/29.

apeired *pp.* damaged 14/18.

apostata *n.* one who leaves a religious order without dispensation 226/3.

apparament *n.* military equipment 234/16.

appechid see **apeched.**

appeled *p.t.* accused 215/18.

appetite *n.* desire 62/29, 164/4.

apposed *p.t.* asked 241/31.

appreued *pp.* sanctioned 220/6; commended 145/19.

aray *n.* show of military force 190/19; magnificence 208/2; supply 247/13; attire 209/1.

arayed *p.t.* adorned 33/3. *pp.* ~ dressed 89/21, 201/25; adorned 77/29; treated 118/20.

arbelasteres *n. pl.* cross-bowmen 166/7.

arblast *n.* missile shot from a cross-bow 115/21.

arestin *v.* arrest 207/14.

Argyues *n. pl.* inhabitants of Argos 25/10. See also *Index*, s.n.

aryue *v.* land 94/25.

Armenes *n. pl.* Armenians 74/5. See also *Index*, s.n. **Armenie.**

armour *n.* military equipment 15/8, 152/8; arms 196/11.

arsbischop *n.* archbishop 213/26.

arsmetrik *n.* arithmetic 8/29.

articule *n.* provision, clause (specified in petition or statute) 136/15. *pl.* **artic(u)les** doctrinal propositions 130/6; charges 193/10; terms (of treaty) 206/13.

asaye *v.* try 132/29. *p.t.* **as(s)ayed** tested 104/7; attempted 159/24.

Ascensioun *n.* Ascension Day 69/11. Cf. **Schere pursday.**

asent *n.* consent 180/17; *be on* ~ through complete agreement 96/4; *be comoun* ~ by unanimous agreement 153/4.

asignament *n.* apportionment 154/14.

asigne *v.* appoint 69/15. *pr. 3 pl.* **asyne** offer 14/10. *p.t.* **assigned** directed 240/20; designated 90/24. *pp.* **assi(g)ned** allocated 154/13; appointed 149/31; consigned 195/15; suggested 12/9.

ask *v.* require 177/11. *p.t.* **axed** asked for 152/1.

asoile *v.* grant absolution 240/10. *p.t.* **as(s)oiled, assoyled** absolved 116/11; released 113/2, 214/4. *pp.* **assoiled** given absolution 240/23.

aspecte *n.* relative positions 14/23.

aspied *p.t.* perceived 111/8, 175/24. *pp.* ~ watched for 115/4; spotted 121/4; detected 154/32; perceived 127/23.

assayed see **asaye.**

assent *v.* agree 131/22.

assi(g)ned see **asigne.**

Assiriis *n. pl.* Assyrians 21/29. See also *Index,* s.n. **Assiry.**

assoiled see **asoile.**

astat(e) *n.* condition 226/14; position 51/7; status 88/29. *pl.* **astatis** (three) social classes constituting the body politic 177/12.

astoyned *pp.* dismayed 132/16. Cf. **stoyned.**

asundir *adv.* apart 245/20; from each other 15/19; in pieces 36/28.

at *prep.* through 127/1; deriving from 14/25; to 142/7; on 158/9; at the time of 224/4; ~ *þe best* of the best kind 65/16.

auctorité *n.* authority 12/29, 141/11.

auctour *n.* prompter 186/12. *pl.* **auctouris** authorities 39/22.

Augustin *adj.* in *a frere* ~ Augustinian friar 170/23. *pl.* (as *n.*) **Austines** Augustinian friars 122/32; *poss.* (absol.) in *þe Frere Austines* Augustinian friary 130/35. See also *Index,* s.n.

aute see **owith.**

auter *n.* altar 18/1, 118/16.

auayle *n.* advantage 126/6.

avayle, availe *v.* be effective 148/32; benefit 230/13. *p.t.* **availed, a-uayled, avayled** was effective 96/26, 140/20; was of advantage 249/7; assisted 189/12.

avayte see **awayte.**

auale *v.* lower 191/24. *p.t.* **avaled** 226/12.

avaunsed *p.t.* promoted 141/18.

avis *n.* in *be his* ~ under his direction 159/14.

avised *p.t.* advised 137/6.

auysed, auised *pp.* warned 246/18; in *be* ~ decide after consideration 147/9.

auisement, avisa- *n.* (time for) consideration 47/13; *put in* ~ held over for further consideration 201/5; *took* ~ considered 194/12.

avoided *p.t.* drove away 232/15. *pp.* ~, **avoyded** rendered ineffectual 123/29; banished 138/18.

avow *n.* solemn promise 12/13, 153/31.

avowid *p.t.* acknowledged 141/23.

awayte, avayte *n.* plot 249/21; *leyd* ~ *upon* set an ambush for 158/6.

awakid *pp.* woken up 91/25.

awte see **owith.**

axed see **ask.**

Bactrianes *n. pl.* people of Bactria, land to east of Caspian Sea 19/8.

bad *p.t.* directed 60/28, 224/2.

bay-salt *n.* sea-salt 178/26.

banechid *p.t.* expelled 116/4. *pp.* **banchid** exiled 151/17; exiled from 146/7.

bank *n.*[1] ridge 116/16.

bank *n.*[2] court of King's Bench 201/30.

baptem *n.* baptism 32/15, 118/15.

baptizeth *pr. 3 sg.* baptizes 70/11.

bare *adj.* without addition 7/25.

bareyn *adj.* unproductive 21/34.

barettoures *n. pl.* malefactors 207/29 n.

barge *n.* ship 183/15.

barn *n.* baron 145/25.

basnet *n.* headpiece 105/7.

bast *n.* bastardy; *of* ~ out of wedlock 107/29.

basulard *n.* dagger 98/30.

bat *n.* stout stick 49/5. *pl.* **battis** cudgels 65/9.

batail(e), batayl(e) *n.* battle 13/20, 121/24; feud 235/28; warfare 73/10; (phr.) *ȝaue* ~ *onto, reysid* ~ *ageyn* attacked 49/26, 184/18, and see also **hald, kepe.** *pl.* **batayles** battalions 169/30.

Bauaris *n. pl.* people of Bavaria 84/24. See also *Index,* s.n. **Bauaré.**

bawmed *pp.* embalmed 26/2.

baxter *n.* baker 44/23.

be *pr. pl.* are 7/19, 12/5, 116/28. *pp.* ~ been 7/7, 36/25, 122/5.

be, by *prep.* through 169/23; via 19/13, 152/29; for (of time) 23/11; in 18/25, 200/29; in accordance with 38/29, 237/11; ~ *ȝere* annually 123/35; as regards 65/26; with 35/13; by means of 234/19;

through the agency of 74/5, 121/28;
by right of 156/30; on account of
45/1.

becomth *pr. 3 sg.* befits 194/3.

bedred *adj.* bedridden 82/9.

befor(e) *prep.* (in preference) to 27/
24.

beforn *adv.* previously 130/30.

begat *p.t. sg.* procreated 11/25,
160/18. *pl.* **begotin** 17/26.

beginner *n.* promoter 91/4. *pl.*
beginneris founders 36/4.

beginning, begynnyng *vbl.n.* in
first ~ coming into existence 11/30.

beginnit(h) *pr. 3 sg.* begins 19/2.
p.t. pl. **begun(ne)** began 12/35,
126/4.

behald *v.* see 23/25.

behest *n.* promise 228/23; in *Lond*
of ~ Promised Land 27/15.

behesting *pr.p.* promising 226/13.
pp. **behestid** promised 192/9.

behite, behote *p.t.* promised 228/22;
gave hope 234/12. *pp.* ~ promised
162/2.

bem *n.* bar 71/14.

benediccion *n.* blessing 90/23.

benedicite *int.* bless my soul! 216/12.

Benedictines *n. pl.* regulations made
by Pope Benedict XII 158/26.

benet *n.* member of third minor order
of secular clergy, exorcist 59/12.

beneuolens *n.* goodwill 193/26.

beqwathe *p.t.* left 57/9, 122/4.

bereth *pr. 3 sg.* carries 9/5. *pr.p.* in
beryng heuyly resenting 211/27. *p.t.*
bar(e), bore(*pl.* only) took, carried
(away) 28/19, 135/33; yielded
14/18; gave birth to 11/8, 220/29;
bare on hand accused 202/13;
bar/bore down pushed to the ground
157/9, defeated 136/5. *pp.* **bor(e)**
carried (away) 34/3; sustained 204/
26; born 12/8, 203/12; *bore of*
driven back 216/30; *bore on hande*
accused 211/15.

bery, beried see **byry**.

bering *vbl.n.* in ~ *up* supporting
28/27.

berk *v.* in ~ *ageyn* denounce 197/24.
pp. **berkid** 188/17.

beside *adv.* by his side 193/27;
nearby 104/11, 188/5.

besynesse see **bysinesse**.

best *adj. superl.* in *at þe* ~ of the
best kind 65/17.

best-beloued *adj.* favourite 82/7.

beþout *p.t.* (refl. w. *of*) recollected
188/4.

betyn *v.* promote 228/29.

betoknyth *pr. 3 sg.* symbolizes 8/22.
p.t. **betok(e)ned** was an omen of
210/28.

beuté *n.* beauty 47/9, 229/13.

bewreyid *p.t.* made known 234/21.
pp. **bewreyed** exposed 151/22.

by *adv.* in *fast* ~ close at hand 163/2.

by *prep.* see **be**.

by(e) *v.* buy 41/12, 124/27. *p.t.*
boute set free by paying a price
85/1, (w. *ageyn*) 248/20. *pp.* **boute**
ransomed 247/24.

biere *n.* buyer 145/21.

bigge *v.* stay 119/31; build 61/24.
p.t. **bigged, -id** stayed 119/32;
built 31/4, 126/20. *pp.* **biggid**
built 122/32; established 113/13.

bikird *p.t.* skirmished 236/17.

byleue *n.* faith 65/15.

bylid, bilid *p.t.* built 68/13 n.;
founded 91/13.

bille *n.* memorandum 240/12. *pl.*
billis letters 225/1; broadsheets
239/5.

bille *v.* indict 219/5.

bynarie *n.* combination of two things
8/37.

byry, bery *v.* bury 60/25–8. *p.t.*
byr-, ber-, biried, byrryed 26/11,
54/1, 85/6, 205/2. *pp.* **byr-, bir-,**
beried, byryed, -id 11/5, 26/4,
51/31, 117/3, 217/12.

biri-, birying, byriyng *vbl.n.* burial
15/14, 130/35; funeral 217/13.

bischop *n.* high priest 43/19.

bisi, bysy, -i *adj.* fully occupied
15/8, 130/18; careful 16/26.

bysi-, bisi-, besynesse *n.* activity
45/5; diligence 134/30; enterprise
146/26; actions 69/24.

bit(h)umen *n.* kind of mineral pitch
20/22.

bityn *pp.* cut 138/33.

blessed *p.t.* (refl.) crossed himself
214/11.

blod-last *n.* blood-letting 125/32–3.

boistous *adj.* ignorant 105/19.
bond *p.t. sg.* tied up 62/15; (refl.) solemnly undertook 211/12. *pl.* **bonde** captured 100/6. *pp.* **bound(e), bownde, bond** held in thrall 41/13; obliged (to agree) 117/27; under obligation 175/20; made surety 248/23.
bondeman *n.* peasant 67/20.
bondis *n. pl.* fetters, chains 30/29.
book *n.* Bible 204/10; chapter 23/33.
bord *n.* table 93/18, 141/17.
borowes *n. pl.* fortified towns 91/9.
bosom *n.* inside breast pocket 240/12.
bound(e), bownde see **bond**.
boute see **bye**.
bowed *p.t.* in ∼ *into* went in the direction of 218/24.
brak(e) see **brekith**.
bras *n.* bronze 36/33.
brast *p.t. sg.* burst 98/12.
brekith *pr. 3 sg.* disrupts 97/7. *p.t. sg.* **brak(e)** broke 30/29, 207/13; wrecked 190/14; burst 196/16; violated 183/29; split open, breached 116/16, 124/12. *pl.* **broke** breached 102/3, 154/17. *pp.* **brok(e), brokyn** broken 97/9; wrecked 114/22; destroyed 165/6; split open 116/17; escaped from 216/16.
brenne *v.* burn 12/3, 182/10. *pr.p.* **brennyng, -ing** 99/5, 186/3. *p.t.* **brent** 23/24, 126/13; was on fire 66/32; started fires 184/15. *pp.* **brent** 40/13, 118/17.
brennyng *vbl.n.* burning 144/18; burn, brand mark 155/1.
breþerin, bretheren, -in *n. pl.* brothers 25/24, 123/10.
bribe *v.* steal 161/32.
brigauntis *n. pl.* foot-soldiers 246/7.
brigge, bregge *n.* bridge 170/9; drawbridge 167/7.
bringith, bryng- *pr. 3 sg.* brings 101/13, 123/28. *subj.* **bryng** 152/18. *pp.* **broute** escorted 82/1; obtained 73/6; *broute in* set in office 92/12.
brynk *n.* shore 94/26.
brithnesse *n.* light 47/15.
Briton *n.* Breton 223/19. See also *Index,* s.n. **(Litil) Bretayn.**
broke, -yn see **brekith**.

broute see **bringith**.
burgeis, -es, burgeys *n. pl.* freemen (of borough) 244/25; members of parliament (for a borough) 154/3, 192/25.
but *adv.* only 33/10, 117/5; no more than 39/8; very 163/2.
but *conj.* except 17/14, 152/12, in ∼ þat 33/12, (*no ferþer* . . .) ∼ þat than (a place whence) 152/6, (*no more* . . .) ∼ þat (nothing) other than that 201/14; unless, if . . . not 54/5, 117/16, in ∼ *if* 54/10, 145/25.
but *prep.* except 23/35, 119/16; *not* (. . .) ∼ only 11/26, 149/22.

cacchid *p.t.* caught 147/11.
cam see **comth**.
Canon *n.* Canon Law 214/2.
Capadoses *n. pl.* Cappadocians 19/23.
capteyn *n.* leader 185/24; commander 144/7. *pl.* **capitanes** 133/4.
caracte *n.* sign 107/7. *pl.* **carectis** distinctive qualities 213/9.
careyn *n.* corpse 138/33.
cariage *n.* baggage 246/8; *coll.* means of transportation 246/18.
carl *n.* (base) fellow 105/19, 118/17. *pl.* **carlis** peasants 121/26.
Carme *n.* Carmelite 191/13.
Carmenes *n. pl.* (?) Carmanians, reported descendants of **Gether** 19/4.
cart *n.* chariot 34/2.
carter *n. poss.* cart-driver's 144/27.
case *n.* incident 146/20.
cassed *p.t.* quashed 119/36.
cast *v.* send forth, cause to spread 54/8. *p.t.* ∼ (refl.) resolved 160/1.
cateloge, cathologe *n.* official list 56/2.
cause *n.* purpose 179/22; charge 62/34, 120/2; blame 176/30; affair 190/2; (phr.) ∼ *why* rational explanation 221/21; ∼ *of* for the sake of 86/25; *for his* ∼ because of him 239/12. *pl.* **causes** lawsuits 59/15; matters of dispute 25/21.
cenewes see **senewis**.
censuris *n. pl.* penalties 210/1.

cerymonie *n.* ceremonial religious usage 53/18.

certeyn *adj.* as *n.* in *in* ~ for sure 17/2, 140/3.

cese see **sese.**

cessacion *n.* retirement from office 213/25.

chalenge *n.* accusation 226/23; claim 168/15.

chaleng(e) *v.* assert (one's right to) 103/14, 176/34. *pr. 1 sg.* ~ lay claim to 214/13. *p.t.* **chalenged** accused 149/24; asserted one's right to 107/17, 129/33 (w. *of* 'from').

chalis *n. pl.* chalices 115/9.

chanon *n.* Augustinian canon regular 219/8; Gilbertine canon 164/17. *pl.* **chanones** secular priests 95/2.

chapuleynis *n. pl.* in ~ *of þe pope* auditors or judges at the papal court 191/16.

charbunculis *n. pl.* rubies 82/15.

chare *n.* chariot 23/31. *pl.* **chares** carriages 206/21.

charmes *n. pl.* incantations 27/10.

Charterhous *n.* in *monkis of* ~ Carthusian monks 242/7 n.

chartour *n.* letter of pardon 208/19; *þe Grete Charter* Magna Carta (1215) 136/31.

cha(u)mbir *n.* room 126/6; suite 47/21, 145/34; bedroom 105/29, 156/2; department of king's household concerned with his private affairs 239/24.

chaumbirleynes *n. pl.* personal attendants 105/17.

chaunceler *n.* official secretary 95/21, 141/30.

chauncelry *n.* court of chancellor of England, chancery 201/30.

chekyr *n.* exchequer 203/9.

cherchȝerd *n.* churchyard 110/24.

chere *n.* disposition 57/8, 213/25; gladness 205/8; *chaunged* ~ altered expression 208/20.

chese *v.* choose 29/32, 127/9. *p.t. sg.* **chase** 48/19. *pl.* **chose(n)** 231/17. *pp.* **chose(n)** 20/16, 123/11.

Chestirreres *n. pl.* men from Chester (see 207/29) 211/23.

cheuesauns *n.* in *make* ~ pawn something (for ready money) 113/32.

cheueteynes *n. pl.* lords 93/11.

child *n.* devotee 235/5. *pl.* **childirn, -yrn** children 11/8, 129/28; **childir, -yr** 18/34, 249/12.

choys *n.* in *put in* ~ forced to choose (between alternatives) 64/30.

cianeus *n.* lapis lazuli 22/5.

cymytery *n.* catacombs 54/5-6.

circumcide *v.* circumcise 118/14. *p.t.* **circumcided** 120/17. *pp.* **circumcidid** 25/8.

circumcision *n.* in *fest of* ~ festival of Christ's circumcision (1 Jan.) 210/24.

circumstauns *n.* ceremony 208/18; instance 40/1.

Cistewis see **Sistewys.**

cité *n.* village 32/11; inhabitants of a city 111/21; *þe* ~ Jerusalem 38/28, Rome 59/4, 231/24.

citeceyn *n.* citizen 152/26.

Cyuyle *adj.* as *n.* Civil Law 71/23.

clausures *n. pl.* fences 186/4.

cleymeth *pr. 3 sg.* (hist.) claimed 246/2.

clene *adj.* undefiled 131/6.

clennes *n.* undefiled quality 14/11.

clepe *v.* summon 81/26, 201/18; call (by the name of) 51/2. *pr. pl.* call 19/14, 118/35. *imper.* summon 9/1. *p.t.* **cleped, -id** summoned 64/11, 138/14; called 13/33, 121/13; *cleped up* appealed to 156/9. *pp.* **cleped, -id, -it** summoned 64/12, 130/4; invoked 233/23; called 8/26, 12/20, 118/8.

clergy *n.* lords spiritual 149/16.

clerk *n.* cleric 62/34, 120/20; scholar 54/31, 119/4; secretary 69/27, 193/15.

clernesse *n.* brightness 75/9.

clientis *n. pl.* followers 62/28, 182/20.

cloystir *n.* monastic precinct 242/22.

clos *adj.* shut off 64/15.

closed *p.t.* in ~ *in* fenced in 164/11. *pp.* ~ set 92/22; bottled up 214/29.

code *n.* systematic collection of imperial statutes made by Justinian 71/23.

colet *n.* acolyte 59/12.

collocucion *n.* conversation 93/14.

colour *n.* complexion 53/7; allegeable reason 236/7; *vndir þe* ~ *of* disguised as 216/5.

comata *n.* comet 176/19.

comaund(e) *p.t.* ordered 41/18, 138/14.

comaundment *n.* instruction 26/9, 118/34; control 175/21; *had in* ~ was under instructions 76/6.

com(e) see **comth.**

com(e)naunt *n.* undertaking 42/11, 238/1; *mad (a)* ~ reached (an) agreement 73/5, 167/2. *pl.* **comnauntis, -es** points of agreement 123/35; terms 132/34; pledges 137/23.

com(e)naunté *n.* the common people 58/3; the Commons 154/10.

comendid *p.t.* entrusted 206/17.

comensale *n.* regular table companion 183/30.

comminacion *n.* threat of punishment 96/34.

commocyon *n.* insurrection 195/1.

comones *n.* *pl.* populace 185/20; common soldiers 246/6.

comorows *adj.* oppressive 92/33.

comoun *v.* have sexual intercourse 12/14. *p.t.* **como(u)ned** had sexual intercourse 17/25; conferred 137/5. *pp.* **comounde** had sexual intercourse 110/7.

comowneres *n.* *pl.* common soldiers 175/1.

compellyng *vbl.n.* power 219/27–8.

compilyng *vbl.n.* compilation 119/2.

compleyned *pp.* mourned 155/32.

complet *pp.* elapsed 8/15.

completori *n.* compline, the last service of the day 82/5.

complexion *n.* temperament 14/11.

comprehended *pp.* understood to be included 8/30.

compromitted *p.t.* agreed to refer (the matter) for settlement 131/20–1. *pp.* ~ referred by agreement for settlement 124/6.

computacio(u)n *n.* method of reckoning 8/3; arithmetical calculation 16/26.

comth *pr. 3 sg.* comes 33/18 (w. *of* 'from'). *p.t.* **com(e)** 11/9, 132/13;

kam 126/15; in *cam oute of* descended from 20/2.

conceyued see **conseyuyng.**

conclusio(u)n *n.* achievement 112/7; proposition 233/8; purpose 145/27.

condempned *pp.* pronounced 195/23.

condescend *v.* accede 146/17. *p.t.* **condescendid** agreed 130/27.

condicion *n.* social position 188/22; disposition, moral nature 65/1. *pl.* **condiciones** behaviour 112/23.

confederacion *n.* in *mad* ~ formed a conspiracy 227/17.

confermed *pp.* sanctioned 113/10.

confusion *n.* discomfiture 31/14–15, 164/1; cause of ruin 144/4.

conjecture *n.* plot 192/17.

consciens *n.* scruples 241/25.

consecrate *p.t.* dedicated 74/30. *pp.* **consecrat(e)** dedicated 36/4; consecrated 159/25; ordained 54/4–5.

conseite *n.* notion 219/1.

conseyuyng *pr.p.* realizing 157/13. *pp.* **conceyued** 204/7.

consent *n.* in *at his* ~ by compliance (with his request) 150/16 n.

consent *v.* assent 76/17, 239/8; allow 136/21. *pr.p.* **consenting, -yng** assenting 70/6; in accord (w. *onto* 'with') 81/24, 243/18. *p.t.* **consented** yielded 232/16. *pp.* **consented** been of one accord (w. *to* 'with') 211/16.

consideracio(u)n *n.* observation 26/17; meditation 8/28; *had* ~ *(at)* paid attention (to) 205/6.

consistory *n.* court 180/25.

conspiracio(u)n *n.* collusion 207/28; conspiracy 162/8.

constauns *n.* steadfastness 141/23.

constitucion *n.* regulation 67/5, 173/30; set of regulations 124/35.

consumed *pp.* destroyed by fire 76/13.

contented *p.t.* paid compensation to *174/25* n.

contracte *pp.* *adj.* shrunk 229/16.

contrari *adv.* in the opposite direction 190/14.

conueniens *n.* appropriateness 9/8.

conuenient *adj.* fitting 150/26.

conueniently *adv.* appropriately 188/16.

conuersacion *n.* behaviour 98/3–4, 159/27.

conuicte *p.t.* proved erroneous 66/8. *pp.* ~ found guilty 120/15.

corage *n.* ferocious anger 105/9.

corown(e) *n.* crown 135/33.

corowned *p.t.* crowned 112/8. *pp.* ~ 112/21, 214/21; **coroned** 127/2.

corporas *n.* corporal, cloth on which consecrated elements are placed during mass 54/8.

correccio(u)n *n.* authority for amending or punishing misconduct 103/26, 168/30; punishment 226/30.

correct(e) *pp.* disciplined 195/2; set right 195/5.

cor(r)upt *pp. adj.* rotten 105/35; infectious 234/20.

cort see **court**.

cosyn *n.* relative 47/4 (grandnephew), 59/9; nephew 145/13; niece 193/24 n. *pl.* in *cosynes in þe þirde degré* second cousins 155/31 n.

cost *n.* expenses 124/4; *ded* ~ spent money 85/8, 232/9. *pl.* in *mad costis* incurred expenses 205/6; *at þe costis of* at the expense of 201/9.

costful *adj.* expensive 72/4.

costfully *adv.* expensively 244/1.

costomable *adj.* usual 29/14.

cote *n.* aliquot part 8/26 n.

cote-armour *n.* garment embroidered with heraldic arms 152/33–4; armorial bearings 153/17.

cothe *n.* fainting-fit 62/32. *pl.* **cothis** labour-pains 87/15.

coude *p.t.* knew 41/13.

coumfort *n.* encouragement 67/15, 222/4; support 145/6; relief 125/26.

coumforted *p.t.* (refl.) encouraged 243/23.

counceleth *pr. 3 sg.* advises 200/30.

councel(l) *n.* secret design 62/20; private matters 164/1; confidence 126/5; *kept* ~ kept secret 62/31; *of* ~ *with* in the confidence of 241/25; *grete of his* ~ intimately acquainted with his secret plans 148/7.

counte *v.* calculate 242/19.

coupled *pp.* married 41/9; in league 114/11.

co(u)rt *n.* imperial court 55/18; papal curia 120/4.

courtesanes *n. pl.* members of the papal curia 168/20.

couent *n.* religious community 47/22, 122/35.

couetise *n.* greed 187/8; avarice 45/26, 235/4.

craft *n.* skill 23/26, 131/6; branch of learning 53/3; occupation 13/17.

crafty *adj.* clever 114/3.

cry(e) *n.* proclamation 117/15; public command 121/14.

crieth *pr. 3 sg.* demands 11/19. *pr.p.* **crying** begging for 229/4. *p.t.* **cried, cryed** begged for 188/7; demanded 208/4; *cried on* appealed to 201/18.

crimes *n. pl.* accusations 84/18.

cristendam *n.* christianity 63/19.

croses *n. pl.* crosiers 106/15.

crosse-staf *n.* staff surmounted by cross 122/12.

crowde *n.* fiddle (erron. for L *chorus* 'music accompanied by dancing') 13/7.

crowet *n.* small bowl 214/30 n.

cruelnes(se) *n.* mercilessness 46/10.

cubiculeres *n. pl.* bedroom attendants 122/14.

cubite *n.* unit of measure approx. half a metre 229/16.

cunnyng *adj.* learned 78/25.

cunnyng *vbl.n.* learning 87/11; wisdom 21/10.

cure *n.* care; *bysy* ~ diligence 248/6; responsibility in spiritual matters 163/30; sphere of ecclesiastical duties 58/23.

cure *v.* cover 50/2.

curtesi(e) *n.* courtly behaviour 105/12, 231/9; goodwill 133/33.

custome *n.* in *of* ~ according to usual practice 213/22.

day *n.* in *many* ~ for a long time 87/23, 138/29. *pl.* **dayes** period of life or office 16/24, 119/4; extent (of life) 16/21; *at/in þese/þo(o) dayes/daies* at this/that time 12/36, 19/14, 53/25, 167/29.

Dam(e) *n.* Madam 73/19; (as title prefixed to name) Lady 130/32.

dampned *p.t.* condemned 51/10. *pp.* ~ 75/13, 194/4; as *adj.* 185/1.

dartis *n. pl.* spears 70/9.

debate *n.* strife, wrangling 45/2, 143/20; dispute 65/31, 235/18.

deceyt(e) *n.* treachery 30/27, 176/15; trick 228/21.

deceyued *pp.* taken unawares 210/30; betrayed 83/21, 187/7; frustrated 216/10; defrauded 174/24.

decerne *pr. 3 pl.* decree 215/20.

declaracio(u)n *n.* description 18/22.

declare *v.* make known 109/24; describe 33/22. *p.t.* declared elucidated 130/15.

ded(e) *adj.* dead; *be* ~ die 35/9, be killed 74/17, 135/9; *was/were* ~ died 48/8, 144/23, was/were killed 59/2, 140/15; *haue* ~ kill 236/21.

ded(e) *p.t.* see **do**.

dede *n.* job 208/22.

defaut(e) *n.* lack 123/7; defect 51/23, 159/26; *put* ~ *on* blamed 188/23. *pl.* defautes misdeeds 193/4.

defendid *pp.* forbidden 247/3.

defensed *pp.* defended 143/28.

defiled *pp.* corrupted 50/31.

degraded *p.t.* deprived of ecclesiastical orders 188/18. Cf. **disgraded**.

degré *n.* way 236/1.

dey(e) *v.* die 50/19, 131/19, **deie** 216/28. *pr. 3 sg.* (hist.) **deieth** 32/10, **deyeth** 34/26. *p.t.* **deied**, **deyed** 11/5, 118/5, **dey(i)d** 26/1, 196/17.

deying *vbl.n.* death 64/6.

dekne *n.* deacon 89/18, 118/13; **diacone** 59/13.

delay *n.* in *put in* ~ deferred 201/1.

delfyn *n.* dauphin, title attached to the seigneury of the Viennois 160/21.

deliberacioun *n.* in *asked* ~ asked for time for consultation 229/28.

delicious *adj.* spiritually delightful 50/24.

delyuer *v.* free 89/4. *pp.* **dylyuered** set free 133/18; **delyueret** saved 190/16.

delue *v.* in ~ *up* exhume 208/31.

deme *pr. 3 pl.* give judgment 215/20. *p.t.* **dempt** determined 124/7; thought 225/5.

deneyed *p.t.* refused to believe in 67/11; repudiated 129/34.

departe *v.* divide up 103/11. *p.t.* **departed** divided 31/20 (w. *to* 'amongst'), 58/20–1; shared 115/2; separated 13/9; (refl.) altered its course 210/26; took leave of each other 111/15. *pp.* **departed** split up 143/20; separated 15/19; distinguished 79/12; divorced 172/27.

depauperat *pp.* impoverished 83/12.

depeyntid *p.t.* painted 80/19. *pp.* **depeynted** portrayed 112/18; as *adj.* depicted 108/32; decorated 78/27; emblazoned 244/1.

deposed *pp.* deprived 149/5; asserted 137/30.

derogacio(u)n *n.* detraction (w. *to* 'from') 139/7; disparagement 211/18.

descense *n.* descent 214/14.

descriued *pp.* described 45/25.

desert *adj.* desolate 173/3.

despiseth *pr. 3 sg.* treats with contempt 226/8.

despite *n.* disgrace 153/20; *had in* ~ held in contempt 150/21; *in* ~ *of* in defiance of 139/12.

destroyed see **distroye**.

detect(e) *pp.* exposed and accused 105/29, 243/20.

determined, determyned *pp.* laid down 17/1; pronounced 109/3–4; decreed 233/11.

deuté, dewté *n.* duty 9/3, 130/22; *be ony* ~ with the maximum deference 7/4; *of* ~ out of obligation 133/32.

deuolute *pp.* transferred 42/21.

deuoute *adj.* devoted 65/12, 181/25.

dew *adj.* due 35/4, 179/15.

diacone see **dekne**.

difficulté *n.* in *mad* ~ showed reluctance 136/14.

digest *n.* collection of Roman laws compiled under Justinian 71/22.

diggid *p.t.* dug 99/19.

dykes *n. pl.* trenches 164/15.

dilate *v.* enlarge upon 7/14.

diligently *adv.* assiduously and eagerly 63/17.

dylyuered see **delyuer**.

dyme *n.* tenth, subsidy equal to one-tenth the value of one's property 203/30.

dymembered *pp.* dismembered 94/30.

directly *adv.* entirely 124/8.

dirige, dyrige *n.* the Office for the Dead beginning with the antiphon at Matins 92/27, 217/10.

dirk *adj.* threatening (of storm) 119/14.

discrepauns *n.* discrepancy 43/23.

disgraded *pp.* demoted, deprived of ecclesiastical status 88/28. Cf. **degraded.**

disherid *pp.* dispossessed 227/26.

disparplied *pp.* scattered 7/8, 177/23.

dispende *pr. pl.* spend 226/20.

dispensacion *n.* in *withoute* ~ without exception 60/3.

dispensid *p.t.* in ~ *with* granted release (from vows) 86/28; granted remission (from penalties) 147/29.

displeasauns *n.* in *ded* ~ offended 37/15.

disposed *p.t.* controlled 114/29; assigned 27/29; (refl.) made up his mind 234/30. *pp.* ~ arranged in order 59/10; as *adj.* constituted 222/4.

disposicio(u)n *n.* control 129/12; direction 237/11; *in þe* ~ *of* at the disposal of 127/10.

dissolute *adj.* remiss 58/4.

dissolue *v.* raise 165/27.

distauns *n.* dissension 103/24, 145/7.

distincte *pp. adj.* in *foure* ~ divided into four (chapters) 38/28.

distribut *p.t.* apportioned 27/30.

distroye *v.* lay waste 11/33, 168/22. *p.t.* **distroyed** ravaged 86/10, 158/18; raised (siege) 71/26 n. *pp.* **distroyed, de-** ravaged 89/2, 143/7–8; taken away 170/20.

dite *pp.* prepared, dressed 131/6; as *adj.* **dith** furnished 28/32.

ditées *n. pl.* poetry 40/9 n.

dyuers *adj.* various 12/5, 129/15; several (different) 13/12 (more than two), 177/23.

diuersité *n.* adversity 219/21.

dyuyded *p.t.* marked out 52/2. *pp.* ~ split (between rival factions) 116/33; set out separately 248/10.

diuision *n.* dissension 116/33.

diuulgid, dyuulged *pp.* made known generally 7/6, 11/19, 175/23.

do *v.* in ~ *upon* dress in 35/24; *auxil.* forming w. inf. periphrastic inf. 209/14. *pr. 3 sg.* **doth** 161/13. *p.t.* **ded(e)** 12/10, 127/18; meted out 226/30; caused (to) 207/14; *auxil.* forming w. inf. periphrastic p.t. 13/17, 128/27. *pp.* **do(o)** 7/17, 28/12, 129/7; completed 119/26; *Aftir þis doo* Later 115/13.

dobbil *adj.* in ~ *festes* important Church festivals 238/30.

docto(u)res, -is *n. pl.* learned men 48/5; Church fathers 66/9, 240/30–1; legal authorities 180/24.

dom(e) *n.* judgment 104/26, 124/6; *þe* ~ day of judgment 32/16, 122/13; *do* ~ administer justice 16/17.

domicelles *n. pl.* young ladies 206/21.

Dominic *adj.* Dominican 170/26; as *n. pl.* **Dominices** 195/19. Cf. **Prechour** and see *Index*, s.n. **Dominic.**

Donatistes *n. pl.* Donatists, N. African heretical Christian sect begun 311 and named after **Donat** 62/1.

dotacion *n.* endowment 188/17.

doutir, -yr, dowtir *n.* daughter 26/26, 118/14; female disciple 82/8; in group gen. *þe kyngis* ~ *Joram* King Joram's daughter 34/17, *þe duke* ~ *of Normandie* the duke of Normandy's daughter 100/11, *Duke Herry* ~ *of Lancastir* Henry duke of Lancaster's daughter 167/27. *pl.* in *þe douteres of men*, name for female descendants of Cain 17/25 (Gen. 6: 2). Cf. **son.**

doutles *adv.* certainly 127/28.

dowarye *n.* portion of husband's estate allowed to widow for life 154/14.

dowe *n.* dove 56/27.

dragones *n. pl.* large snakes 73/31.

drautes *n. pl.* deceitful practices 45/2.

drawe *v.* pull 66/20; drag behind a horse 142/31. *pr.p.* **drawyn(g)** borrowing 107/3; resorting (to) 63/16. *p.t.* **drow(e), drew** pulled 38/29; went 113/20; *drow (on)to*

drawe (*cont.*):
joined the side of 148/33. *pp.*
draw(e), drawen pulled up 89/21,
167/7; dragged behind a horse
120/24, 134/26.

drawyng *vbl.n.* punishment of being
dragged behind a horse 147/28.

dred(e), dreed *n.* awe 9/3; fear 21/23,
155/7.

drede *v.* in *to* ~ to be feared 40/6.
p.t. **dred** regarded with awe 32/14;
feared 71/5, 194/11.

dredful *adj.* terrifying 208/26.

dreid *pp.* dried 168/6.

drenchid *p.t.* flooded 73/31, 227/2;
scuttled 131/15. Cf. **dronchin.**

dryuyth *pr. 3 sg.* conducts 139/17.
p.t. **drof** drove 115/19; **droue**
deduced 14/1 (w. *oute*), 109/8.
pp. **dryue** 168/26.

dronch(in) *pp.* drowned 59/27, 176/
11. Cf. **drenchid.**

ducheries *n. pl.* duchies 82/29.

duke *n.* leader 185/23; military commander 58/5; governor 201/17.

dured *p.t.* lasted 22/16, 166/19; continued in office 93/35.

durst *p.t. subj.* would have dared
111/14.

dwelle *v.* stay 213/5. *pr. 3 sg.* **dwellith** remains 24/27. *p.t.* **dwelled,
dwelt** was staying 96/33; stayed
238/4. *pp.* **dwelled** stayed 73/3.

dweller *n.* inhabitant 19/2. *pl.*
dwelleres residents 191/8.

ech *adj.* as *pron.* (phr.) ~ *aftir opir*
one by one 95/18; ~ *to opir* one
another 243/23; ~ *with othir*
against each other 39/12.

edifie, -ye *v.* provide with buildings
39/18; establish 119/28. *p.t.* **edified** built 69/16, 121/35; set up
20/30. *pp.* **edified** built 38/6.

edifieres *n. pl.* builders 20/29.

edifiyng *vbl.n.* building 171/22.

effect *n.* in *to þis effect* for the following purpose 215/1.

egel, -il *n.* flask in shape of an eagle
214/29.

eydir *adv.* either 156/30.

eyeledes *n. pl.* eyelids 131/3.

eyer, eyir, eir, eyre *n.*[1] heir 46/1,
144/25.

eyer, eyir, eyr(e) *n.*[2] air 23/27,
172/32.

eyne see **y3e.**

eject *pp.* expelled 89/14.

eke *conj. adv.* also, moreover 7/21,
11/32, 117/12.

eld(e) *adj.* old 7/7, 20/5, 125/19;
ancient 114/31, **olde** 69/22.

eldfader *n.* ancestor (here 'great-
grandfather') 23/2.

eleccion *n.* in *had* ~ was the choice
70/24.

eleuacion *n.* lifting up of the Host
107/33.

eleuene *adj.* eleventh 190/27.

ellis, -es *adv.* else 12/22, 119/30;
otherwise 246/24.

elmesse *n.* alms 15/2, 242/20; works
of charity 82/10.

empire *n.* rule 61/14; position of
emperor 50/14; reign of an emperor 55/17.

enbassiatour *n.* envoy 132/9. *pl.*
em-, enbass(i)atouris 220/24.

encense *n.* incense 54/8.

encensed *p.t.* offered incense before
60/19.

enchete *v.* confiscate for the royal
treasury 226/16.

enchetyng *vbl.n.* confiscation for the
royal treasury 232/31.

encres *n.* augmentation 14/6.

encresed *p.t.* caused to grow 139/
8–9; enriched 127/24.

ende *n.* furthest point 21/33; last
part (of life) 62/6, *last* ~ 93/29,
169/27; death 67/8, *last* ~ 33/4,
199/25; *mad a* ~ died 96/8, 125/8;
mad a ~ *of* killed 126/9.

endented *pp. adj.* having serrated
edge to tally with copy 240/12.

endewe *v.* put 200/27. *pp.* **endewid**
endowed 50/15, 118/26.

ending *vbl.n.* death 24/27.

endited *p.t.*[1] dictated 56/6.

endited *p.t.*[2] charged (w. *of* 'with')
149/32. *pp.* ~ 193/11.

endith *pr. 3 sg.* (hist.) died 38/1. *pp.*
ended dissolved 209/15.

endytment *n.* indictment 193/16.

endure *v.* continue 226/8.

enfeffed *p.t.* put in possession (of) *151/7.*

engynes *n. pl.* siege machines for casting objects over walls 234/19.

enormes *n. pl.* wicked acts 118/16.

ensaumple *n.* in *gyue* ~ set an example 123/5. Cf. exaumple.

entended *p.t.* applied oneself assiduously 18/21.

entent *n.* wish 81/16; desire 226/4; attention 23/26; purpose 13/16, 130/18.

enterdite *n.* interdict 116/11.

enterdited *pp.* put under interdict 116/9.

enterditing *vbl.n.* interdict 148/24.

entering *vbl.n.* entry (to office) 131/30.

enterly *adv.* earnestly 244/12.

entyr, -ir *v.* take up (possession of lands) 119/31; take up (office) 108/4, 214/16. *p.t.* entered, ent(i)red took possession of 22/13, 128/23; came to (office) 9/10, 78/8; *entered into* came into possession of 138/13; *entred upon* began to attack 124/12; put out to 152/23. *pp.* entered come to (office) 131/26.

entirmeting *pr.p.* interfering *180/23.*

entitiled *p.t.* dedicated 119/23.

entré *n.* right of entry 52/10.

envye *n.* unpopularity 55/18; had ~ *with* were jealous of 235/10.

ephiphani(e) *n.* epiphany (6 Jan.) 153/26.

epitafi *n.* epitaph 99/8.

er *conj.* before 212/26. Cf. or.

erde *n.* earth 9/17, 11/31, 166/31.

erdeli *adj.* earthly 14/21.

erdqwaue *n.* earthquake 127/17.

ereyne *n.* spider 234/6.

Eri(s)ch *adj.* Irish 203/5.

Erisch *n.* Irish people 203/6.

erldam, herldam *n.* territory governed by an earl or count 80/13, 150/32.

erl(e), herl *n.* earl 119/19; European nobleman such as count or marquis 90/13, 120/13.

erred *p.t.* went astray 62/5, 223/30.

erroneous *adj.* misguided 197/25.

ese *n.* in *wel at* ~ in comfortable

circumstances 225/18; *more at* ~ with less annoyance 97/31.

esy *adj.* propitious 113/19; lenient 56/13.

Estern *n.* Easter 141/15. Cf. Pase.

ete *p.t.* ate 14/15, 159/23. *pp.* ~ eaten 141/3.

eterne *adj.* eternal 59/19.

Ethiopes *n. pl.* Ethiopians, Cushites 19/11.

euangelie *n.* gospel 49/8.

euasion *n.* escape 241/18.

euel *adj.* wicked 195/23.

euel *adv.* wrongfully 103/35; wickedly 130/26; badly 194/3.

euel-beloued *adj.* out of favour 211/28.

euel(e) *n.* in *seid* ~ *of* made unfavourable remarks about 74/16; *þe falling* ~ epilepsy 75/7.

euen *n.* evening 111/17; eve 84/11, 179/2; *at* ~ in the evening 208/31.

euene *adv.* fully, completely 57/3, 168/6; namely 213/24; indeed 238/19; (phr.) ~ *as* just as 9/2, 240/26, at the moment when 119/13; ~ *(on)to* right up to 144/30.

euensong *n.* sunset 173/9.

euery *adj.* any 55/5.

euyr, -ir *adv.* perpetually 44/9; always, at all times 8/2, 15/8, 136/15; continually 63/17, 136/12, unceasingly 152/24; progressively 229/15; proportionately 100/6.

euyrlesting *adj.* eternal 65/22.

ex *n.* axe 34/5.

exaumple *n.* precedent 113/29. Cf. ensaumple.

excite *v.* incite 121/18.

excuse *n.* in *to his* ~ to his defence 177/28.

excuse *v.* (refl.) allege by way of excuse 133/12; try to obtain release (from obligation) for 150/5. *p.t.* excused (refl.) sought to be released (from duty) 110/33, 158/5. *pp.* excused exonerated 208/18; released (from obligation) 149/14.

execucion *n.* in *do* ~ inflict punishment 148/13.

exempcion *n.* freedom from jurisdiction of local bishop 130/8.

exempt *adj.* not subject to a higher authority 204/28.

expenses *n. pl.* charges incurred 179/27.

expert *adj.* experienced 185/12.

exposiciones *n. pl.* interpretations 84/31; commentaries 7/7.

expouned *p.t.* interpreted 39/10.

expresse *v.* describe 79/12. *pr.p.* **expressing** stating 203/29. *p.t.* **expressed** mentioned 11/26; described 116/21. *pp.* **expressed** described 17/14–15.

expression *n.* explicit mention 7/29.

face *n.* outward appearance 114/7.

faderhood *n.* in *his holy* ~ the pope 134/3.

failed *p.t.* lacked 223/9; ~ *of* came short of obtaining 81/18. *pp.* in ~ *of* come short of catching 138/29.

fayn *adj.* content 26/30, 144/19; obliged 29/3, 124/27; disposed 68/22.

fayre, faire *adj.* handsome 58/9; eloquent 108/22; morally good 32/11.

fayre *adv.* suitably 118/29.

falle *v.* come to pass 200/28; ~ *on* attack 216/4. *p.t.* **fel, fell(e)** collapsed (through illness) 75/8, 199/10; became 87/14; occurred, came about 7/30, 39/25, 119/12; came as a result 141/4; *fel(le) in* met with 147/7, joined 191/19; *fel in lecherie* committed adultery 94/7; *fell(e) fro* revolted against 177/33, gave up 145/31; *fel(l) upon* came over 62/28, attacked 149/3; *fell on* came on 97/12. *pp.* ~ 27/18; ~ *in* become subject to 148/25.

fals *adj.* disloyal and detestable 83/21, 139/14; dishonest 138/2; wicked 183/15.

fals *adv.* untruthfully 88/5.

falshed *n.* deceitfulness 194/4.

fame *n.* widely circulated report 108/8.

famed *pp.* rendered famous by talk 232/7.

familiar *adj.* in ~ *deuel* attendant demon 23/29.

fast *adv.* in prep. phr. ~ *be* close to 12/24, 117/25. Cf. **by.**

fastid *pp.* observed as time for abstinence 61/5, 186/27.

faut(e), fawt(e) *p.t. (sg. & pl.)* fought 89/2, 121/31. *pl.* **foutyn** 39/12.

fautour *n.* supporter 81/24, 233/14; abettor 240/2.

fauour *n.* support 203/23; *for* ~ *of* out of goodwill towards 201/3; *do* ~ show goodwill 128/23; *gaf* ~ *to* supported 156/16.

fe *n.* perquisite 104/11.

fedir-beddis *n. pl.* down-filled mattresses 209/13.

fe(e)r *n.* fire 13/18, 234/11.

feyer *n.* fair 130/16.

feyne *pr. pl.* invent (unfavourable stories) 41/4. *p.t.* **feyned** made out 21/7, 158/32; (refl.) pretended to be 120/21. *pp.* in *feyned on* falsely alleged against 155/28.

feyned *adj.* fictitious 134/4.

feyning *vbl.n.* dissembling 45/26.

feith *n.* in *mad* ~ gave a pledge 63/18.

felauchip, felaw- *n.* company 65/20–1; group of companions 192/20; force of armed men 83/19, 121/33.

felaw(e) *n.* colleague 188/5; accomplice 243/18; equal 87/8. *pl.* **felawes, -is, felaues** companions 74/9, 194/9; members 137/32.

feld *n.* open country 121/23; plain 11/2; victory 245/24.

fer *n.* 'fire' see **feer.**

fer-forth *adv.* in *so* ~ to such an extent 50/31, 133/11.

ferme *adj.* fixed 200/2.

ferme *adv.* steadily 8/20.

fer(r) *adv.* far 127/20.

ferþer *adv.* further 116/13, 152/6.

ferþermore *adv.* moreover, in addition 9/8, 97/1, 146/12.

ferþest *adj. superl.* most distant 135/16.

ferþing *n.* in ~ *of gold* quarter-noble 121/13.

festful *adj.* in ~ *day* religious holiday 188/4.

fiftene *n.* tax of one-fifteenth levied on property 203/31.

fifti *adj.* fiftieth 180/11.

figure *n.* typological prefiguration

24/30; symbol 99/22; *in þe ~ of* as a symbolic prefiguration of 25/9.

figured *pp.* expressed figuratively 8/21.

fikil *adj.* deceitful 148/10.

filt *pp.* stuffed 234/18.

fynde *v.* provide for 137/11. *p.t.* **fond(e)** found 7/28, 36/11, 129/2; met with 157/3; discovered 13/15. *pp.* **found(e)** invented 13/14.

fynder *n.* deviser 13/4; inventor 13/13.

firmament *n.* heavens 28/27.

fischeres *n. pl.* fishermen 89/23.

fischid *p.t.* caught by fishing 129/21.

flagellid *p.t.* scourged 76/17.

flay *p.t.* flayed 28/17 n. *pp.* **flayn** 49/7.

fley *p.t.* fled 109/30.

fle(s)ch *n.* meat 14/16, 245/18.

flete *v.* float 34/5.

flewme *n.* mucus 78/23.

flix see **flux**.

flood *n.* river 19/13, 144/12.

florenis *n. pl.* Florentine florins (54 grams in weight and supposed to circulate in England at 3*s.* in 1344) 172/17.

flour *n.* supreme example 66/9. *pl.* **floures** state of greatest eminence 56/3.

floured *p.t.* were distinguished (in) 41/22.

flux *n.* in *þe ~ of blood* excessive bleeding 50/18. **flix** 64/32.

folk *n.* members of the royal household 105/17.

folowand *pr.p.* following 244/27. *p.t.* **folowid** accompanied 111/1; went in pursuit 127/1.

folowand *pr.p. adj.* that comes next in time 111/23, 129/11; that is/are now to be set forth 237/18.

fond see **fynde**.

fonnednesse *n.* folly 118/20.

for *conj.* because 7/20, 24/29, 123/2.

for *prep.* as 37/3, 249/27; because of 22/3 (2nd), 117/12; from 63/9, 123/6; through 9/19; as a precaution against 13/18; ~ *to* (introd. inf.) (in order) to 7/35, 13/5, 119/28.

forbarre *v.* deprive (of) 107/23; exclude 160/32.

forbedyng *pr.p.* prohibiting 211/6. *pp.* **forbode** forbidden 160/6.

forby *adv.* past 29/17.

forbreke *v.* break in two 185/7.

forfet *n.* crime 146/11.

forfète *pp. adj.* subject to seizure (by) 140/26.

forgaf *p.t.* pardoned 173/19.

forgete *pp.* forgotten 51/1.

forgifnesse, forgeuenesse *n.* pardon 114/15, 124/29.

forgo *v.* forfeit 215/27.

forme *n.* manner 187/17; method 8/5; prescribed course 83/6; formal agreement 172/3; *vndir þis ~* on these terms 168/13.

fors *n.* in *with ~* by the employment of military strength 73/2.

forsake *v.* refuse to undertake 111/6; give up 175/19; renounce 63/19, 234/10. *pr. 2 sg.* **forsakest** refuse to undertake 111/3. *3 sg.* **forsakith** deserts 198/8. *p.t.* **forsok(e), forsook** repudiated 36/16; declined 33/8; gave up 127/9; broke off from 37/1; renounced 64/31; left 20/14.

forseid, -said, -seyd *adj.* previously mentioned 13/22, 137/3.

forsoth *adv.* truly 7/26, 162/25.

forth *adv.* onwards 8/4; away 156/7; (w. ellipsis of v.) set out (on) 130/1; out 229/10; ~ *anon* promptly 196/27.

fosteres *n. pl.* foresters; in *~ of þe kyng of Frauns* title given to governors of Flanders 87/33.

foule *adv.* grievously 109/9. Cf. **fowler**.

foules *n. pl.* birds 11/31.

founde see **fynde**.

fourt(e) *adj.* fourth 9/9, 14/19, 121/9.

fourty *adj.* fortieth 23/23.

foutyn see **faute**.

fowler *adj. compar.* uglier 229/15. Cf. **foule**.

fray *n.* attack 236/25.

frech *adj.* freshly blooming 161/17.

frely *adv.* at liberty 125/15; with absolute possession 88/22.

Frensch *n pl.* Franks 82/2.

frend *n.* supporter 89/11; ally 15/16; ~ *of God* person of exeptiona

frend (*cont.*):
piety 23/31. *pl.* **frendis** relatives 54/10.

frendchip *n.* reconciliation 205/7.

frenesi *n.* in *fel in a* ~ had a fit of madness 199/10.

frentik *adj.* insane 120/21.

frere *n.* friar 7/2, 118/35. See also **Augustin, Carme, Menouris, Prechour.**

fret *p.t.* gnawed 89/5.

Frises *n. pl.* Phrygians 37/30. See also *Index*, s.n. **Frise**. [prob. L *Phryx* adj. confused w. L *Frisi* 'Frisians']

fro *prep.* from 7/17, 11/2, 116/29; of 21/31; away from 205/19; severed from 50/8.

fructuous *adj.* edifying 107/2.

frustrat(e) *pp.* rendered ineffectual 217/25; balked 190/15, as *adj.* 119/11.

frute *n.* children 12/18, 198/15. *pl.* **frutes** crops 14/18.

ful *adv.* very, exceedingly 7/21, 14/33, 124/30; quite 32/16.

fulfille *v.* carry out 241/24; do 97/18. *pr. 3 sg. subj.* ~ complete 9/19. *p.t.* **fulfillid** put into effect 82/27, 119/26; carried out 164/17. *pp.* **fulfillid** imbued 65/16; carried out 11/20 (w. *in* 'on'), 178/12.

fulleres *n. sg. poss.* belonging to one who beats cloth for the purpose of cleaning and thickening it 49/5.

fully *adv.* in *not* ~ not quite 77/23, 180/20.

funt *n.* font 175/13.

gader(e), -ir *v.* (refl.) assemble 194/14; (absol.) accumulate wealth 226/6; compile 7/7; collect (w. *to* 'for') 184/8. *p.t.* **gadered** (refl.) assembled 126/21; compiled 118/35. *pp.* **gadered** collected 221/18.

gaderingis *n. pl.* collections of money 207/8.

gaf see **geue**.

Galadite *n.* Gileadite 30/5.

galey-halfpenies *n. pl.* galley-halfpennies, silver coins introduced by Genoese traders 247/3.

galow *n.* gallows 153/16.

gan *p.t. sg.* as auxil. in ~ *remembre* remembered 97/22.

gat see **gete**.

geaunt *n.* giant 28/26.

gelde *v.* castrate 110/1.

genelogie *n.* lineage 24/26; pedigree 109/24.

generacion *n.* offspring 15/20; descendants 15/28–9.

gentil *adj.* courteous 96/31.

gentilmen *n. pl.* men of high (but not noble) birth 186/11.

gentilnes *n.* courtesy 133/34.

gere *n.* warlike equipment 234/21.

gete *v.* capture 237/16; (refl.) procure for oneself 73/19; beget 18/8. *pr. subj. pl.* ~ would catch 138/30. *p.t. sg.* **gat** (refl.) won 71/26; procured 103/33, 204/27. *p.t. pl.* **gote** 157/1. *pp.* **get** caught 184/23; **gote** acquired 121/5.

geue *v.* give 15/2. *p.t. sg.* **gaf** 23/25, 119/28; (refl.) devoted himself (to); inflicted upon 167/7; **gaue** in *gaue aboute* distributed 224/28. *pp.* **goue** 14/11, 122/28. Cf. **ȝiuing**.

giftis *n. pl.* bribes 87/28.

gilty *adj.* at fault 204/13; in ~ *of/to* to blame for 156/14, 195/23.

gise *n.* usual practice 206/23.

gladed *p.t.* delighted 216/18.

glorious *adj.* illustrious 59/28; shining 39/1.

go *v.* in ~ *with* support 241/20; ~ *owte* die 103/36. *pr. 1 sg.* ~ move about 164/11. *3 sg.* **goth** travels 87/17; leads 87/20; passes 46/25; *goth up* passes 80/13. *pp.* **go(o)** passed 103/32, 192/9; departed 73/9, 243/24; *go ouyr* crossed 147/15. For *p.t.* see **went**.

gong *n.* latrine 62/30.

good, gode *n.* possessions 103/34, 130/19; money 83/13, 139/16; merchandise 132/14; (phr.) *a myty man of* ~ a man of vast wealth 91/30; *gret* ~ a large sum of money 137/10.

goodly *adj.* appropriate 73/23; (phr.) *in moost* ~ *hast* with the utmost speed 97/29; *in al* ~ *maner* (1) in the most suitable way 203/24, (2) in the most friendly way 198/6.

goot *n. pl.* goats 13/10.

gored, -id *p.t.* stabbed deeply 93/19, 147/21.

gote see **gete**.

Gothis *n. pl.* Visigoths 65/7; Ostrogoths 71/27. See also *Index*, s.n.

goue see **geue**.

gouernauns, -aunce *n.* management 146/2; mode of behaviour 9/20, 33/20, 155/33; (phr.) *vndir* ~ subject to control 196/24; *had in* ~ was in charge of 221/11.

gouerne *v.* take control of 96/13. *p.t.* regulated 55/32. *pp.* **gouerned** commanded 177/19.

grace *n.* favour 113/21, 138/24; pardon 9/6, 193/8; (phr.) *of* ~ as a favour 147/29; *take to* ~ look favourably upon 139/22; *stand in* . . . ~ be favoured by 145/25; *þe ʒere of* ~ the year of Our Lord 181/27. *pl.* **graces** privileges 191/ 15.

gracious *adj.* benevolent 141/10; endowed with divine grace 181/24.

grate *n.* gridiron 58/19.

graunt *n.* consent 37/5; promise 143/15.

graunted *p.t.* agreed 114/25, 150/28. *pp.* ~, **-id** agreed to 149/9; in *had* ~ would have allowed 236/21; **graunte** granted 160/3.

graue *n.* (?) mausoleum 23/30.

grauing *pr.p.* incising 21/9.

grauing *vbl.n.* incision of lines to form design 13/21.

Greces *n. pl.* Greeks 19/20.

grecis *n. pl.* steps 62/15.

gres(se) *n.* grass 140/21.

gret(e) *adj.* massive 20/16; pregnant 161/2; swollen 158/20; big 15/20, 123/1; many 103/12, 139/29; severe 232/17; noble 192/1. *superl.* **grettest** largest 80/4.

grete *adv.* greatly 105/19.

grete-named *adj.* prominent 87/32.

grete-wittid *adj.* shrewd 138/28.

greued, -id, -yd *p.t.* troubled 125/ 12; hurt 199/13; vexed 208/28; annoyed 143/31.

greuous *adj.* burdensome 177/34; arduous 168/28; injurious 174/27; severe 11/22; grave 241/2.

greuously *adv.* in an oppressive manner 63/25.

Grew *n.* Greek (language) 81/12.

grew *p.t.* see **growith**.

grifes *n. pl.* griffins 22/4.

Griphones *n. pl.* Greeks 114/12.

groped *p.t.* felt 48/34.

grotes *n. pl.* groats (4*d.*) 167/16.

ground(e) *n.* basis 71/23; territory 151/32; (phr.) *be þe* ~ *on the* ground-floor 242/16.

growith *pr. 3 sg.* grows 14/16. *p.t.* **grew** in *grew(on)to* developed 46/10, 191/20; *grew in* passed into a state of 197/18. *pp.* **growe** vitally united (w. *to* 'with') 208/29; **grown** 97/21; (phr.) *growe to mannes age* grown up 26/28.

grucching *vbl.n.* grumbling 68/21, 207/19.

gruch *v.* be discontented 192/11. *p.t.* **grucchid** complained (w. *ageyn* 'about') 233/26.

gummes *n. pl.* aromatic gums 26/3.

guttis *n. pl.* bowels 62/30.

ʒald see **ʒelde**.

ʒaue see **ʒiuing**.

ʒe *pron. 2 pl.* you 98/11, 138/29. *obl.* **ʒou** 226/19. *poss. adj.* **ʒoure** 138/29. Used as polite form to one person **ʒe** 7/16, 18/25, 116/29; **ʒou, ʒow** 7/16, 101/19, 194/29; **ʒour(e)** 8/33, 195/2; **ʒoureselue** (refl.) yourself 226/7. Cf. **þou**.

ʒelde *v.* surrender 232/14; (refl.) 246/26. *imp. sg.* **ʒeld** 246/24 (refl.). *p.t. sg.* **ʒald** 213/15 (refl.). *p.t. pl.* **ʒold(e)** 145/29 (refl.). *pp.* **ʒoldyn** 125/27; **ʒolde** 180/2.

ʒer(e) *n.* year 7/18, 20/7, 117/18. *pl.* ~ 7/25, 11/4, 151/29.

ʒeringis *n. pl.* yearlings 13/12.

ʒerli, ʒerly *adv.* annually 38/20, 189/10.

ʒet *adv.* also 9/8; still 12/24, 218/12, (w. neg.) 237/28.

ʒiuer *n.* giver 14/13.

ʒiuing *pr.p.* giving 82/29; **ʒeuing** proclaiming 66/30. *p.t. sg.* **ʒaue** 49/25. *p.t. pl.* **ʒoue** 20/34. Cf. **geue**.

ȝok *n. pl.* pair of animals coupled by a yoke 66/20.

ȝold(-) see ȝelde.

ȝong *adj.* young 33/9, 118/14; (*of*) ~ *age* (in) youth 21/16, 54/29, 195/24; *vndir* ~ *age* below the age of maturity 157/17. *compar.* ȝonger 46/9, 124/13; (absol.) 178/23; þe ~ (after person's name) junior 67/10, 145/17. *superl.* ȝongest 182/3.

ȝou, ȝow, ȝour- see ȝe.

ȝoue see ȝiuing.

ha (= *haue*) see schal, wil(l) *v.*

habite *n.* article of clothing 140/8.

habundauns *n.* abundance 22/3.

had see hath.

hald *v.* hold, observe 53/19; be held, have title derived (w. *of* 'from') 128/9. *pr.p.* haldyng celebrating 205/8. *p.t.* held joined (battle) 23/23, 129/30. *pp.* hald convened 102/22, 123/8; held, considered 41/4; hold convened 77/8, 183/7; holden 179/14; holdyn 88/8.

haliwatir *n.* holy water 52/14.

halowid *pp.* consecrated 102/21.

halp see help.

hambir *n.* hammer 13/8, (fig.) 66/27. *pl.* hamberes 13/23.

handelyng *vbl.n.* handle 92/21.

hange *v.* put to death by hanging 142/31. *pr.p.* hanging in position of suspension (at crucifixion) 111/16. *p.t.* hing 44/11, 131/11; was suspended (in crucifixion) 241/6. *pp.* hang(e) 126/17; hanged 120/24; hangid 127/29; hangged 144/29; hangen 148/8; hangin 153/18.

happed, -id *p.t.* (it) came about 36/6; (w. indir. obj.) 82/14, 129/7; happened by chance (w. pers. subj.) 144/4.

harmles *adj.* unharmed 223/5; unpunished 228/23.

harneys *n.* trappings of a horse 223/11.

hast *n.* in *in al* ~ as quickly as possible 221/27. Cf. ᵹoodly.

hast *pr. 2 sg.* see hath.

hastid *p.t.* made haste (refl.) 203/23.

hate *n.* hatred 81/30, 178/13; *in* ~ *of* out of hatred for 185/32.

hath *pr. 3 sg.* has 8/19, 22/5, 163/30; *auxil.* 9/19, 93/22, 214/15. *2 sg.* hast *auxil.* 41/1, 131/28. *p.t.* had in *had in age* was . . . (years) old 24/7; *auxil.* in *had take* took 167/4; *auxil. subj.* would have 34/16, 120/22 (2nd); in *had seid* said (w. ref. to poss. fut.) 52/24, sim. 130/12. *pp.* had held 150/20. See also lef, wers, word *n*¹.

haunted *p.t.* employed habitually 23/29.

he *pron. 3 sg. masc.* it 8/17, 21/31, 129/19. *obl.* him himself 85/16, 161/27; it 8/17, 129/21. himself itself 28/23. *poss. adj.* his its 7/18, 22/19, 127/26.

Hebrak *adj.* Hebraic 19/32.

Hebrev *n.* Hebrew 52/17.

hed see he(e)d.

heded *p.t.* beheaded 185/25. *pp.* ~, -id 49/7, 155/25.

hedyng *vbl.n.* decapitation 147/28.

hedir *adv.* (to) here 54/15.

he(e)d *n.* head 27/18, 185/28; life 55/18; (= *pl.*) lives 203/4; *for her* ~ per head 184/32 n.

he(e)r *n.* hair 50/2, 129/19.

heggis *n. pl.* hedges 164/14.

hey(er) see hie.

heil *int.* greetings! 98/32.

heilsom *adj.* wholesome 243/2.

heith *n.* height 20/16, 153/17.

held see hald.

help *v.* cure 89/4. *p.t. sg.* halp went to the assistance of 26/29. *p.t. pl.* holp(e) assisted 112/14, 141/26. *pp.* holpen cured 127/16.

helth *n.* salvation 116/26.

hem *pron. 3 pl. obl.* them, those 7/9, 11/32, 116/33; *of* ~ on their part 85/26. hemself, -selue themselves 13/11, 127/24 (refl.); *be hemself* in their own right 156/30. *poss. adj.* her(e) their 7/11, 11/27, 117/17; the inhabitants' 67/27; (absol.) theirs 97/21. Cf. þei.

hepis *n. pl.* hips 65/27.

her *poss. adj.* see hem.

her *n.* see he(e)r.

heraudis *n. pl.* messengers 121/23.

herby *adv.* in connection with this 110/1.

herborow *v.* cherish privately 24/9. *p.t.* **herborowid** lodged 146/27.

herd *pp.* heard of 224/8.

hered *p.t.* employed 56/18.

heres *n.*[1] *pl.* armies 234/31.

heres *n.*[2] *pl.* wages 196/10.

heried *pp. adj.* ploughed 245/23.

heritage *n.* hereditary succession 138/10.

herl(dam) see **erl(e), erldam.**

hert *n.*[1] stag 104/12 (1st).

hert *n.*[2] purpose 243/17; *with mery* ~ full of happiness 218/12. *pl.* **hertis** heart-shaped ornaments 224/27.

hertly *adv.* devoutly 24/9.

heruest *n.* harvest season 141/1.

hethen *adj.* Mohammedan 204/18.

heuene *n.* heaven 8/22, 20/34, 122/10.

heuy *adj.* sad 40/9, 213/3. *compar.* **heuyer** heavier 13/24.

heuynesse *n.* sadness 111/30, 139/5.

hew *p.t.* in ~ *on* struck 188/2.

hy *adv.* high 45/23. *superl.* **hiest** 98/34.

hid *pp.* concealed 11/28, 243/25; shielded 195/2.

hie *adj.* high 22/12, 218/24; **hy(e)** 34/16, 122/10, tall 99/5; **hey** 36/25. *compar.* **hier** 155/7; **heyer** 171/25. *superl.* **hiest** 18/18. Cf. **hy.**

hillis *n. pl.* exalted persons, 9/18 n.

him(self) see **he.**

hing see **hange.**

hir(e) *pron. 3 sg. fem. obl.* her 42/11, 131/1. **hirselue** herself 46/22. *poss. adj.* ~ 21/10, 128/22. Cf. **sche.**

hirun see **yrun.**

his see **he.**

hys *n.* ice 158/17.

hite *v.* (1) *act. p.t.* promised 135/28. *pp.* called 29/20, 131/23. (2) *pass. pr. 3 sg.* is called 22/6. *p.t.* 11/9, 122/21.

hodid *adj.* in ~ *men* Lollards 191/22.

hok *n.* oak-tree 110/25.

hol *adj.* hollow 110/25.

hold *n.* in *in* ~ in custody 137/19. *pl.* **holdis** strongholds 147/12.

hold(en), holdyn see **hald.**

hol(e) see **ho(o)l.**

holy *adj.* reverently set apart (from) 155/10.

holp(e), holpen see **help.**

homage *n.* in *make, took* ~ render, received homage 150/6, 103/3; **omage** 126/31.

hom(e)ly, -li *adj.* as one of the household 126/3; intimate 87/12, 156/23.

homward *adj.* on his way home 132/31.

honour *n.* in *ded* ~ paid respects 138/5.

honoured *p.t.* paid respects to 210/17; **honovrid** worshipped 37/2.

ho(o)l *adj.* in sound condition 66/15; intact 131/1; healthy 68/34; restored to health 75/20; *mad* ~ healed 77/17, 126/12; complete 8/27, 60/9.

ho(o)st *n.* army 28/32, 117/22; **o(o)st** 37/9, 222/2.

hooth *n.* oath 204/11; **oth** 107/18.

hopen see **ope.**

hordam *n.* illicit sexual indulgence 55/22.

horibil *adj.* excessive 121/21.

horologe *n.* sun-dial 37/4; clock 159/15.

horrock *n.* hold 183/18 n.

hors *n.* in *take* ~ proceed on horseback 58/1. *coll. pl.* ~ horses 142/12; mounted soldiers 201/9; *grete* ~ chargers 135/6.

horsmen *n. pl.* mounted soldiers 157/25.

hoselid *p.t.* gave consecrated host to 68/19. *pp.* (h)oseled 79/3.

hosen *n. pl.* stockings 56/10.

hospital *n.* hostel, hospice 112/10–11, 174/31.

host(is) see **ho(o)st.**

hostel *n.* lodging 217/29.

houres *n. pl.* prayers to be said at stated times of the day 100/30.

hous *n.* room 63/8 n. *pl.* in phr. *lond and* ~ land and property 56/16 n.

hucch *n.* coffer 243/9.

hundred *adj.* hundredth 16/30.

hungir *n.* famine 73/28, 122/34.

hurt *n.* force, blow 162/19.

hurt *p.t.* struck 104/10. *pp.* ~ inflicted 127/14.

ierark *n.* archbishop 228/30.

yȝe *n.* 197/2 n. *pl.* **eyne** 27/17, 249/13.

yld(e), ild(e) *n.* island 35/13, 125/24; **yle** 135/16. *pl.* **yles** 196/6. See also *Index* s.nn. **Ylde, Man, Wite.**

illuded *pp.* tricked 168/21.

ymage *n.* portrait 108/32; figure, apparition 204/15.

ymaged *p.t.* conceived 59/17. *pp.* ~ planned 156/9.

ymaginacion *n.* scheme 192/7.

Ymbir-dayes *n. pl.* Ember-days 55/27–8.

impetous *adj.* violent 219/24.

ympne *n.* hymn 70/22.

in *n.* house 195/27; (guest-)house 249/22 (2nd); *kept it as his* ~ took up residence there 145/34. *pl.* **innes** houses 216/23.

in *prep.* (of position) on 12/1, 153/17 (2nd); at 212/1; among 45/2 (2nd), 136/2; (of manner) to 13/6; (of means) with 77/10, 168/28; (of constituent) on 39/9; (of time) at 11/30, 117/12; on 37/9, 120/13; during 12/10, 151/3 (2nd); for 12/14; (pregnant uses) through 21/1; in the case of 174/5; on peril of 163/26; (of motion) into 13/28, 134/27; (in constructions) with regard to 95/14 (2nd), 174/24 n.; on 206/26; ~ *so fer þat* to the extent that 222/18.

in-as-mech *adv.* in so far (as) 175/19.

inconuenientis *n. pl.* improprieties 219/17.

incorporate *pp. adj.* united in one body (w. *to* 'with') 16/13.

incubus *n.* demon descending upon people (esp. women) in their sleep 42/2.

indignacion *n.* contempt 224/18–19.

induccioun *n.* installation (w. *of* 'in') 237/5.

induct *pp.* persuaded 242/30.

indulgens *n.* relaxation of the full rigour of the law 241/16. *pl.* ~ indulgences 199/24.

infamynde *p.t.* starved to death 132/4 n.

infect(e) *pp.* imbued with a pernicious belief (w. *in* 'with') 69/2, 121/33.

infortunat *adj.* unfortunate 230/29–30.

infortune *n.* misfortune 158/2.

inhabitable *adj.* uninhabitable 22/2.

inhabited *p.t.* peopled 19/9.

inhibite *pp.* forbidden 127/22.

innoumbirabel *adj.* innumerable 121/24.

innoumbred *adj.* countless 92/28.

inobediens *n.* disobedience 116/5.

inow *adv.* enough 104/4, 208/22.

inpenetrabel *adj.* impenetrable 105/7.

inquisicio(u)n *n.* in *make* ~ *of*/*upon* carry out official investigation into 35/4, 193/3–4.

inqwyred *pp.* asked 214/7.

insolens *n.* arrogance 31/11; overbearing governance 227/18.

in-so-mech *adv.* since, in as much as 131/33; ~ *þat* to such an extent that 36/17, 145/19.

instauns *n.* urgent entreaty 83/17, 130/15.

institucioun *n.* system of regulation 95/20.

insufficiens *n.* incapacity 116/1.

insufficient *adj.* unfit 153/27.

insulane *n.* islander 161/13.

into *prep.* to the number of 175/32.

intronized *pp.* installed 92/15, 197/26.

intrusion *n.* usurpation 9/9.

inuasif *adj.* offensive 13/20.

ypocrisie *n.* hypocrisy 188/11.

yrun *n.* in *with fire and* ~ with violently waged warfare 88/18; **hirun** appliance made of iron 218/18. *pl.* in *in yrunnes* in fetters 142/33.

issew *n.* discharge 62/29; children, descendants 14/20, 160/22; decision 187/13.

Januense *n.* Genoese 167/4.

jewelis, -es *n. pl.* costly ornaments 103/12, 138/35; **joweles** 154/17.

jogulour *n.* player, minstrel 141/16.

joy(e) *n.* state of happiness 111/4; *had* ~ (*of*) was delighted (with) 139/4; ~ *was mad* there was rejoicing 242/31.

joyned *pp. adj.* in ~ *with him* together with 88/9.

joyntis *n. pl.* gaps between inter-woven canes in basketwork 26/24.

jornay, jornai *n.* in *took his ~* set out and proceeded on his way 76/21, 139/31; military enterprise, campaign 60/8, 129/4; *make a ~* undertake an expedition 211/1; battle 153/12.

jorned *pp.* adjourned 209/14.

joweles see **jewelis.**

juge *n.* judge 27/34, 122/10.

juged *pp.* sentenced 147/28.

jugement *n.* decision 137/24.

Jule July 181/29; **Julii** 247/16.

Juni June 181/2.

just *adj.* righteous 17/31; honourable (in social dealings with) 58/3.

justeres *n. pl.* mounted knights who joust with lances 136/4.

justing *pr.p.* jousting 198/21.

justis *n. pl.* jousts 136/5.

justise *n.* jurisdiction 127/13; fair judicial decision 132/22.

kalend(e) *n.* (after ordinal number) the Nth day before the 2nd of the following month (i.e. including the 1st in the count) 108/18, 135/20. *pl.* **kalendis** 1st day of the month 99/16, 190/12.

karikis *n. pl.* galleons 247/21.

kep *n.* notice 215/3.

kepe *v.* continue to occupy 141/13; guard 52/3. *p.t.* **kept(e)** continued to occupy 70/25; (refl.) remained 43/1, 189/2; waged (war) 71/24; offered (battle) 165/15. *pp.* **kept** held 179/13.

keper *n.* governor 143/30; regent 153/4.

kyn *n.* ancestral stock 31/18; **ny of . . . kyn** closely related (to) 239/11.

kynde *n.* nature (in general) 24/1. *pl.* **kyndis** separate natures 77/12.

kynrod, -red, kinrod *n.* family, clan 15/8, 198/23; descendants 14/28; pedigree 19/5; stock 17/10; family, relatives 214/16. *pl.* **kynrodis** tribes 20/2.

knyt(e), knite *n.* (applied to person in ancient history, viewed as holding position similar to that of a medieval knight) 99/13; soldier (trans. L *miles*) 64/3. *pl.* in *knytes of þe parlement* gentlemen representing a county in parliament 227/24.

knyt(e)hod *n.* military profession 64/30; military service 44/6.

knites-mete *n.* 'knights' measure', a tax of 20s. on each knight's fee 231/6.

know(e) *v.* become acquainted with, ascertain 164/1. *pr. 2 sg.* **knowist** 164/10. *3 sg.* **knowith** 110/20, 163/30. *p.t.* **knew(e)** became aware of 167/5. *pp.* **knowe** discovered 215/29.

knowyn *pp. adj.* recognized (w. *to* 'by') 25/29.

knowyng *vbl.n.* knowledge 11/27, 222/29.

knowlech *n.* acquaintance 94/26; knowledge 72/3, 193/18; condition of understanding 14/6.

labour *n.* trouble 229/25; exertion of influence 239/19.

labour *v.* use one's influence (w. *to* 'with') 117/30. *p.t.* **laboured** trudged on 246/20.

laden *pp.* loaded 132/13.

lay see **ly.**

layd see **ley.**

lay-fe *n.* laity 81/23, 149/16.

langage *n.* talk 218/29.

langaged *pp.* enfeebled 181/26 n.

lap *n.* part of garment folded to form receptacle 208/24.

large *adj.* munificent 108/22; abundant 217/30; broad, open 9/1.

largely *adv.* generously 180/17; extensively 56/17; fully 11/19.

largenes *n.* generosity 78/1.

lasse *adj. compar.* less 185/8; **lesse** inferior (w. *þan* 'to') 61/32.

lasse *adv.* in *þe ~* the less 155/32.

last *adj. superl.* as *n.* in *at þe ~* finally, eventually 23/28, 126/4.

lastid see **lest(id).**

lat *imper.* let 8/9. *p.t.* **let(e)** leased 182/21; caused 186/2, *let(e) make* caused to be made 21/16, 121/12.

late *adv.* recently 172/25; a very short time 167/6.

laude *n.* paean of praise 157/28.

lawe *n.* general practice 9/6; *þe* ~, *Moyses* ~ Pentateuch 40/13, 35/7; *þe Elde* ~, *þe* ~ *of God* Old Testament 55/11, 43/13.

lawh *v.* laugh 57/9. *p.t.* **low** 23/34.

lawhing *vbl.n.* laughter 23/35.

leche *n.* medical practitioner 53/1; spiritual adviser 106/18.

leddir *n.* skin 29/18.

lede *v.* take 138/28; convey 94/22, 171/11; escort 206/19. *pr. 3 sg.* **ledith** *leads* 8/39. *p.t.* **led(de)** took 38/22, 138/26; conveyed 81/8, 131/10; escorted 192/11; accompanied 87/12. *pp.* **led** taken 23/31, 124/20; escorted 201/8.

lederis *n. pl.* counsellors, guides 195/24.

leed *n.* leaden coffin 176/27.

lef *adj.* in *I had as* ~ . . . *as* I would just as soon . . . as 111/10.

le(f)ful *adj.* permissible, lawful 93/15, 235/28.

left(e) *p.t.*, *pp.* see **leue** *v.*, **lift(e)**.

leftenaunt *n.* regent 102/12.

legacion *n.* request 203/30.

legatis, **-es** *n. pl.* envoys 44/17, 237/3.

legauns *n.* allegiance 221/14; **ligauns** 192/31.

legittimat *pp.* legitimized 205/13.

ley *v.* in ~ *plegges* give up as hostages 244/22. *pr. 2 sg. subj.* put 8/19. *p.t.* in *leid aboute* (*refl.*) surrounded 194/21. *pp.* **leyd(e)**, **leid**, **layd** buried 81/6; put 142/33; imposed 178/1; (phr.) *leyd in plegge* given as hostages 115/7; *leyd to a contribucion* compelled to make a payment 149/18 n.; *leyd to* placed in juxtaposition with 110/25.

leiser(e) *n.* opportunity 44/24; time 47/11.

lende *v.* grant 199/5. *p.t.* **lent** 117/32.

lenger *adj. compar.* longer 37/3. *adv.* ~ 41/19, 140/28.

length *n.* in *o* ~ in distance 210/27.

lengthid *pp.* added on 37/5.

Lenton *n.* Lent 82/4, 187/27.

lepre, **-er** *n.* leprosy 34/6.

lerned *pp.* taught 83/26; educated 103/23.

lese *v.* lose 97/7, 137/17.

lesing *vbl.n.* loss 152/16.

lesse see **lasse**.

lest *pr. 2 sg. subj.* wish 60/24.

lest(id), **-ed** *p.t.* lasted 23/11, 180/20; **lastid** continued 184/25.

letanie *n.* litany 75/24.

let(e) see **lat**.

let(te) *v.* stand in way of, prevent 64/2, 135/27, (w. inf. 'from') 212/15, (w. *of* 'from') 212/2. *pr.p.* **letting** 188/15. *p.t.* **lette(t)** 50/27, 151/2, **letted**, **-id** 95/16, 147/16. *pp.* **lettid** 24/13, 181/21.

letter *n.* preventer 249/3.

lettered *pp. adj.* educated 65/15.

letterure *n.* learning 164/2.

lettyng *vbl.n.* prevention 180/4.

lettir *n.* writing 116/19. *pl.* **letteres** inscription 110/26.

leue *n.* in *took* ~ obtained permission 208/8.

leue *v.* abandon 70/19; raise (siege) 180/6; desist from 175/18. *pr. pl.* ~ discontinue 42/17. *p.t.* **left(e)** abandoned 44/5, 129/4; desisted from 45/1, 130/25; remained 20/3, 166/22.

leue live, **leuyng**, **leued**, **-yd** see **lyue** *v.*

leuene *n.* (flash of) lightning 23/31, 130/29.

lewed *adj.* in ~ *men* lay-brothers 242/14.

ly *v.* be in a prostrate position 57/31. *pr. 3 sg.* **lith** is buried 58/15, 125/33; (hist.) died 75/25 n.; rests 8/20; remains 7/31. *pl.* ~ are buried 95/28. *pr.p.* **lyand** situated 21/31. *p.t.* **lay** lodged 104/7, 166/10; was staying 144/2.

licens *n.* permission 103/33.

license *v.* release 242/17.

lich *adj.* like 9/11, 21/17, 129/17.

lich *adv.* like 87/7, 124/23; ~ *as* as though 194/22.

lichmen see **ligeman**.

lycour *n.* liquid 99/6.

lif see **lyue** *n.*

lyflod(e), **liflod** *n.* means of living 213/10; stipend 150/22; property yielding income 154/15.

lift *adj.* left 28/11.

lift(e) *p.t.* lifted 34/5; **left** raised

175/13; ~ *up* removed 57/15. *pp.*
lift taken up and removed 11/5; in
lift, left up raised up 26/27, 131/3.
ligauns see **legauns.**
lige *n.* vassal 106/4.
ligeman *n.* vassal 101/25. *pl.* **lige-men** 126/22; **lichmen, lych-** 116/
8, 211/28.
liknes *n. pl.* likenesses 28/24.
lym-whiting *n.* whitewash 181/13.
lynand *adj.* linen 108/32, 131/5. *n.*
50/2, 242/15.
lyne *n.* supporting cord 107/33. *pl.*
lines degrees, marks on a sun-dial
37/4.
lystir *n.* reader 183/30.
lite *n.* (coll. sg.) candles 21/19.
litely *adv.* easily 138/31.
lith see **ly.**
lithnes *n.* agility 42/2.
litil *adj.* small 53/7.
litil, lytyl *n.* in *a ~ fro* not far from
74/13, 167/11.
lityng *pr.p.* alighting 56/28.
lyue *n.* life 8/29, 48/23, 247/11; **lif**
in *haue lif* remain alive 148/9; *his*
~ during his lifetime 137/15; *for*
his ~ for the remainder of his lifetime 114/2.
lyue *v.* live; **leue** 116/23; ~ *and*
dey(e) risk death 139/18, (w. *on*
'against') 145/22. *pr. 3 sg.* **lyueth**
is living 33/30. *pr.p.* **lyuand** 225/
15, **leuyng** 72/27. *p.t.* **leued, -yd**
22/1, 134/15. *pp.* **leued** 16/26.
lyuyng *vbl.n.* manner of life 36/32,
125/3.
lo *int.* look 240/14.
loke *v.* see 221/8. *imper.* ~ make
sure 8/35. *pr.p.* **lokyng** seeing
212/1. *p.t.* in *loked aftir* sought
for 240/24.
lomb *n.* lamb 114/7.
lond *n.* land 7/6, 19/2, 117/6; tract
of land 245/23. *pl.* **londis** ground
158/21.
londe *v.* land 165/4. *p.t.* **londid,**
-ed, -yd 102/1, 151/30. *pp.*
londed 157/4.
londyng *vbl.n.* landing 182/23.
lone *n.* forced contribution 200/9.
long(e) *v.* be appropriate 7/12; be a
part (w. *to* 'of') 188/3. *pr. 3 sg.*

longith, -eth pertains 8/16, 13/30;
(it) is fitting 117/14; is the property (w. *to* 'of') 203/5. *pl.* ~,
longyn, -in pertain 13/9, 145/4;
belong 204/2; are the property (of)
140/32. *pr.p.* **longing** pertaining
44/1; dependent (w. *to* 'on') 184/6;
being the property (of) 137/16.
p.t. **longid, -ed** was appropriate
189/19; pertained 34/29; was dependent (on) 133/22; was the
property (of) 159/30.
Long(o)bardis, Lumbardes *n. pl.*
Lombards 73/1, 174/23. See also
Index, s.n. **Lumbardi.**
lordchip *n.* rule 60/7; lord's domain
138/33; territory of ruler 76/13,
176/1–2.
losed *p.t.* released 173/18; dispensed
with 116/11.
lost *p.t.* got no return for 229/25.
loude *adv.* loudly 74/19, 249/16.
low see **lawh.**
lowd *adj.* noisy 119/14.
Lumbardes see **Long(o)bardis.**

may *pr. 2, 3 sg./pl.* can 7/16, 15/1,
216/13; were to 215/29. *p.t.* **myte,**
mite, mith could 25/2, 118/27.
mayde *n.* girl 206/17; young unmarried woman 36/6; virgin (of the
Virgin Mary) 47/16, 166/16; male
virgin 11/16.
mayden *n.* young unmarried woman
36/4; ~ *Marie* Virgin Mary 175/28.
maydenhod *n.* virginity 220/6.
maistir, maystir *n.* leader 121/32;
master 21/19, 174/31; tutor 41/26;
spiritual leader 27/21, 140/8; quali-
fied teacher 181/7; as title prefixed
to name of man of learning or high
(ecclesiastical) rank 109/5, 119/35.
pl. **maistires** scholars 87/10.
makith *pr. 3 sg.* offers 48/12; ~
mencioun, mynde mentions 16/14,
107/14; hist. in ~ *an ende* came
to the end 38/10.
malandryn *n.* brigand 243/7.
malapert *adj.* presumptuous, im-
pudent 113/24, 180/22.
malice, malys *n.* wickedness 69/31,
191/20; harmful action 189/25;

malice (*cont.*):
spite 130/25; malicious conduct 111/21, 145/4.
malicious *adj.* wicked 86/16.
malle *n.* heavy hammer 29/5.
malt *p.t. sg.* melted 13/25. *pp.* **molten** 13/28, 115/9.
maner *n.* form 172/7; *be no ~ ne no weye* not at all 205/28; usual way 99/13; custom 142/3; sort, kind in *what ~ what* kind of 8/11, *al*(*l*) *~* all kinds of 18/10, 50/4, 129/20, *no ~ no* . . . at all 226/29; *in ~* so to speak 116/31, to a considerable degree 193/26; *in swech ~* for such a reason 149/18. *pl.* **maneris, -es** habitual (moral) behaviour 45/25.
manhod *n.* courage 69/19, 202/27.
Manichees *n. pl.* adherents of Manichaeism 59/16.
manly *adv.* valiantly 131/13.
mansion *n.* house 118/9.
manslauth, -slawth *n.* manslaughter 44/7, 116/6, 144/18.
mantel, -il *n.* cloak 34/23.
marc see **mark.**
march *n.* in *~ of Wales* Welsh border lands 145/10. *pl.* **marches** 128/33.
marchale *n.* master of ceremonies 95/24.
marchaund, -t *n.* merchant, wholesale trader 249/15, 207/10.
marchaundise *n.* business transaction 174/24; saleable commodities 183/2.
mariages *n. pl.* (royal right to exact) fines for marriage of vassals 156/23.
marices *n. pl.* marshes 148/2.
mark, marc *n.* monetary unit of value of 66⅔*p.* (160*d.*) 103/19, 123/35; *VIIId. of þe ~* levy of one-twentieth of valuation 142/19.
markeis, -eys *n.* marquis 95/23, 189/6.
market *n.* market-place 25/23; *kepe ~ trade* 132/8.
markyd see **merked.**
mateyns *n. pl.* canonical hour, prop. a midnight office 100/30.
mater *n.* topic 21/13; business 148/28. *pl.* **materis** affairs 139/17.
mavment *n.* idol 36/18.

maumentrie *n.* idolatry 21/6; idols 36/17.
Mauritanes *n. pl.* people of Morocco 19/13.
Maurus *adj.* Moorish, from Africa 173/15.
mech *adj.* big 104/4; great 12/36, 124/9, **mechil** 164/12; much 7/10, 15/5, 136/12; *~ folk, puple* a large number of people 21/32, 165/19; *~ þing* many things 17/26, 117/26; (absol.) as *n.* 19/9, 132/27.
mech *adv.* much, greatly 8/16, 14/24, 194/11.
meditaciones *n. pl.* thoughts 8/12.
meyhir *n.* Roman prefect 58/7; mayor 144/27, **meir** 186/7.
meynteyneres *n. pl.* supporters (of wrongdoers) 204/4.
meynten *v.* maintain 226/11; aid and abet 202/15; uphold 204/9. *pr.p.* **meyntenyng** aiding and abetting 249/4. *p.t.* **meynte(y)ned** aided and abetted 12/36; upheld 77/10, 170/22. *pp.* **meynteyned** advocated 236/2; upheld 65/13.
meke *adj.* compassionate 52/27.
membris *n. pl.* limbs 66/15, 129/20; penises 219/16; branches of the body politic 214/14.
mende *n.* recollection 154/14; *in ~* remembered 159/12.
mendinauntis *n. pl.* mendicants 205/22.
mene *adj.* moderate 53/7.
mene *n.* compromise 132/30; *be swech/þis ~* thus 137/7, 232/4; *be ~ of* through 189/2. *pl.* **menes** intermediaries 202/16; opportunities 236/6; *fynde menys of* secure 132/32; *be ony menis* at all 232/16.
meneth, -yth *pr. 3 sg.* means 21/22, 166/16.
meny *n.* retinue 97/12; followers 121/5; company of armed men 121/28, **mené** 177/23.
Menoures, Menowres *n. pl.* Franciscans 113/5, 123/4.
Menouris *adj. pl.* in *Frere ~* Franciscan friars 47/22, 120/35.
mercy *n.* in *was take to ~* was pardoned 72/22.
mery *adj.* cheerful 213/25.

merily, meryly *adv.* pleasantly 150/17; agreeably 193/22.

merk *n.* sign 214/11; appearance (indicating impending death) 11/21.

merked *p.t.* observed 99/18. *pp.* **merkyd** invested with the sign of the cross (as token of joining a crusade) 121/16; **markyd** 186/29.

merour *n.* (fig.) exemplar 188/11.

merth see **myrth**.

merueile, merueyle *n.* astonishing occurrence 210/28; wonder 109/33, 245/14; *had ~ of* were astonished at 237/30. *pl.* **merueyles** miracles 172/30.

merueyle *pr. 2 pl.* wonder 7/19. *p.t.* **merue(i)led, merueyled, -id** was filled with wonder (w. *of* 'at') 41/15, 200/17.

meruelous *adj.* remarkable 29/26, 119/12.

meruelously *adv.* in a manner to be wondered at 39/11.

message *n.* business 146/13.

messager(e) *n.* messenger 65/27, 180/5; envoy 26/34, 200/20, **messanger** 210/13.

messe *n.* mass 49/21, 172/22.

mesure *n.* upper limit 29/14 (of river level), 110/30 (of human stature).

mesured *pp.* restrained 65/15.

mete *n.* food 18/12, 123/7; *at (his) ~* at the/his meal table 93/18, 176/15; *at tyme of ~* at meal time 113/24; *went to ~* sat down at the meal table 206/22; *aftir ~* after the meal 206/25.

mete *v.* in *~ with* encounter 144/16. *pr. 1 sg.* sim. 115/17. *p.t.* **met(te)** joined 162/15; *met(te) with* met (face to face) 171/13, encountered 132/14.

meve *pr. pl.* propound 14/9. *p.t.* **meued** influenced 221/24. *pp.* **meued, -yd, mevid** angered 138/8; influenced 222/8; urged 119/22.

meuyng *vbl.n.* impulse 8/36. *pl.* **meuyngis** movements 159/15.

myd *adj.* middle of (the) 53/19, 190/14.

myddis *n.* middle 121/24.

Myhilmesse *n.* Michaelmas, feast-day of St. **Michael** the archange (29 Sept.) 143/16; **Mihelmesse Day** 213/24.

myn *poss. adj.* my 7/26, 98/24, 226/20.

ministres *n. pl.* attendants 39/13.

mynstralsie *n.* musical instrument 29/10–11.

myrth *n.* joke 57/9; **merth** fun 114/3.

mischef *n.* misfortune 66/33; distress 141/4; trouble 241/16; injury 164/4.

myscheuous *adj.* harmful 116/5.

mysel *n.* leper 75/19.

Missomyr *n.* attrib. in *~ Euen* day before Midsummer Day (24 June) 179/2.

mysti *adj.* spiritual 84/31.

mysused *p.t.* dishonoured 156/10.

myte *n.* power 204/20.

myte, mith, see **may**.

myty *adj.* powerful 83/19, 175/1; imposing 66/27; *with ~ hand* with a strong army 187/2.

mo *adj.* more 199/31; *no ~ . . . but* only 246/27. Cf. **more.**

mo(o) *adv.* besides 153/11.

mo(o) *quasi-pron.* more 162/14; others 181/19, in *many ~* 47/14, 127/30, *no ~* 178/18 could also be *adv.* 'besides'.

mocions *n. pl.* inclinations 238/20.

Moises-werk *n.* mosaic designs 78/26.

molten see **malt**.

Monalechites *n. pl.* Monothelites 76/18.

mony *n.* coin 121/12; coinage 127/25.

monstrows *adj.* unnatural 24/1.

morder *n.* slaughter 85/18.

more *adj. compar.* bigger 38/7; greater 160/7; *þe ~ part* the majority 60/16. *superl.* **most** in *þe~ part* nearly all 72/2, 142/17. Cf. **mo(o).**

more *adv. compar.* furthermore 127/8. *superl.* **most** mostly 144/22.

mored *p.t.* enlarged 53/5.

morow *n.* morning 52/25, 172/32; next day 37/11, 206/1.

morown *n.* morning 224/1.

morownyng, -ing *n.* morning 37/10, 246/20.

most see **more**.

mote *pr. pl.* must 222/16; (hist.) had to 207/10.

mount *n.* hill 35/16.

multiplied *p.t.* augmented 51/13; accumulated 43/17; brought together an abundance of 185/3–4. *pp.* ~ increased by procreation 16/2.

mummeres *n. pl.* actors in Christmas play 216/5.

munkys *n. pl.* in **blake** ~ Benedictines 118/1.

murmour *n.* discontent 211/20.

mussel *n.* morsel 101/20.

nacio(u)n *n.* country 108/12; nationality 51/30. *pl.* **naciones** Gentiles 23/8.

nay *adv.* no 202/15.

naked *adj.* unsheathed 74/18.

name *n.* existence 39/24. *pl.* **names** titles 215/22.

named *pp. adj.* renowned 202/27.

namely *adv.* in particular 62/24.

natif *adj.* (w. *to*) born (in) 108/9.

nature *n.* physical strength 126/12; in *of* ~ by virtue of his very character 235/29.

naue, nauy *n.* fleet 125/23, 177/6.

nawt see **nowt**.

Nazareis *n. pl.* Nazarites 31/30.

ne *conj.* nor 14/16, 117/16; and (w. neg. following) 141/26; and . . . not 137/2.

necligens *n.* negligence 31/10.

nede *adv.* of necessity 222/16. **nedis** 246/19.

nede *n.* emergency 231/28; (phr.) *for* ~ by necessity 55/5; *is* ~ is necessary 241/5; *had* ~ was in straits 180/16.

nedist *pr. 2 sg.* require 41/1. *pr. 3 sg.* **nedith** is under a necessity 180/14.

nest *adj. superl.* following 233/1.

nether *adj.* lower 65/26.

neue *n.* nephew 107/15, 221/12; grandson 68/1; descendant 19/32 n.

neuyrþelasse *adv.* nonetheless 119/23.

new *adv.* afresh 40/17, 215/7; newly 13/28, 139/4.

newly *adv.* very recently 235/4.

new-schaue *pp. adj.* newly shaved 104/8–9.

next *adv. superl.* (as *prep.*) closest to 131/5; nearest to 48/25, 156/6; immediately after 56/26.

ny *adj.* related by blood 193/24.

ny *adv.* (as *prep.*) near 190/18; (w. *at, be, onto*) close to 142/7, 200/4, 15/21; closely related 239/10; almost 7/11, 23/3, 124/15. *compar.* **nyher** nearer 161/8.

nygromancer *n.* necromancer 94/29.

nigromancie, -y *n.* necromancy 63/24, 219/27.

nyhyng *vbl.n.* neighing 40/23.

no *adj.* (in double neg. constructions) (not) any 24/28 (2nd), 127/23 (2nd).

nobil *n.* noble, English gold coin worth 33½p. (6s. 8d.) 172/18.

noble *adj.* outstandingly skilful 45/15.

noye *v.* trouble 37/9, 236/5.

noyse *n.* report 74/20; common talk 160/14.

noyse *v.* spread rumours 224/25; defame 221/21. *p.t.* **noysed** spread rumours 78/16, 144/26. *pp.* **noysed** reported 190/10.

noyseres *n. pl.* spreaders of rumour 218/30.

non *adj.* (not) any, no 54/8, 199/20.

norched, -id *p.t.* reared 36/10; fostered 55/32, 141/18. *pp.* ~ nurtured 26/26; promoted 56/1.

norcher *n.* promoter 188/11.

Normanndes *n. pl.* Normans 89/2, 131/14; **Normanntes** 132/7.

northen *adj.* northern 213/17.

not *adv.* (redundant after v. of forbidding) 174/3.

not *n.* nothing 32/4, 137/11.

notarie *n.* secretary 69/12.

noten *v.* in *is for to* ~ is to be noticed 39/21 (sim. 17/9). *pp.* **noted** stigmatized 152/27.

noþing *adv.* not at all 123/12.

noþing *n.* (in double neg. construction) (not) anything 193/21.

notwithstand(ing) *conj.* although 211/8; ~ *þat* 7/27, 182/18.

noumberes *n. pl.* consecutive natural numbers beginning with one 8/26 n.

now *adv.* in *as* ~ at this time 108/28.

nowil *n.* navel 65/25.

nowt *adj.* worthless 212/13 (1st).

nowt *adv.* not at all 141/26; not 12/9, 149/11.

nowt *n.* nothing 83/8, 212/13 (2nd); *rith* ~ nothing at all 103/21, 154/19, sim. **nawt** 221/8; *for* ~ in vain 171/19.

o see **o(f)** *prep.*; **on** *adj.*; **o(n)** *prep.*

obediens *n.* rule 177/33; respectful submission 7/3; *do* ~ show reverence 183/6; *mad* ~ did homage 182/19.

obe(y)chauns *n.* authority 116/8, 202/20; **obejauns** submission 133/14 n.

obey(e) *v.* allow 235/17; ~ *to* be obedient to 242/21. *p.t.* in *obeyed/-id (on)to* 60/18, 187/16.

objecciones *n. pl.* charges 149/26.

occean *n.* prop. name of great outer sea surrounding the mass of land of the E hemisphere 14/18. See also **se(e)**.

occupacion *n.* use 83/27; exercise 44/6.

octaue *n.* eighth day after a festival 202/11.

Octones *n. pl.* Ottos (I, II, and III) 95/18. See *Index*, s.n. **Octo**.

of *adv.* cut off 83/1.

o(f), off *prep.* (of liberation and privation) from 28/14, 122/7; (of source) after 18/28, from 24/16 (1st), 124/27, on 93/34 (2nd), 149/30; (of reason or motivation) on 143/24, out of 69/31, 130/25, ~ *himself* of his own volition 155/26, on account of 20/31, 125/26 (2nd); (of agent) by 11/16 (3rd), 117/35; (of means) with 103/34 (1st); (of concern) as regards, in respect of 81/18, 138/29, with regard to, about 12/5, 123/17; (in *v.* phr.) at 126/10, for 68/22, 124/29, subject to 126/32 (1st), over 28/25, 121/29; (for gen. of quality) in 99/4 (2nd), 210/27; (in loc. and sim. uses) on 88/22 (1st), 174/22, to 121/31 (2nd).

offir *v.* make sacrifices 15/30; show 7/4. *p.t.* **offered** made presentation of 86/26, 166/9; proposed 180/16.

o-fire *adv.* on fire 234/23.

ofte *adv.* often 93/27, 221/3.

oftentyme *adv.* many times 146/10.

oft-tyme *adv.* many times 74/17.

oyle *n.* (fig.) soothing words 12/31.

olde see **eld(e)**.

Olimpias *n. pl.* Olympiads 30/18 n.

o-lyue *adj.* alive 16/8, 196/5.

olyue-tre *n.* olive-wood 21/9.

omage see **homage**.

omelies *n. pl.* sermons 91/6.

on *num. adj.* one 7/19, 12/1, 122/32. **o** 7/8, 11/8, 118/25; same 101/20. ~ *and fifty* fifty-first 181/22; *al* ~ the same 228/14; used predic. in *be her* ~ alone together 126/6.

on *pron.* one 21/5, 119/10; someone 40/3, 137/30; a man 29/20.

o(n) *prep.* (of time) during 96/25, in ~ *a tyme* on one occasion 92/26, ~ *a/o day* one day 109/28, 162/23; (of manner) in 72/15 (1st), 116/31; (of direction) against 44/29, 249/21, at 139/32, ~ *peces* into pieces 107/32; unto 92/1, with regard to 155/28; with 101/30, of 238/9.

onbiried *pp. adj.* unburied 60/27.

onbrent *pp. adj.* unburnt 26/34.

onclennes *n.* moral impurity 38/2.

onde *n.* breath 53/8.

ondo *pp.* opened 77/28, 140/6.

ones *adv.* on one occasion 32/29; at any time 223/14.

ongentyly *adv.* roughly 154/27.

ony *adj.* any 14/21, 122/8; (absol.) either 233/13.

ony *pron.* any persons 194/29.

o-nites *adv.* at night 82/9.

onyþing *pron.* anything 68/26.

onkende, -kynd, vnkynde *adj.* ungrateful 45/7, 216/2; **onkind** hostile 113/1.

onknowe *pp. adj.* unknown 192/7.

onknowyng *pr.p. adj.* ignorant of 87/14.

onleful *adj.* illicit 94/7.

onmanerly *adv.* disrespectfully 114/23.

onrithfully *adv.* wrongly 163/9–10; **vnritefully** 168/14.

onto *prep.* to 7/4, 12/30, 117/23; towards 176/20; until 53/18, 119/32; under 202/20; into 41/10, 137/31; up to 222/23; down to 88/29, 178/2; against 49/26; in

onto (*cont.*):
honour of 51/21; upon 179/1; for 113/19, 161/27.

ontretable *adj.* intractable 129/3.

ontrew(e) *adj.* unfaithful 157/14; unjust 199/11. Cf. **vntreuly.**

oost see **ho(o)st.**

ope *adj.* open 98/12, 161/29; **hopen** 25/23.

openly *adv.* plainly 32/16.

opinion *n.* in *ageyn þe ~ of many men* despite general disapproval 205/12; *was in swech ~* had such a reputation 87/9.

oppresse *v.* quell 45/4; suppress 203/20. *p.t.* **oppressed** crushed 31/2; bore down 29/1. *pp.* **oppressed** smothered 209/13.

oppressing *vbl.n.* oppression 227/28.

opteyned *p.t.* secured agreement (that) 184/6.

or *conj.* before 16/27, 119/26; ~ *þat* 109/12. Cf. **er.**

or *prep.* before 31/28, 151/8.

ordeyne *v.* provide 147/3. *imper.* **ordeyn** arrange 97/25. *p.t.* **ordeyned** instituted 52/14; set up 58/21; equipped 131/13; appointed 60/30; enacted 131/17; determined 136/21. *pp.* **ordeyned** instituted 75/15; devised 227/27; equipped 187/19; assigned 235/3; enacted 86/18.

order, -ir *n.* ecclesiastical position 225/30; condition (regarded as equivalent to holy orders) 225/31.

ordinacioun *n.* divine decree 14/27.

ordinarie *n.* person of ecclesiastical authority 239/14.

ordinauns, ordenauns *n.* literary plan 248/11; contrived plan 155/2; military device 234/18; established rule 97/30; injunction 140/20; prescribed usage 231/19.

orgo(u)n *n.* musical (wind) instrument 13/7; agent 188/9.

orison, -en *n.* prayer 86/33; praying 66/11.

o-rowe *adv.* in a line 7/23.

oseled see **hoselid.**

o-side *adv.* away from consideration 118/29.

ost see **ho(o)st.**

oterauns *n.* statements 204/14.

oth see **hooth.**

oþir, othir *adj.* rest of the 54/25; another 146/27; different 53/6; others who were 143/9; *a ~* another 102/26; ~ *many/thre* many/three others 192/16, 131/23; ~ *to* the two remaining 109/32. *absol.* the other 39/12, 157/9; second 238/10; others 7/22, 38/18, 119/29; *a ~* another 41/3, 122/33; *no/ony ~* no-/anyone else 149/19, 122/8.

oþir, othir *pron.* others 106/6, 152/4.

oþirwise, -wyse *adv.* differently (w. *þan* 'from') 151/5; in another way 177/14.

oure *poss. adj.* (used of single person by himself) my ('editorial') 33/17, 116/30. *absol.* ours 228/14. See also **us, we.**

oute *adv.* abroad 71/8; extinguished 99/8. *prep. phr.* ~ *of* from: (w. ellipsis of v. of motion) gone from 79/8, coming from 221/26; (as v.) depart from 122/19.

outelawed *pp.* banished 120/25.

outeward *adv.* externally 155/1; outwardly 205/8-9.

ouyr *adv.* too 95/3, 127/30.

ouyr *prep.* in addition to 181/13.

ouircomer *n.* conqueror 65/16.

ouyrcured *p.t.* covered up 158/21.

ouyrflew *p.t.* inundated 18/17. *pp.* **ouirflowe** 29/13.

ouirlyued *p.t.* outlived 103/19.

ouyrryde *pr. 3 pl. subj.* crush by riding all over 175/28. *p.t. pl.* **ouyrrydin** 175/17. *pp.* **ouyrrydyn** 171/5.

ouyr-sone *adv.* too readily 134/4.

ouirthrowe *pp.* defeated 219/15.

ouir-wel *adv.* too much 21/15-16.

owith *pr. 3 sg.* is under obligation to acknowledge/render 103/1. *pl.* **owe** 202/21. *p.t.* **aute** 130/1, **awte** 133/6.

pay *pr. 3 sg. subj.* (absol.) make recompense 152/16. *p.t.* in *payed rite not* made no recompense at all 211/2.

paynymes *n. pl.* infidels 174/28.

paleis, -eys *n.* palace 25/1, 135/31.

palle *n.* woollen vestment conferred by pope on archbishop 102/27.

Panormitanes *n. pl.* citizens of Palermo, Sicily 129/25–6.

parable *n.* fictitious allegorical narrative 29/31 n.

paralisé *n.* paralysis 125/33; **paralsie** 188/12 n.

parch *n.* parish 118/9.

parfit(e) *adj.* fully accomplished 17/32; faultless 48/13; completely excellent 220/7.

parfitely *adv.* thoroughly 8/6.

park *n.* deer-park 164/12.

parlement *n.* attrib. in *in þe ~ tyme* during the parliament 232/20.

part *n.* side, party, faction 133/10; (phr.) *þe betir ~* the upper hand 232/25.

party, -ie *n.* ellipt. for *in ~* (18/18) partly 29/18; state of mind 127/13; *on o ~* on the one hand 137/13. *pl.* **partyes** regions 152/10; *on both ~* as far as both sides are concerned 132/23.

particuler *adj.* constituent 8/25 n.

pascale *n.* Easter candle 67/20.

Pase *n.* Easter 49/18.

Pas(e)-day *n.* Easter Day 53/19, 192/8.

Pase-tyme *n.* period of the Easter festival 139/32.

passage *n.* movement 160/6; way 127/1; ford 165/11.

passes *n. pl.* paces, (approx.) yards 18/13.

passid *prep.* more than 169/29.

passing *adv.* exceedingly 82/13, 125/9.

passing *prep.* more than 245/13.

passio(u)n *n.* martyrdom 91/21; bodily disorder 33/17.

passith *pr. 3 sg.* surpasses 54/22. *p.t.* **passed** exceeded 30/28.

past *n.* dough 74/30 n.

patentis *n. pl.* letters patent 211/8.

patently *adv.* openly 175/23.

pax *n.* plate used to convey the kiss of peace 77/19.

pe(e)s *n.* peace 24/25, 117/7; friendly recognition 124/34; protection 47/9;(phr.) *þe ~ the law of the land* 202/14; *hold his ~* keep quiet 197/9.

peyn(e) *n.* punishment 193/9; penalty 124/31; *up ~ of* on peril of losing 152/18.

peyned *p.t.* starved 217/7.

peisid *p.t.* weighed; in *~ heuyly* resented 114/36.

Pelagianes *n., poss. pl.* followers of **Pelagius** 66/24.

peloure *n.* fur 174/6.

pelow *n.* pillow 90/14.

penauns *n.* penitence 37/19; *do ~* repent 241/15.

peny *n.* in *~ of gold* gold coin issued in 1257 and worth 20 silver pennies 121/13; *þe x ~* tax of one-tenth of valuation (of) 160/3. *pl.* in *pens of too pens* half-groat 167/16 n.

penytauncer *n.* Grand Penitentiary, confessor who assigns penance in unusual cases 118/34.

pension *n.* fee 182/22.

Pent(e)cost *n.* Whitsun 170/7. As *adj.* in *þe Moneday in ~ weke* Whit-Monday 229/5.

perauenture *adv.* perhaps 53/5.

perch *v.* cease to exist 13/17. *p.t.* **perchid** died 246/16.

percid *pp.* stabbed 222/18.

perel *n.* in *þe ~ of* the danger caused by exposure to 224/3; *it was ~ it* was dangerous 163/32.

peres *n. pl.* equals 243/20.

perfeccion *n.* completion 8/16.

perjure *adj.* perfidious 233/7.

Perses *n. pl.* Persians 39/16, 55/13 n.

pes[1] see **pe(e)s**.

pes[2] *n.* coin 210/21.

pesibel *adj.* peaceable 95/1.

pesibyly *adv.* without dispute 168/13; **pesabely** amicably 224/13.

Petir-peny *n.* Peter's pence, ecclesiastical tax formerly paid in England to the pope 108/16; also called **Rome-scot** 86/27.

Pharao *n., poss. sg.* Pharaoh's 26/26. *pl.* **Pharaones** 22/15.

philisofer, -sophre *n.* philosopher 40/5. *pl.* **philisoph(e)res** learned men 14/25.

Philisteis *n. pl.* Philistines 31/14.

Picardis *n. pl.* inhabitants of Picardy 190/8.

pike *n.* point 122/12.

pilgrimage *n.* journey 35/12. *pl.* **pylgrimages** places of pilgrimage 158/1.

pilgrime *n.* traveller 24/13.

pilled *pp.* plundered 229/28.

pité *n.* in *had ~ on* was compassionate towards 234/9.

pix *n.* pyx, vessel in which consecrated bread is kept 107/33.

place *n.* square 25/23; buildings 185/33; lodging-place 146/27; palace 186/1; religious house 113/12, 126/14; house of worship 33/21, 137/31; portico 77/4; *strong ~* fortified position 236/15. *pl.* **places** shrines 108/34.

play *n.* sport (general) 30/25. *pl.* **playes** games 30/23; **pleyes** sports 196/12.

playstir *n.* curative plaster 37/7.

planetis *n. pl.* heavenly bodies which (acc. to Ptolemaic system) rotated around the earth 14/26.

ple *n.* law-suit 184/6.

plegge *n.* person who goes surety 124/19.

pleyes see **play**.

pleyn *adj.* level with the ground 164/14; clear 127/21.

pleynes *n. pl.* sides, flat surfaces 8/19.

pleynly *adv.* openly 221/1.

plener *adj.* absolute 189/22.

plenté *n.* abundance 33/18, 183/2; large number 22/3.

plenteuously *adv.* fully 29/11; generously 32/31.

plesauns *n.* delight 13/21; will 12/17, 129/13; pleasantness 162/4; enjoyment (w. *of* 'gained from') 33/3; (phr.) *do ~ to* please 142/30; *(was) ~ (on)to* pleased 25/29, 238/23.

plesaunt *adj.* pleasing 24/14.

plese *v.* appease 236/2. *pp.* **plesed** 236/4.

plete *v.* argue (for or against) 180/25. *pp.* **pleted** been advocate (for) 122/5; formally pleaded 25/21.

plowmen *n. pl.* farm-labourers 106/12.

pluralités *n. pl.* benefices held together 173/30.

podegra *n.* gout in the feet 33/17.

poyntelis *n. pl.* writing instruments 86/16.

poyntment *n.* coming to terms 166/10.

polled *pp. adj.* tonsured 183/11.

pored *p.t.* poured 13/27.

porely *adv.* in frugal style 102/32, 150/29.

porged, -id see **purgith**.

porrect *pp.* presented 209/18.

porsewe see **pursewe**.

port *n.* estuary 161/4. *pl.* in *þe v portes* the Cinque Ports (between Hastings and Sandwich) 146/14.

possession *n.* wealth 56/17 n.; (phr.) *þe regal ~* the occupancy of the Crown 108/3.

possibilité *n.* capability 7/6–7.

postiled *p.t.* wrote comments on 121/1.

postis *n. pl.* upright supports 31/1.

potestates *n. pl.* rulers, kings 9/5, 22/12.

pouert *n.* poverty 44/22.

pound *n. pl.* pounds (weight) 71/15; (money) 96/21, 117/32.

power *n.* physical strength 30/22; might 41/31; legal authority 209/18; military strength, army 33/24, 117/12; (phr.) *aftir her ~* according to their ability 236/3; *with al her ~* to the utmost of their ability 119/10.

practik *n.* policy 60/1.

practized *pp.* put into practice 218/6.

pray *n.* spoil 111/15 n., haul of booty 190/8.

pray *v.* entreat, ask 210/14. *pr. 1 sg. ~* 134/20. *imp. sg.* **prey** 164/13. *pr.p.* **pray(i)ng** 85/33, 203/20. *p.t.* **prayed, praied** 41/19, 132/8; invited 206/14.

prayer, praier *n.* earnest supplication 7/3; request, entreaty 86/14, 138/17.

praysed *pp.* valued 8/25.

precept *n.* order 52/8, 131/7.

prechid *p.t.* proclaimed 144/24.

prechyngis *vbl.n. pl.* sermons 61/25.

Prechour *n.* in *a Frere ~* Dominican friar 118/33. *pl.* **Prechoures** Dominicans 113/4, 120/36; (poss.) 113/5, 124/3–4. Cf. **Dominic** and see also *Index*, s.n. **Dominic**.

precious *adj.* expensive, of the highest quality 154/28.

prees *n.* crowding together 170/9.

prefecte *n.* senior office-holder 55/18.

preferre *v.* advance 27/24. *p.t.* **preferred** assigned 56/30.

prefixed *pp.* arranged beforehand 179/9.

prey see **pray** *v.*

prejudise *n.* in *do* ~ *to* impair the rights of 117/13.

Premonstracense *n.* (for pl.) White Canons, Norbertians 101/5.

prentise *n.* inexperienced barrister-at-law 217/20.

preserue *v.* keep alive 14/22.

president *n.* governor 48/9.

pres(s)ed *pp.* run through 222/18; (w. *down*) reduced to straits 40/4.

prestod *n.* the order of priest 220/6.

pretending, -yng *pr.p.* claiming 156/27; alleging as a pretext 109/15, 177/13. *p.t., pp.* **pretendid** put forward as a pretext 154/29, 178/18.

pride *n.* splendour 62/28.

prince *n.* king, ruler 78/20, 204/18; commander 22/18; leader 27/21.

princesse *n.* chief priestess 33/21.

principalis *n. pl.* most prominent men 124/25.

pris, prys *n.* value 200/9; *set more* ~ *be* had greater esteem for 160/7.

Priscilianistes *n., poss. pl.* followers of Priscillian (d. 385) 66/23.

prisoned *p.t.* put in prison 100/23, 169/5. *pp.* ~ 93/32.

prisonment *n.* imprisonment 163/26.

priuacioun *n.* deprivation 211/27.

pryue *v.* deprive 163/29; strip 176/1. *p.t.* **pryued** stripped 199/5; cut off (w. *of* 'from') 63/25. *pp.* **pryued** stripped 223/11; **pryuyd** divested 78/31.

pryuy *adj.* on intimate terms 225/10; personal 8/12; privately aware 8/11; secret 14/21, 126/5; surreptitious 45/3.

pryuyleged *pp.* granted particular immunities 113/12.

pryuyly *adv.* secretly 96/25, 161/20.

probleme *n.* enigma, riddle 40/24.

processe *n.* sequ ntial progression 7/11; series of events 241/14; story 87/6, 249/18.

procuracie *n.* letter of attorney 237/8 n.

procuracion *n.* careful management 151/25.

procure *v.* bring about 150/19. *p.t.* **procured** contrived 151/20; brought about 99/32, 137/28; induced 118/17. *pp.* **procured** brought about 165/31.

profered *p.t.* offered 41/11, 127/7. *pp.* ~ 105/2.

profession *n.* taking vows on entry to a religious order 242/17.

profir *n.* proposal, offer 47/21, 187/16.

profitable *adj.* beneficial 184/19.

profite *n.* revenue 139/30.

profiteth *pr. 3 sg.* is advantageous 14/24.

progenie *n.* family 131/31.

promitting *pr.p.* undertaking to give (in marriage) 235/25. *pp.* **promittet** promised 108/4.

promote *v.* help forward 179/16.

pronounce *v.* produce vocally 40/15.

Propiciacioun *n.* in *þe* ~ Day of Atonement (Lev. 25: 9) 35/23.

propir *adj.* own particular 241/4; full, whole 242/12.

propirté *n.* distinctive quality 116/22; intrinsic nature 222/18.

proporcioned *p.t.* fashioned 13/22.

proporciones *n. pl.* dimensions 13/23.

proue *n.* fulfilment 242/4.

proue *v.* test 149/13; find out 225/19.

proued *pp. adj.* known 152/4.

prouidens *n.* wise government 44/1.

prouynce, -uince *n.* county 114/1; diocese 204/26.

prouision *n.* divine ordination 9/10. *pl.* **prouysiones** appointments to bishoprics 201/4; letters of appointment 163/26.

pulled *p.t.* in ~ *in* brought in 197/1; ~ *hom* brought back 205/22.

punche *v.* punish 205/17. *p.t.* **punchid** 52/6. *pp.* **punchid** 31/12, 126/16.

punchid *pp.* stabbed 86/16.

puple, -il *n.* (1) *coll. sg.* nation, tribe

puple (*cont.*):
18/28, 163/30; company of armed men 60/7, 121/30; (2) as *pl.* people 16/3, 121/19; troops 68/7, 121/23; the laity 158/15. *poss. sg.* (as *pl.*) **puples** common people's 167/15.

puplischid *p.t.* issued 143/1.

purchace *v.* obtain 137/7. *p.t.* **purchased** obtained 193/6; obtained (the right) 102/18–19.

purgith *pr. 3 sg.* drives out 241/5. *p.t.* **porged, purged** rid 38/11; purified 45/10; exonerated 84/17. *pp.* **porgid** purified 36/27.

purpil *n.* purple robes 60/6.

purpos *n.* in *in* ~ intending 41/25; *of* ~ purposely 114/35; *upon þat* ~ to that end 160/2, sim. 176/34.

purpos(e) *v.* put forward for consideration 136/15; plan 193/21. *pr.p.* **purposing** intending 76/21, 132/32. *p.t.* **purposed** intended 78/19, 137/27; resolved 17/27; (*refl.*) was bound (w. *into* 'for') 162/7. *pp.* **purposed, -it** put forward for discussion 40/24, 176/32; put forward for acceptance 139/18.

pursewe, por- *v.* chase after 229/21; try to obtain 101/31, 145/27. *p.t.* **pursewid, -ed, porsewid** persecuted 62/22; chased, went after 29/3, 139/12; tried to obtain 115/30. *pp.* **pursewid, -ed** chased 141/21; made their objective 145/31.

puruey(e) *v.* supply 115/8, 200/5. *p.t.* **purueyed** prepared in advance 179/28; requisitioned and collected 211/2.

puruyauns *n.* divine direction 29/30; provision 229/26.

puruioures, -uyouris *n. pl.* official suppliers 173/27; domestic officers 146/26.

put *v.* expel (w. *fro*) 136/32; deprive (w. *fro* 'of') 192/26; ~ *vndir* subject to 36/20. *pr.p.* in *puttyng upon* alleging against 134/13. *p.t.* ~ dismissed 78/11, 122/16; affirmed 59/18; (phr.) ~ *in choys* forced to choose 64/30; ~ *of* repulsed 76/23; ~ *on a crosse* crucified 120/18;

~ *oute of* expelled from 89/19; ~ *vndir* subjected to 46/26. *pp.* ~ deprived (w. *fro* 'of') 225/27; (phr.) ~ *in delay* deferred 201/1; ~ *on* imputed against 240/15; ~ *on þe cros* crucified 49/2; ~ *oute of* expelled from 106/29, 141/5; ~ *vndir* subjected to 163/7.

qualité *n.* nature 13/10.

quantité *n.* size 18/10; amount 167/17 n.

quarel *n.* cause 222/5.

quarter *n.* measure of capacity for grain: 8 bushels = 291 litres 174/17. *pl.* **quarteres** the four parts, each containing a limb, of a human body divided after execution 129/15.

quartered *pp.* cut in quarters (as prec.) 129/14; **qwartered** 134/26.

question *n.* in *mad* ~ raised discussion 241/20.

qwan see **whan(ne)**.

qwenchid *pp.* extinguished 99/6; stifled 225/5.

qwer(e) *n.* choir (eccl. and mus.) 64/19; chancel 141/13.

qwerne *n.* hand-mill 44/23.

qwest *n.* team of persons appointed to carry out an official inquiry 149/31.

qwiet *adj.* free from mental agitation 208/33.

qwik *adj.* alive 28/17.

raced *p.t.* erased 97/27. *pp.* **rased** 68/27.

ransake *v.* make a thorough examination of 129/8.

raunson *n.* ransom 85/2, 125/15.

raunsond *pp.* set free on payment of ransom-money 121/21.

raueyn *n.* robbery 130/28.

raueschid *p.t.* carried off by force 30/12.

real *adj.*[1] royal 153/21; magnificent 93/29; noble, large 22/5.

real *adj.*[2] actual, genuine 237/5.

rebel(le) *adj.* rebellious 52/6, 158/13.

rebuk(e) *n.* shameful defeat 177/19; in *put to* (*a*) ~ defeated shamefully 117/23.

rebuked *pp.* repulsed 187/8.

receyued *p.t.* showed respect to 169/25.

receyuing *vbl.n.* hospitality 206/26.

receyuoures *n. pl.* collectors of dues 211/7.

recorded *p.t.* told 229/15.

recure *v.* redress 237/20; recover 176/3. *p.t.* **recured** recovered 78/22. *pp.* **recured** restored 166/33.

redempcion *n.* atonement (for offence) 211/9.

redy *adj.* prepared (w. *to* 'for') 50/4, 121/31; (phr.) *make hem* ~ prepare (refl.) 216/20, sim. (p.t.) 158/14. *compar.* **redier** more prepared 15/2.

redith *pr. 3 sg.* reads 45/27. *p.t.* **red** taught 87/9.

reforme *v.* re-establish 141/31; convert 53/17. *pp.* **reformed** in ~ *to* brought to accept 71/21.

reformeres *n. pl.* persons disposed to change the attitude of others 160/13.

refrecchid *p.t.* provided with refreshment 29/4, 224/2.

refused *p.t.* rejected 108/10, 120/1; divorced 191/32. *pp.* ~ rejected 208/15.

regalie, -y *n.* kingship 101/27, 213/8; royal prerogative 193/1.

region *n.* kingdom, country 35/16.

regne *n.* sovereignty 35/4; monarchical state, kingdom 21/28, 175/28; reign 8/3, 23/23, 116/29.

regne *v.* reign, rule 20/12, 126/28. *pr. 3 sg.* (historic) **regneth, -ith** reigned 46/14; began to reign 43/26; ceased to reign 39/15. *p.t.* **regned** reigned, ruled 22/11, 117/5; flourished 28/15; was prevalent 144/22. *pp.* **regned** reigned, ruled 22/14, 238/6.

regner *n.* ruler 42/18.

reherse *v.* repeat 104/1. *pr. 3 sg.* **rehersith** states 21/13. *p.t.* **rehersed, -id** repeated 101/16; related 47/12; stated 240/9; recounted in order 134/7; mentioned 117/36. *pp.* **rehersid** gone over repeatedly 117/26; mentioned 228/9.

reyn *n.* shower of rain 125/12.

rejecte *pp.* rejected 70/27, 164/3.

rejoyse *v.* have full possession of 88/22, 227/13. *p.t.* **rejoysed** 42/20.

relacion *n.* report 221/20.

relesed *p.t.* granted remission 42/24. *pp.* **relesid** cancelled 39/17.

religio(u)n *n.* religious vows 205/21; religious order 235/3; religious conduct 91/4; in *houses of* ~ religious houses 242/6.

relik *n.* precious object 215/4.

remayne *v.* pass 198/15.

remanent *n.* remainder 242/20.

rem(e) *n.* kingdom 113/20, 117/15; **rewme** 142/16.

rememberauns *n.* recollection 21/18; power of recollection 40/17; memory 40/18; record 7/13.

remembir *v.* (refl.) bear in mind 226/10 (w. *of*). *imper. sg.* ~ 226/5.

remeue *v.* transfer 103/33; raise, relieve 157/20; get rid of 92/6; move off 41/19. *p.t.* **remeued** moved 171/16; dismissed 197/1; raised 191/5. *pp.* **remeued** taken away 73/23; moved 118/10; compelled to go 180/22; dismissed 178/10.

renegate *n.* apostate 226/2.

reneye *v.* renounce 108/25. *p.t.* **reneyed** 118/15.

rennith, -yth *pr. 3 sg.* flows 19/13, 210/25. *pl.* **renne** hasten along 9/1; continue 7/25; *renne togidir* coincide 7/32. *pr.p.* **renning** running 221/6. *p.t. sg.* **ran** 13/26, 171/20. *pl.* **runne** ran 55/26; ~ *awey* fled 119/15.

rent *p.t.* tore in pieces 29/1, 186/5.

rentis *n. pl.* income (from land) 166/30.

repayred *p.t.* renewed 40/13.

reparacion *n.* in *mad* ~ did repair-work 34/31, 118/31.

repast *n.* sustenance 118/22.

repent *v.* (refl.) be contrite 238/8. *p.t.* ~ 74/20 (w. *of* 'on account of').

reported *p.t.* related 56/6–7.

reproue *v.* condemn 193/29.

reputacion *n.* in *wer in no* ~ had no recognition 141/20.

requirith *pr. 3 sg.* demands 70/14.

rere *v.* elevate 155/29. *p.t.* **rered** originated 199/11. *pp.* **rered** collected 225/26; raised 194/26.

resigned *pp.* abdicated 154/10.

reson *n.* in *be* ~ through logical thought 14/1.

resonable *adj.* rational 14/1.

responses *n. pl.* responsories 95/31 n.

restauracion *n.* general renovation 34/32–3.

retenew *n.* followers 237/29.

returne *v.* revert 151/9.

reule *n.* rule 12/28, 130/15; conduct 205/23; government 152/36; (phr.) *set in* ~ established in good order 23/4; *set* ~ *in* established good order in 42/23; *withoute* ~ in a disordered state 161/32.

reuled *p.t.* ruled 145/24. *pp.* ~ influenced, controlled 14/26, 153/1.

reuerens *n.* (phr.) *ded* ~ (*to*) showed deep respect for 78/3, 226/27; *hauyng* ~ *to* displaying respect for 188/5; *at* ~ *of* out of respect for 175/31; *for* ~ *of* for the sake of 104/25, 191/14.

reuocacion *n.* recantation 99/25.

reuoke *v.* retract 99/24. *p.t.* **reuoked** 163/16.

reuoluing *vbl.n.* conversion back (of an aliquot part to the original integer) 8/27.

rewme see **rem(e)**.

ri(c)chesse *n.* opulence 33/3; wealth 57/10, 165/5.

rich *adj.* powerful 21/14.

ride *v.* go on an expedition 223/8; go on horseback in procession 231/24. *p.t. sg.* **rod(e), rood** went on an expedition 106/33, 146/30; went in procession 104/23, 206/2. *p.t. pl.* ~ 142/7, **ryde** 142/3, **riden** 184/14, **ridyn** 132/26, **rydyn** 213/13.

ridyng *vbl.n.* making forays on horseback 175/18.

rise *v.* recover 241/2, take up arms 152/12. *pr. 3 sg.* **riseth** is increased (through addition) 8/17. *p.t. sg.* **ros(e)** set 46/11; took up arms 38/4, 185/29; became exalted 191/32; arose 136/1; became current 160/14. *p.t. pl.* ~ 85/17, 142/8 (w.

coll. sg. subject); **ryse** took up arms 171/19; **risen** 68/10, 154/16, took up arms 190/4, came into circulation 207/7; **risin/rysin** 51/24, 129/23, took up arms 121/26; **rysyn** 154/21.

riseris *n. pl.* insurrectionists 186/22, criminal types 207/29.

rite, rith *adj.* right 28/11, 206/22; true 65/14; lawful 227/14.

rite, rith, ryth *adv.* straight 50/19, 176/20; very 15/21, 119/20; absolutely 103/20, 139/7.

rite, ryte *n.* law 138/14; justifiable claim 101/11, 119/36, (w. *of* 'to') 169/21; legal entitlement 163/29; territory 43/6; (phr.) *of* ~ by rights 202/21; *in þe kyngis* ~ in accordance with the king's justifiable claim 150/13.

rithful(l), riteful *adj.* upright 54/23; just 16/16, 188/11; lawful 160/15.

rithfully *adv.* uprightly 33/19; lawfully 92/13.

ryueling *vbl.n.* plundering 185/16.

rode *n.* crucifix 197/22.

rolle *n.* register in form of scroll 218/30.

Rome-scot see **Petir-peny**.

rosyn *n.* resin 131/4.

round *n.* round object (= circular coin) 128/30 n.

row *adj.* rough 129/19.

rowe *n.* in *be* ~ in order 134/7.

saccis see **sak**.

sacramental *adj.* (of oath) corporal, ratified by touching a sacred object 195/30.

sacrarie *n.* place where church valuables were kept, sanctuary 77/26.

sacre *v.* consecrate (to office) 197/19.

sacri *n.* consecration of the eucharistic elements at mass 52/19; **sacre** 109/27.

sad *adj.* of reliable judgment 238/7.

say see **se** *v.*, **sei**.

sak *n.* in *a* ~ *wolle* a bale of wool 173/25. *pl.* **saccis** pieces of sackcloth 17/15.

same *adj.* in *þe* ~ *tyme* the time presently under consideration 248/19.

Sarasin(e) *n.* infidel 111/11, 126/6. *pl.* **Sarasines** Arabs 72/1; Moslems 75/7.

sat *p.t.* dwelt 115/18; ~ *(up)on* sat in judgment on 147/25.

saunctuarie *n.* consecrated graveyard 170/32.

saute *n.* sudden onslaught 167/7. *pl.* **sawtes** 187/12.

sauter *n.* Book of Psalms 71/33; copy of the psalms 116/20.

sauacion *n.* deliverance from sin 49/16, 118/20.

saue *conj.* except that 33/13, 208/17; ~ *þat* 181/25; ~ *only for* except for 185/6.

saue *prep.* (1) with the exception of 14/21, 132/14; (2) but for 7/31, 105/19.

saued *p.t. pl.* allowed to live 100/6; *pp.* 228/23.

sauour *n.* scent 67/15.

Saxones *n. pl.* Anglo-Saxons 74/9; continental Saxons 92/6.

scape *pr. 3 sg. subj.* get safely out of 138/30. *p.t.* **scaped** gained liberty by flight 68/4, 132/15; avoided (threatened evil) 31/12, 183/14; **skaped** 218/20.

scarse *adv.* barely, only just 229/16.

scarsly *adv.* barely, only just 66/20, 166/22; *ful* ~ 206/20; *ful scarcely* 154/15.

schaberk *n.* scabbard 92/19.

schadow *n.* phantom 208/27.

schal *pr. 1 sg.* shall, will 27/24, 164/15. *2 sg.* ~, **schalt** 246/24; shall, will 27/15, 131/29. *3 sg.* ~, **schul, schall** 98/25; will have to 7/26; is to 8/13, 17/14; shall, will 8/6, 16/16, 116/30; should 200/31. *pl.* ~, **schul**, ought to 76/3, 135/30; have to 242/20 n.; are to 8/20, 79/10, 116/29; shall, will 7/10, 16/9, 123/27. *p.t.* **schuld(e), schul, schud** 74/17. (1) ought to 7/4, 41/5, 117/20, (with inf. of motion understood) 122/19; had to 28/12 n., 121/18 (1st); was to 11/33, 137/34; was about to 98/7, 138/13; should 12/17, 117/15; (forming condit. fut.) 96/32, 124/31; would

12/14, 117/13. (2) *w. inf.* (of uncertified report) *schuld sey* said 109/36, sim. 224/4 (cf. 145/25); (in indirect question) *schuld rise* rose 241/21, (w. inf. of motion understood) were going 241/32; (forming condit. fut. perf.) *schuld have* would have had 186/13. (3) *w. p. inf.*: *schul(d) a* (= *haue*)+*pp.* was to 70/13; (of uncertified report) had, is presumed to have 12/30; would 192/9; (forming condit. fut. perf.) would have 186/10.

scharp *adj.* in ~ *of witte* sagacious 59/17.

scharply *adv.* with keen intelligence 192/24.

sche *pron. 3 sg. fem.* 11/14, 120/31. Cf. **hir(e).**

scheperde *n.* shepherd 36/11. *pl.* **schepherdis** 13/5; **schippardes** the Shepherds, rebellious French peasants 121/27.

schep-kepyng *n.* tending of sheep 13/16.

Schere þursday *n.* Holy Thursday 56/28–9. Cf. **Ascensioun.**

schette *imp.* shut 98/11.

schewe *v.* show 138/4. *p.t.* **schewid** 11/17, 122/27.

schip *n.* (Noah's) Ark 17/32; *within* ~ on board 183/16; *to take* ~ go on board 230/1. *pl.* in *grete schippis* ships-of-war 167/12.

schipmen *n. pl.* sailors 94/21.

schippid *pp.* embarked 94/21.

schon *n. pl.* shoes 56/11.

schot *n.* action of shooting 86/11; discharged projectiles 244/18.

schotyng *vbl.n.* sport of shooting with a bow 196/12.

schreue, schryue *n.* sheriff 183/13, 232/23; governor 105/17. *pl.* **scryues** 192/22.

schriue *pp.* confessed and absolved 241/4; **schryue** 199/25.

schul(-) see **schal.**

Scicilianes *n. pl.* Sicilians 129/25.

sciens *n.* knowledge 14/19. *pl.* ~ fields of knowledge 63/23, **sciencsi** 14/29; *þe Liberal Sciens* the Liberal Arts 87/8.

scilens see **silens.**

scip *n.* point on ground where jump ended 50/9.

scippit *p.t.* jumped 83/1.

scisme *n.* division in Church 97/34, 188/11; state of divided spiritual allegiance in Church caused by disputed election to the papacy 63/5.

Scitas *n. pl.* Scythians 21/28.

scole *n.* institution of higher learning 119/2; organized body of teachers and scholars 89/28.

scoler *n.* pupil 242/2. *pl.* **scoleres** students 130/25.

scorne *n.* in *had* ~ entertained a feeling of contempt 97/15.

scryues see **schreue.**

scrowis *n. pl.* notices 204/1.

se *n.* throne 214/19; diocese 202/1.

se(e) *n.* in *þe* ~ *occean* the sea 79/33; *kepte þe* ~ kept it clear of foreign vessels 131/8; *Amirelis of þe* ~ Commanders-in-Chief of the Navy 183/1; *þe grete* ~ the Mediterranean 21/32; *þe Scotisch* ~ the sea north of Northumberland (? Firth of Forth) 80/14; *be þe* ~ by sea 114/7, 138/20; *in þe* ~ on the sea's surface 39/10, 162/17, aboard ship 146/14; *ouyr þe* ~ abroad 136/12; *went, cam (in)to þe* ~ went on a sea voyage 115/18, 131/14, 211/29; *take þe* ~ set out on a sea-voyage 216/30, (with p.t. *tok, entered*) 157/1, 152/23; *passe þe* ~ go abroad 183/29; *þe myd* ~ halfway on a sea voyage 190/14. See also **occean.**

se *v.* see 7/16, 15/1, 139/18; watch over 93/28. *pr. 1 sg.* ~ 226/2. *pr. pl.* ~ 98/11. *pr.p.* **seing** 40/29, 209/5; **seyng** 62/31, 147/16. *imper. pl.* ~ 15/28. *p.t.* **sey** 23/18, 137/22; **say** 37/11, 148/32; **sei** 39/3. *pp.* **seyn** 47/21, 118/18; **sey** 91/5; **seyne** 221/7.

se(a)l *n.* seal 126/25; (as mark of office) 196/26; *pryuy* ~ Lord Privy Seal 178/11.

se-bank *n.* sea-coast 131/10.

secrete *adj.* secluded 120/17.

secte *n.* body of followers 218/11; adherents of one of the principal world religions 65/32; system of belief or observance differing from the orthodox one 239/8.

seculer *adj.* (of clergy) not living in monastic seclusion 95/2, 184/30; in ~ *hand*, ~ *power* civil power as 'invoked' by the Church to punish offenders 72/26, 218/5; in ~ *man* layman 242/22; (of knowledge) relating to non-religious subjects 63/23.

seculeris *n. pl.* secular clergy 185/29.

secundary *n.* church dignitary of second rank 230/18–19.

sed *n.* semen 220/9 n.

seek, seke *adj.* sick, ill 174/12, 226/25.

sege *n.* privy 98/29; *go to a* ~ go to stool 62/29.

sei, sey(e), seyn, say *v.* say 11/22, 135/32; deliver (sermon) 121/18; express (praise) 248/8; ~ *of* speak (critically) of 109/36; *herd* ~ heard tell 20/11, 161/8; *is to* ~ signifies 12/21, (in parenthetic phr.) 22/12. *pr. 1 sg.* **sey** (w. pron. in obl. case) 226/20. *pr. 2 sg.* **seist** 111/14. *3 sg.* **seith** 9/5, 12/6, 128/29. *pr. pl.* **sei, sey** 12/7, 120/24. *pr.p.* **seying** 92/26, 194/24; **seyng** 41/30; **seiand** 27/23. *p.t.* **seid(e), said(e), seyd(e), sayd(e)** 16/15, 138/29; *seid ageyn* made (unfriendly) remarks about 97/1, 122/11; *seid euel of* spoke ill of 74/16; *saide onto . . . þat . . .* told (a person to do something) 100/17. *pp.* **seid(e), said(e), seyd** 8/30, 11/14, 120/18; called (by name) 32/3; commemorated 199/2; *seid of* remarked (critically/favourably) about 211/18, 125/4; *seid ageyn* told (in criticism) about 146/11.

Sey-euel *n.* 'Speak-with-abusive-words', name attributed to Pope Benedict XI 134/21.

Seyn *adj.* (prefixed to names) Saint 53/16, 176/26; **Seynt** in *Seynt Spirit* the Holy Spirit 112/11.

Sey-wel *n.* 'Speak-with-friendly-words', name attributed to Pope Benedict XI 134/20.

seke *adj.* see **seek.**

seke *v.* in ~ *oute* pursue with hostile

intent 190/28. *pr.p.* in *sekyng of* trying to find out 7/11. *p.t.* **soute** 7/27, 113/28 (pursued), 137/21 (resorted to); **sowte** in *sowte oute* pursued with hostile intent 115/27; *soute aftir* pursued 128/4.

sek(e)nes, seknesse *n.* illness, malady, disease 34/6, 199/12.

sekirly *adv.* without doubt 144/9.

sel see **seal**.

seld *p.t.* sold 113/33, 140/25; sold treacherously 143/30; (refl.) 41/10; **sold** 115/3. *pp.* ~ 140/21; **sold** 25/24, 174/17.

seled *p.t.* approved (by placing seals on a document) 193/11.

semeth *pr. 3 sg.* befits 50/19; seems 16/3, 205/13.

senatoure *n.* member of the ancient Roman senate 71/32; civil head of city government in Rome, appointed by the pope 129/16. See also *Index*, s.n. Senate.

sendith *pr. 3 sg.* sends (dutiful respects) 7/3. *pr. 3 sg. subj.* **send** (of God) ordain as a blessing (something for someone) 9/19. *p.t.* **sent** (w. compl. n.) sent as 82/26, 132/9; *sent ageyn* sent to meet 244/26; *sent down* sent instructions 118/23; *sent oute* dispatched (persons) 239/13.

sene *n.* synod 103/25.

seneschal *n.* governor (of city) 122/17.

senewis *n. pl.* sinews 39/5; **cenewes** 29/16.

sense *v.* perfume with odours from burning incense 35/24.

sentens *n.* sentence of excommunication 142/16; sense, substance 43/23, 133/15; insight 33/2. *pl.* pithy sayings 248/2.

sepulcur *n.* sepulchre 100/28.

sepulture *n.* burial 11/18, 208/30.

sercle *n.* ring 99/14; **serkil** 210/21.

serjaunt *n.* serjeant-at-law 193/12.

serue *v.* perform divine service 58/22. *pr. 2 sg.* **seruist** 248/6. *3 sg.* **seruith** 7/33. *pp.* **seruyd** stricken 116/14.

seruise, seruyse *n.* state of submission to foreign power 57/30; allegiance 129/33, in *ded* ~ *to*

professed allegiance to 133/32; worship 74/29; (prob.) the daily office of the breviary 70/19; *to his* ~ at his disposal 237/10. *coll. pl.* ~ friendly assistance 161/5.

ses(e), cese *v.* cease; ~ *of* discontinue 133/29. *p.t.* **sesed, -id, cesed** became extinct 43/6, 116/31; caused to desist 56/13.

seside *n.* in *on þe* ~ on the coast 131/12.

seson *n.* in *took* ~ *in* took possession of 128/21.

sete *n.* throne 36/25; position (of pope) 87/10, 139/26; (of king) 214/9. *pl.* **setes** thrones (symbolizing royal authority) 32/1.

set(te) *v.* (with double meaning) cause to be situated, place in estimation 98/34; deal with 42/19; apply (remedy) 192/6; appoint (a parliament) 195/4; establish (peace) 142/1; ~ *in* insert 7/32. *pr. 1 sg.* ~ write down 7/23. *p.t.* ~ placed (circlet on head) 117/12; put (in prison) 104/14, 124/26; dealt with 42/18; ~ *ope* opened 161/29; brought about 100/25; imposed (penalties) 210/3; appointed 38/19, (a parliament) 129/13; established (good government) 42/23; wrote 42/1; assessed 161/25; ~ *in* installed (in office) 85/6. *pp.* ~ mentioned 8/2; (of penalty) prescribed 124/30; (of a parliament) appointed 136/16; established (peace) 247/18; placed (in estimation) 48/25; (of value) ~ *at* fixed at 172/17.

seuene *adj.* seventh 12/28, 247/5.

seuenet *adj.* seventh 186/28.

sex *adj.* six 8/19, 15/34, 159/8.

sex *n.* six 8/15.

sext(e) *adj.* sixth 14/27, 118/12.

sextene *adj.* sixteen 233/14; sixteenth 181/29.

sexti *adj.* sixty 15/27, 132/13; sixtieth 8/14.

side *n.* one of the two divisions of a choir 64/19 (cf. 141/13).

signe *n.* miracle 111/17.

sikir *adj.* safe 144/3; reliable 26/17; indubitable 24/30.

sikirnes(se) *n.* security (sense of) 74/25, (condition of) 181/3, (for performance of treaty) 172/14.

silens *n.* in *put to* ～ silenced by prohibition 130/10; **scilens** reticence 105/12.

siluir *n.* in *no* ～ something not made of silver 77/28.

similitude *n.* similarity 9/11, 43/31; likeness 129/19. *pl.* **similitudes** effigies 20/31.

simonianes *n. pl.* those who practised simony 100/17.

simpil *adj.* inconsequential 130/4; (in apologetic formula) deficient in learning 8/8.

sinagog *n.* (disparagingly, of Church) in *þe* ～ *of Sathanas* the religious organization of Satan 220/12.

singe *v.* say mass 102/19. *pr. 3 sg.* **singith** chants 9/12. *p.t. pl.* **songin** 51/24. *pp.* **songe** 58/29; **songen** 77/25; **sunge** 52/19.

singulerly *adv.* individually 214/6.

Sistewys, -is, *n. pl.* (order of) Cistercians 101/4, 121/34; **Cistewis** 91/28.

sistir *n.* in *þe kingis* ～ *of Ynglond* the king of England's sister 156/19.

site, sith *n.* sight 13/21, 142/34; vision 47/19; *at þe first* ～ immediately upon seeing (him) 41/27.

sith *prep.* since 215/26.

sith(e) *adv.* afterwards 118/10; at any time since 14/19.

sith(e) *conj.* from the time when 57/3; seeing that 228/14.

sithis *n. pl.* (of multiplication) times 8/31; **sithe** orig. *gen.* 8/27.

sixte see **sext(e).**

skaped see **scape.**

skil *pr. 3 sg. impers.* in *It* ～ *þou not* It makes no difference to you 241/21.

Slauis *n. pl.* Slavs 87/24.

sla(u)ndir *n.* discredit 92/4, 180/26; **slaundre** opprobrium 82/18.

slaundiring *pr.p.* vilifying 191/21. *pp.* **slaundered** disgraced 105/20; accused 145/2.

sle *v.* kill 24/12, 186/13. *pp.* **slayn** 15/22, 120/22.

slepe *p.t.* slept 29/5.

smaragdis *n. pl.* emeralds 22/5.

smite, smyte *v.* strike 113/25, 239/16. *p.t.* **smet** 29/17, 198/22. *pp.* **smet** (with *with* 'by') 38/12, 188/12.

smok *n.* woman's undergarment 84/7.

snybbed *p.t.* rebuked 204/8.

socour *n.* military assistance 78/21, 217/27.

socour *v.* furnish with military assistance 90/4.

sodeyn *adj.* unexpected 237/29.

sodeynly *adv.* without warning 37/9, 130/17; at once 75/19, 241/26.

soile *n.* district 137/16.

solaced *pp.* entertained 29/23.

sold see **seld.**

solemply *adv.* ceremoniously 61/5; earnestly 87/9.

solemp(ne) *adj.* serious and important 67/2; ～ *daies* feast-days 247/10.

solempnité *n.* observance of ceremony 124/4.

somyr *n.* summer 221/5.

somnour *n.* officer bearing summons 239/25.

somoun *v.* issue a summons against 239/20. *pp.* **somound** summoned (to parliament) 178/17.

somounis, somownes *n.* summons 239/27; *make* ～ issue a summons 132/24.

son *n.* in group gen. *þe kyngis* ～ *of Frauns* the king of France's son 117/7. *pl.* in *þe sones of God*, name for male descendants of Seth 17/24 (Gen. 6: 2). Cf. **doutir.**

sond *n.* sand 125/10.

sone *adv.* shortly 94/16, 163/14; without delay 138/31.

songe(n), songin see **singe.**

soper *n.* supper 49/33, 190/24.

sore *adj.* aching 33/17.

sore *adv.* intensely 143/31; bitterly 154/5; grievously 106/15; hard 203/21; greatly 12/35.

sores *n. pl.* tumours 31/17.

sori *adj.* sad 14/33.

soth *n.* truth 106/17, 225/19; (in emph. phr.) *in veri* ～ in fact 12/23.

sotil(l) *adj.* acute 65/1; treacherously cunning 126/1.

sotil(l)y *adv.* cunningly 209/17;

treacherously 99/32; insidiously 131/30.

sotilté *n.* acuteness 42/3; trickery 248/16.

soudan, soudon *n.* Aghlabid emir 85/33; Zangid Sultan 108/34; Ayyubid Sultan 121/21; Mamluke Sultan 126/1, 175/9; Jalayrid Sultan 175/2; Ottoman Sultan 218/9.

soudioures, soudyoures *n. pl.* soldiers 40/28, 234/22.

soule *n.* life 234/6; spiritual part of man (as opposed to emotions and intellect) 8/33 n.

Soule-masse Day *n.* All Souls' Day (2 Nov.) 155/10.

soundith *pr. 3 sg.* signifies 13/34. *p.t.* sounded tended (with *in* 'towards') 204/3.

souereyn *adj.* supreme 7/1, 101/19, 194/28.

souereynes *n. pl.* monarchs 22/12.

souereynté *n.* supremacy 8/36.

Spaynard *n.* Spaniard 104/19.

spak see spekith.

spare *v.* exercise forbearance 222/8. *pp.* spared allowed to go untaxed 183/8.

spech(e) *n.* general talk 105/24; term 43/31 n.

special *adv.* in *in* ~ in particular 18/27; especially 238/9.

speciali *adv.* exclusively 128/9.

spede *v.* succeed 150/27; accomplish 132/31; go with speed 243/13. *pr. 3 sg. subj.* ~ cause to succeed 130/2. *p.t.* sped succeeded 148/27. *pp.* sped helped 156/16; expedited 118/27.

speker *n.* in ~ *of þe parlement* Speaker in the House of Commons 180/14.

spekith *pr. 3 sg.* speaks 9/4, 24/29. *pl.* speke (with *of*) are discussing 66/10. *p.t.* spak 24/10, 238/2; spoke 60/2. *pp.* spoke 11/18, also as *adj.* fayre-spokyn eloquent 65/1.

sperd *p.t.* fastened 126/7; closed 64/13; sealed up 34/1. *pp.* ~ closed 241/30; shut up 63/8; caged in 234/8.

spere *n.* spear 48/35, 147/21. *pl.* speres spearmen 211/31.

spete *n.* spit 154/33.

spoile *v.* strip of possessions 223/15. *p.t.* spoiled robbed 114/22, 168/25; plundered 76/15, 163/1. *pp.* spoiled stripped of possessions 83/13.

spores *n. pl.* spurs 135/33; *gilt sporis* (the distinctive mark of a knight) 242/5.

spring *n.* place of rising 19/10.

sprong *p.t. pl.* arose 66/23.

stabil *adj.* durable 200/3.

stabil *n.* cattle-shed 61/1.

stal *p.t. sg.* stole 135/6. *pl.* stole kidnapped 249/12. *pp.* stole 246/19; kidnapped 120/16.

stand(e) *v.* face (with *into* 'towards') 72/20; ~ *to* obey 127/13; ~ *with* agree with 138/14. *pr. 3 sg.* standith 159/15; stant is situated 22/11, 202/6; is 7/25. *pl.* in ~ *in fredam* are free 41/14. *p.t.* in *stood drye* dried up 210/27.

stapil *n.* town whose merchants have exclusive rights to purchase goods for export 196/12.

state *n.* exalted office (of king) 139/7; dignitary 214/6. *pl.* states, -is delegates 209/17.

stature *n.* build 20/16.

statute *n.* decree, law 54/4, 131/17.

stauns *n.* dispute 74/15.

stede *n.* in *in* ~ *of* in exchange for 121/15; *in his* ~ as his successor 122/17.

stedis *n. pl.* high-mettled horses 242/4.

stepil *n.* tall-towered church 204/16.

stere *v.* exhort 200/20; stir 163/2. *pr. 3 sg.* stereth 235/4. *p.t.* stered 193/8 (tried to persuade). *pp.* stered 226/16 (tried to persuade).

stereris *n. pl.* instigators (with *to* 'of') 126/23.

stering *vbl.n.* prompting, instigation 31/1, 231/25.

sterlyngis *n. pl.* silver pennies 167/17.

sterre *n.* star 176/19.

steward *n.* controller of the royal household, office held by an important nobleman 110/6, 195/14.

stille *adv.* (w. *dwelled, abod(e), lay*)

stille (*cont.*):
without change of place 15/22, 58/11, 144/3; (w. *hold*) motionless 109/29; in future as up to now 215/28.

stith *n.* anvil 13/8.

stoyned *p.t.* stunned, amazed 200/12; crashed, shattered 98/13 n. Cf. **astoyned**.

stok *n.* tree trunk deprived of its branches 124/23.

stole *p.t.* and *pp.* see **stal**.

story *n.* historical event 39/25. *pl.* **stories** 7/13; historical episodes 40/9; historical works 53/31.

strangil *pr. 3 sg. subj.* choke 101/20. *p.t.* **strangild** suffocated 90/14. *pp.* **strangillid** 64/15.

straunge *adj.* foreign 45/6, 155/4.

streit(e), streyt(e) *adv.* without delay 60/26, 133/2; **streith** 157/22.

streyt *adj.* tight-fitting 201/25; **streite** narrow and difficult to proceed along 8/39; **streith** strictly conducted 127/27.

streytid *p.t.* pressed hardly upon 232/13; **streited** subjected to hardship 93/12. *pp.* ~ forced into a confined space 246/23; subjected to hardship 235/11.

strenger see **strong**.

strength *n.* (coll. sg.) troops 138/20; a military force 147/18; *be* ~ *by force* 74/10, 134/1. *pl.* **strengthis** fortresses 133/11.

strength *v.* confirm 193/17; strengthen with military reinforcements 110/33. *p.t.* **strengthid** (refl.) 221/15.

strete *n.* road 50/6.

stringis *n. pl.* ligaments 29/18.

strok *n.* wound 122/14; impact 219/26.

strong *adj.* in *he mad him* ~ *he* consolidated his military strength 241/19 n.; *with* ~ *hand* by force 98/7, with a powerful army 179/4 n. *compar.* **strenger** 59/4, 228/4.

studye *v.* be perplexed 23/28. *p.t.* **studied** endeavoured 43/14.

studier *n.* student 7/12.

stuf *n.* military supplies, baggage 177/7.

stuffid *p.t.* furnished 152/8. *subj.* **stuf** 138/22.

suasiones *n. pl.* arguments 133/30.

subdiacone, -diacoun *n.* subdeacon 59/13, 225/30.

subjeccio(u)n *n.* overlordship 102/38; homage, submission 7/4, 96/29, 161/12.

sublimat *pp. adj.* exalted 74/24.

subsidy, subsidi(e) *n.* pecuniary aid granted by parliament to the king 178/7.

successio(u)n *n.* series of persons in genealogical order 19/26; series of items in order 248/10; followers (of religious leader) 123/2.

sudarie *n.* napkin which was about Christ's head in the tomb 84/6.

sufficiens *n.* sufficient means 73/20.

sufficiently *adv.* as *n.* sufficient means 242/19.

suffir *v.* endure 119/17; permit 238/16.

suffocat *pp.* killed by suffocation 210/6.

suggestiones *n. pl.* false statements 134/4.

sum(me) *adj.* some 13/16, 129/25.

sum(me) *pron.* one 90/6; some 13/23, 122/24; (w. *n.* in apposition) an indefinite number 177/25; in ~ . . . *þan* ~ some . . . than others 15/2.

sumtyme *adv.* sometimes 7/24–5, 19/33, 120/21; (correl.) 173/4–5; once 57/19; formerly 15/12, 117/28; (passing into adj.) 215/30; at some future time 192/6.

sumwhat *adv.* somewhat 7/6, 33/30, 172/6.

sumwhat *n.* a certain amount 38/24–5.

sundri, sundry *adj.* various 43/21, 87/28; different 7/9, 16/24, 127/5.

superaltarie *n.* portable altar-slab 102/20.

suppose *v.* think, believe 186/12. *pr.* ~ 9/17, 14/3, 179/3. *pr.p.* **supposing, -yng** 23/28, 136/14; expecting 149/2. *p.t.* **supposed, -id** 21/1, 119/14; expected 147/8. *pp.* **supposed** 70/30, 166/29.

supprioure *n.* prior's deputy 115/35.

surfetis *n. pl.* illegal actions 139/22.

suruiour *n.* architectural super-intendent 171/23.

suspecio(u)n *n.* in *had ~ to* entertained a suspicion of 101/17, 216/21.

suspect *adj.* in *hald ~* suspected 113/18.

susteyned *p.t.* provided for 54/31. *pp. ~* 102/31.

sware *adj.* cube-shaped 8/18.

swech(e) *adj.* such (a) 8/3, 13/30, 119/17; this/these, having the following matter 27/23, 133/30; *and ~ oþir* and the like 117/28; *no ~* no (person) of the kind 87/23; *~ on* such a person (as that specified) 231/15; *~ maner* of such a kind 121/30.

swerd *n.* sword 9/5, 66/11, 208/20.

swete *adj.* pleasing 236/2.

swetith *pr. 3 sg.* exudes moisture 95/29.

swier(e), swyere *n.* young nobleman attendant upon a knight 180/8; (placed after the surname as a designation of rank) 193/15; personal attendant 76/5; follower 249/22.

swyn *n.* pig 140/22.

swore *pp.* sworn 172/21; bound by oath 123/9; bound by oath of allegiance (to) 133/7; **sworne** 35/13.

tabard *n.* sleeveless upper garment of coarse material 140/6.

tabernacle *n.* portable wooden sanctuary of Israelites 31/10.

tabil, -el *n.* slab 73/21; index 121/2; in *round ~* form of tournament (1345) derived from ideal of Arthurian Round Table 164/26.

tayl *n.* buttocks 241/11.

tayle *n.* (fig.) reckoning, retaliation in kind 223/21 n.

take *v.* mount (for a journey) 58/1; seek refuge in 235/10; *~ dayes* fix times (for repayment) 248/23. *p.t.* **took, tok(e)** occupied 119/29; exacted (oath) 204/10; fell into 229/18; gave 122/25; *took onto him* took into his own keeping 161/27; *took to* (refl.) became an adherent

of 72/21. *pp.* **tak(e)** taken refuge in 216/15; given 14/12, 179/1; handed over 234/7; *~ up* taken into protection 26/25.

taliages *n. pl.* levies 207/9.

talked *p.t.* gossiped 208/29.

talkyng *vbl.n.* conversation 213/12.

targe *n.* in *þe grete ~* king's most important document-stamp 142/28.

taried *p.t.* waited 177/2; continued 229/6. *pp. ~* delayed 132/10; stayed 236/12.

task(e) *n.* tax 184/28.

taute, tawt *p.t.* taught 25/28.

telle *v.* say 109/33. *pr. 3 sg.* **tellith** gives an account (of) 36/23; states 24/22. *p.t.* **teld** related 32/16.

temperauns *n.* self-restraint 14/14.

tempest *n.* (fig.) downpour 176/10.

Templaries *n. pl.* Templars, members of Christian military order suppressed in France in 1312 137/25.

temporal *adj.* bodily, earthly 31/12.

temporaltés *n. pl.* worldly possessions 225/27.

temporat *adj.* self-restrained 83/25.

ten *adj.* tenth 17/32, 129/5.

tent *adj.* tenth 208/30.

tercian *n.* fever involving paroxysms every third (i.e. every alternate) day 229/18.

terment *n.* funeral service 238/28.

ternaries *n. pl.* sets of three 8/31.

ters *n.* canonical office said at third hour of day (9 a.m.) 52/24.

testament *n.* will 101/23-4.

tetis *n. pl.* breasts 131/2.

tewhel *n.* rectum 154/33.

Tewisday *n.* Tuesday 244/10.

þai see **þei.**

þank *n.* in *had ~* was thanked 8/10.

þan(ne), than(ne) *adv.* at that time 7/32, 12/13, 119/30; subsequently 12/32, 117/14; consequently 24/24, 140/7.

þat *conj.* in that 9/8, 31/10, 124/6.

þat *pron. rel.* that which, what 7/28 (2nd), 34/28, 161/32; those who 141/18.

þe, the *pron. 2 sg.* see **þou.**

þe *pron. 3 pl.* see **þei.**

Thebees *n. pl.* Thebans, Christians from Upper Egypt 60/9.

þedir see þidir.

þeef n. robber 230/12; theef scoundrel 177/22. pl. þeues freebooters 191/1.

þei, also thei, they pron. 3 pl. they, those 7/10, 11/31, 117/9; þai 228/10; þe 120/10. obl. þem 190/8. Cf. hem.

þens adv. (from) there 58/9, 126/32.

þere adv. rel. where, in which 66/21, 208/20; in the place where 71/7.

þereaboute adv. near there 30/24.

þerfor adv. for that reason, on that account 40/6, 129/1.

þerof adv. of it 22/2, 166/11; from it/them 13/26, 141/3; about it 18/13, 112/16; to it 163/19; into it 128/12.

þeron adv. on it 108/5, 138/4.

þerto(o) adv. to that place 22/4; to it 34/29, 191/17; to that 116/4, 117/30; of it 215/3; in honour of it 21/19; also 23/5, 121/6.

þes adj. demons. pl. see þis.

þi(n), thi poss. adj. and pron. see þou.

þidir adv. (to) there 81/6, 129/18; thidir 192/19; þedir 136/17.

þing n. in al(l) ~ everything 82/27, 137/1, (construed w. sg. v.) 243/16. pl. þingis, -es writings 102/35, 136/31; see also 122/7 n.

þird adj. in þe ~ part one-third 51/14, 127/27.

þirtene adj. thirteenth 74/8.

þis, this adj. demons. this; þus 97/32. pl. ~ these 30/23, 122/13; þes 99/27.

þiself see þou.

þo(o), tho adj. demons. pl. those 8/39, 12/36, 122/28. See also 137/29 n.

þo(o), tho pron. demons. pl. they 131/5; those 7/8, 50/26, 215/27.

tho, þo(o) adv. at that time 214/9; after that, thereupon 68/22, 126/24.

Tholomei n. pl. Ptolemies, Macedonian Gk rulers of Egypt from Alexander the Great to Cleopatra 22/25.

þor(o)w prep. through 27/25, 154/33; throughout 62/23, 117/15.

þor(o)woute prep. right through 132/4; throughout 60/4, 145/1.

þou, thou pron. 2 sg. you 27/15, 123/22; (indef.) anyone 8/19. obl. þe, the 27/24 (1st), 123/21 (2nd). þiself yourself 60/24. poss. adj. þi, thi your 41/16, 123/22; þin 204/12. poss. pron. þin yours 98/25. Cf. ȝe.

þou(ȝ) conj. although 7/20, 14/5, 121/4, thow 12/20, þow 162/13, þow þat 163/2, even if 175/28; (after neg.) that 109/33, 225/29, ~ þat 40/16; as ~ as would have been the case if 36/24, 140/7, so as to suggest the notion that 106/13, 143/14.

þoute p.t. planned 192/8. pp. ~ 241/24.

þretyng pr.p. threatening 106/16. p.t. þrette 63/33.

threw p.t. shot 104/9; þrew cast violently 127/20. pp. þrow(e) 49/4.

thries adv. three times in succession 50/8; þries 138/4; threes three times as much as 8/28.

þundir n. thunder-clap 119/14.

thurifie v. offer incense 60/32.

þus adj. see þis.

tiding n. a report 168/22. pl. tydannes news 190/5; tidyndis 126/29.

til conj. in ~ þat until 35/12.

tyl n. burnt clay 12/2.

tilmen, tyl- n. pl. men who cultivate the soil 21/34, 166/31.

tyme, time n. end of gestation period 36/7, 87/15; (phr.) long ~ for a long time 237/32; in þe ~ of during 246/7; þat/that ~ during the period under consideration 14/13, 132/28; for þat ~ for the time being 129/4; þis/this ~ at this period of time 30/4, 172/30; in elde ~ in ancient times 114/31; on a ~ on one occasion 92/26; þat ~ at that point in time 147/30, on that occasion 219/17; whech ~ at which point in time 34/17; the same ~ during the same period 158/1.

tyraunt n. villain 149/3. pl. tyrauntis rulers 45/11.

tithe v. pay one-tenth to the Lord 15/30.

tithes n. pl. payments of one-tenth to the Church 166/30.

tithing *n.* offering of one-tenth to the Lord 11/18.

titil, -el, -le *n.* inscription 82/7; grounds (w. *of* 'for') 235/28; legal right 117/9; cardinal church, parish 85/8, 188/19. *pl.* **tytiles** certificates of presentation to a benefice 163/25.

to *prep.* before 149/22; with regard to 240/20; on behalf of 180/13.

tobroken *pp.* broken to pieces 31/16.

togidir *adv.* together 7/33, 20/19, 126/21.

tok(e) see **take.**

tokne *n.* sign of God's power 29/27. *pl.* **toknes** omens 107/34.

tongis see **tunge.**

to(o) *adj.* two 7/32, 11/8, 120/3.

too *n.* two 7/19.

touch *n.* reference (w. *of* 'to') 7/14.

touch(e) *v.* write about 33/30; tell 25/13. *p.t.* **touchid** told 39/11. *pp.* **touchid** treated 7/17; told 18/8.

touching *prep.* concerning 240/15.

tour *n.* (fig.) stronghold 220/12.

tow *adj.* of viscous consistency 20/21.

trace *n.* in *þou tredis þi* ~ you pursue your course of action 123/22.

tractes *n. pl.* treatises 70/16.

trayn(e) *n.* stratagem 142/29.

trajedi *n.* writer of tragedy 40/8.

translacion *n.* feast of removal of remains (of saint) to another burial place 135/17.

translat(e) *p.t.* removed 82/6; transferred 82/2, 135/2; translated 43/13. *pp.* ~ removed 26/9; transferred 201/30; conveyed to heaven without death 11/10; translated 43/19.

tre *n.* wood 114/16, in *sawe of* ~ wooden saw 36/29; cross (made of wood) 9/14, 84/5. *pl.* **trees** gallows 153/19.

trede *v.* trample 73/24. *pr. 2 sg.* **tredis** see **trace.** *pp.* **trode** 114/36.

treso(u)re *n.* (transf.) precious relics 94/16; treasury 43/15.

trespas *n.* offence 74/20, 124/29.

trespasin *pr. 3 pl.* do wrong 181/12. *p.t.* **trespased** sinned 9/13; offended 124/31.

trete *v.* negotiate 178/14; persuade 129/2; **tretyn** try to arrange 228/29. *p.t.* **tretid** negotiated 125/13.

trety *n.* discussion of terms 117/26; **treté** 179/21; settlement 89/31.

tretyng *vbl.n.* discussion 135/24.

tretis, -ys *n.* negotiation 200/8; settlement 168/27.

tretour *n.* traitor 101/12, 142/24.

treuly *adv.* truly; faithfully 70/19, 248/21; honourably 153/15; (emph.) indeed 115/15, 144/5.

treuth *n.* truth; solemn promise 214/4; agreement 141/33; uprightness 200/14; (phr.) *for a* ~ as a fact 226/7; *þe veri* ~ *of my consciens* a full and accurate account of my feelings in conscience 238/12.

trew(e) *adj.* true, faithful, loyal 9/14, 11/18, 126/21; upright 53/21, 212/14. *compar.* **trewer** 12/26. *superl.* **treuhest** 21/13.

trews, treus *n.* truce; *take* ~ make temporary peace 144/19, sim. (p.t.) 77/13.

tribus *n. pl.* tribes (of Israel) 20/4.

trode see **trede.**

Troian *n.* native of Troy 47/4. See also *Index,* s.n. **Troye.**

trone *n.* throne 39/1.

trost *n.* trust; (w. *to* 'in') 221/2.

trost *v.* trust. *pr.p.* **trosting.** *p.t.* **trosted** relied 239/8.

trosti *adj.* trustworthy 82/8.

trouble *n.* public disturbance 56/2, 184/21.

troubled *p.t.* harassed 189/29.

trumpis *n. pl.* trumpets 29/29.

tuycioun *n.* safe keeping 150/2.

tunge *n.* speech 108/22. *pl.* **tongis** advisers 139/6.

tunne *n.* (coll. sg.) barrels 187/23; tub 41/17, 234/8.

turne *v.* read through 7/16; convert 108/14; ~ *ageyn* go back 179/8. *pr. 1 sg.* ~ return 166/17. *imper.* ~ change 134/21. *p.t.* **turned** passed 189/13; went over 163/17; was changed 179/10; led (to) as a consequence 180/26; transpired 151/5; *turned ageyn* went back 58/11, 142/14, reverted 202/8. *pp.* **turned** converted 48/24.

tutour *n.* guardian 151/10 n.

twyes, twies *adv.* twice 8/28, 32/28, 126/8.

Vfforthis *n. pl.* members of the **Vfford** family, viz. Robert (1st earl of Suffolk) and Ralph 156/5.

vndir *prep.* during 38/23; at the hands of 140/14; on 171/14; as 155/31.

vndirstand *pp.* understood 96/2.

vndirtake *v.* rebuke (w. *of* 'for') 16/17. *p.t. sg.* **vndirtook** 73/18. *pp.* ~ 11/21.

vnkynde see **onkende**.

vnritefully see **onrithfully**.

vnsowid *pp. adj.* unstitched 74/13.

vntillid *pp. adj.* uncultivated 166/31.

vntreuly *adv.* treacherously 81/16. Cf. **ontrew(e)**.

up *adv.* open 126/10; up in arms 121/30; ~ *to* to the top of 27/13 n.

up *prep.* upon 56/22, 152/16.

vphap *adv.* perhaps 68/15.

upon, vpon *prep.* over 20/17; on peril of 132/25; against 190/8; with reference to 181/15; ~ *þis* on this subject 163/27.

uprysyng *vbl.n.* rising 99/17.

us *pron. 1 pl.* (used by single person of himself) me ('royal') 110/36, 148/12.

usage *n.* established practice 192/24.

vse *n.* custom 206/24.

vse, use *v.* observe 235/7; enforce 103/26; have sexual intercourse with 54/9; partake of 174/8. *pr. 3 sg.* **vsith** follows 220/6. *p.t.* **vsed** carried out 98/6; practised 27/9; accustomed 219/13. *pp.* **used** engaged in 196/12.

vsure *n.* usury 127/24.

vsurped *p.t.* claimed 106/34.

vttir *adj.* absolute 243/24. *superl.* used absol. in *to þe vtterest* as severely as possible 229/21.

valew *n.* worth 226/18; equivalent (in material worth) 152/15.

variacioun *n.* discrepancy 39/22.

veynes *n. pl.* in ~ *of þe erde* small channels in the ground through which liquid flows 13/26.

velim *n.* vellum 7/31.

venge *v.* (refl.) inflict retributive punishment 17/27, 175/23; avenge

50/17, 129/32. *p.t.* **venged** 78/22 (refl.); **vengid** 72/3. *pp.* **vengid** 27/29 (refl.), 147/6; **venged** 114/37.

venim, venym *n.* poison 42/25, 126/7.

venjabil *adj.* vengeful 57/13.

venjauns *n.* vengeance 11/20, 131/12.

veri, very *adj.* true 19/26, 117/10; real 59/20; actual 13/14; veritable 73/16, 199/18.

very *adv.* really 99/22; truly 137/4.

verili, -ly, veryly *adv.* in truth 23/16, 166/24; in reality 199/24.

vernicle *n.* woman's cloth used to wipe Christ's face and on which his features were impressed 50/17.

vers *n. pl.* lines of verse 45/16, 134/16.

vertu, uertu *n.* power inherent in divine being 41/29; high merit 50/32.

vestimentis *n. pl.* ecclesiastical vestments 58/14, 154/18.

vexacioun *n.* harassment 95/17.

viage *n.* military expedition 121/31; *holy* ~ crusade 121/19; *took his* ~ journeyed 126/30.

vicarie *n.* vicar 183/13.

viciat *pp. adj.* spoiled 7/21.

vigil(e) *n.* eve of church festival 167/29.

vileny, vilony(e) *n.* insult 114/36; dishonour 157/23; discredit 180/26.

vilens *adj.* offensively opprobrious 97/1.

vilensly *adv.* vilely 182/26.

vine *n.* vineyard 116/17.

vyntage *n.* (?) fleet 187/22 n.

visibily *adv.* in a visible form 111/16.

visitacioun *n.* in *þe* ~ *of oure Lady* the day (2 July) on which the visit paid by the Virgin Mary to Elizabeth is commemorated 199/2.

uisite *v.* visit (w. *with* 'bringing') 82/10. *p.t.* **visit(e)** 83/28; **visited** 42/24, 157/32.

vitail(e) *n. coll. sg.* food, provisions 114/11, 138/22; naval provisions 247/13; **vitale** 169/11. *pl.* **vitailes** supplies 245/17.

vitailed *p.t.* furnished with provisions 189/1.

voide *adj.* worthless 21/33.

voide, voyde *v.* evacuate 98/30;
depart 194/7. *p.t.* voyded, voided
quit 113/30; spat 191/28; departed
195/26. *pp.* voyded emptied (w. *fro*
'of') 203/6.

waged *pp.* remunerated with pay
236/11.

wagis *n. pl.* soldiers' pay 241/22.

wayte *v.* in ~ *upon* escort 228/18.

walkith *pr. 3 sg.* is leading 226/2.
p.t. walkid traversed 63/16.

walnotes *n. pl.* walnuts 245/18.

Walsch *adj.* Welsh 219/15.

Wal(s)chmen *n. pl.* people of Wales
91/10; Welsh soldiers 129/7.

wan see wyn.

want *pr. 1 sg.* lack 7/11. *p.t.* wanted
47/6.

wantyng *vbl.n.* lack 165/33.

war *adj.* aware 107/23, 241/29; prepared 45/27.

ward *adv.* in *fro him* ~ away from
him 115/16.

wardeyne *n.* governor 199/7.

wardes *n. pl.* wardships, the guar-
dianship and custody of the persons
and lands of minors with all profits
accruing during minority 156/22;
divisions of fortress 150/15.

warned *p.t.* told, instructed 106/18.
pp. ~ 12/17, 239/22.

waschid *pp.* whitewashed 64/14.

waspis *n. pl.* in *a greuous sekenes of*
~ *in his nose* ? irascibility 50/16 n.

wasted, -id *p.t.* devastated 66/30,
140/30; diminished and disappeared
(w. *oute of* 'from') 66/28.

water, -ir *n.* stream 59/27; river
27/25, 210/24; (w. *of*) 73/30, 165/8.
pl. wateres rain-water as collected
in the clouds 18/20; floods 158/20;
see also *Index*, s.n. Scipping.

wax *v.* become 236/13. *p.t.* wex
111/8, 137/11.

we *pron. 1 pl.* (used by single person
of himself) I ('royal') 110/36, 144/5;
('editorial') 8/22, 11/25, 117/36.
See also oure, us.

wech see whech.

wedde *n.* pledge, in *laid to* ~ mort-
gaged 202/9.

wedded *p.t.* in ~ *a wyf* got married
109/25.

wedding *vbl.n.* married state 46/1.

wed(d)ir *n.* weather 166/17; wedyr
storm 119/14.

wedlak *n.* marriage 225/31.

we(e)l *adv.* well 28/12, 125/24; with
good fortune 103/36; readily 145/
30; very 43/20; ~ *at ese* comfortably
placed 225/17.

weel-wyllid *adj.* favourably disposed
(w. *to* 'towards') 192/20.

wey(e) *n.* street 50/5; passage 156/3;
(in phr.) way 144/1; journey 223/
30; *be þe* ~ in the course of his
journey 85/1, 216/19; course of
life 8/38, 74/4; see also maner.
adv. gen. weyes along routes 121/4.

weye *v.* weigh 172/17. *p.t.* weied
127/26; weyed 71/15.

welle *n.* river 32/29; miraculous
spring, fountain 50/9.

welowes *n. pl.* willow-trees 161/17.

wene *pr. 3 pl.* think 37/4. *pr.p.*
wenyng 106/17, 161/31.

went *p.t.* departed 20/14; was proceeding 73/21, 226/24; were going
around 106/10; went about 240/26;
was filled 95/19; was transferred
90/2, 202/2; was current 56/9, 229/
14; (phr.) cohabited (w. *with*) 56/24;
~ *on his feet* proceeded on foot
83/28; ~ *bak* backed out 145/28;
~ *of* was severed 208/23.

wepyng *pr.p. adj.* in ~ *teres* abundant
weeping 198/7.

wepun *n. pl.* arms 15/8; wepenes
13/20.

were[1] *p.t. pl.* lived 43/12; had existed
113/10; (ellipt.) there were 21/23;
(w. pp.) had 203/6. *subj. sg.* was
24/1, 186/12. See also be.

were[2] *p.t.* wore 82/15; wered 56/11,
247/10.

werk *n.* act 9/11; deed 155/4; work
114/8; task 188/5; building 126/20;
building operation 171/24; literary
work 7/16, 71/30, 119/5. *pl.*
werkis skills 13/9.

werk *v.* see wondir.

werking *vbl.n.* effectiveness 14/22.

werkman *n.* man who practises a
skill 114/3.

werre *n.* war 45/1, 124/9.

werriour *n.* warrior 107/6, 177/8; commander 74/6 n.

wers *compar. adj.* worse 111/12, 196/22; as *n.* in *had þe* ~ *was defeated* 89/30. *superl.* **werst** 145/17.

wete *v.* find out 140/2; **wite** 106/20, 150/11; *doyng to* ~ informing 183/4. *p.t.* **wist, wyst** 122/19; knew 97/11, 165/1.

wex see **wax**.

whan(ne) *conj.* when 7/13, 11/4, 117/5; **qwan** 209/3.

whas *p.t.* was 130/4.

what *adj. interrog.* which 97/31, 140/10. *indef.* any . . . who 40/1, 241/1; whatever 28/12, 211/17.

what *pron. interrog.* who 91/25.

whech *adj. rel.* which 8/30, 11/9, 117/10.

whech *pron. interrog.* which 60/22. *rel.* which 7/29, 11/27, 117/27; **wech** 60/32; who 7/10, 17/25, 117/2; ~ *þat* 38/15; whom 13/33, 131/22; (after co-ordinate *same* or *swech*) as 42/2, 91/23, 161/25; ? such as 166/28.

whedir see **whidir**.

wheythir *conj.* whether 163/12 n.

whidir *adv. interrog.* to what place 165/1, **whedir** 241/32. *rel.* to which place 220/25.

whil *adv. rel.* during which 211/26.

whil *conj.* when 38/27, 126/2; **whill** while 162/33.

whilis *conj.* while 132/10.

white *adj.* fair 53/7; **wite** white 56/27. See also *Index*, s.n. **White Felauchip**.

white *n.* weight 167/17.

who *adv. interrog.* how 17/14, 130/8; ~ *þat* 157/15; that 110/1, 134/10; ~ *þat* 154/4. *rel.* however 114/34; ~ *it be of þat* however that may be 105/33.

who *pron. rel.* anyone who 152/18; ~ *þat* 97/7 (w. correl. pron.); the one who 103/19. *obl.* whom anyone whom 68/34; which 117/14. *gen.* **whos** of which 27/27.

wich *n.* magician 75/7.

Wiclefistis *n. pl.* followers of Wiclef 191/20.

wif, wyf *n.* wife. *poss.* **wyues** 128/22. *pl.* **wyues** mistresses 105/28.

wykyris *n. pl.* wickerwork 26/24.

wil(l) *n.* desire, wish 71/10, 193/21; *with good* ~ voluntarily 213/25; *þe bettir* ~ more goodwill 163/5; *aftir* (or *ageyn*) *þe kyngis* ~ according (in opposition) to the king's wish 115/37, 193/3; *in* ~ purposing 220/9.

wil(l) *pr. pl.* choose to 7/32; are determined to 139/18; *we* ~ let us 98/24, 140/4. *p.t.* **wold(e)** would 44/24, 118/20; desired 41/18, 132/20; wished for 131/22; ordained 14/27, 218/20; wished to 47/10, 127/9; intended to 104/12; (w. inf. of motion understood) intended to go 165/2; (w. neg.) could 201/3; *wold not be* was all in vain 234/13; *2 sg. subj.* **woldist** would like 226/3; *auxil.* (subj.) w. p. inf. *wold* (*h*)*a* (= *haue*) + pp. would have 71/4, 126/2.

wyn *v.* subdue and take possession of, capture 121/29. *p.t. sg.* **wan** 22/19, 163/20. *p.t. pl.* **wonne** 107/13, 157/27. *pp.* **wonne** 144/5; **wunne** 121/22.

wynd *n.* forceful puff of breath 62/16.

wyntir, -yr *n. pl.* years 12/7, 173/17.

wisdam *n.* knowledge, understanding 32/31.

wis(e) *adj.* knowledgeable 32/11 (w. *in* 'with regard to').

wise *n.* in various phr.: *in no* ~ not at all, by no means 37/8, 105/28; *in þe best* ~ well 56/1; *on þis* ~ as follows 98/32; *on þe moost malicious* ~ very vindictively 191/22.

wist, wyst see **wete**.

wit see **wit(te)**.

wite *adj.* see **white**.

wite *v.* see **wete**.

with, wit3, wyth *prep.* against 39/12, 191/2; in favour of 180/25; by the use of 56/17; by 11/5, 125/18; at 42/8, 124/4; in 23/31, 198/18; on 133/20; through 56/12, 150/30; ~ *þe best* from among the most distinguished 244/22; ~ *him* in his possession 155/26.

withdrawe *v.* withhold 221/14; (refl.) withdraw 236/4. *p.t.* **withdrow** refrained from proceeding with 204/13; (refl.) 144/8.

withoute *adv.* outside 126/9.

withoute *prep.* outside, beyond 41/25; (absol.) 83/10; **withouten** without 9/5, 24/25, 140/23.

withstood *p.t.* opposed 163/25.

witnesseth *pr. 3 sg.* attests 21/21.

wit(te) *n.* intellect 41/33; mental ability, skill 59/17, 239/9.

wyues see **wif**.

wodnes *n.* violent anger 185/21.

wodwous *n.* wild man of the woods 201/25.

wolkom *adj.* welcome 160/5.

wolland *n.* cloth made of wool 242/15.

wolle *n.* wool 29/27, 140/23; þe *occupacion of* ~ the employment of working in wool 83/27. *pl.* **wolles, -is** supplies of wool 160/6. See also **sak**.

wombe *n.* abdomen 62/30.

wondir *n.* in *it is not grete* ~ it is not very surprising 40/16, (sim. without neg.) 161/9; *haue* ~ be greatly surprised 16/12, (sim.) 221/21. *pl.* in *werk wonderes* perform miracles 17/16.

wone *adj.* wont 87/13, 136/17.

wonne see **wyn**.

wont *n.* custom 135/30.

wood *adj.* mad 134/22 n. in *Be-cursed-and-wood*, tr. L *maledic[it]e* 'a curse upon you', appellation used of Pope Benedict XI.

worcheped *p.t.* worshipped 36/17. *pp.* **worchipid** honoured 156/16.

worchip, -chep *n.* renown 71/27, 177/5; credit 209/9; dignity 63/25,

149/5; honour 84/16, 136/20; *to/in* þe ~ *of* in honour of 32/4, 113/14; *do* ~ *to* pay respects to 140/10.

worchipful(l) *adj.* distinguished 103/34, 157/11.

worchip(p)fully *adv.* with due honour 64/10, 150/7.

worchiphing *vbl.n.* worshipping 20/27.

word *n.*[1] speech 243/16; statement 144/4; saying 103/36. *pl.* **wordis, -es** ? form of the text 43/24; *had* þe *wordis* spoke as their leading representative 194/27.

word *n.*[2] world 15/6. *pl.* **worldis** regions of the earth 116/23.

worthi, -y, worþi *adj.* of high standing 53/27, 180/3; *were* ~ deserved 193/6. *compar.* **worthier** of higher standing 103/17.

woue *pp.* woven 159/18.

wrecchidhest *adj. superl.* most contemptible 50/4.

wrechid *pp.* avenged 243/27.

wryte *n.* carpenter 188/2.

writeres *n. pl.* scribes 7/21, 56/5.

writith *pr. 3 sg.* writes 23/20, 49/24 (hist.). *pl.* **writyn** 104/30. *p.t. sg.* **wrote** in ~ *down* sent written instructions 121/17. *pl.* **writyn, -in** 92/5, 134/9. *pp.* **wretin** 99/8; **wrytin** inscribed 45/16.

wrong *adj.* unlawful 176/7.

wrong *adv.* erroneously 68/26.

wroth *adj.* very angry, stirred to wrath 17/27, 132/16.

wroute *p.t.* did 131/33; carried out 34/28; worked 13/8.

wunne see **wyn**.

zelator *n.* defender, supporter 244/4. *pl.* **zelato(u)ris** 152/3.

GLOSSARIAL INDEX

THE main purpose is to provide an index to the varied material contained in the work as well as to gloss unfamiliar forms and provide brief explanatory notes when appropriate. Completeness is aimed at, but, while titles are given as fully as possible, no attempt has been made to record all orthographic variants and (unless a line reference is essential) references are to pages only. For names of persons containing *at/of (þe)* or *de (la)* see the word following (except when the word following *þe* is an ordinal number or other descriptive adjective). Titles of books are to be found under the first noun or adjective in the title. In the alphabetical arrangement Latin and English forms of a name (e.g. *Antonius* and *Antony*) are often treated as equivalent.

The following special abbreviations are employed:

a	abbot	k	king
ab	archbishop	l	lord
b(ps)	bishop(s)	m	mother
br	brother	mq	marquis
c	count	p	prince
da	daughter	q	queen
dk(s)	duke(s)	s	son
e	earl	sr	sister
emp	emperor	vc	viscount
f	father	w	wife
fd	feast-day		

Abacuch Habakkuk; (body of) 66.

Abbreuiacion of Cronicles 'Abridgement of Chronicles', title given by C to the present work 248. Cf. *Glossary*, s.v. abreuiacioun.

Abda, putative f of **Daniel** 39.

Abdon 30.

Abel 11, 12.

Aberden Aberdeen 217.

Abessem see **Esebon**.

Abgarus Abgar V (4 BC–AD 50), k of Edessa 108.

Abia Abijam, k of Judah (959–956 BC) 33/12 n.

Abimelech 29.

Abyngdon Abingdon, Berks. 216; (monastery at) 95.

Abyngdon, Maistir Edmund, also **Seint Edmund** of Abingdon (Ed-mund Rich), ab of Canterbury (1233–40) 120; (fd of, 26 Nov.) 126. *gen.* in *Seynt Edmund day þe archbischop* 153.

Abra(h)am 15, 19, 22, 23, 24, 26, 27. *poss.* ~ 15/16, 23/22.

Abrustwith Aberystwyth, Cardigan-shire; (castle of) 232.

Absalon *poss.* of Abishalom 33.

Aburre erron. for Alboïn, k of Lom-bards (561–72) 73.

Achay Achaia = Greece 48/27 n.

Achaz Ahaz, k of Judah (742–726 BC) 36. *poss.* ~ 37.

Achildes, name of monster reported to have been killed by Hercules 28.

Acon, Acris Acre, Palestine 84, 101, 114, 125, 126, 130.

Acris, Dame Jone Joan of Acre, da of Edward I 130.

Actus Apostolorum L for Acts of the Apostles; (verse commentary on by Arator) 71.

Ada Adah 13.

Adam 11–12, 14, 15; (as head of 1st generation of Jewish patriarchs) 15, 19; (of 7th, 10th, 20th generations) see **Ennok, Noe, Abraham;** (as figure standing at beginning of time) 7, 47–8, 116; (as 1st sinner) 9.

Adam Orleton, b of Hereford (1317–27) 146, 149–50, 151, 153.

Adam, Ser see **Eston.**

Adamarius Aymardus, a of Cluny (942–8) 91.

Adelida Adela, q to Henry I 105.

Adelstan see **Athelstan.**

Adelwolf Æthelwulf, k of W Saxons (839–55) 86; (erron.) **Adelwold** 89.

Adrian Hadrian, emp (117–38) 52.

Adrianus Ius Adrian I, pope (772–95) 82–3, 84.

Adrianus IIus, pope (867–72) 88.

Adrian þe þirde, pope (884–5) 88.

Adrianus IIus, erron. for Adrian IV, pope (1154–9) 108.

Adriane þe V, pope (1276) 127–8. See also **Octobone.**

Aduentinus, Mons Aventine hill, Rome 35.

Adventinus, Siluius see **Siluius.**

Aella¹ ? Aelle, k of Deira (559–88) erron. attrib. to Mercia 80/8.

Aella² prob. Adda, k of Bernicia (559–67) 80/14.

Affrik Africa 26, 44, 61, 71, 85; (people of) 19; (Vandal kingdom in: (a) Hunneric, k of; (b) churches in) a 69, b 70.

Agapitus St. Agapetus I, pope (535–6) 71, 72.

Agapitus Agapetus II, pope (946–55) 91.

Agas St. Agatha 60.

Agaton St. Agatho, pope (678–81) 77.

Agenes Agenais, France 169.

Ageny Agen, France; (lordship of) 128.

Agnes, (Seynt) 60; (church of, Rome) 75.

Agnus Dei L for 'Lamb of God', 1st words of communion prayer said while celebrant receives host 77, 96.

Ayoth Ehud 28.

Alba Longa, Latium 31.

Albanactus 31.

Albania Scotland 31.

Albanie Albanopolis 49.

Albemarle see **Awmarle.**

Albericus Alaric, k of Visigoths (395–410) 66.

Albert¹ Alberic, c of Tusculum (932–54) 91.

Albert² Adalbert, joint-k of Italy (950 ff.) 92.

Albinus Alcuin 83.

Albon, (Seynt) St. Alban (3rd cent.) 140.

Alcoran The Koran 75.

Aldred Ealdred, ab of York (1060–9) 102.

Alenconye gen. of Alençon; (count) see **Jon³.**

Alexander Mammeas Alexander Severus, emp (222–35) 55/30 n.

Alexander/Alisaunder II, k of Scotland (1214–49) 133.

Alisaundre Paris of Troy, called *Alexander* 30.

Alisaundre, (Kyng) Alexander the Great (355–323 BC) 22, 41, 42, 43; (time of) 8, 22. *poss.* ~ 43/1.

Alisaundre St. Alexander I, pope (105–15) 52.

Alexander IIus, pope (1061–73) 99; **Alisaundre** 101, 102.

Alisaundre, (þe Pope) Alexander IV (1254–61) 119/27 n., 122–3.

Alisaundir þe Fift Alexander V, pope at Pisa (1409–10) 233, 234.

Alisaundre Alexandria, Egypt 43, 44, 53, 54, 64, 69, 175; (people of) 44; (Church council at) 55; (b of) see **Cirille.**

Alfrik Ælfthryth, 3rd q of Edgar, m of Ethelred the Unready 95.

Alisaundre indexed with **Alexander.**

Al(l)-halow feast of All Saints (1 Nov.) 74, 174; **Halowmesse** 201/2.

Almagest Arabic name meaning 'Great Work' given to Ptolemy's *System of Mathematics* 53.

Almayn (Holy Roman Empire of) Germany 58, 90, 91, 93, 112; (knights of) 164; (alleged emp of) see **Richard**[5]; (persons from = **Almanes**) 90, 93. See also **Germanie**.

Almaricus Amalric, scholastic philosopher (d. *c*.1207) 112.

Al Seintis feast of All Saints (1 Nov.) 242. Cf. **Al(l)-halow**.

Alum, Maystir Robert Robert Hallum, b of Salisbury (1407–17) 233, 242.

Aluerne Auvergne, France 179; (c of) see **Jon**[11].

Alured[1] Alfred, k of W Saxons (871–99) 86, 89; (s of) 91.

Alured[2] Alfred (d. 1036), br of Edward the Confessor 99–100, 101.

Amalthea name of Sibyl of Cumae, Italy 37.

Amasias Amaziah, k of Judah (838–808 BC) 35.

Ambianense see **Amyas**.

Ambri Amram 26.

Ambrisbury Amesbury, Wilts.; (convent at) 95.

Ambrose, Seint, b of Milan (374–97) 62, 64, 65, 66.

Amyas Amiens, France 124; **Ambianense** 201.

Amon[1], k of Judah (642–640 BC) 38/1 n.

Amon[2] Ammon 41.

Amphibalus, 3rd cent. martyr 140.

Anaclete St. Anacletus I, pope (78–90) 51/29 n., 50/26.

Anastace, Seint St. Anastasius the Persian (d. 628); *Seint Anastace at þe Scipping Wateris*, church of St. Vincent and St. Anastasius, EUR, Rome 82–3.

Anastase St. Anastasia, 3rd cent. martyr 60.

Anastase Anastasius, patriarch of Constantinople (730–53) 81.

Anastasius I, emp of E (491–518) 70/4.

Anastasius Secundus, emp of E (713–15) 80.

Anastasius I, pope (399–401) 66.

Anastasius II, pope (496–8) 70/18.

Anastasius III[us], pope (911–13) 90.

Anastasius IIII, pope (1153–4) 108.

Anatoth Anathoth 38.

Ancelme Anselm, prior and a of Bec (1063–93), ab of Canterbury (1093–1109) 103.

Andrew, (Seynt), apostle 48; (body of) 63.

Androche Androgeus, nephew of **Cassebelian**, overlord of London and Kent 46.

Angliseye Anglesey 128.

Angoye Anjou 123; (c of) see **Charlys, Herri þe Secunde, Plauntgenet**; (Louis, dk of) 179, 184.

Angolisme, Richard of Guichard d'Angle, e of Huntingdon (1377–80) 182.

Aniane, Seynt St. Anianus of Orléans (1st half 5th cent.); (fd of, 17 Nov.) 96.

Anicetus, pope (155–66) 54.

Anyslé, Ser Jon Sir John Annesley 180.

Anlaf[1] Olaf Guthfrithson, k of Norse kingdom of Dublin (d. 941) 92.

Anlaf[2] Olaf Tryggvason, k of Norway 96.

Anne Hannah 31.

Anne, (Qwen) of Bohemia, sr of Emperor Wenceslas, q of Richard II 186, 202.

Antecrist Antichrist 16/10 n., 17, 33, 116, 220; (name for pope) 241.

Anteros Anterus, pope (235–6) 56.

Anthé Antaeus 28.

Anthemius Anthimus, b of Trebizond (533–5), patriarch of Constantinople (535–6) 81.

Antigonus, k of Asia Minor and Syria (323–301 BC) 43.

Antioche Antioch, Asia Minor 43, 49, 52, 71, 101; (b of) see **Gregorie, Ignace, Paule**[4] (erron. for Ancona).

Antiochus (Magnus) Antiochus III, the Great, k of (Seleucid) Asia (223–187 BC) 44.

Antoni (þe Meke) Antoninus Pius, emp (138–61) 52–3.

Antoni(e) = Marcus Antoni þe Trewe see **Marcus**.

Antonius Carcalla Caracalla, emp (211–17) 55.

Antonius Aurelius Heliogabalus, emp (218–22) 55.

Antony, (Seynt), of Egypt (3rd–4th cent.) 63, 113.

Anwerp Antwerp 161.

Apocalipse, þe The Revelation of John 48, 109.

Apocripha Apocrypha 16.

Apocriphum Gk for 'hidden (thing)', name given to **Penauns of Adam** q.v.

Appia, Porta, now Porta San Sebastiano, Rome 52.

Appollo Apollo 29, 37.

Aput Aquas Saluias see **Scipping Wateres.**

Aquila 52.

Aquitense gen. erron. for *Aquense* of Aachen 210; see **Bosco.**

Arabes, þe see **Damask.**

Ara Celi L for 'Altar of Heaven', church of S. Maria in Aracoeli, Rome 47.

Aragon 242; (k of) 235, 249 (Ferdinand I, 1411–16), and see **Petir³.**

Aram 18.

Arath Ararat 108/24 n.

Araxen R Araxes (Aras), Armenia 22. Cf. **Fasiden.**

Arbe (city of) Arba, see **Cariatharbe.**

Archadie Arcadia, country in middle of Gk Peloponnesus 23, 28.

Archadius Arcadius, emp of E (395–408) 66.

Arderne Arden, War.; **þe Blak Dog** of ~, abusive name for **Gy of Warwik.**

Ardyngnete, site of Augustinian house near Sens 113.

Argyues, þe kyngdom of þe Argos 25; (k of) see **Ymacho, Phoroneus.**

Aristotoles Aristotle 41–2.

Armachan, name given to Richard FitzRalph, ab of Armagh (1346–60) 170.

Armenak Armagnac; (Bernard VII, c of) 235, 246; title used erron. of **Jon³** 237/1 n.

Armenie Armenia 19, 49; (k of) 189; (men of = **Armenes**) 74.

Arnulphus Arnulf, k of Germans (887–), emp (896–9) 89.

Aron Aaron 26.

Arphaxat Arphaxad 18, 19; (descendants of) 19.

Arpie Harpies 28.

Arry, Arrian Arius, heretic 61, 62, 70; (followers of = **Arrianes**) 61, 62, 65, 69, 70, 71.

Arsanius Arsanes 42/6 n.

Arstulf Aistulf, k of Lombards (749–57) 81.

Artharxerses Artaxerxes I, k of Persia (464–425 BC) 40.

Artarxerses Artaxerxes II, k of Persia (404–358 BC) 41/8.

Artarxerses called **Othus** Artaxerxes III surnamed *Ochus*, k of Persia (358–337 BC) 22, 41/21.

Arthure¹ Arthur, putative k of the British 69, 134, 164; (body of) 110. poss. **Arthures** 110.

Arthure², s of Geoffrey of Brittany, nephew of Richard I and John 115, 117. poss. ~ 117/9 n.

Arthure³, br of **Jon Mountforth,** e of Richmond (1372–84, 1398–9) 246.

Arundel, Thomas, ab of York (1388–96), of Canterbury (1396–7, 1399–1414), Chancellor (1391–6) 202, 203, 206, 208, 211, 213, 214, 215, 223, 226, 229, 230, 235, 239–41.

Arundel, þe Erle Thomas FitzAlan, e of Arundel (1400–15) 229, 230, 236, 237, 245. For other earls see **Edmund, Richard** FitzAlan.

Aruigarus Arvirargus or Armoger, British chief (AD 43 ff.) 49/27 n.

Asa, k of Judah (956–915 BC) 33.

Ascanius 31.

Ascor ?R Cyrus (Kura) 22.

Asie Asia Minor 23, 51, 53; (kingdom of under **Antigonus**) 43; (bps of) 53.

Asseles erron. for Atholl; (e of) see **Dauid.**

Assiry Assyria; (kingdom of) 21, 22–3; (k of) 24, and see **Senacherib;** (army of) 37; (people of = **Assirianes**) 18, and see *Glossary,* s.v. **Assiriis.**

Assisé Assisi 113.

Assuerus Ahasuerus 41. [Esther 1: 1]

Assur Asshur 18.

Atenes see **Attenes.**

Athalia Athaliah, q of Judah (883–877 BC) 34.

Athanasius, b of Alexandria (328–73) 62–3, 64.

Athelford erron. for Ethelfrith, k of Bernicia and Deira (593–616) 80.

Athelstan, k of W Saxons (924–39) 92; (half-br of) 93, 94.

Athelwold erron. for Æthelwalh, k of S Saxons (fl. 674–80) 79.

Athla(n)s Atlas, k of Mauritania 26/14, 28.

Athlans, The Mount Mt Atlas 26/15.

Athlantis *poss.* prob. for the Atlantides (confused w. Hesperides) 28.

Attenes Athens 21, 28, 41, 42, 53, 87.

Audré, Seynt St. Audrey (Etheldreda) of Ely; (fd of, 23 June) 179.

Au(gu)stin, Seynt, b of Hippo (396–430) 23–4, 65–7, 71, 122–3; (tomb of) 176; (rule of) 181; (Order of Hermits of) 7, 113, 119, 141; (members of OESA = Austines) 122, 170, 191, 208; (houses of OESA) 119, 122, and see **Clare, Lenne;** (Augustinian Canons) 141, 158. *poss.* ~ 81/5, 107/3, 242/10.

Aungel Angelo Correr, Pope **Gregorius XII,** q.v.

Aungel, (þe) Castel (of) Castel Sant'Angelo, Rome 93, 94, 210, 231.

Aungeles, Seynt Mary of S. Maria degli Angeli, Assisi 113.

Aurea, name of street in Borgo area of Rome 50.

Aurely Aureolus, general who tried to become emp 58.

Aurelianense Orléans 59; (university of) 233.

Aurelianense *gen.* in *þe Duke* ~ Louis, dk of Orléans (d. 1407) 206/3. See also **Charlis.**

Aurelianus Aurelian, emp (270–5) 58–9.

Austin (of Hippo) see **Augustin.**

Austin, Seint St. Augustine, ab of Canterbury (597–604) 74, 79. *poss.* in *Seyn Austyn day* (26 May) 93/17.

Auallone isle of Avalon, legendary burial place of Arthur 69, 110.

Auinioun Avignon 135, 158; (b of) see **Johannes XXII.**

Awdlé/Haudlé, (Ser) Hew Hugh Audley, e of Gloucester (1337–47) 147, 159.

Awmarle/Albemarle Aumale; (dk of) see **Edward 'of York'.**

Azuba Azubah 33.

Baal *poss.* 34. Cf. **Bel.**

Babilonie Babylon 37–9, 42, 51; (k of) see **Nabugodonosor;** (sultan of) see *Glossary,* s.v. **soudan.**

Bacheler, William William Bachelor, member of chapter of Lincoln cathedral 164.

Bagot, Sir **William** 208, 212.

Baylol, see **Baliol.**

Bayon Bayonne 133, 179; erron. for Bayeux 102.

Baldak, the Kyng ruler of Baghdad 175.

Baldewyn[1] Baldwin, a of Bury St. Edmunds 102.

Baldewyn[2] Baldwin, ab of Canterbury (1184–90) 113.

Baldok, Robert Robert Baldock, Chancellor (1323–6) 148, 152, 153.

Baliol/Baylol, Edward (de) Edward Balliol, titular k of Scots (1332–6) 156–8, 169.

Balthasar see **Jon XXIII.**

Balthasardan, also called **Morettus** Bajazet I, sultan of Ottoman Turks (1389–1403) 204; (s of) 218.

Banborow[1] for Brunanburh, OE name for unknown site of battle (937) 92.

Banborow[2] Bamborough, Northumberland 157.

Banburgense *gen.* of Bamberg 96.

Bangor (Llywelyn Bifort, b of, 1405–8) 232.

Barabas, reported Arian b (c.500) 70.

Barach Barak 29.

Bardolf, Lord/Ser Thomas, l of Wormegay (1386–1406) 227, 229, 232.

Baré Bari; (Vrbane þe Sexte, b of, 1377–8) 182.

Barlaam, legendary saint 64.

Barnabé, Seynt Barnabas, apostle; (body of) 69.

Barry see **Berry.**

Bartholomé, (Seynt) St. Bartholomew, apostle 49; (body of) 94; (church of, Smithfield) 233.

Bas Île de Batz 196.

Basile St. Basil, b of Caesarea (370–9) 63–4.

Basili Basle erron. for Constance 249.

Bassan, s of Bajazet I Ottoman sultan, ? erron. for Bassak 218.

Basset, Raf¹ Ralph Basset of Drayton 124.

Basset, Raf² Sir Ralph Basset, seneschal of Gascony 150.

Batayle Battle, Sussex; (abbey of) 102.

Bateman, William, b of Norwich (1344–55) 164, 168.

Bathe Bath; erron. for Bayeux 102; (Nicholas Bubwith, b of ∼ and Wells, 1407–24) 242.

Batilesmere, Bartholomé Bartholomew Badlesmere, steward of royal household (1318–21) 146, 147.

Bauaré Bavaria; (Lewis IV, dk of and emp, 1314–47) 161; (people of = **Bauaris**) 84.

Bauer Bar; (Edward, dk of) 245.

Beamount, (Ser) Herry Henry de Beaumont, titular e of Buchan (1312–40) 142, 156, 158.

Beamount, Lodewik Lewis de Beaumont, b of Durham (1317–33) 142.

Beamunde erron. for Bohemond (s of Robert Guiscard), c of Apulia (1085–1128) 100.

Bech, Matheus de la erron. for Sir Nicholas Beche, constable of the Tower (1340) 161.

Bede 47.

Bedforth Bedford 221; (dk of) see **Lord Jon.**

Bedforthschire (river in) 210.

Bek Bec; (abbey of) 102, 103.

Bel form of Baal, god of Babylon 23.

Belchaump, Ser Thomas Thomas Beauchamp, e of Warwick (1329–69) 177.

Belknap, Sir **Robert,** CJKB 192.

Belleiocy the Beaujolais; (l of) see **Jon⁵.**

Bellemount Beaumont-sur-Sarthe; (vc of) see **Charlis.**

Belmaryn, þe Kyng 175.

Bel-phegor Baal-peor, god of Israelites' opponents 23. [Num. 25: 3]

Belus Menpronides/Menprotides Belus, ancient k of Babylon (before Assyrians broke away) 23.

Belzebul prob. for Baal-zebub, god of Israelites' opponents 23. [2 Kgs 1: 2]

Bem Bohemia 192; (dk of) see **Spigreuus, Herry þe First** (erron. for Bavaria); (k of) 95; (John of Luxembourg, k of, 1310–46) 141, 165; (p of) see **Nycenlaus.** See also **Anne.**

Bemound, þe Lord John, Lord Beaumont (1369–96) 187, 195/20 n. See also **Beuchamp, þe Lord.**

Bemount see **Beamount.**

Benedicte Benedetto Gaetani; see **Bonefacius** VIII.

Benedictus þe First, pope (575–9) 73.

Benedictus IIᵘˢ, pope (684–5) 77.

Benedictus IIIᵘˢ, pope (855–8) 87.

Benedictus IIIIᵘˢ, pope (900–3) 89.

Benedictus V, pope (964) 92.

Benedictus VI, pope (973–4) 94.

Benedict þe VII, pope (974–83) 94.

Benedictus VIII, pope (1012–24) 97.

Benedictus IX, pope (1032–44, 1045, 1047–8) 97–8, 102.

Benedictus Xᵘˢ, pope (1058–9) 99.

Benedicte XI, pope (1303–4) 134.

Benedictus XII, pope (1334–42) 158, 163.

Bene(dic)t XIII, also called **Petir de Luna** Pedro de Luna, pope at Avignon (1394–1423) 233, 242, 249; (party of) 233, 242.

Benerles, James erron. for Sir James Berners 195.

Benet, Seynt St. Benedict of Nursia (d. c.550) 72; (body of) 77, 81; (rule of) 181. *poss.* ∼ 242/8.

Beneuent(ane) Benevento 76, 94; (duchy of) 82.

Bentlé, Ser Raf 167.

Beouille, þe Lord 148.

Berengarius Primus, also erron. called **Berengary þe Secunde,** ~ **Tercius** Berengar I (of Friuli), k of Italy (888–), emp (915–24) 90, 90/28 n., 92.

Berengary the Fourte erron. for Berengar II (of Ivrea), k of Italy (950–62) 92–3.

Berengarie Berengar of Tours, 11th-cent. theologian 99, 102, 185.

Bergeueny, Lord (William Beauchamp) Lord Abergavenny (1389–1411) 213.

Bergeueni, þe Lord (Richard Beauchamp) Lord Abergavenny (1411–22) 243.

Berkyng Barking, Essex; (abbess of) see **Mary.**

Berklé, Berkley (castle of) Berkeley, Glos. 152, 154.

Berklé, Ser Mauris Maurice, Lord Berkeley (1321–6) 147.

Berklé, Ser Thomas Thomas III, Lord Berkeley (1326–61) 152, 154.

Berklé, Thomas/þe Lord Thomas IV, Lord Berkeley (1368–1417) 213, 230.

Bernard, Seint (1090–1153) 101, 109–10. *poss.* ~ 107/8.

Bernwelle Barnwell, Cambs. 196.

Ber(r)y, Barry Berri 169; (dk of) see **Jon⁴.**

Bersabe¹ Bathsheba 32.

Bersabe² Beersheba 34.

Berwik¹ Berwick upon Tweed 133, 140, 143–4, 157, 168, 169, 222 (prob. allusion), 225, 229; (castle of) 113; (walls of) 135; (governor of) 143/30, 157/31.

Berwik² Barwick, Norfolk 159.

Berwik³ Great Berwick, Salop 222.

Besibarius erron. for Belisarius 71.

Bethlem Bethlehem 32, 47, 52, 64, 65, 67.

Bethsaida 48–9.

Beucham, William Sir William Beauchamp 185.

Beuchamp, Jon/þe Lord Lord John Beauchamp of Kidderminster or Holt, Steward of the King's Household (1387) 195/13.

Beuchamp, þe Lord erron. for

John, Lord Beaumont 195/20. See **Bemound.**

Beuforth, Herry Henry Beaufort, b of Lincoln (1398–1404), of Winchester (1404–47) 210, 212, 240.

Beuforth, Ser Thomas erron. for John Beaufort, mq of Dorset (1397–9), e of Somerset (1397–1410), mq of Somerset (1397–9) 207, 209/25 n., 215, 229.

Beuforth, (Ser) Thomas Thomas Beaufort, e of Dorset (1411–), dk of Exeter (1416–26), Chancellor (1410–11) 235, 237, 244–5, 246, 249.

Beuirlé Beverley, E Riding of Yorks. 143.

Bias of Priene (fl. 566 BC) 39.

Bible, þe 16, 43, 54, 121. Cf. **Eld(e) Testament.**

Bica = Wodous 119/30 n.

Bierne, Gaske/Gascon of Gaston, vc of Béarn (1229–90) 127.

Bikilliswade Biggleswade, Beds. 221.

Bynham (abbey of) Binham, Norfolk; (prior of) 146.

Byryn, (Seint) St. Birinus, b of Dorchester (634–50) 79, 80.

Birstane, Seynt Beornstan, b of Winchester (931–4) 92.

Biturie = **Berry.**

Bizans Byzantium; see **Constantinople.**

Blake, Jon John Blake, clerk to Tresilian 193.

Blakeheth, þe Blackheath 186, 217.

Blanc erron. for Isabella of Angoulême, q of **(Kyng) Jon** 115.

Blaunch Blanche (of the Tower) (d. 1341) 163.

Blaunche, Dam Blanche, duchess of Lancaster (1361–9) 171, 172.

Blesens (*adj.* of) Blois; (c of) see next and **Charlis, (Kyng) Steuene.**

Bloys, Charles de Charles, c of Blois (d. 1364), would-be dk of Brittany 163, 166, 174.

Bloys Blaye (Gironde) 133.

Blundy, Maystir Jon John Blund, ab-elect of Canterbury (1232–3) 119–20.

Boys Boethius 70, 71.

Bokes of Sentens, þe iiii, the *Sententiarum libri quatuor* by Peter Lombard, a compilation of the opinions of the Fathers on questions of Christian doctrine 109.

Bokyngham Buckingham; (e of) see **Wodstok.**

Boloyne Boulogne 172; (c of) see **(Kyng) Steuene.**

Bonefas Boniface I, pope (418–22) 67.

Boneface þe Secunde, pope (530–2) 72.

Bonefas þe III, pope (607) 74.

Bonefas þe IIII, pope (608–15) 74.

Bonefas þe Fifte, pope (619–25) 75.

Bonefacius þe Sexte, pope (896) 89.

Bonefacius þe Sexte erron. for Boniface VII, pope (974, 984–5) 94.

Bonefacius VIII, called **Benedict** Benedetto Gaetani, pope (1294–1303) 131–2, 133–4.

Bonifacius þe IX, pope (1389–1404) 197, 199, 227.

Bononie Bologna; (university of) 233; (bps of) see Popes **Innocent þe VII, Jon XXIII.**

Borbon, James James de Bourbon, s of Jon[6] 170.

Borboun see **Burbon.**

Bordews see **Burdews.**

Borgayn, -goin see **Burgeyn.**

Borouhbrigge Boroughbridge, W Riding of Yorks. 147.

Borow[1] Peterborough; (abbey at) 95.

Borow[2] Bourg (Dordogne) 133.

Borow, Fulco of erron. for Hubert de Burgh, e of Kent (1227–32, 1234–43), Chief Justiciar (1215–32) 119.

Borow, Dame Ysabel of ? Elizabeth de Burgh, w of Lionel, dk of Clarence 131.

Borow, William of Sir William Burgh 192.

Bosco, Petrus de ? Petrus d'Agoult, b of Aix (Aachen) (1395–7) 210.

Boston, Lincs. 130.

Boteuyle see **Stuteuyle.**

Bothulp, Seynt St. Botulph (7th cent.); (fd of, 17 June) 120.

Bowan Buchan; (countess of) 135 (w of John Comyn, earl 1290–1308).

Bown, Humfrey[1] Humphrey de Bohun, e of Hereford (1299–1322) 136, 145, 146, 147.

Bown, Humfrey[2], e of Hereford (1363–73) 177; (da of) see **Mary.**

Braban Brabant 161; (John III, dk of) 161, 162; (Anthony, dk of) 245.

Bradborne, Herry Henry de Bradbourne 147.

Branburgense Brandenburg; (mq of as imperial elector) 95.

Brandane, Seynt St. Brendan the Voyager 72.

Bresith, reported burial place of Joseph son of Jacob before his bones were removed to Shechem 26.

Brest 191; (castle of) 180, 189.

Bretayn, (Grete) Britayn Great Britain 31, 60, 61; (k of) see **Arthure[1], Lucius;** (people of = **Britones**) 69, 134, 184.

Bretayn/Britayn, (Litil) Brittany 163, 174, 177, 180, 182, 189, 220, 223, 232; (John VI, dk of) 235, and see next, **Bloys, Mountforth;** (governor of) 167; (men of = **Britones**) 187, 223, 224.

Bretayn, Ser Jon (of) John II de Bretagne, dk of Brittany, e of Richmond (1306–34) 144, 149, 150, 151.

Brews, Ser William William de Braose 145.

Brian, Gy Sir Guy Brian 168.

Bryce, Seynt *poss.* St. Brice's (day, 13 Nov.) 96, 173.

Bride, Seynt *poss.* St. Bridget's 242/10 n.

Bridlington, E Riding of Yorks. 197.

Bridlington, Jon, also called **Seynt Jon** John (prior of Austin canons) of Bridlington 224, 228.

Brigerak Bergerac 164.

Bristow Bristol 80, 107, 152, 212, 217; (castle of) 152, 195, 212.

Brokas, Jon 182.

Bronbrigge ? Bridgenorth, Salop 91.

Bronbury unidentified Mercian fortress town, poss. Bromborough, Cheshire 91. [Prob. corr. to OE *Bremesburh*]

Brounfeld, Edmund Edmund Bromfield 183.

Brucegald John II de Boucicaut, marshal of France (1391–1415) 246. Cf. **Bursigalde.**

Bruges 179; (men of) 162.

Brus, Edward Edward Bruce, br of next 140, 143.

Brus, Robert Robert I (Bruce), k of Scots (1306–29) 135, 140, 141, 142, 143, 148, 149. *poss.* **Robard** 135/8.

Brute Brutus, legendary founder of Britain 31. *poss.* **Brutes** 79.

Bulgaris *n. pl.* people of Bulgaria 77.

Burbage, Jon John Burbage, DCL (Oxon.), (d. 1402) 214.

Burbon, Duke see **Jon⁵.**

Burburgh Bourbourg 187.

Burdews Bordeaux 132, 133, 161–2, 169–70, 175, 179; (lieutenant of) see **Mountforth;** (ab of) 119 (Gerald of Malemort, 1227–61), 233 (F. Uguccione, 1384–1412, cardinal 1405–), and see **Clemens Vᵘˢ.**

Burdine Maurice Bourdain, Antipope Gregory VIII (1118–21) 104.

Burgeyn, Burgundy 171, 173, 179; (dks of: Philip de Rouvres, 1349–61) 171, (John the Fearless, 1404–19) 234, 235–6, 237, 248, (erron. of Charles VI of France) 184/17 n., and see **Philip** (the Bold); (da of dk of = Margaret, q of Louis X of France) 160; (p of, erron.) see **Wiliam¹.**

Bury St. Edmunds 96–7, 185; (monastery at) 183; (a of) 185, and see **Baldewyn¹, Brounfeld;** (townspeople of) 154.

Burlé, Symon Sir Simon Burley 191, 195.

Burnel, (Hew/þe) Lord Hugh Lord Burnell (1383–1420), 195, 213.

Bursigalde John I le Meingre de Boucicaut, marshal of France (d. 1367) 172. Cf. **Brucegald.**

Burton upo Trent, Staffs. 147.

Burwayche, Herry Henry Burghersh, b of Lincoln (1320–40) 151, 153, 164; erron. called **Ser Water Burwage** 162/13–14 n.

Bussy, Jon Sir John Bussy 208, 212.

Bussy, þe Lord 206.

Butler, Jon 239.

Cades Kadesh 25.

Cadmus, founder of Boeotia 28.

Cayn Cain 11, 12, 15; (descendants of) 15, 16, 17. *poss.* in ~ *douteris* 17/25.

Caynan Kenan 14–15, 16, 17, 19/27. See also **Chanaan.**

Calabir Calabria, S Italy 94, 109.

Calcidony Chalcedon, city of Bithynia, nearly opposite Constantinople; (council of, 451) 68.

Caleys Calais 165, 166, 167, 169, 171, 184, 190, 196, 200, 201, 205, 206, 207, 209, 210, 227, 234, 245, 246, 248; (governor of) 167; (garrison of) 234/22.

Caleph Caleb 28/2 n.

Calmana 11/9 n.

Caluirlé, (Ser) Hew/Hugo Sir Hugh Calveley 175, 182–3, 184.

Cam see **Cham.**

Camber, putative 1st ruler of Wales 31.

Cambises Cambyses, k of Persia (529–521 BC) 22.

Cambria Wales 31.

Cambrige Cambridge 196; (parliament at, 1388) 196; (earls of) see **Langlé, Richard.**

Cambrigschire Cambridgeshire 79.

Campanie Campania (S of Rome) 93.

Camuse, þe Lord Thomas Lord Camoys (1383–1421) 195.

Canaan see **Chanaan.**

Cane, Kame Caen 103, 165.

Capadoce Cappadocia 63.

Capgraue, in the author's signature 9.

Capitol, þe, Rome 47, 210.

Captiuité (of þe Jewis), þe Babylonian Captivity (587–530 BC) 38–9.

Carcalla see **Antonius ~.**

Cariath-arbe, Arbe Kiriath-arba (= Hebron) 15, 24. [Gen. 35: 27; Judg. 14: 15]

Carlil, Carlyle see **Karlhill.**

Carmele, þe Mount Mt Carmel, Palestine; (hermits of) 113/9–10 n.

Carmentis, Arcadian prophetess 27.

Carnotense *adj.* as *n.* Chartres; (b of) see **Fulbert.**

Cartage Carthage 32, 44–5; (Church Council at, 416) 67; (bps of) see **Cipriane, Olimpius.**

Cassebelian Cassivellaunus, k of Catuvellauni (55 BC) 46.

Cassilense *adj.* of Cashel; (Philip of Torrington, bishop 1373–81) 183.

Cassine, þe Mount of (monastery of) Montecassino 77. **Cassinense** *adj.* as *n.* (monks of) 81.

Cassiodre Cassiodorus 71.

Castel, ? in Brittany; (lord of) 223–4.

Castel, Castile, in Spain; (k of) 130, 110 (Alphonso VIII, 1158–1214), 117, 198 (John I, 1379–90), 198 (Henry III, 1390–1406, as s of prec.), 200, and see **Herry⁴, (Kyng) Petir;** (sr of k of) see **Helianore⁵.** See also **Spayne.**

Cath Kohath 26.

Caundisch, John Sir John Cavendish, CJKB 185.

Cauntirbury Canterbury 119, 127, 146, 238; (citizens of) 143; (see of) 102–3, 115, 117; (cathedral priory of **Crist Cherch** at) 210; (prior of) 213; (ab of) 149, 96 (Sigeric Serio 990–4), 128–9, 130 (John Pecham 1279–92), 160 (John Stratford 1333–48), 172 (Simon Islip 1349–66), and see **Abyngdon, Ancelme, Arundel, Austin, Baldewyn, Courtné, Lamfrank, Langdon, Odo, Robert, Simon, Stigand, Sudbury, Theobald, Theodre, Thomas, Walden, Walter, Wiliam², Wynchilseye;** (ab's cross of) 149. For **Thomas of ~** see **Thomas.**

Caus, ylde of Caux (Seine estuary) 171.

Cecile see **Cicile.**

Celestinus Iᵘˢ, pope (422–32) 67.

Celestinus II, pope (1143–4) 108.

Celestinus III, pope (1191–8) 112.

Celestin þe Fourte, pope (1241) 121.

Celestinus þe Fifte, pope (1294) 131.

Celestines, house of the order of prec. at Sheen 242.

Celum Aureum, L for 'gilded vault', church of San Pietro in Ciel d'Oro, Pavia 81/10 n.

Cenomaine county of Maine 123; (c of) see **Herri þe Secunde.**

Censius, Cencius or Cinthius, s of John Tiniosus, city prefect of Rome (1072) 100.

Centilogie for *Centiloquy,* work containing 100 aphorisms of astrology attributed to Ptolemy 53.

Ceorlus Cearl, k of Mercia (early 7th cent.) 80.

Cerberus 28.

Cesaré Caesarea, Palestine 72.

Cesarie Caesaria, Cappadocia 63; (b of) see **Basile.**

Chaldé, Chaldea 18, 24; (people of) 40. *adj.* Chaldean 27/3.

Chalkhul, place near Calais 177.

Chalomes Châlus (Haute-Vienne); (castle of) 115.

C(h)am Ham 18, 19; (descendants of) 20; also name for **Zorastes.**

Chana Cana-in-Galilee 49.

C(h)anaan, Caynan 19, 19/28. **(lond of)** ~ Palestine 19, 24, 26.

Chanones see **Augustin.**

Charles, (þe) Grete, also **Karolus Magnus/þe First** Charlemagne, k of Franks (771–), emp (800–14) 80, 81, 82, 83–4; (s of) see **Lodwicus;** (descendants of) 89; (ref. to reign of) 107.

Charles (þe Secund), called **Caluus** Charles II, the Bald, k of France (843–77) emp (875–6) 87; (Judith, da of) 86.

Charles þe þirde, called **Grossus** Charles III, the Fat, emp (876–87) 88.

Charles, Kyng Charles IV, k of France (1322–8) 148, 150–1, 155, 160.

Charles V, k of France (1364–80) 168 (as heir to throne), 172 (as regent), 175, 177, 182, 183, 184. For Charles VI see **Frauns.**

Charlys of Anjou, k of Sicily (d. 1285) 125/8 n.

Charles of Valois (d. 1325) 131.

Charlis Charles, dk of Orléans (1407 ff.), c of Blois and Valois, vc of Beaumont-sur-Sarthe 235–8, 245.

Charneys, Geffrey 167.

Cheyne, Ser Thomas 182.

Chelmisforth Chelmsford, Essex 217.

Chelricus Ceol(ric), k of W Saxons (591–7) 80.

Chene, Ser Jon Sir John Cheyne, Speaker in Coventry parliament (1404) 225.

Cheny, William William Cheyny 147.

Cherborow Cherbourg 182, 202.

Chestir Chester 105, 212; (castle of) 213; (e of) see Edward (Black Prince), Herri V, Ranulf, Richard⁴, Richard II (also styled p of); (diocese of = Coventry and Lichfield) 210; (b of) 217 (John Burghill, 1398–1414), see (Richard) Scrop, erron. for Chichester see Russoc, erron. for Exeter see Stafford, and cf. Couentré.

Chestirschere Cheshire 194, 202, 208; (men of) 222.

Cheulingus Ceawlin, k of W Saxons (560–91) 80.

Chichestir Chichester; (John Langton, b of, 1305–37) 146, and see also Chestir.

Chymegundis Kunigunde, empress of Henry II 96.

Chorus noue Jerusalem, L for 'Choire of new Jerusalem', 1st line of Easter hymn by Fulbert of Chartres 95/32 n.

Chus Cush.

Cicetir Cirencester, Gloucs. 216.

Cicile see Scicile.

Cicile, (Seint) St. Cecilia (2nd or 3rd cent.) 56, 85; (cardinal church of, S. Cecilia in Trastevere, Rome) 188.

Cicrops Cecrops 21.

Cylon Chilon, Spartan ephor (6th cent. BC) 39.

Cimerea, name of 4th Sibyl, who was 'of Cumae' 37/24 n.

Cipir Cyprus 46, 114, 125; (Peter I, k of) 174, 175.

Cipriane St. Cyprian, b of Carthage (d. 258) 57, 58.

Cyriacus, reported pope elect (235), ? Hippolytus, 1st antipope 56.

Ciricus Siricius, pope (384–99) 65.

Cirille St. Cyril, patriarch of Alexandria (412–44) 67.

Cirille, Seint St. Cyril of the Slavs (d. 869) 87.

Cyrophanes Syrophanes 21.

Cirus Cyrus the Great, k of Persia (547–529 BC) 22, 39.

Cisara see Sisara.

De Ciuitate Dei, L for 'Concerning the City of God', by St. Augustine of Hippo 23–4, 67.

Clayanger Clayhill Farm, Tottenham; (house of Augustinian friars at) 119/29 n.

Claykyn, Bertran Bertrand Du Guesclin 175–6.

Clambowh, John Sir John Clanvowe 191.

Clare, Suffolk; (house of Augustinian friars at) 119/29 n., 130, 176.

Clare, Seynt (d. 1253) 122.

Claremount Clermont(-Ferrand); (Church council at, 1095) 100; (c of) see Jon⁵.

Clarens Clarence; (dk of) see Leonel, Thomas.

Claringdoun Clarendon, Wilts. 141.

Claudius¹, emp (41–54) 49–50.

Claudius², emp (268–70) 58.

Cley, Norfolk; (men of) 231.

Cleykyn see Claykyn.

Clement, (Seynt), pope (90–9) 51; (body of) 87. poss. in Seynt ~ cherch church of S. Clemente, Rome 87.

Clement þe Secund, pope (1046–7) 98.

Clement þe þirde, pope (1187–91) 112.

Clemens IIII, pope (1265–8) 125.

Clemens Vᵘˢ, also Pope Clement (1305–14), previously ab of Bordeaux (1299–) 134–5, 139, 141, 143.

Clemens VI, also Pope Clement (1342–52), previously ab of Rouen (1330–) 163, 167.

Clement VII, pope at Avignon (1378–94) 182.

Clementins, þe the Clementines, collection of decretals added to canon law by Pope Clement V

Clementins, þe (*cont.*):
promulgated (1317) by John XXII 143.

Cleobolus Cleobulus, a tyrant of Rhodes (d. 564 BC) 39.

Cleopatra I, q of Egypt (d. 176 BC) 44.

Cleopatra, (þe Qween) Cleopatra III, w and sr of Ptolemy VIII of Egypt, m of Ptolemy IX and X 46.

Cleopatra VII, q of Egypt (51–30 BC) 46/19.

Cleophas, Simon see **Simon.**

Clere, þe Lord l of Clères 244.

Clerkenwelle Clerkenwell, Middx. 186.

Cletus prob. the same as **Anaclete** q.v.

Clifforth, Jon (erron.), also **Richard,** Richard Clifford, dean of York, archdeacon of Canterbury, later b of Worcester (1401–7), of London (1407–21), keeper of the great wardrobe (1390–8) 195, 240.

Clifforth, Lodewic Sir Lewis Clifford 191, 204, 220.

Clifforth, (Ser) Roger Roger Lord Clifford (1314–22) 147.

Clifforth, þe Lord Thomas Lord Clifford (1389–91) 195.

Clifforth, (Ser) William Sir William Clifford 225.

Clynton, William William Clinton, e of Huntingdon (1337–54) 159.

Cloyne Cluny; (abbey of) 90; (a of) 171 (Adrian) and see **Adamarius, Majolus, Odo;** (order of) 103.

Cnapwelle, Richard Richard Knapwell OP 130.

Cobbam see **Oldcastell.**

Cobbam/Cobham, Regnald/Ser Reynald Sir Reginald Cobham 162, 179.

Cokayn, William, royal judge 230.

Colchester (a of) 224; (da of Coel, k of) see **Heleyn.**

Coleyn, Coloyne Cologne 83, 161, 219; (b of as imperial elector) 95.

Collisé, þe Colosseum, Rome 87.

Coln Colne, Essex 205.

Colpepir, Thomas 146.

Columpnes, þe Colonna family 131.
Nicholas of ~ Nicolo Colonna 231.

Commestor, Maister Pers Peter Comestor (d. *c.*1179) 111.

Compostel Compostela; (diocese of) 104/24 n.

Concha Concessa 67.

Concionat, Lord see **Charlis** of Orléans.

Conrardus Conrad I, k of Germans (911–18) 90.

Conrardus Primus Conrad II, k of Germans (1024–39) 97.

Conrard þe Secund Conrad III, k of Germans (1138–52) 107.

Conrardis, þe German kings by the name of Conrad 96/3.

Constance, Constauns (Church Council at, 1414–18) 242–3, 249/25 n.

Constant, Constauns Constans, emp (337–50) 62–3.

Constantin (þe þird) Constans II, emp (641–68) 74, 76.

Constantine Constantius Chlorus, emp (305–6) 61/8, 13.

Constancius Constantius II, emp (337–61) 62. *poss.* **Constans** 64.

Constantine, Grete, emp (306–37) 38, 61–2; (sons of) 62; (weapons belonging to) 92. *poss.* in ~ *modir* 85, 210; ~ *broþir* 63; ~ *dowtir* (Constantia) 63.

Constantine II, emp (337–40) 62.

Constantinus IIII, Constantine IV, emp (668–85) 77.

Constantinus V^{us}, emp (741–75) 80–1.

Constantyn Constantine, k of Scots (defeated 937) 92.

Constantine, pope (708–15) 78–9, 80.

Constantinus II, pope (767–8) 82.

Constantine erron. for Octavian, name of Pope **Johannes XII,** q.v.

Constantyn, ylde of, apparently Coutances (Manche) 180.

Constantinople 38, 62, 63, 66, 68, 69, 71, 72, 73, 79, 81, 83, 94, 112; (as capital of Byzantine empire) 83, 84; (Manuel II, emp of) 204, 217, 218; (Church Council at) 65 (381), 77 (680), 81 (754), 88 (prob. erron. for Photian synod, 879–80); (patriarch of) see **Anastase, Paule^{2};** (people of) 76.

Constantinopolitan *adj.* of Constantinople; (Emperor John V Palaeologus) 184.

Constauns Constance of Brittany, m of **Arthure**² 115.

Constauns, (Dam) Constance of Castile, w of **Jon of Gaunt** (1371–94) 178, 185, 189, 198, 202.

Conweye Conway; (castle of) 213.

Cornelius, pope (251–3) 57.

Cornwayle Cornwall 120, 183; (dk of) see **Edward** (Black Prince), **Herri V, Richard II**; (e of) see **Edmund, Eltham, Richard**⁵.

Corporis Cristi Corpus Christi, feast of body of Christ (Thursday after Trinity Sunday) 143, 172.

Cosdre Chosroes II, k of Persia (d. 628) 75.

Cosmas, St. 60.

Coulyng Cooling, Kent; (castle of) 239.

Courtné, Maistir William William Courtenay, b of London (1375–81), ab of Canterbury (1381–96) 181, 204–5, 206.

Courtnei, Maistir Richard Richard Courtenay, b of Norwich (1413–15) 239, 245.

Couentré Coventry 120; (parliament at, 1404) 225; (Roger Northburgh, bishop 1321–58, Treasurer 1340) 153, 161, and cf. **Chestir.**

Crakow Kraków, for (and capital of) Poland; (Ladislaus II, k of, 1386–1434) 234–5.

Cremense, Jon John of Crema, cardinal legate in England (1125) 105.

Crescens Crescentius 95.

Cressi Crécy-en-Ponthieu 165.

Crete 35, 68.

Crisantus St. Chrysanthus (d. 283) 59.

Crisping, William erron. for William Clito, s of **Robert** (Curthose) 105.

Crist(e), (oure Lord Jesu) Jesus Christ 8, 9, 14, 31, 37, 47–9, 51, 53, 55, 60, 61, 64, 66–8, 72, 79, 108, 116, 118, 123, 137–8; (duality of) 67, 69, 76–7, 240; (bread as body of) 59, 99, 185, 234, and see also **Corporis Cristi**; (pre-figura-

tion of) see **Ysaac, Melchisedech**; (sepulchre of) 100, 108; (relic(s) of) 74, 84; (pictures of) 81, 244; (vision of) 111; (infidel enemies of) 107; (time of = years AD) 7/32. *poss.* **Cristis, -es** 32, 36, 50, 67, 83, 92, 99, 100, 185, 197, 205, 227, 234–5, 240.

Crist Cherch see **Cauntirbury.**

Cristofer Christophorus, pope (903–4) 89.

Crotey Le Crotoy (Somme) 165.

Cruce, Seint church of S. Croce in Gerusalemme, Rome 94–5.

Cuda Creoda, k of Mercia (6th cent.) 80.

Cunstauns see **(Dam) Constauns.**

Curthose see **Robert.**

Cusan-rasathaim Cushan-rishathaim, k of Aram-naharaim 28. [Judg. 3: 8–11]

Dagon 31.

Dagworth, þe Lord Sir Thomas Dagworth 166.

Dagworth, Nicholas Sir Nicholas Dagworth 195.

Dayncourt, William William Deyncourt 166.

Dalyngbrig, Edmund Sir Edward Dallingridge 199.

Dalmacie Dalmatia 59.

Daluida erron. for Adelaide, w of (1) Lothair III of Italy, (2) Emperor Otto I, 93.

Damask Damascus 18; **feld of** ~ garden of Eden 11; (people of = **Arabes**) 77.

Damasus, pope (366–84) 64.

Damasus þe Secund, pope (1048) 98.

Damian erron. for ? Duvian 54/16 n.

Damian, Seynt pres. St. Peter Damian (d. 1072); (assoc. with St. Clare and Franciscans) 122/31 n.

Damiane, St., twin br of Cosmas 60.

Danes see **Denemarc.**

Daniel 38–9, 106.

Danubie R Danube 21.

Dardani erron. for the Ardennes 89. [medL *Ardenna*]

Daria, St. (d. 283) w of **Crisantus** 59.

Darius I, k of Persia (521–485 BC) 39.

Darius II (Nothus), k of Persia (425–404 BC) 40.

Darie, Darius III (Codomannus), k of Persia (337–331 BC) 42.

Dauy Dafydd ap Gruffudd, p of Wales (1282–3) 129.

Dauid¹ David, k of Jews (d. 1016 BC) 31–2, 38.

Dauid² David de Strathbogie, e of Atholl (1326–35) 156, 158–9.

Dauid³ David II, k of Scots (1329–71) 156, 165, 170, 174; (Joan, w of) see **Edward þe pirde.**

Decius, emp (249–50) 57.

Decius, called **Minor,** city prefect of Rome, prob. prec. before he became emp 58.

Decrées de Consecratione, document containing Berengar of Tours's retraction (1079) 99.

Decretales, (þe) collection of papal decrees 109, 119, 132, 135.

Dee, R (Cheshire) 80.

Delbora¹ 11/13 n.

Delbora² Deborah, Israelite judge 25, 28–9.

Delphis Delphi; (sibyl of) 37.

Demetrius, titular k of Asia Minor and Syria (301–286 BC) 43.

Demoratus Demaratus, banished k of Sparta (5th–4th cent. BC) 40.

Demostenes Demosthenes 41.

Dene Denia, Spain; (c of) 176.

Denemarc, Denmark 69, 98, 214; (k of) 229 (Eric IX), and see **(Kyng) Herri, Knowt;** (men of = **Danes,** i.e. Vikings) 86, 88, 89, 91, 93, 96.

Denise/Dionise, Seynt St. Dionysius (Denis) of Paris (c.250) 51/5 n.; (works of, erron. for those by Dionysius the Pseudo-Areopagite (c.500)) 84, 86.

Deodatus II, pope (672–6) 76–7. Cf. **Deusdedit.**

Derby 93; (earldom of) 80; (e of) see **Herry IV, Herry of Lancastir;** (countess of) see **Mari.**

Derlyngton Darlington 142.

Dertemouthe Dartmouth 224; (men of) 187.

Desideri Desiderius, k of Lombards (757–74) 82–3.

Deusdedit Deodatus I, pope (615–18) 75. Cf. **Deodatus.**

Dialoges *Dialogues* by Gregory the Great tr. from L into Gr. by Pope Zacharias 81.

Diapolitani L *n. pl.* Thebans 22/14–15 n.

Dictes 'Maxims', name of work attrib. to Robert Grosseteste 120.

Dido, legendary q of Carthage 32.

Dignum et justum est equum et salutare, L for 'It is meet and just, right and availing unto salvation', 1st words of preface to eucharistic prayer of L mass 70.

Dinastines, name for rulers of Egypt 22.

Dindimus erron. for Didymus the Blind (d. 398), theologian 64.

Dioclecian Diocletian, emp (285–305) 59–60; (persecution of) 58, 60, 81.

Diogenes the Cynic 41.

Diomede Diomedes, mythical k of Thrace who kept man-eating horses 28.

Dionise Dionysius, pope (259–68) 58.

Dionise, Seynt see **Denise.**

Dionisie þe Tyraunt Dionysius I (d. 367 BC), tyrant of Syracuse 40.

Dioscorus, patriarch of Alexandria (d. 454), disciple of Eutyches 69.

Dys, Maystir erron. for Walter (of) Diss, O.Carm. 191.

Dodington erron. for Dadlington, Leics. 138.

Domician Domitian, emp (81–96) 50–1.

Domine de Pace, [Capella] Nostre Chapel of our Lady of Peace, to be built near Calais at place of Anglo-French meeting in 1395 206.

Dominic, Seint 113, 118; (Order of = OP) 113, 118, 123, 124; (members of OP) 118, 120, 127, 130, 134; (houses of OP) see **Langlé, Norwich, Oxenforth.** See also *Glossary,* s.vv. **Dominic, Prechour.**

Donat either (1) Donatus, b of Casae Nigrae (e. 4th cent.) or (2) Donatus the Great, Donatist b of Carthage

(4th cent.) 61; (followers of) 61–2, and see *Glossary*, s.v. **Donatistes.**

Donate[1] Aelius Donatus, grammarian (4th cent.) 63.

Donate[2] Donatus, b of Nicopolis (*c.*425) 66.

Donus[1], pope (676–8) 77.

Donus[2], erron., alleged pope for one year after Benedict VII (94/18) 94/28 n.

Donwich Dunwich, Suffolk; (b of) see **Felice.**

Dorcet, Dorset (mq, e of) see **Beuforth.**

Dordraute Dordrecht, Netherlands 248.

Dorham Durham 165; (province of = sheriffdom of Northumberland) 114; (b of) 113–14 (Hugh de Puiset 1153–95), 150/151 (erron. for **Dulyn**), 201 (Walter Skirlaw 1388–1406), and see **Beamount, Fordam.**

Dorsete Dorchester, Oxon.; (b of) see **Byryn.**

Dortmouth see **Dertemouthe.**

Douyr Dover 31, 111, 174, 246; (castle of) 195.

Downfermelyn Dunfermline; (abbey of) 157.

Duglas, þe Erl Archibald, e of Douglas (1400–24) 220, 222.

Duglas, William Sir William Douglas, later e of Douglas (d. 1384) 165.

Dulyn Dublin; (nominal parliament at, 1395) 203; (mq of) see **Ver**; (ab of) see **Robert**; (b of) see 150/5 n., 151/34 n.

Dunbar 133, 195.

Dunkirk 187.

Dunstable 111, 242.

Dunstan, Seynt, ab of Canterbury (959–88) 94; (fd of, 19 May) 238.

Ebron see **Hebron.**

Ecclesiasticus 43.

Edenborow Edinburgh 159.

Edgare Edgar, k of England (959–75) 93, 94–5, 134; (q of) see **Alfrik.**

Edissa Edessa (mod. Urfa) 55, 108.

Edyngton, William William Edington, b of Winchester (1346–66), Treasurer (1344–56), Chancellor (1356–63) 167.

Edmund, k of W Saxons (939–46) 93–4; (q of) see **Elgiue.**

Edmund (Yrunside) Edmund Ironside, k of England (1016) 98, 134. *gen.* **Edmundis** 98.

Edmund, Kyng/Seint, k of E Angles (855–70) 86, 97; (town of) see **Bury.** *gen.* in *Seint Edmund Fosse* ? Devil's Dyke (Cambs.) 79.

Edmund, Seint, þe archbischop see **Abyngdon.**

Edmund FitzAlan, e of Arundel (1306–26) 147.

Edmund *erl of Cambrig, duke of Jork* see **Langlé.**

Edmund 'of Almaine', e of Cornwall (1272–1300) 132–3.

Edmund *erle of Cornwaile* erron. for **Jon Eltham** 155/17.

Edmund, e of Kent, half-br of Edward II see **Woodstok.**

Edmunde erron. for **Edwyn** 93/7.

Edred prob. Ethelred, ealdorman of the Mercians (d. 911) 91/12–13 n.

Edred, k of W Saxons (946–55) 94.

Edrede prob. erron. for Eadric, ealdorman of Mercia (d. 1017) 98.

Edward, called *Senior* 'the Elder', k of W Saxons (899–924) 91; (s of) 92.

Edward (þe) Martir, k of England (975–8) 96, 134.

Edward, Kyng/Seynt Edward the Confessor, k of England (1042–66) 100, 101; (objects revered for their former association with) 135–6; (q of) see **Ydani**; (parish of) St. Edward's parish, Oxford 118/10 n. *gen.* ~ 101/15; in *Seint Edward day* (13 Oct.) 214.

Edward (þe First), (Kyng), k of England (1272–1307) 120–1, 122, 124–6, (reign) 126–35, 138/9; (q of) see **Helianore**[5], **Margaret**; (s of) 144/25. *gen.* ~ 126/4.

Edward (þe Secund), (Kyng), k of England (1307–27), (reign) 135–54, 154–5; (q of) see **Ysabell.** *gen.* **Edwardes** 156/15.

Edward (þe þirde), (Kyng) k of England (1327–77) 139, 150/31 (2nd), 151–2, 153, (reign) 154–81

Edward (þe pirde) (*cont.*):
and 203; (q of) see **Philip¹**; (sr of) 156 (Joan); (party of) 168. *gen.* in *Kyng Edward dowtir* 192/2.

Edward þe Fourt, k of England (1461–70, 1471–83) 7, 9.

Edward, Prince Edward the Black Prince, e of Chester (1333–), dk of Cornwall (1337–), p of Wales (1343–76) 156, 159, 169–70, 171, 172, 175–6, 177–8, 181, 215; (w of) see **Jone³**.

Edward, s of Black Prince 175.

Edward 'of York', e of Rutland (1390–1415), dk of Aumale (1397–9), dk of York (1402–15) 203, 206, 207, 209, 211, 212, 215, 237, 246.

Edwyn Edwy, k of England (955–9) 94, **Edmunde** (erron.) 93/7.

Edwyne Edwin, k of Bernicia, Deira and Northumbria (616–32) 80.

Effraim (hill-country of) Ephraim 27, 30. [Josh. 24: 30]

Effrem prob. Ephrath(ah) 15/23 n.

Egbrite Egbert, k of W Saxons (802–39) 86. *gen.* ∼ 86/25.

Egecippus Hegesippus (2nd cent.) 53.

Egipte Egypt 15, 21, (ancient kingdom) 22, 25, 27, 38, (Ptolemaic kingdom) 42–6, 49, 69; (k of) 53/4 n.; (people of = **Egipcianes**) 19, 26, 27; (Israelites in) 26.

Eglon, Kyng, k of Moab 28. [Judg. 3]

Elam 18; (sons of Aram attrib. to) 18/34; (people said to be descended from = **Elamites**) 18. [Gen. 10: 23]

Eld(e) Testament Old Testament 43, 52. Cf. **Bible**.

Eleazar, Jewish high priest (3rd cent. BC) 43.

Elesponcia, name of Sibyl of Marpessa on the Hellespont 37.

Eleutheri Eleutherus, pope (175–89) 54.

Elgiue Ælfgyfu, q of **Edmund** k of W Saxons 93.

Eliogabelum Heliogabalus, Phoenician god 55/21 n.

Elle Ælle, k of S Saxons (477 ff.) 79.

Elman/Helman, (Ser) William Sir William Elmham 187, 195.

Eltham, Kent 241.

Eltham, (Ser) Jon John of Eltham, 2nd s of Edward II, e of Cornwall (1328–36) 152, 155, 159, **Edmund** (erron.) 155/17.

Emaus Emmaus 65/25 n.

Emericus Eormenric, k of Kent (d. *c.*560) 79.

Emme Emma (d. 1052), 'the brooch of Normandy', da of **Richard¹**, q of (1) **Ethelthredus**, (2) **Knowt** 96, 100.

Eneas Aeneas; (descendant of) 31, 47. *gen.* in ∼ *kyn* 31/18.

Engelysyn Angoulême; (Audemar, c of) 115.

Englischmen see **Inglond**.

Ennok Enoch, s of Jared 16–17, 19.

Enok Enoch, s of Cain 11, 13/1; (city of same name named after) 12/37.

Enos Enosh 13–14, 15, 17, 19.

Ephese Ephesus 48, 51; (Church council at, 431) 67.

Ephron 24. [Gen. 25: 10]

Epiphanius, St., b of Salamis (4th cent.) 63.

Eraclius¹ Heraclius, emp (610–41) 74–6.

Eraclius² Heraclius, patriarch of Jerusalem (1180–91) 110–11.

Erico ? Erech 49.

Erithea name given to Erythraean Sibyl 37/25 n.

Erkynwyn Erchenwin (= Æscwine), reputed k of E Saxons (6th cent.) 79.

Erlond, Yrland Ireland 7, 67, 108, 136–7, 140, 143, 186, 189, 192, 195, 201–2, 203, 207, 210–11, 212, 215; (k of) see **Anlaf**; (dk of) see **Ver**; (ab of) see **Armachan**; (men of = **Erischmen**) 203, 210.

Erpingham, (Ser) Thomas 214, 244.

Erudite ? name for Arsinoë III, sr and w of Ptolemy IV 44.

Erwaldus Earpwald, k of E Angles (early 7th cent.) 79.

Esau 25.

Esdras 40.

Esebon Ibzan 30. [Judg. 12: 8]

Esk Oeric surnamed Oisc, k of Kent (488–?512) 79.

Essex, Estsex 144, 207, 216; (AS kingdom of) 79, 91.

Ester Esther 41.

Est-Ynglond E Anglia; (AS kingdom of) 79, 91.

Eston, Ser Adam Adam Easton, cardinal of Santa Cecilia in Trastevere, Rome (1381–6, 1389–97) 188, 199.

Ethe Heth 24. [Gen. 25: 9–10]

Ethelbert, k of Kent (560–616) 79.

Ethelbrite Ethelbert, k of W Saxons (860–5) 86.

Ethelfled Æthelflæd 'lady of the Mercians' (d. 918) 91.

Ethelthrede Ethelred, k of W Saxons (865–71) 86.

Ethelthredus Ethelred (*Unræd*), k of England (978–1013, 1014–16) 96, 99; (q of) see **Emme.**

Ethelwold[1] Ethelbald, k of W Saxons (855–60) 86.

Ethelwold[2] Æthelweald I, b of Winchester (963–84) 95.

Ethimilogies *Etymologiae* by Isidore of Seville 29.

Ethiop Ethiopia; (k of) see **Zaram.**

Eubony, þe Ylde of see **Man.**

Eugeni Eugenius, b of Ostia (878 ff.) 88.

Eugenius Primus, pope (655–7) 76.

Eugenius II[m], pope (824–7) 85.

Eugenius III, pope (1145–53) 108.

Euripides 40.

Europe 23.

Eusebie Eusebius, b of Nicomedia (d. *c*.342) 62.

Eusebius[1], pope (309–10) 61.

Eusebius[2], b of Caesarea (d. *c*.340) 23, 63/1 n.; (chronicle by) 7.

Eusebius[3], Roman priest killed for calling Pope Liberius an Arian 63/8.

Eustace, reputed Christian martyr (2nd cent.) 51.

Eustochium, St. Julia (d. *c*.419) 65.

Euticen Eutyches (d. 454), founder of Monophysitism 68.

Eutician Eutychianus, pope (275–83) 58.

Euander Evander, Arcadian k of Latium region 99.

De Euangelica Uita, L for 'Concerning The Evangelical Life', by Geoffrey Hardeby OESA 170.

Euaristus Evaristus, pope (99–105) 52.

Eue Eve 11, 12.

Euerwik (= **ʒork**) York(shire); (sheriff of) 232/23 n.

Euesham Evesham, Worcs.; (battle of, 1265) 124.

Euyrlastyng Gospell the 'Eternal Evangel', work containing excerpts from writings of **Joachim** of Fiore and used by Spiritual Franciscans 123/31 n.

Ew Eu, Normandy; (Charles d'Artois, c of) 246.

Exaltacion of þe Cros feast of Exaltation of the Cross (14 Sept). 75.

Excetir Exeter 96, 102; (dk of) see **Beuforth, Holland;** (b of) 164 (John Grandisson, 1327–69), and see **(Edmund) Stafford, Stapilton.**

Exston, Richard Richard Exton, mayor of London 190.

Ezechie Hezekiah, k of Judah (726–697 BC) 36–7.

Ezechiel Ezekiel 38–9.

Fabian, monophysite heretic (1st half 5th cent.) 68.

Fabian, St., pope (236–50) 56; (fd of, 20 Jan.) 120.

Fallisle, Ser Jon Sir John Fallesley 182.

Faringdoun, William Sir William Faringdon 187.

Fasiden ? Phasis, name used by Xenophon for R Araxes 22. Cf. **Araxen.**

Fastulus Faustulus, shepherd of Amulius, k of Alba 36.

Fekenham perhaps John Feckenham OESA 208/23 n.

Felice Felix, 1st b of E Anglia (Dunwich) (630–47) 79.

Felix I, pope (269–74) 58.

Felix II, antipope (355–65) 63.

Felix III, pope (483–92) 70.

Felix þe IIII, pope (526–30) 72.

Fenise, Phenice Phoenicia; (people of) 21.

Ferby, William William Ferriby, chancery clerk 214.

Ferreres Ferrers, name for earldom of Derby; (Thomas of Lancaster reported e of) 138.

Feuersam Faversham, Kent; (Benedictine house at) 108.

Filgeriarum Fougères (Ille-et Vilaine); (l of) see **Jon³**.

Fynian Finan, b of Lindisfarne (651–61) 80.

FitzWalter, þe Lord Walter Lord FitzWalter (1361–86) 177.

Flaundres Flanders 69, 87, 137, 163, 171, 187, 227; (c of) 160/22; (men of = **Flemingis**) 107, 160, 161, 178, 183, 187, 191; (supporters of Avignon pope Clement VII from) 186/29; (weavers of) 160/5.

Flynt Flint; (castle of) 213.

Flisco, Lucas de Luca Fieschi, cardinal legate in England (1317) 141.

Florens Florence; (Church council at, 1056) 98.

Florens, (Ser) Andrew (of) 148.

Floriacense gen. of Fleury 77, 81.

Floriane Florian, emp (276) 59.

Focas Phocas, emp (602–10) 74.

Forcius, Seynt erron. for Pothinus, b of Lyon (d. 177) 53.

Fordam, Jon John Fordham, b of Durham (1381–8) 193, 195.

Forestis Forez (Loire and Puy-de-Dome); (c of) see **Jon⁵**.

Formosus, pope (891–6) 88–9.

Foroneus see **Phoroneus**.

Fowey, Cornwall; (ship from) 183.

Fraunceys, Seint St. Francis of Assisi (d. 1226) 113; (rule of) 181; (member of the order of) 122.

Frauns France 53, 59, 60, 61 (as part of Roman empire), 69, 71, 81, 82–3, 84–5, 87–90, 100, 107, 110, 117, 119, 121, 122, 128, 133, 137, 139, 149–51, 155, 158, 160–1, 162–3, 164–5, 166, 168, 171–2, 173, 175–7, 179, 182, 184, 187, 189, 190, 195, 197, 201, 202, 204, 206, 214, 218, 230, 231, 232, 237, 243; (coast of) 131. (English lands in, subject to k of France's overlordship) 126. (Kings of) 160,

(Charles the Simple, 893–929, also his da) 88, (Charles VI, 1380–1422) 184, 187, 190, 199–201, 202, 205–6, 233, 235, 244–5, 247–8, (his s) 247 (John), (his da) see **Helianore⁶**, (his house) 225, and see **Charles, Jon⁶, Lodewik, Lotharie, Philip(pe), Pipine, Robert**; (br of k of) see **Charles** of Valois. (Q of) see **Helianore¹**; (dauphin of) 160, 245, 247, and see **Philippe IV**; (steward of) 172, 230, and see **Plauntgenet**; (marshal of) 167, and see **Brucegald**; (constable of) 245, and see **Bursigalde**; (chancellor of, imperial elector) 95; (council of) 171. (Lords of) 139, 172, 206; (knight of) 105. (Church of) 82, 99; (crusaders from) 107; (supporters of Avignon Pope Clement VII from) 186; (English priories dependent on abbeys of) 226; (people of) 19, 132, 183; (people of, living in England) 150; (men of, i.e. Franks) 86, 88, 90; (men of = **Frenschmen**) 112, 114, 122, 129, 132, 133, 161, 162, 168, 169, 174, 176, 177, 178, 179, 182, 187, 189, 191, 198, 223, 224, 236, 245, 246, 247; (merchants of) 132; (laws of) 150; (English prisoners in) 133. (English claim to crown of) 160–1, 163, 164, 168; (Edward IV of England titular k of) 7; (émigré knights from) see **Charneys, Harecort**.

Fraxineto, Gilbertus de Gilbert of Fresney OP, prior provincial of the order in England (1221 ff.) 118.

Frederik þe First Frederick I (Barbarossa), k of Germans (1152–), emp (1155–90) 108, 115, 116/32 n.

Frederik þe Secund, k of Sicily (1198–), k of Germans (1212–), emp (1220–50) 112–13.

Frenschmen see **Frauns**.

Frise (? erron. for) Phrygia 49. [See *Glossary*, s.v. **Frises**]

Frunsak Fronsac (Gironde); (castle of) 122.

Fugan 54/15 n.

Fulbert, St., b of Chartres (1007–28) 95.

Fulgens Fulgentius Mythographus (*fl.* 480–500) 21.

Fulþorp, Roger Sir Roger Fulthorp 192.

Futh P(h)ut 19; (unknown N African river reported to be named after) 19/14.

Gabba Galba, emp (68–9) 50.

Gabriel 75.

Gad, prophet 32.

Gaynysborow Gainsborough, Lincs. 97.

Gayus¹ Caius Caligula, emp (37–41) 49.

Gayus² Gaius, pope (283–96) 59, 60.

Galerius, emp (305–10) 61.

Galgalis Gilgal 27. [Josh. 9]

Galiene¹ Galen, ancient physician 53.

Galiene² Gallienus, emp (253–68) 57–8.

Galilé ? Galilean 64. [Cf. Acts 2: 7]

Gallus Trebonianus Gallus, emp (251–3) 57.

Galon, Edmund 185.

Galowey Galloway 158.

Gamme, Dauy David Gam (David ap Llewelyn) 246.

Ganerion Ganelon 83.

Gascoyne, William Sir William Gascoigne, CJKB 229.

Gascon, Gascoyne Gascony, France 121, 122, 176, 178, 237; (men of) 235.

Gauceline Cardinal Gaucelin of Eauze 141–2.

Gaucort, þe Lord Ralph, l of Gaucourt 244.

Gaunt Ghent, Belgium 162; (men of) 162.

Gaunt, (Ser) Jon/Jon of John of Gaunt, e of Richmond (1342–72), dk of Lancaster (1362–99) 162, 169, 171, 172, 177, 178–9, 181, 182, 187, 188–9, 191, 197–8, 201, 202, 205–7, 210, 211; (Catalina, da of) 198/12; (children of by Katharine Swynford) 206–7. *gen.* in *þe duke of Lancastir place* 186/1. See also **Blaunche, Constauns,** and **Swynforth.**

Gauerstoun, Petir Peter Gaveston, e of Cornwall (1307–12) 135–7 138–9 (139/24 n.).

Gedeon Gideon 29.

Gelasius Gelasius I, pope (492–6) 70.

Gelasius (þe Secund) Gelasius II, pope (1118–19) 101, 104; **Gelase** 104/20.

Genabum erron. for *Cenabum,* Roman name for Orléans 59.

Gene, Jene Genoa 81; (cardinal of) 188.

Genofepha, Seynt St. Geneviève 68.

George, Seynt (fd of, 23 Apr.) 238; (statue of) 247. *poss.* **Georges** 247.

Gera, f of **Ayoth** 28.

Gerard, b of Sées (1082–91) 110.

Geraris Gerar 25.

Germanie Germany 21, 88; (chancellor of, imperial elector) 152; (people of = **Germanes**) 84. See also **Almayn.**

Geround R Gironde, France 133.

Geruase St. Gervase 60; (fd of, 19 June) 158.

Gether 18–19.

Gy Guy, mq of Tuscany 90.

Gy, Marchio Guy, dk of Spoleto 86/3 n.

Gy (of Warwik) Guy Beauchamp, e of Warwick (1298–1315) 138. *poss.*

Gyis 138.

Gian, Gyane Guienne (Aquitaine) France 117, 122, 126–7, 132, 148, 159, 164, 171, 176, 177–9, 198, 238; ('king' of) see **Pipine**; (duchy/lands of) 150, 151, 155, 168–9, 237; (dk of) 109 (= William, f of **Helianore¹**), 109 (= Henry II), 153 (= Edward III), 205 (= **Jon of Gaunt**), 215 (= Henry V); (men of) 119, 235.

Giffard, Robert erron. for Lord Robert Clifford 135.

Gilbert¹ Gerbert of Aurillac (= Pope **Siluestir** II) 94.

Gilbert² Clare, e of Gloucester (1217–30) 119.

Gilbert³ (of Gloucetir) Gilbert Clare, e of Gloucester (1263–95) 124, 125, 126, 130.

Gilbert⁴ Clare, e of Gloucester (1307–14) 136/8–9 n.; (sr of) 137.

Gildeforth Guildford, Surrey 100.

Gilis, (Doctour) Giles of Rome, medieval philosopher 119.

Gilis Feld see **Seint** ~.

Gynes Guînes, France 205.

Gion R Gihon (at Jerusalem) 32.

Giraldus Gerald of Wales 110.

Glasconbury Glastonbury, Somerset 110, 127; (abbey of) 95; (burial at) 98.

Gledesmore app. for (battle of) Dupplin Moor (near Perth) 157/5 n.

Glendor, (Howeyn) Owain Glyn Dŵr 217, 218–19, 221, 229, 230, 232; (military strength of) 227.

Gloria in Excelsis [Deo] L for 'Glory to God in the Highest', the Gloria 70.

Gloucestir Gloucester 49, 152; (coronation at) 117; (e of) see **Awdlé, Gilbert, Richard, Robert, Spencer**; (youngest da of 2nd e of, Isabel, 1st w of King John) 115; (dk of) see **Humfrey, Wodstok**.

Gloucetirschire Gloucestershire 147.

God 7, 8, 9, 11, 12, 13, 14, 15, 16, 17, 18, 23, 24, 25, 26, 27, 28, 29, 32, 33, 34, 36, 37, 58, 59, 64, 65, 66, 68, 73, 74, 76, 82, 84, 87, 89, 101, 103, 104, 108, 125, 130, 136, 149, 153, 154, 162, 174, 188, 191, 198, 205, 214, 218, 220, 221, 224, 237, 240, 245, 247, 248, 249; as **Juge** 122, 140; (representations of) 14; (Son of) see **Crist(e)**; (descendants of Seth as sons of) 12, 17; (arke of = Ark of the Covenant) 31; (lawe of) see **Bible**; (Temple of) see **Temple**; (word of, i.e. Christian faith) 123; (worshipers of) 37, 76, 89; (enemies of) 27. *gen.* **Goddis** 9, 14, 27, 47, 97, 139, 157. See also **Crist(e), Holy Go(o)st, Trinité**.

Godrus Guthrum, k of the Danelaw 89.

Godwyn Godwin, e of Wessex 99–100, 101.

Golgatha Golgotha 11.

Goly Goliath 32.

Golofir, Jon Sir John Golafre 195.

Gomer 18, 19.

Gordian III, emp (238–44) 56.

Gorganye ? Georgia; (k of) see **Seward**.

Gorgialis *Gorgias*, dialogue by Plato 41.

Gorgony St. Gorgonia 60.

Gothis *n. pl.* Goths 19, 58; Visigoths 65, 66, 68; (k of) see **Albericus, Theodoricus**; (Teias, k of) Ostrogoths 71.

Gouernauns of Princes, Of tr. *De Regimine Principum* 'Concerning Government by Rulers' by **Gilis** of Rome (c.1285) 119.

Gower Londis Gower, S Wales 145.

Gracian Gratian, emp (367–83) 65.

Graunson, þe Lord Thomas, Lord Grandison (1369–75) 177.

Grauening Gravelines, Flanders 187.

Grece, Grecia Greece 23, 30, 45, 61; (k of) see **Ymacho**; (people of = **Grekis**) 19, 25, 30, 40, 62, 82, 94; (scholars of) 21; (monks from) 85.

Grego Nazanzene St. Gregory of Nazianzus 64.

Gregori erron. for Georgius, patriarch of Constantinople (678–83) 77.

Gregorie Gregory, b of Antioch (569–84) 74.

Gregori, (Seynt/þe Pope) St. Gregory the Great, pope (590–604) 62, 74, 87. *poss.* in *Seynt Gregory day* (12 Mar.) 171.

Gregorius Secundus Gregory II, pope (715–31) 80.

Gregorius IIII^us Gregory IV, pope (827–44) 85.

Gregori þe V, pope (996–9) 95.

Gregorius VI, pope (1045–6) 98.

Gregorius VII^us, pope (1073–85) 100.

Gregorius VIII, pope (1187) 111. Cf. **Burdine**.

Gregorius IX, pope (1227–41) 118.

Gregori þe X, pope (1271–6) 125.

Gregori þe XI, Gregorius XI, pope (1370–8) 177, 182.

Gregori(us) (XII), called **Aungel**, Angelo Correr, pope (1406–15) 231, 233, 242; (party of) 233, 242.

Grey, Thomas Sir Thomas Grey of Hetton 214, 243

Grey Riffyn, Ser Reynald Lord Reginald Grey of Ruthin 217.

Grene, Thomas erron. for Sir Henry Green 208, 212.

Grimbald, unidentified interpreter of dreams to Henry I 106.

Grinnaldus Grimoald, dk of Benevento and k of the Lombards (662 ff.) 76.

Grisogonus (for) St. Chrysogonus 60.

Grymisby Grimsby, Lincs. 212.

Groyne La Coruña, Spain, 189.

Grostede, (Maistir) Robert, also Bischop Robert Robert Grosseteste, b of Lincoln (1235–53) 120, 122.

Guallo Gualo, papal legate in England 117.

Guychardy see Robert ~.

Gurnay, Mathew Sir Matthew Gournay 185.

Gurnay, Thomas Sir Thomas Gurney 155.

Gwynderyn Guiderius, British chief (AD 43) 49.

3ermoth Great Yarmouth, Norfolk 162.

3ork York 61, 140, 142–3, 201–2, 223, 229, 232 (walls of) 144; (castle of) 102; (keeper of) 147; (men of) 144, 227; (parliament at) 158/4 (1334), 158/31 (1335); (see of) 102–3; (ab of) 153 (= William Melton, 1316–40), see also Aldred, Arundel, Neuyle, Pauline, (Richard) Scrope, Souch, Thomas; (duchess of) see Ysabell; (dk of) see Edward, Langlé. See also Euerwik.

Hay, Petir de la 232.

Hailes (monastery of), Cornwall 117, 121; (burials at) 125.

Hakevile, þe Lord William II of Hacqueville, near Fresles, France 244.

Hales, Ser Robert, Treasurer (1381), prior of the Hospital of St. John of Jerusalem in England 185.

Halowmesse see Al(l)-Halow.

Hampton see Southamptoun.

Hamptschire Hampshire 79.

Haraldus Harold Godwinson, k of England (1066) 101–2. poss. Haraldis 102.

Hardeby, Geffrey Geoffrey Hardeby OESA, Prior Provincial of the Order in England (1360) 170/23 n.

Harecort, N. Geoffrey of Harcourt, l of St. Sauveur-le-Vicomte 165/3 n.

Hareflw Harfleur, France 244, 245, 247.

Haryngey Hornsey, Middx. 194.

Harleswode, unidentified place in Beds. 210.

Hasting, Jon John Hastings, e of Pembroke (1375–89) 198.

Hastingis Hastings, Sussex 102.

Hastingis, Ser Jon John Hastings, e of Pembroke (1348–75) 178.

Hatspor, Herry Henry Hotspur, name given to Herry Percy þe 3onger 190.

Haudlé see Awdlé.

Haukwood, Ser Jon Sir John Hawkwood 177, 202.

Heber Eber 19. poss. ~ 19.

De Hebraicis Questionibus, The Liber quaestionum hebraicarum in Genesim by Jerome 16/25 n.

Hebrewis n. pl. Israelites, Jews 19, 26; ancient Jewish scholars 14, 16; (biblical Epistle to) 24. Cf. Jewis.

Hebron, Ebron capital of Judah 11, 12, 15, 24, 32. Also called Cariatharbe.

Heleyn, Seynt St. Helen 61; (body of) 85, (treasure left by) 210.

Heleyne Helen of Troy 30.

Heli Eli, high-priest 23, 31. gen. Hely 31.

Hely Ely 100, 139–40, 185, 197; (John Hotham, bishop 1316–37)146, 151, 153, and see Lyle; (church at) 170, 179.

Helianore[1] Eleanor of Aquitaine, q to King Henry II (formerly married to Louis VII of France) 109, 110.

Helianore[2] Eleanor, da of Henry II and prec. 110.

Helianore[3] Eleanor, da of Geoffrey of Brittany, niece of Richard I and John 115.

Helianore[4] Eleanor of Provence, q to King Henry III 120.

Helianore[5] Eleanor of Castile (half-sr of Alfonso X), q to Edward I 122, 127, 144.

Helianore[6] (erron.), da of Charles VI of France, see **(Qween) Ysabell.**

Helie Elijah 16, 17, 33, 34.

Helys, Robert Robert Ellis 232.

Helise Elisha 33, 34; (body of) 69.

Helius see **Pertinax.**

Helman see **Elman.**

Helwolphus (erron. for) Ceolwulf, k of W Saxons 80/2 n.

Hengist, k of Kent (c.455–c.488) 79.

Hennon (valley of) Ben-hinnom, Jerusalem 36.

Hennow (c of) Hainault 151, 162; (da of c of) 151.

Henry, Henrius Henry I (the Fowler), dk of Saxony, k of Germans (919–36) 90, 91; **Herry** in þe othir Herry 96.

Herclé, Sere Andrew Andrew Harclay, e of Carlisle (1322–3) 147, 148–9.

Hercules 28.

Herford, Herforth Hereford 153; (b of) 242 (Robert Mascell, 1404–16), and see **Adam, Jon**[1] and **Maydeston**; (dk of) see **Herry (þe Fourte)**; (e of) erron. for Thomas FitzAllen (later e of Arundel, 1400–15) 211/30 n., and see **Bown.**

Herforthscire Herefordshire 219.

Hermes Hermas 53.

Herry (= Henry I) see **Henry.**

Herry þe First Henry II, dk of Bavaria (985–), emp (1014–27) 95–6; (reign of) 97.

Herry þe Secund Henry III, emp (1039–56) 99; also the child in the story 97.

Herry þe þird Henry IV, emp (1056–1105) 100.

Herri (þe Fourte) Henry V, emp (1111–25) 104, 105; (w of) see **Maute**[3].

Herry (þe V) Henry VI, emp (1191–7) 112.

Herri (þe First), (þe King), also **Herry Clerk** 'Henry the Scholar', Henry I, k of England (1100–35) 103, (reign) 104–6, 107; (q of) see **Adelida, Maute**[2]. gen. **Herry** 105/30.

Herri (þe Secunde), (Kyng/Duk) Henry II, k of England (1154–89), dk of Normandy etc. 107, 108, (reign) 109–11, 113, 122; (q of) see **Helianore**[1].

Herri (þe þird), (King) Henry III, k of England (1216–72), (reign) 117–26, 133; (q of) see **Helianore**[4]; (issue of) 214/15.

Herry (þe Fourte), (King); previously **Herri ((of) Lancastir), (Duke/Ser)** Henry IV, k of England (1399–1413), e of Derby (1377–99), dk of Hereford (1397–9), dk of Lancaster (1399) 9, 192, 199, 206, 209/22, 211–14, (reign) 214–38; (1st w of) see **(Dam) Mary**; (Joan, 2nd w and q of) 220, 230; (Blanche, da of) 219.

Herri (þe V), (Prince) Henry V, k of England (1413–22), e of Chester (1399–), dk of Cornwall (1399–), p of Wales (1399–) 211/24, 214/24, 215/12, 230, 232, 234, (reign) 238–49.

Herri Henry, e of Lancaster (1326–) and of Leicester (1324–45) 151, 153.

Herry (of Lancastir (þe ʒonger)), (Duke) Henry of Grosmont, e of Derby (1337–61), of Lancaster (1345–51), dk of Lancaster (1351–61), s of prec. 159, 164, 168–9, 171, 172, 214/30; (da of) see **Blaunche.** gen. in Duke Herry doutyr (Maud) 167/27.

Herry[1] prob. Henry V, dk of Bavaria (1004–9, 1017–26) 97/19.

Herry[2] Henry, s of King Henry II 110/8.

Herry[3] Henry of Almaine, s of **Richard**[5] 125.

Herry[4] Henry II (of Trastamara), k of Castile (1369–79) 176.

Herri, Kyng Eric IV, k of Denmark (1241–50) 91/22 n.

Hertforth (erron. for **Herforth**) Hereford (b of) see **Maydeston.**

Herwich Harwich, Essex 151.

Heth, Haymo at þe Hamo Hethe (prop. 'of Hythe'), b of Rochester (1317–52) 167.

Hewe Hugh of St.-Cher, OP, cardinal of S. Sabina, Rome (d. 1263) 120–1.

Hiberi see **Spayne.**

Hildebrande Hildebrand, (later Pope Gregorius VII[us]) 100.

Hillari Hilary, pope (461–8) 69.

Hillari, Seynt St. Hilary of Poitiers (d. 367); (eight-day period following fd (13 or 14 Jan.) of) 202; **Hillarius** 63.

Hillarion St. Hilarion (d. 371) 63.

Hingwar Ingwar 86.

Historia Scolastica *Historia Scholastica* by Peter Comestor 111/27 n.

Hogges St. Vaast-de-la-Hogue, Normandy 165.

Holland, Ser Jon John Holand, e of Huntingdon (1388–1400), dk of Exeter (1397–9) 207, 209, 211, 212, 215, 216–17; (w of) 206.

Holland[1], Ser Thomas Thomas Holand, e of Kent (1360) 172.

Holland[2], Ser Thomas Thomas Holand, e of Kent (1397–1400), dk of Surrey (1397–9) 207, 209, 212, 215, 216.

Hollond Holland 227; **Holland** (William c of and his da Jacqueline) 247. Cf. **Seland.**

Holt (castle of) Holt on the Dee, Denbighshire 202.

Holt, Jon of Sir John Holt 192.

Holy Go(o)st 8, 24, 31, 43, 70, 233, 234.

Holy Lond Palestine 26, 100, 107, 113, 114, 121, 125, 130; as **Lond of Behest** 27. Cf. **Palestine.**

Honorius, emp (395–423) 66–7.

Honorius Primus Honorius I, pope (625–38) 75.

Honorius þe Secund Honorius II, pope (1124–30) 106.

Honorius, (þe Pope) Honorius III, pope (1216–27) 112–13, 118; **Honory** 112.

Hormisda Hormisdas, pope (514–23) 71.

Hostiense[1] (for L *Via Ostiensis*) Ostian Way, road from Rome to Ostia 50, 57.

Hostiense[2] (b) of Ostia, see **Eugeni, Steuene.**

Hubba Ubba 86.

Huys, France (c of) 235.

Humbir, -yr R Humber 31, 80, 195.

Humfrey, dk of Gloucester (1414–47) 214, 248; **Vmfrey** 230.

Hungari(e) Hungary; (k of) see **Jon[7], Sigemund, Totila;** (Clementia, da of k of = q to Louis X of France) 160.

Huntingdon 230; (e of) see **Angolisme, Clynton, Holland;** (countess of) see **Ser Jon Holland.**

Ida, k of Bernicia (547–59) 80.

Ydani Edith, q to Edward the Confessor 99/31 n., 101.

Ydapsis Hystaspes, f of Darius I of Persia 40.

Ydida Jedidiah, name given to Solomon at birth 32. [2 Sam. 12: 25]

Ydras Hydra, a monster 28.

Ieraple Hierapolis 49.

Yginius Iginus, pope (136–40) 53.

Ignace, Seint St. Ignatius, b of Antioch (67–107) 51.

Ylde, (Ser) Waryn of þe Sir Warin Delisle 147.

Illiricum Illyria (mod. Albania and Yugoslavia) 58.

Ymacho, Ynachi Inachus, k of Argos 25, 27/7–8 n.

Inde Asia 15, 19, 21, 39; India 23, 48, 51.

Yngham, Ser Olyuere of Sir Oliver Ingham 161.

Inglond England 79–80, 86, 89, 91, 93, 94–5, 96, 98, 99, 101–2, 103, 104–5, 107, 109, 111, 118, 119, 121, 122, 124, 125, 127, 129, 132–3, 137, 139, 141, 151, 154, 155, 156, 157, 159–60, 163, 166, 168, 169, 170, 173, 175, 177–8, 179–80, 183, 185–7, 189, 190, 197, 200, 202–3, 205, 213, 214–15, 217–18, 220, 232, 237, 243,

Inglond (*cont.*)
247–8; (crown of) 101, 104–5, 140, 175, 214; (k of) 79/7, 124/1 and see under k's name; (heir(s) to crown of) 144, 227; (reigns of kings of) 116; (regent of) 153, 203; (Church of) 118, 122; (bp(ric)s of) 163, 179; (pilgrims from) 223; (notary from) 148; (lords of) 139, 143 (their Scottish lands), 172; (knight from) 150; (men of = **Englischmen**) 100, 107, 129, 131, 132, 133, 135, 136, 140, 157, 158, 161, 162, 165, 171, 175, 176, 178, 179, 183, 187, 191, 201, 220, 223, 235, 236, 238, 246; (poets of) 105; (shires of) 147, 154, 192; (towns of) 143, 225; (Jews of) 130. Cf. **Saxones.**

Innocent Innocent I, pope(401–17)67.

Innocent, (Pope) Innocent II, pope (1130–43) 106.

Innocencius III Innocent III, pope (1198–1216) 112; **Pope Innocent** 112.

Innocent þe IIII Innocent IV, pope (1243–54) 121; **þe Pope Innocent** 122; (papacy of) 113.

Innocent þe V Innocent V, pope (1276) 127.

Innocent þe Sext Innocent VI, pope (1352–62) 167; **Pope Innocent** 173.

Innocent þe VII Innocent VII, pope (1404–6) 227, 231.

Ionicus Javan 20/13 n.

Ypon Hippo 67, 81.

Ypres, France 187; (men of) 162.

Yrad Irad 11, 13.

Yradone erron. for Heraclonas (Heracleon), emp (641) 76.

Yreneus St. Irenaeus, b of Lyon (d. *c.*201) 54.

Yrland see **Erlond.**

Ysaac Isaac 15, 19, 21, 24, 25.

Ysabel erron. for Philippa de Coucy, da of Isabella of Woodstock 192.

Ysabell Isabella of France, q of Edward II 135, 137–9, 144, 146, 150–6, 160.

Ysabell, (Dame) Isabella of Castile, w of **Edmund Langlé,** dk of York 178, 185, 198, 202, 219.

Ysabell, Qween Isabella, da of Charles VI of France, q of Richard II 216, 218, 224; **Helianore** (erron.) 206.

Ysabelle, þe Lady Isabella Marshal 119.

Ysaie Isaiah 36–7.

Ysider St. Isidore of Seville; (chronicle method of) 8; (statement by) 29, 62.

Ys(id)is Io (identified with Isis) 25/11 n., 27.

Ysidre ? St. Isidore of Pelusium 64/27 n.

Ismael Ishmael 21.

Israel, name for Jacob 19/33.

Israel (nation) 19, 25, 28, 31, 32; (ten tribes of) 20; (judge(s) of) 8, 27–30, and see under judge's name.

Itaile, Itale Italy 27, 36, 37, 65, 66, 71, 73, 76, 83, 87, 88, 90–1, 93, 106, 177; (kingdom of) 73; (ruler of) 70, 71, 84; (chancellor of as imperial elector) 95; (noble titles of) 200; (people of) 19, 64; (native of) 53, 102, 103; (bps of) 71, 82.

Jabel Jabal 13.

Jacob 15, 19, 25–6.

Jacob(us) James 'the Less' (identified with James 'the Lord's brother') 49/3; (church of) 73. Cf. **Jame.**

Jael 29.

Jayr Jair 30.

Jame, Seynt James 'the Great'; **Jacobus** 48/29; (act in honour of) 104; (hand of) 105.

Januensis *n. pl.* Genoese 184.

Japhet(h) 18, 19; (s of) 21; (descendants of) 20.

Jared, Jareth 15, 16, 18, 19.

Jeconias Jechonias, Gk form of Jeconiah, another name for **Joachim** 38.

Jectan Joktan 19, 20.

Jene see **Gene.**

Jeremie Jeremiah 38.

Jericho 27.

Jerom, (Seynt) St. Jerome 63, 64, 65, 67; (chronicle by) 7; (statement by) 16, 56, 103–4; (fd of, 30 Sept.) 214. *poss.* ~ 25.

Jerusalem 17, 20, 24, 32–9, 43, 48, 50, 52, 57, 68, 74, 75, 83, 101, 111, 223; (b of) see under b's name; (patriarch of) see **Eraclius²**; (crown of) 105; (k of) 137; ((proposed) crusade to) 111, 121. See also **Cruce, Temple**.

Jesse 32.

Jesu¹ Joshua, s of Jehozadak 39. [Hag. 1: 1]

Jesu² Jesus Christ, our Lord; (name of) 51; (revelation through) 121; (year of) 238. *poss.* ~ 84. See also **Crist**.

Jesus, s of Sirach 43.

Jethro, f-in-law of Moses 26.

Jewis *n. pl.* Jews 8, 65, 145, (in Jerusalem) 52, 63, 138, (in Crete) 68, (in Caesarea, Palestine) 72, (in England) 113, 118, 127, 130, (in Norwich) 120; (Babylonian captivity of) see **Captiuité**; (rebellion of against Romans) 50; (persecution of) 52, 66; (ancient Jewish scholars) 21; (usage of *re* date of Easter) 53. See also **Israel, Jerusalem**; cf. **Hebrewis**.

Joachim Jehoiakim, k of Judah (609–599 BC) 38.

Joachim, (Abbot) Joachim (d. 1201/2), a of Fiore in Calabria 109; (republication of works of) 123.

Joaden Jehoaddin 35.

Joas Joash, k of Judah (877–838 BC) 34.

Joathan Jotham, k of Judah (756–742 BC) 35–6.

Job 19.

Joiada Jehoiada 34.

Jon Joan, legendary pope (855 ff.) 87.

Johannes Crisostomus St. John Chrysostom (d. 407) 63.

Johannes Patricius John, a Roman patrician (mid 4th cent.) 68/14 n.

Jon Baptiste, (Seynt) John the Baptist 31; (feast of nativity of, 24 June) 158, 166, 177, 197, 202, 225. *poss.* in ~ *day* 143/12.

Jon (þe) Euangelist, (Seyn) John, apostle 48, 51; (follower of) 53.

Jon John I, pope (523–6) 71.

Jon þe Secunde John II, pope (533–5) 72.

Jon þe pird John III, pope (561–74) 73.

Jon þe Fourt John IV, pope (640–2) 75.

Johannes Vᵘˢ John V, pope (685–6) 77.

Jon þe Sexte John VI, pope (701–5) 78.

Johannes VII John VII, pope (705–7) 78.

Johannes VIIIᵘˢ John VIII, pope (872–82) 88; **Jon** 88.

Johannes IXᵘˢ John IX, pope (898–900) 89.

Johannes Xᵘˢ John X, pope (914–28) 90.

Johannes XII John XII, pope (955–64) 91–2; **Jon** 93.

Johannes XIIIᵘˢ John XIII, pope (965–72) 93.

Jon þe XVII erron. for John XVI, pope (997–8) 95.

Johannes XII erron. for John XVII, pope (1003) 96.

Johannes XIII erron. for John XVIII, pope (1004–9) 96.

Johannes XX erron. for John XIX, pope (1024–32) 97.

Jon þe XXI John XXI, pope (1276–7) 128.

Johannes XXII John XXII, pope (1316–34), previously b of Avignon (1310–) 139; **Pope Jon** 143; **Jon þe XXII** 141, 158; (time of) 135; (bulls from) 141.

Jon John XXIII, called **Balthasar** Baldassare Cossa, pope at Pisa (1410–15), previously erron. styled b of Bologna 234, 242–3.

Jon¹ John Trefnant, b of Hereford (1389–1404) 213.

Jon² John Buckingham, b of Lincoln (1362–98) 210.

Jon³ John, c, then dk of Alençon, l of Perche and Fougères 236–7, 245.

Jon⁴ John, 3rd s of John II of France, dk of Berri, c of Auvergne 205–6, 235, 236.

Jon⁵ John, dk of Bourbon, c of Clermont, of Ferez, l of the Beaujolais 206, 236, 246.

Jon⁶ John II, k of France (1350–64) 168–71, 172, 174.

Jon⁷ John, name attributed to k of Hungary in middle of reign of Louis II (1342–82), ? John VI, k of Bulgaria (1331–71) 174.

Jon⁸ John (Balliol), k of Scotland (1292–6) 133–4.

Jon⁹ John, name of Pope **Gelasius** II 104.

Jon¹⁰ in *Paule and* ∼ SS. John and Paul, Roman martyrs 63.

Jon, (Kyng) John, k of England (1199–1216) 110, 115, 116, 122; (q of) see **Blanc** (erron.). *poss.* **Kyng Jones** 117.

Jon, (Lord) John, s of Henry IV, dk of Bedford (1414–35) 214, 228, 247.

Jon, Seynt, see **Bridlington.**

Jon Postumus John, posthumous s of Louis X of France by Clementia of Hungary 160.

Jon þe Scot John Scotus Eriugena 86.

Jonas, reported name of boy revived by Elijah (1 Kgs. 17: 17–24) 33.

Jone¹ Javan 19/19 n.

Jone² Joan, da of Henry II 110.

Jone³ Joan, heiress to earldom of Kent (1353 ff.) and m of Richard II 172, 189.

Jones, Seynt ellipt. for Hospital of St. John of Jerusalem 186; (prior of) 185.

Joram, k of Judah (889–885 BC) 34; (da of) 34.

Jordan R Jordan, Palestine 27.

Josaphat¹ Jehoshaphat, k of Judah (915–889 BC) 33.

Josaphat² St. Josaphat or Joasaph, s of Abenner an Indian king 64.

Joseph¹, s of Jacob 25, 26.

Joseph² St. Joseph, reputed f of **Jacob(us)** 49.

Josephus, Jewish historian; (statement by) 24.

Josias Josiah, k of Judah (640–609 BC) 38.

Josue Joshua 27–8. *poss.* ∼ 26.

Jouiniane Jovian, emp (363–4) 64.

Jozabeth Jehoshabeath or Jehosheba 34.

Jubal 13.

Jubanense *gen.* of Geneva 182/17 n.

Juda Judah; (tribe of) 20, 32; (king(s) of) 8, 33.

Judas Judas Iscariot 49/14.

Judas Machabeus Judas Maccabaeus 45.

Judas (Thadeus) St. Judas Thaddaeus, apostle 49/12; (Letter of) 16; **Jude** (fd of, 28 Oct.) 206. See also **Thade.**

Jude Palestine 45; (governor of) 48.

Juliane Julian the Apostate, emp (361–3) 63–4; **Julianus (Apostata)** 63, 64.

Julius (Cesar) Julius Caesar (d. 44 BC) 46–7.

Jupitir Jupiter 21.

Justine Justin, emp of E (518–27) 71; (time of) 69.

Justiniane (þe First) Justinian I, emp of E (527–65) 71–2.

Justiniane (þe Secunde) erron. for Justin II, emp of E (565–78) 72–3.

Justiniane (þe Secund), Justinianus Secundus Justinian II, emp of E (685–95, 705–11) 77–9. *gen.* ∼ 78.

Justus, Seynt, b of Vienne (d. 168) 53.

Kayerglau Gloucester 49/31 n.

Kalixt(us) St. Callistus I, pope (217–22) 55; (catacombs of) 54, 59. *poss.* **(Seynt) Kalixte** 58 (catacombs), 102 (fd, 14 Oct.).

Kalist (þe Secund), Kalixtus II^{us} Callistus II, pope (1119–24) 101, 104.

Kame see **Cane.**

Karine Carinus 59.

Karington, Thomas Thomas Catterton 180.

Karlhill, Karlile, also **Carlil** Carlisle, Cumberland 140, 149; (governor and e of) see **Herclé**; (b of) 212 (Thomas Merks).

Karolus see **Charles.**

Karus Carus, emp (281–3) 59.

Katerine St. Catherine of Alexandria 60.

Kech, William erron. for William Keith 157.

Kemperlé Quimperlé, France 180·

Kenelworth Kenilworth, War. 153, 249.

Kent (AS kingdom of) 79; (county of) 227; (towns in) 227; (**Godwyn**, reported dk of) 99; (e of) see **Holland, Woodstok**; (countess of) see **Jone²**.

Kidkaus Chef de Caux, Normandy 244.

Kym Kyme, Lincs.; (Gilbert Umfraville, wrongly styled e of) 236.

Kynderton, þe barne of Sir Richard Venables, l of Kinderton, Cheshire 222.

Kyngeston, Maistir William erron. for William de Kyngescote, chancellor of Oxford University (1289) 130.

Kingeston (upon Temse) Kingston on Thames, Surrey 94, 117.

Kyngilis Cynegils, k of W Saxons (611–43) 80.

Kyngis, þe first book of 1 Sam. 31.

Kynricus Cynric, k of W Saxons (534–60) 80.

Knollis, (Ser) Robert Sir Robert Knollys 177, 184, 232.

Knowt Cnut, k of England (1016–35), k of Denmark (1019–35) 96, 98; (q of) see **Emme**.

Kredicus Cerdic, k of W Saxons (519–34) 80.

Krownwell, Ser Jon Sir John Cromwell 150.

Labdon see **Abdon**.

Lacedomy Sparta, also called Lacedaemon; (k of) see **Ligurgius**.

Lacy, (Ser) Herry Henry de Lacy, e of Lincoln (1272–1311) 132, 138.

Lady, oure The Blessed Virgin Mary 64, 68, 72, 74, 78, 116, 166, 175, 214, and see *Glossary*, s.v. **mayde(n)**; (undergarment of as relic) 84; (feast of immaculate conception of, 8 Dec.) 155; (feast of nativity of, 8 Sept.) 105, 169, 176, 186, 196, 203, 208, 219; (feast of annunciation to, 25 Mar.) 191, 234; (feast of visitation of to Elizabeth, 2 July) 199; (feast of assumption of, 15 Aug.) 122, 167, 219, 232, 237, 244; (church of) 84 (at Acre), and

see **Transtibir, Viuiane**; (pictures of) 80; (statues of) 81; (responsories of) 95; (phr.) *mateyns and houres of* ~ Little Office of our Lady 100/30. See also **Domine**.

Lagidi Ptolemies of Egypt who took the surname *Lagides* after next 22.

Lagus, stepfather of Ptolemy I 42.

Lambhithe Lambeth 247.

Lameth¹ Lamech, s of Methushael 11, 13, 17.

Lameth² Lamech, s of Methuselah 16–17, 19.

Lamfrank Lanfranc, prior of Bec (1045–63), ab of Canterbury (1070–89) 102–3.

Lancastir Lancaster 143; (dks of) see **Gaunt, Herry** (of Grosmont), **Herry þe Fourte**; (earls of) see **Herri, Thomas**.

Lancastirschere Lancashire 194.

Lancecrone Agnes Lancecrona 192.

Lando Landonius, pope (913–14) 90.

Langdon, (Maystir) Steuene Stephen Langton, ab of Canterbury (1206–28) 116, 117–19.

Langlé Kings Langley, Herts. 205, 219; (Dominican house at) 217.

Langlé (Ser) Edmund Edmund of Langley, 5th s of Edward III, e of Cambridge (1362–), dk of York (1385–1402), regent (1399) 173, 178, 179, 185, 189, 198, 203, 212, 219; (w of) see **(Dame) Ysabell**; (s of) 198.

Lanson Alençon; (dk of) see **Jon³**.

Laodicia Laodicea (Ladik), city south of Antioch 43.

Lateran The Lateran (Rome), palace of popes 87. *gen.* **Lateranense**; (church of St. John Lateran) 89, 95, 106; (palace) 70, 112.

Latinorum Latium 35.

Latymer, þe Lord William, Lord Latimer, Chamberlain to Richard II 180.

Latymer, Thomas Sir Thomas Latimer 191, 204.

Laudunense *gen.* of Laon (Aisne); (cathedral spire) 204.

Laurens¹ Acca Laurentia, called *Lupa* 36.

Laurens[2] Laurentius, antipope (498–505), b of Nocera (499–501) 70.

Laurens, (Seynt) St. Laurence (d. 258) 57, 58; (body of) 68, 69, 72; (fd of, 10 Aug.) 157, 223. **Seynt Laurens (oute of þe Wallis)** church of S. Lorenzo fuori le Mura, Rome 62, 63, 87, 112. *gen.* in *Seint Laurens gate* Porta S. Lorenzo, Rome 231.

Lawne Launde, Leics.; (head of priory of Augustinian Canons at) 219.

Ledis Leeds, Kent; (castle of) 146, 240.

Leycetir Leicester 80, 93, 143; (house of Augustinian Friars at) 122; (e of) see **Herri, Mountforth, Thomas**.

Lemouica, Lemouicense see **Lymozin**.

Lemustre prob. erron. for Ile de Noirmoutier 196.

Lenne Lynn, now King's Lynn 217, 230, 249; (Friary of Augustinian Hermits at) 7; (fishermen of) 217/15.

Lenton, Notts.; (manor-house at) 156.

Leon, (Seint) Leo I the Great, pope (440–61) 68–9.

Leo II[us], pope (682–3) 77.

Leon þe IIII erron. for Leo III, pope (795–816) 84.

Leon Leo IV, pope (847–55) 86–7.

Leo V[us], pope (903) 89.

Leo þe Sext, pope (928) 90.

Leon þe VII, pope (936–9) 90.

Leo(n) VIII, pope (963–5) 92.

Leo X[us] erron. for Leo IX, pope (1049–54) 98.

Leon, Petir Pierleone, antipope Anacletus II (1130–8) 106.

Leo þe First, emp of E (457–71) 69.

Leo (þe Secund), also called **Patricius** 'patrician', Leontius, emp of E (695–8) 78.

Leo Tercius, also **Leon,** emp of E (717–41) 80–1; (s of) 81.

Leo þe IIII, emp of E (775–80) 82.

Leon Leo, s of **Zenon** 69.

Leoncius Leonidas, f of Origen 54.

Leonell Lionel, 3rd s of Edward III, dk of Clarence (1362–8) 161, 169, 173, 176; (w of) see **Borow**.

Leonyne, þe cité The Leonine city (L *Civitas Leonina*), area adjacent to and including the Vatican, now the *Borgo*, fortified by Pope Leo IV 86, 87.

Lettow Lithuania; (grand p of) 175, 199, 218.

Leuy Levi 26.

Leulyne Llywelyn ap Gruffudd, p of Gwynedd (1246–), of Wales (1258–82) 128–9. *gen.* ~ 129.

Lews Lewes; (battle of, 1264) 124; (head of Cluniac priory at) 182.

Liberius, pope (352–66) 63; (time of) 68.

Libi Libya; (people of) 19; (giant of) see **Anthé**; (sibyl of) 37.

Ligurgius Lycurgus, k of Sparta (898–873 BC) 35.

Lyle, Frere Jon erron. for Thomas de Lisle, b of Ely (1345–61) 170.

Lymozin, Lemouica Limousin 169; (lordship of) 128. *gen.* in *þe cité Lemouicense* Limoges 178.

Lincoln 93, 107, 117, 140, 205; (e of) see **Lacy**; (bps of) 130 (Oliver Sutton, 1280–99), 170 (John Gynwell, 1347–62), and see **Beuforth, Burwayche, Grostede, Jon**[2], **Welle**; (cathedral chapter of) 164/16; (Gilbertine Canons of) 164/13. *gen.* **Lyncolniense** 120/9.

Lincoln, Jon 195.

Lyndesey Lindsey, district of Lincs. 96.

Linus of Thebes, musician 28.

Linus, pope (67–78) 50.

Lister, Jak erron. for Geoffrey Litster 185.

Lodwicus, also (þe **Emperour**) **Lodewik,** Louis I (the Pious), emp (814–40) 84/19, 26, 29, 31, 34, 86/4.

Lodewic þe Secunde Louis II, s of Lothair I, k of Italy and emp (855–75) 85, 86/6.

Lodewik þe þirde Louis III (the Blind), k of Provence (887–928), emp (901–5), 90 (see 90/1 n.).

Lodwik[1] Lewis I (the German), s of Louis the Pious, k of Germans (843–76) 84/22, 87.

Lodewik² Lewis III (the Child), k of Germans (899–911) possibly 90. See 90/1 n.

Lodewik³ Louis IV, k of France (936–54) 93.

Lodewik⁴ Louis VI, k of France (1108–37) 105, 107.

Lodewik⁵ Prince Louis of France (later Louis VIII, 1223–6) 117.

Lodewik, Kyng/Seynt Louis IX of France (1226–70) 120–1, 123–5, 160/15; (q of) see **Margarete**.

Lodewik⁶ Louis X, k of France (1314–16) 140, 160 (except for prec. at 160/15).

Loegria England 31.

Loegrius Locrinus 31.

Logon, Ser Robert Sir Robert Logan 217.

Lokton, Jon 193.

Lol(l)ardis *n. pl.* Lollards 191, 203–5, 216, 220, 239, 241, 243, 248; (law against) 218.

Lond of Behest see **Holy Lond**.

London 94, 98, 102, 113, 117, 119, 124, 127–8, 134, 142, 146, 149, 151–2, 153, 156, 170, 171, 174, 181–2, 185–6, 190, 194, 201–2, 216, 217, 225, 231, 232, 241, 246–7, 249; (Tower of) see **Tour**; (gates of) 241; (royal council at) 106 (1127), 142/22 (1317); (= Westminster, parliament at) 136/16 (Apr. 1309), 136/24 (1310), 139 (1313), 140 (1315), 143 (1318), 149 (1324), 158 (1334), 161 (1339), 174 (1363), 179 (1373), 180 (1376), 186/28 (May 1382), 189 (1384), 202/12 (1394), 203 (1395), 206 (Jan. 1397), 208 (Sept. 1397), 213 (30 Sept. 1399), 218 (1401), 220 (1402), 224 (Jan. 1404), 232 (1407), 234 (1410), 238 (1414), 248 (Oct. 1416); (mayor of) see **Exston, Walworth**; (citizens of) 117, 124/26, 143/18, 146/30, 152, 178, 181/20, 190, 194/23, 199, and see **Wolleman**; (Church council at) 105, 155, 233, 238, 239; (bps of) Robert Braybrooke (1381–1404) 193–4, 203, 212, Stephen Gravesend (1318–38) 146, and see **Arundel, Jon** (= Richard) **Clifforth, Courtné, Maurice, Melite**; (coronation at) 104, 181, 220; (Carmelite house at) 232; (Dominican chapter at) 124; (country around) 79. See also **Paule, Westminster**.

London Brigge 134.

Longe, William William Long of Rye 235.

Longobardis see **Lumbardi**.

Longspere, Steuene Stephen Longespée 122.

Longswerd, William William Longsword, dk of Normandy (931–42) 88/23, 93.

Lopham, Dyonise Denis Lopham 214.

Losinga, Herbert, a of Benedictine house at Ramsey (1087–91), b of Thetford/Norwich (1091–1119) 103.

Lotharinge Lotharingia (Brabant and Alsace-Lorraine) 88–9; (crusaders from) 107; (c of) 105 (Godfrey VII of Brabant); (dk of) 165 (Raoul *the Valiant* of Alsace-Lorraine, 1329–46).

Lotharius Primus Lothair I, emp (840–55) 84–5.

Lotharie Lothair II, 2nd s of prec., k of Lotharingia (855–69) 88/2 n.

Lotharius þe Secunde Lothair III, k of Italy (945–50) 92; (w of) see **Daluida**. *gen.* **Lothari** 93/1.

Lotharius þe Fourt, also þe **Emperour Lotharie**, Lothair IV, emp (1133–7), previously dk of Saxony (1106–25), k of Italy (1125–37) 106.

Loua(y)n Louvain 199, 224.

Louel, þe Lord John Lord Lovel of Titchmarsh (1361–1408) 195.

Lownde, Alexander Sir Alexander Lounde 232.

Luce see **Luk**.

Lucery Lucera, Italy 188.

Lucinie Licinius, emp (308–24) 61.

Lucy, (Seynt) (d. *c*.303) 57, 60. *gen.* in *Seynte Lucye day* (13 Dec.) 171/12.

Lucy, Ser Antony Sir Anthony Lucy 149.

Lucye Lucius Verus, emp (161–9) 53.

Lucius, putative k of Britain (*c.*180) 54.

Lucius I, pope (253–4) 57–8.

Lucius II, pope (1144–5) 108.

Lucius III, also þe **Pope Lucius** (1181–5), 110, 111.

Lucius erron. for Julius I, pope (337–52) 62–3.

Ludi Lud (whence the Lydians) 18.

Ludlow (house of Augustinian Friars at) 122.

Lugdune(nse) Lyon; (bps of) see **Forcius, Yreneus.**

Luidbrande Liutprand, k of Lombards (712–44) 81.

Luk, Luce Luke, evangelist; (body of) 63; (paintings reported to be by) 80. *gen.* in *Seint ~ day* (18 Oct.) 249/1.

Lumbard, Maystir Pers þe Peter Lombard, theologian and b of Paris (1160) 109.

Lumbardi Lombardy; (kings of) see **Aburre, Arstulf, Desideri, Luidbrande, Rotharie**; (people of = **Longobardis**) 73, 76, 81, 82, 86, 90; (merchants of) 174.

Luna, Petir de see **Benedict XIII.**

Lundy 120.

Lupold, unidentified German count, reported f of Emperor Henry III (actual father Conrad II) 97.

Maacha Maacah 33. [1 Kgs. 15: 2]

Macedonie Macedonia 30, 49, 58; (kingdom of) 42.

Macharies, þe too St. Macarius of Alexandria (4th cent.) and St. Macarius of Egypt (4th cent.) 64.

Machomet Mohammed 75.

Madian Midian 26.

Magdalen see **Mari.**

Magog 19, 21.

Maydenborow Magdeburg 93.

Maydeston, Maystir Richard erron. for Ralph Maidstone, b of Hereford (1234–9) 120.

Maioricarum *gen.* of Majorca 165, 175.

Majolus, a of Cluny (948–94) 91.

Malaleel Mahalalel 15–16, 19.

Malcolyn Malcolm III, k of Scotland 103, 104.

Maluerne Great Malvern 243.

Maluerne, þe hillis of Malvern Hills 179.

Mambre Mamre 15. [Gen. 35: 27]

Mamert ? erron. for St. Mauritius; (b attached to cathedral of, Vienne) see **Justus.**

Mamert, Seint St. Mamertus (5th cent.) 69.

Mammael Mehujael 11, 13.

Mammea Julia Mammaea 56. See also 55/30–1.

Man, þe Ilde of, Isle of Man 182, 202, 209, 215; **Eubony** 202.

Manasses Manasseh, k of Judah (697–642 BC) 36–8.

Manes, Maniche Manes, also called Manichaeus 59, 65.

Mar, Petir de la Sir Peter de la Mare, Speaker in Good Parliament (1376) 180.

Mar, Thomas de la Thomas de la Mare, a of St. Albans (1349–96) 184.

Marcelle Marcellus I, pope (308–9) 60.

Marcelline Marcellinus, pope (296–304) 60.

March (earls of) 169 (Roger Mortimer, 1354–60), and see **Mortimer.**

Marchale, þe Erle Earl Marshal; (Thomas of Brotherton, e of Norfolk 1312–38) 151; (John Mowbray, dk of Norfolk 1413–32) 245; and see **Mounbray.**

Marchale, Jon John the Marshal, supposed spy of Despenser's 152.

Marcian, emp of E (450–7) 68.

Marcyle Marseilles 155.

Marcus Antoni þe Trewe erron. for Marcus Aurelius, emp (161–80) 53–4.

Mardoche Mordecai (apparently confused with Marduk, name for Babylonian god Bel) 38.

Mare Ionicum Ionian Sea 19.

Margarete, Seinte St. Margaret (lived 3rd cent.); (fd of, 20 July) 130.

Margarete, infant da of Louis VII of France 110.

Margarete of Provence, q to Louis IX of France 120.

Margarete of France, q to Edward I 133.

Mari Miriam 26. [Num. 26: 59]

Mary, abbess of Benedictine convent at Barking (1173–5) 111.

Mari Magdelen St. Mary Magdalene; (fd of, 22 July) 222, 233.

Mari Major, Seynt S. Maria Maggiore, Rome 68, 70, 76.

Mary, (Dam) Mary Bohun, w of Henry IV when styled e of Derby (d. 1394) and da of **Humfrey Bown²** 202, 214.

Mary, oure Lady see **Lady.**

Marys, William William de Marisco 120.

Mark, St., evangelist; (body of) 69.

Markam, Jon John Markham 213–14.

Mars 36.

Martyn, Seynt St. Martin of Tours (d. 397) 64; (fd of, 11 Nov.) 184/27 n.; (feast of translation of, 4 July) 212. *gen.* ~ 67/26. ~ *in Montibus* S. Martino ai Monti, Rome 85.

Martin þe First, pope (649–55) 76; (fd of, 12 Nov.) 189/4 n.

Martinus IIᵘˢ, pope (882–4) 88.

Martinus IIIᵘˢ, pope (942–6) 88/30, 91.

Martyn þe Fourt, pope (1281–5) 129.

Mate-grifon, name of siege-tower used by Richard I 114.

Matheu Matthias 49/14.

Mathew, (Seint) Matthew, apostle 49; (gospel acc. to) 69; (fd of, 21 Sept.) 208, 240.

Mat(h)usael Methushael 11, 13.

Mathusale(m) Methuselah 16–17, 18, 19.

Matrinus Macrinus, emp (217–18) 55.

Maudut, Thomas Thomas Mauduit 147.

Mauntrauers, Ser Jon Sir John Maltravers 154–5.

Maurice, Seynt 60.

Mauricius, emp (582–602) 74.

Maurice, b of London (1085–1107) 104.

Mauron ? Montmuran, Brittany 167.

Maurus, St. (6th cent.) 72.

Maut Matilda, da of Henry II 110.

Maute¹ Matilda, q to William the Conqueror 102.

Maute² Matilda, 1st q to Henry I 104–5.

Maute³ Matilda, da of prec., empress to Henry V (1114–25), w of Geoffrey of Anjou, m of Henry II 105–6, 107–8, 109.

Mawny, Ser Walter Sir Walter Manny 162.

Maxencius Maxentius, emp (306–12) 61.

Maximiane¹ Maximinus, emp (235–8) 56.

Maximiane² Maximian, emp (286–305) 59–60.

Medai Madai 19.

Medes *n. pl.* 19, 39.

Medewey R Medway 232.

Melan Milan 66, 73, 176/22 n.; (b of) see **Ambrose.**

Melan, Seynt Petir of erron. for St. Peter Martyr, of Verona (d. 1252) 121/10–11 n.

Melchiades, pope (311–14) 61.

Melchisedech Melchizedek 24.

Meleyn Malines; (vc of) 206.

Melite Mellitus, b of London (601–24) 79.

Menoures *n. pl.* Franciscans 47, 113, 120, 122, 123, 130, 219.

Mens Mainz 56, 87; (b of) 95 (as imperial elector), and see **Rabanus.**

Mer Mash 18–19.

Merce(orum) Mercia; (AS kingdom of) 80, 91; (ealdormann of) see **Edred.**

Mercury 29.

Mercurie, soldier said to have killed Emperor Julian the Apostate 64.

Merlyn Merlin 128.

Mesopotamy Mesopotamia (mod. Iraq) 57.

Mesram Mizraim 19.

Messane Messina 114.

Methodius of Olympus, St. (d. c.311) 15, 17.

Metles, Jewet Juet (diminutive of Juliana) Meat-less (abstainer from food) 159.

Michael, (Seynt), archangel 12; (chapel of, on Glastonbury Tor,

Michael, (Seynt) (*cont.*):
destroyed by landslip 1271) 127;
(fd of, 29 Sept.) 128, 166, and see
Glossary, s.v. **Myhilmesse.**

Michael I Rhangabe, emp of E (811–13) 83.

Michael II, emp of E (820–9) 84.

Miche Micah 33; (body of) 66.

Micherius erron. for Nocera, Italy;
(b of) see **Laurence.**

Mydilborow Middelburg, Zeeland
195, 196.

Mydilton, Gilbert of Sir Gilbert
Middleton 142.

Mildnale Mildenhall, Suffolk 186.

Mylforth Haue Milford Haven 230.

Minerue Minerva (Pallas Athene) 21.

Mithforth Mitford, Northumberland; (castle of) 142.

Mithologiis *Mitologiarum libri iii*,
work by Fulgentius Mythographus
21.

Moises Moses 7–8, 26–7, 37;
(time of) 34; (devil in likeness of)
68; (= Pentateuch) 11–12; (1st
book of = Gen.) 108. *gen.* **Moyses**
35/7, and cf. *Glossary*, s.v. **Moises-
werk.**

Moyne, þe Lady Joan Lady Mohun
(d. 1404), widow of John Lord
Mohun 195.

Moleyns, þe Lady Margery Lady
Moleyns (d. 1399), widow of
William Lord Moleyns 195.

Monstreworth, Ser Jon John Menstreworth 177.

Morettus prob. 'the Mohammedan'
(Moor) = **Balthasardan.**

Moris, þe Lord erron. for John
Randolph, e of Moray (1332–46)
159.

Morlé, Ser Robert Sir Robert
Murley 240.

Morlé, William William Murley 242.

Morley, Ser Robert Robert, Lord
Morley, admiral of the northern
fleet (1339–42) 162.

Morpath Morpeth, Northumberland
142.

Mortimer, Edmund, l of Wigmore
(d. 1304) 129.

**Mortimer (þe ȝonger), (Ser)
Roger** Roger Mortimer of Wig-

more, s of prec., e of March and
of Kent (1328–30) 145, 147, 150,
151–2, 155–6, 157.

Mortimer, Roger, l of Chirk (d.
1326), uncle of prec. 145, 147,
150/17.

Mortimer, Edmund, e of March
(1360–81) 179, 186.

Mortimer, Roger, e of March
(1394–8) 203, 210.

Mortimer, Edmund, e of March
(1413–25) 219, 227, 245.

Mortimeres, þe too Roger Mortimer of Chirk and Roger Mortimer
e of March (1328–30) 147.

Mosaca (city of), prob. Mushki,
name of country and people 19.

Mosok Meshek 19.

Mounbray, (Ser) Jon John Mowbray, l of Axholme and Gower 145,
147.

Mounbray, Thomas, erron. for
John Mowbray, e of Nottingham
(1377–83) 182.

Mounbray, (Ser) Thomas Thomas
Mowbray, e of Nottingham (1383–),
dk of Norfolk (1397–9), Earl Marshal 190–1, 192, 203, 206, 207,
209–10.

Mounbray, Thomas, Earl Marshal,
s of prec. 227–8.

Mountagew, (Ser) William¹ William Montague, e of Salisbury
(1337–44) 158, 159.

Mountagew, (Ser) William², e of
Salisbury (1349–97) 172, 179, 202.

Mountagu, (Ser) Jon John Montague, e of Salisbury (1397–1400) 191,
204, 207, 216.

Mounte-pesulane Montpellier;
(university of) 233.

Mountforth, Jon John IV de Montfort, dk of Brittany and poss. e
of Richmond (1341–5) 163. Cf.
Bretayn.

Mountforth, (Ser) Jon John V de
Montfort, dk of Brittany, e of
Richmond (1372–84, 1398–9) 174,
179, 182, 184, 199; (Joan, widow
of) 220; (br of) see **Arthure³.** *gen.*
Jon 174/22.

Mountforth, Petir Peter de Montfort, l of Beaudesert (War.) 124.

Mountforth, Simund/Symon Simon de Montfort, e of Leicester (1231–65) 122, 124; (Eleanor, da of) 128.

Mountforth, Simon, s of prec. 124/13.

Muylla, Goselyne of erron. for Jocelyn Dayville 147/33 n.

Mutforth, Richard Richard Mitford 195.

Naaman, Syrian (Aramaean) commanding officer 34.

Nabugodonosor Nebuchadnezzar, k of Babylon 38, 106; (dreams of) 39; name attributed to **Cirus** 22.

Nachor Nahor 19, 22.

Naȝar (battle of) Nájera, Spain 176.

Naples 99, 106, 112, 232; (Ladislas, k of) 231–2; (people of) 86.

Narciscus Narcissus, b of Jerusalem (d. *c.212*) 54.

Narses, general under Justinian I (erron. assigned to reign of Justin II) 72–3.

Nathan 32.

Natures of al þing, Of tr. *De Universo* 'Concerning the Essential Qualities of all Things' by **Rabanus Maurus** 84.

Nauern Navarre; (Charles II, k of) 182; (Charles III) 202, 235.

Necenlaus see **Nycenlaus.**

Nectanabus Nectanebo II, k of Egypt (359–341 BC) 22.

Ned, Seint St. Neot (9th cent.) 89.

Neda erron. for Sledda, poss. k of E Saxons (*c.*600) 79.

Nembrot Nimrod 20.

Neptunus, alternative name for **Pandion** (? confused with Poseidon) 28.

Nero, emp(54–68), 48, 50. *poss.* ~ 57.

Nerua Nerva, emp (96–8) 51.

Nestorius, founder of Nestorianism (d. *c.*451) 67.

Neuyle, Alexaundir Alexander Neville, ab of York (1373–88) 192, 193, 195.

Neuyle, Raf¹ Ralph Neville, l of Raby (1331–67) 166.

Neuyle, Raf² Ralph Neville, e of Westmorland (1397–1425), held earldom of Richmond (1399–1425) 209, 212, 213, 215, 223, 228.

Neuyle, William Sir William Neville 191.

Neuport Nieuport, Flanders 187.

Newcastell (upo(n) Tyne) Newcastle upon Tyne 138, 139, 158, 188.

Newe Forest New Forest 104.

Newgate, prison in London 153.

Nycene erron. for Nicea, Bithynia; (Church council at, 325) 61, 62.

Nycenlaus erron. for Wenceslas, p of Bohemia (d. 929) 91.

Nicheforus Nicephorus I, emp of E (806–15) 83.

Nicholas, (Seynt), b of Myra, Lycia (4th cent.) 61, 63; (fd of, 6 Dec.) 167, 200.

Nicholas (Primus), pope (858–67) 87, 88.

Nicholas (II^us), pope (1059–61) 99.

Nicholas þe Fourt erron. for Nicholas III, pope (1277–80) 128.

Nicholace Nicholas IV, pope (1288–92) 130.

Nichomedi Nicomedia; (b of) see **Eusebie.**

Nylus R Nile 29.

Nyniue Nineveh 23, 37.

Ninus 23–4.

Noe Noah 16–18, 19, 20, 24; (descendants of) 18, 24; (time of) 7.

Noema Naamah 13.

Normandie, -mannie Normandy 93, 96, 101, 102, 106, 115, 117, 165, 182, 237; (duchy/lands of) 103, 151 (erron. for Poitou); (dks of) 88, and see **Herry (þe Secunde), Longswerd, William;** ('brooch of') see **Emme;** (leaders of) 93, 162; (men of = **Normannes**) 88, 100, 119, 131, 132, 162, 171, 191, and see *Glossary*, s.v. **Normanndes.**

Nor(t)hampton 144, 249; (battle of, 1264) 124; (parliament at, 1380) 184; (William Bohun, e of) 165, 169.

Nor(th)folk 79, 145, 231; (dk of) see **Marchale, Mounbray;** (Margaret, countess of 1338–97, duchess of 1397–9) 209/25; (mq of, erron.

Nor(th)folk (*cont.*):
for **Somirsete**) see **(Thomas) Beuforth.**
Northumbirlond Northumberland; (AS kingdom of = Bernicia+ Deira) 80; (earls of) see **Percy, Vtred.**
Norwey Norway 69.
Norwich 96, 120, 126, 185, 238; (diocese of) 103, 184; (church at) 111; (Dominican house at) 238; (bps of) 115–16 (John Gray 1200–14), 150 (John Salmon 1299–1325), 153 (William Ayermine 1325–36, Chancellor 1326–7), and see **Bateman, Courtney, Spenser, Totyngton, Wakeryng, William**[3]; (monk(s) of) 123, 188, 199; (men of) 126, 178; (Jews of) 120.
Nothus, surname of **Darius** II of Persia erron. given to **Artharxerses** I 40.
Notingham Nottingham 93, 192, 207; (castle of) 102, 156, 180, 192, 195; (parliament at) 156 (1330), 160 (1336); (earldom of) 80; (e of) see **Mounbray.**
Numerian, emp (283–4) 59.
Numeus Narmer, first ruler of united Egypt (*c.*2850 BC) 22.
Nun 27.

Occa Octa, k of Kent (6th cent.) 79.
Occhozie Ahaziah, k of Judah (885–883 BC) 34; (s of) see **Joas.**
Octauian[1] Octavianus Augustus, emp (27 BC–AD 14) 46–7.
Octauian[2] Octavius, f of prec. 47/3.
Octo (þe First), (þe Emperour) Otto I the Great, k of Germans (936–73), emp (962–73) 92–3, 95/18; (w of) see **Daluida**; (time of) 90.
Octo þe Secund Otto II, emp (973–83) 94, 95/18.
Octo þe þirde Otto III, emp (983–1002) 94, 95.
Octo þe Fourte Otto IV, emp (1209–18) 112.
Octobone Ottobono de' Fieschi, cardinal legate, later Pope **Adriane þe V** 124, 127.
Ode/Odo, (Seynt) St. Odo, a of Cluny (927–42) 91, 92.

Odiham, Hants; (castle of) 170.
Odo[1], ab of Canterbury (942–58) 94.
Odo[2], b of Bayeux (1050–97) 102.
Offa Wuffa, poss. k of E Angles (? 571–8) 79.
Oldcastell, (Ser Jon) Sir John Oldcastle, Lord Cobham 236, 239–42, 243; (follower of) 249.
Olimpe Mount Olympus 30.
Olimpius Olympius, Arian ? bishop (d. at Carthage 498) 70.
Olyuere Oliver, companion of **Rouland** 83.
Oloferne Holophernes 22.
Olorum Ile d'Oléron, France 196.
Olun Ile d'Olonne, France 196.
Omere Homer 32. *poss.* ∼ 37.
Orator Arator, 6th-cent. biblical epic poet 71.
Orcey erron. for Auray, France; (castle of) 180.
Orgliauns see **Aurelianense.**
Origene Origen 54, 56.
Orkeney Orkney; (Henry Sinclair, 3rd e of) 231.
Ormesta Mundi ? *Or[osii] m[undi] ist[ori]a* (+*Mundi* repeated erron.), *Historia adversus Paganos* 'World History contradicting the Pagans' by Orosius (417) 65.
Ormund Ormond, Ireland; (James Butler, 1st e of) 155.
Orosius 65.
Orphé Orpheus 29.
Osney, Oxon. 118.
Ostrich Austria 243; (dk of) 95 (as imperial elector), 114–15 (Leopold I), 189–90 (Leopold III), 242–3 (Frederick of Tyrol) 231. *poss.* in þe *duk of* ∼ *men* 115.
Oswyn, Seynt Oswine, k of Deira (644–51); (fd of, 20 Aug.) 188.
Otho Otto, cardinal deacon of S. Nicola in Carcere, papal legate in England 120–1, 124.
Othoniel Othniel 27–8.
Othus see **Artarxerses** III.
Ouyde Ovid 48.
Oxenforth Oxford 89, 118, 144, 170, 194; (parliament at) 123 (1258); (inhabitants of) 168; (mayor of) 144; (Benedictine chapter at) 118; (Dominicans of) 118, 138;

(Franciscans of) 120, 122; (university of) 130, 227 (New College), 235; (MA of) 181; (countess, earls of, see **Ver**.

Ozias Uzziah = Azariah, k of Judah (808–756 BC) 35. [2 Kgs. 15: 1, 13]

Pafnucius St. Paphnutius (d. *c.*360) 63.

Pay, Herry Henry Pay 230.

Palestine 50, 55, 72. Cf. **Holy Lond**.

Pallas 99/12 n.

Pandion, k of Athens (d. 1477 BC) 28.

Panonie Pannonia (Hungary) 73.

Pantheon, Rome 74 and see 74/27 n.

Papie see **Pauye**.

Paradisus Sancti Petri 'Paradise', name given to great quadrangular colonnaded portico at entrance to original church of St. Peter's, Rome 77.

Paris 51, 68, 83, 107, 112, 126, 132, 137, 171, 179, 197, 236; (men of) 236; (university of) 233; (b of) see **Lumbard**.

Pascale Paschal I, pope (817–24) 85.

Pascale Paschal II, pope (1099–1118) 104; **Paschasius** erron. for same 101.

Pathmos Patmos 48.

Patrik, Seint St. Patrick 67.

Patteshul, Petir Peter Patteshulle 191.

Paula St. Paula (347–404) 65.

Paule[1] (Roman martyr) see **Jon**[10].

Paule[2] Paul II, patriarch of Constantinople (641–54) 76.

Paule[3] Paul I, pope (757–67) 82.

Paule[4] Paulus, b of Ancona (878–87) 88.

Paule/Poule, (Seint) St. Paul the Apostle 48; (martyrdom of) 50; (head of) 82–3; (body of) 57; (church of S. Paolo fuori le Mura, Rome) 85 and see *poss*.; (church of SS. Pietro e Paolo, Rome) 62; (church of, London) 136, 197 (north door) and see *poss*.; (feast of conversion of, 25 Jan.) 154. *poss*. ~ 35, 82; **Poules** 50. *poss*.

absol. **Paules/Poules** S. Paolo fuori le Mura, Rome 87; St. Paul's, London 191 (attrib.), 204, 233, 240, 243; **Seynt Paules/Poules** 119, 211, 217.

Pauline[1] Paulinus, b of York (625–33) and of Rochester (633–44) 80.

Pauline[2] Paulinus, b of Aquileia (787–802) 95.

Pauye Pavia, Italy 70, 141, 176; **Papie** 81, 82.

Peytris Poitiers; (battle of, 19 Sept. 1355) 169–70.

Pelagius, heretical theologian (early 5th cent.) 67.

Pelagius I, pope (556–61) 72.

Pelagius þe Secund, pope (579–90) 73.

Penauns of Adam, þe, extracanonical Book of Adam 12.

Penbrok Pembroke, Wales; (earls of) see **Hasting(is), Valauns**.

Penda, k of Mercia (? 626–54) 80.

Penitencial, manual relating to penance, usu. attrib. to Theodore, ab of Canterbury (668–90) but here erron. assoc. with Pope Theodore I 76.

Pennarch Penmarch, Brittany 223.

Percy, Herry Henry Lord Percy (1299–1314) 135.

Percy, Herry Henry Lord Percy (1314–52), s of prec. 166.

Percy, (Ser) Herry Henry Percy, e of Northumberland (1377–1406) 182, 206, 212–13, 215, 221–3, 224, 225, 227, 229, 232.

Percy, (Ser) Herry, (þe ȝonger) Henry Percy the younger (Hotspur) 190, 212, 221–2; (army of, at Shrewsbury) 222/2.

Percy, Ser Herry, e of Northumberland (1416–55) 247.

Percy, (Ser) Thomas Sir Thomas Percy, e of Worcester (1397–1403) 182–3, 184, 209, 221–2.

Peregor Périgord, France 169.

Pereres, Dame Alis Alice Perrers, mistress to Edward III 180.

Pernel, Seynt St. Petronilla, Roman virgin (1st cent.) 82.

Perse Persia 18, 59, 75; (kingdom of) 42; (people of = **Perses**) 39, 55,

Perse (*cont.*):
56, 63, 71, 74; (kings of) 8, 39–42
and see **Artarxerses, Cirus,
Cosdre, Darius, Sapor, Xerses;**
(governors of) 40; (sybil of) 37.
Persida erron. for Persis, province
of Persia 49.
Perspectif for *Optics* by Ptolemy 53.
Pertica Perche (Orne, Eure-et-
Loire); (l of) see **Jon³**.
Pertinax, Helius, emp (193) 54.
Pes, þe Temple of Temple of
Concord, Rome 50.
Petir¹ Cardinal Peter, leader of
Roman delegation to Photian Synod
at Constantinople (879–80) 88.
Petir², city prefect of Rome (966)
93.
Petir³ Peter III, k of Aragon (1276–
85) 129.
Petir, (Kyng) Peter the Cruel, k of
Castile (1350–69) 176; **(Con-
stauns** and **Ysabell,** daughters of)
178, 185, 189, 198, 202, 219.
Petir, (Seynt) St. Peter, apostle 48,
49, 60, 68, 82, 181; (martyrdom
of) 50; (body of) 57, 60; (fd of
chains of, 1 Aug.) 68; (church of
= S. Pietro in Ciel d'Oro, Pavia)
81; (church of = S. Pietro in
Vaticano, Rome) 53, 85, 108, and
see *poss.*; (church of SS. Pietro e
Paolo, Rome) 62; (br of) 48. *poss.* in
Seint ~ cherch and sim. (Rome) 63,
67, 68, 71, 73, 75, 77, 78, 82, 86,
89, 98, 112. *poss. absol.* ~ St.
Peter's, Rome 71/15; **Seynt
Peteres** 83, 87.
Petrigoricum Périgueux, France;
(lordship of) 128.
Phalech, Phalegh Peleg 19, 20.
Phasga Pisgah 27. [Deut. 3: 27]
Phedron Phaedrus 41.
Phenice see **Fenise.**
Philadelphia, in Lydia 53.
Philip(pe), apostle 49; (church of)
73.
Philippicus Philip I, emp (244–9) 57.
Philip Philip II, emp (247–9) 57.
Philip (þe Secunde), Philippicus,
emp of E (711–13) 79, 80.
Philip II, Augustus, k of France
(1180–1223) 111, 114–15.

Philip(pe) III, k of France (1270–85)
127, 128, 129/24, 29, 160/16–17.
Philip(pe) (þe Fayre) Philip IV, k
of France (1285–1314) 119 (as
dauphin), 129/33, 131–4, 137, 139,
140, 160/17–18; (da of) see **Ysabel;**
(sr of) see **Margarete.**
Philip V, k of France (1316–22)
148, 160/20, 23, 29.
Philip, (Kyng) Philip VI, k of
France (1328–50) 159, 160/10–11,
161–3, 164–6, 168; (arms of) 161;
(galleys of) 159.
Philip(pe) (the Bold), fourth s of
Jon⁶ k of France 170, later dk of
Burgundy (1363–1404) 200, 206,
248/19.
Philip¹ Philippa of Hainault, q of
Edward III 151, 157, 161, 162,
163, 169.
Philip² Philippa, da of Henry IV
229–30.
Philippe, name for Aridaeus, illegiti-
mate half-br of Alexander the
Great 42–3.
Phoroneus, Foroneus, k of Argos
25.
Picardie Picardy, France 123, 165,
171.
Pilate Pontius Pilate 48.
Pipine¹ Pepin III, k of Franks 81–2.
Pipine² Pepin, s of Emperor Louis
I 84.
Pire province of Epirus (now N
Albania) 66.
Piriandus Periander, tyrant of
Corinth 39.
Pise Pisa; (council of, 1409) 233, 234.
Pitacus Pittacus (of Mitylene) 39.
Pitharas ? Protagoras 41.
Pius St. Pius I, pope (140–55) 53.
Plasché Pleshey, Essex 207, 217.
Plato 40–1.
Plauctus Plautus 44.
Plauntgenet, Gefrey Geoffrey V,
Plantagenet, c of Anjou (1131–51)
106, 107, 109–10; (w of) see
Maute³.
Plumerel Ploërmel, Brittany 167.
Plummouthe Plymouth 223.
Plutarc Plutarch 51/20 n.
Pollicarp St. Polycarp, b of Smyrna
(d. *c.*155) 53.

Poncian, (Seynt) Pontianus, pope (230–5) 56, 57.

Ponciane Ponza 72.

Pool, Michael at þe or de la Michael de la Pole, Chancellor (1383–6), e of Suffolk (1385–8) 189, 190–1, 192–4, 195, 197.

Pool, Michael at þe Michael de la Pole, e of Suffolk (1398–1415) 245.

Portesmouthe Portsmouth; (men of) 187.

Portingale Portugal 185; (people of) 185; (Ferdinand I, k of) 185; (da of prec.) 185; (da of John I, k of) 230.

Postumus see Jon.

Potencian St. Pudentiana 54.

Poule see Paule.

Poumfreite, Pountfract Pontefract, W Riding of Yorks. 142/26–7 n., 147, 171, 225, 232; (castle of) 189, 217.

Pounte Poitou, France; (earldom of) 150, 155; (k of England's lands in) 176. Pounteys (Eleanor of Castile, countess of) 128/22 n. Pountuey 165/16 n.

Powningis, þe Lady Isabel Lady Poynings (d. 1394), prob. widow of Richard Lord Poynings 195.

Praxede, (Seynt) St. Praxedes 54; (church of = Santa Prassede, Rome) 85.

Precian Priscian 71.

Premunire facias, medL for 'lest you cause to warn', title of statute designed to protect rights claimed by the English crown against encroachment by the Papacy 200.

Prendirgest, Jon John Prendergast 235.

Priscille Priscilla; (catacombs of, Via Salaria, Rome) 61.

Probus, emp (276–82) 59.

Promotheus Promethius 21.

Prophetys, Upon þe XII, commentary by Stephen Langton 119.

Prosper St. Prosper of Aquitaine (d. c.463) 69.

Prothase St. Protasius 60; (fd of, 19 June) 158.

Prouince Provence, France; (Ray-

mund[3], c of, Helianore[4], Margarete, daughters of) 120.

Prouynce Provence; erron. for Nice 57/7 n.

Prus Prussia 199; (armies of Teutonic Order of Knights in) 234–5; (master of Teutonic Order in) 199/28.

Psalme, Upon þe XIII, pres. Explanatio super psalmos xii by Ambrose 62.

Ptholome(us), surnamed Sother Ptolemy I Soter, satrap/king of Egypt (323/311–285 BC) 42–3.

Ptholomeus Philadelphus Ptolemy II Philadelphus, k of Egypt (285–246 BC) 43.

Ptholomeus Euergetes Ptolemy III Euergetes, k of Egypt (246–221 BC) 43.

Ptholomeus Philopater Ptolemy IV Philopator k of Egypt (221–203 BC) 44; (w of) see Erudite.

Ptholome, surnamed Epiphanes Ptolemy V Epiphanes, k of Egypt (203–180 BC) 44.

Ptholomeus Philometor Ptolemy VI Philometor, k of Egypt (180–145 BC) 44.

Ptholome, surnamed Euergetes þe Secunde Ptolemy VIII Euergetes (Physcon), k of Egypt (145–116 BC) 45; (q of) see Cleopatra.

Ptholome, surnamed Sother or Phiscon Ptolemy IX Soter II (Lathyrus), k of Egypt (116–106 BC and 88–81 BC) 45/29, 46/8, 46/14.

Ptholome Alisaundre Ptolemy X Alexander I, k of Egypt (105–87 BC) 46/9–10.

Ptholome Dionisius Ptolemy XII Auletes or Dionysius, k of Egypt (80–51 BC) 46.

Ptholome Ptolemy, astronomer (2nd cent.) 53.

Quare impedit, L for 'whereby he obstructs', title of statute enabling a writ to be issued in cases of disputed nomination to a benefice, requiring the defendant to state why he hinders the plaintiff from

Quare impedit (*cont.*):
being installed in the benefice 200, 210.

Quicunque vult, L for 'Whosoever wishes', opening words of, and alternative name for, the Athanasian Creed 62.

Quintine St. Quentin (d. *c.*287) 60.

Rabanus Maurus, ab of Mainz (847–56) 84.

Rachel, w of Jacob 25.

Radyngis see **Redyngis**.

Radyngton, Baldewyn Sir Baldwin Raddington 199.

Ragau (Gk form of) Reu 19, 20, 21.

Raymund¹ erron. for Rainolfus, c of Apulia (1137) 106.

Raymund² St. Raymond of Penafort (d. 1275) 118.

Raymund³ Raymund-Berengar IV, c of Provence (d. 1245); (**Helianore⁴, Margarete**, daughters of) 120.

Ramatha Ramah 31, 32.

Ramsey, Hunts.; (a of) 103, 230.

Ranulf Ranulph II, de Gernon, e of Chester (1129–53) 107.

Rasin Rezin, k of Syria 36.

Rauenesporne Ravenspur, Yorks. 212.

Rauenne Ravenna 71. **Rauen** erron. for Rome; (Church council at, 501) 70; (**Cassiodre**, senator of) 71.

Ré Île de Ré, France 196.

Rea Rhea Sylvia, also called Ilea 36.

Reatinense *gen.* of Rieti, Italy; (B. Mezzavacca, b of Rieti 1376–80, cardinal 1378, d. 1396) 188.

Rebec Rebecca, w of Isaac 26.

Reding, Simon Simon Reading 153.

Redyngis, Reding Reading, Berks. 216, 249; (monastery at) 106.

Register tr. L *Registrum* (*Epistolarum*) 'Collected Letters' by Gregory the Great 62.

Reglan La Réole (Gironde); (castle of) 122.

Reymes¹, erron. for *Reynes*, Rennes, France 167.

Reymes² Rheims, France 171.

Remigius, Seynt, (d. *c.*533) 'apostle of the Franks' 70.

Remus 36.

Renauges erron. for Benagues (Ariège) 122.

Rene, þe R Rhine 83.

Richard¹ Richard I, dk of Normandy (942–96) 88/24 (1st), 93; erron. called ~ þe Secund 96.

Richard² Richard II, dk of Normandy (996–1027) 88/24 (2nd).

Richard³, illegitimate s of Henry I (d. 1120) 105.

Richard⁴, e of Chester (1101–20) 105/17.

Richard⁵, e of Cornwall (1227–72), k of Romans (1257–), br of Henry III 117, 119, 121–2, 123, 124, 125.

Richard⁶, k of Majorca, godfather of Richard II 175.

Richard, (þe) Kyng Richard I, k of England (1189–99), 109, 110, 113–16 (reign), 122, 134. *poss.* **Richard** 114/10, 12, 14.

Richard (of Burdews), (þe) Kyng Richard II (of Bordeaux), k of England (1377–99), e of Chester (1376–), dk of Cornwall (1376–), p of Wales (1376–) 175, 178, 181–214 (reign), 215, 216, 218, 221, 224, 225, 230, 238; (q of) see (**Qwen**) **Anne**, (**Qween**) **Ysabell**; (m of) see **Jone³**. *poss.* **Richard** 194, 206; **Richardis** 181, 212, 217.

Richard Clare, e of Gloucester (1243–62) 119/26.

Richard Clifford, b of London, see **Clifforth, Jon**.

Richard 'of Conisburgh', e of Cambridge (1414–15) 243.

Richard FitzAlan, e of Arundel (1330–76) 168.

Richard FitzAlan, e of Arundel (1376–97), admiral of England (1386–9) 190, 192, 196, 202, 207, 208–9; (income of) 209.

Richemund Richmond, Yorks.; (earldom) of) see **Arthure³, Bretayn, (Jon of) Gaunt, Mountforth, (Raf²) Neuyle**.

Riffyn see **Grey Riffyn**.

Ripon, Jon John Ripon 193.

Robert¹, known as Rollo, dk of Normandy (911–31) 88/23.

Robert², illegitimate s of Henry I, dk of Gloucester (1122–47) 107.

Robert II, k of France (996–1031) 96.

Robert Champart of Jumièges, ab of Canterbury (1051–2) 102.

Robert (Curthose), also **Duk Roberd**, dk of Normandy (1087–1106) 103, 104–5.

Robert Guychardy Robert I, called 'the Devil', dk of Normandy (1027–35) 88.

Robert Kilwardby, ab of Canterbury (1273–8) 127.

Robert Wikeford, b of Dublin (1376–90) 193.

Roboam Rehoboam, k of Judah (976–959 BC) 33. *poss.* ~ 20.

Rochel La Rochelle 178; (wine from) 223; Ile de Rochelle 196.

Rodis Mediterranean island of Rhodes 53; (Grand Master of Knights Hospitaller of) 174, 204.

Rodwaldus Redwald, k of E Angles (d. *c.*620) 79.

Roger II, k of Sicily (1101–54) 106.

Rokby, Ser Thomas Sir Thomas Rokeby, sheriff of Yorkshire 232.

Rokisborow Roxburgh 158, 169; (castle of) 113.

Romaynes *n. pl.* ancient Romans 44, 45, 46, 47; Christians of ancient Rome 57, 61, 80.

Romanes *n. pl.* inhabitants of Rome (after AD 800) 90, 92, 95, 100, 104, 112, 142. *poss.* ~ 9.

Romanus, pope (897) 89.

Rome 31, 32, 35, 36, 37, 44, 47, 48, 49, 50, 51, 53, 56, 57, 58, 59, 60, 61, 62, 65, 66, 67, 69, 70, 71, 74, 75, 76, 79, 82, 83, 85, 86, 87, 92, 93, 94, 95, 99, 103, 104, 106, 112, 116, 118, 122, 126, 132, 135, 158, 182, 183, 189–90, 196, 210; (walls of) 73, 83; (St. Paul's gate) 87; (laws of) 37; (rulers/emperors of) 45, 90; (prefect of) 93, 100; (people of) see **Romaynes, Romanes**; (rule of) 60; (empire of) 68; (papal see at) 200/25; (pope at) 51, 53, 54, 55, 78, 83, 87/4, 89, 97, 242; (Church of) 108/16, 133, 148, 168, 181, 200; (cardinals of) 93; (clergy living in) 201/3; (church

in) 73, 108/21; (hospice in) 112; (burial at) 71/17, 72; (plague in) 74/2. See also **Senate, Vaticanus**.

Romulus 36.

Rone Rouen, Normandy 93, 123; (ab of) see **Clemens VI**.

Ros, Lord William Lord Roos of Helmsley (1394–1414) 213.

Rotharie Rothari, k of Langobards (636–52) 73.

Rotyngdene Rottingdean, Sussex 182.

Rouchestir Rochester, Kent 232; (see of) 167; (gates of monastery at) 239.

Rouland Roland 83.

Rupibus, Petrus de Peter des Roches, b of Winchester (1205–38) 118, 120.

Russel, Jon Sir John Russell 212.

Russoc, Frere Thomas Thomas Rushook OP, b of Chichester (1385–8), of Kilmore (1389–93), confessor to Richard II 195 and see 195/19 n.

Ruthland Rutland; (e of) see **Edward** 'of York'.

Sabelly Sabellius, African heresiarch, 55.

Sabine (Seynt) St. Sabina, Roman martyr 52; (church of S. Sabina, Rome) 85.

Sabrine Sabrina, L name for R Severn 80.

Sacra Priapi L for 'the shrines of Priapus' 33. [See Vulgate 1 Kgs. 15: 13]

Sadoch Zadok 32.

Sagiense *gen.* of Sées (Orne) 110.

Sala Shelah 19.

Salamon Solomon, k of Jews (1016–976 BC) 32–3. *gen.* **Salamones** 43.

Sale Sheleph 19/7.

Salem¹ name for Jerusalem 24/32 (1st).

Salem² Salim 24.

Salisbury, Wilts. 95, 96; (parliament at, 1328) 155; (diocese of) 197; (bps of) 146 (Roger Martival 1315–30), and see **Alum**; (cathedral treasurer of) 120; (earls of)

Salisbury (cont.):
  see Mountagew; (Henry de Lacy, reported e of) 138.
Salesbury, Jon Sir John Salisbury 195.
Salle, Ser Robert 185.
Saloigne erron. for Saintonge 169.
Salome m of St. James and St. John, the sons of Zebedee 48. [See Matt. 27: 56 and Mark 15: 40]
Saluatour, cherch of þe ? San Salvatore in Onde, Rome 62.
Samarie Samaria, district of Palestine 20, 34.
Samia name of Sibyl of Samos 37.
Samson 30–1.
Samuel 31–2; (time of) 28.
Sancer Sancerre (Cher); (l of) 206.
Sancti Spiritus assit nobis gratia, L for 'May the grace of the Holy Spirit be with us', 1st line of sequence by Robert II of France 96/16–17 n.
Sancto Martino, Laurens de, a knight of Wiltshire 191.
Sancto Victore, Hugo de Hugh of St.-Victor 107; (statement by) 18.
Sanctone Saintes; (lordship of) 128.
Sanctus L for 'holy', title and 1st, 2nd, and 3rd word of 'angelic hymn' which concludes the eucharistic preface 36, 52. [See Isa. 6: 3]
Sanir Shamir 30.
Sapor I, k of Persia 57.
Sapor II, k of Persia 64.
Sarasines n. pl. Arabs 72, Moslems 75/7, infidels 75/29, 76, 77, 81, 83, 85, 86, 108, 110, 111, 121, 125, 126, 145, 166, 189, 234.
Sardinia 69, 81.
Sare Sarah 24, 25, 26.
Saruch, Sarugh Serug 19, 21–2; (time of) 23.
Sathanas Satan; (Church as religious organization of) 220.
Saueye the Savoy Palace, London 174, 186.
Sauinian Sabinian, pope (604–6) 74.
Sauyour, Seynt St. Sauveur-le-Vicomte; (castle of) 180.
Saul 31.
Saxone Saxony 93; (dk of) 95 (as imperial elector), 110 (Henry the

Lion, 1142–95), and see Henry; (people of = Saxones) 92, 112.
Saxones n. pl. Anglo-Saxons 74, 79. Cf. Inglond.
Scala Celi (L for 'Ladder of Heaven') church of S. Maria Scala Coeli, Rome 83.
Scarborow Scarborough; (castle of) 138.
Schaftisbyry Shaftesbury; (abbey at) 95.
Schene Sheen, Surrey, old name for Richmond 181, 242.
Schepey, Maystir Jon John Sheppey, b of Rochester (1352–60) 167/23.
Schirborne Sherburn in Elmet, W Riding of Yorks. 145/27.
Schrouesbury Shrewsbury 80, 221; (parliament at) 129 (1283), 209 (1398); (a of) 222; (battle of) 218, 222–3, 224; (house of Augustinian friars at) 122.
Scicile, Cicile Sicily 72, 76, 94, 104, 114; (k of) 110 (William II, 1166–89), 188 (Charles III, k of Naples, 1382–6), and see Frederik; (people of) 129.
Sciciniis n. pl. Sicyonians, people of Sicyon (now Basilico), city of Peloponnesus 22–3; (q of) see Zeucippe. [Dat./abl. of L Sicyōnii pl.]
Scicopolin Scythopolis 25.
Scipio Affricanus Publius Cornelius Scipio, surnamed Africanus for conquering the Carthaginians 44–5.
Scipping Wateres, At þe tr. of L Aput Aquas Saluias, place where St. Paul was martyred 50. See also Anastace.
Scithia Scythia, ancient land comprising mod. E Europe, Russia and Mongolia 21–2; (people of) 19.
Scone (abbey of) 135, 157.
Scot, Jon þe see Jon.
Scotlond 31, 72, 103, 134–5, 141, 148, 156–7, 158–9, 187, 195, 225, 229, 232, 247; (kingdom of) 133–4; (crown of) 156, 169; (k of) 134, (William I, 1165–1214) 113, and see Alexander, Baliol, Brus, Constantyn, David³, Jon⁸,

Malcolyn; (s of k of) 156, 231; (regent of) 157; (bps of) 158; (people of = **Scottis**) 91, 92, 133, 140, 141, 143–4, 148, 156–8, 165, 168, 169, 187, 190, 202, 220, 231; (ships from) 217.

Scroop, Herry Henry Scrope, 1 of Masham (1341–92) 166.

Scrop, Henry Henry Scrope, 1 of Masham, Treasurer (1410–11) 243.

Scrop, Maistir Richard Richard Scrope, b of Coventry and Lichfield (= Chester, 1386–98), ab of York (1398–1405) 193, 213, 227–8, 231, 238.

Scrop, Ser William William Scrope, Vice Chamberlain (1393–9), 1st e of Wiltshire (1397–9), Treasurer (1398–9) 202, 207, 209, 212.

Sebastian, Seynt 60; (church of, Rome) 55, 58; (fd of, 20 Jan.) 120.

Sebertus (reported 4th k of E Saxons) ? Sæweard 79.

Sebra Zibiah 34.

Secundus, Roman philosopher 52.

Sedechie Zedekiah, tributary p of Judah (599–588 BC) 38.

Seyn-Clo St.-Cloud 236.

Seyn-Omeres St.-Omer 169, 234.

Seyne R Seine 88, 165.

Seynt Albone(s) St. Albans, Herts. 108, 212, 249; (monastery at) 108, 139–40, 145–6, 154, 184, 186; (a of) 159, 217; (people of) 154.

Seint-Denys St.-Denis 174.

Seint Germyn St. Germain, France 86.

Seint Gilis Feld St. Giles's Fields (outside London) 241.

Seint Jon, Ser Jon Sir John St. John 198.

Seint-Mathew St.-Mathieu, Brittany 223 (town); (castle of) 180.

Seynt Osithes St. Osyth, Essex; (a of) 224.

Seir (wilderness of) Shur, S of Gaza 25.

Seland Zeeland 227; (William II, c of Hainault, Holland, and Zeeland) 167. Cf. **Hollond.**

Selby, Walter 142.

Seleuce Seleucia, city in ancient Syria 43.

Seleucus surnamed *Nicator*, founder of Seleucid empire 43.

Sella Zillah 13.

Sem Shem 18–20, 24.

De Seminibus Literarum, unidentified work attrib. to Joachim of Fiore, perhaps the *Liber figurarum* 109.

Senacherib Sennacherib, k of Assyria 37.

Senar Shinar 20.

Senate, þe ancient Roman Senate 44, 47.

Senys Sens 113. *gen.* **Senonense** (Guilielmus de Melun, bishop 1345–75) 170.

Sephath Zephath 74.

Sephora Zipporah 26.

Seraphia Serapia 52.

Sergius, adviser of Mahomet 75.

Sergius I, pope (687–701) 77.

Sergius IIᵘˢ, pope (844–7) 86.

Sergius þe þirde, pope (904–11) 89.

Sergius IIII, pope (1009–12) 98.

Serle, supporter of Richard II 225.

Seth 11–12, 13, 15–16, 19; (descendants of) 15–16, 17.

Seuerinus Severinus, pope (638–40) 75.

Seuerus Septimius Severus, emp (193–211) 54.

Seward k of ? Georgia 174.

Sibertus Sæberht, k of E Saxons (?603–?616) 79.

Sibille 37 and see under sybil's name.

Sichem Shechem 26.

Sidingborn Sittingbourne, Kent; (house of Augustinian friars at) 119/29 n.

Sigbertus Sigeberht I, k of E Saxons (?617–?652) 79.

Sigebertus Sigeberht, k of E Angles (?631–?637) 79.

Sigemund Sigismund, k of Hungary (1387–), emp of E (1411–37) 243, 247–8, 249.

Silo Shiloh 31.

Siluery Silverius, pope (536–7) 72.

Siluestir, Seynt Sylvester I, pope (314–35), 61–2; (time of) 56. *poss.*

Siluestir, Seynt (*cont.*):
in (*Seynt*) *Siluestir day/fest* (31 Dec.) 188.

Siluestir þe Secund, pope (999–1003) 94, 95. See also **Gilbert**[1].

Siluius Aduentinus Aventinus (Silvius), k of Latium 35.

Simachus Symmachus, translator of the OT into Gr. 54.

Simachus Symmachus, pope (498–514) 70.

Simeon, Seynt; (arm of, as relic) 84. [See Luke 2: 25–35]

Simon, apostle 49/10 n.; **Symund** (fd of, 28 Oct.) 206.

Simon Walton, also **Simund,** b of Norwich (1257–66) 123.

Simon Mepham, ab of Canterbury (1327–33) 155.

Simon Cleophas Simeon, son of Cleophas, 2nd b of Jerusalem (*c.*62) 51.

Simpliciane St. Simplicianus 66.

Simplicius pope (468–83) 69.

Simund see **Simon.**

Sirac *gen.* of Sirach 43.

Sisara, Cisara Sisera 28–9.

Sisinnius pope (708) 78.

Sistewis *n. pl.* (order of) Cistercians 91, 101, 121, 158.

Sixte, Seynt, Sixte þe First, Sixtus I, pope (115–25) 52, 57, 58/8.

Sixte, Seynt, Sixtus II, pope (257–8) 58; (church of, Rome) 112.

Sixtus III, pope (432–40) 68.

Slake, Nicholas, chaplain to Richard II 195.

Slus Sluys 162, 190.

Smythfeld Smithfield, Middx. 218, 233–4.

Snelleston ? Shelton, Beds. 210.

Snowdon Snowdonia 129, 217.

Socrates 40.

Solem justicie, 1st words of versicle by **Fulbert** of Chartres 95/32 n.

Solon Greek legislator 39.

Somirsete Somerset; (e and mq of) see **(Thomas) Beuforth.**

Sophie Sophia, empress of E (565–78) 72.

Sophie, Seint church of S. Sophia, Constantinople 72.

Sophodes Sophocles 40/7 n.

Sother Soter, pope (166–75) 54.

Sother, Ptholome see **Ptholome(us).**

Sotherey see **Suthrey(e).**

Souch, Lord William Zouche, 1 of Harringworth (1382–96) 195.

Souch, William, Lord, also **Ser Wylliam la Souch** William Zouche, ab of York (1340–52) 153, 166.

Southampton, Hants. 159, 243; **Hampton** 103.

Southsex Sussex 79, 182; (AS kingdom of) 79.

Spayne Spain 48, 58, 61, 68, 83, 116, 122, 175–6, 178, 189, 191, 198, 232; (as part of Roman Empire) 61; (kingdom of = **Castile**) 198; (regent of) 84; (people of = **Spaynardis,** L *Hiberi*) 19, (Castilians) 176, 185, 189; (men of, i.e. Castilians) 167, 178, 191. See also **Castile.**

Spalding, Petir of, governor of Berwick 143.

Spencer, Ser Thomas/Lord Thomas, Lord Despenser (1375–1400) 207; (as e of Gloucester, 1397–9) 209, 215, 217.

Spenser, (Ser) Herry Henry Dispenser 177; (as b of Norwich, 1370–1406) 184, 186–7, 231.

Spenser, Hewe/þe Lord Hugh, Lord Despenser (1338–49) 164, 165.

Spenser, þe Lord Edward, Lord Despenser (1357–75) 179.

Spenser, Hugo/(Ser) Hewe Hugh Despenser, the elder 144, 146, 148, 152; (as e of Winchester, 1322–6) 147.

Spenser, Hugo/Ser Hewe/Hewe þe Hugh Despenser, the younger, Chamberlain 1313–21, 145, 146, 147, 152–3, 156.

Spenseres *pl.* the Hugh Despensers, elder and younger 145–6, 147, 148, 151.

Spigreuus Spitigniev I, dk of Bohemia 91.

Spolet (duchy of) Spoleto, Italy 82.

Stafford, Stafforth 91; (Anne, countess of, d. 1438) 206; (Hugh Stafford, e of, 1372–86) 179.

Stafford, Raf Ralph Stafford, e of Stafford (1351–72) 164, 168, 169.

Stafford, Ser Edmund Edmund Stafford, b of Exeter (1395–1419), Chancellor (1396–9) 212/6 n.

Stanpark (military confrontation between English and Scots at) Stanhope Park, Durham 156.

Stapilton, Maystir Walter Walter Stapledon, b of Exeter (1308–26) 152, 155.

Staumforth, Staunford Stamford, Lincs. 93; (abbey at) 95; (council at) 201.

Steuene, Seynt St. Stephen I, pope (254–7) 58; (bones of) 72.

Stephanus II Stephen II, pope (752–7) 81–2.

Stephanus IIIus, pope (768–72) 82.

Stephanus IIIIus, pope (816–17) 84.

Steuene þe V, pope (885–91) 88.

Stephanus þe Sexte, pope (896–7) 89.

Stephanus VIIus, pope (929–31) 90.

Steuene þe VIII, pope (939–42) 90.

Stephanus IX, pope (1057–8) 98.

Steuene Etienne d'Aubert, b of Ostia (1352) 167. See also **Innocent þe Sext**.

Steuene, (þe) Kyng Stephen, k of England (1135–54) 106 (as c of Boulogne and Blois), (reign) 107–8, 109.

Steuene, þe Abbot St. Stephen Harding, a of Cîteaux (1109–34) 101.

Stigand(us) Stigand, ab of Canterbury (1052–70) 102.

Stirps Jesse, 1st words of response by **Fulbert** of Chartres 95/31 n.

Stoke, Thomas 214.

Storry, Richard see **Sturry.**

Straw, Jon Jack Straw 186.

Stryuelyn Stirling; (battle of = Bannockburn) 140.

Strogoil Chepstow 152.

Sturry, Richard Sir Richard Stury 191; **Storry** 204.

Stuteuyle, þe Lord, also called **þe Lord Boteuyle**, John, l of Estouteville 244/15 n.

Sudbyry, Simon Simon Sudbury, ab of Canterbury (1375–81), Chancellor (1380–81) 179, 181, 185.

Suffene, ? erron. for Sumer, putative founder of Sumerians 20.

Suffolk, Suthfolk 79, 122; (earls of) 246 (Michael de la Pole, 1415), and see **Pool, Vfford.**

Summe R Somme 165.

Surek ? Surrex, Essex; (house of Augustinian friars at) 119/28 n.

Surré, Surry Syria (and Mesopotamia) 18, 43, 111, 124, 127; (k of) see **Cusan-rasathaim, Rasin, Seleucus;** (commanding officer of) see **Naaman.**

Susanne Susanna 39.

Sutbyry see **Sudbyry.**

Suthfolk see **Suffolk.**

Suthreye, Sotherey Surrey 79; (dk of) see **Holland**[2]; (e of) see **Wareyn.**

Swayn Swegn Forkbeard, k of Denmark (987–1014) 96–7.

Swale R Swale, Yorks. 144.

Swyn R Zwyn, Flanders 161.

Swynborn, Ser Thomas Sir Thomas Swinburn 230.

Swyneshede Swineshead, Lincs. 116.

Swynforth, (Dame) Katerine Katharine Swynford, mistress and w of John of Gaunt 205, 206; (children of Gaunt by) 206–7, 210.

Swynmouth name attributed to Sergius II before he became pope 86. [Tr. of L *Os Porci* 'pig's mouth']

Swithine, Seynt St. Swithun; (translation of remains of) 117/33.

Tafnes Tahpanhes, Egypt 38.

Talbot, (Ser) Richard Richard, Lord Talbot (1332–56), 156, 158, 159.

Tamary, Roger erron. for Sir Roger Damory 144.

Tamnath-sare Timnath-serah 27.

Tamworth, Staffs. 91.

Tankeruyle, þe Erl John II (d. 1382), c of Tancarville (Seine et Marne), Grand Chamberlain of France (1347–) 172.

Tarquinius Priscus 5th k of Rome 37.

Tartaré ? khanate of Turkestan 175.

Tebes[1] Thebes, Egypt; (rulers from) 22.

Tebes[2] Thebes, Greece 28.

Te Deum laudamus 'We praise You, Lord', title of L hymn to the Father and Son 246.

Tempil-barre Temple-bar, gateway marking entrance to City of London from Strand 185.

Templaries see *Glossary* s.v.

Temple (of God), þe Jewish Temple, Jerusalem 32, 33, 34, 36, 38, 42, 45, 48, 49, 52, 63.

Temse, (þe) R Thames 79–80, 158.

Terculian Tertullian, early Christian Latin writer 54.

Terrencius Terence, early Roman comedy-writer 45.

Tersone erron. for *Cersone* Chersonese, Thracian peninsula W of Hellespont 78.

Teutonye country inhabited by Teutons, Germany; (regent of) 84.

Thade = Judas Thadeus (q.v.), erron. for Addai, one of the Seventy (Luke 10: 1) 108.

Thales of Miletus, Greek philosopher (b. c.624 BC) 39.

Thanaus ? Tammuz, Babylonian deity 21.

Thanis Tanis, Lower Egypt 15.

Thare Terah 19, 22–3.

Thasis unidentified monster killed by Hercules (? erron. for Geryon) 28.

Thebea, unidentified reported b of Jerusalem (end of 6th cent.) 74.

Thelophorus St. Telesphorus, pope (125–36) 52.

Theobald of Bec, ab of Canterbury (1138–61) 109, 110.

Theodoricus Theodoric I, k of Visigoths 68.

Theodorik Theodoric the Great, k of Ostrogoths 70.

Theodorus þe First Theodore I, pope (642–9) 76.

Theodorus II, pope (897) 89.

Theodosie Theodosius I, emp (378–95) 65–6.

Theodosius þe Secunde, emp of E (408–50) 67–8.

Theodosius Tercius, emp of E (716–17) 80.

Theodre Theodorus, ab of Canterbury (668–90) 76.

Theophilus, unidentified archdeacon of Sicilian town who gave himself to devil c.540–50 72.

Thetforth Thetford, Norfolk 96; (Benedictine monastery at) 103; (b of) see **Losinga.**

Thimeus *Timaeus*, dialogue by Plato 41/2.

Þirnyng, William Sir William Thirning, CJKB 213.

Thobie Tobit 38.

Thola Tola 30.

Tholomayda, -maide, reported ancient name for Acre 114, 126.

Tholous Toulouse, France 110, 113; **Tholosane** (university of) 233.

Thomas St. Thomas, apostle 48. *gen.* in *Seint ~ day þe apostil* (21 Dec.) 217.

Thomas of Bayeux, ab of York (1070–1100) 102.

Thomas (of Cauntirbury), Seint St. Thomas Becket, Chancellor (1155–62), ab of Canterbury (1162–70) 110, 111, 214–15; (translation of, 1220) 118; (feast of translation of, 7 July) 135, 161; **(Mary, sr of)** 111. *gen.* in *Seint Thomas day* (29 Dec.) 188.

Thomas ((of) Lancastir), (Ser/þe Erle) Thomas, e of Lancaster and Leicester (1298–1322) 136, 138, 142, 144, 145, 147, 148; (trial of) 198; (tomb of) 171; (canonization of) 198; (member of household of) 148.

Thomas, 2nd s of Henry IV, dk of Clarence (1412–21) 214, 230, 237–8, 244–5.

Thorney, Cambs.; (foundation of abbey at) 95.

Thrisk Thirsk, N Riding of Yorks. 232.

Tiberius, emp (AD 14–37) 48.

Tiberius þe Secund, emp (578–82) 73.

Tiberi(us) III, emp of E (698–705) 78.

Tibir R Tiber, Rome 31, 36, 73, 89, 94.

Tiburce St. Tiburtius, reputed br of Valerian; (body of) 85, 86.

Tiburtina, name given to the Sibyl of Tibur (Tivoli) 37; Sibille Tiburtine 47.

Tyes, Herry Sir Henry Tyes 147.

Tyler, Wat, leader in Peasants' Revolt (1381) 185–6.

Tille, Frere Jon John Tille, ? O. Carm. 238/7 n.

þe Tymes, Jon of John of the Times 107.

Tynla ? for Pybba, putative 6th-cent. k of Mercia 80.

Tynmowth Tynemouth, Northumb. 138, 188.

Tiras 19.

Tyrel, Water Walter Tyrrell, 1 of Poix in Ponthieu 104.

Tyrel, Ser Hewe Sir Hugh Tyrrell 182.

Titilinus Tytili, putative 6th-cent. k of E Angles 79.

Titus, emp (79–81) 50.

Tollete Toledo, Spain 116.

Tollouse see Tholous.

Tophet 36.

Torneacense Tournai, Belgium 162.

Totila erron. for Attila, ruler of Huns in E Europe (433–53) 68.

Totyngton, Alisaundre Alexander Tottington, b of Norwich (1406–13) 231, 239.

Tour of Confusion, þe Tower of Babel 20.

Tour/Towre (of/at London), þe Tower of London 103, 124, 129, 146–7, 152, 161, 163, 174, 183, 194, 213, 216, 235, 241; (governor of) 161, 240; (jailers of) 150.

Trace Thrace, ancient country now European Turkey 19, 38; (mythical k of) see Diomede.

Traconides Trachonitis (mod. Iraq), identified (by Josephus) with land of Uz 19.

Trajan, emp (98–117) 51–2.

Transamunde Thrasamund, k of Vandals (496–523) 70.

Transtibir, cherch of oure Lady in S. Maria in Trastévere, Rome 55.

Tresilian, Robert Sir Robert Tresilian, CJKB 192.

Treuer Trier; (b of as imperial elector) 95.

Trinité, þe 8, 23, 24, 70, 109, 234; in þe secund ~ 220.

Tripolim Tripolis (now in Lebanon) 101.

Tryuet, (Ser) Thomas Sir Thomas Trivet 187, 195, 196.

Troye Troy 30–1, 37; (siege of) 30, 32; (men of = Troianes) 30, and see also Eneas.

Tubal 19. Cf. next.

Tubal-cayn Tubal-cain 13; (sr of) 13. poss. Tubal 13/22.

Turkye Turkey; (plain of = Maritza) 174–5; (p of, i.e. khan of the Khazars) 78; (k of) 175; (men of = Turkis) 217, 248.

Turnus, k of the Rutuli, Italy 99.

Tussie Tuscany, Italy 86.

Vfford, Robert Robert Ufford, e of Suffolk (1337–69) 159. See also Glossary, s.v. Vfforthis.

Vl Hul 18–19.

Vmfrey see Humfrey.

Vmfreuile, (Ser) Gilbert Gilbert Umfraville, titular e of Angus (1331–81) 156, 166.

Vphowel, Maistir Reson Rhys ap Howel 153/8.

Vrbane, (Seynt) St. Urban I, pope (222–30) 56, (body of) 85, 86.

Vrbanus IIus, pope (1088–99) 100.

Vrbanus Tercius, pope (1185–7) 111.

Vrbane, þe Pope Urban IV (1261–4) 143.

Vrban(us Quintus), (Pope) Urban V (1362–70) 173, 177.

Vrbane (þe Sexte), (þe Pope) Urban VI (1378–89) 182–4, 186–7, 188, 189, 197, 199.

Vrcines, Paule of þe Paolo Orsini 231–2.

Vry Uriah 32.

Vs Uz, s of Aram 18–19. [Gen. 10: 23]

Vs ? île d'Aix 196.

Vtred Uhtred, e of Northumbria (d. 1016) 96.

Vulpinianus Ulpinianus Domitius 56.

Vurbane see Vrbane (þe Sexte).

Valauns/Valens, Aymer/Eymer of Aymer of Valence, e of Pembroke (1307–24) 135, 136, 147, 198.

Valens, emp (364–78) 65; **Valent** 64.

Valens *gen.* of Valois; (dk) see **Charles, -is.**

Valentinian[1] Valentinian I, emp (364–75) 64–5.

Valentinian[2], **Ualentinian** Valentinian II, emp (375–92) 65.

Valentiniane Valentinian III, emp in W (425–55) 68; **Valentinus** 68/29.

Valentinus Valentine, pope (827) 85.

Valerian, husband of St. Cecilia 56; (body of) 85.

Valeriane Valerian, emp (253–60) 57–8.

Vanes Vannes, Brittany 163.

Vaticanus Ager Vaticanus (now the Borgo), Rome 50; (after *in*) **Vaticano** (burial at) 50, 51, 52, 54, 55; **Vatican** 57.

Velamensse *gen.* ? of Valence; (bishop) 206.

Vendone (Louis de Bourbon, c of) Vendôme 246.

Veneraca ? Guinevere 110/29 n.

Veniades, master of Diogenes 41.

Venys, Venice 69; (cardinal of) 188; (men of = **Venecianes**) 112.

Ver, (Ser) Robert Robert de Vere, e of Oxford (1381–8), mq of Dublin (1385–8), dk of Ireland (1386–8) 189, 191–2, 193, 194, 195, 199; (body of) 205; (m of, countess of Oxford) 224–5.

Ver, Ser Albré de Aubrey de Vere, e of Oxford (1393–1400) 202.

Vernon, Ser Richard Richard de Vernon 222.

Verone Verona, Italy 57, 90.

Vescal *n.* the cult of Vesta, female Roman deity 36/5 n.

Vespasian, emp (69–79) 50.

Via Appia (patrician cemetery forming first part of) Appian Way (now Via Appia Antica), Rome 55.

Via Lata L for 'wide street', now Via del Corso, Rome 60.

Via Tiburtina (here *able.*) L for 'on the road to Tivoli', now Highway 5 from Rome 68.

Victor I, pope (189–99) 55.

Victor II[us], pope (1055–7) 98.

Victor III[us], pope (1086–7) 100.

Victorius Victorinus Afer, rhetorician and theologian (4th cent.) 63.

Vienne (Church council at, 1311–12) 137; (dauphin of) 160.

Vigilius, pope (537–55) 72.

Vilentynge another name for **Wodous.**

Vincent St. Vincent of Saragossa 58.

Vitalianus Vitalian, pope (657–72) 76.

Viterbe Viterbo, Italy 125; (conclave at) 125.

Viuiane, Seint (church of our Lady and) St. Viviana (= S. Bibiana, Rome) 69.

Uolucianus Volusianus, s of **Gallus** 57.

Wade, Baldewyn erron. for Baldwin Wake (d. 1281/2) 124.

Wake, þe Lady Blanche, Lady Wake (d. 1380) 170.

Wakeryng, Jon John Wakeryng, b of Norwich (1415–25) 245.

Walden, Roger, Treasurer (1395–8), ab of Canterbury (1397–9), b of London (1404–6) 208, 230–1.

Waleys, Wyliam William Wallace, Scottish leader 134.

Wales 31, 74, 120, 128–9, 153, 192, 217, 219–20, 221, 223, 227, 229–30, 232; see also *Glossary,* s.v. **march;** (p of) see (Prince) **Edward, Herri V, Leulyne, Richard II;** (men of = **Walschmen**) 129, 153, 213, 219; (people of) 91; (rebellion by people of) 217.

Walingforth, Richard Richard Wallingford 159.

Walkfare, Robert 145.

Wallingford, Walingforth, Berks. 136, 153, 216; (castle of) 147.

Walsingham, Norfolk 159; (place of pilgrimage at) 197.

Walter Reynolds, ab of Canterbury (1313–27) 149–50, 151/34 n., 153, 154.

Waltham Waltham Holy Cross, Essex; (a of) 217.

Walworth, William, mayor of London 186.

Wandalis *n. pl.* Asding Vandals, Germanic tribe who set up kingdom in N Africa 70/5 n. [L *Vandalus*; see n.]

Warde, Ser Symund Simon Ward, governor of York 147.

Ware, Herts. 218.

Wareyn/Warenne, Johan John de Warenne, e of Surrey (1306–47) 136, 147.

Warenne, Jon count of John de Warenne, e of Surrey (1240–1304) 126.

Warwic Warwick 91, 138; (earls of) see **Gy, Belchaump**; (Thomas Beauchamp, earl 1370–97 and 1399–1401) 179–80, 192, 197, 207, 209, 209 (his living); (Richard Beauchamp, earl 1403–39) 242.

Watirton, Robert Sir Robert Waterton 223.

Welle, Maistir Hewe Hugh of Wells, b of Lincoln (1209–35) 120.

Werwell Wherwell, Hants; (convent at) 95.

Westbrom, Robert 185.

Westminster, Westmester (often implying the abbey, hall or palace at) 115, 120, 143, 170, 204, 235, 241; (abbey at) 118; (burial at) 100, 125, 126, 135, 163, 202; (coronation at) 102, 117, 127, 135, 154, 238; (a of) 211, 213, 242; (k's palace at) 247; (hall at) see next entry; (parliament at) 172 (1361), 176 (1369).

Westminster Halle, formerly the seat of the High Court of Justice 103, 104, 139, 146, 153, 214.

Westmorland (e of) see **Neuyle**.

Westsex (AS kingdom of) Wessex 79.

West Wade ? Langwade Cross; (miracle at) 197.

White Felauchip, þe the White Company 177/11 n.

Wicetir see **Wissetir**.

Wiclef, (Jon) John Wyclif 170, 181, 185, 188; (followers of) 197. See also *Glossary*, s.v. **Wiclefistis**.

Wikham/Wikkam, Maystir/Ser William William Wykeham, Chan-

cellor (1367–71, 1389–91), b of Winchester (1366–1404) 171, 178, 196, 227.

Wilbey, Lord William, Lord Willoughby (1396–1409) 213.

Wilforth, William William de Wilford 223.

Wiliam[1] William the Pious, dk of Aquitaine (d. 918) 90/19 n.

Wiliam[2] William of Corbeil, ab of Canterbury (1123–36) 107.

William[1], s of Henry I (d. 1120) 105.

William[2], name of child abducted by Norwich Jews 120.

William[3] William Middleton, b of Norwich (1278–88) 128; see also **Bateman**.

William[4] erron. for **Walter Reynolds**.

William, (Duk/Kyng), also ~ **Bastard,** ~ **Conqwerour** William I, k of England (1066–87), dk of Normandy (1035–87) 101, (reign) 102–3, 134; (called *Notus*, for *Nothus*, L for 'illegitimate') 88; (his right to English throne) 101; (q of) see **Maute**[1]; (Henry I, 3rd s of) 104. *gen.* Wiliam 102/2.

William (þe) Rede), (þe Kyng) William II, called *Rufus* 'red-haired', k of England (1087–1100) 103–4.

William Longswerd see **Longswerd**.

Williamson, William William Fitz-William 147.

Wiltens erron. for Fulda, Germany 84.

Wilton, Wilts. 96.

Wiltschere (e of) see **Scrop (William)**.

Wymundam Wymondham, Norfolk 197.

Wynchestir Winchester, Hants. 103, 127, 220, 227 (Winchester School); (see of) 102; (abbey of) 86; (burial at) 91; (coronation at) 100; (Church council at, 1070) 102; (parliament at) 155 (1330), 178 (1371), 201 (1393); (Henry Woodlock, bishop 1305–16) 135; (John Stratford, bishop 1323–33; Treasurer 1326–7) 150, 153; (other bps of) see

Wynchestir (*cont.*):
　Beuforth, Birstane, Edyngton, Ethelwold, Rupibus, Wikham; (e of) see **Spenser.**

Wynchil(is)sey Winchelsea, Sussex 171; (naval battle off) 167.

Wynchilseye, Maistir Robert Robert Winchelsey, ab of Canterbury (1293–1313) 135, 136.

Wyndesore Windsor 105, 124, 164, 216, 247; (castle of) 171, 227.

Wyndesore, William Sir William of Windsor 184.

Wissetir, Wircetir Worcester; (council at, 1404) 229; (prior of) 242; (e of) see **Percy.**

Wite, þe Ilde of Isle of Wight 207, 224.

Witot Vitold, grand p of Lithuania (1392–1430) 199.

Wodous Woodhouse, Salop.; (house of Augustinian friars at) 119.

Wodstok Woodstock, Oxon. 120.

Wodstok, (Ser) Thomas Thomas of Woodstock, e of Buckingham (1377–97), dk of Gloucester (1385–97), Chief Governor of Ireland (1392), 169 (born 7 Jan. 1355), 182, 184, 187, 189, 190, 192–5, 196–7, 201, 203, 206–7, 209, 210, 215, 217, 225; (expenses of) 201; (property of) 209, 215; (w of) 206; (s of) 211. See also **Woodstok.**

Wolf, tr. L *Lupa*, name given to **Laurens¹** 36/12 n.

Wolinster Ulster; (supposed da of e of) 136/9 n.

Wolleman, Benedict Benedict Wulleman 248.

Woodstok, (Ser) Edmund, also **Edmunde of** Edmund of Woodstock, e of Kent (1321–30) 138, 150, 151–2, 155. See also **Wodstok.**

Wormancie ? erron. for Norway (L *Norwagensis*) 108.

Wraw, Jon John Wrawe 185, 186.

Wrecchid Kynde of Man, Of the tr. *De Miseria Humanae Conditionis* 'Concerning Man's unhappy Condition' by **Innocencius III** 112.

Xerses¹ Xerxes I, k of Persia (485–464 BC) 39–40.

Xerses² see **Arsanius.**

Zacari Zacharias, patriarch of Jerusalem (d. 631) 75.

Zacharie Zacharius, pope (741–52) 81.

Zaram Zerah, k of Ethiopians 33. [2 Chr. 14: 9]

Zebede Zebedee 48. See **Salome.**

Zeno (erron. for) Conon, pope (686–7) 77.

Zenocrates Xenocrates 42.

Zenon Zeno, emp of E (474–91) 69.

Zepherine Zephyrinus, pope (199–217) 55.

Zeucippe Zeuxippe, q of Sicyonia 23. See **Sciciniis.**

Zorastes Zoroaster 23–4.

Zorobabel Zerubbabel 39.

Zozime Zosimus, pope (417–18) 67.